VERSION 2003

INSIDE MICROSOFT® VISUAL STUDIO® .NET

Brian Johnson
Craig Skibo
Marc Young

PUBLISHED BY
Microsoft Press
A Division of Microsoft Corporation
One Microsoft Way
Redmond, Washington 98052-6399

Library of Congress Cataloging-in-Publication Data pending.

Printed and bound in the United States of America.

1 2 3 4 5 6 7 8 9 QWE 8 7 6 5 4 3

Distributed in Canada by H.B. Fenn and Company Ltd.

A CIP catalogue record for this book is available from the British Library.

Microsoft Press books are available through booksellers and distributors worldwide. For further information about international editions, contact your local Microsoft Corporation office or contact Microsoft Press International directly at fax (425) 936-7329. Visit our Web site at www.microsoft.com/mspress. Send comments to *mspinput@microsoft.com*.

Acquisitions Editor: Danielle Bird Voeller
Project Editor: Sally Stickney
Technical Editor: Jack Beaudry

Body Part No. X08-99931

For Will, Hunter, and Buffy, who waited very patiently while Daddy finished his chapters.

–B.J.

To my parents, Al and Jan; my brother, Brian; and all my friends.

–C.S.

To Julia and Max—time to write more new chapters of our life together.

–M.Y.

Contents at a Glance

Table of Contents

Acknowledgments

We need to thank a huge number of people for helping us put this book together.

First, we'd like to thank our acquisitions editor, Danielle Bird Voeller, who worked very hard to get this book rolling. She introduced Brian and Marc to Bill Chiles, who in turn introduced us to Craig, which marked a turning point in our development of the book. Bill was absolutely tireless in his efforts to get us the information that we needed early on, and for that effort we are especially grateful.

We would also like to thank our project editor, Sally Stickney, for her work on this book. She's an excellent editor, but perhaps more important for us as writers, she's an outstanding teacher. Jack Beaudry worked as our technical editor and was instrumental in helping us hone the book into a complete, finished product. Ina Chang was our copyeditor. We're very grateful to her for turning our sometimes incoherent babbling into easy-to-understand, grammatically correct sentences. Tess McMillan put together the book's Web page, and Tim Kim tested our companion content installer. We'd also like to thank Michael Kloepfer for his work on the book's art and Jason E. Fish for taking our author photo.

Ken Hardy provided us with invaluable technical assistance and review. Kalpana Sanghrajka and Natalie Wells helped us highlight the most exciting user features of Microsoft Visual Studio .NET. In addition, we'd like to thank Greg DeCicco, Kipper York, Kenny Kerr, and Sam Henry for their assistance.

Finally, Brian and Marc would like to thank Mary DeJong for giving us the go-ahead to work on the book. Brian would like to thank his wife, Kathryn, for her help, support, and motivation through the whole process; Craig would like to thank his parents, his brother, and his friends for their support. Marc would like to thank the Big Bang, without which none of this would have been possible.

Introduction

In the fall of 2000, Marc Young and I (Brian Johnson) attended an event that introduced Microsoft Visual Studio .NET to computer writers and editors from around the world. We were both amazed to see how easy it was going to be to create Windows and Web applications using this tool in the context of the .NET Framework. As I watched the demonstrations, it became pretty clear to me that this new tool deserved a book of its own. I took a few notes and jotted down an outline for the book I had in mind. At the top of my outline, I wrote *Inside Visual Studio .NET*.

About a year later, I was still toying with the idea of writing this book, but other commitments were keeping me busy enough that I kept putting it off. One day, Marc asked me if I would be interested in doing some writing and I showed him the material I had put together for *Inside Visual Studio .NET*. I told him I was interested in writing about the Visual Studio .NET automation object model, about the IDE, and about the macros facility. Marc took this information and spent nearly every night for three or four months writing add-ins and getting to know the internal workings of the IDE.

In the spring of 2002, we took a proposal to our acquisitions editor, Danielle Bird Voeller, who got us in touch with a few people on the Visual Studio .NET team. The first person she introduced us to was Bill Chiles, a program manager responsible for many of the features that we were planning to write about.

Meeting Bill Chiles was probably the best thing that could have happened to us because he in turn introduced us to Craig Skibo. Craig is the developer who wrote most of the automation API that we cover in the book. Craig offered to help us out with the book as best he could. At some point in our early conversations with Craig, he told us that he was also working on a book about the automation object model. In fact, he had already written four chapters but wasn't sure he was ever going to have time to finish a book.

We read through Craig's chapters and found that they were exactly what we were looking for and asked him if he would be willing to become a coauthor with us on *Inside Microsoft Visual Studio .NET 2003*. He agreed, and Marc and I couldn't have been more pleased.

What you're reading now is the result of a very close collaboration between Craig, Marc, and me. What we wanted to produce was a book that would help developers to use Visual Studio .NET 2003 more effectively, to customize and extend the IDE, and finally, to see the tremendous productivity gains that they can expect by moving their development efforts to Visual Studio .NET 2003 and the .NET Framework.

Target Audience

The target audience for *Inside Microsoft Visual Studio .NET 2003* is any developer who is interested in learning the ins and outs of Visual Studio .NET. We wrote the book using Visual Studio .NET 2003, but nearly everything that we discuss in the book also applies to Visual Studio .NET 2002.

This book won't teach you programming, but it will help you understand the solution and project paradigm used to organize the application projects that you'll work with using Visual Studio .NET. That said, if you're a student who is just learning a programming language, you might find the initial chapters of the book very helpful as you go about programming in this IDE.

If you're interested in extending and customizing the Visual Studio .NET IDE, this book is for you.

Book Layout

Inside Microsoft Visual Studio .NET 2003 is divided into three parts:

- In Part I, Visual Studio .NET as a Development Tool, we discuss the Visual Studio .NET user experience and how developers can make the most of the features of the IDE to become as productive as possible. If you're a developer who is very experienced with the IDE, you can probably breeze through the first part of the book fairly quickly, though we've tried to add enough surprises so that most developers will learn something new for their efforts. The subjects covered in Part I include a discussion of the history of the IDE, managing solutions and projects, using the code editor, and an introduction to the macros facility.
- Part II of the book, Extending Visual Studio .NET, provides an in-depth discussion of Visual Studio .NET 2003 add-ins and the automation object model. In these chapters, you'll get an overview of the extensibility API, architectural information about add-ins and commands; a discussion of programmatic solution and project

management; and information about building Visual Studio .NET wizards, programming the Visual Studio .NET user interface, controlling the text editor, and using the code model to parse your source files.

- In Part III of the book, we grouped together a number of topics that tend not to get covered in most programming books because they're not usually central to the language that's discussed. These topics include an in-depth look at how to build deployment projects using the Visual Studio .NET Help facility and building your own Help into Visual Studio .NET. Finally, we devote some space to command-line options used to build and test Visual Studio .NET 2003 solutions and to using Microsoft Visual SourceSafe for version control.

The book also includes an appendix that provides you with some reference material for the code object model discussed in Chapter 12.

Companion Content

You can find the book's companion content on the Web at *http://www.microsoft.com/mspress/books/6425.asp*. Click the Companion Content link in the More Information box to bring up the companion content page. From this page, you can download the installer for the sample files. The installer was written using Visual Studio .NET, as described in Chapter 13 of the book. This installer places a number of files on your machine in specific places. For example, utility code is added to the Program Files\Microsoft Visual Studio .NET 2003\Common7\IDE\PublicAssemblies folder, sample code is installed in My Documents\Microsoft Press\InsideVSNET, and macros are placed in your Visual Studio .NET 2003 macros directory to make them available to you as you read and work through the book. You can uninstall the samples and utilities from Add Or Remove Programs in Control Panel. The Web page for the companion contents includes more details about what gets installed on your machine.

> **Note** We wrote the samples in this book specifically for Visual Studio .NET 2003, but most of the projects will work if you create new project files and import the source back into Visual Studio .NET 2002. We can't make any promises about what will work in Visual Studio .NET 2002, but most of the examples should give you little trouble. We recommend upgrading if you're able to do so.

System Requirements

You can use any system that will run Visual Studio .NET 2003 efficiently to build and run most of the most of the examples in the book. We targeted Visual Studio .NET 2003 Professional Edition, so if you have that, it should be enough. If you're using one of the standard edition products such as Visual C# .NET, Visual Basic .NET, or Visual C++ .NET, all of the macros discussed in the book should work, but because we wrote the add-ins in all three languages, you'll need the language specific to a particular add-in to compile.

Tracking Down an Author

If you have comments about the book, feel free to send them along to me at *brianjjo@hotmail.com*. I most likely won't be able to answer technical questions regarding building your add-ins, but I would like to get any feedback or suggestions that you have for future editions of the book. For announcements about changes to source code, please feel free to subscribe to the MSN community at *http://groups.msn.com/insidevsnet/*. For bug reports, please use the Microsoft Press Support information in the next section.

If you have technical questions about using Visual Studio .NET, writing macros, or building your add-ins, the best place to ask is probably in one of Microsoft's newsgroups. The server is *news://msnews.microsoft.com*, and the Visual Studio .NET groups all begin with *microsoft.public.vsnet*. In addition, there's a Yahoo group devoted to add-ins at *http://groups.yahoo.com/group/vsnetaddin/* that all three of us monitor regularly.

Microsoft Press Support

Every effort has been made to ensure the accuracy of the book and it's companion content. Microsoft Press also provides corrections for books through the World Wide Web at the following address:

http://www.microsoft.com/mspress/support/

To query the Knowledge Base for book and companion content corrections, visit *http://www.microsoft.com/mspress/support/search.asp*.

In addition to sending feedback directly to the authors, if you have comments, questions, or ideas regarding the presentation or use of this book or the companion content, you can send them to Microsoft using either of the following methods:

Postal Mail:
Microsoft Press
Attn: Inside Microsoft Visual Studio .NET 2003 Editor
One Microsoft Way
Redmond, WA 98052-6399

E-mail:
mspinput@microsoft.com

Please note that product support isn't offered through the above mail addresses. For support information regarding Microsoft Visual Studio .NET 2003, go to *http://msdn.microsoft.com/vstudio/*. You can also call Standard Support at (425) 635-7011 weekdays between 6 a.m. and 6 p.m. Pacific time, or you can search Microsoft's Support Online at http://support.microsoft.com/support.

Part I

Visual Studio .NET as a Development Tool

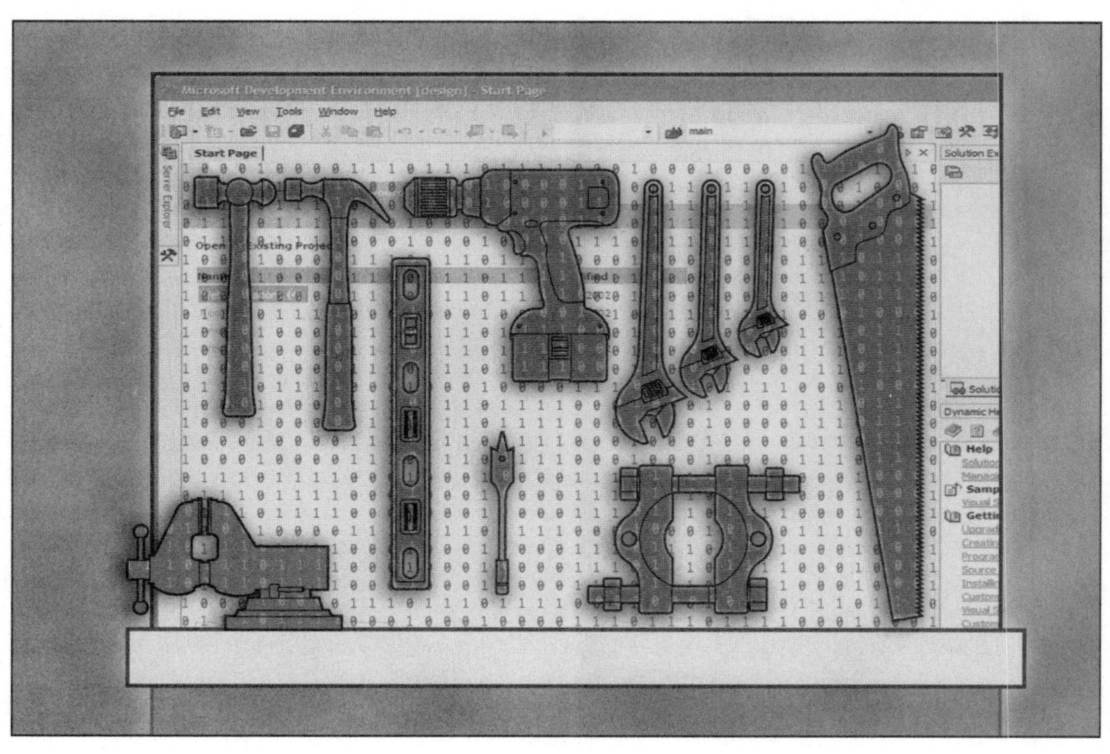

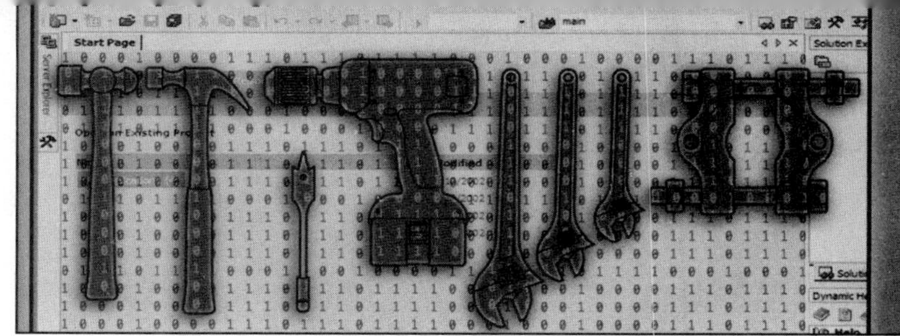

1

The Evolution of Visual Studio .NET

The normal development cycle for a Microsoft product is about two years. Microsoft Visual Studio .NET, which was released in February 2002, took more than three years to develop. The reason this product revision took longer than usual was .NET, Microsoft's technology for managed applications and XML Web services, which was also released in 2002. Visual Studio .NET 2003, the focus of this book, was released nearly a year after .NET. It was revised to be released in tandem with Microsoft .NET Server 2003; both use the .NET Framework version 1.1.

In this chapter, we'll provide a brief overview of .NET and unmanaged development in Visual Studio .NET. We'll then introduce some of the features of the integrated development environment (IDE) to provide some context for the extensibility and customization discussion throughout the rest of the book. And finally, we'll discuss the extensibility features that make Visual Studio .NET an extremely compelling tool for programmers who are really looking to customize and extend their development environment.

Moving to Visual Studio .NET

The evolution of development tools at Microsoft has always been focused on emerging technologies. The release of a new tool is often concurrent with the introduction and release of a new technology. In 1993, Microsoft C/C++ was at version 7 when Microsoft introduced Visual C++ 1.0. Microsoft C/C++ was a truly refined MS-DOS product. In fact, Microsoft C/C++ was so refined that a good number of programmers were reluctant to upgrade to Visual C++. In the end, though, the fully Windows-hosted IDE with its integrated editor, debugger, build engine, and source browser made Visual C++ a compelling upgrade. The introduction of the Microsoft Foundation Classes (MFC) 2.0 in Visual C++ also helped to further boost the product's popularity. Visual C++ made it possible to quickly create Win32 and MFC-based Windows applications without having to pop in and out of MS-DOS. Looking back, this made perfect sense: using a Windows application to build Windows applications. But back then, the logic wasn't quite as clear.

Fast-forward about nine years, to the introduction of .NET. This technology makes it possible to deploy extremely efficient managed applications and XML-based Web services. At the .NET launch, Visual Studio, which was first released in 1998, was at version 6. This tool, which is really a combination of products—Visual C++, Visual Basic, Visual InterDev, and Visual J++—is the most popular application development suite on the planet. Visual Studio 6 does it all. It targets Win32, MFC, COM, ActiveX, Active Template Library (ATL), Java, DirectX, and the Web; if you can do it in Windows, you can probably build it in Visual Studio 6. Again, we had a very mature product with an extremely loyal following. Visual Studio 6 is to Visual Studio .NET what Microsoft C/C++ was to Visual C++ 1.0. In retrospect, it's easy to see why developers migrated from MS-DOS-based tools to Windows-based tools. Because the XML Web services infrastructure is still being built out, it might be less apparent why a move to .NET and Visual Studio .NET is needed.

To answer that question, we should probably talk about what makes .NET an attractive technology for developers and why Visual Studio .NET is the right tool to use for targeting that environment.

Developing for .NET

When we were all developing programs in MS-DOS, you could look at a Windows 3.1 screen and see that this was how computing was supposed to be: lots of color, beautiful fonts, and a high-resolution windowing system that took care of most of the nasty stuff that made MS-DOS development hard. Because the differences are more architectural than visual, it's a little more difficult to see the advantages of .NET, but for developers, most of the features of .NET are at least as compelling as those of Windows compared to MS-DOS.

One purpose of the .NET Framework is to simplify application development and deployment in the distributed Internet environment. This extends to applications that are run locally or remotely or that are distributed over the Internet. This simplification is achieved through a common language runtime (CLR) that provides a managed execution environment available to any language that targets the runtime. The functionality this execution environment provides is made available to these languages through the .NET Framework class library. Figure 1-1 illustrates how the CLR relates to the .NET Framework.

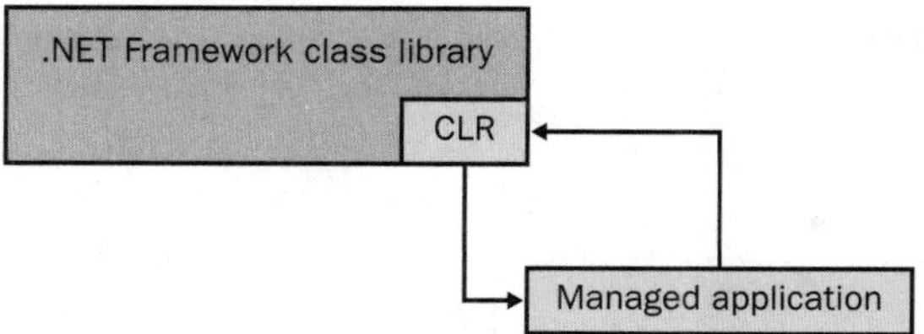

Figure 1-1 The CLR and the .NET Framework class library are the two major components of the .NET Framework.

The Common Language Specification (CLS) defines what a .NET-compliant language must provide to the system. The common type system (CTS) ensures that any types created by a language conforming to the CLS can be consumed by any other CLS-compliant language.

Languages that target the CLR are compiled to Microsoft Intermediate Language (MSIL). These applications are compiled as PE (portable executable) files and DLLs, so to users they look just like any Windows-based applications. The MSIL code in these files is then JIT-compiled to machine instructions locally at run time. All of this means that any CLS-compliant language that targets the CLR will look like any other language to the runtime and can act and be treated as a first-class citizen. For example, a Visual Basic .NET program will have the same base functionality as a Visual C# program or even a managed C++ program.

> **Tip** For a detailed look at the architecture of .NET, take a look at *Applied Microsoft .NET Framework Programming* by Jeffrey Richter (Microsoft Press, 2002).

The managed CLR environment provides some other significant advantages. It's designed to help eliminate versioning conflicts—the infamous DLL Hell. It's designed to provide an environment that ensures that code is executed safely. And finally, it's designed with an API that is targetable from both Windows-based and Web-based applications.

You don't need to think about the .NET Framework as a monolithic virtual machine that requires constant care and feeding. The .NET Framework provides an environment that can be hosted by unmanaged components. The unmanaged components (such as Internet Explorer and the ASP.NET runtime) load the CLR and execute the managed code. The managed CLR provides garbage-collection services and security on a number of levels.

For corporate developers, this runtime solves a huge problem. In many shops, the Visual Basic programmers, the C/C++ programmers, and the COBOL programmers are all segregated. They meet to figure out how to functionally interoperate, but in a number of ways they work as individual teams inside the same space. In a shop that targets the CLR, development becomes a little more manageable. The same .NET Framework class library is available across languages. The CTS in the class library ensures that components can be easily shared between .NET languages, as shown in Figure 1-2. These components can even be exposed as XML Web services.

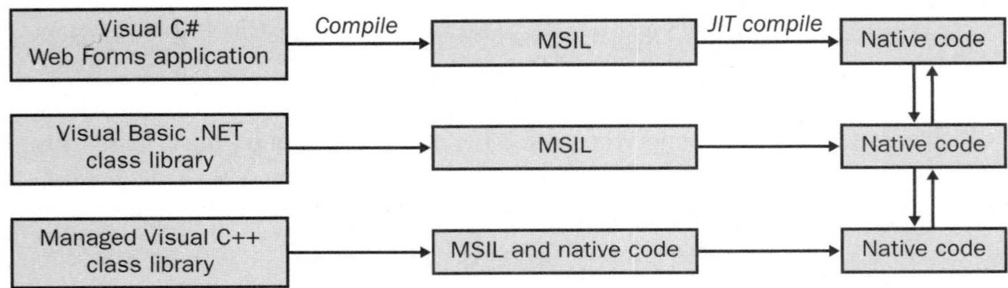

Figure 1-2 .NET allows different languages to target a managed environment and to interoperate securely and efficiently.

The CLR provides a target that's available from most of the major programming languages used today. Visual Studio .NET has support for Visual C++, Visual Basic .NET, Visual J# .NET, and Visual C# out of the box. You can add support for a growing number of languages that are available from third-party software vendors, including COBOL, Eiffel, Python, and Perl.

Unmanaged Development Enhancements

For Visual C++ programmers writing unmanaged code, Visual Studio .NET offers enhancements that make it a good upgrade. We'll discuss the IDE-specific features a bit later in the chapter. Here, we'll give a brief overview of the version 7 compiler and library features.

New Compiler Options

Visual C++ .NET, the C++ component of Visual Studio .NET, has been enhanced in a number of ways to help C++ programmers write robust, secure, and efficient code. Much of this improved functionality has been achieved through the version 7.1 compiler. Microsoft has added 17 new compiler switches and 12 new linker switches to Visual C++ .NET. The following are some of the more compelling new compiler switches. Even without the new features of the IDE and .NET, for some developers these enhancements alone would justify an upgrade.

Code optimization: */GL* The */GL* switch performs whole-program optimization on a project. This optimization usually results in measurable performance improvements, but you should be sure to read the cautionary notes in the documentation regarding the use of this switch.

What the */GL* switch essentially does is optimize the whole program based on information from each of the modules. This type of optimization allows for the use of registers across function boundaries. It also allows for the generation of inline functions, even when the functions are defined in separate modules.

> **Note** When the compiler team at Microsoft tests switches such as this internally, they're actually able to do so against real-world code. For example, they used the */GL* switch on the game engine that Ensemble Studios uses in the Age of Empires titles. This switch produced a 10 percent increase in the performance of the engine.

Buffer overrun checks: */GS* Nearly any application you write today has the potential to be used over the Internet. The most common technique for exploiting applications over the Internet is the buffer overrun. When a hacker takes advantage of a buffer overrun, he uses memory past the boundary that the function's programmer thought would be necessary for the execution of the routine. All a hacker needs is a tiny bit of space to enter some assembly code, and then he can usually call any function that's available to the hacked program. The */GS* compiler switch can help prevent this sort of compromise by injecting security checks into the target modules at compile time.

The security code works by allocating some memory on the stack just before a function's return address. When the function is entered, a security cookie is placed in that space. When the function is exited, the cookie is checked; if it's been changed, a security error handling routine kicks in. By default, this means that the user is notified of the potential compromise and the process is exited. You can change this default behavior of the error handling routine using the *_set_security_error_handler* function.

> **Note** When I was tech editing the second edition of *Writing Secure Code*, I ran across a slight problem with the samples designed to demonstrate buffer overruns. I was using Visual Studio .NET and I found that I couldn't duplicate the examples in the way described. As you can guess, the checks that were set by default in version 7 of the compiler were blocking the buffer overrun hacks. It's fairly clear that without even trying, code compiled in Visual Studio .NET will be safer code. There's no panacea for preventing security problems in code, but Visual C++ .NET can get you off to a pretty good start.

Run-time error checks: /*RTCn* The run-time error checks are designed to help you catch bugs that are normally hard to detect. The */RTCn* switches help you detect problems with stack corruption (*/RTCs*), dependencies on uninitialized variables (*/RTCu*), and data loss that can occur when you assign larger data to a smaller variable and array overruns (*/RTCc*).

Like the */GS* switch, the run-time error checks inject code at compile time. The /RTC*n* switches aren't used with optimized */O* builds, and you'll get an error if you try. The /RTC*n* switches have integrated support in the Visual Studio .NET debugger. If a run-time error check condition is detected, the application will break into the debugger by default.

You can set any of these compiler switches inside the Visual Studio .NET IDE through the Property Pages dialog box available from Solution Explorer. Just right-click on the project you want to set the options for, and choose Properties. We'll discuss the project's Property Pages dialog box in more detail in Chapter 2.

Updated Class Libraries

Visual C/C++ .NET lets developers continue to use the class libraries that they've targeted over the years. Microsoft has stated that it is committed to supporting developers who use the unmanaged class libraries that ship with Visual Studio .NET for the foreseeable future. This support includes updates for future versions of Windows.

Note Microsoft is also moving to managed code internally at a fairly rapid pace. We encourage you to learn and explore the .NET Framework because it is destined to become the native API for Windows-based applications.

The major class libraries that ship with Visual Studio .NET have been versioned to match the build number of Visual Studio .NET, so these libraries are now at version 7. These libraries include MFC 7, which features native support for Windows XP, Windows 2000, and ATL 7. A new MFC feature is DHTML dialog boxes, which allow you to create active, compelling dialog boxes for your MFC applications. Finally, ATL and MFC now share some commonly used classes, such as *CString*, that allow ATL programmers to take advantage of MFC functionality without having to load all of MFC.

A new feature of ATL is ATL Server. ATL Server is used to create high-performance, ISAPI-based Web applications and XML Web services. You can use ATL Server to build unmanaged XML Web services solutions or to integrate legacy ATL code into your .NET solutions.

Other class libraries that have been updated include the Standard Template Library (STL) and the C runtime (CRT).

C++ Attributes

C++ attributes allow programmers to add Interface Definition Language (IDL)–style attributes to C++ source files. These attributes are different from the attributes that you can add to managed code. Attributes reduce the amount of code that you have to write by hand by providing specific ATL functionality that the compiler emits when the application is built.

Standards Conformance

Something that the Visual C++ team has worked extremely hard on over the last couple of years is ANSI/ISO C++ standards compliance. In Visual C++ .NET 2003, the C++ compiler has reached a compliance level of more than 98 percent, making this compiler one of the most standards-compliant you can buy.

A New IDE

Microsoft's shift to .NET has required a new set of tools to make it easy for developers to target the environment. Visual Studio .NET provides a number of compelling features for developers who are writing code and for Windows and Web developers moving to .NET.

First, Visual Studio .NET unifies the IDEs of the major languages that were available in Visual Studio 6. Developers can now move freely between the different languages hosted by the same IDE. Developers working in different languages in Visual Studio .NET can work together more seamlessly and efficiently than they've ever been able to.

Second, the languages that ship with Visual Studio .NET are all able to target the CLR. More specifically, Visual Basic .NET and Visual C# both target the CLR exclusively. Visual C++ .NET can target both the managed CLR and the unmanaged Windows environment. Because all .NET code eventually becomes MSIL and then JIT-compiled binaries, the runtime operates in basically the same way whether you're working in Visual C# or Visual Basic .NET. It might be easier for certain languages to access functions outside the CLR, but languages that target the CLR are functionally virtually identical. Developers are acutely aware of the language chauvinism that tends to exist between programmers who specialize in one language or another. With .NET, those lines start to blur and can cause developers to see a once-dismissed language in a whole new light.

Finally, Visual Studio .NET provides editing and extensibility features that make this IDE a best-of-class tool, regardless of the target platform. The advanced features built into the designers and editors in Visual Studio .NET make creating Windows-based and Web applications a breeze. A managed-code macros facility and IDE make recording and running macros easy and seamless. And an updated extensibility API exposes parts of the IDE that have never before been available to Visual Studio developers.

Visual Studio .NET Features

In this section, we'll present an overview of the Visual Studio .NET feature set. We'll look at some of these features in more detail in the next few chapters of the book. Here we'll define some common terms that we can use to describe the different parts of the IDE. Visual Studio .NET is a fairly large and complex product. The terms used to describe the IDE are helpful for developers who are working to understand the tool and, perhaps more important, for developers who will eventually extend the IDE through macros and add-ins.

Editors, Designers, and Tool Windows

The windows in the Visual Studio .NET IDE fall into two major groups. *Document windows* are windows that usually appear tabbed in the center of the IDE and that contain editors, designers, Web pages, or Help topics. *Tool windows* are windows in the IDE that present utility functions to the programmer. The tool windows include Solution Explorer, the Class View window, and the Properties window, among others. Tool windows are distinct from editors and designers in the way they dock around the sides of the IDE.

> **Note** The extensibility API built in to Visual Studio .NET allows programmers to create tool windows for use with language packages installed into the IDE. The editors and designers in the IDE can be accessed through this API, but the extensibility model doesn't allow the creation of new document window types. For that you'll need to look into the Visual Studio Integration Program (VSIP), which we'll describe at the end of this chapter.

Figure 1-3 shows a typical developer setup with the different window types labeled.

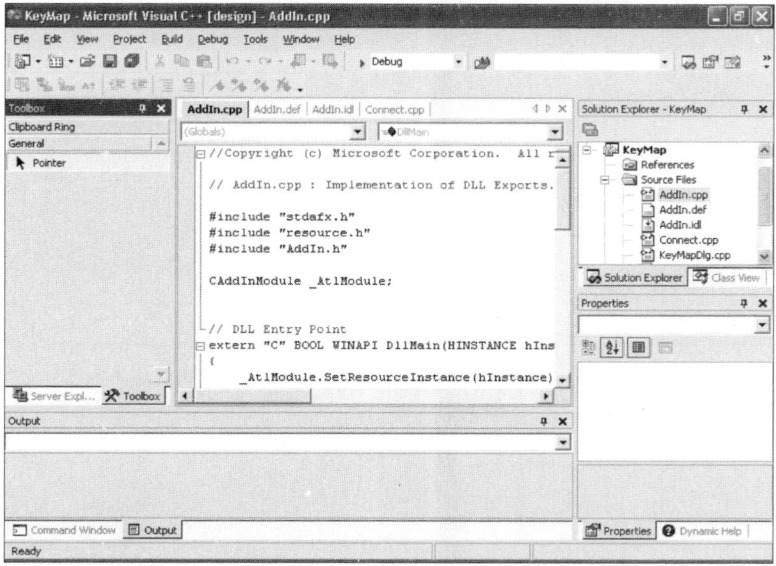

Figure 1-3 A typical solution in Visual Studio .NET

> **Note** All of the managed languages that ship with Visual Studio .NET 2003 feature designer support in the IDE.

The Start Page

The first time you run Visual Studio .NET, you're presented with a Start Page open to the My Profile tab, as shown in Figure 1-4. A profile is a window, keyboard, and Help layout that's tailored to a specific type of programmer. The My Profile tab allows you to select the profile that best describes the type of programmer that you are and to apply those characteristics to the IDE. In general, this page is designed to help you apply a window and keyboard layout that lets you easily transition from your preferred Visual Studio 6 language into Visual Studio .NET. If you're moving to .NET from Visual Studio 6, it's probably worth your time to spend a few minutes viewing the available profiles.

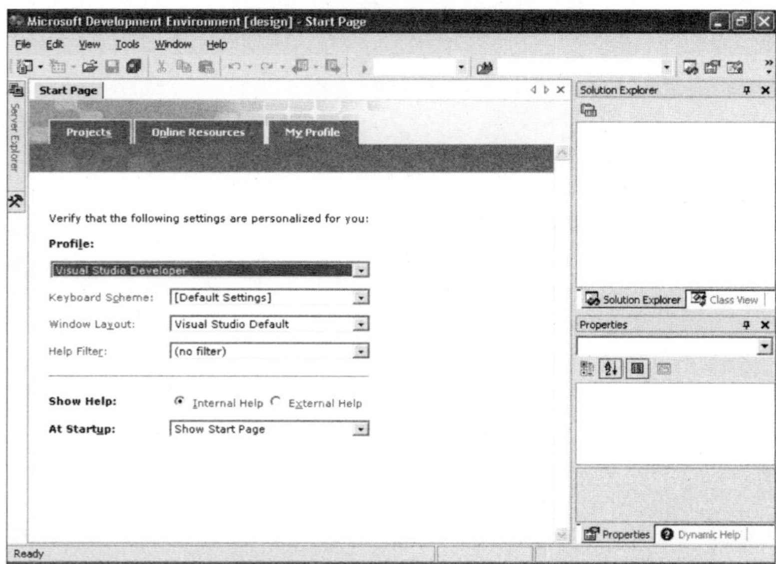

Figure 1-4 Setting the preferred initial profile from the Visual Studio .NET Start Page

Tip If you can live with it, we suggest going with the default Visual Studio Developer profile. You'll find that most of the books on Visual Studio .NET use this profile and that it lays out the various tool windows in a logical, efficient manner. You'll probably also find yourself spending less time messing with the layout as you rebuild machines and move from one machine to another in your work environment.

In addition to affecting the window layout, the profile you choose affects the keyboard shortcuts that are set in the IDE. For the most part, you'll find that the Visual Basic 6 and Visual InterDev shortcuts have been employed in the appropriate profiles. If you're a C++ programmer who's used to the keystrokes in Visual C++ 6, you might notice some changes that can affect the way you work. For example, in the Visual Studio Developer profile, the Alt+7 Disassembly window keystroke is replaced with Ctrl+Alt+D. If you're finding that the keystrokes you're used to aren't doing what you want in the IDE, we suggest you check the profile you're using and adjust the Keyboard Scheme setting accordingly. In Chapter 3, we'll discuss customizing and saving a keyboard mapping scheme.

Lab: Using a Custom Profile in a Macro

As you delve into Visual Studio .NET extensibility, you'll use the Macros IDE a lot to experiment with the Visual Studio .NET extensibility APIs. We'll discuss macros in detail in Chapter 4, but let's take a minute to try out the macros facility right now. To get started, press Alt+F11 to open the Macros IDE. Take a look in the Project Explorer tool window in the Macros IDE. If you installed the samples for this book, you should see a Macros project named InsideVSNET. In that project, you'll find a module named Samples, which contains macros that demonstrate concepts described in the book.

In this case, the macro we're going to run is named *AutoHideToggle*. What *AutoHideToggle* does is to toggle the state of the tool windows in Visual Studio .NET. It does this by calling the *Window.AutoHideAll* named command that's available from the Visual Studio .NET main menu.

The problem with calling *Window.AutoHideAll* is that there's no *Window.AutoUnhideAll* command, so you have to reset the window layout using the Reset Window Layout button in the Options dialog box,reselect your profile from the My Profile tab on the Start Page, or tack open the tool windows you want to see by hand. Our little macro takes care of all this in true hacker style.

We want to keep our carefully customized window layout, so we'll create a temporary profile that stores the positions of all the open tool windows. We'll do this through the *DTE.WindowConfigurations* object. Our macro will then apply this profile and call the *Window.AutoHideAll* named command. To get back to where we were, we'll check whether the temporary configuration is the active configuration. If it is, we'll use *Apply* again, which will load all the tool windows back into place.

Here's the code:

```
Sub AutoHideToggle()
    Static aTemp As WindowConfiguration = Nothing
    Dim cmdobj As Command
    ' Create a variable to hold the AutoHideAll command.
    cmdobj = DTE.Commands.Item("Window.AutoHideAll")
    With DTE.WindowConfigurations
        ' Check if whether we're using our temporary configuration.
        ' If we aren't create one and save it out.
        If aTemp Is Nothing Then
            ' If we're not in the aTemp config, create a new
            ' aTemp and apply it to save it.
            aTemp = .Add("aTemp")
            aTemp.Apply()
            ' Call AutoHideAll.
            DTE.Commands.Raise(cmdobj.Guid, cmdobj.ID, Nothing, Nothing)
        Else
            ' The second time this is run, the windows are put back
            ' the way they were the first time it was run.
            aTemp.Apply()
            aTemp = Nothing
        End If
    End With
End Sub
```

When you run this macro, you'll notice that it works but that it might be too painfully slow to use. (Then again, it's no slower than getting things back together by hand, so go ahead and use it if you feel so inclined.) What it's doing is loading the configuration profile a number of times (whenever the *Apply* method is called). In Chapter 4 we'll show you how to speed up this little macro by turning it into an add-in. Chapter 3 provides some techniques you can use to make this macro accessible through a menu command or a keyboard shortcut.

The Help Filter setting lets you filter the information that the Visual Studio .NET Help system presents to you by default as you work. If you're a specific type of developer, such as an MFC or ATL C++ programmer, you can save some time and clock cycles by having Visual Studio .NET filter the Help to the main topics you're interested in. The Help Filter setting affects the Filtered By combo box in the Search window, making what you set on the My Profile tab the default. We'll explain how you can create your own custom Help filters in Chapter 14.

The final option on the My Profile page sets the way that Visual Studio .NET opens when you run the program. If you set At Startup to Show Start Page (the default), you'll get the Get Started tab on the Start page when the IDE loads. The Start Page offers some compelling features, but it's not everyone's cup of tea. Keep in mind that this option is enabled in every profile and that if you want to change how the IDE loads, you must set this option separately.

The Editor

In talking with members of the team that developed the base editor in Visual Studio .NET, it's clear that they understand that programmers live in the editor. It's where the most important programming work is done. To this end, the Visual Studio .NET team worked hard to create a code editor that's on par with the best commercial and free editors available today. To a great extent, they have succeeded in this goal, largely due to new enhancements to the macros facility. These enhancements include an extremely powerful extensibility model, a new macro recording facility, and a dedicated Macros IDE. The Visual Studio .NET extensibility model is a major focus of the book because it's what we use to customize and to add functionality to the IDE.

Other new features in the editor include outlining, line numbering, and a really outstanding search and replace facility, all of which are discussed in detail in Chapter 3.

Designers

Visual Studio .NET offers four major types of designers: Windows Forms designers, which let you create Windows Forms applications visually; Web Forms designers, which help you create WYSIWYG ASP.NET Web Forms applications; the Component Designer, which is used to build server-side components for enterprise solutions; and the XML Designer, which makes it easy for programmers to work with XML Schema Definition (XSD) files.

In Visual Studio .NET 2003, all languages provide designers for .NET application creation. This means that you can design your Windows Forms and Web Forms in the same language you use to write your most important algorithms. In the past, it was common for developers to create the front end of their application using a visual tool such as Visual Basic and to write the back end in Visual C++. Because of the way that .NET assemblies interoperate, you're still free to do your forms layout and library writing in different languages, but you're no longer forced to work that way.

Tool Windows

Tool windows are the nondocument windows in the IDE that provide you with information and utility functionality as you work. The IDE has a large number of tool windows, and you can access them easily using keyboard shortcuts, the Command Window, and menu commands. The following are the most commonly used tool windows in Visual Studio .NET. These tool windows are presented with their associated default keyboard shortcuts.

Solution Explorer (Ctrl+Alt+L) The Solution Explorer window is arguably the most important tool window in Visual Studio .NET. In Visual Studio .NET, nearly all the work done by a programmer revolves around a solution. A solution is a collection of projects, which are themselves collections of files. It's through Solution Explorer that you'll get access to the files in your projects. Here you'll add new classes and files to projects, and even new projects to larger solutions. Figure 1-5 shows a project in the Solution Explorer tool window.

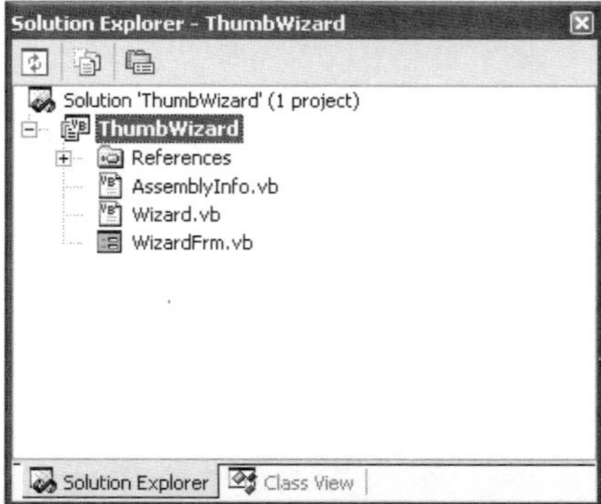

Figure 1-5 A managed project in Solution Explorer

Class View (Ctrl+Shift+C) The Class View window provides you with a hierarchical view of the classes in your solution. If you're working with larger projects, you might find it easier to navigate your solutions using Class View than using Solution Explorer. Figure 1-6 shows the extensibility solution from Figure 1-5 in Class View.

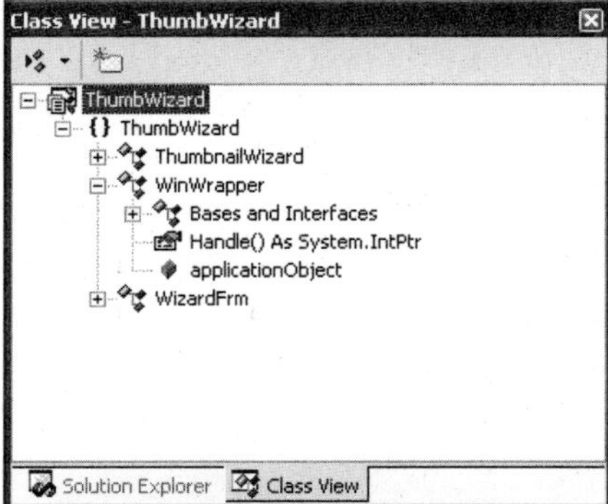

Figure 1-6 The Class View window gives you an alternative view of the objects in your solution.

Properties window (F4) In the Properties window, you can get and set properties for the user interface items that you add to Windows Forms and Web Forms applications. You can also use this window to set properties for solutions, projects, and files that you have selected in Solution Explorer. Figure 1-7 shows the Properties window for a setup project that's part of an extensibility solution.

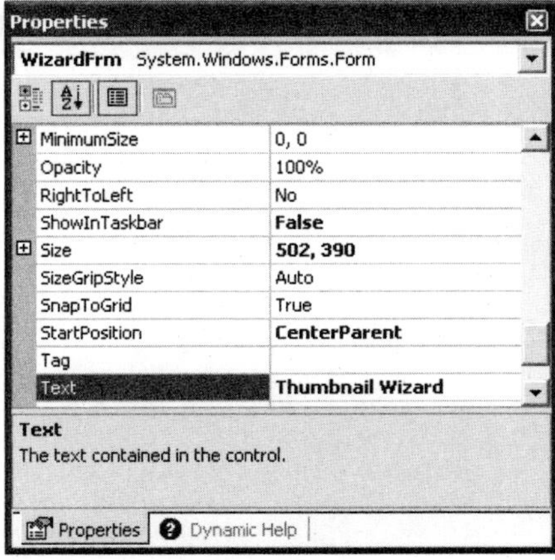

Figure 1-7 You can use the Properties window to set properties of components, projects, and solutions.

Server Explorer (Ctrl+Alt+S) You use the Server Explorer tool window to access data sources and information on your local machine and on remote servers. Through this window, you can make data connections, access performance counters and event logs, and even manage system services. Even when used locally, this tool can save you a ton of time, letting you easily start and stop system services that you're testing and access system logs. In Figure 1-8, you can see two machines available in Server Explorer. The first machine is the local machine on which Visual Studio .NET is running. The second machine is a remote test server.

> **Note** Keep in mind that you'll need the proper level of access on a particular server to access system information.

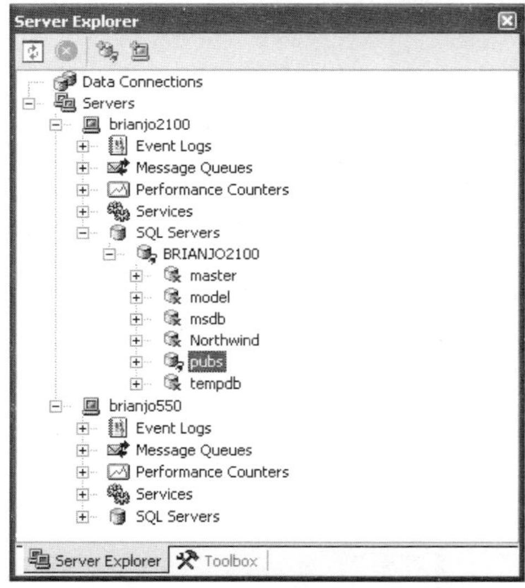

Figure 1-8 The Server Explorer window provides you with remote access to the machines you're working with.

Toolbox (Ctrl+Alt+X) For the most part, the Visual Studio .NET Toolbox window is used to hold the controls that you add to your Windows Forms and Web Forms applications. That part is probably fairly familiar to you. What you might not be aware of is that you can use the Toolbox to hold code fragments that you use frequently or fragments you want to keep as you read through the Help files or Web pages. The Clipboard Ring makes it possible for you to go back and access previously copied text. You can add your own custom tabs to the Toolbox to help organize your code and controls. You can see a custom tab in the Toolbox in Figure 1-9. This tab is installed by the Visual Studio .NET guided tour (available from *http://msdn.microsoft.com/vstudio/productinfo/tour.asp*).

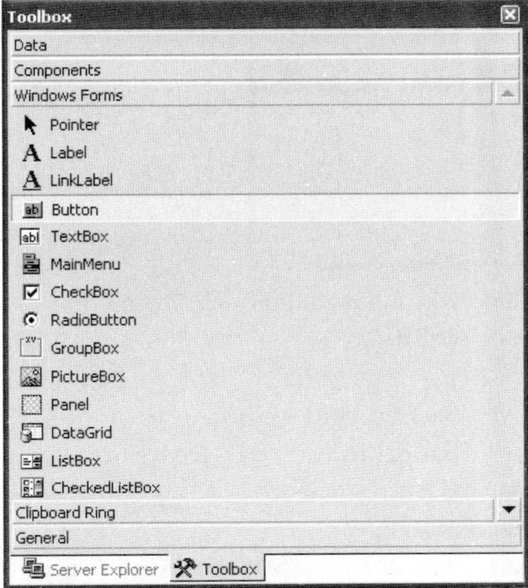

Figure 1-9 The Toolbox window gives you access to controls and code snippets.

Command Window (Ctrl+Alt+A) The Command Window is a new feature of Visual Studio .NET. It combines some of the best features of the Immediate window from Visual Basic with the power of a command line. Chapter 2 covers the Command Window in detail. You use the Command Window to enter and execute *named commands* directly in Visual Studio .NET. A named command is essentially any IDE command that you can run through a menu, toolbar button, or shortcut. Many of the named commands in Visual Studio .NET aren't mapped to a keystroke or available through a menu by default. The only way to access these commands without mapping them or adding them to a toolbar is to type them directly into the Command Window.

The Command Window has two modes of operation. In Command mode, the window acts as a command-line tool. In Immediate mode, the Command Window is used for debugging. In Immediate mode, you can execute statements, change variables and print their values, and evaluate expressions. To get to Immediate mode from Command mode, type **immed**. To get to Command mode from Immediate mode, type **>cmd**.

> **Tip** In Command mode, the > prompt will be visible on the line where you're typing in your commands. Immediate mode shows no prompt.

Figure 1-10 shows the Command Window in Command mode.

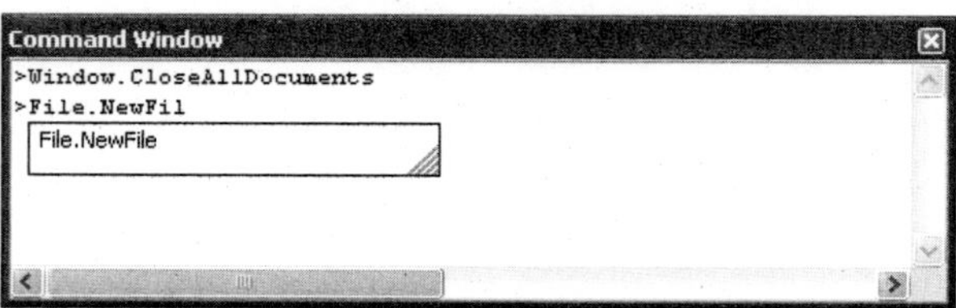

Figure 1-10 The Command Window in Visual Studio .NET provides easy access to named commands in the IDE.

Macro Explorer (Alt+F8) The Macro Explorer window provides a view of the macro projects that are currently loaded in the IDE. Keep in mind that a macro project needs to be loaded in order for the macros in the project to be available for use or for editing in the Macros IDE.

When you record a temporary macro by pressing Ctrl+Shift+R, that macro becomes available through the MyMacros\Recording Module\TemporaryMacro item in Macro Explorer. You can rename the temporary macro to save it, or you can copy the code from the macro into another module in the Macros IDE. We'll discuss using recorded macros in more detail in Chapter 4. The Macro Explorer window is shown in Figure 1-11.

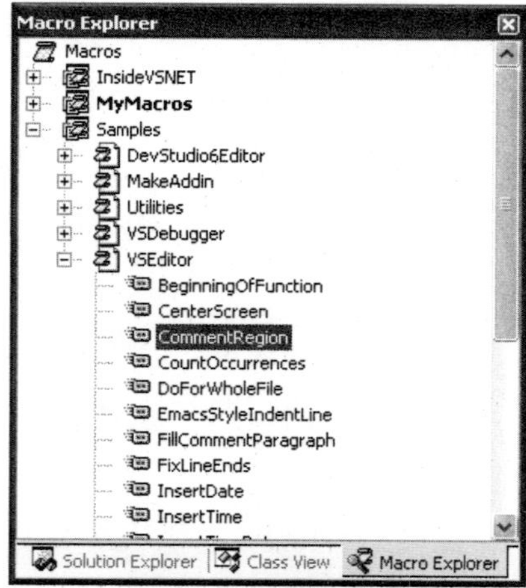

Figure 1-11 Macro Explorer gives you easy access to the macros available for use.

The IDE has a number of other important windows, which we'll talk about more fully in the next couple of chapters. Among these are the various debugging windows, the Help windows, and the Object Browser.

Visual Studio .NET File Paths

In this section, we'll tell you a little bit about where Visual Studio .NET places its important files. We'll cover this subject in more detail throughout the book, where it applies, but for now you should be aware of the locations of the files that you can manipulate to enhance the IDE and make automation a bit easier. The default base folder for the Visual Studio .NET 2003 installation is \Program Files\Microsoft Visual Studio .NET 2003. Most of the folders we'll talk about in this section are subfolders under the Microsoft Visual Studio .NET 2003 folder (unless we provide the full path).

Installing Visual Studio .NET also installs the .NET Framework SDK in the SDK\v1.1 subfolder. All the .NET Framework tools and samples are available in this folder, so it's a good place to start digging around if you're just getting to know .NET. Check out the StartHere.htm file in the SDK\v1.1 folder for the full story on the .NET Framework SDK.

The various languages that ship with Visual Studio .NET all have their own subfolders that contain the project and solution templates for their respective project types. These folders are all named appropriately. Visual C++–specific files are found in VC7, C#-specific files are in VC#, and Visual Basic .NET files are in Vb7. We'll use these folders to create and add custom projects to the various languages in the IDE.

> **Tip** You'll notice a file named Samples.vsmacros in the IDE folder. The sample macros for Visual Studio .NET that run in your IDE are actually stored in your My Documents\Visual Studio Project\VSMacros folder. The version in the IDE folder is a backup copy. You can edit the Samples.vsmacros file in your My Documents\Visual Studio Project\VSMacros\Samples folder, but try to keep the version in your IDE folder clean. If you ever run into a macro corruption problem, you can usually copy the Samples.vsmacros file from your IDE folder to your VSMacros folder to get rid of the problem.

The IDE executable itself is Devenv.exe. This file is available in the Common7\IDE subfolder. The IDE folder contains a number of subfolders that you'll be using throughout the book. These folders include the PublicAssemblies and PrivateAssemblies folders, which you'll use to add custom assemblies that are available to macros in the IDE. You'll use the HTML folder to customize the Start Page. The templates for the macro projects are stored in the MacroProjectItems and MacroProjects folders. Generic item templates (those not associated with a particular project type) are stored in the NewFileItems and NewScriptItems folders.

Adding an IDE Folder Shortcut to Your Tools Menu

If you do a lot of extensibility work, you might want to add a shortcut to the IDE folder to your Visual Studio .NET Tools menu. To do this, follow these steps:

1. Press Ctrl+Alt+A to open the Command Window, and then type **Tools.ExternalTools**. This will open the External Tools dialog box.
2. Click Add to add a new tool to the menu, and type **IDE Folder** as the Title.
3. In the Command text box, type **Explorer.exe**.
4. In the Arguments text box, add the path to your Visual Studio .NET IDE subfolder. (This is usually C:\Program Files\Microsoft Visual Studio .NET 2003\Common7\IDE.)
5. Click OK.

If all that works, your IDE folder should open when you choose IDE Folder from the Tools menu. We'll use the External Tools feature to create some more time-saving shortcuts later in the book.

If you do command-line builds or if you simply like to work from the command line, you'll want to set environmental variables for Visual Studio .NET when you launch Cmd.exe. You have a couple of options for setting these variables. First, you can simply open the Start menu and choose the Visual Studio

.NET Command Prompt. You'll find that command prompt in the Visual Studio .NET Tools folder, which is in the Microsoft Visual Studio .NET 2003 folder.

> **Tip** We suggest pinning the Visual Studio .NET Command Prompt link to the Start menu so you'll have easy access to it as your primary command prompt.

The Visual Studio environmental variables are available in a file named vsvars32.bat, which is in the Common7\Tools subfolder. If you want access to these variables from every instance of Cmd.exe on your machine, you can add C:\Program Files\Microsoft Visual Studio .NET 2003\Common7\Tools to your system path. (Alternatively, you can copy this file to a folder in your path.) Then you can just type **vsvars32** from any command prompt and you'll have a Visual Studio .NET working environment from your current command prompt.

You can take this one step further by creating a Command item on the Tools menu. You create a new menu item from the External Tools dialog box by clicking Add, making the Title of the new item Command Prompt, and making the Command item cmd.exe. If you want, you can set the Initial Directory box to $(ProjectDir). Setting the Initial Directory to your project directory will open the command prompt to that directory. This can make it very convenient to work with your project files from the command line.

Finally, consider adding the Common7\IDE path to your system variables. The full path is C:\Program Files\Microsoft Visual Studio .NET 2003\Common7\IDE. This will make Devenv.exe available from any command prompt on your system. This path is added by the vsvars32.bat command, but sometimes you just need access to Devenv.exe.

> **Tip** Consider using Devenv over Notepad when you're editing files for command-line builds. Even though you might not get access to the build and project facility without a solution, you still have access to your custom tools and to your macros.

Visual Studio .NET Extensibility

Visual Studio .NET builds on an extensibility model that was first developed for Visual C++ 5. In Visual Studio .NET, the *DTE* object (*DTE* stands for Development Tools Extensibility) sits at the top level of an automation model that features nearly 200 objects.

The functionality provided by the DTE object model can be described as user-defined customization. The DTE API is available to developers who are programming macros, wizards, and add-ins. Even more functionality is exposed to commercial-language developers who are part of the Visual Studio Integration Program (VSIP). (We'll discuss this program in more detail shortly.)

The following sections describe the automation mechanisms available to developers who are customizing Visual Studio .NET.

Macros

The macros facility in Visual Studio .NET provides programmers with easy access to the features available through the automation APIs. The macros facility features its own Macro Explorer tool window (described earlier in the chapter), an extremely powerful macro recording facility, and a full-blown Macros IDE that is itself extensible through the DTE object model. We'll use macros to illustrate concepts relating to extensibility throughout the book. Chapter 4 covers creating and editing macros in the Macros IDE in detail.

Macros in Visual Studio .NET are written in Visual Basic .NET. Because the macros facility takes advantage of .NET, macro programmers have access to the entire .NET Framework as well as to custom assemblies built in any other .NET language.

To open the Macros IDE, just press Alt+F11 from inside Visual Studio .NET. The Macros IDE will open in a new window. The first thing you'll notice about the Macros IDE is that its layout is extremely similar to the layout of Visual Studio .NET itself. In fact, you'll find that most of the features available to you as a Visual Studio .NET programmer are available to you as a macro programmer.

Figure 1-12 shows the Macros IDE in its default layout. This layout features a Project Explorer window that shows all of your currently loaded macro projects.

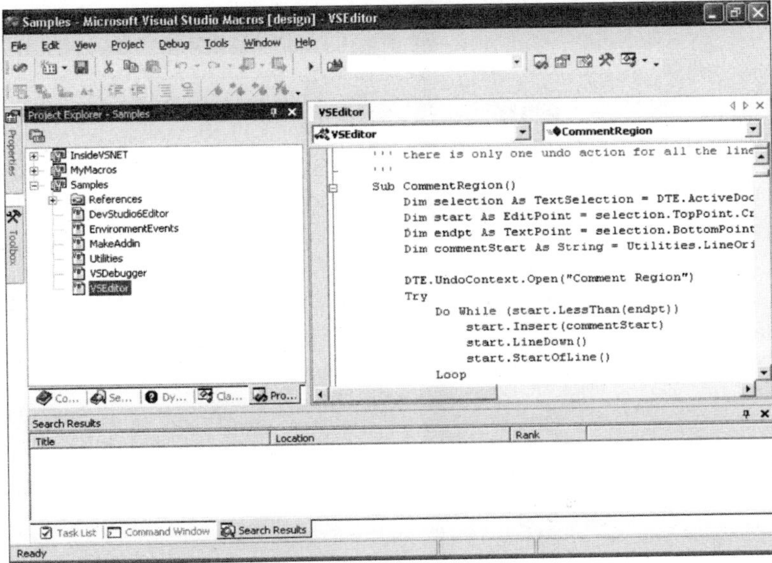

Figure 1-12 The Visual Studio .NET Macros IDE

Add-ins

Add-ins allow developers to create extensions to the Visual Studio .NET IDE and to the Macros IDE. In general, compiled add-ins provide better performance than Visual Studio .NET macros. Add-ins also provide functionality that integrates seamlessly into the environment. Independent software vendors (ISVs) and individual programmers can extend the IDE through add-ins in a way that makes the use of the add-in look just like a built-in part of the IDE.

Add-ins can be written in any .NET language, or they can be written as native COM components in unmanaged Visual C++. Add-ins are required to implement the *IDTExtensibility2* interface. Most of the add-in samples in this book will be shown in Visual C#. The book samples installed from the Web will be available in both C# and Visual Basic .NET.

Microsoft makes available a number of add-in samples that you can use to explore the extensibility object model or simply to add functionality to your Visual Studio .NET IDE. The samples are available at *http://msdn.microsoft.com/vstudio/downloads/automation.asp*. We'll use a few of these add-ins in the early chapters of the book to add specific features to Visual Studio .NET. Starting with Chapter 5, we'll provide all the details you need to build your own custom add-ins.

Wizards

Visual Studio .NET wizards are similar to add-ins, but they are created using the *ITDWizard* interface. Wizards are fairly simple constructions that are designed to take a user step by step through a specific task.

Wizards are used in Visual Studio .NET for a variety of purposes. Project wizards help get you started on a particular type of Visual Studio .NET project. Other wizards in the IDE, such as the MFC Event Handler Wizard shown in Figure 1-13, walk you through adding code to an existing project.

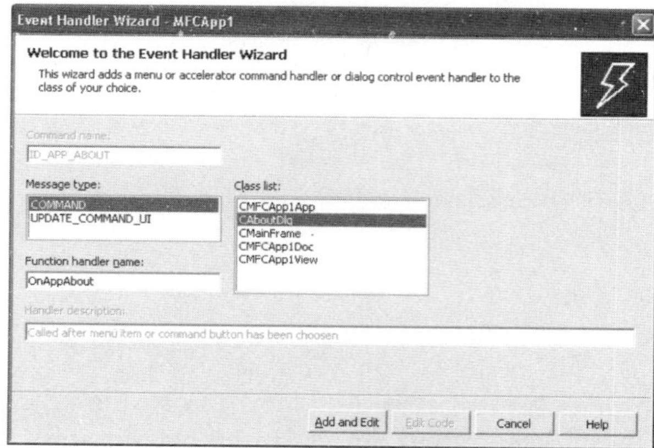

Figure 1-13 The Event Handler Wizard helps you add code to existing projects.

The Visual Studio Integration Program (VSIP)

We won't discuss VSIP much in this book because it's a specialized program with fairly substantial licensing fees. The program makes available to licensees APIs that are not part of the extensibility API discussed in this book. Developers who are part of the program can build custom editors and designers to integrate new .NET languages and high-end tools into the IDE.

Companies that make specific integrated products include ActiveState (makers of Visual Perl .NET and Visual Python .NET), Compuware (which makes DevPartner Profiler), and Fujitsu (which makes NetCOBOL for .NET).

You can find out more about VSIP at *http://msdn.microsoft.com/vstudio/vsip/*.

Looking Ahead

In Chapter 2, we'll continue our discussion of Visual Studio .NET, focusing on the project management facilities of the IDE. The chapter will provide some insight into one of the great strengths of Visual Studio .NET: the ability to host projects based on different programming languages in a single solution.

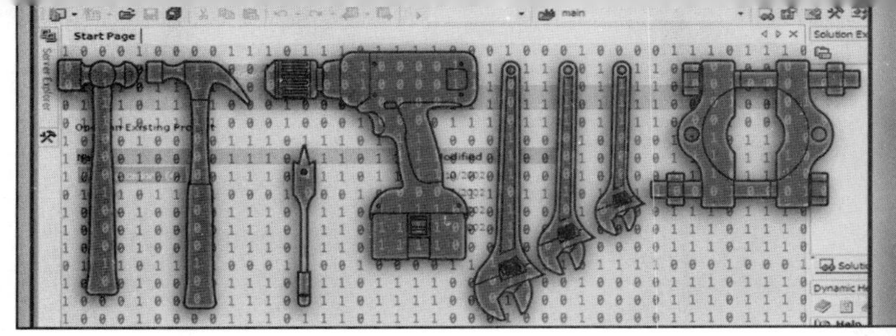

2

Project Management in Visual Studio .NET

Nearly everything you do in Microsoft Visual Studio .NET revolves around solutions and projects. In this chapter, we'll talk about solutions and projects in detail and give you a good handle on what those terms really mean. We'll also describe project management in Visual Studio .NET and explain how you can organize your software projects to maximize the features of the integrated development environment (IDE).

Overview of Solutions and Projects

Managing complex software projects can be a difficult and messy affair. Visual Studio .NET helps by organizing programming projects along the lines of solution (groups of projects) and projects and by handling references to assemblies and to components outside this structure. This organization and reference feature helps promote code reuse by allowing you to take advantage of related projects, existing assemblies, COM components, and source code. The easiest way to reuse .NET code is through references to assemblies in your projects and solutions.

> **Important** Visual Studio .NET organizes software projects on two conceptual levels. *Solutions* contain projects and solution items. *Projects* contain the source files that are compiled into executables and assemblies.

The most important tool for project management in Visual Studio .NET is Solution Explorer (Ctrl+Alt+L), shown in Figure 2-1. Solution Explorer is a tree-view window that provides access to all the projects and files that are part of the currently open solution. Visual Studio .NET can host one solution at a time, but you can run multiple instances of Visual Studio if you want to work with multiple solutions concurrently.

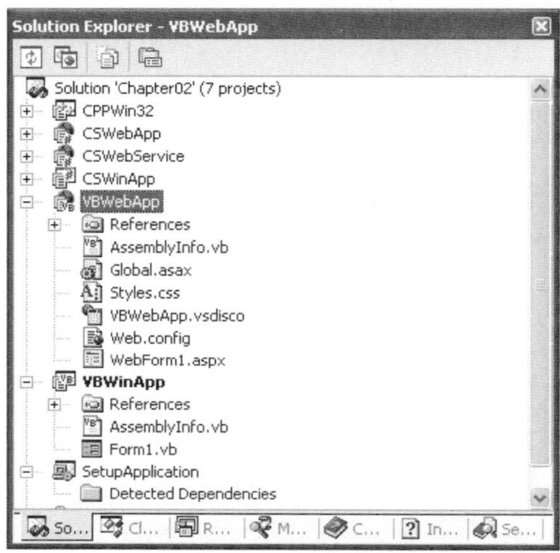

Figure 2-1 Solutions act as containers for projects and solution items.

Most new projects in Visual Studio .NET are created using a template developed by a language integrator. For example, Visual Studio .NET 2003 ships with support for Microsoft Visual Basic .NET, Visual C#, Visual J#, and Visual C++ .NET. Each of these languages features a number of project types that programmers can choose from when creating a new project. A new project is created as part of a new solution by default. You can also add projects to existing solutions.

For Windows Forms applications and unmanaged Windows-based applications, the solution file for a project is by default stored in the same folder as the project. For Web Forms applications, solution files are typically stored in a folder in the Visual Studio Projects folder in your My Documents folder and point to the Web server that's hosting the application.

A single project can be a member of many different solutions. Because it's so easy to reorganize your projects in Visual Studio .NET, you should feel free to create your initial projects with default solutions. Later on, you can move your projects around and add them to new solutions if you want.

Lab: Playing with Solutions

The best way to get comfortable with solutions and projects is to spend some time playing with them. Let's say you're writing a book (like this one!). You've got a bunch of samples, and you want to make it easy for the reader to see all the samples from a single chapter in a single solution.

To get started, create a new folder named Chapter02. This folder will hold the various project folders in the solution. Next, create a Visual C# Windows Application project and call the new project Sample01.csproj. Save the project, and name the solution Sample01.sln. Save the solution in the same folder as the project, Sample01.

With the solution file selected in Solution Explorer, choose Save Sample01.sln As from the File menu to save the file to the Chapter02 folder, naming it Chapter02.sln.

At this point, you've got two solutions: one in the Chapter02 folder and one in the Sample01 folder. The Chapter02.sln file is the one that's currently open. Let's add another project to the solution. Press Ctrl+Alt+A, and enter **File.AddNewProject** in the Command Window. This should bring up the Add New Project dialog box. Create a C# Windows application, and name it Sample02. You now have a solution file named Chapter02 and two projects. Close the Chapter02 solution file and click Yes if you're prompted to save.

If you go into the new folder created for Sample02, you'll notice that there's no solution file for that project. No problem—just open the Sample02.csproj file. You can work on that project alone and save a new solution file in the Sample02 folder if you want. You can close that project and go to the Chapter02 folder; again, you'll see the two projects. As you can see, a project can be a member of a number of different solutions. This is an important concept to understand as you plan team development projects. As you explore the solution concept further, you'll also see that it can be an integral part of code reuse in Visual Studio .NET.

Understanding Solutions

In Visual Studio .NET, a solution is a thin wrapper that contains a project or a number of projects. Every project in Visual Studio .NET is part of a solution by default, and even if you open a lone project file for editing, you'll be prompted to save a new solution file for the project at some point in your editing session. The solution concept is important because much of what you can do in Visual Studio .NET revolves around accessing functionality that's exposed in different projects.

Solution Items and Miscellaneous Files

Solutions can contain solution items and miscellaneous files in addition to projects. Solution items can consist of HTML files, bitmaps, icons, XML files, templates, and schemas, among others. Miscellaneous files can be a bit of a mystery. First of all, you need to make the Miscellaneous Files folder visible in Solution Explorer to take advantage of these kinds of files. To see this folder, you select the Show Miscellaneous Files In Solution Explorer check box on the Documents page in the Environment folder of the Options dialog box, as shown in Figure 2-2. Keep in mind that you won't see the Miscellaneous Files folder until you open a nonproject item in the IDE using *File.OpenFile*.

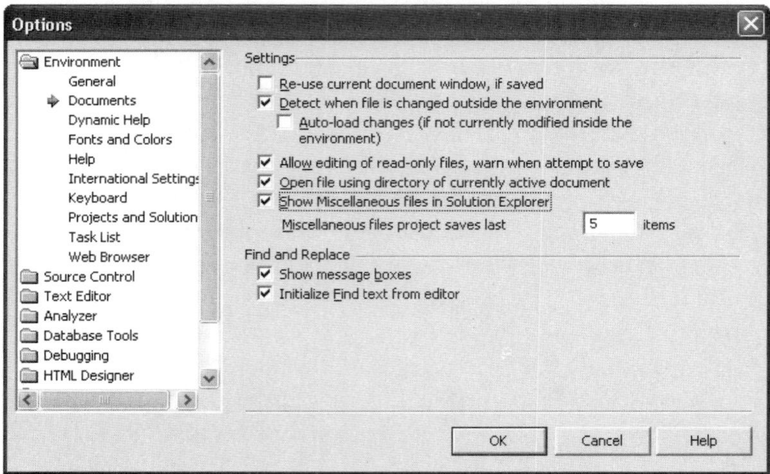

Figure 2-2 You can enable the Miscellaneous Files folder in the Options dialog box.

Miscellaneous files are files that you might open in the IDE for reference purposes—for example, if you want to review some code in a listing that you don't want to make part of your project. Opening such a file in the IDE without importing it into your solution automatically places the file into the Miscellaneous Files folder. The linked file is aggregated into the Miscellaneous Files folder in a solution.

Keep in mind that any file you open from Visual Studio .NET gets a link in the Miscellaneous Files folder. This folder persists your items between sessions if you set Miscellaneous Files Project Saves Last to something like five items. This means you can open specifications, schedules, and notes and have those files at your fingertips every time you open your project, as shown in Figure 2-3.

Figure 2-3 You can use the Miscellaneous Files folder to store links to documents relating to your projects.

Solution Properties

The Solution Property Pages dialog box gives you easy access to the settings that apply to an entire solution. Among the options that you can control include the startup project or projects for your solution, the locations for files and symbols used for debugging, and the configuration settings that apply to the different projects in your solution.

You can get to the Solution Property Pages dialog box by making sure that the solution name is selected in Solution Explorer, pressing Ctrl+Alt+A, and entering **Project.Properties** in the Command Window, or by right-clicking on the project and then choosing Properties. Most of the major programming projects in Visual Studio .NET present you with the Property Pages dialog box shown in Figure 2-4.

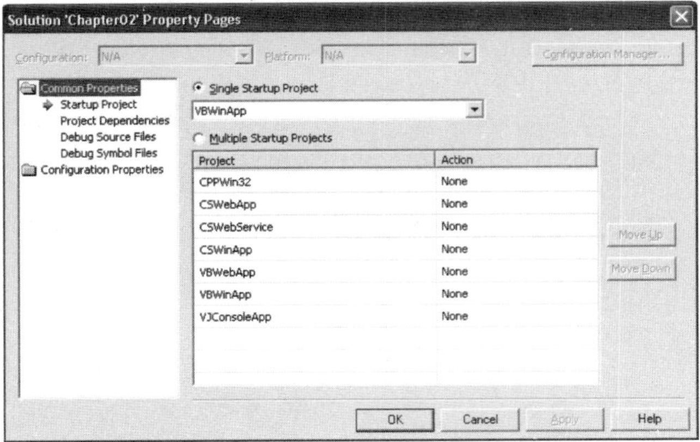

Figure 2-4 The Solution Property Pages dialog box gives you access to solution settings.

Common Properties

Clicking the Common Properties folder in the folder pane on the left exposes a number of options. The first option is Startup Project. In multiple-project solutions, you can select which project launches when the solution is run from the Debug menu. You'll most often set this option on the fly by right-clicking on a project name in Solution Explorer and then choosing Set As StartUp Project from the project shortcut menu.

If you want to run more than one solution when you choose Start or Start Without Debugging from the Debug menu, you can select the Multiple Startup Projects option. Selecting this option lets you select the behavior of each of the projects in your solution when you invoke *Debug.Start* or *Debug.StartWithoutDebugging*. You can select Start, Start Without Debugging, or None. The Move Up and Move Down buttons to the right of the list of projects lets you set the order in which the programs are started.

In a number of scenarios, running multiple projects concurrently might be useful. You might want to test some interprocess communication features between various assemblies in your solution. You might use a second project to do some profiling or instrumentation. Another use might be to run a utility that takes control of another assembly for automated testing purposes.

The second option in the Common Properties folder is Project Dependencies. When some assemblies in a solution depend on others in the same solution, the build order for the different projects in the solution is critical. The Project Dependencies settings let you specify which projects need to be built before others in order to get the entire solution up and running.

The last two options in the Common Properties folder let you set file paths for source files and debug symbols that might come up in your application. These settings allow you to step into the source code for libraries that are referenced by your projects but that aren't part of your project. If you're debugging a project that's referencing a debug version of a .NET assembly, Visual Studio .NET is usually able to find the source for the assembly if it's available. If the source is stored in a different location, you can specify the location of the source files and the debug symbols so that you can debug into that source.

Configuration Properties

Solutions can have multiple configurations that give you quick access to preset options relating to your solution. The Debug and Release configurations are available to new projects by default, but you can create your own configurations using the Configuration Manager, which is accessible from the Solution Property Pages dialog box or from the Build menu (*Build.ConfigurationManager*).

Visual Studio .NET offers two types of configurations: solution configurations and project configurations. Solution configurations are for configuring different build setups within a particular solution. For example, you can create and save a specific solution that allows you to select a different configuration for each project in your solution.

The second type of configuration is the project configuration. We'll discuss custom project configurations in detail later in the chapter, but for now consider how different projects might relate to one another in a solution. Project configurations let you change some very specific build characteristics. These characteristics include code optimizations, debugging switches, and even the location of the project's compiled files. If you have five projects with different custom settings in a single solution, you should use custom solution configurations to save and manage the different build scenarios that might come up.

Solution and Solution User Options Files

The solution source .sln file is a plain-text document that describes the solution. The solution file contains links to the projects contained in the solution. It also contains version information about the format of the solution file itself. Solution files created with Visual Studio .NET 2002 carry the signature *Microsoft Visual Studio Solution File, Format Version 7.00*. Solution files created with or converted to Visual Studio .NET 2003 read *Microsoft Visual Studio Solution File, Format Version 8.00*.

> **Important** Once you convert a file to Visual Studio .NET 2003, you can no longer open it in Visual Studio .NET 2002.

The .sln file also contains information on the various configurations that have been set up in the solution. Information about the different solution configurations is stored in this file, along with information about how the different project configurations are organized in those solution configurations. Listing 2-1 was used to organize a number of different project types for this chapter.

Chapter02.sln

```
Microsoft Visual Studio Solution File, Format Version 7.00
Project("{F184B08F-C81C-45F6-A57F-5ABD9991F28F}") = "VBWinApp",
    "VBWinApp\VBWinApp.vbproj",
    "{D7AFF922-38D5-461C-A07B-859080BFCFBF}"
EndProject
Project("{F184B08F-C81C-45F6-A57F-5ABD9991F28F}") = "VBWebApp",
    "http://localhost/VBWebApp/VBWebApp.vbproj",
    "{D654F4FC-7144-457A-9D73-A149ECD0DB40}"
EndProject
Project("{FAE04EC0-301F-11D3-BF4B-00C04F79EFBC}") = "CSWinApp",
    "CSWinApp\CSWinApp.csproj",
    "{9D585FB1-AA56-4227-AB14-23F16E4F07E4}"
EndProject
Project("{FAE04EC0-301F-11D3-BF4B-00C04F79EFBC}") = "CSWebApp",
    "http://localhost/CSWebApp/CSWebApp.csproj",
    "{AB66D7EB-DB6F-45E8-AE7D-B972D2A652F1}"
EndProject
Project("{8BC9CEB8-8B4A-11D0-8D11-00A0C91BC942}") = "CPPWin32",
    "CPPWin32\CPPWin32.vcproj",
    "{912ECF9E-5ABA-4E85-8955-2B0DC464C377}"
EndProject
Project("{E6FDF86B-F3D1-11D4-8576-0002A516ECE8}") = "VJConsoleApp",
    "VJConsoleApp\VJConsoleApp.vjsproj",
    "{2022B3FD-6AFB-4912-8687-4B09257A48A1}"
EndProject
Project("{FAE04EC0-301F-11D3-BF4B-00C04F79EFBC}") = "CSWebService",
    "http://localhost/CSWebService/CSWebService.csproj",
    "{22A37BFE-687D-44E6-9C0C-711735BC5018}"
EndProject
Global
```

Listing 2-1 An example solution file

```
GlobalSection(SolutionConfiguration) = preSolution
    ConfigName.0 = Debug
    ConfigName.1 = Debug1
    ConfigName.2 = PostCMD
    ConfigName.3 = PostExplorer
    ConfigName.4 = Release
EndGlobalSection
GlobalSection(ProjectDependencies) = postSolution
EndGlobalSection
GlobalSection(ProjectConfiguration) = postSolution
{D7AFF922-38D5-461C-A07B-859080BFCFBF}.Debug.ActiveCfg = Debug|.NET
{D7AFF922-38D5-461C-A07B-859080BFCFBF}.Debug.Build.0 = Debug|.NET
{D7AFF922-38D5-461C-A07B-859080BFCFBF}.Debug1.ActiveCfg = Debug|.NET
{D7AFF922-38D5-461C-A07B-859080BFCFBF}.Debug1.Build.0 = Debug|.NET
{D7AFF922-38D5-461C-A07B-859080BFCFBF}.PostCMD.ActiveCfg = Release|.NET
{D7AFF922-38D5-461C-A07B-859080BFCFBF}.PostCMD.Build.0 = Release|.NET
{D7AFF922-38D5-461C-A07B-859080BFCFBF}.PostExplorer.ActiveCfg =
    Release|.NET
{D7AFF922-38D5-461C-A07B-859080BFCFBF}.PostExplorer.Build.0 =
    Release|.NET
{D7AFF922-38D5-461C-A07B-859080BFCFBF}.Release.ActiveCfg = Release|.NET
{D7AFF922-38D5-461C-A07B-859080BFCFBF}.Release.Build.0 = Release|.NET
{D654F4FC-7144-457A-9D73-A149ECD0DB40}.Debug.ActiveCfg = Debug|.NET
{D654F4FC-7144-457A-9D73-A149ECD0DB40}.Debug.Build.0 = Debug|.NET
{D654F4FC-7144-457A-9D73-A149ECD0DB40}.Debug1.ActiveCfg = Debug|.NET
{D654F4FC-7144-457A-9D73-A149ECD0DB40}.Debug1.Build.0 = Debug|.NET
{D654F4FC-7144-457A-9D73-A149ECD0DB40}.PostCMD.ActiveCfg = Release|.NET
{D654F4FC-7144-457A-9D73-A149ECD0DB40}.PostCMD.Build.0 = Release|.NET
{D654F4FC-7144-457A-9D73-A149ECD0DB40}.PostExplorer.ActiveCfg =
    Release|.NET
{D654F4FC-7144-457A-9D73-A149ECD0DB40}.PostExplorer.Build.0 =
    Release|.NET
{D654F4FC-7144-457A-9D73-A149ECD0DB40}.Release.ActiveCfg = Release|.NET
{D654F4FC-7144-457A-9D73-A149ECD0DB40}.Release.Build.0 = Release|.NET
{9D585FB1-AA56-4227-AB14-23F16E4F07E4}.Debug.ActiveCfg = Debug|.NET
{9D585FB1-AA56-4227-AB14-23F16E4F07E4}.Debug.Build.0 = Debug|.NET
{9D585FB1-AA56-4227-AB14-23F16E4F07E4}.Debug1.ActiveCfg = Debug1|.NET
{9D585FB1-AA56-4227-AB14-23F16E4F07E4}.Debug1.Build.0 = Debug1|.NET
{9D585FB1-AA56-4227-AB14-23F16E4F07E4}.PostCMD.ActiveCfg = Debug1|.NET
{9D585FB1-AA56-4227-AB14-23F16E4F07E4}.PostCMD.Build.0 = Debug1|.NET
{9D585FB1-AA56-4227-AB14-23F16E4F07E4}.PostExplorer.ActiveCfg =
    Debug1|.NET
{9D585FB1-AA56-4227-AB14-23F16E4F07E4}.PostExplorer.Build.0 =
    Debug1|.NET
{9D585FB1-AA56-4227-AB14-23F16E4F07E4}.Release.ActiveCfg = Release|.NET
```

```
{9D585FB1-AA56-4227-AB14-23F16E4F07E4}.Release.Build.0 = Release|.NET
{AB66D7EB-DB6F-45E8-AE7D-B972D2A652F1}.Debug.ActiveCfg = Debug|.NET
{AB66D7EB-DB6F-45E8-AE7D-B972D2A652F1}.Debug.Build.0 = Debug|.NET
{AB66D7EB-DB6F-45E8-AE7D-B972D2A652F1}.Debug1.ActiveCfg = Debug|.NET
{AB66D7EB-DB6F-45E8-AE7D-B972D2A652F1}.Debug1.Build.0 = Debug|.NET
{AB66D7EB-DB6F-45E8-AE7D-B972D2A652F1}.PostCMD.ActiveCfg = Release|.NET
{AB66D7EB-DB6F-45E8-AE7D-B972D2A652F1}.PostCMD.Build.0 = Release|.NET
{AB66D7EB-DB6F-45E8-AE7D-B972D2A652F1}.PostExplorer.ActiveCfg =
    Release|.NET
{AB66D7EB-DB6F-45E8-AE7D-B972D2A652F1}.PostExplorer.Build.0 =
    Release|.NET
{AB66D7EB-DB6F-45E8-AE7D-B972D2A652F1}.Release.ActiveCfg = Release|.NET
{AB66D7EB-DB6F-45E8-AE7D-B972D2A652F1}.Release.Build.0 = Release|.NET
{912ECF9E-5ABA-4E85-8955-2B0DC464C377}.Debug.ActiveCfg = Debug|Win32
{912ECF9E-5ABA-4E85-8955-2B0DC464C377}.Debug.Build.0 = Debug|Win32
{912ECF9E-5ABA-4E85-8955-2B0DC464C377}.Debug1.ActiveCfg = Debug|Win32
{912ECF9E-5ABA-4E85-8955-2B0DC464C377}.Debug1.Build.0 = Debug|Win32
{912ECF9E-5ABA-4E85-8955-2B0DC464C377}.PostCMD.ActiveCfg =
    PostCMD|Win32
{912ECF9E-5ABA-4E85-8955-2B0DC464C377}.PostCMD.Build.0 = PostCMD|Win32
{912ECF9E-5ABA-4E85-8955-2B0DC464C377}.PostExplorer.ActiveCfg =
    PostExplorer|Win32
{912ECF9E-5ABA-4E85-8955-2B0DC464C377}.PostExplorer.Build.0 =
    PostExplorer|Win32
{912ECF9E-5ABA-4E85-8955-2B0DC464C377}.Release.ActiveCfg =
    Release|Win32
{912ECF9E-5ABA-4E85-8955-2B0DC464C377}.Release.Build.0 = Release|Win32
{2022B3FD-6AFB-4912-8687-4B09257A48A1}.Debug.ActiveCfg = Debug|.NET
{2022B3FD-6AFB-4912-8687-4B09257A48A1}.Debug.Build.0 = Debug|.NET
{2022B3FD-6AFB-4912-8687-4B09257A48A1}.Debug1.ActiveCfg = Debug|.NET
{2022B3FD-6AFB-4912-8687-4B09257A48A1}.Debug1.Build.0 = Debug|.NET
{2022B3FD-6AFB-4912-8687-4B09257A48A1}.PostCMD.ActiveCfg = Release|.NET
{2022B3FD-6AFB-4912-8687-4B09257A48A1}.PostCMD.Build.0 = Release|.NET
{2022B3FD-6AFB-4912-8687-4B09257A48A1}.PostExplorer.ActiveCfg =
    Release|.NET
{2022B3FD-6AFB-4912-8687-4B09257A48A1}.PostExplorer.Build.0 =
    Release|.NET
{2022B3FD-6AFB-4912-8687-4B09257A48A1}.Release.ActiveCfg = Release|.NET
{2022B3FD-6AFB-4912-8687-4B09257A48A1}.Release.Build.0 = Release|.NET
{22A37BFE-687D-44E6-9C0C-711735BC5018}.Debug.ActiveCfg = Debug|.NET
{22A37BFE-687D-44E6-9C0C-711735BC5018}.Debug.Build.0 = Debug|.NET
{22A37BFE-687D-44E6-9C0C-711735BC5018}.Debug1.ActiveCfg = Debug|.NET
{22A37BFE-687D-44E6-9C0C-711735BC5018}.Debug1.Build.0 = Debug|.NET
{22A37BFE-687D-44E6-9C0C-711735BC5018}.PostCMD.ActiveCfg = Release|.NET
```

```
    {22A37BFE-687D-44E6-9C0C-711735BC5018}.PostCMD.Build.0 = Release|.NET
    {22A37BFE-687D-44E6-9C0C-711735BC5018}.PostExplorer.ActiveCfg =
        Release|.NET
    {22A37BFE-687D-44E6-9C0C-711735BC5018}.PostExplorer.Build.0 =
        Release|.NET
    {22A37BFE-687D-44E6-9C0C-711735BC5018}.Release.ActiveCfg = Release|.NET
    {22A37BFE-687D-44E6-9C0C-711735BC5018}.Release.Build.0 = Release|.NET
    EndGlobalSection
    GlobalSection(ExtensibilityGlobals) = postSolution
    EndGlobalSection
    GlobalSection(ExtensibilityAddIns) = postSolution
    EndGlobalSection
EndGlobal
```

If you take a look at an .sln file in which solution items have been enabled and added, you'll notice that there's no information about these files. Solution items are considered user items, so links to these files are stored in the solution user options (.suo) file. If you pass a folder containing an .sln and an .suo file to another user on another machine, much of the information in the .suo file will become useless to the second user and will be ignored.

Some important items are stored in the .suo file that you can choose to pass to another person. Breakpoints that you set in your solution are stored in the .suo file, as are tasks that have been added to the Task List window. If you want to share that information with the person you're sharing the solution with, you should be sure to keep the .suo file with the .sln file. If you don't need to share such information, we recommend deleting that file because the file can contain personal and confidential data such as the paths to network shares and even your e-mail alias.

Projects

Projects are the second type of container used in Visual Studio .NET. Projects are used to maintain the source files associated with individual assemblies, Web sites and services, and applications. As with solutions, Solution Explorer is the primary tool for managing projects in Visual Studio .NET.

Project Items

Projects in Visual Studio .NET consist primarily of file items. These items can be links to files or source files in the same folder as the project file. Whether an item is a link or an actual file depends on the type of project you're working with. The files associated with Visual C++ projects are links displayed in Solution Explorer. It just so happens that these files are usually in the same folder as the projects. Deleting a link to a file in a Visual C++ project doesn't necessarily delete the file that's opened by the link. It's a rather fine distinction, but if you've ever moved a Visual C++ project and found yourself missing a project file, it might be that the file existed outside the project folder. Windows Forms projects can consist of a mix of links and actual file items. Web Forms projects generally contain the actual files in the folder structure that hosts the project file. Table 2-1 shows the possible relationships between project type and file items in Visual Studio .NET 2003.

Table 2-1 Project Items in Visual Studio .NET 2003

Project Type	Associated Items
Visual C++	Links to items
Visual Basic .NET (Web)	Items in the project folder
Visual C# .NET (Web)	Items in the project folder
Visual Basic .NET	Links and actual items
Visual C# .NET	Links and actual items
Visual J#	Links and actual items

If you take a look at Solution Explorer for a Windows Forms application written in Visual C# or Visual Basic .NET, you can see the mix of project items and file structure items using *Project.ShowAllFiles*. Files that are part of the project will appear normally. Files that are not part of the project but are in the project folder will appear slightly grayed. The *ShowAllFiles* command is available from the Project menu and via toolbar buttons in Solution Explorer. In addition, you'll see a number of files that are kept hidden from the user by default. These include some types of configuration files and the code-behind files used in ASP.NET applications. In Figure 2-5, most of the items in the project shown are project items.

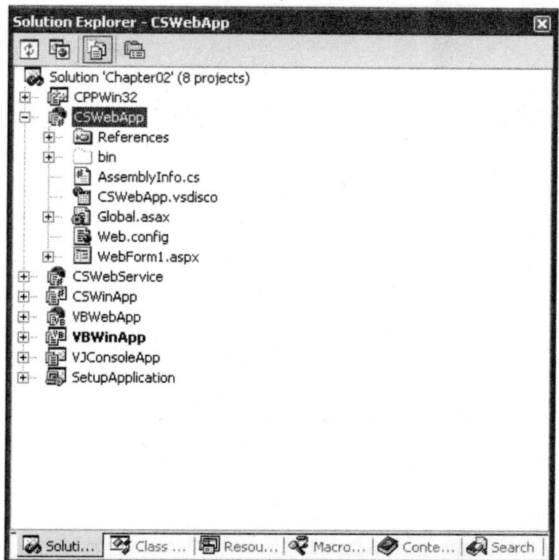

Figure 2-5 Links and files in a Visual C# solution

In addition to the items, a project stores the configuration metadata associated with the project. Information stored includes configuration data that you specify in the IDE as well as build and debugging data. The nature of this data differs from project type to project type. All .NET languages compile to Microsoft intermediate language (MSIL), but the compilers themselves are written by different teams, so the available options differ from language to language.

Project Properties

You set the options for a project in the Property Pages dialog box. (In Solution Explorer, right-click on a project and choose Properties from the shortcut menu.) The Property Pages dialog box looks a lot like the Solution Property Pages dialog box we discussed earlier. However, the project Property Pages dialog box has a lot more options that you can configure in a project. Most of these options are settings that you would otherwise have to specify at the command line when compiling a project; these settings match particular command-line options.

Between the four major languages that ship with Visual Studio .NET and the different types of projects that you can create, we're talking about a lot of compiler options. This is where project configuration in Visual Studio .NET gets fun. By creating custom project configurations, you can try out a lot of different types of builds and save those configurations for future use and reference.

Saving a Custom Configuration

You can access the Configuration Manager dialog box by clicking the Configuration Manager button in the Property Pages dialog box, or you can enter **Build.ConfigurationManager** in the Command Window. To create a new project configuration, click the drop-down button adjacent to the desired project in the Configuration column of the Project Contexts grid and then click New. You'll see the New Project Configuration dialog box (shown in Figure 2-6).

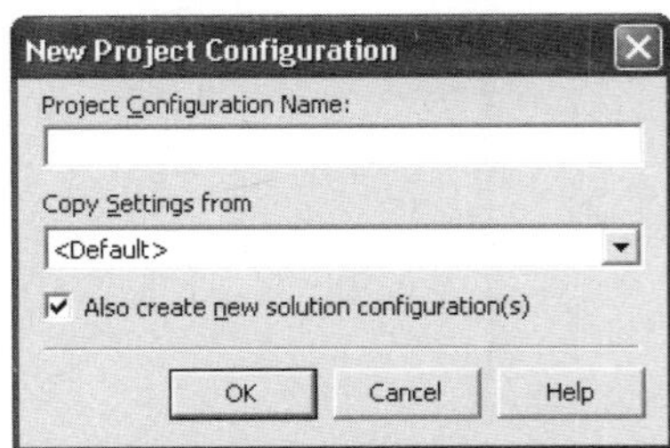

Figure 2-6 The New Project Configuration dialog box

Give your new configuration a name, and set the base settings for the configuration by selecting an existing configuration from the Copy Settings From drop-down list. As with the New Solution Configuration dialog box, you can create a new solution configuration automatically to match your new project configuration by selecting the Also Create New Solution Configuration(s) check box. At this point, you should be ready to play with some settings in your project. Just create a new test configuration that you can play with and leave all the default settings in the two default configurations.

Let's look at the different types of projects and some of the settings you can configure in each.

Managed Application Projects

Managed applications, such as Visual Basic .NET, Visual C#, and Visual J#, all use somewhat similar layouts in the Property Pages dialog box. Different folders are available depending on whether you're creating a Windows Forms application or a Web Forms application.

Common Properties

Figure 2-7 shows the General page for a Visual Basic .NET Windows Forms application that's located in the Common Properties folder. This page is different from the General page in the Configuration Properties folder. Notice that the Configuration combo box, Platform combo box, and Configuration Manager button are all unavailable when items from the Common Properties folder are open. You can't save these settings separately when you save a new build type.

The settings in this folder set properties such as Assembly Name, Output Type, and Namespace. Other Common Properties settings include Page Layout, which lets you specify either a Flow or Grid type layout for your Web Forms and Windows Forms applications; Target Schema, which lets you specify the level and type of Web browser that your application will be compatible with; and the Scripting Language for your application.

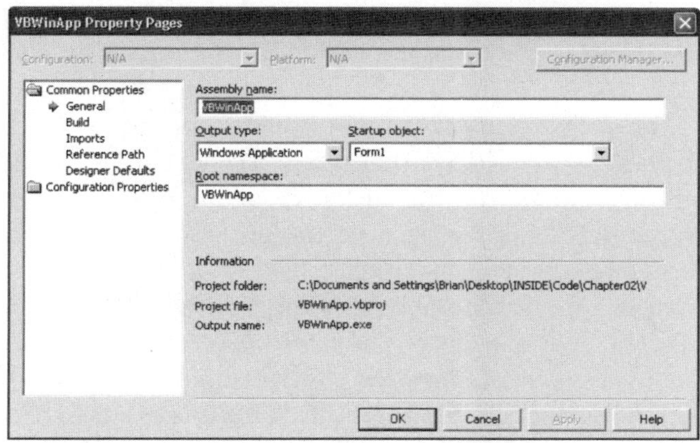

Figure 2-7 The General page in the General folder for a Visual Basic .NET Windows Forms application

Contrast this dialog box style with that shown in Figure 2-8, which shows the General page for a Visual C# Web Forms application. The Visual Basic .NET page uses controls to configure the same types of settings that are set in Visual C# using a grid.

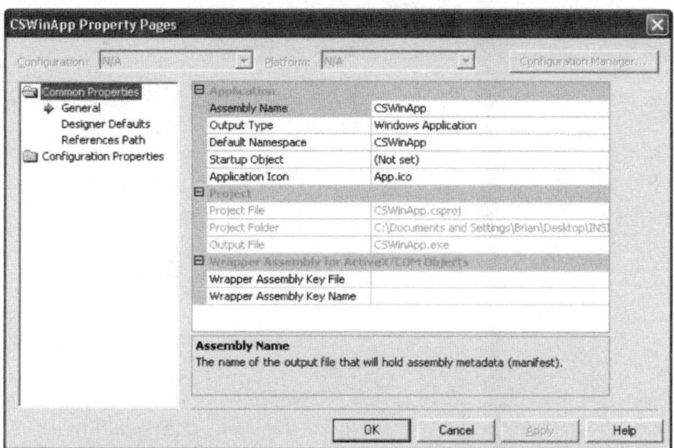

Figure 2-8 The General page for a Visual C# Windows Forms application

These two types of property page styles are consistent for each language. Even though these page types are visually different, they provide access to the same kinds of settings.

Configuration Properties

The Configuration Properties folder for a project is the place where you can play with settings and save them out in separate build types. You can easily create and save new build types for almost any kind of Visual Studio .NET project and compile them from inside the IDE or from the command line, as we'll show you in Chapter 15.

In this section, we'll point out a few of the important Configuration Properties settings in the Property Pages dialog box for Visual C# projects. You can get to most of these settings in a Visual Basic .NET Property Pages dialog box as well, but we're using Visual C# because the grid style for these pages makes them a little more concise.

Figure 2-9 shows the Build page from the Configuration Properties folder for a Visual C# project. You can save any of these settings to a custom build type. One of the most useful settings for configuring for a custom build type is the Output Path. The default output path for a Visual C# Debug build is \bin\Debug\. The release build is \bin\Release\ by default. When you create a custom build type, you get one of these two paths, depending on which type of build you get your initial settings from. If you're creating a custom build, it might make sense to copy the output of that build to a new folder so you can compare the output assemblies. For cases like this, you can create a new build path to match your build name. For example, if you have a build named DebugOverflow (to indicate that you've enabled overflow checks for this build type), you can change the output to \bin\DebugOverflow.

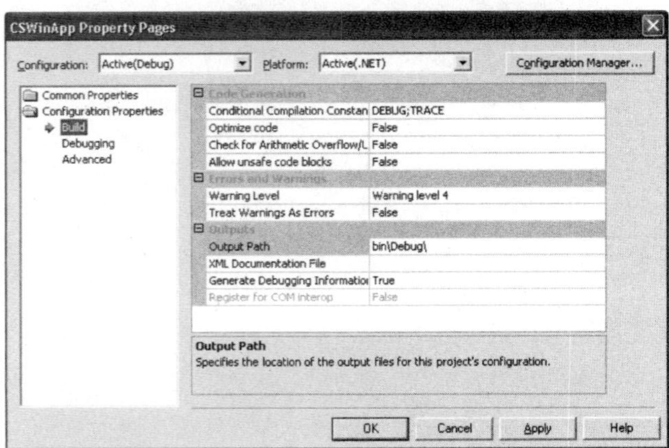

Figure 2-9 The Build page for a Visual C# Windows Forms application

The Debugging page, shown in Figure 2-10, can be especially useful when you're building class library, Web Forms, and XML Web services projects. You can play with a lot of settings on this page, but one of the most useful to our discussion is the Start URL option. Using different build types, you can specify particular URLs that you want to test your XML Web service against. You can use the Start Application option in the same way to test your libraries. It lets you easily debug your service or library against a number of test applications.

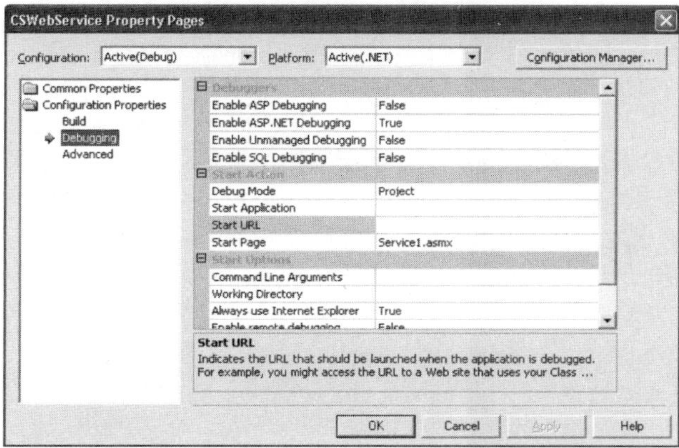

Figure 2-10 The Debugging page for a Web Forms application

Command-Line Settings

One setting I often use custom builds for is Command Line Arguments. By creating a custom build type and setting a command-line argument for that build type, I can save a lot of time that I'd normally spend fiddling with scripts and the command shell. This setting came in handy when I was tech-editing a security book and needed to test a number of different strings in buffer overrun scenarios. By creating three or four different build configurations, I was able to quickly debug and test applications using different command-line arguments. Most important, I was able to create these build types, move on to something else for a while, and come right back to the security project and get straight into it because I had already saved all my test scenarios as custom builds.

The Advanced page, shown in Figure 2-11, has some equally useful settings, especially for testers. Notice that on the Visual C# Advanced page in the Configuration Properties folder you can specify the offset for a DLL, which can be useful for debugging. You can also set the section size of your output file. This size is normally 4 KB in Windows, but you can specify 512, 1024, 2048, 4096, 8192, or 16384 in .NET. The Incremental Build option is important if you're using the */doc* option to generate documentation from the comments in your source code. The */doc* option is ignored when you're doing an incremental build, so you might want to create a custom documentation build and set the Incremental Build property to False in that build type to ensure that your documentation is updated when you debug.

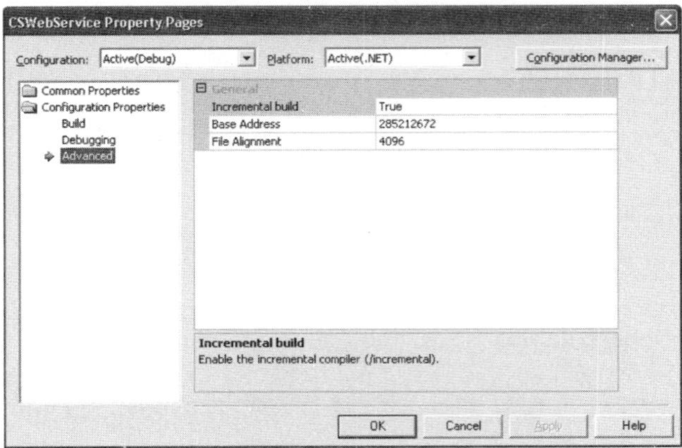

Figure 2-11 The Advanced page for a Web Forms application

Visual C++ Projects

The Property Pages dialog box for Visual C++ projects has a huge number of settings because of the large number of compile and link options available. The custom build options that we've talked about in this chapter apply to Visual C++ as well. In fact, because of the many properties available, you should find custom settings for unmanaged projects very useful, especially in testing and teaching scenarios.

Figure 2-12 shows the Property Pages dialog box for a Visual C++ Win32 project. You should notice right away that there's only one root folder in the folder list on the left. Everything in that folder can be customized and saved in a unique project configuration.

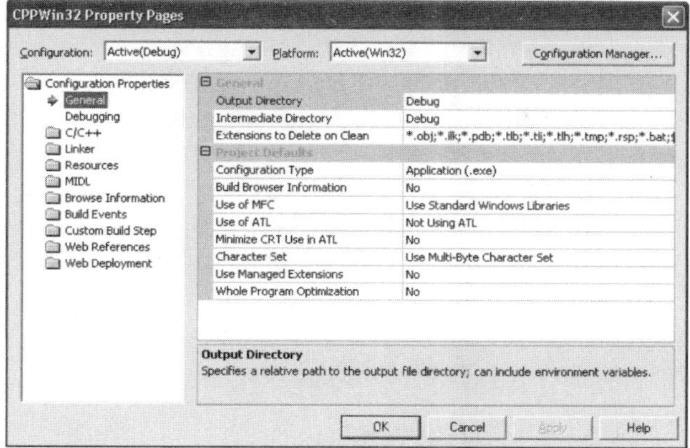

Figure 2-12 A custom configuration in Visual C++

The Property Pages dialog box for a Visual C++ project has a number of subfolders under the Configuration Properties folder. Table 2-2 contains a list of these folders and the general property types that you can set from each.

Table 2-2 Configuration Properties Subfolders in Visual C++

Subfolder	Properties
C/C++	Compiler options, preprocessor definitions, paths to some output files, and command-line compile options
Linker	Link options, debug options, and command-line link options
Resources	Resource filename and path, culture, and resource compiler command line
MIDL	Microsoft Interface Definition Language (MIDL) compiler options, output paths, and compiler command line
Browse Information	Options relating to BSCMAKE (browser files)
Build Events	Commands that you can run during the build process
Custom Build Step	Properties for configuring an additional task you specify when building a file or a project. For example, you might pass an input file to a tool that returns an output file.
Web References	Properties that determine how an XML Web service proxy class will be created when you reference an XML Web service in your project
Web Deployment	Specifies how a Web deployment tool will install your application

If you're an experienced Visual C++ programmer, you'll find most of these settings fairly straightforward. The Web References folder is interesting in that you can reference an XML Web service in Visual Studio .NET and the IDE creates an appropriate proxy class that allows you to easily access the functionality in the service.

The Build Events folder allows you to do a few interesting things with your custom builds. You can see the Post-Build Event page in Figure 2-13. If you're working with multiple projects and builds, you can use the Build Events folder to run applications and scripts during your build process. In this case, we've added a call to Regsvr32.exe as the command line for the Post-Build Event in the project. After this project is built under this configuration, the target file is registered with Windows.

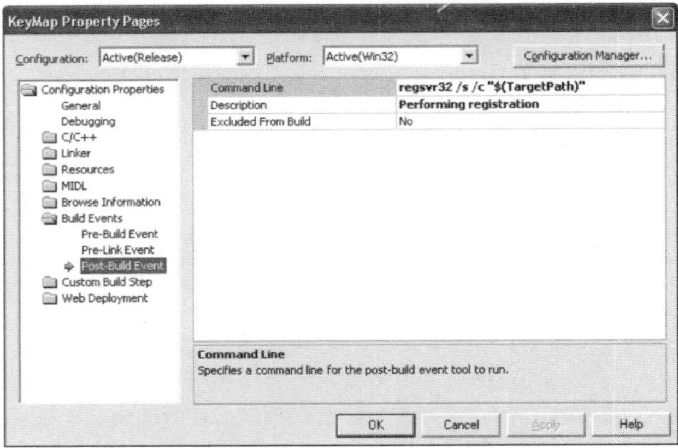

Figure 2-13 Build events let you run applications during your build process.

Lab: Adding a Build Event

This is sort of a homework scenario, but I still find this kind of build trick useful when I'm playing around with code. Let's say you're working on some problems in C and you want to open the folder in which you've built your new file. You could add a new tool to the Tools menu in Visual Studio .NET that would let you open Windows Explorer to the current project's build folder. (You should add such a tool because it's an easy way to get a folder where you want it.) But let's be really lazy and create a post-build event that launches Explorer.exe to the folder where our build is being placed:

1. Create a custom build called PostExplorer.
2. Add the following Command Line to the Post-Build Event:

```
Explorer.exe $(TargetDir)
```

3. Rebuild your project.

You'll see the build process take place normally. After the build is finished, you should see Windows Explorer open to your target folder. You can now double-click the executable to run it, examine the files created in the build, and read the BuildLog.htm file.

The Property Pages dialog box accepts a number of commonly used macros, which are described in Table 2-3.

Table 2-3 Macros Used in Property Pages

Macro	Description
$(ConfigurationName)	Current project configuration
$(DevEnvDir)	Visual Studio .NET installation folder
$(FrameworkDir)	.NET Framework installation folder
$(FrameworkSDKDir)	.NET Framework SDK installation folder
$(FrameworkVersion)	.NET Framework version number
$(Inherit)	Specifies the order of the inherited properties at the command line created by Visual Studio .NET
$(InputDir)	Input file folder is equivalent to the project file folder
$(InputExt)	Extension of the input file
$(InputFileName)	Name of the input file (name + extension)
$(InputName)	Input filename
$(InputPath)	Input file path
$(IntDir)	Intermediate file path
$(NoInherit)	Forces properties to not be inherited
$(OutDir)	Output folder
$(PlatformName)	Name of the project platform, usually Win32 or .NET
$(ProjectDir)	Folder containing the project files
$(ProjectExt)	Extension of the project (.vcproj)
$(ProjectFileName)	Full name of the project (CPPWin32.vcproj)

Table 2-3 Macros Used in Property Pages *(continued)*

Macro	Description
$(ProjectName)	Name of the project (CPPWin32)
$(ProjectPath)	Full path to the project file
$(RemoteMachine)	Remote machine (when debugging remotely)
$(SolutionDir)	Folder containing the solution file
$(SolutionExt)	Extension of the solution file (.sln)
$(SolutionFileName)	Full name of the solution (Chapter02.sln)
$(SolutionName)	Name of the solution (Chapter02)
$(SolutionPath)	Full path to the solution file
$(TargetDir)	Output folder for the project
$(TargetExt)	Extension of the output target (.exe)
$(TargetFileName)	Target filename (CPPWin32.exe)
$(TargetName)	Name of the target (CPPWin32)
$(TargetPath)	Full path to the target
$(VCInstallDir)	Visual C++ .NET installation folder
$(VSInstallDir)	Visual Studio .NET installation folder

Project Source Files

Project source files have different extensions, based on the language specific to the project. The extensions and the project types that they hold are listed in Table 2-4. Adding languages developed by Visual Studio Integration Program (VSIP) vendors adds new project types.

Table 2-4 Project Types and Extensions

Project Type	Extension
Visual Basic .NET	.vbproj
Visual C#	.csproj
Visual C++	.vcproj
Visual J#	.vjproj
Deployment	.vdproj

Listing 2-2, CSWinApp.csproj, is a Visual C# project file from Visual Studio .NET. You can see that it contains many of the settings we discussed earlier.

CSWinApp.csproj

```
<VisualStudioProject>
    <CSHARP
        ProjectType = "Local"
        ProductVersion = "7.10.2215"
        SchemaVersion = "2.0"
        ProjectGuid = "{9DC32270-2155-414F-9BE5-C593ADE47FFD}"
    >
        <Build>
            <Settings
                ApplicationIcon = "App.ico"
                AssemblyKeyContainerName = ""
                AssemblyName = "CSWinApp"
                AssemblyOriginatorKeyFile = ""
                DefaultClientScript = "JScript"
                DefaultHTMLPageLayout = "Grid"
                DefaultTargetSchema = "IE50"
                DelaySign = "false"
                OutputType = "WinExe"
                PreBuildEvent = ""
                PostBuildEvent = ""
                RootNamespace = "CSWinApp"
                RunPostBuildEvent = "OnBuildSuccess"
                StartupObject = ""
            >
                <Config
                    Name = "Debug"
                    AllowUnsafeBlocks = "false"
                    BaseAddress = "285212672"
                    CheckForOverflowUnderflow = "false"
                    ConfigurationOverrideFile = ""
                    DefineConstants = "DEBUG;TRACE"
                    DocumentationFile = ""
                    DebugSymbols = "true"
                    FileAlignment = "4096"
                    IncrementalBuild = "false"
                    NoStdLib = "false"
                    NoWarn = ""
                    Optimize = "false"
                    OutputPath = "bin\Debug\"
                    RegisterForComInterop = "false"
                    RemoveIntegerChecks = "false"
                    TreatWarningsAsErrors = "false"
                    WarningLevel = "4"
```

Listing 2-2 An example project file

```
            />
            <Config
                Name = "Release"
                AllowUnsafeBlocks = "false"
                BaseAddress = "285212672"
                CheckForOverflowUnderflow = "false"
                ConfigurationOverrideFile = ""
                DefineConstants = "TRACE"
                DocumentationFile = ""
                DebugSymbols = "false"
                FileAlignment = "4096"
                IncrementalBuild = "false"
                NoStdLib = "false"
                NoWarn = ""
                Optimize = "true"
                OutputPath = "bin\Release\"
                RegisterForComInterop = "false"
                RemoveIntegerChecks = "false"
                TreatWarningsAsErrors = "false"
                WarningLevel = "4"
            />
            <Config
                Name = "Debug1"
                AllowUnsafeBlocks = "false"
                BaseAddress = "285212672"
                CheckForOverflowUnderflow = "true"
                ConfigurationOverrideFile = ""
                DefineConstants = "DEBUG;TRACE"
                DocumentationFile = ""
                DebugSymbols = "true"
                FileAlignment = "4096"
                IncrementalBuild = "false"
                NoStdLib = "false"
                NoWarn = ""
                Optimize = "false"
                OutputPath = "bin\Debug\"
                RegisterForComInterop = "false"
                RemoveIntegerChecks = "false"
                TreatWarningsAsErrors = "true"
                WarningLevel = "3"
            />
        </Settings>
        <References>
            <Reference
                Name = "System"
```

```
                AssemblyName = "System"
                HintPath =
"C:\WINDOWS\Microsoft.NET\Framework\v1.1.4322\System.dll"
            />
            <Reference
                Name = "System.Data"
                AssemblyName = "System.Data"
                HintPath =
"C:\WINDOWS\Microsoft.NET\Framework\v1.1.4322\System.Data.dll"
            />
            <Reference
                Name = "System.Drawing"
                AssemblyName = "System.Drawing"
                HintPath =
"C:\WINDOWS\Microsoft.NET\Framework\v1.1.4322\System.Drawing.dll"
            />
            <Reference
                Name = "System.Windows.Forms"
                AssemblyName = "System.Windows.Forms"
                HintPath =
"C:\WINDOWS\Microsoft.NET\Framework\v1.1.4322\System.Windows.Forms.dll"
            />
            <Reference
                Name = "System.XML"
                AssemblyName = "System.Xml"
                HintPath =
"C:\WINDOWS\Microsoft.NET\Framework\v1.1.4322\System.XML.dll"
            />
        </References>
    </Build>
    <Files>
        <Include>
            <File
                RelPath = "App.ico"
                BuildAction = "Content"
            />
            <File
                RelPath = "AssemblyInfo.cs"
                SubType = "Code"
                BuildAction = "Compile"
            />
            <File
                RelPath = "Form1.cs"
                SubType = "Form"
                BuildAction = "Compile"
```

```
                />
                <File
                    RelPath = "Form1.resx"
                    DependentUpon = "Form1.cs"
                    BuildAction = "EmbeddedResource"
                />
            </Include>
        </Files>
    </CSHARP>
</VisualStudioProject>
```

Visual Basic .NET, Visual C#, and Visual J# projects also contain user option files. These files take the form *ProjectName.ProjectExt*.user.

A Visual Basic .NET user options file has the extension .vbproj.user. These project user files are in XML and contain information specific to the custom builds that you've created. The Visual C# project user file in Listing 2-3 is matched to the .csproj file from Listing 2-2. Notice that there's an extra configuration named Debug1. This is a custom configuration that was added to the project during development. Unlike the binary .suo file, the .user files are intrinsic to the custom build and should usually be kept with a project.

CSWinApp.csproj.user

```
<VisualStudioProject>
    <CSHARP LastOpenVersion = "7.10.2215" >
        <Build>
            <Settings ReferencePath = "" >
                <Config
                    Name = "Debug"
                    EnableASPDebugging = "false"
                    EnableASPXDebugging = "false"
                    EnableUnmanagedDebugging = "false"
                    EnableSQLServerDebugging = "false"
                    RemoteDebugEnabled = "false"
                    RemoteDebugMachine = ""
                    StartAction = "Project"
                    StartArguments = ""
                    StartPage = ""
                    StartProgram = ""
                    StartURL = ""
                    StartWorkingDirectory = ""
                    StartWithIE = "true"
                />
```

Listing 2-3 An example project user options file

```
                <Config
                    Name = "Release"
                    EnableASPDebugging = "false"
                    EnableASPXDebugging = "false"
                    EnableUnmanagedDebugging = "false"
                    EnableSQLServerDebugging = "false"
                    RemoteDebugEnabled = "false"
                    RemoteDebugMachine = ""
                    StartAction = "Project"
                    StartArguments = ""
                    StartPage = ""
                    StartProgram = ""
                    StartURL = ""
                    StartWorkingDirectory = ""
                    StartWithIE = "false"
                />
                <Config
                    Name = "Debug1"
                    EnableASPDebugging = "false"
                    EnableASPXDebugging = "false"
                    EnableUnmanagedDebugging = "false"
                    EnableSQLServerDebugging = "false"
                    RemoteDebugEnabled = "false"
                    RemoteDebugMachine = ""
                    StartAction = "Project"
                    StartArguments = ""
                    StartPage = ""
                    StartProgram = ""
                    StartURL = ""
                    StartWorkingDirectory = ""
                    StartWithIE = "true"
                />
            </Settings>
        </Build>
        <OtherProjectSettings
            CopyProjectDestinationFolder = ""
            CopyProjectUncPath = ""
            CopyProjectOption = "0"
            ProjectView = "ProjectFiles"
            ProjectTrust = "0"
        />
    </CSHARP>
</VisualStudioProject>
```

Project Dependencies

If you're building complex solutions that contain a number of assemblies with interproject dependencies, you can take advantage of Solution Explorer to help you manage these dependencies. Solution Explorer makes it really easy to add file, project, and Web references to your projects. For solutions with dependencies between projects, you'll want to use project references.

To add a project reference, open the Add Reference dialog box by selecting a project in Solution Explorer and entering **Project.AddReference** in the Command Window. On the Projects tab, you'll see a list of the projects in your solution, as shown in Figure 2-14.

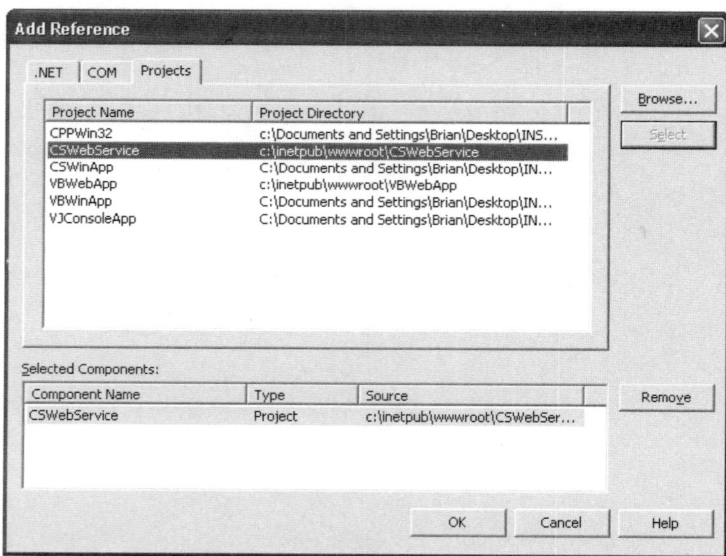

Figure 2-14 Adding a project reference to a project in a solution

After you add a project reference, the functionality available from the referenced project becomes available to the project adding the reference. At this point, build order becomes important because the referenced assembly must be built before the project that references it. To help you manage dependencies such as this, Visual Studio .NET provides a Project Dependencies dialog box (*Projects.ProjectDependencies*), as shown in Figure 2-15. This dialog box lets you specify a dependency, and it then changes the build order of affected projects in a solution accordingly. The dialog box was updated automatically with the dependency information when we added the project dependency. (If we had added the output of this project as a standard dependency, Visual Studio

.NET wouldn't have changed this option for us.) Once the dependency was specified, the XML Web service we referenced was added to the top of the build list on the Build Order page.

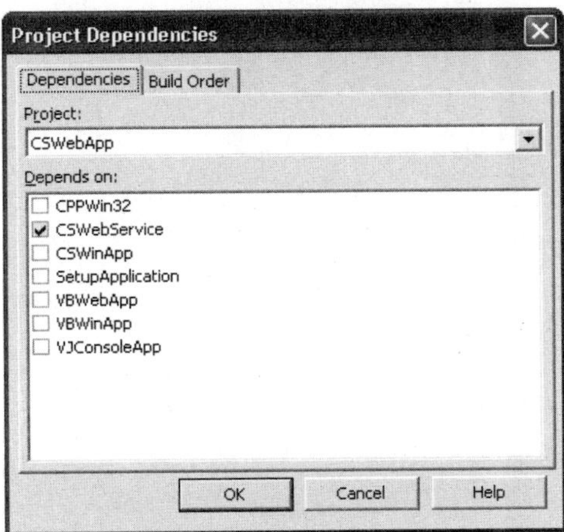

Figure 2-15 Configuring build dependencies for a project

Building Projects and Solutions

Once the projects, custom build configurations, and references are set in a solution, you can begin to work out the build scenarios that you want to run with the different configurations. To specify which projects in the solution should be built, you can use the Configuration Manager dialog box (shown in Figure 2-16). You can easily exclude projects that might give you problems, or you can simply save some time when you want to concentrate on a specific build in a solution.

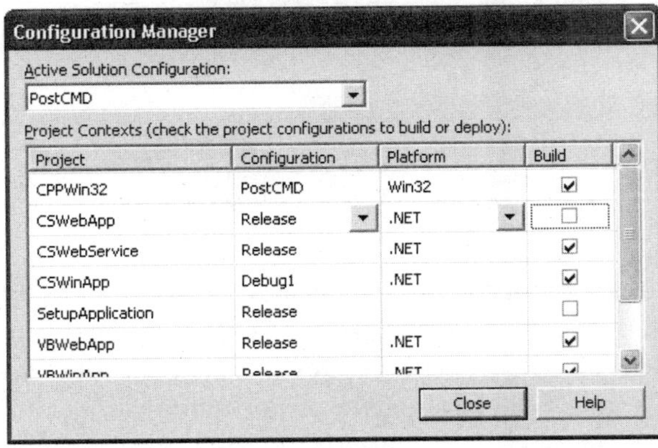

Figure 2-16 Determining which project to build for a given build configuration

There's one more powerful build dialog box you can use to batch-build multiple-build configurations in a single go. The Batch Build dialog box (*Project.BatchBuild*), shown in Figure 2-17, isn't available for every solution type, but you can use it if your project consists of non-Web applications.

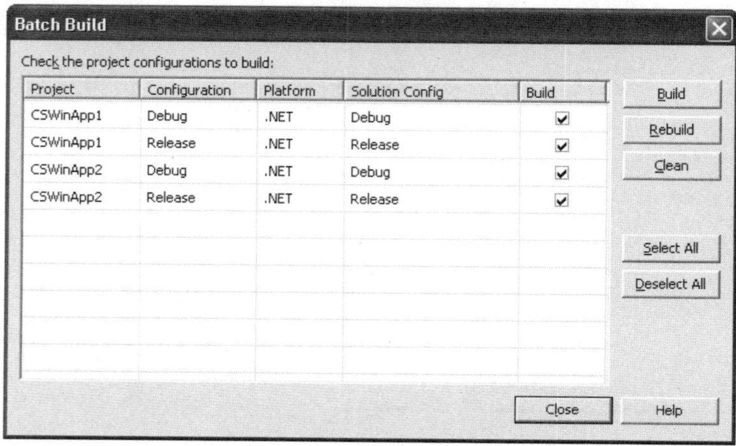

Figure 2-17 The Batch Build dialog box

The Batch Build dialog box lets you perform a number of important actions, including building, rebuilding, and cleaning your projects. Clicking the Build button initiates an incremental build for projects that are configured for such a build. The Rebuild button initiates a Rebuild All for all of the selected projects. Clicking the Clean button deletes the files that are output by a build so you can start clean or share your projects without unnecessary bulk. Note that in Visual Studio .NET the Clean command doesn't actually do anything for Visual Basic .NET and Visual C# projects. The Visual Basic .NET and Visual C# teams decided that this kind of functionality wasn't really necessary for managed projects, so it was left out.

Looking Ahead

While the project management facilities in Visual Studio .NET are formidable, the usability of the IDE for developers also relies on the editor features in the IDE. In Chapter 3, we'll discuss the code editor in detail and discuss techniques that can help you become more productive as you write code.

3

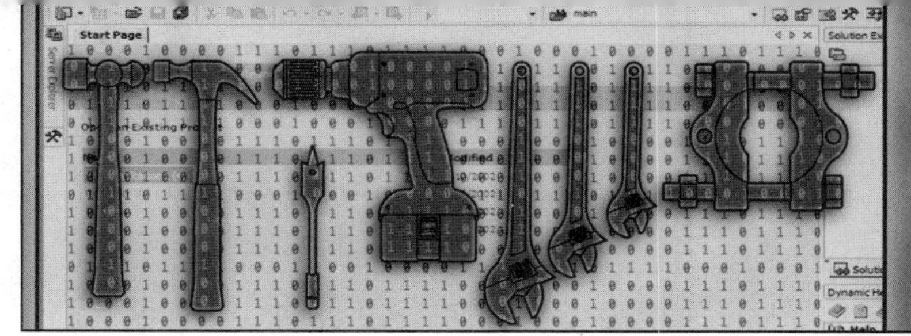

The Visual Studio .NET Editor

The editor is the heart of any development environment. Programmers live in their editors, and the editor in Microsoft Visual Studio .NET was designed to be a programmer's editor. In this chapter, we'll take a close look at the editing tools built into Visual Studio .NET. If you're an experienced programmer, the information in this chapter will help you become even more productive in Visual Studio .NET; if you're new to Visual Studio .NET, this chapter will serve as introduction to its new and enhanced features. We'll show you how to access editor features that make your job easier, and we'll describe some of the features of the integrated development environment (IDE) that make working in Visual Studio .NET a real pleasure.

Documents in the IDE

In Visual Studio .NET, everything you do revolves around the solution and the projects in the solution. In that way, Visual Studio .NET becomes your project management tool. What you're managing, for the most part, are source documents that comprise your projects and the tool windows that provide functionality inside the IDE. To create and edit the documents themselves, you use the Code Editor and the designers in the IDE. The source files you're editing show up in windows that open to the center of the IDE and become part of the tabbed view. The windows that contain these files are known collectively as *document windows*, and they can be designers, editors, the Web browser, and Help windows.

Dockable Tool Windows

Not all the tabbed windows in the IDE are document windows. You can add a tool window to the tabbed windows at the center of the IDE by selecting the window and toggling off the window's Dockable value on the Window menu. The Object Browser window (Ctrl+Alt+J) is undocked by default, making it a tabbed window in the IDE. The benefit of adding a tool window to the set of tabbed windows at the center of the IDE is that you can display a large amount of information at once. Alternatively, you can undock a tool window by dragging it away from the edge where it's docked and leave its Dockable setting on, essentially making the window a floating window. This technique is especially handy if you're working with multiple monitors.

Visual Studio .NET has a huge number of additional Code Editor features in the 7.0 and 7.1 versions. Among the new and enhanced features are outlining, code formatting, and my personal favorite, line numbering.

All of these features can be accessed using named commands either from the Visual Studio .NET Command Window (Ctrl+Alt+A) or through menu commands or keyboard shortcuts. Master these commands and you master Visual Studio .NET.

It's All About Text

The place where you write your code in Visual Studio .NET goes by one of two names, depending on the context of the file being edited. When you're working on a file that's been saved as a programming language type recognized by Visual Studio .NET, the editor you're working in is called the Code Editor. The functionality that you'll find attached to the Code Editor will depend on how your language was integrated into the IDE. When you're working on a text file or a file type that's not been recognized by the IDE, you're working in the Text Editor. This editor has less functionality than the Code Editor, but it's still fairly powerful. It's important to note that you can run macros in either editor, although the Code Editor hosts a much larger feature set. For the most part, we'll refer to these editors collectively as the Code Editor, but we'll make a distinction where appropriate.

Figure 3-1 shows the various parts of the Code Editor in the IDE. Take a look at the names used in the figure. The parts are probably familiar to you from a usage standpoint, but you might not be aware of their names. Depending on which language you're using, you might find some slight naming differences in the Code Editor, but the functionality is fairly consistent between languages.

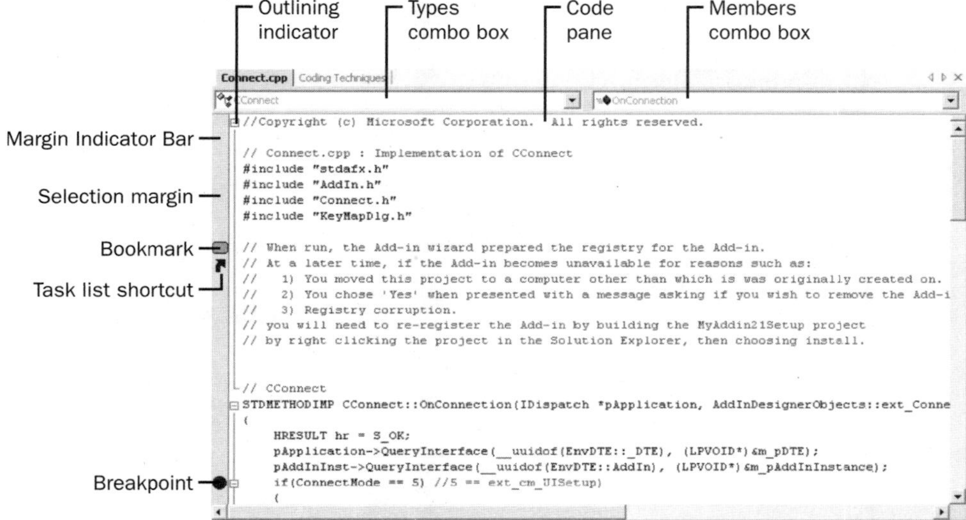

Figure 3-1 The parts of the Code Editor window

The Code Editor is where you type in code and text. Most of the other features shown in the figure can be toggled off to give you an unfettered view of the Code Editor. You can click and drag just above the scrollbar on the right side of the Code Editor to break the view into two separate Code Panes. By using multiple Code Panes with a single file, you can look at different parts of your code concurrently.

The Navigation Bar contains the two boxes at the top of the Code Editor. In Visual C#, these are the Types drop-down list and the Members drop-down list. In Visual Basic .NET, these boxes are called the Class Name and Method Name combo boxes. You can use the Navigation Bar to quickly jump to different parts of your code. In Visual Basic .NET, you can also use these boxes to add methods to the current source file.

The light vertical line to the left of the code is the outlining indicator. By clicking the + and – boxes along this line, you can hide and show blocks of code within a source file. We'll discuss this feature in some detail later in the chapter.

The area between the rightmost part of the outlining indicator and the Margin Indicator Bar is the selection margin. Clicking in the selection margin selects the adjacent line of code. When your mouse pointer is in the area of the selection margin, it changes from an arrow pointing northwest to one that's pointing northeast. By clicking and dragging down or up in this area, you can select complete blocks of code, as shown in Figure 3-2. The benefit of doing this is that you end up selecting the same amount of white space in each line of code, giving you a nice clean block. (Trust me: for editors and writers, this feature is huge.) Using the selection margin to select an entire line with a single click can help reduce selection errors and can make it much easier to keep your code formatting when you copy text between files.

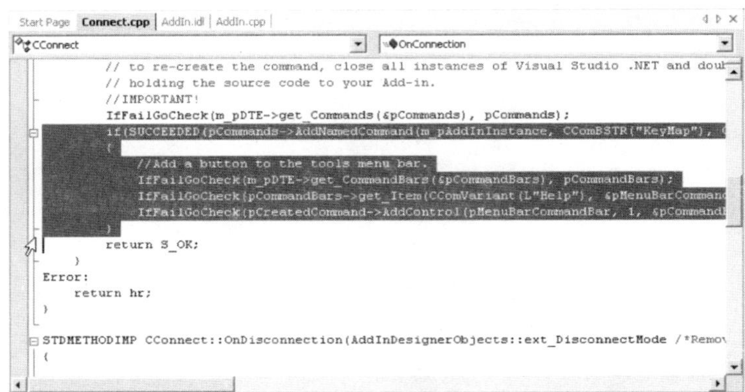

Figure 3-2 Selecting text using the selection margin

The Margin Indicator Bar is a tool that serves many purposes. It's used to set and delete breakpoints in your code, to indicate bookmarks in code, and to hold Task List shortcuts. During debugging, you'll see an indicator in this margin. When a breakpoint is hit, the breakpoint indicator will contain a yellow arrow that points to the current line of code. This line of code is highlighted in yellow by default. As you step through the code, the yellow indicator shows you where you are in the code, and that line is highlighted in the Code Editor.

Notice the tab at the top of the Code Editor window. When you're in tabbed view, you'll see a tab like this for every document and nondockable tool window that you have open. These tabs let you navigate easily between multiple source files and forms in your project. If you prefer working with multiple document interface (MDI) windows, such as the ones in Visual Studio 6, you can turn off the tabs in the Options dialog box.

Now that we've reviewed the Code Editor window, let's take a look at the kinds of things we can do inside the Code Editor to make programming and editing tasks easier.

Lab: Navigating Between Views and Windows

Let's loosen up our fingers and take a look at how to quickly navigate between the Code Editor, the Designer window, Solution Explorer, and Class View.

Let's say we're in a project and that we're working on some code and some user interface design. Using the keyboard, press Ctrl+Alt+L to pop into Solution Explorer. Navigate to a C# code file, and press Enter. By default, any Windows Forms or Web Forms associated with the file will open; otherwise, the source file will open. To see the source code for the C# file, press F7. To pop back to the form, press Shift+F7.

Now click Ctrl+Alt+L again to pop back into Solution Explorer. Navigate to another file, and press Enter. You should have at least three tabs showing in the IDE. To jump between these open files, press Ctrl+Tab or Ctrl+F6.

Finally, to jump into Class View, use Ctrl+Shift+C.

These are all important keystroke combinations. They let you move around in the IDE without taking your hands off the keyboard. If you're the kind of programmer who likes to stick close to the keyboard, these shortcuts can save you a ton of time.

Typing and Shortcuts

If good editors are about anything, they're about efficient typing and text manipulation. If you're new to programming, you might not be aware of the ferocious battles being fought in chat rooms and newsgroups and on Web sites between factions of programmers who prefer one editor over another and who will argue incessantly about what makes their editor better than another. (Not that I'm above the fray, given my belief that Visual Studio .NET is the One True Editor.)

So what is it about text editing that causes such a strong reaction among programmers? I think it has to do with the idea that programmers like to find the most efficient way to do anything, and if a specific editor allows them to accomplish their goals they become very attached to that editor. A secondary reason is that it takes some time to master an editor, and once a programmer masters an editor, he's less likely to want to learn things all over again unless a better editor comes along.

The sections that follow are designed to show you how Visual Studio .NET can work for a programmer who likes to keep her hands on the keyboard. I've noticed that many of the most productive programmers I work with rarely take their hands off the keyboard to perform routine tasks that less experienced programmers go to the mouse for. The idea behind these shortcuts is to improve your speed in the IDE, and they take some time and practice to learn. The information that follows is provided as a quick reference for programmers who are experienced with Windows shortcuts and as a tutorial for programmers who are used to working in a UNIX editor such as Vi or Emacs.

Common Editing Shortcuts

Applications written for Microsoft Windows use a number of standard keyboard shortcuts that you're probably familiar with. These shortcuts are known as Common User Accessibility (CUA) shortcuts and are based on work done at IBM that has standardized shortcuts across a number of platforms. The biggest advantage of using this particular set of shortcuts is that once you learn them, you can apply them in almost any Windows application, including Microsoft Office. These shortcuts have also been labeled on a number of popular keyboards, including most of the Microsoft keyboards.

> **Tip** For more information about Windows keyboard shortcuts, see the book *Microsoft Windows User Experience* (Microsoft Press, 1999), which details how shortcuts such as these should be used in Windows applications.

The tables that follow group the common editing shortcuts for Visual Studio .NET based on function and on when you're likely to use them in an editing session. Table 3-1 lists the file shortcuts. You'll use these to open a new file or existing files and to save files as you work.

Table 3-1 Common File Shortcuts

Command	Keystroke	Named Command
New	Ctrl+N	*File.NewFile*
Open	Ctrl+O	*File.OpenFile*
Save	Ctrl+S	*File.SaveSelectedItems*
Save All	Ctrl+Shift+S	*File.SaveAll*
Print	Ctrl+P	*File.Print*

You'll notice that you're presented with a New File dialog box when you try to create a new file in Visual Studio .NET. This might take a little getting used to if you prefer to see a new text document appear immediately. By selecting a specific file type when you create the new file, you enable much of the functionality associated with a particular language before you save the file. You can save some time when creating a new file by using the Command Window and adding the name and extension of the file you want to create. For example, if you want to create a file named UserMotion.cpp, you press Ctrl+Alt+A to open the Command Window and then enter **File.NewFile UserMotion.cpp**. Later in this chapter, in the section "Using the Command Window," we'll show you how to alias commands like this one so you can easily create the files you use most often. In Chapter 4, we'll show you how to create a macro that creates a new file of the type you're most likely to be interested in when you press Ctrl+N.

Navigating in a document using keystrokes is one of those skills you tend to learn without actually picking up a book or reading an article. We'll review the common navigation and selection keys and shortcuts here. They are listed in Table 3-2. Notice that selection involves holding down the Shift key and that moving to a larger selection for a particular key usually involves holding down the Ctrl key.

Table 3-2 Common Navigation and Selection Shortcuts

Movement	Movement Keystroke(s)	Selection Keystroke
Character	Right Arrow	Shift+Right Arrow
	Left Arrow	Shift+Left Arrow
Word	Ctrl+Right Arrow	Ctrl+Shift+Right Arrow
	Ctrl+Left Arrow	Ctrl+Shift+Left Arrow
Line	End	Shift+End
	Home	Shift+Home
	Down Arrow	Shift+Down Arrow
	Up Arrow	Shift+Up Arrow
Code Pane	Page Down	Shift+Page Down
	Page Up	Shift+Page Up
Document	Ctrl+End	Ctrl+Shift+End
	Ctrl+Home	Ctrl+Shift+Home

Once you've selected text, you can copy or cut it to the Clipboard and you can paste it back into the Code Editor. The common editing shortcuts are listed in Table 3-3.

Table 3-3 Common Editing Shortcuts

Command	Keystroke	Named Command
Cut	Ctrl+X	*Edit.Cut*
Copy	Ctrl+C	*Edit.Copy*
Paste	Ctrl+V	*Edit.Paste*
Undo	Ctrl+Z	*Edit.Undo*
Redo	Ctrl+Y	*Edit.Redo*
Select current word	Ctrl+W	*Edit.SelectCurrentWord*
Select all	Ctrl+A	*Edit.SelectAll*

Lab: Using the Clipboard Ring

The Clipboard Ring is a tool you can use to track and use multiple copy operations in the IDE. The Clipboard Ring is available as a tab in the Toolbox. To practice with the Clipboard Ring, pin open the Toolbox and click the Clipboard Ring Toolbox tab. Open a code listing, and select some text. Copy that text to the Clipboard, and watch the Clipboard Ring. Copy a few more bits of text and notice that the most recently selected text is always at the top. You can double-click any of the Clipboard items to insert them into a file, but there's a much cooler way to use this tool. Press Ctrl+Shift+Insert, holding down Ctrl+Shift. This will insert the text at the top of the stack. Notice that the inserted text is still selected. Press Insert again, and the second item on the stack replaces the selected text. Press Insert a third time, and the text from the first copy operation is inserted. (You get the idea.) Press Insert a final time, and you're back to the text you last selected. You can cycle through the Clipboard Ring to easily find the copied text you're looking for.

Finally, let's take a look at the shortcuts that you can use to transpose letters, words, and lines. You can use the shortcuts shown in Table 3-4 to swap the position of two items in the Code Editor. For example, if the cursor is positioned before the letters *AB*, pressing Ctrl+T will cause the letters to switch their order to *BA*. Typing Ctrl+Shift+T with the cursor adjacent to or in the word *go* in the string *go boldly* will result in a transposition to *boldly go*. The most useful shortcut in this group runs the command *Edit.LineTranspose*. Using the shortcut Alt+Shift+T swaps the line where the cursor is located with the next line, making it really easy to move a line of code down the page.

Table 3-4 Transposition Shortcuts

Command	Keystroke	Named Command
Transpose character	Ctrl+T	*Edit.CharTranspose*
Transpose word	Ctrl+Shift+T	*Edit.WordTranspose*
Transpose line	Alt+Shift+T	*Edit.LineTranspose*

These shortcuts should provide you with the functionality you need to perform a fair number of editing tasks without the mouse if you choose to work that way. There's nothing wrong with using the mouse for editing. It's not really much slower to use the mouse than to use shortcuts, but the extra second or two that it takes to go to the mouse can take you out of that creative groove you can get into when you're editing. For me, transitioning from using a mouse back to the keyboard takes a little more time than using a shortcut, so I try to use shortcuts whenever possible.

Custom Keyboard Shortcuts

Earlier we talked about toggling a window's Dockable state to add it to the center of the IDE. There's no shortcut assigned by default to the *Window.Dockable* command, but you might find that adding one would be handy for making a very data-heavy window easier to read.

To create a new shortcut in the IDE, press Ctrl+Alt+A to open the Command Window and enter **Tools.Options**. This will bring up the Options dialog box (shown in Figure 3-3). Click the Keyboard item in the Environment folder to bring up the Keyboard page. This page lets you do a number of things with shortcuts in the IDE, such as create and edit shortcut keys, change the keyboard mapping scheme, and save a custom mapping scheme. The first time you add a custom shortcut to the IDE, you'll be prompted to save your mapping scheme with a custom name.

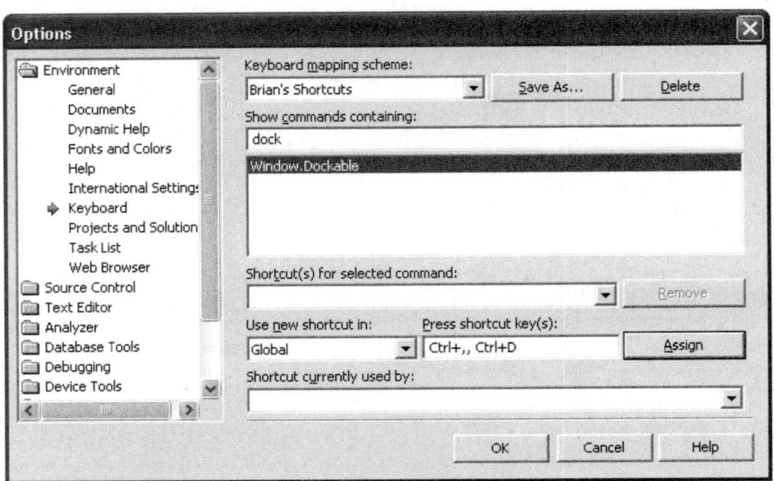

Figure 3-3 The Keyboard page of the Options dialog box

To find the command you want to assign the new shortcut to, type part of the command name in the Show Commands Containing box. In this case, type **dock**, and Window.Dockable will show up in the command list.

Here's the tricky part. Nearly every possible keystroke shortcut has been taken in Visual Studio .NET. You can overwrite keystrokes that you think you'll never use, but that isn't always the most satisfactory solution. For one thing, if you go to work on a different machine and you haven't updated the shortcuts, you might end up keying the wrong command, which can be both annoying and potentially harmful to whatever you're typing in at the moment. You're best bet is to find an available keystroke and take maximum advantage of it.

Visual Studio .NET now allows you to create chorded shortcuts. To start a chord, you hold down the Ctrl key and press another key. The IDE then waits for another stroke to determine which command to execute. I've found that Ctrl+, (Ctrl+comma) hasn't been taken in Visual Studio .NET by default. So I can chord all my personal commands off this key sequence and assign the second key sequence to one that matches the command I'm trying to execute. For the *Window.Dockable* command, I assign the sequence Ctrl+,, Ctrl+D (Ctrl+comma, Ctrl+D) by typing that combination in the Press Shortcut Key(s) box. Be sure to save the new shortcut by clicking the Assign button.

While I have the Options dialog box open, I can add a keystroke shortcut for the Options dialog box itself by typing **Tools.Options** in the Show Commands Containing box and assigning the keystroke Ctrl+,, Ctrl+O. Now I can open the Options dialog box quickly at any time to customize my IDE.

You can assign keystroke shortcuts to named commands in the IDE, to add-ins that you create or install, and to macros that you create and save.

Using the Keybindings Table Add-in

The only way to determine what shortcuts are assigned in Visual Studio .NET without resorting to code is to look at the commands assigned in the Options dialog box. That isn't the easiest way to map out what's going on, so Craig wrote a nice little add-in that lists all of the named commands and currently assigned shortcuts in the IDE.

The Keybindings Table add-in is available from the Visual Studio .NET Web site at *http://msdn.microsoft.com/vstudio/downloads/automation.asp*. Because this add-in is written in C++, you need to compile it using Visual Studio .NET or Visual C++ .NET. The compiled add-in is registered in Visual Studio .NET during the build process. After you restart Visual Studio .NET, you'll find that the add-in loaded by the IDE.

On the Visual Studio .NET Help menu, you'll find a new command named KeyMap. Choosing this command brings up the Keyboard Help dialog box, shown in Figure 3-4.

Keyboard Help

Copy | View: Bound Commands

Command Name	Scope	Key Binding
Build.BuildSolution	Global	Ctrl+Shift+B
Build.Cancel	Global	Ctrl+Break
Build.Compile	Global	Ctrl+F7
Database.Run	Global	Ctrl+E
Database.RunSelection	Global	Ctrl+Q
Database.StepInto	Global	Alt+F5
Debug.ApplyCodeChanges	Global	Alt+F10
Debug.Autos	Global	Ctrl+Alt+V, A
Debug.BreakAll	Global	Ctrl+Alt+Break
Debug.Breakpoints	Global	Ctrl+Alt+B
Debug.CallStack	Global	Ctrl+Alt+C
Debug.ClearAllBreakpoints	Global	Ctrl+Shift+F9
Debug.Disassembly	Global	Ctrl+Alt+D
Debug.EnableBreakpoint	Global	Ctrl+F9
Debug.Exceptions	Global	Ctrl+Alt+E
Debug.Immediate	Global	Ctrl+Alt+I
Debug.Locals	Global	Ctrl+Alt+V, L
Debug.Memory1	Global	Ctrl+Alt+M, 1
Debug.Memory2	Global	Ctrl+Alt+M, 2
Debug.Memory3	Global	Ctrl+Alt+M, 3
Debug.Memory4	Global	Ctrl+Alt+M, 4
Debug.Modules	Global	Ctrl+Alt+U
Debug.NewBreakpoint	Global	Ctrl+B
Debug.QuickWatch	Global	Shift+F9

Figure 3-4 The Keyboard Help dialog box

The Keybindings Table add-in performs a number of useful functions. You can use this add-in to browse the keystroke shortcuts assigned to named commands in the IDE, or you can just browse all the commands available. You can also copy the table entries to the Clipboard. Just select an entry and click the

Copy button. If you want to select multiple entries, hold down the Ctrl key and click another item in the list to select a range of entries. Once on the Clipboard, these entries can be pasted into Microsoft Excel for easier reading and sorting.

The Zen of Tabs and Code Formatting

Code formatting is another one of those issues that developers tend to feel strongly about. When it comes to code formatting, the bottom line for most organizations is that some sort of standard should exist. The formatting options for each of the languages supported in the Visual Studio IDE are set in the Text Editor folder of the Options dialog box. When you set options for All Languages, as shown in Figure 3-5, you override the settings for each individual language listed in the Text Editor folder.

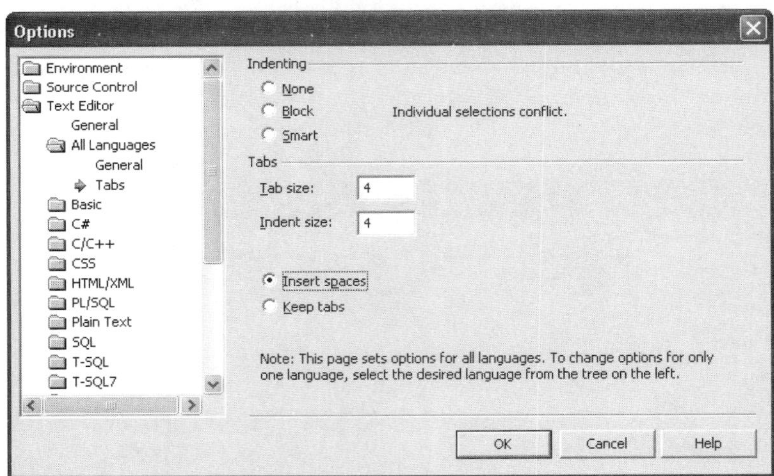

Figure 3-5 Setting global Tabs options

As you can see in the figure, you can set Indenting to None, Block, or Smart. The behavior of these options is determined by the language and the Tabs settings below them. When None is the selected Indenting type, pressing Enter at the end of a line will start the next line at the leftmost space in the Code Editor. Block indenting sets the indent to the same space as the first character in the current line. This is a common generic setting that lets you indent manually but doesn't force you to key a lot of extra tabs to get to where you want to be. The Smart setting applies an indent by context. For example, pressing Enter after an open brace ({) in C# will automatically indent the next line.

The choice between using spaces or tab characters for indenting is usually a matter of personal preference or of the coding standard you want to apply. If you prefer that all the code you deal with consists of spaces rather than tabs, you can set that option globally when you customize your IDE. If you prefer spaces to tabs, keep in mind that Visual C# specifies tabs for indentation by default. You can view the white space in the document by using the *Edit.ViewWhitespace* command (Ctrl+R, Ctrl+W). Figure 3-6 shows a document in which the white space is visible. If you use tab characters in your source code, they will show up as right arrows. If you use spaces in your code, a single dot will show up for every space.

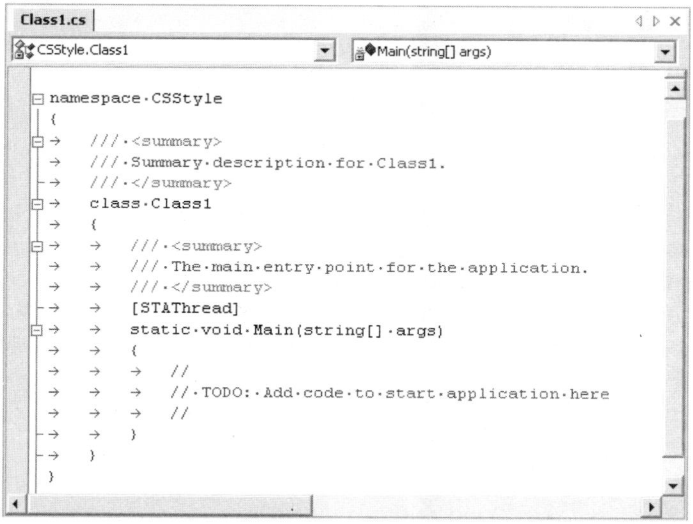

```
Class1.cs
CSStyle.Class1                    Main(string[] args)

namespace·CSStyle
{
→	///·<summary>
→	///·Summary·description·for·Class1.
→	///·</summary>
→	class·Class1
→	{
→	→	///·<summary>
→	→	///·The·main·entry·point·for·the·application.
→	→	///·</summary>
→	→	[STAThread]
→	→	static·void·Main(string[]·args)
→	→	{
→	→	→	//
→	→	→	//·TODO:·Add·code·to·start·application·here
→	→	→	//
→	→	}
→	}
}
```

Figure 3-6 Displaying white space in the Code Editor

If you want to convert existing files from tabs to spaces or vice versa, select the desired option on the Tabs page of the Options dialog box and then click OK to close the dialog box. Then simply select all the code in the file by pressing Ctrl+A. Press Ctrl+K, Ctrl+F (*Edit.FormatSelection*) to apply the new formatting to the selection.

The Formatting page of the Options dialog box, shown in Figure 3-7, controls a number of characteristics of code typed into a Code Pane. This page is available for most of the major languages supported in the IDE, but under Basic, the VB Specific page handles the customizations. The page in the figure shows the C# formatting options.

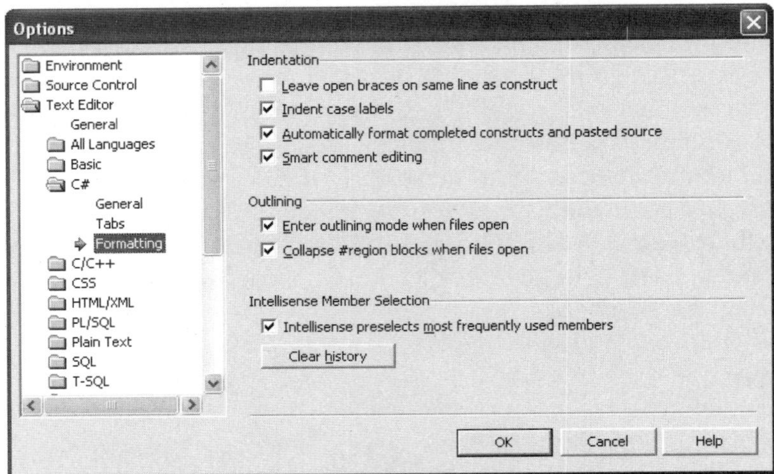

Figure 3-7 The C# Formatting page

Different options are available for different languages. The option to notice in Figure 3-7 is the Leave Open Braces On Same Line As Construct check box. In C#, this check box is clear by default. This setting forces an open curly brace added at the end of a line to be moved to the next line in the Code Editor and to be aligned with the beginning of the statement. The following line is then indented like this:

```
static void Main(string[] args)
{
    //
    // TODO: Add code to start application here
    //
}
```

Selecting the Leave Open Braces On Same Line As Construct option causes your code to be formatted in slanted style, which is often called *K&R* for the style adopted by Kernighan and Ritchie in *The C Programming Language* (2nd ed., Prentice-Hall, 1988). In this style, the first brace in the block is located at the end of the statement, as in the following:

```
static void Main(string[] args) {
    //
    // TODO: Add code to start application here
    //
}
```

Once you decide on the style characteristics you want to apply to your code, you can use the *Edit.FormatSelection* command to apply the style.

You might have noticed that the C# Language Specification employs a mixed style, similar to strict K&R styling, in which methods use the slanted style and classes use the straight style. When you use *Edit.FormatSelection* to apply your desired formatting, your style is applied to every selected block in your code. If you use the *Edit.FormatDocument* command, every block in the document is modified to match the selected style. To use a mixed style, select the Leave Open Braces On Same Line As Construct check box, but make sure that you don't apply your formatting to the entire document.

Syntax Coloring, Line Numbering, and Outlining (or, What the Compiler Saw)

None of what we're talking about in this chapter has anything to do with what happens when you build your applications. Depending on the language you use, compilers remove formatting and white space when a file is processed. At the editor level, however, even the small features provided in the IDE can have a profound effect on your productivity and comfort when you're working with code.

Syntax Coloring

To change the colors used in the Text Editor, go to the Fonts And Colors page located in the Environment folder in the Options dialog box. This page, shown in Figure 3-8, lets you change settings for most of the windows used in the IDE. The settings include printer settings, tool window settings, and the query and view designer settings.

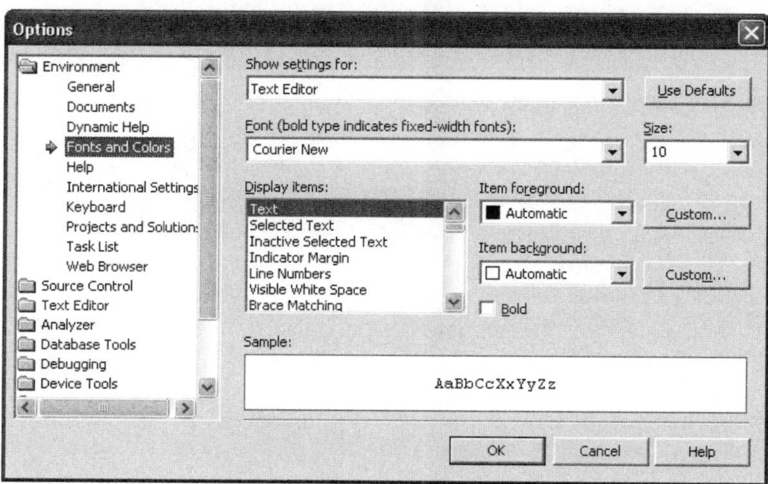

Figure 3-8 The Fonts And Colors page

To customize an item in your Text Editor windows, select the item in the Display Items list and select the Item Foreground color and Item Background color you want the item to use in the editor. Select the Bold check box if you want an item to appear in bold. The Text item governs the overall look of the Text Editor, so if you want to make a drastic change, such as displaying white text on a black background, set those colors first and then customize the rest of your items. This will let you see in the Sample window how other items with the Item Background or Item Foreground settings set to Automatic will look with the custom color you've selected for Text. For example, in Figure 3-9, the Text item is set to display white text on a black background. Clicking the Comment item will show an Automatic background and a Dark Green foreground. You can change the foreground to Green and get much better visibility for the item.

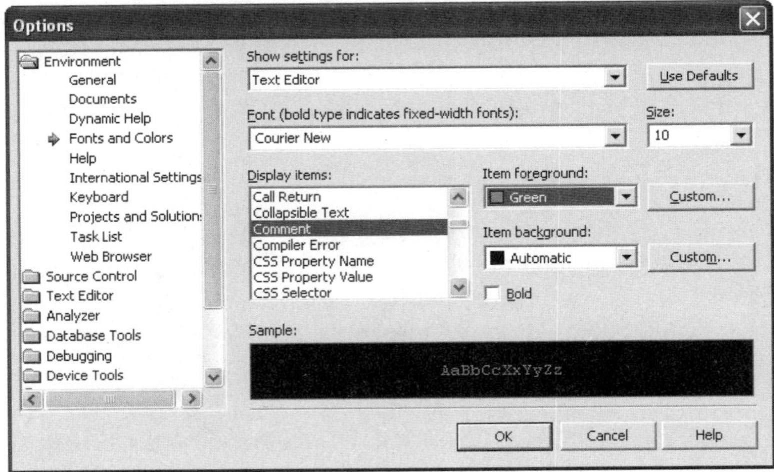

Figure 3-9 Customizing the Text Editor

You can also use the Fonts And Colors page to change the default font used in the dialog boxes and on the Start Page of the IDE. Figure 3-10 shows a tool window after Dialogs And Tool Windows has been customized to use a custom font. You can easily get back to the Visual Studio .NET defaults by clicking the Use Defaults button on the Fonts And Colors page.

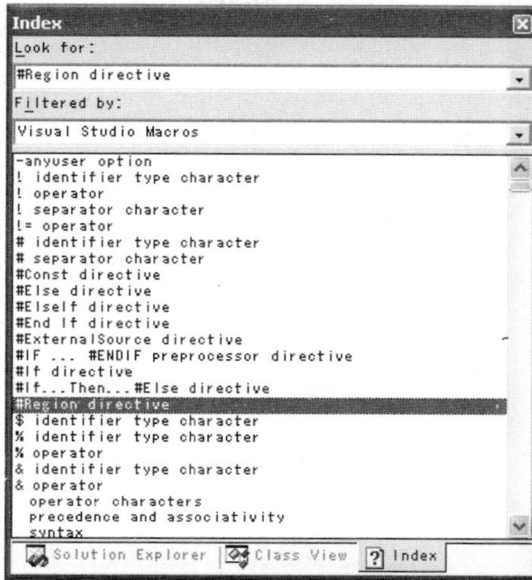

Figure 3-10 The Index tool window after the Dialogs And Tool Windows option has been customized

There's one customization on the Fonts And Colors page that can be very useful if you use a standard black-and-white printer to print your code listings or if you do a lot of customization of the Text Editor in the IDE. You can select Printer in the Show Setting For list box to set the fonts and colors used when you print a document. The Use button replaces the Use Defaults button in this circumstance to allow you to use a different set of font and color options when you print. If you're displaying white text on a black background, for example, you probably don't want to print your pages in that format. The Printer settings are kept separate from those for the Text Editor by default. If you want, you can use your custom Text Editor settings for printing by selecting Text Editor Settings from the list shown in Figure 3-11.

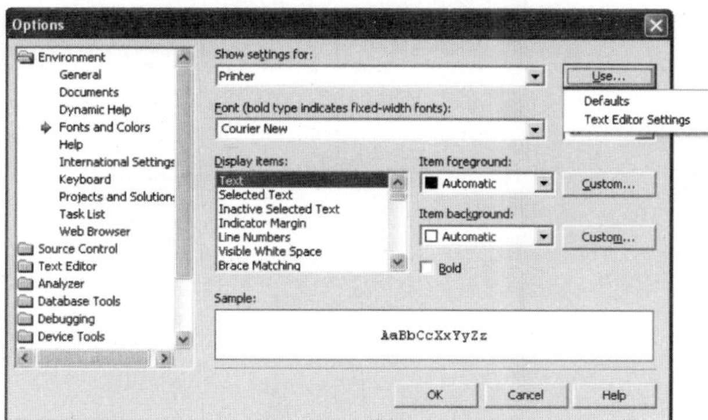

Figure 3-11 Customizing printer settings

Here we'll use settings that are separate from those in the Text Editor. By customizing Printer output, you can improve the readability of the code that you're printing. Figure 3-12 shows some printer output after the comments have been set to Bold on the Fonts And Colors page. Keep in mind that this setting doesn't affect the appearance of the code in the Text Editor.

```
c:\Documents and Settings\brianjo\Desktop\KeyMap\KeyMap\AddIn.cpp
//Copyright (c) Microsoft Corporation.  All rights reserved.

// AddIn.cpp : Implementation of DLL Exports.

#include "stdafx.h"
#include "resource.h"
#include "AddIn.h"

CAddInModule _AtlModule;
```

Figure 3-12 Printed source code with comments in bold

Customizing at Microsoft

If you've been to any conferences where Microsoft employees have demonstrated products, you might have noticed that they don't do much customization of the user interface or the Windows environment in which they work. There's a reason for this. There's an informal understanding at Microsoft that if you *need* to customize your environment (and you want to show that to customers), you should file a bug and argue that the feature you're customizing should be set to your preference by default. (Of course, a customization such as temporarily making the font in the Text Editor larger so audience members can read more easily is exempt from this guideline.) It's not that it's wrong to customize things—it's just that we strive to always provide the customer with the best experience out of the box. If something *needs* to be changed to make that experience better, then that setting should be made the default if possible.

If you spend a lot of time customizing the colors and fonts in your IDE, you might want to back up those settings so you can apply them on a different machine or have them in case you need to rebuild. You can back up your custom settings by using Regedit to export the following registry key to a REG file on your machine.

Visual Studio .NET 2002

```
HKEY_CURRENT_USER\Software\Microsoft\VisualStudio\7.0\FontAndColors
```

Visual Studio .NET 2003

```
HKEY_CURRENT_USER\Software\Microsoft\VisualStudio\7.1\FontAndColors
```

Once you've saved the registry key, you can import the REG file using Regedit if you need to. Restarting the IDE after importing your custom settings will apply the imported settings.

Line Numbering

You can set line numbering on the General page for any of the languages available in the Text Editor folder in the Options dialog box. You can set this option for any specific language, or you can set it for all languages. You can toggle this setting in the Options dialog box, but there is no named command associated with this setting.

To toggle this setting without opening the Options dialog box, you have to run a macro or an add-in to automate that functionality. Two of the macros that are part of the Samples macros set included with Visual Studio .NET were designed to turn line numbering on and off. You can customize these macros yourself, or you can use them from the Command Window, from shortcuts, or by creating new menu commands or toolbar buttons.

The line-numbering macros are *Macros.Samples.Utilities.TurnOnLineNumbers* and *Macros.Samples.Utilities.TurnOffLineNumbers*. Either of these can be a finger buster to type into the Command Window, even with the aid of IntelliSense, so we'll create an alias for each of these commands. An alias is a short command name that's used to represent a longer command in the Command Window. To create an alias for the *TurnOnLineNumbers* macro, open the Command Window by pressing Ctrl+Alt+A and enter the following command:

```
>alias  lnon Macros.Samples.Utilities.TurnOnLineNumbers
```

Now when you enter **lnon**, line numbering will be turned on (if it's currently off). To turn line numbering off, we'll create an alias for the *TurnOffLineNumbers* macro by typing the following into the Command Window:

```
>alias lnoff Macros.Samples.Utilities.TurnOffLineNumbers
```

The *TurnOffLineNumbers* macro is now mapped to *lnoff.*

Suppose you now want to map these macros to keyboard shortcuts. That's not a problem—you just search for the word *Numbers* on the Keyboard page in the Environment folder of the Options dialog box, as we did earlier. Select the macro that you want to map to a keystroke, type your keystroke, and click the Assign button. We use the following mapping for the line-numbering macros. For *TurnOnLineNumbers* we map the keys Ctrl+,, Ctrl+N. (The *N* stands for numbering.) We've mapped the *TurnOffLineNumbers* macro to Ctrl+,, Ctrl+Shift+N. Figure 3-13 shows how that shortcut looks after we've assigned it to the macro.

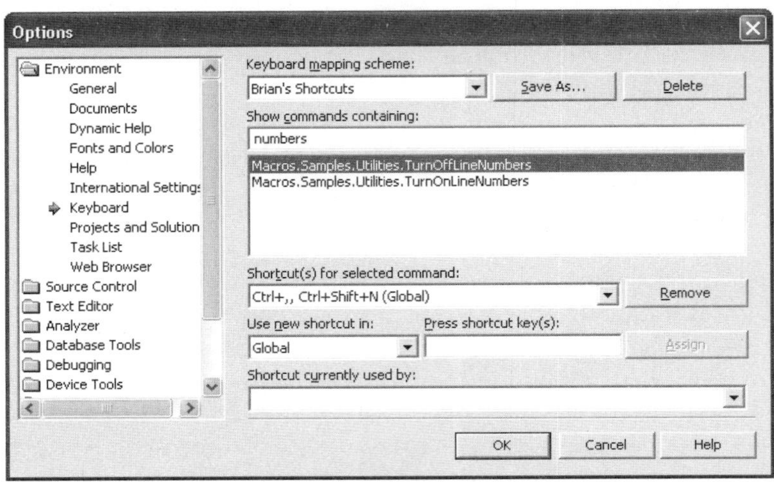

Figure 3-13 The *TurnOffLineNumbers* macro with a shortcut key assignment

Setting up line numbering is fairly straightforward, but will we want to toggle line numbering often enough to justify the brain cells it'll take to remember the aliases and the shortcuts we just created? Maybe. But if not, we can store these commands on a menu and then find them there when we need them. To add these macros to a menu, right-click on a toolbar in Visual Studio .NET and choose Customize. On the Commands tab of the Customize dialog box, you'll find a Macros category. With Macros selected, scroll through the Commands list until you find Samples.Utilities.TurnOnLineNumbers. Choose that command and drag it to a menu. The menu you drag it to will expand, and you can place your selected command precisely where you want it.

To customize the new menu command, right-click on it to bring up a shortcut menu. (The Customize dialog box must remain open.) You can rename the new command Turn On Line Numbers to make it a little more readable. Do the same with the *TurnOffLineNumbers* macro, as shown in Figure 3-14.

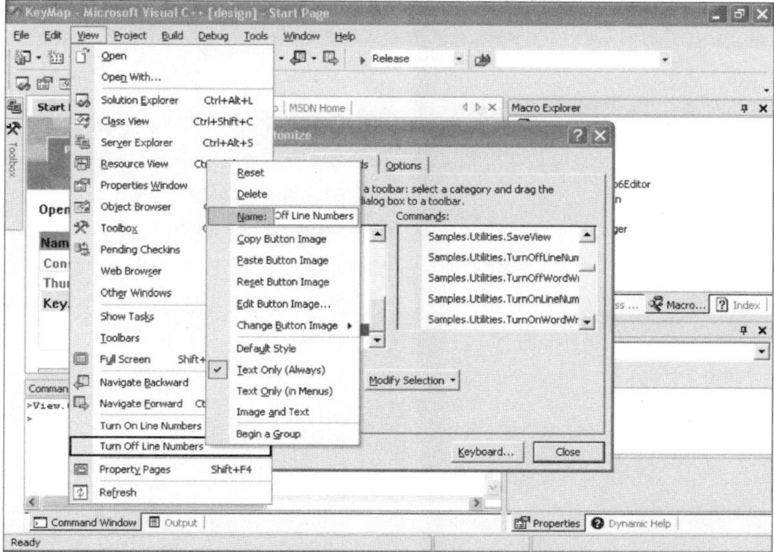

Figure 3-14 Adding the *TurnOffLineNumbers* macro to a menu

You can add a macro like this one to a toolbar in just the same way. In that case, you'll probably want to specify a button image to use with the macro that you're adding.

Outlining

The Visual Studio .NET outlining feature is probably familiar to programmers who've used other advanced editors. The idea is to group code by functionality to make it easier to navigate the code in the Code Editor. Figure 3-15 shows a code file in which the outline has been collapsed to the methods in the file. At the end of each collapsed line you'll see a box with ellipses in it. Hover your mouse pointer over that box to display a ToolTip that shows some of what's in the collapsed node.

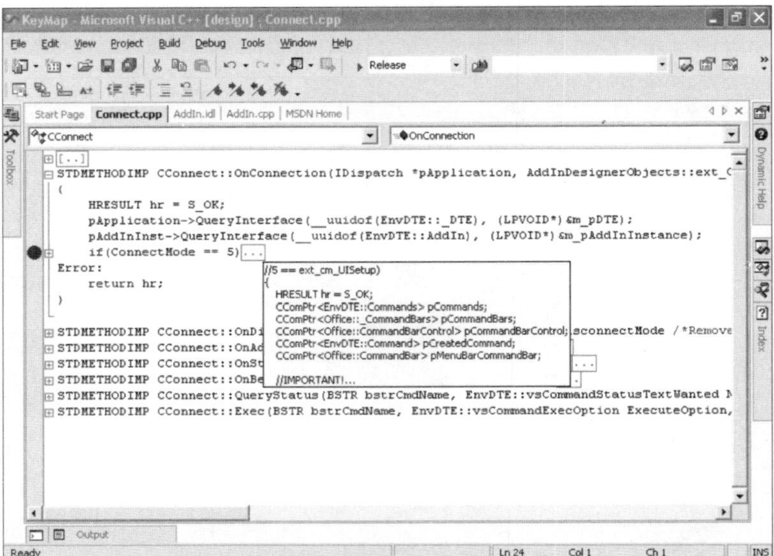

Figure 3-15 A ToolTip indicates the contents of a collapsed node when Outlining is enabled.

You can turn off outlining by pressing Ctrl+M, Ctrl+P (*Edit.StopOutlining*). Turning off outlining makes the outlining indicators along the side of the Code Editor disappear completely. You can restart outlining by pressing Ctrl+M, Ctrl+O (*Edit.CollapsetoDefinitions*). The *CollapsetoDefinitions* command will restart outlining in the Code Editor and will collapse each code block in the file. Pressing Ctrl+M, Ctrl+L (*Edit.ToggleAllOutlining*) will open all the collapsed blocks in the Code Editor.

In addition to hiding logical code blocks in the Text Editor, you can collapse an arbitrary selection by selecting some text and pressing Ctrl+M, Ctrl+H (*Edit.HideSelection*). This function can be very handy for collapsing some code between two distant points in a code file, and it even works to collapse lines in a plain text file. If you want to expand the collapsed selection, press Ctrl+M, Ctrl+U (*Edit.StopHidingCurrent*).

Table 3-5 lists the shortcuts associated with outlining in the Text Editor.

Table 3-5 Outlining Shortcuts

Command	Keystroke	Named Command
Stop outlining	Ctrl+M, Ctrl+P	*Edit.StopOutlining*
Toggle outlining	Ctrl+M, Ctrl+L	*Edit.ToggleAllOutlining*

Table 3-5 Outlining Shortcuts *(continued)*

Command	Keystroke	Named Command
Toggle expansion	Ctrl+M, Ctrl+M	*Edit.ToggleOutliningExpansion*
Hide selection	Ctrl+M, Ctrl+H	*Edit.HideSelection*
Stop hiding selection	Ctrl+M, Ctrl+U	*Edit.StopHidingCurrent*

Programming Help

A number of features in the IDE make it easier for programmers to write code. You should be familiar with Help in the IDE, so we won't talk too much about it. Help in Visual Studio .NET is dead simple—you just select what you don't understand and press F1. You almost always get what you're looking for. In this section, we'll go over some of the features of the IDE that you've probably used but that you might not be so familiar with.

The Power of F1

A true story: A guy called me a few years ago and told me he'd been trying to find out why he was getting a Visual Basic error code when he was running some function (in Visual Basic 4, I think). He told me he'd been searching for an answer for hours and then finally called me for help. He e-mailed me his project, and I ran it while we talked. Sure enough, I got the same error. He heard my machine ding, and about 10 seconds later I told him what the error message meant. "How did you find that?!" the caller asked in amazement. I told him that I pressed F1 while the message box was still open.

IntelliSense

IntelliSense is one of those features that you start to rely on utterly as a programmer. It's a time-saving feature that can really help you do the right thing when you're typing code into the IDE. What IntelliSense does is provide statement completion in the form of context-sensitive member lists that appear automatically as you type code into the Code Editor. These lists can save you a ton of time when you're programming an unfamiliar API, and they can help you reduce errors that would normally be caught only at build time.

IntelliSense works by parsing the code you type into the Code Editor based on the project type context. This means that your source file needs to be part of a project or a solution before IntelliSense kicks in. IntelliSense is mostly automatic. It works on code that's part of the .NET Framework, and it works on external methods from references you've added to your project. It even works on XML Web services references that have been added to a project.

IntelliSense provides four major types of functionality when you're working with a supported language. Most programmers will use four of these features—statement completion, parameter information, word completion, and code comments—in their automatic form; that is, they'll take the information as presented in the IDE without thinking too much about what's being shown. That's an absolutely valid way to use the technology. If this approach works for you and doesn't get in your way, IntelliSense is doing exactly what it's designed to do. You can also employ IntelliSense more deliberately by using the shortcuts associated with displaying IntelliSense information.

You might want to turn statement completion and parameter information off if you find them distracting, in which case you'll need to use the shortcuts, named commands, or toolbar buttons associated with the various IntelliSense features to display this information. To turn off statement completion in the Code Editor, go to the Text Editor folder in the Options dialog box. Select the language you want to apply your changes to, or select All Languages if you want to apply your changes universally. Open the General page, and in the Statement Completion section clear Auto List Members check box. You can also toggle the Parameter Information setting from this page.

> **Note** You can increase the number of options returned in a member list by clearing Hide Advanced Members. Hide Advanced Members is the default setting for Visual Basic .NET, so you might be missing a number of possible completions if you leave that setting checked.

With statement completion turned on, IntelliSense presents you with information as soon as you type an operator as part of a statement. If you have statement completion turned off or if you want to display this information immediately, press Ctrl+J. The result is shown in Figure 3-16.

```
        static void Main(string[] args)
        {
            //
            // TODO: Add code to start application here
            //int
            Console.
        }
    }
}
```

```
Equals
Error
In
OpenStandardError
OpenStandardInput
OpenStandardOutput
Out
Read
ReadLine
ReferenceEquals
```

Figure 3-16 Forcing statement completion by pressing Ctrl+J

To select an entry to complete a statement, use the up and down arrow keys to navigate to the desired completion and then press Tab.

> **Note** In Visual Studio .NET 2003, you can set an option to make IntelliSense preselect the most frequently used member for a particular statement in Visual C#. You'll find this option on the Formatting page in the C# folder in the Options dialog box.

To force parameter information like that shown in Figure 3-17, press Ctrl+Shift+Spacebar. This gives you a list of the parameter overloads you can choose from for a particular method. With the parameter information showing, use your up and down arrow keys to view the available parameters.

```
        static void Main(string[] args)
        {
            //
            // TODO: Add code to start application here
            //int
            Console.Write(
        }
    }
}
```

```
▲17 of 18▼ void Console.Write (string format, object arg0, object arg1)
format: The format string.
```

Figure 3-17 Viewing the parameter information for a method by pressing Ctrl+Shift+Spacebar

Use the parameter information provided by selecting the item that best suits your needs and then type the parameters into your method. You'll notice that after you type each parameter, the next parameter in the list appears bold. Watching for this pattern helps ensure that every parameter in the list is entered correctly.

You might not be too familiar with the word completion feature if you're used to using IntelliSense automatically. Word completion lets you type in a few characters of a particular statement and get a list of possible completions for that statement. This functionality is a bit different from statement completion, which gives you a member list based on context. Word completion simply gives you a list of all the possible completions for the letters you've typed in. The shortcut for word completion is Alt+Right Arrow, but the statement completion shortcut (Ctrl+J) also works.

Finally, you might have noticed that when you hold your mouse pointer over an identifier in the Code Editor, ToolTip information appears. This ToolTip information is part of the Quick Info feature of IntelliSense, which contains the declaration for the identifier and any associated code comments. You can force this information using Ctrl+K, Ctrl+I. You can add code comments to any method in Visual C# by typing /// on the line directly above the method definition. Even if you're not going to create documentation for your methods, IntelliSense makes code comments such as these helpful for letting another developer figure out how to use your code.

Brace Matching

Automatic brace matching is an IntelliSense feature that helps you determine whether braces in your code are matched properly. Brace matching works in Visual C# and Visual C++ and goes into effect when you type a closing brace into the Code Editor. The brace types affected include parentheses *()*, brackets *[]*, and braces *{}*. In addition, the conditional macro expressions *#if*, *#else*, and *#endif* are matched as you type the closing expression, and quotation marks are matched when you type the closing set.

You can't turn off brace matching—but why would you want to? Well, you might want to, and we'll show you a way to at least hide this feature so it doesn't bother you while you're typing. To customize the way that braces are matched, go to the Fonts And Colors page in the Environment folder of the Options dialog box. Select Brace Matching from the Display Items list. If you clear the Bold check box for Brace Matching and leave the Foreground and Background settings as Automatic, you no longer see the matched braces when you type in the Code Editor. Of course, you can also change the colors and settings to make the brace matching stand out even more. Making the background

Yellow while keeping the text Bold really makes the braces pop out (and is my preferred work setting).

Dynamic Help

Dynamic Help is one of those awesome features that's easy to overlook when you're working with a complex tool such as Visual Studio .NET. Dynamic Help is a tool window in the IDE that constantly serves up help suggestions based on what you're doing in the IDE. If you select a designer, you see suggestions for designer help. If you select a tool window, you see help for that particular tool window.

More important, Dynamic Help serves up information based on code context in the IDE. If you open a Visual C# Code Editor window and you type *Console*, you'll see a Dynamic Help window that looks like the one in Figure 3-18. This window provides links to the help topics appropriate to the *System.Console* class. This is extremely significant because I can't even begin to tell you how many times I've typed Ctrl+Alt+F3 (*Help.Search*) and then proceeded to type the same thing I've already typed into the Code Editor.

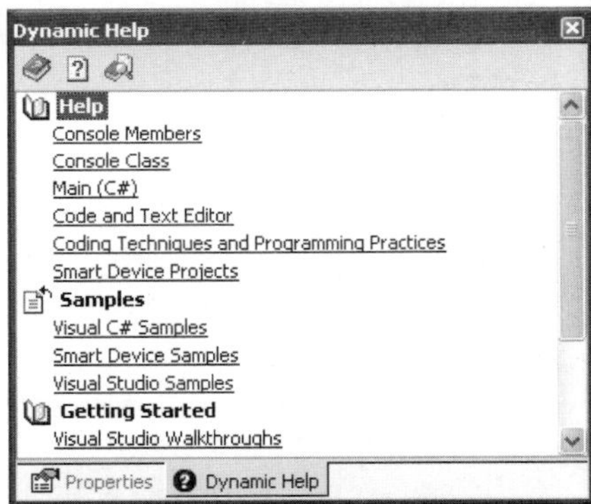

Figure 3-18 The Dynamic Help window

I think this feature isn't talked about more often because of limited space in the IDE. Developers need to use the Properties tool window frequently, so Dynamic Help gets left behind (literally). Using the appropriate shortcuts, you can change that a little bit and make it easier to use this window.

To bring up the Dynamic Help window, press Ctrl+F1. To get a feel for how this will work when you're using the IDE, open a project and be sure the Properties window is obscuring the Dynamic Help window. Navigate to someplace in one of the code files for the project and consider how you can get information about the different elements in your source file. You can place the cursor in a particular statement and press F1 to bring up the associated Help topic. You can press Ctrl+Alt+F3 to open the Search window and then type in the subject that you're looking for help on, or you can press Ctrl+F1 and choose from one of the suggestions from Dynamic Help. In my experience, the Dynamic Help window provides the information I'm looking for well over 90 percent of the time. Using this window takes a little practice, but when you get used to it you'll probably save a significant amount of time.

Using the Command Window

If you've used a modal editor such as Vim (Vi improved) for a number of years and are used to typing editor commands in at a command line, the Command Window in Visual Studio .NET will come as a welcome surprise. I've already referred to using the Visual Studio .NET Command Window a number of times (in both Chapter 1 and Chapter 2), but it's worth considering the various ways you can use this tool in your everyday work.

If you've installed and played with the Keybindings Table add-in, you'll find that more than 1100 commands are available in the IDE. Of those commands, nearly 400 are bound to keyboard shortcuts by default. That leaves a huge number of commands that are available only through menus, toolbars, or the Command Window.

The Command Window in Visual Studio .NET supports two modes of operation. In *Command Mode*, the Command Window runs named commands. In *Immediate Mode*, the Command Window evaluates expressions related to the code you're working with. You can toggle between Command Mode and Immediate Mode using a couple of commands. Typing **immed** will put the Command Window into Immediate Mode. You can switch back to Command Mode by typing **>cmd**. In fact, you can do some expression evaluation in Command Mode while debugging by prefixing your command with a ? (question mark), as shown here:

```
>? i
4
>? i = 7
7
>? i + i
14
```

Conversely, you can easily enter a command while you're working in Immediate Mode by prefixing your command with a > (greater than) character:

```
i
7
```

```
i + i
14
>Edit.Find i
>immed
```

You'll notice that as soon as you enter a completed command, the Command Window switches into Command Mode. You'll need to enter the **immed** command to get back to Immediate Mode. Certain commands, such as *Edit.Find*, open a dialog box and return you to Immediate Mode.

> **Tip** You can clear the Command Window by entering the **cls** command. You can do this from either Command Mode or Immediate Mode; the Command Window will be returned to the mode that it was in when you entered this command.

As you've probably noticed by now, the named commands in Visual Studio .NET generally map to menu commands in the IDE. So if you want to use a named command from the Command Window, all you usually need to do is to type the name of the menu containing the command and then the dot operator and the name of the command. For example, if you want to search using the Command Window, you first bring the window to the front by pressing Ctrl+Alt+A. To open the Find dialog box, you enter **Edit.Find** into the Command Window. You'll notice that some commands, such as the *Edit.Find* command, can take arguments. This means you can search from the Command Window without having to deal with a dialog box. Whether or not you find this approach better is a matter of taste. Now let's take a look at an idea that we introduced a little earlier in the chapter, aliasing, and look at how we can use that feature to make our work in the Command Window a little easier.

We'll use the *Edit.Find* command as an example here. For this command to be really useful, you need to be able to quickly type the command and the search parameters. Entering **Edit.Find** takes a little more effort than you would normally want to expend on a command that you can already perform efficiently in a number of different ways. So let's map this command for a reason other than convenience. Let's say you're used to working in the Vi editor and you find yourself wanting to type \ (backslash) to search for items in the Text Editor. You can alias the backslash character to *Edit.Find* using the following command sequence:

```
>alias \ Edit.Find
```

To use the new alias, you type your command just as if you were using the actual named command. The following shows using the new \ alias to search in the Text Editor for a couple of terms:

```
>\ main|args /regex
```

This implementation of the \ search character isn't perfect. You need to type a space between the character and the term or expression you're searching for. This feature does the job, though, and it makes converting to the new editor just a little easier.

You'll probably find that aliasing commands is most useful for macros that you've written. The paths to these macros can get pretty long, and an alias can save you a lot of work. We'll talk about macros and how to employ them in the IDE in Chapter 4.

There are two ways to get to a command prompt in Visual Studio .NET. The way that we've described in the book so far is to open the Command Window using the Ctrl+Alt+A shortcut. You can also type commands into the Find combo box on the Standard toolbar by pressing Ctrl+D (*Edit.GoToFindCombo*). Normally, typing text in the Find combo box simply gives you a quick way to search the currently open document for a term or phrase. When you type a > (greater than) character into the box, the box changes to one capable of taking commands. You can then type named commands in the box that you would usually type in the Command Window. Because both the Command Window and the Find combo box support IntelliSense, you can simply type a named command to see all the possible completions for the command. You can see the list of completions in Figure 3-19.

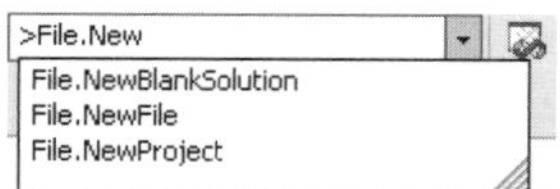

Figure 3-19 Command completion in the Find combo box

Search, Replace, and Regular Expressions

If you can't easily search for and replace text in your editor, you're probably not working with a very good editor. It's great to be able to type in code easily, but finding and fixing code problems is something you must do often as a programmer, and the search functions built into the editor are what make that work easy (or difficult). Visual Studio .NET offers a number of ways to search in the Text Editor, and it offers a powerful regular expressions facility that allows you to do extremely complex searches.

First let's take a look at the named commands and shortcuts associated with the Find and Replace operations in Visual Studio .NET. These might be familiar to you because they're mapped to the Common User Accessibility (CUA) shortcuts that you might have used in Windows or in Office.

To bring up the Find dialog box, press Ctrl+F. You can see this dialog box in Figure 3-20. The options in this dialog box are fairly straightforward. You can specify case (Match Case), whole word searches (Match Whole Word), and the direction of your search (Search Up). An interesting option on this dialog box is Search Hidden Text. When this check box is left clear, text that is hidden in a collapsed node of an outline won't be searched.

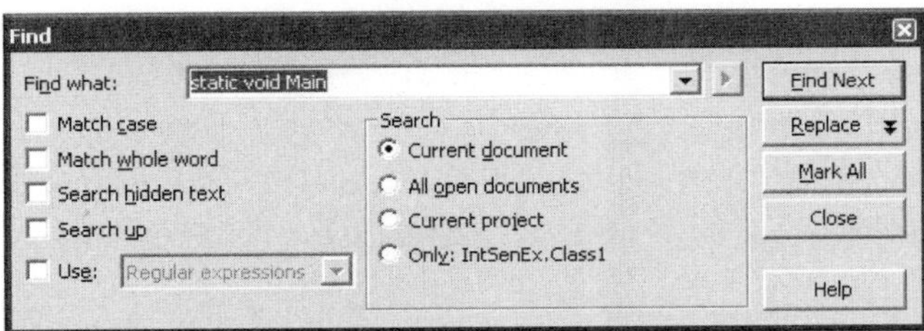

Figure 3-20 The Find dialog box

The Find dialog box in Visual Studio .NET is actually a tool window, so you can dock it in the IDE or even toggle off the Dockable option on the shortcut menu available from the title bar to make it a tabbed window in the center of the IDE.

You can dock the Find dialog box by dragging it to a side of the IDE. But making it a floating dialog box might be preferable because it's easy to accidentally dock the window when you're trying to get it out of your way. You can turn off docking by choosing Floating on the shortcut menu for the dialog box. (Right-click the Close button on a dialog box to open its shortcut menu.) Doing so will let you drag the Find dialog box around the screen with impunity.

You can bring up the Replace dialog box by pressing Ctrl+H. This dialog box (shown in Figure 3-21) is nearly identical to the Find dialog box, except that it contains a combo box for the Replace With text.

Figure 3-21 The Replace dialog box

Using the Find and Replace dialog boxes is straightforward. Especially handy are the Search options, which let you choose between the current document, all open documents, the current project, and specific selections or blocks in the editor.

The Find In Files dialog box (Ctrl+Shift+F), shown in Figure 3-22, and the Replace In Files dialog box (Ctrl+Shift+H) make it fairly easy to find text within a project or a directory structure. Setting up these file searches takes a little more work than performing a standard find command. You might find this facility easier to use than the Windows search facility, but it's usually not quite as fast. (It depends on how wide your search is.) The most important button in this dialog box is the … button, which opens the Look In dialog box. You can use this dialog box to narrow your search to your project or to a directory structure on your machine. The output from the Find In Files search is sent to the Find Results window by default.

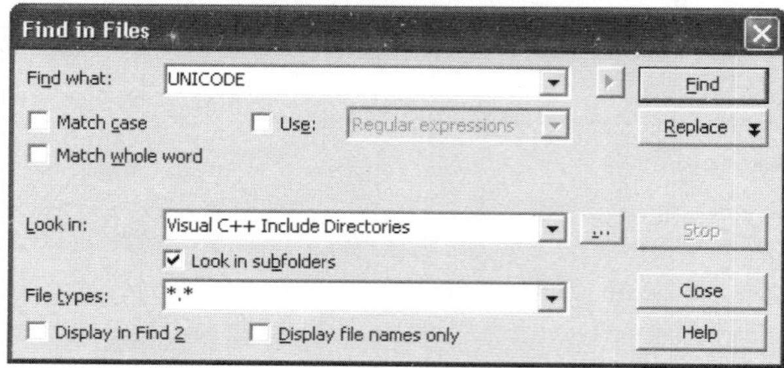

Figure 3-22 The Find In Files dialog box

The Visual Studio .NET Find and Replace shortcuts are listed in Table 3-6.

Table 3-6 Common Search Shortcuts

Command	Keystroke	Named Command
Find	Ctrl+F	*Edit.Find*
Replace	Ctrl+H	*Edit.Replace*
Find in files	Ctrl+Shift+F	*Edit.FindinFiles*
Replace in files	Ctrl+Shift+H	*File.ReplaceinFiles*

Wildcards

The Use check box in the Find and Replace dialog boxes lets you choose between using regular expressions in your search strings and using wildcard characters. If you're not used to regular expressions, the Wildcards option can provide you with a lot of extra functionality with a very short learning curve. The wildcard characters let you fine-tune your search parameters.

Let's take a look at how this works. If you want to search for a pattern of characters in a file that contains a number if incremented values such as H03XA01, H03XB02, H03XC03, H03XD04, and so on, you can use the # wildcard character to match any digit that comes up in the pattern and use the ? to match any character. To perform a search for these values, select Use in the Find dialog box and select Wild Cards from the adjacent combo box. The search string would then be something like *H03X?0#*.

The simplest wildcard search allows you to search for a match while disregarding an ending character or group of characters. The * wildcard character provides this functionality. Continuing with the example in the previous paragraph, a more general search string that matches the same pattern might actually be *H03X**. If the body of the pattern isn't widely used in a file, you can expand the pattern to make things a little easier.

Be aware that searches using the * character can extend beyond the end of the term(s) you're searching on, so you can end up with more selected than you had intended. For example, if you're looking for the term *class* in the Code Editor and you're using *cla** as your search term, one of the returned selections might be *class Class1*. When you're performing a replace operation, you're probably not looking for a string like this. If you know the pattern of the item you're searching for, it's best to use specific parameters when possible.

To search for a string that does *not* contain certain values, you use the [!] wildcard. For example, working with the same list, let's say you want to match all the characters in the H03X?0# series except those that contain A or C as the fifth letter in the series. In such a case, the search string *H03X[!AC]0#* will return the values you're searching for while filtering out the items you don't want to see.

The [ ] wildcard works by matching any of the characters inside the brackets as part of the search. To return only the items that contain *A* and *D*, the search string would look like *H03X[AD]0#*.

Wildcards aren't as powerful as the regular expressions that we'll talk about in the next section, but they can be a lot easier to remember if you don't use regular expressions that often. You'll find the list of wildcard characters supported in Visual Studio .NET Find and Replace operations in Table 3-7.

Table 3-7 Wildcard Characters Supported in Visual Studio .NET

Character	Description
?	Searches for any single character in the pattern
#	Searches for any single digit in the pattern

Table 3-7 Wildcard Characters Supported in Visual Studio .NET *(continued)*

Character	Description
*	Searches for one or more matching characters in the pattern
[!]	Searches for characters that do not match the items in this list
[ ]	Searches for characters that match the characters in this list

Regular Expressions

Whole books have been written about regular expressions, and it would take at least a chapter to do the subject justice, but because this is a book about Visual Studio .NET, we'll explain just enough about regular expressions in Find and Replace operations to get you started. Visual Studio .NET supports about 70 regular expressions that you can use in Find and Replace operations. We'll talk about a few of these and how you can use them to improve your searches. To enable regular expressions in a search, you must select the Use check box and select Regular Expressions in the Use combo box.

The set expression [ ] is similar to the wildcard expression we described earlier. This expression is used to include a number of different characters in a search. One powerful feature of this expression is that you can specify a range of characters to search for by placing a dash between two characters. For example, to search for any character in the series *a* through *d* in a regular expression, you can specify *[a-d]* in the Find What combo box. The expression *[a-d]b* searches for any of the following character sets in the Text Editor: *ab*, *bb*, *cb*, and *db*.

Wherever there's a Find option, you'll have a Don't Find option—in this case, the expression [^] weeds out the matches you don't want to see. For example, the expression *[^t-v]s* returns a match for *as*, *bs*, *cs*, *ds*, and so on. It skips *ts*, *us*, *vs*, and so forth.

If you want to find something at the beginning of a line, you can place the ^ character at the beginning of your search string. Using this expression alone will match the beginning of each line in a file. The *$* character indicates a search at the end of a line. Two other expressions match the beginning and the end of a particular word. The < character matches the beginning of any word in the search string, and the > character matches the end of any word. These expressions must appear in a logical place in your search string. For example, if you want to search for all instances of the word *int* in a file, you can specify *<int* as your search string. This returns *int* as part of a larger word as long as *int* is at the beginning of the word. *Integer* and *int* both match, but *mint* doesn't match.

If you want to take this a step further and search only for the word *int*, you can just add a closing > expression.

You can create some pretty complex expressions with all the regular expression tools at your disposal. You might want to use these types of expressions to search your code for patterns that match a statement of a particular form. For example, if you want to search for C# *MessageBox* statements that provide only one string argument to the function, your expression might look something like this:

```
<MessageBox.Show\(:q|(<.>)\);
```

That expression is somewhat complex, but it contains elements we've already discussed. The < expression indicates the beginning of a word. The words *MessageBox.Show* are what we're looking for. The \ expression indicates that the next character is a literal and not a regular expression element. The *:q* expression is interesting. It's a quoted string expression. It represents the same thing as typing _((“[^”]*”)|(‘[^’]*’))_. The | expression that follows *:q* is an *or* expression. The string you find in *MessageBox.Show* might be a string variable, so you can test for any single word by putting <.> in parentheses. The . represents any character, and you use parentheses to contain the *or* operation. Finally, you check for a closing semicolon.

There's a problem with this expression, though, and it has to do with how the method calls are formatted in the Code Editor. If the programmer of the method call that you're searching for left white space between the end of the parameter and the closing parenthesis, you lose your match. You can adjust for that by adding the *:Wh* expression followed by the * expression, which will match any or no instance of the preceding expression. So now you're up to _<MessageBox.Show\(:q|(<.>):Wh*\);_. But what about space before the quoted string, _<MessageBox.Show\(Wh*:q|(<.>):Wh*\);_? What about before the semicolon? It goes on and on. Regular expressions are excellent tools for searching for text, but you really need to spend some quality time learning to work with them effectively. To that end, we recommend two books that cover regular expressions nicely. The first is *Mastering Regular Expressions* by Jeffrey E. F. Friedel (O'Reilly, 1997). The second book is *Writing Secure Code*, Second Edition, by Michael Howard and David LeBlanc (Microsoft Press, 2003). The Friedel book does a good job of explaining regular expressions, and *Writing Secure Code* gives you some insight into uses for regular expressions that you might not have considered before.

Table 3-8 contains the expressions we've discussed in this chapter. See Visual Studio .NET Help for the complete list. (Click Help in the Find dialog box, and on the help page that opens, you'll find a link to all the regular expressions supported in Visual Studio .NET.)

Table 3-8 Casual Regular Expressions

Expression	Description
[ ]	Find using provided set of characters. You can express a range using the - character.
[^]	Find not including the provided set of characters.
< *or* >	Find the beginning of a word or find the end of a word.
^ *or $*	Find at the beginning of a line or find at the end of a line
.	Match any single character.
\	The next character in the search string is a literal character and not a regular expression.
*	Match regardless of character or characters.
:q	Match a quoted string.
:Wh	Match any type of white space .

Searching from the Command Window

Putting this all together, you might find it easier to perform a complex search operation from the Command Window. The Command Window gives you a lot more room for your search strings, especially if you're using wildcards or regular expressions in your searches.

To use the Find command from the Command Window, type **Edit.Find** followed by the string you want to search the current file for and press Enter. If you want to specify any of the switches associated with this command, type them *after* the search string you're entering. For example, if you want to use a wildcard in your search, your command might look something like this:

```
Edit.Find  Class# /Wild
```

The rest of the Find command switches match the options in the Find dialog box that we described earlier. Unless you reset them, these switches stick after each search as if you selected them in the dialog box. So you don't have to specify them every time you perform a search from the command line. To find out what Find options are currently set, enter **Edit.Find /options**, as shown here:

```
>Edit.Find /options
/wild /doc /names /sub
>
```

Table 3-9 lists most of the switches that apply to the Find command in Visual Studio .NET. You'll find that these are similar for *Edit.Replace*, *Edit.FindinFiles*, and *Edit.ReplaceinFiles*. To get the full list, enter **help Edit.Find** in the Command Window.

Table 3-9 Find Command Switches

Switch	Short Form	Description
/case	/c	Case-sensitive
/doc	/d	Search current document
/hidden	/h	Search hidden code
/markall	/m	Marks each occurrence in the Margin Indicator Bar
/open	/o	Search all open documents
/options	/t	Display the current Find options
/proc	/p	Search current procedure only
/sel	/s	Search the currently selected text only
/up	/u	Search up
/regex	/r	Search with regular expressions
/wild	/l	Search using wildcards
/word	/w	Search for whole word only

Note The *Edit.Find* command also contains a */reset* switch that is supposed to reset the Find options to a default setting. This switch currently has a bug that requires you to enter a parameter with the switch.

Incremental Searching

Incremental searching is a feature of Visual Studio .NET that's a real timesaver. An incremental search is performed one character at a time, matching each word in the search string from the top of the file. You can start an incremental search by pressing Ctrl+I. You'll see the mouse pointer transform into a down arrow like the one shown in Figure 3-23.

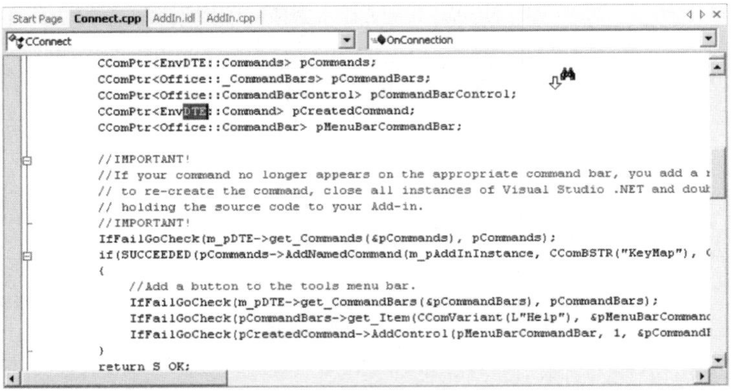

```
Start Page | Connect.cpp | AddIn.idl | AddIn.cpp
CConnect                                OnConnection
        CComPtr<EnvDTE::Commands> pCommands;
        CComPtr<Office::_CommandBars> pCommandBars;
        CComPtr<Office::CommandBarControl> pCommandBarControl;
        CComPtr<EnvDTE::Command> pCreatedCommand;
        CComPtr<Office::CommandBar> pMenuBarCommandBar;

        //IMPORTANT!
        //If your command no longer appears on the appropriate command bar, you add a 
        // to re-create the command, close all instances of Visual Studio .NET and dou
        // holding the source code to your Add-in.
        //IMPORTANT!
        IfFailGoCheck(m_pDTE->get_Commands(&pCommands), pCommands);
        if(SUCCEEDED(pCommands->AddNamedCommand(m_pAddInInstance, CComBSTR("KeyMap"), 
        {
            //Add a button to the tools menu bar.
            IfFailGoCheck(m_pDTE->get_CommandBars(&pCommandBars), pCommandBars);
            IfFailGoCheck(pCommandBars->get_Item(CComVariant(L"Help"), &pMenuBarComman
            IfFailGoCheck(pCreatedCommand->AddControl(pMenuBarCommandBar, 1, &pCommand
        }
        return S_OK;
```

Figure 3-23 Starting an incremental search by pressing Ctrl+I

With the down arrow showing, start typing the term you want to search for. As you type, words that match the letters are matched starting from the top. When you've completed the pattern you want to search for, press Ctrl+I again to move to the next match. You can continue to press Ctrl+I until you reach the end of the document to match every instance of the term you're searching for. If you want to search upward, just press Ctrl+Shift+I. It works in just the same way. You can exit the incremental search by pressing Enter or Esc.

Looking Ahead

This chapter should have given you a pretty good idea of how named commands apply to the Code Editor in the IDE and how you can customize the IDE by using alias commands in the Command Window, through keyboard shortcuts, and by adding menu items associated with named commands and macros. In Chapter 4, we'll take a look at how you can start to extend the IDE by creating your own Visual Studio .NET macros.

4

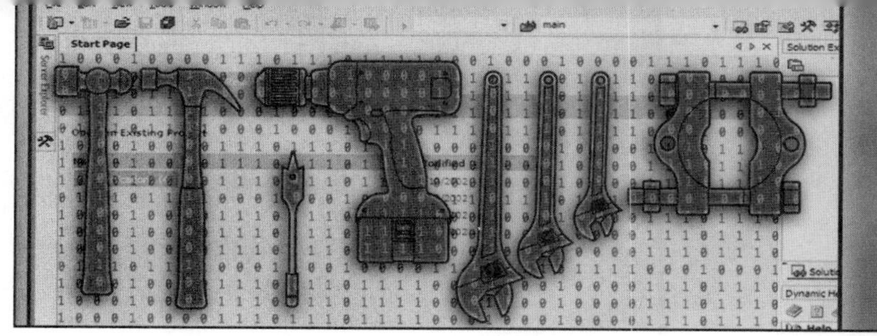

Visual Studio .NET Macros

The macros facility in Microsoft Visual Studio .NET is arguably one of the most compelling reasons for using the IDE. This facility exposes almost all the functionality that you can access through the automation object model, but in an easy-to-use, scriptable form.

In this chapter, we'll introduce you to macros in Visual Studio .NET. We'll show you how to record macros and how to edit macro projects in the Macros IDE. We'll also show you how you can extend macros using .NET assemblies and how to share your macros with others. In addition, we'll explain how you can turn a macro project into a full-fledged Visual Studio .NET add-in, using a macro that ships with the Visual Studio .NET samples.

Macros: The Duct Tape of Visual Studio .NET

The macros facility of Visual Studio .NET uses Visual Basic .NET as its macro language. This fit has a much better feel to it than the Visual Basic Scripting Edition (VBScript) facility built into Microsoft Visual C++ 6.0. The Visual Basic .NET language can take full advantage of the .NET Framework and its own automation object model, so it offers an extremely powerful and compelling set of features that you can use to automate tasks in the IDE. In fact, you can convert any macro into a Visual Basic .NET–based add-in that you can compile and share with other developers.

As we mentioned in Chapter 1, Visual Studio .NET macros are saved into files with a .vsmacros extension. These macros are stored in the VSMacros71 folder in your default Visual Studio .NET projects folder. You can specify the Visual Studio .NET projects folder in the Options dialog box, on the Projects and Solutions page in the Environment folder. By default, this path is My Documents\Visual Studio Projects. Macros are stored in the VSMacros71 subfolder.

Visual Studio .NET macros are usually created in one of two ways. You can record a macro in the IDE (Ctrl+Shift+R); the code generated during the recording session will be stored in the *MyMacros.RecordingModule.TemporaryMacro* method. Alternatively, you can open the Macros IDE (Alt+F11) and create a new method by writing it from scratch. One of the best things about macros is that they're designed to automate functionality in the Visual Studio .NET IDE. This means you can often simply record a macro, copy the generated code to a new method, and use that as the basis for your own automation project. You can also use this technique to get code for the add-ins you create for Visual Studio .NET.

Visual Studio .NET macros are accessed in the IDE just like any other named command. You can enter the name of the macro in the Command Window (Ctrl+Alt+A), you can add the macro to a toolbar or a menu, you can assign the macro a keystroke shortcut, you can run the macro by double-clicking it in Macro Explorer, and you can run the macro directly from the Macros IDE.

> **Note** When you run a macro by double-clicking it in the Macro Explorer window, the focus returns to the last active window. As a result, you can set the active document, open Macro Explorer, double-click the macro and have it affect the last active document.

We consider macros the duct tape of Visual Studio .NET—in the best sense of the term. Duct tape is made of an extremely strong material and can help you accomplish tasks quickly and easily. We would describe macros in the same way: they're extremely powerful tools in the IDE that you don't have to spend a ton of time thinking about. You can create your macro to perform your task and then tuck it away. If the macro is sufficiently important and powerful, you can turn it into a full blown add-in and then polish that code to your heart's content.

Recording Visual Studio .NET Macros

To record a Visual Studio .NET macro, first press the Ctrl+Shift+R keyboard shortcut. This combination brings up the Recorder toolbar and creates a macros module named *RecordingModule* if one doesn't already exist. You can see the

Recorder toolbar in Figure 4-1. Notice that you can pause, stop, or even cancel the recording session that you've started.

Figure 4-1 The Recorder toolbar

The easiest way to get going with macros is to record a simple macro that you might want to use repeatedly. For example, let's say you want to find the word *Connects* in your code files. You would normally use the Find or Find In Files command for this purpose. But by using one of these commands in the context of a macro, you can gain more flexibility and use the macro in later sessions.

Here are the steps for recording the macro we have in mind:

1. Press Ctrl+Shift+R to start the macro recorder.
2. Press Ctrl+F to open the Find dialog box.
3. Type **Connect** in the Find What box.
4. Click Find Next.
5. Press Ctrl+Shift+R to stop recording.

We now have a *TemporaryMacro* method saved in the module *Recording-Module*. You can see that macro in Figure 4-2.

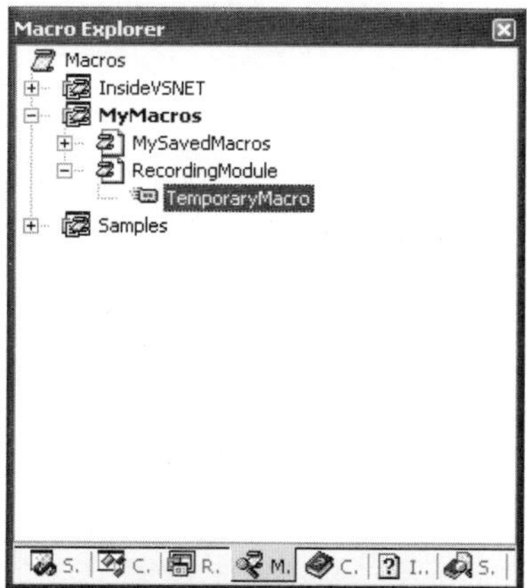

Figure 4-2 The Macro Explorer window

Here's the listing that's generated by the preceding series of steps. Notice that mouse movements and keystrokes (such as Tab for navigating to the Replace dialog box) aren't recorded. Visual Studio .NET limits macro recording to actual named commands that are called during the recording session.

```
Imports EnvDTE
Imports System.Diagnostics
Public Module RecordingModule
    Sub TemporaryMacro()
        DTE.ExecuteCommand("Edit.Find")
        DTE.Find.FindWhat = "Connect"
        DTE.Windows.Item("Connect.cpp").Activate()
        DTE.Find.FindWhat = "Connect"
        DTE.Find.Target = vsFindTarget.vsFindTargetCurrentDocument
        DTE.Find.MatchCase = False
        DTE.Find.MatchWholeWord = False
        DTE.Find.Backwards = False
        DTE.Find.MatchInHiddenText = False
        DTE.Find.PatternSyntax = _
            vsFindPatternSyntax.vsFindPatternSyntaxLiteral
        DTE.Find.Action = vsFindAction.vsFindActionFind
        DTE.Find.Execute()
    End Sub
End Module
```

To play back this macro, press Ctrl+Shift+P, which is simply a shortcut to the *Macros.Macros.RecordingModule.TemporaryMacro* command. You should see the Find dialog box open with the first instance of the word you're searching for selected. In our case, this is the first instance of *Connect* in a file named Connect.cpp.

Take a look at the line *DTE.Windows.Item("Connect.cpp").Activate()*. If Connect.cpp isn't already open, this line will bring it into focus in the IDE, so this macro won't be very useful if you want to save it for use with a number of different files or projects. Commenting out or removing this line from the listing will cause the macro to work with the currently active document.

To save the recorded macro, you can either rename *TemporaryMacro* to something else in Macro Explorer or you can copy and paste the recorded code into another macro module or method.

Macro Commands

Macro Explorer lets you manage your macros from inside the Visual Studio .NET IDE. You can access the commands related to macros in the IDE from the Macros submenu of the Tools menu or through the shortcut menus within Macro Explorer.

Macros are divided into projects containing modules, which in turn contain methods. Projects are represented hierarchically in Macro Explorer below the Macro icon. Right-clicking the Macro icon brings up the shortcut menu containing commands for creating and loading macro projects. You can access the same functionality as named commands in the Command Window. Table 4-1 lists the macro commands related to macro projects.

Table 4-1 Macro Project Commands

Command	Description
Tools.LoadMacroProject	Brings up the Add Macro Project dialog box, where you can select a macro project file.
Tools.NewMacroProject	Brings up the New Macro Project dialog box, where you can save your macros into specific projects.
Tools.MacrosIDE	Brings up the Macros IDE. This command is mapped to Alt+F11.

You can navigate to Macro Explorer by pressing Alt+F8. Most commands available from the shortcut menus in Macro Explorer are also available from the Command Window (because the items in Macro Explorer lose focus when you change to the Command Window). You can rename a macro project by right-clicking on the project in Macro Explorer and then clicking Rename. Doing so will allow you to edit the name of the macro project in place. You can delete a macro project by choosing Delete from the shortcut menu. The same basic shortcut menu items are available for renaming and deleting modules and methods from within Macro Explorer.

Table 4-2 lists a few of the commands available from within a particular macro project.

Table 4-2 Macro Project Commands

Command	Description
Tools.Newmodule	Brings up the New Module dialog box, where you can create a new module from within Macro Explorer
Tools.Newmacro	When enabled, this command brings up the Macros IDE with a new macro method
Tools.Edit	Brings up the Macros IDE open to the currently selected project or module

By right-clicking on a macro in Macro Explorer, you can bring up a shortcut menu that lets you work with the macro directly. The Run command executes the *Tools.Run* command on the currently selected macro. The Rename command allows you to edit the name of the macro in place. The change you make to the name is reflected in the method name in the Macros IDE. The Delete command deletes the currently selected macro. And finally, the Edit command opens the current macro in the Macros IDE.

Macro Explorer is a powerful tool for organizing the macros you've created. You'll find that you can do quite a bit in Macro Explorer without having to go to the Macros IDE. For example, you can record a macro, rename that macro to save it, and even add that same macro to a toolbar or a menu in the IDE, all without having to go to the Macros IDE. You'd probably find it limiting not to use the IDE, but it is possible. To really get the most out of Visual Studio .NET macros, you'll want to be able to create and edit them from within the Macros IDE.

Editing Macros in the Macros IDE

Working with the Macros IDE is similar to working in Visual Studio .NET. Many of the same shortcuts work in the Macros IDE. The Macros IDE editor features IntelliSense, and the Help system for macros is integrated right into the IDE.

One difference you'll notice right away is that all your loaded macro projects show up in the Project Explorer window. Visual Studio .NET ships with an extremely useful set of macros out of the box. You can see these macros if you expand the Samples project in Project Explorer in the Macros IDE (as shown in Figure 4-3).

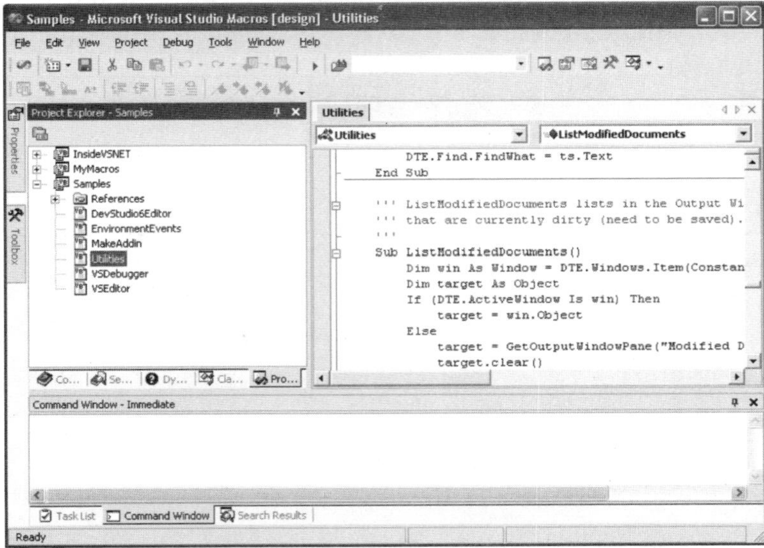

Figure 4-3 The Samples project in the Macros IDE

The memory space for macro projects is separated, so if you want to utilize functionality between different macros or if you want to take advantage of a common set of environmental events, you must keep the macros that you write inside the same project. If you want to access functionality from another macro project, you simply copy the macros you want to access into the project you're working on. For example, you can copy modules from the Samples project into your own project to take advantage of the functionality exposed by those macros.

To create a new macro project, you need to start from the Visual Studio .NET IDE. You can use the New Macro Project command on the shortcut menu in Macro Explorer or you can enter **Tools.NewMacroProject** into the Command Window to open the New Macro Project dialog box (shown in Figure 4-4). Enter a name and location for your project, and then click OK. Pressing Alt+F11 will toggle you back to the Macros IDE, where you can work on the code in the new project.

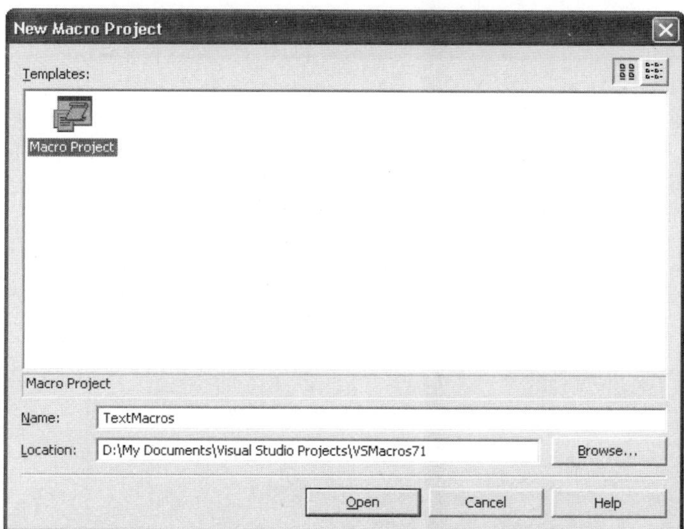

Figure 4-4 The New Macro Project dialog box

If you take a look at the new macro project created in Project Explorer, you'll notice that a number of features are added to your project by default. The References folder works similarly to the References folder in the Visual Studio .NET IDE. Two new modules are added to get your macros up and running. The *EnvironmentEvents* module contains generated code that gives you access to the events in the IDE. The *Module1* module provides a place where you can start writing code.

Lab: Navigating Between IDEs

To shift from the Macros IDE to the Visual Studio .NET IDE, you can click the Visual Studio button on the Macros IDE toolbar. There's no such button on any of the default Visual Studio .NET toolbars, so you'll need to add one if you want to get back to the Macros IDE in the same way. To do so, right-click on a toolbar in the Visual Studio .NET IDE and click Customize. On the Commands tab, find the Macros IDE command in the Tools category and drag it to the toolbar you want to use it from. The button will have the same infinity image used in the Macros IDE. This makes it easy to navigate between the two IDEs while you work on your macros.

If you'll be doing a lot of macro development, a better solution is to run your machine with two monitors, keeping the Macros IDE in one screen and Visual Studio .NET in the other.

Adding a reference to a macro project is slightly different from adding one to a standard Visual Basic .NET project. If you look at the Add Reference dialog box that's used in the Macros IDE Project Explorer (shown in Figure 4-5), you'll notice that it doesn't offer a way to add custom assemblies.

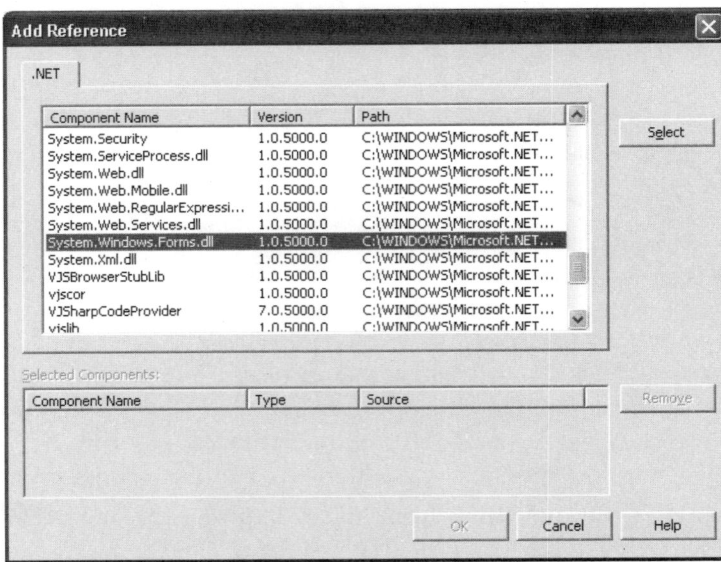

Figure 4-5 Add Reference dialog box

To add references to your own assemblies, you must copy them to the C:\Program Files\Microsoft Visual Studio .NET 2003\Common7\IDE\PublicAssemblies folder. You can then add your own reference to the assembly from the Add Reference dialog box. Using assemblies, you can write your macro functionality in any language you want and then access that functionality from a fairly simple macro. You can also write assemblies that call to unmanaged code and assemblies that act as COM wrappers to access COM functionality from within your macros.

Let's go over a few examples built from a new project.

A Simple Macro

Earlier in the book, we touched on the behavior of the *File.NewFile* command in Visual Studio .NET. Some programmers haven't been pleased that this command displays a dialog box by default, forcing them to resort to the mouse or to a series of keystrokes to get an empty file up and running. But the solution is simple: you just create a macro that does exactly what you want and then assign that macro an alias in the Command Window. The following code is all you really need to create a new text file in the IDE:

```
Imports EnvDTE
Imports System.Diagnostics

Public Module NewFile

    Sub NewTextFile()
        DTE.ItemOperations.NewFile("General\Text File")
    End Sub

End Module
```

As you can see, this macro has been created in a module named *NewFile*. It consists of a single method, *NewTextFile*. The single line of code in this macro simply creates a new file of the type Text File in the General folder of the New File dialog box. We'll talk about the *NewFile* method that creates the new text file in a minute. What's important right now is that we have a macro that will add just the functionality we want to the IDE. To make this macro a tool we're willing to spend some time with, we'll want to make the macro as easy to get to as possible.

To get to a macro you want to execute, you've got a few choices. One approach is to run the macro from Macro Explorer in the Visual Studio .NET IDE. This works fine, but it's probably not the optimal solution for a macro that you're planning to use often. The second choice is to create an alias for the macro in the Command Window. This is probably the best choice for a command that you want to use while you're typing. To alias this command, you can type the alias command followed by the name of the macro. IntelliSense will kick in when you start to type a macro, so the whole alias line might look something like this:

```
>alias nf Macros.InsideVSNET.Chapter04.NewFile.NewTextFile
```

Now you've got a new command you can use from the Command Window: *nf*. To create a new text file, you can simply press Ctrl+Alt+A and then type *nf* to get your new file. Of course, if you want to take it a step further, you can assign the macro a keystroke shortcut from the Options dialog box. In keeping with the Ctrl+, initial chord introduced earlier in the book, Ctrl+,,Ctrl+N might make a good shortcut. Finally, you can add a button to the toolbar that initiates the macro (as described in Chapter 3).

The *Imports* statement in this sample is important. The API associated with the Visual Studio .NET automation object model is contained in the *EnvDTE* namespace. The automation object model is discussed in depth in Chapter 5 through Chapter 12. Here we simply want to familiarize you with this object model and get you up and running with some of the more common functionality that you'll use in your macro projects. Most of the subjects covered in the chapters that comprise Part II of the book apply to both macros and add-ins. In fact, you can use macros to quickly test add-in functionality that you're writing. You'll save time because you normally test an add-in by compiling the add-in and loading a second instance of the IDE. Using a macro, you can get to the automation object model, write and test your routines, and then add them to your add-in projects.

Working with Macros

The macros you build will use the automation object model to access and automate the different parts of the IDE. In this section, we'll demonstrate how you can use macros to automate some simple tasks and we'll talk a bit about the automation object model as it applies to documents and windows in the IDE. We'll also discuss events and provide some simple examples to help you get going right away. Much of the material we'll cover here is discussed in detail in Part II of the book.

Manipulating Documents and Text

Some of the most useful tasks you can perform with macros involve working with text in documents. You might want to search for text, change a selection in some way, or just insert text into a document. The *Document* object in the *DTE* provides a good deal of functionality that makes it easy to manipulate text in code documents.

Macros are often run on the document with the current focus. To get the currently active document in the IDE, you use the *DTE.ActiveDocument* property, which returns a *Document* object. (Recall that a Visual Studio .NET document is an editor or a designer window that opens to the center of the IDE.) If the document is an editor, it has an associated *TextDocument* object.

The *TextDocument* object has three properties of interest for programmers who want to manipulate text inside the object. The *StartPoint* property returns a *TextPoint* object that points to the beginning of the document. The *EndPoint* property returns an object that points to the end of the document. And finally, the *Selection* property returns a *TextSelection* object, which offers a number of properties and methods you can use on selected text.

The *TextPoint* object provides location information for the editing functionality inside a document. You create a *TextPoint* in a document whenever you want to insert or manipulate text in the document or when you want to get some information about a particular document. *TextPoint* objects aren't dependent on text selection, and you can use multiple *TextPoint* objects in a single document.

Let's look at a couple of examples that use the objects we've mentioned. You should become familiar with this code because much of the macro automation code you'll write will depend on it.

First, let's get the *ActiveDocument*, create a couple of *EditPoint* objects, and add some text to the *ActiveDocument* using that information:

```
Sub CommentWholeDoc()
    Dim td As TextDocument = ActiveDocument.Object
    Dim sp As TextPoint
    Dim ep As TextPoint
    sp = td.StartPoint.CreateEditPoint()
    ep = td.EndPoint.CreateEditPoint()

    sp.Insert("/* ")
    ep.Insert(" */")

End Sub
```

Running this sample on a Visual C# or a Visual C++ code document will comment out the entire document, unless the source already contains comments. The macro isn't very practical, but it does show you how to put those parts together. You can use IntelliSense to make your way through the objects created to experiment with some of the other functionality.

Let's take a look at a second, more useful, example that inserts text into a document based on a selection. The following example creates an HTML comment in a document. This functionality doesn't exist in Visual Studio .NET 2003, so you might find this simple macro useful enough to add to your own toolbox. Here we'll declare *ts* as a *TextSelection* object and assign it the current selection using *DTE.ActiveDocument.Selection*:

```
Sub HTMLComment()
    Dim ts As TextSelection = DTE.ActiveDocument.Selection
    ts.Insert("<!-- ", vsInsertFlags.vsInsertFlagsInsertAtStart)
    ts.Insert(" -->", vsInsertFlags.vsInsertFlagsInsertAtEnd)
End Sub
```

This macro uses the *TextSelection Insert* method to insert text around the *Selection* object. The *Insert* method takes two arguments. The first argument is the string that you want to insert into the selection. The second argument is a *vsInsertFlags* constant that defines where the insertion is to take place. The first *Insert* call in the example uses *vsInsertFlagsAtStart*. The second uses *vsInsertFlagsAtEnd*. Table 4-3 lists these constants.

Table 4-3 *vsInsertFlags* Constants

Constant	Description
vsInsertFlagsCollapseToStart	Collapses the insertion point from the end of the selection to the current *TextPoint*
vsInsertFlagsCollapseToEnd	Collapses the insertion point from beginning of the selection to the current *TextPoint*
vsInsertFlagsContainNewText	Replaces the current selection
vsInsertFlagsInsertAtStart	Inserts the text before the start point of the selection
vsInsertFlagsInsertAtEnd	Inserts text just after the end point of the selection

With a *Selection*, a *TextPoint*, and the methods available through the *DTE*, you should have a good basis for the types of operations you can perform with macros on source code.

Moving Windows

Windows in Visual Studio .NET are controlled through the *Window* object, which is part of the *DTE.Windows* collection. The *Window* object provides functionality based on the window type. Specifically, the *CommandWindow*, *OutputWindow*, *TaskList*, *TextWindow*, and *ToolBox* derive from the *Window* object.

Of the window objects, *OutputWindow* is among the most practical for macro writing. You can use it to display and hold messages in much the same way you would use *printf* or *Console.Write* in a console application, or in the same way that you use *MsgBox* or *MessageBox.Show* in a Windows-based application.

To use the *OutputWindow* object to display messages, you must create a new method that takes a string argument. You can then call the method with the argument in same way you use the *MsgBox* method to display a message. The following example is a method named *MsgWin*. It takes only a string as an argument. You can use this method in place of *MsgBox* when you want to quickly see a bit of text information.

```
Sub MsgWin(ByVal msg As String)
    Dim win As Window = DTE.Windows.Item(Constants.vsWindowKindOutput)
    Dim cwin As Window =
        DTE.Windows.Item(Constants.vsWindowKindCommandWindow)
    Dim ow As OutputWindow = win.Object
    Dim owp As OutputWindowPane
    Dim cwp As CommandWindow = cwin.Object
    Dim i As Integer
    Dim exists As Boolean = False
    ' Check to see if we're running in the Command Window. If so,
    ' we'll send our output there. If not, we'll send it to a Command
    ' window.
    If (DTE.ActiveWindow Is cwin) Then
        cwp.OutputString(msg + vbCrLf)
    Else
        ' Determine if the output pane name exits. If it does, we need
        ' to send our message there, or we end up with multiple windows of
        ' the same name.
        For i = 1 To ow.OutputWindowPanes.Count
            If ow.OutputWindowPanes().Item(i).Name() = "MsgWin Output" Then
                exists = True
                Exit For
            End If
        Next
```

```
        ' If our output pane exits, we'll use that to output the string,
        ' otherwise, we'll add it to the list.
        If exists Then
            owp = ow.OutputWindowPanes().Item(i)
        Else
            owp = ow.OutputWindowPanes.Add("MsgWin Output")
        End If
        ' Here we set the Output window to visible, activate the pane,
        ' and send the string to the pane.
        win.Visible = True
        owp.Activate()
        owp.OutputString(msg + vbCrLf)
    End If
End Sub
```

MsgWin uses a pretty cool feature that's found in the samples that ship with Visual Studio .NET. The method determines whether the calling method was invoked from the Command Window. If it was, the output is directed right back to the user in the Command Window. If it's called from a macro that was run from a menu, shortcut, or button, *MsgWin* sends the output to an Output window named MsgWin Output.

Tip The Samples macros project that ships with Visual Studio .NET contains a lot of really good, functional macro code that you can use in the macros you write.

To use the *MsgWin* macro, you must call it from another method. For this example, we've created a method that lists all the currently open windows in the IDE:

```
Sub MsgWinTest()
    Dim wins As Windows = DTE.Windows()
    Dim i As Integer

    For i = 1 To wins.Count
        MsgWin(wins.Item(i).Caption.ToString())
    Next
End Sub
```

Figure 4-6 shows what the Visual Studio .NET IDE looks like after it has been invoked from the *MsgWinText* macro in the IDE.

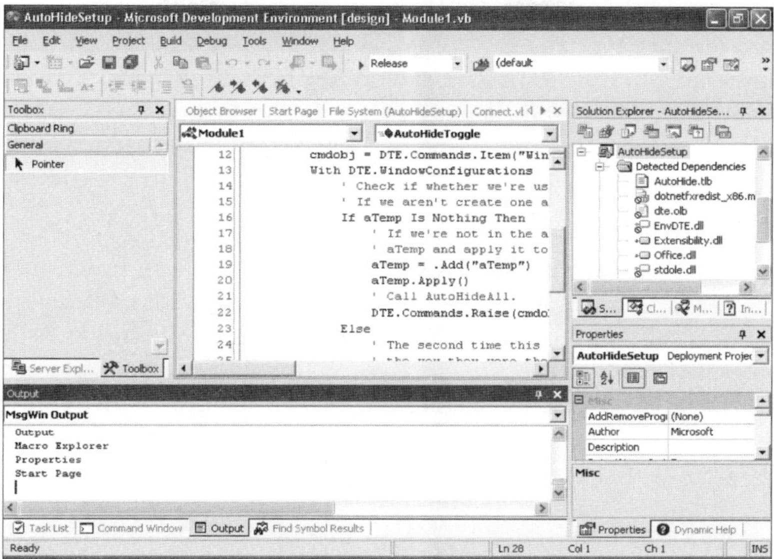

Figure 4-6 The MsgBox Output window in the IDE

You can do a lot of things with this basic *MsgWin* macro to improve it. It would be pretty trivial to overload the *MsgWin* method to allow for such actions as clearing the output pane or adding a heading to the list. For example, to create an overload for the *MsgWin* function that clears the output pane, you can make the method look something like this:

```
Sub MsgWin(ByVal msg As String, ByVal clr As Boolean)
        ⋮
        ' If clr is True then we'll clear the output pane.
        If clr = True Then
            owp.Clear()
        End If
        ' Here we set the Output window to visible, activate the pane,
        ' and send the string to the pane.
        win.Visible = True
        owp.Activate()
        owp.OutputString(msg + vbCrLf)
    End If
End Sub
```

Of course, this overload won't do you much good if you call the macro the way we did in *MsgBoxTest*, but as you can see it's easy enough to do what you want with the macro.

Another way to add this kind of functionality to your macros is to create an assembly in the language of your choice and then reference that assembly from within your macro project. We did this with the *CommandWindowPaneEx* object.

Using Assemblies in Your Macros

A couple of things become apparent when you start to use macros a lot. The first is that you can use macros as a place to test the functionality of .NET assemblies. For example, if you want to test some bit of functionality in the framework, all you need to do is reference the appropriate assembly and then call the methods from within a macro. With a little practice, you'll find that the Macros IDE can work as a little laboratory that lets you try out functionality without having to mess around with rebuilding your projects.

The second thing you'll notice is that you have to write all this cool stuff in Visual Basic, and if that's not your preferred language, you might be spending a lot of time performing tasks you already know how to accomplish quickly in another language. As we mentioned earlier, there is a way to write macro functionality in languages other than Visual Basic—by building your functionality into an assembly and then referencing that assembly from within your macro project.

We wrote a base set of utility functions for the book that you can take advantage of in your own macros and add-ins. In the Utilities folder of the companion content, you'll find the Utilities solution. This solution contains the *OutputWindowPaneEx* object. Build the solution and copy the InsideVSNET.Utilities.dll file from the bin\debug folder for the project into the C:\Program Files\Microsoft Visual Studio .NET 2003\Common7\IDE\PublicAssemblies folder.

Once you've copied that file into your Public Assemblies folder, you can add a reference to the assembly from your macro project in the Macros IDE by right-clicking on the References folder in the Project Explorer window and choosing Add Reference, or by selecting the References folder and typing **Project.AddReference** into the Macros IDE Command Window. On the .NET tab of the Add Reference dialog box, you should see the new InsideVSNET.Utilities assembly. Select it in the list, click Select, and then click OK. You'll see the new assembly in the list of references if you expand the References folder.

After you add the reference to your project, it's helpful to add the appropriate *Imports* statement to your module. In this case, you'll add the following to the top of the module:

```
Imports InsideVSNET.Utilities
```

Once you add the reference, IntelliSense kicks in automatically as you create an *OutputWindowPaneEx* object and use it. The really cool thing about this object is that it lets you specify whether to send your output to the Output window in the Visual Studio .NET IDE or to the Macros IDE. In this example, we specified the Macros IDE, passing *DTE.MacrosIDE* when we created the object. We also changed the test a bit by enumerating the open windows in the Macros IDE rather than the Visual Studio .NET IDE, as we did earlier.

```
Sub OutputWindowPaneExTest()
    Dim owp As New OutputWindowPaneEx(DTE.MacrosIDE)
    Dim wins As Windows = DTE.MacrosIDE.Windows()
    Dim i As Integer

    owp.Activate()

    For i = 1 To wins.Count
        owp.WriteLine(wins.Item(i).Caption.ToString())
    Next
End Sub
```

In addition to letting you perform the tasks that you're able to perform with the *OutputWindowPane* object, *OutputWindowPaneEx* lets you do a number of things with text that you want to send to an Output window. As we mentioned, you can specify the IDE to which you want to send your output. The *Write* method has three overloads, letting you specify an object, a string, or a formatting string/parameter array. Using these overloads, you can specify formatting options, much like using the *System.Console.Write* and *System.Console.WriteLine* methods in the .NET Framework.

Macro Events

One of the most powerful features of macros in the IDE is an event model that lets you fire macros based on events that take place in the IDE. You can use events to fire macros that create logs, reset tests, or manipulate different parts of the IDE in the ways we've already talked about in this chapter. In this short section, we'll show you how to create event handlers for different events in the IDE. Using this information and the detailed information about the different parts of the automation API discussed throughout the rest of the book, you should have a good idea how to take advantage of events in your own projects.

The easiest way to get to the event handlers for a macros project is through the Project Explorer window in the Macros IDE. Expand a project, and you'll see an *EnvironmentEvents* module listed. Open that file, and you'll see a block of code that's been generated automatically by the IDE. Here's the important part of the block. (The attributes have been removed to make this fit the page.)

```
Public WithEvents DTEEvents As EnvDTE.DTEEvents
Public WithEvents DocumentEvents As EnvDTE.DocumentEvents
Public WithEvents WindowEvents As EnvDTE.WindowEvents
Public WithEvents TaskListEvents As EnvDTE.TaskListEvents
Public WithEvents FindEvents As EnvDTE.FindEvents
Public WithEvents OutputWindowEvents As EnvDTE.OutputWindowEvents
Public WithEvents SelectionEvents As EnvDTE.SelectionEvents
Public WithEvents BuildEvents As EnvDTE.BuildEvents
Public WithEvents SolutionEvents As EnvDTE.SolutionEvents
Public WithEvents SolutionItemsEvents As EnvDTE.ProjectItemsEvents
Public WithEvents MiscFilesEvents As EnvDTE.ProjectItemsEvents
Public WithEvents DebuggerEvents As EnvDTE.DebuggerEvents
```

As you can see from this listing, there are a lot of event types you can take advantage of in the IDE. In fact, you can use all the DTE events, though they're not included by default. You can add these other events to this list to get to the events that you're interested in. To create a new event handler, you select the event type you want to handle from the Class Name list at the top of the code window. You can see how this looks in Figure 4-7.

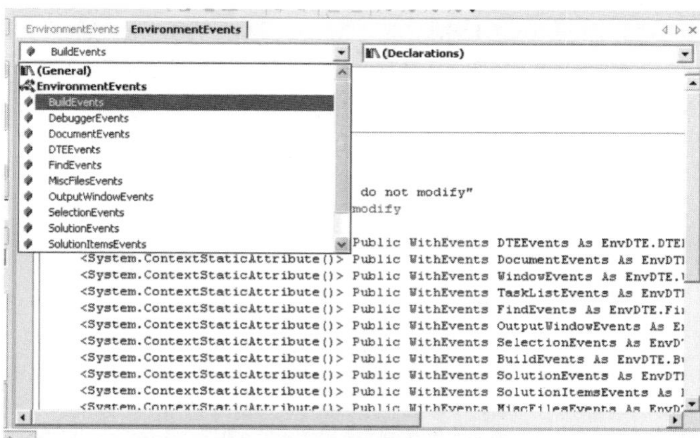

Figure 4-7 Selecting the event type you want to handle from the Class Name list

After you select an event type, the Method Name list in the upper-right portion of the code pane will list the events you can handle, as shown in Figure 4-8.

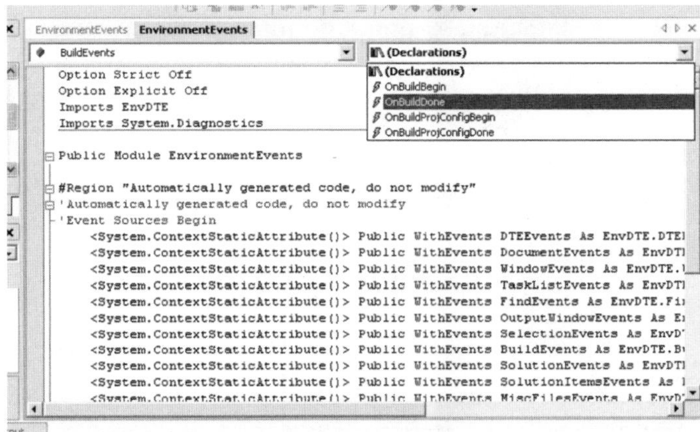

Figure 4-8 Selecting the event you want to handle from the Method Name list

Select the event you want from the list, and your event handler will be generated automatically. From this generated event handler, you can call a method that you've created in the project, or you can add your event handling functionality directly to the event handler code. In this example, we'll call the *MsgWin* function that we worked through earlier to display a message that indicates that the build has completed.

```
Private Sub BuildEvents_OnBuildDone(ByVal Scope As EnvDTE.vsBuildScope, _
    ByVal Action As EnvDTE.vsBuildAction) _
    Handles BuildEvents.OnBuildDone
        MsgWin("Build is done!")
End Sub
```

As you can imagine, these events open up all sorts of possibilities for automation and customization in the IDE. One thing you should keep in mind when working with events is that all the code in a single macro project shares the same event module. This means that if you want to create different event handlers for the same event, you'll need to create the other event handlers in other projects.

Event Security

As you can imagine, executing event code in a powerful macros facility such as the one in Visual Studio .NET has some potential security implications. The first time you load a macro project that contains event-handling code, you see a dialog box that looks like this:

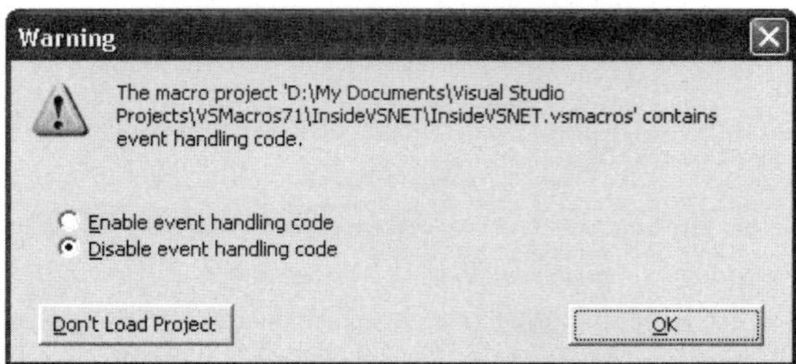

You should be sure you know where your macros come from when you load macro projects. If you're not sure of the event-handling code in the project, click Disable Event Handling Code in the Warning dialog box and review the code in the module before you use it.

Sharing Macros with Others

If you want to share the macros that you've created, you have a number of choices to make. Do you want to share the source? Do you want to share the whole project or just part of it? The answers to these questions will determine how to best share your work. Let's take a look at the different ways that you can share your macro functionality with others.

Exporting Modules and Projects

The easiest way to share your macros with other developers is to simply cut and paste your source code into e-mail messages and Usenet postings. This approach works well if the methods you're sharing are fairly short and if they don't span multiple modules. If they do span multiple modules, you'll probably want to export the modules you want to share or simply pass on the whole project.

To export a macro module in Visual Studio .NET, you must open the Macros IDE and select the module you want to export from the Project Explorer window. Pressing Ctrl+E will invoke the *File.SaveSelectedItemsAs* command, which brings up the Export File dialog box. This command is listed on the File menu as Export.

The Export File dialog box lets you save the module as a .vb file that you can easily import into another project using the *File.AddExisitingItem* command (Shift+Alt+A). Don't forget to include the code from the *EnvironmentEvents* module if your macros rely on some sort of event functionality.

If your macros are very complicated, you might want to share an entire macro project. You can do this in a couple of ways. You can copy the .vsmacros file for the project and pass it along, or you can save your macro project as a text-based project and share those files.

To make a macros project text-based, you change the *StorageFormat* property in the Visual Studio .NET IDE for the project that you want to change. Select the project in Macro Explorer and then change the *StorageFormat* property in the Properties window from Binary (.vsmacros) to Text (UNICODE). This change will create a number of files in the macro project's folder that looks much like a regular Visual Studio .NET project folder. In Figure 4-9, you can see the folder for the Samples project after it has been converted to Text format.

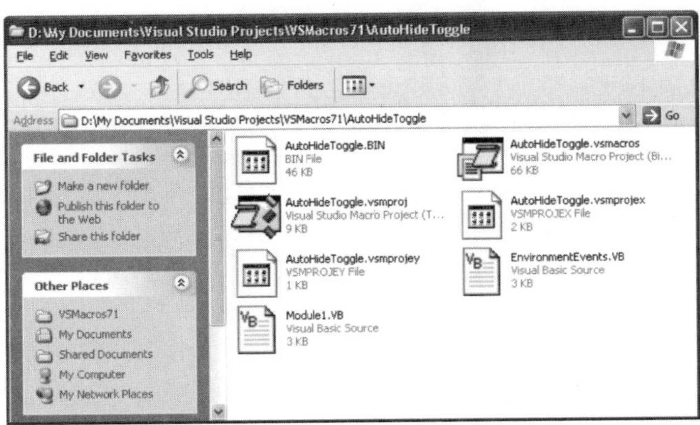

Figure 4-9 A macro project that has been stored in Text format

The advantage of passing along a text-based project is that it allows other programmers to look at the source files in your project before loading them into their IDE.

There's always a security risk in opening unknown macro projects in any application. Be sure you know where any binaries you open came from. At the very least, check the EnvironmentEvents.vb module to make sure it doesn't include any unexpected code.

Also keep in mind that shipping a binary macro project does nothing to safeguard your source code. To do that, you're better off adding your functionality to an assembly that gets called from a macro, as we demonstrated earlier. An even better solution, where appropriate, is to turn your macro project into an add-in.

Turning Macros into Add-ins

Visual Studio .NET ships with a macro in the Samples project that lets you turn a macro project into a Visual Studio .NET add-in, complete with an installer. The macros in the *MakeAddin* module take a macro and turn it into an add-in project that you can compile and install into your environment. Macros that have been turned into add-ins can be shipped as binaries that are installed on a user's machine. Keep in mind, though, that you really should test the add-ins that you create in this way to make sure they do what you expect.

For this example, we'll take the *AutoHideToggle* macro that we created in Chapter 1 and turn it into an add-in using the *MakeAddin* macros. To get started, copy the macro you want to turn into an add-in into a new macro project. You can give the project the same name as the method if you want. Just be sure to build the new project to test it before you use it.

Next, you create a new add-in project in Visual Studio .NET by pressing Ctrl+Shift+N to open the New Project dialog box. Expand the Other Projects folder and then open the Extensibility Projects folder to get to the Visual Studio .NET Add-in project template, as shown in Figure 4-10.

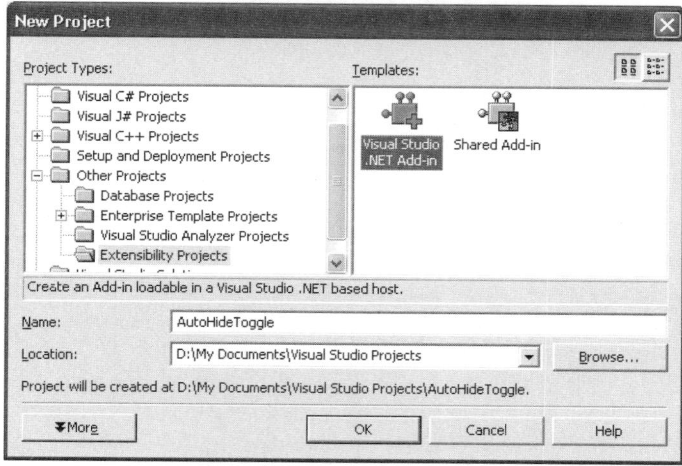

Figure 4-10 Creating a new add-in project

Give your new add-in an appropriate name, and then go through the wizard to create a Visual Basic .NET add-in project that installs a menu command in the IDE.

After your new add-in project is complete, press Ctrl+Alt+A to bring up the Command Window and then type **Macros.Samples.MakeAddin.MakeAddinFromMacroProj**. This will bring up the input box shown in Figure 4-11. In the box, type the name of the macro project you want to turn into an add-in, and then click OK.

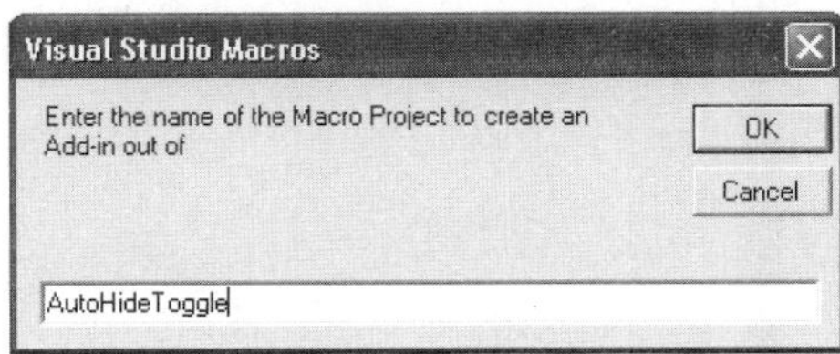

Figure 4-11 Specifying the macro project you want to turn into an add-in

At this point, if all the projects are of the right type, you should see a message asking you to confirm that you want to run the macro on the current project. Click OK, and the *MakeAddin* macro project will complete its work. When the macro is finished, you'll see the dialog box shown in Figure 4-12. What the *MakeAddin* macro has done is add the macro functionality from your project to the new add-in.

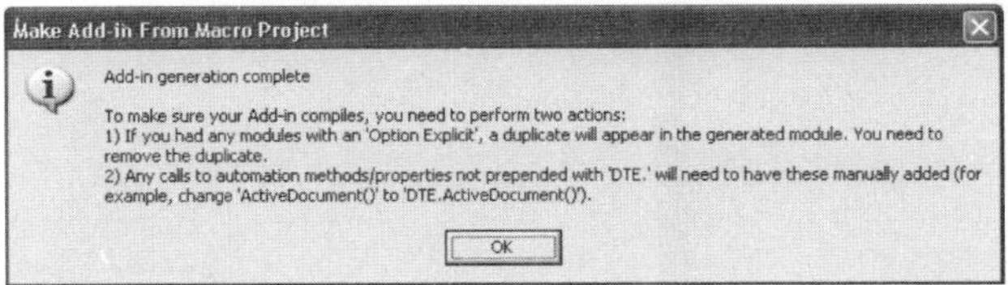

Figure 4-12 The message box confirming completion and final instructions for the *MakeAddin* macro

To test the new add-in, press F5 to start debugging; you should see a second instance of the Visual Studio .NET IDE open. On the Tools menu of that second instance of the IDE, you should see a menu containing the name of your project and the name of the macros that were in your original macro project. You can see in Figure 4-13 that the AutoHideToggle add-in is ready to go. Choosing this menu command does exactly what running the macro in the IDE did in Chapter 1.

> **Note** If you use this add-in or the macro described in Chapter 1, keep in mind that the layout you have open will become your default layout. It won't overwrite the layouts that ship with Visual Studio .NET, but if you want to get back to one of those, you'll need to go back to the My Profile tab on the Start Page and select an alternative layout in the Windows Layout list. Then select the layout you chose when you originally created your profile and your windows should return to that layout.

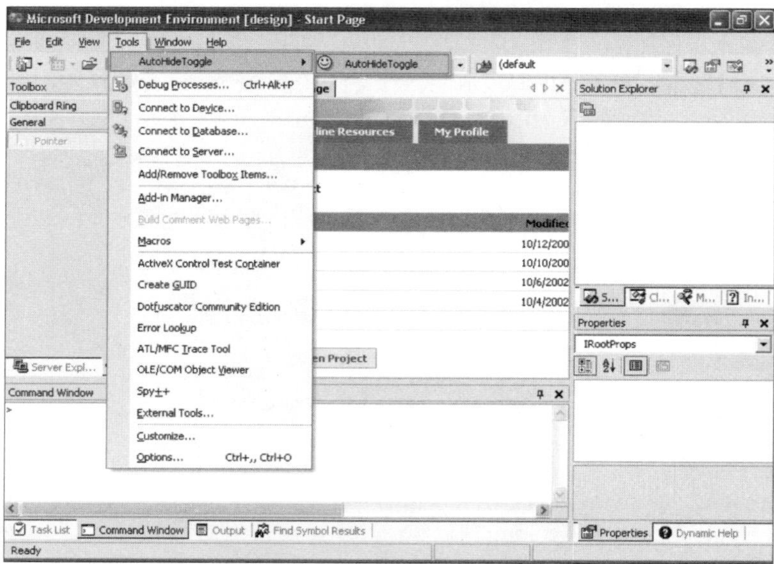

Figure 4-13 The new AutoHideToggle add-in in the IDE

To use this new add-in in Visual Studio .NET, you build a release version of the setup project that's generated for the add-in and then you navigate to the folder containing the setup program. Close all your instances of Visual Studio .NET and run the Setup.exe program. When you open the IDE, you'll find that your new add-in has been installed and is ready for use.

Looking Ahead

This chapter gave you some information about using the Visual Studio .NET macro facility to perform some simple automation tasks. Part II of the book should provide you with enough information to do just about anything you want with automation in Visual Studio .NET.

Part II

Extending Visual Studio .NET

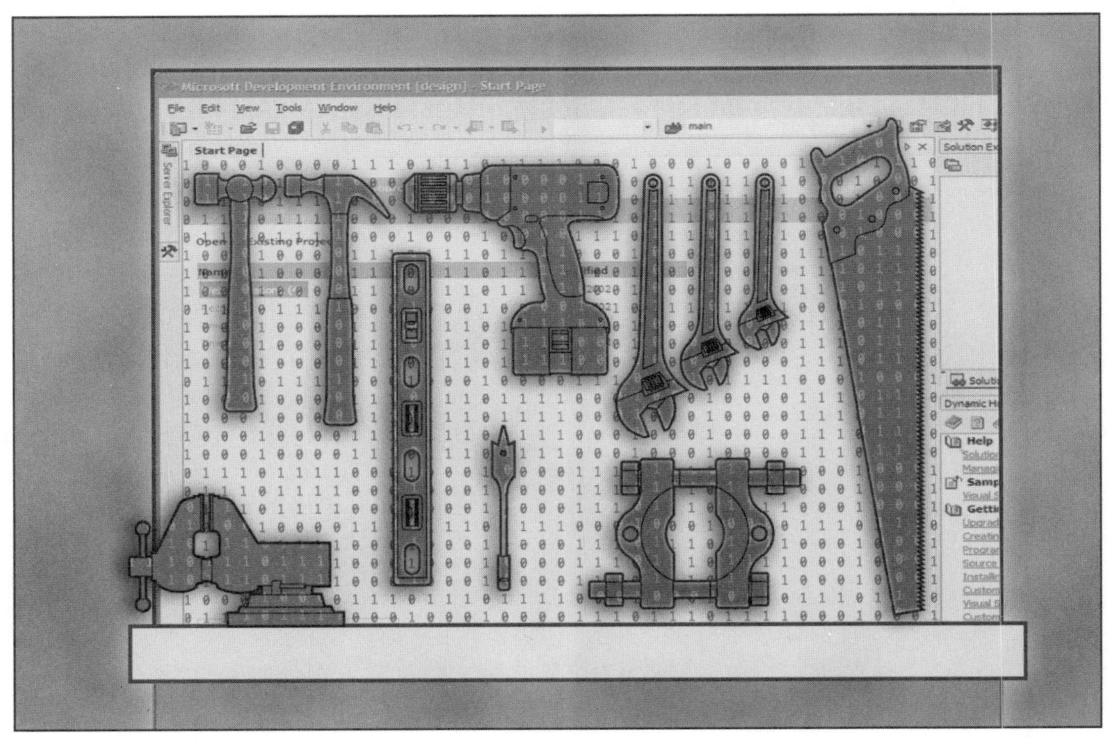

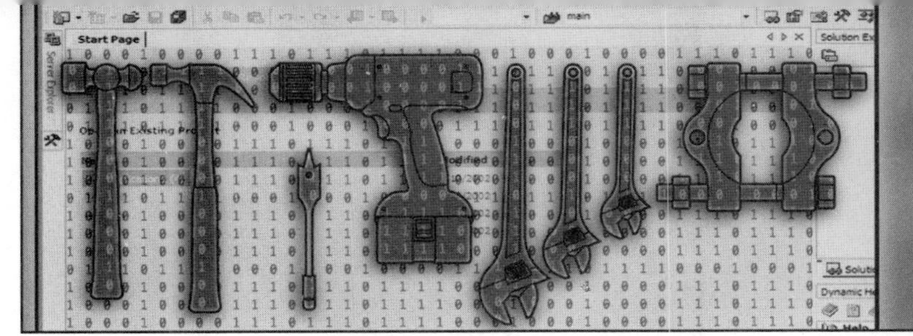

5

The Add-in Wizard and the Automation Object Model

The Add-in Wizard provided by Microsoft Visual Studio .NET makes creating add-ins as easy as taking a Sunday drive—just choose a few options, and the wizard generates a road-ready add-in that you can take for a spin in the integrated development environment (IDE). Of course, you won't drive very far if you can't find the add-in's clutch, stick shift, and steering wheel (not to mention the gas pedal), so in the first half of this chapter we'll show you how the different parts of an add-in work together to make it go. Think of it as "driver's ed" for wizard-generated add-ins.

There's no point in taking your add-in out on the road without a worthwhile destination in mind, so we've chosen one for you. In the second half of this chapter, we'll map out a scenic route through Visual Studio .NET's programming interface: the automation object model.

The Add-in Wizard

You learned in Chapter 4 that macros provide a convenient way to automate tasks within Visual Studio .NET, and we encourage you to write macros as a first resort when customizing the IDE. But for some purposes, such as writing commercial software, you might find that macros are a poor choice in terms of performance and protection of intellectual property. In such cases, the appropriate vehicle is an *add-in*, which is a compiled DLL (providing increased protection) that runs within the IDE (providing increased performance). And the fastest way to get started as an add-in programmer is through the Add-in Wizard, which gathers your requirements in six easy steps and creates an add-in project tailored to your needs.

Running the Add-in Wizard

When you choose File | New | Project, Visual Studio .NET offers its selection of project types in the New Project dialog box. By expanding the Other Projects node and selecting Extensibility Projects, you'll find the Visual Studio .NET Add-in template shown in Figure 5-1; double-clicking its icon launches the Add-in Wizard.

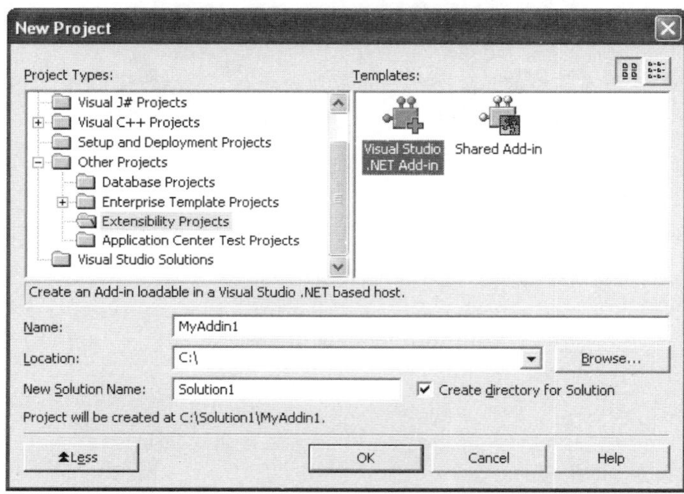

Figure 5-1 The Visual Studio .NET Add-in template

The six pages of the Add-in Wizard collect your choices about the final form of your add-in. The wizard gives you control over the following areas:

- **Programming language** The Add-in Wizard generates the add-in source code in one of three programming languages—C#, Visual Basic .NET, or Visual C++ (using the Active Template Library [ATL]). You're not restricted to these languages when you write add-ins by hand, however; any language that supports the creation of COM objects will suffice.
- **Application host** Add-ins can run in the Visual Studio .NET IDE, the Macros IDE, or both. With few exceptions, the rules that apply to an add-in running in the Visual Studio .NET IDE also apply to an add-in running in the Macros IDE. (We'll point out differences between the two hosts when appropriate.)

- **Name and description** These settings let you associate a meaningful name and description with your add-in. The wizard stores these values in the registry so that any interested client can find them.
- **Menu command** The Add-in Wizard can generate code that creates a new menu item for your add-in, giving users a convenient way to load your add-in and execute a command.
- **Command-line build support** You can mark your add-in as being safe for use with unattended builds. Such an add-in promises that it won't display user interface elements that require user intervention (such as modal dialog boxes).
- **Load at startup** Add-ins can request that they be loaded automatically when Visual Studio .NET starts up.
- **Access privileges** You can make an add-in available to all users on a machine or just the user who installs the add-in.
- **About box information** You can provide support information for your add-in that Visual Studio .NET will display in its About dialog box.

When the Add-in Wizard finishes, it generates two projects: an add-in project that builds the add-in DLL and a setup project that builds a Windows Installer (MSI) file that you can use to distribute your add-in.

The Add-in Project

Add-ins are DLLs, so the Add-in Wizard creates a Class Library project for your add-in. This project contains a source file named Connect, which defines the add-in class, also named *Connect*. The *Connect* class implements the *IDTExtensibility2* interface, which serves as the main conduit for add-in/IDE communication. (*Connect* also implements *IDTCommandTarget* if you select the user interface option in the Add-in Wizard.) Table 5-1 lists the five methods of the *IDTExtensibility2* interface.

Table 5-1 *IDTExtensibility2* Interface

Method	Description
OnConnection	Called when the add-in is loaded.
OnStartupComplete	Called when Visual Studio .NET finishes loading.
OnAddInsUpdate	Called whenever an add-in is loaded or unloaded from Visual Studio .NET.

Table 5-1 ***IDTExtensibility2*** **Interface** *(continued)*

Method	Description
OnBeginShutdown	Called when Visual Studio .NET is closed.
OnDisconnection	Called when the add-in is unloaded.

The Connect.cs file in Listing 5-1 shows the code (minus some comments) that the Add-in Wizard generates for a typical C# add-in with a menu command. We'll walk through the source code, pointing out any interesting features along the way.

Connect.cs

```
namespace MyAddin1
{
    using System;
    using Microsoft.Office.Core;
    using Extensibility;
    using System.Runtime.InteropServices;
    using EnvDTE;

    /// <summary>
    ///   The object for implementing an add-in.
    /// </summary>
    /// <seealso class='IDTExtensibility2' />
    [GuidAttribute("BA857E49-7873-45D2-8335-FCCD4123739E"),
        ProgId("MyAddin1.Connect")]
    public class Connect : Object, Extensibility.IDTExtensibility2,
        IDTCommandTarget
    {
        /// <summary>
        ///   Implements the constructor for the add-in object.
        ///   Place your initialization code within this method.
        /// </summary>
        public Connect()
        {
        }

        /// <summary>
        ///   Implements the OnConnection method of the
        ///   IDTExtensibility2 interface.
        ///   Receives notification that the add-in is being loaded.
        /// </summary>
        /// <param term='application'>
```

Listing 5-1 The add-in source code generated by the Add-in Wizard

```
///   Root object of the host application.
/// </param>
/// <param term='connectMode'>
///   Describes how the add-in is being loaded.
/// </param>
/// <param term='addInInst'>
///   Object representing this add-in.
/// </param>
public void OnConnection(object application,
    Extensibility.ext_ConnectMode connectMode,
    object addInInst, ref System.Array custom)
{
    applicationObject = (_DTE)application;
    addInInstance = (AddIn)addInInst;

    if (connectMode ==
        Extensibility.ext_ConnectMode.ext_cm_UISetup)
    {
        object []contextGUIDS = new object[] { };
        Commands commands = applicationObject.Commands;
        _CommandBars commandBars =
            applicationObject.CommandBars;

        try
        {
            Command command = commands.AddNamedCommand(
                addInInstance, "MyAddin1", "MyAddin1",
                "Executes the command for MyAddin1", true, 59,
                ref contextGUIDS,
                (int)vsCommandStatus.vsCommandStatusSupported +
                (int)vsCommandStatus.vsCommandStatusEnabled);
            CommandBar commandBar =
                (CommandBar)commandBars["Tools"];
            CommandBarControl commandBarControl =
                command.AddControl(commandBar, 1);
        }
        catch(System.Exception /*e*/)
        {
        }
    }
}

/// <summary>
///   Implements the OnDisconnection method of the
///   IDTExtensibility2 interface.
///   Receives notification that the add-in is being unloaded.
```

```
/// </summary>
/// <param term='disconnectMode'>
///   Describes how the add-in is being unloaded.
/// </param>
/// <param term='custom'>
///   Array of parameters that are host-application specific.
/// </param>
public void OnDisconnection(
    Extensibility.ext_DisconnectMode disconnectMode,
    ref System.Array custom)
{
}

/// <summary>
///   Implements the OnAddInsUpdate method of the
///   IDTExtensibility2 interface.
///   Receives notification that the collection of add-ins
///   has changed.
/// </summary>
/// <param term='custom'>
///   Array of parameters that are host-application specific.
/// </param>
public void OnAddInsUpdate(ref System.Array custom)
{
}

/// <summary>
///   Implements the OnStartupComplete method of the
///   IDTExtensibility2 interface.
///   Receives notification that the host application has
///   completed loading.
/// </summary>
/// <param term='custom'>
///   Array of parameters that are host-application specific.
/// </param>
public void OnStartupComplete(ref System.Array custom)
{
}

/// <summary>
///   Implements the OnBeginShutdown method of the
///   IDTExtensibility2 interface.
///   Receives notification that the host application is
///   being unloaded.
/// </summary>
```

```
        /// <param term='custom'>
        ///   Array of parameters that are host-application specific.
        /// </param>
        public void OnBeginShutdown(ref System.Array custom)
        {
        }

        /// <summary>
        ///   Implements the QueryStatus method of the
        ///   IDTCommandTarget interface.
        ///   This is called when the command's availability is updated.
        /// </summary>
        /// <param term='commandName'>
        ///   The name of the command to determine state for.
        /// </param>
        /// <param term='neededText'>
        ///   Text that is needed for the command.
        /// </param>
        /// <param term='status'>
        ///   The state of the command in the user interface.
        /// </param>
        /// <param term='commandText'>
        ///   Text requested by the neededText parameter.
        /// </param>
        public void QueryStatus(string commandName,
            EnvDTE.vsCommandStatusTextWanted neededText,
            ref EnvDTE.vsCommandStatus status, ref object commandText)
        {
            if (neededText ==
EnvDTE.vsCommandStatusTextWanted.vsCommandStatusTextWantedNone)
            {
                if (commandName == "MyAddin1.Connect.MyAddin1")
                {
                    status =
(vsCommandStatus)vsCommandStatus.vsCommandStatusSupported |
vsCommandStatus.vsCommandStatusEnabled;
                }
            }
        }

        /// <summary>
        ///   Implements the Exec method of the IDTCommandTarget interface.
        ///   This is called when the command is invoked.
        /// </summary>
        /// <param term='commandName'>
```

```
        ///   The name of the command to execute.
        /// </param>
        /// <param term='executeOption'>
        ///   Describes how the command should be run.
        /// </param>
        /// <param term='varIn'>
        ///   Parameters passed from the caller to the command handler.
        /// </param>
        /// <param term='varOut'>
        ///   Parameters passed from the command handler to the caller.
        /// </param>
        /// <param term='handled'>
        ///   Informs the caller whether the command was handled.
        /// </param>
        public void Exec(string commandName,
            EnvDTE.vsCommandExecOption executeOption, ref object varIn,
            ref object varOut, ref bool handled)
        {
            handled = false;
            if (executeOption ==
                EnvDTE.vsCommandExecOption.vsCommandExecOptionDoDefault)
            {
                if (commandName == "MyAddin1.Connect.MyAddin1")
                {
                    handled = true;
                    return;
                }
            }
        }
        private _DTE applicationObject;
        private AddIn addInInstance;
    }
}
```

At the top of the listing, you'll see that the Add-in Wizard generates a set of *using* statements for the programmer's convenience. (A quick look through Connect.cs reveals that the Add-in Wizard eschews the *using* statements in favor of fully-qualified types—a practice that proves invaluable when you're trying to figure out where all the weird add-in types come from.) The two most important namespaces in the *using* statements are *EnvDTE* and *Extensibility*; the former defines the types used by *IDTExtensibility2*, and the latter defines the types in the automation object model. (A close third in the namespace contest is *Microsoft.Office.Core*, which defines types for manipulating command bars in the IDE.)

The first method in the listing, *OnConnection*, wins the prize for "most important add-in method." Visual Studio .NET calls this method when it loads the add-in, and it passes the add-in a reference to the root object of the automation object model through the *application* parameter. The code generated by the Add-in Wizard casts the *application* parameter to the *EnvDTE._DTE* type and stores the result in a private variable named *applicationObject*. All further interaction between the add-in and the automation object model takes place through the *applicationObject* variable.

Visual Studio .NET also passes the add-in a reference to its corresponding *AddIn* object through the *addInInst* parameter; the add-in stores this reference in a private variable named *addInInstance*.

The rest of the code in *OnConnection* creates an add-in menu command on the Tools menu. (This code is absent if you forgo the user interface option in the Add-in Wizard.) The menu-creation code executes conditionally, depending on the following *if* statement:

```
if (connectMode == Extensibility.ext_ConnectMode.ext_cm_UISetup)
```

The *connectMode* parameter holds a value that describes how the add-in was loaded. For add-ins that create a menu command, Visual Studio .NET passes in the *Extensibility.ext_ConnectMode. ext_cm_UISetup* value the first time the add-in loads after being installed, which signals to the add-in that now is as good a time as any to add its commands to the IDE.

The Add-in Wizard doesn't generate any code in the bodies of the other four *IDTExtensibility2* methods: *OnStartupComplete*, *OnAddinsUpdate*, *OnBeginShutdown*, and *OnDisconnection*. The two *IDTCommandTarget* methods, *QueryStatus* and *Exec*, have some boilerplate code that helps manage the add-in's menu command and menu command clicks, respectively. To handle menu command clicks, you add code to the *Exec* method in the second *if* statement, which begins with

```
if (commandName == "MyAddin1.Connect.MyAddin1")
```

There isn't much code in Connect.cs, even if you've selected every option in the Add-in Wizard, but the code that's there creates a fully-functional add-in that you can build on.

Installing and Loading the Add-in

The easiest (and best) way of installing your new add-in is to build the add-in setup project and install the MSI file that it creates. The MSI file is a completely self-contained package that can be deployed on any Windows machine, with one caveat: the target machine must have the .NET Framework installed. (If you need to, you can distribute the .NET Framework along with your add-in. Chapter 13 explains how.) This single-package distributable makes installing the add-in as simple as double-clicking the MSI file's icon in Windows Explorer. If you like, you also can install the add-in from within Visual Studio .NET. After you build the setup project, choose the Install command from the project's shortcut menu, as shown in Figure 5-2. After you launch the setup, an installer wizard steps you through the setup process.

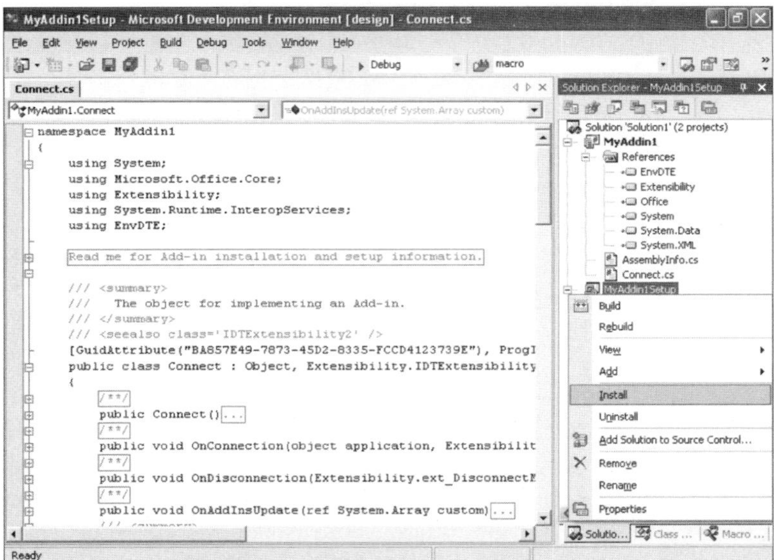

Figure 5-2 Installing the add-in from within Visual Studio .NET

The way you load your add-in into Visual Studio .NET can vary, depending in part on the options you selected in the Add-in Wizard. If you chose to have your add-in load on startup, Visual Studio .NET will load the add-in automatically each time it runs. If you chose to have a user interface item for your add-in, the next time Visual Studio .NET runs, you'll be able to load the add-in by choosing its command from the Tools menu, as shown in Figure 5-3.

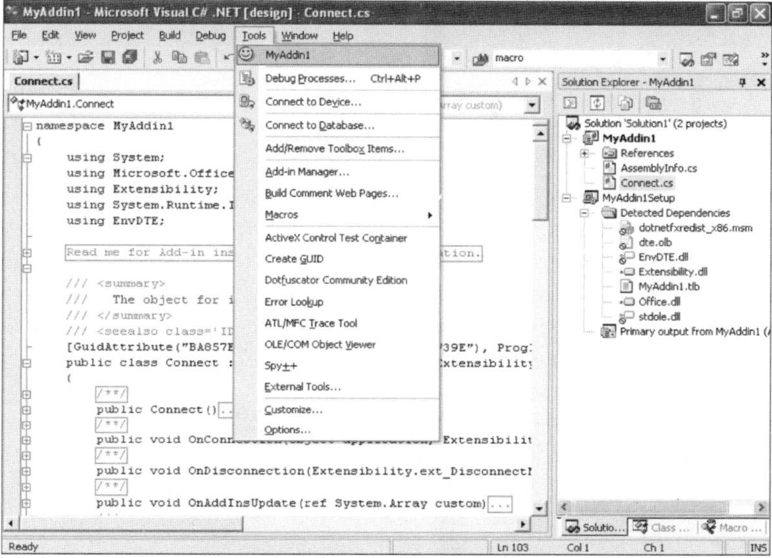

Figure 5-3 A default add-in menu command

If you didn't choose either of these options, you can load the add-in by choosing Tools | Add-in Manager, which launches the Add-in Manager (shown in Figure 5-4). The Add-in Manager gives you control over all the registered add-ins, allowing you to load them, unload them, and mark them to load on startup and during command-line builds.

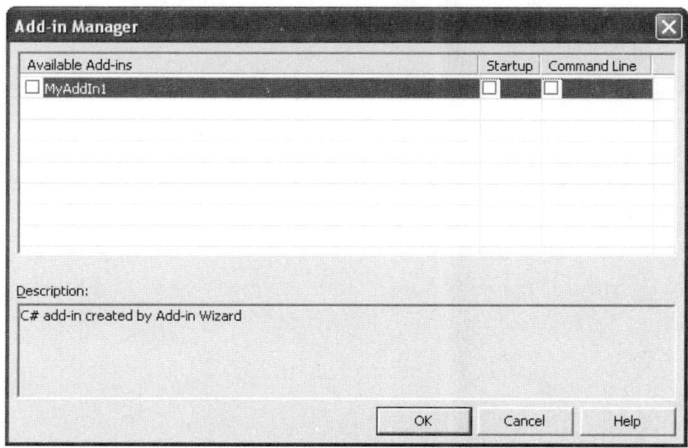

Figure 5-4 The Add-in Manager dialog box

Debugging the Add-in

An add-in is just a DLL, so debugging an add-in project is no different from debugging any other Class Library project. Because a DLL can't run on its own, it needs a host application; for an add-in, that host is Visual Studio .NET (devenv.exe) or the Macros IDE (vsaenv.exe). The Add-in Wizard sets the debugging properties of the add-in project so that Visual Studio .NET is the host. You can examine and modify the project's debugging properties by right-clicking the add-in project in Solution Explorer, choosing Properties from the shortcut menu, and selecting Configuration Properties | Debugging in the Property Pages dialog box (shown in Figure 5-5). For most purposes, however, the default settings work just fine.

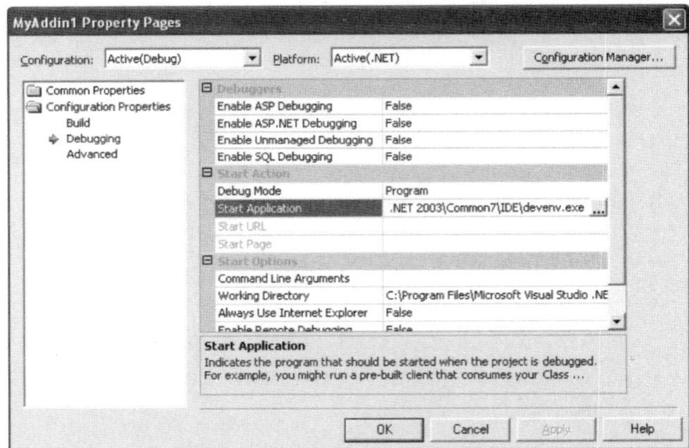

Figure 5-5 The add-in project's debugging properties

In a typical debugging session, you open the add-in project in Visual Studio .NET, set breakpoints in the add-in source code, and then start the debugger by choosing Start from the Debug menu (or pressing F5). The debugger, in turn, launches a second instance of Visual Studio .NET and attaches itself to this new process. You load the add-in to be debugged in the second instance of Visual Studio .NET, and when the add-in code hits a breakpoint, execution passes to the debugger running in the first instance of Visual Studio .NET. From there you can step through the code, examine the contents of variables and registers, and perform other sundry debugging tasks.

Debugging add-ins in the Macros IDE is almost as easy as debugging add-ins in Visual Studio .NET. The one catch is that you can't just open the Macros IDE from an instance of Visual Studio .NET and then attach the debugger from that instance to the Macros IDE. Why not? Because the two processes will deadlock if Visual Studio .NET fires a macro event while execution is stopped in the debugger. Instead, the recommended way to debug add-ins in the Macros IDE is similar to the way you debug add-ins in Visual Studio .NET: open the add-in project in Visual Studio .NET, start a second instance of Visual Studio .NET, open the Macros IDE from the second instance of Visual Studio .NET, attach the debugger from the first instance of Visual Studio .NET to the Macros IDE process, load the add-in in the Macros IDE, and then debug as normal. (And don't forget to breathe.)

Finally, you shouldn't feel obligated to run the Visual Studio .NET debugger if you have a favorite debugger you'd rather use. Any debugger that can handle delay-load DLLs will do (such as the Microsoft CLR Debugger that comes with the .NET Framework SDK, shown in Figure 5-6).

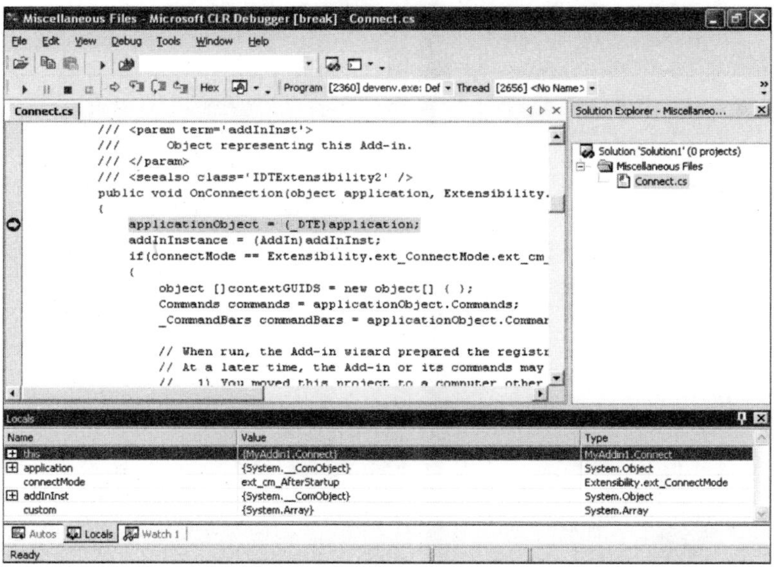

Figure 5-6 Using the CLR Debugger to debug an add-in

The Automation Object Model

One look at the automation object model chart and you'll agree that the Visual Studio .NET designers are serious about letting developers customize their programming environment. With over 140 different objects, the automation object model gives you unprecedented control over the IDE, from the solution level all the way down to a single parameter in a function.

Automation Objects

Just as its name suggests, the automation object model exposes its functionality through objects—a programming paradigm familiar to most programmers today. Each object in the model encapsulates some small part of Visual Studio .NET and offers programmatic access to it through a set of methods, properties, and events. The objects are arranged in a hierarchy, with the methods and properties of one object allowing access to its child objects below and to its parent object above.

The *DTE* object sits atop this automation object model hierarchy and serves as the entrance to its furthest recesses. Add-ins get their *DTE* reference from the *application* parameter of their *OnConnection* event; macros use the *DTE* reference in the predefined global variable named *DTE*. From this *DTE* reference, you can reach all the other objects in the automation object model. If you're wondering what objects you might want to reach, the following short list should get your imagination working:

- *Solution*, *Project*, and *ProjectItem* objects give you programmatic control over all aspects of project management.
- *Document* and *TextDocument* objects let you manipulate documents in the IDE.
- *TextSelection* and *TextPoint* objects let you edit text as viewed in an editor window; *EditPoint* objects let you make changes directly to the text buffer.
- *FileCodeModel*, *CodeNamespace*, *CodeInterface*, *CodeVariable*, *CodeFunction*, and similar objects let you manipulate code constructs at a level independent of the underlying programming language.
- *CommandWindow*, *TaskList*, *OutputWindow*, *ToolBox*, and other similar objects give you control of specific tool windows within the IDE.
- *Command* objects let you access environment commands.
- *Debugger*, *Process*, *Program*, *Thread*, *StackFrame*, and other related objects give you control over the Visual Studio .NET debugger.

Of course, the objects in the previous list are only the beginning. The remainder of the book covers these objects and more in exhaustive detail, teaching you everything you need to know to turn your copy of Visual Studio .NET into the coolest IDE on your block.

Object Model Guidelines

Whenever possible, the automation object model design follows a few simple guidelines, shown in the following list. (Keep these rules in mind while you program, and you won't waste time agonizing over why *AddIns(0)* throws a *COMException* or why *Activate* won't display your @#&%*! output window.)

- All objects use Automation types only.
- All objects have a *DTE* property that returns the *DTE* object.
- Collections have names that are the plural form of the objects they contain. For example, *Documents* is the collection of *Document* objects.
- Collections are accessed through properties that have the same name as the collection.
- Collections have an *Item* method—not a property—for accessing their contained items.
- The *Item* method for a collection takes an object when you're using a managed language; it takes a *VARIANT* when you're using an unmanaged language.
- The *Item* method on a collection takes a numerical index or the name of a collection item.
- Numerical indexes into a collection are 1-based.
- Collections have a *Count* method that returns a *System.Int32* when you're using a managed language or a *long* when you're using an unmanaged language.
- Collection items have a *Collection* property that returns the owning collection; all other objects have a *Parent* property that returns its parent object.
- You add an item to a collection by using the *Add* method on the collection; you remove an item from a collection by using the *Remove* or *Delete* method on the item. (*Delete* applies to user interface items, such as *ToolBoxTab* objects; *Remove* applies to non–user interface items, such as *AddIn* objects.)
- The *DTE.Events* object provides access to all event interfaces.
- A general object can return one or more specific objects through its *Object* property, which takes the case-insensitive name of the specific object.

- Creating a window doesn't automatically make that window visible; instead, you make a window visible by setting its *Visible* property to *True*.
- Properties that return a complete path to a file on disk are called *FullName*.
- The *Activate* method sets the focus on a visible user interface item; if the item isn't visible, *Activate* won't necessarily make its container visible.

Automation Events

If automation objects tell you what you can do within Visual Studio .NET, automation events tell you when you can do it. Each of the functional groups within the automation object model defines events that allow you to listen in on Visual Studio .NET's activities and take action based on what you hear. Together with automation objects, automation events allow you to achieve hands-free control over every important aspect of Visual Studio .NET.

Connecting to Automation Events

Connecting to automation events is pretty simple, although the syntax for doing so differs dramatically between the languages supported by Visual Studio .NET. We'll begin our events overview with C# because the C# syntax reveals everything we care to know about the mechanics of events.

The *DTE.Events* property is the first stop on the way to automation events. This property returns an *EnvDTE.Events* interface, which defines the read-only properties shown in Table 5-2. Each of the *Events* properties returns an event interface with the same name as the property; each event interface, in turn, defines a set of events to which you can subscribe.

Table 5-2 *EnvDTE.Events* Properties

Property	Events
BuildEvents	*OnBuildBegin*
	OnBuildDone
	OnBuildProjConfigBegin
	OnBuildProjConfigDone
*CommandEvents**	*AfterExecute*
	BeforeExecute

Table 5-2 *EnvDTE.Events* Properties *(continued)*

Property	Events
DebuggerEvents	*OnContextChanged* *OnEnterBreakMode* *OnEnterDesignMode* *OnEnterRunMode* *OnExceptionNotHandled* *OnExceptionThrown*
*DocumentEvents**	*DocumentClosing* *DocumentOpened* *DocumentOpening* *DocumentSaved*
DTEEvents	*ModeChanged* *OnBeginShutdown* *OnMacrosRuntimeReset* *OnStartupComplete*
FindEvents	*FindDone*
MiscFilesEvents (returns *ProjectItemsEvents*)	*ItemAdded* *ItemRemoved* *ItemRenamed*
*OutputWindowEvents**	*PaneAdded* *PaneClearing* *PaneUpdated*
SelectionEvents	*OnChange*
SolutionEvents	*AfterClosing* *BeforeClosing* *Opened* *ProjectAdded* *ProjectRemoved* *ProjectRenamed* *QueryCloseSolution* *Renamed*

Table 5-2 *EnvDTE.Events* Properties *(continued)*

Property	Events
SolutionItemsEvents (returns *ProjectItemsEvents*)	*ItemAdded* *ItemRemoved* *ItemRenamed*
TaskListEvents[*]	*TaskAdded* *TaskModified* *TaskNavigated* *TaskRemoved*
TextEditorEvents[*]	*LineChanged*
WindowEvents[*]	*WindowActivated* *WindowClosing* *WindowCreated* *WindowMoved*

[*] C# won't allow you to reference these properties using property syntax because their *get* accessors take parameters. Use explicit calls to the *get* accessors instead.

Before you can subscribe to one of the events in Table 5-2, you need to define the function that will handle the event, and to do that you need the event's signature. The Visual Studio .NET documentation contains all the signature information for the automation events; once you have that information, you can define an event handler function whose prototype matches that of the corresponding event.

Next you need the delegate that's defined for the event. In the .NET Framework event model, a *delegate* is a class that wraps a callback function (such as an event handler) and provides type-safe access to it. The delegates for the automation events have names that follow this pattern: *_disp<event interface>_<event name>EventHandler*. To add your event handler to the event's list of subscribers, you create a new instance of the event's delegate, passing the event handler to the delegate's constructor, and then you assign the delegate to the event using the += syntax. If you've never done this before, it's easier than it sounds. Let's look at an example.

Suppose the software company you work for logs its daily builds and you would like to inject custom information into those logs, such as the name and department of the person performing the build. One way to do that would be to write an add-in that intercepts the *BuildEvents.OnBuildBegin* event—which fires just before a build takes place—and write the custom information into the log from the event handler. A quick peek at the documentation reveals the event's signature:

```
void OnBuildBegin(vsBuildScope scope, vsBuildAction action);
```

When this event fires, Visual Studio .NET passes along information about the impending build through the *scope* and *action* parameters: the *scope* parameter tells you the extent of the build that is about to begin (solution, batch, or project), and the *action* parameter tells you the kind of build that is about to begin (build, rebuild all, clean, or deploy). The event handler that you create must have the same signature as this event; you can name the handler anything you like, but the event's name is as good as any other:

```
public class Connect : Object, Extensibility.IDTExtensibility2
{
    ⋮
    private void OnBuildBegin(vsBuildScope scope, vsBuildAction action)
    {
        // Log the builder's information
        ⋮
    }
}
```

Now that the event handler is in place, it's time to wire it up to the event. From Table 5-2, you know that build events belong to the *BuildEvents* interface, so the delegate you need for the *OnBeginBuild* event has the name *_dispBuildEvents_OnBeginBuildEventHandler*. The following code wires up the event handler:

```
public class Connect : Object, Extensibility.IDTExtensibility2
{
    ⋮
    public void OnConnection(object application,
        Extensibility.ext_ConnectMode connectMode,
        object addInInst,
        ref System.Array custom)
    {
        applicationObject = (_DTE)application;
        addInInstance = (AddIn)addInInst;

        buildEvents = applicationObject.Events.BuildEvents;
        buildEvents.OnBuildBegin +=
            new _dispBuildEvents_OnBuildBeginEventHandler(
                this.OnBuildBegin);
        ⋮
    }
    ⋮
```

```
    public void OnDisconnection(
        Extensibility.ext_DisconnectMode disconnectMode,
        ref System.Array custom)
    {
        buildEvents.OnBuildBegin -=
            new _dispBuildEvents_OnBuildBeginEventHandler(
                this.OnBuildBegin);
        ⋮
    }
    ⋮
    private void OnBuildBegin(vsBuildScope scope, vsBuildAction action)
    {
        // Log the builder's information
        ⋮
    }
    ⋮
    private _DTE applicationObject;
    private AddIn addInInstance;
    private EnvDTE.BuildEvents buildEvents;
    ⋮
}
```

The pattern is simple: *OnConnection* hooks up the *OnBuildBegin* event handler to the event when the add-in loads, and *OnDisconnection* unhooks the same event handler when the add-in unloads.

> **Important** If you don't unsubscribe from all events before the add-in unloads, you're in for a good old-fashioned memory leak. Under normal circumstances, the add-in becomes fair game for the garbage collector when Visual Studio .NET unloads it. But when the add-in doesn't unsubscribe from its events, it never gets garbage collected because the events still hold references to it. And like the ghosts in the movie *The Sixth Sense* who "don't even know they're dead," the add-in will behave as though nothing is wrong and will continue to process events long after it has passed on from the realm of Visual Studio .NET.

Macro Event Handlers

Connecting to events from add-ins is easy, and connecting to events from macros is easier still. Every new macro project begins life with a module named *EnvironmentEvents*. This module defines an event variable for each of the event interfaces listed in Table 5-2, and these event variables are initialized automatically by the Macros IDE. When the *EnvironmentEvents* module is open in an editor window, you can add a new event handler by selecting the event variable from the Class Name drop-down list and then selecting the event you want to connect to from the Method Name drop-down list (as shown in Figure 5-7). The Macros IDE generates an empty event handler—all you have to do is add the code.

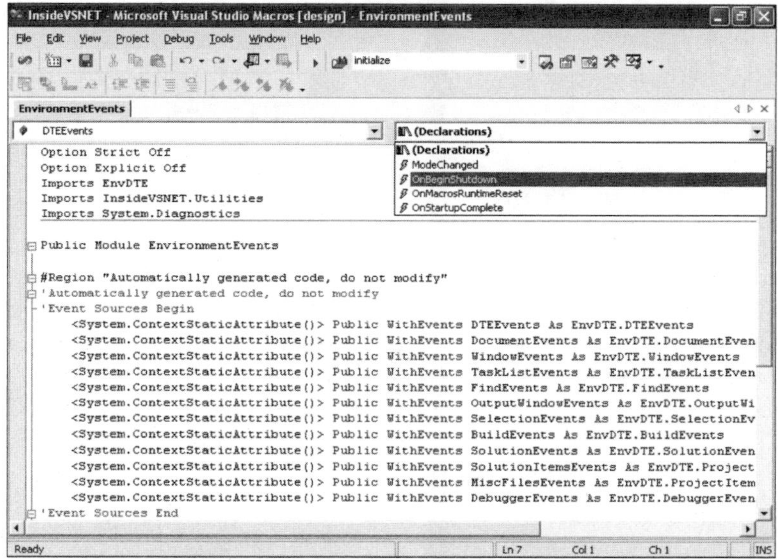

Figure 5-7 Adding a macro event handler

To unsubscribe from an event, you just delete its event handler from the *EnvironmentEvents* module. Be careful not to modify or delete the event variables located within the region marked "Automatically generated code, do not modify," because doing so might prevent the macro project from building.

Defining Your Own Event Variables

Although the *EnvironmentEvents* module is a convenient place to create and manage your macro event handlers, you might have reason to define some of your event handlers in other modules (if only to keep *EnvironmentEvents* from growing too large). To create an event handler in an arbitrary module, you first need to declare an event variable in that module. The following declaration creates the *MyWindowEvents* variable for handling window events:

```
<System.ContextStaticAttribute()> Public WithEvents _
    MyWindowEvents As EnvDTE.WindowEvents
```

If you open the module containing this declaration in an editor window, you can generate an empty event handler just as you would in the *EnvironmentEvents* module by selecting the *MyWindowEvents* variable from the Class Name drop-down list and then selecting the event you want to handle from the Method Name drop-down list. Unlike the *EnvironmentEvents* module, however, the new event handler won't receive events automatically. That's because the Macros IDE initializes the event variables in *EnvironmentEvents* for you—when you create your own event variables, you have to initialize them yourself.

To initialize an event variable, you assign the appropriate *DTE.Events* property to it:

```
MyWindowEvents = DTE.Events.WindowEvents
```

You can put the assignment in a regular macro and run the macro by hand, which works well enough for some situations, but your handler will miss all events up to the time you run the macro. If the event handler has to intercept events right from startup, you need to automate the assignment somehow. The *DTEEvents* interface defines the two events you'll need for this purpose: *OnStartupComplete*, which fires when Visual Studio .NET finishes loading, and *OnMacrosRuntimeReset*, which fires when a macro project is reloaded into memory. By creating handlers in *EnvironmentEvents* for both of these events and performing the assignment within each handler, you achieve automatic initialization of your event variable:

```
Public Module EnvironmentEvents
    ⋮
    Public Sub DTEEvents_OnMacrosRuntimeReset() _
            Handles DTEEvents.OnMacrosRuntimeReset
        MyModule.MyWindowEvents = DTE.Events.WindowEvents
    End Sub

    Public Sub DTEEvents_OnStartupComplete() _
            Handles DTEEvents.OnStartupComplete
        MyModule.MyWindowEvents = DTE.Events.WindowEvents
    End Sub
    ⋮
End Module
```

Filtered Events

In general, you should use events sparingly because too many event handlers will degrade the performance of Visual Studio .NET. By creating a *filtered event*, however, you can have your event and eat it, too. Essentially, a filtered event lets you handle the events of some objects and ignore the events of others. For example, instead of receiving *WindowClosing* events for every window, you can choose to receive *WindowClosing* events for the Task List window only. The *DTE.Events* properties listed in Table 5-3 allow you to create filtered events.

Table 5-3 Properties for Filtered Events

***DTE.Events* Property**	**Filtered By**
CommandEvents	*Command* name
DocumentEvents	*Document* object
OutputWindowEvents	Output window pane name
TaskListEvents	Task List category
TextEditorEvents	*TextDocument* object
WindowEvents	*Window* object

Suppose you want to handle events from a specific window in the IDE. From Table 5-3, you see that the *WindowEvents* property accepts a *Window* object as its filter. You retrieve the *Window* object you want from the *EnvDTE.Windows* collection by passing its *Item* method the associated *EnvDTE.Constants.vsWindowKindxxx* constant. Pass this *Window* object to the *WindowEvents* property and you'll receive an event interface for that particular window. The following code shows how to narrow down window events to the Macro Explorer window only:

```
' Event variable declaration
<System.ContextStaticAttribute()> Public WithEvents _
    MacroExplorerWindowEvents As EnvDTE.WindowEvents

Sub InitializeMacroExplorerFilter()
    Dim macroExplorerWindow As EnvDTE.Window

    macroExplorerWindow = _
        DTE.Windows.Item(EnvDTE.Constants.vsWindowKindMacroExplorer)
    MacroExplorerWindowEvents = _
        DTE.Events.WindowEvents(macroExplorerWindow)
End Sub

Sub MacroExplorerWindowEvents_WindowActivated( _
        ByVal GotFocus As EnvDTE.Window, _
        ByVal LostFocus As EnvDTE.Window) _
        Handles MacroExplorerWindowEvents.WindowActivated
    ' Description: Tracks each time the Macro Explorer window
    '              is activated
    ⋮
End Sub
```

Lab: Unfiltered and Filtered Events

Want to see the difference between unfiltered and filtered events? Then open the Output window and try the following experiment, which uses macros in the *FilteredEvents* module:

1. Run the *InitializeUnfilteredEvents* macro, which initializes *DocumentEvents* and *TextEditorEvents* event variables without filters. *FilteredEvents* defines event handlers that process *DocumentSaved* and *LineChanged* events for these two event variables.
2. Create two new text files.
3. Type a line of text, and press Enter in both of the files you created. The Output window displays a "LineChanged fired" message for each new line.
4. Save both of the files. As you save each file, the Output window displays a "DocumentSaved fired" message.

Because the *DocumentEvents* and *TextEditorEvents* event variables were initialized without filters, the corresponding event handlers receive events for all documents. Now, leave open the two files you created and try a similar experiment using filtered events:

1. Run the *InitializeFilteredEvents* macro. This macro creates a file named New File and initializes the *DocumentSaved* and *LineChanged* event variables so that they target events for this file only.
2. In the New File file, enter a line of text and press Enter. The Output window displays a "LineChanged fired" message.
3. Switch to each of the text files you created, and repeat the previous step. Notice that the Output window doesn't display "LineChanged fired" for either of these files.
4. Save both of the text files. Again, notice that the Output window doesn't display "DocumentSaved fired" messages.
5. Save New File. This time, you'll see "DocumentSaved fired" in the Output window.

Late-Bound Events

Programming languages integrated into Visual Studio .NET can offer late-bound events that monitor the status of their own project types—you can think of them as filtered events for projects. These project-specific events are shown in Table 5-4.

Table 5-4 Late-Bound Events

Language	Event Interface
Visual C#	*CSharpBuildManagerEvents*
	CSharpProjectsEvents
	CSharpProjectItemsEvents
	CSharpReferencesEvents
Visual Basic	*VBBuildManagerEvents*
	VBImportsEvents
	VBProjectsEvents
	VBProjectItemsEvents
	VBReferencesEvents
Visual C++	*CodeModelEvents*
	VCProjectEngineEventsObject

The event interface names are the same as the interfaces they derive from, but with a language-specific prefix: *VBProjectsEvents*, *CSharpProjectItemsEvents*, and so on. (The Visual C++ event interfaces are the exceptions because they derive from a different code base.) You retrieve the event interface you want by passing its name to the *DTE.Events.GetObject* method. For example, the following code initializes an event variable with the interface that handles all the C# project events:

```
<System.ContextStaticAttribute()> Public WithEvents _
    CSharpProjectsEvents As EnvDTE.ProjectsEvents

Sub InitializeCSharpProjectsEvents()
    CSharpProjectsEvents = DTE.Events.GetObject("CSharpProjectsEvents")
End Sub
```

After the previous code executes, any event handlers you created for the *CSharpProjectsEvents* variable will receive C# project events only.

Looking Ahead

Our Sunday drive is over. We've toured the Add-in Wizard countryside and cruised past the shores of the automation object model—now it's time to get to work. Pull your add-in into the garage, pop the hood, and roll up your sleeves. In the next chapter, we're stripping the add-in down to the frame and reassembling it piece by piece.

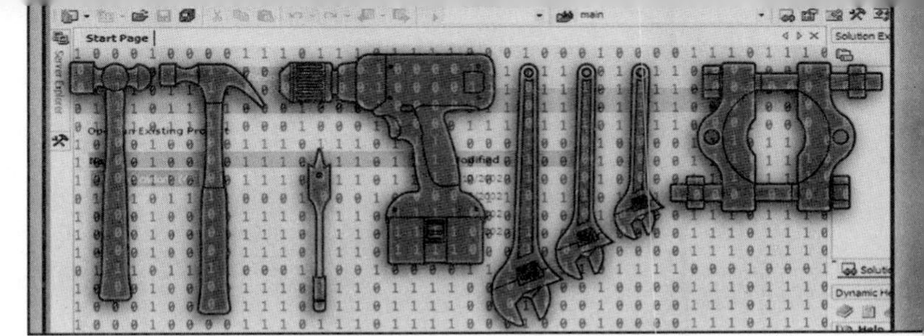

6

Add-in Architecture

As you learned in Chapter 5, the easiest way to create an add-in is by running the Add-in Wizard included with Microsoft Visual Studio .NET. The easiest way isn't always the best way, however, especially when you're trying to learn an unfamiliar technology. In this chapter, we'll hold to the ideal that good wizards are tools, not crutches, and that you should use them as a convenience only after you're capable of writing the equivalent code. Of course, we don't expect you to reach that goal without a little help—in the pages that follow, we'll teach you everything you need to know to write the equivalent of a wizard add-in. By the end, if you pay attention, you just might be able to write your own Add-in Wizard.

If that sounds like fun, then put your IDE away, open up a Command Window, and let's get started. In the next section, you'll learn the fundamentals of add-in construction by writing add-ins the old-fashioned way—by hand, from scratch.

Writing an Add-in from Scratch

Listing 6-1 shows the source code for our first add-in, named Basic. You can think of Basic as a wizard-generated add-in with all its clothes removed—the naked add-in that's left is the smallest one possible that still does something useful. And, as you can see from the listing, the smallest possible add-in is small indeed. That's because add-ins have one requirement only: a public class that derives from and implements the *Extensibility.IDTExtensibility2* interface. Basic.cs satisfies this requirement by defining a single, public class, named *Basic*, that derives from *IDTExtensibility2* and implements the interface's five methods—*OnConnection*, *OnStartupComplete*, *OnAddInsUpdate*, *OnBeginShutdown*, and *OnDisconnection*. There's no *Main* method because Basic, like all add-ins, is destined to become a DLL. Instead, the *OnConnection* method serves as the add-in's entry point, and the Basic add-in implements that method by displaying its own name in a message box.

Basic.cs

```
using System;
using System.Windows.Forms;
using Extensibility;

public class Basic : IDTExtensibility2
{
    public void OnConnection(object application,
        ext_ConnectMode connectMode,
        object addInInst,
        ref Array custom)
    {
        MessageBox.Show("Basic Add-in");
    }

    public void OnStartupComplete(ref Array custom)
    {
    }

    public void OnAddInsUpdate(ref Array custom)
    {
    }

    public void OnBeginShutdown(ref Array custom)
    {
    }

    public void OnDisconnection(ext_DisconnectMode removeMode,
        ref Array custom)
    {
    }
}
```

Listing 6-1 The Basic add-in source code

Compiling the Basic Add-in

If you add the source code in Listing 6-1 to a text file named Basic.cs, you can compile the Basic add-in from the command line by using the following command:

```
csc /t:library /r:"c:\program files\microsoft visual studio .net 2003\
common7\ide\publicassemblies\extensibility.dll" basic.cs
```

The */t:library* flag directs the C# compiler to create a DLL (Basic.dll) from the source file, and the */r:"c:\program files\microsoft visual studio .net 2003\common7\ide\publicassemblies\extensibility.dll"* flag points the compiler to the assembly that contains the *Extensibility* namespace (Extensibility.dll). The *Extensibility* namespace defines three types, which all add-ins use: the *IDTExtensibility2* interface and the *ext_ConnectMode* and *ext_DisconnectMode* enumerations, which define values passed to the *OnConnection* and *OnDisconnection* methods, respectively.

> **Tip** Typing long references at the command line invites both carpal tunnel syndrome and boredom. As an alternative, you can add a reference to the list of default references in the global CSC.rsp file, located at <WinDir>\Microsoft.NET\Framework\<Version>\CSC.rsp. For example, if you add */r:"c:\program files\microsoft visual studio .net 2003\common7\ide\publicassemblies\extensibility.dll"* to the global CSC.rsp file, you can compile the Basic add-in with the following command:
>
> ```
> csc /t:library basic.cs
> ```

Registering the Basic Add-in with COM

At this point, you have an add-in in a file named Basic.dll. To be more precise, you have a managed add-in that is defined in an assembly stored in a file named Basic.dll. Now comes the grand irony of Visual Studio .NET add-ins: Without some help, Visual Studio .NET can't host the managed add-ins that it builds—not even the ones created by its own Add-in Wizard. The reason is that Visual Studio itself is mostly an unmanaged application. Visual Studio .NET inherited much of its functionality from Visual Studio 6, including its ability to host add-ins. Because Visual Studio 6 dealt with COM add-ins only, Visual Studio .NET won't host any other kind, either.

Fortunately, COM interoperability comes to the rescue. The .NET Framework designers knew from the beginning that the world wasn't about to throw away its enormous investment in COM and start all over with managed code, so they made sure that COM classes and .NET classes would be able to interact seamlessly. All it takes for a .NET class to make itself available to COM is for the .NET class to register itself as a COM class. In particular, managed add-ins require the following registry entries:

- **HKEY_CLASSES_ROOT\<ProgID>** A key whose name is the ProgID of the class that implements *IDTExtensibility2*
- **HKEY_CLASSES_ROOT\<ProgID>\CLSID** A key whose default value is the CLSID of the class that implements *IDTExtensibility2*
- **HKEY_CLASSES_ROOT\CLSID\<CLSID>** A key whose name is the CLSID of the class that implements *IDTExtensibility2*
- **HKEY_CLASSES_ROOT\CLSID\InprocServer32** A key whose named values identify the class that implements *IDTExtensibility2* and the assembly in which that class is defined

Figure 6-1 shows the registry entries for the Basic add-in.

> **Note** Visual Studio .NET isn't the only beneficiary of COM interoperability. As long as your managed add-in is registered correctly, any environment that can host COM add-ins, such as Visual Basic 6, can host your managed add-in (provided, of course, that the .NET Framework is installed on the same machine).

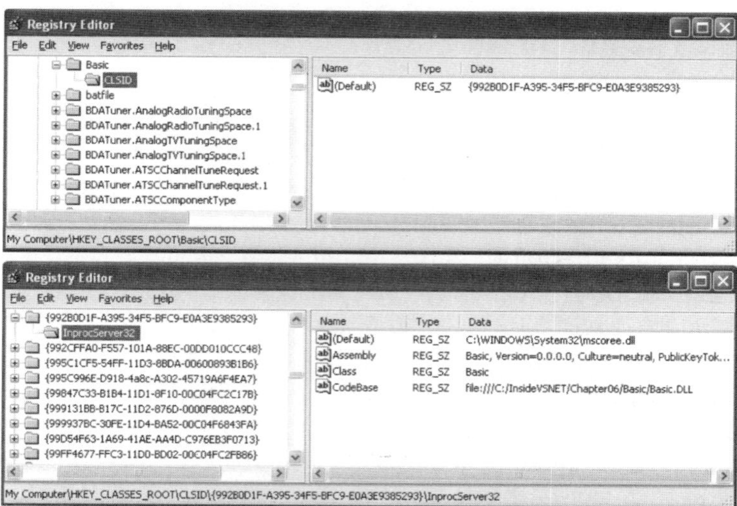

Figure 6-1 The COM interoperability registry entries for the Basic add-in

Thankfully, there's no need to add these registry entries by hand. They're created automatically when you register your add-in using the .NET Framework Assembly Registry utility (RegAsm). The following command registers the *Basic* class as a COM class:

```
regasm /codebase basic.dll
```

> **Note** Ignore RegAsm when it complains that the */codebase* flag should be used only with strongly named assemblies. The */codebase* flag generates the *CLSID\InprocServer32\CodeBase* named value—without this value, the CLR won't be able to locate your add-in's assembly.

RegAsm generates a default ProgID and CLSID for each class it encounters in an assembly. (See the upcoming sidebar "GUIDs and FUIDs" for more information about the default CLSID.) The default ProgID is the same as the class's fully qualified name. For example, the code

```
namespace Outer
{
    namespace Inner
    {
        public class MyClass ()
        {
        }
    }
}
```

produces the default ProgID, *Outer.Inner.MyClass*. Because the *Basic* class doesn't belong to a namespace, its ProgID is simply *Basic*.

GUIDs and FUIDs

Traditionally, a CLSID is a globally unique identifier (GUID)—a 16-byte number that's guaranteed to be unique in time and space. However, close inspection of the default CLSID that RegAsm generates reveals a number that's a GUID in appearance only. In fact, RegAsm always generates the same CLSID when given the same fully qualified class name, regardless of where or when the number is generated. (We'll call this number a FUID—for-the-most-part unique identifier—which ranks just below a GUID.)

This means that if two different programmers, at two different times, on two different machines, on two different continents, register a class named *Basic*, their classes will have the same FUID: 992B0D1F-A395-34F5-BFC9-E0A3E9385293.

Well, you might not be able to stop others from co-opting your carefully chosen class name, but you don't have to accept the off-the-rack FUID that RegAsm hands out to your class. That's where *System.Runtime.InteropServices.GuidAttribute* comes in handy. When applied to a class, *GuidAttribute* overrides the default FUID and lets you assign a GUID of your own choosing. (And there are lots of GUIDs to choose from—just run the Create GUID utility [GuidGen] to create an honest GUID that your class can call its own.)

Registering the Basic Add-in with Visual Studio .NET

Basic.dll is a fully functional add-in, but Visual Studio .NET won't know of its existence yet. Add-ins signal their availability to the Visual Studio .NET integrated development environment (IDE) through one of the following registry entries

- HKEY_LOCAL_MACHINE\SOFTWARE\Microsoft\VisualStudio\7.1\AddIns\<ProgID>
- HKEY_CURRENT_USER\Software\Microsoft\VisualStudio\7.1\AddIns\<ProgID>

And they make themselves known to the Macros IDE through one of the corresponding *VSA* registry entries:

- HKEY_LOCAL_MACHINE\SOFTWARE\Microsoft\VSA\7.1\AddIns\<ProgID>
- HKEY_CURRENT_USER\Software\Microsoft\VSA\7.1\AddIns\<ProgID>

> **Note** From here on out, we'll refer only to add-ins in the Visual Studio .NET IDE. However, the information in the rest of the chapter applies equally well to add-ins in the Macros IDE.

The Add-in Manager populates its add-ins list from these two *AddIns* keys. An HKEY_LOCAL_MACHINE entry makes the add-in available to all users on a machine; because modifying the HKEY_LOCAL_MACHINE hive requires administrator privileges, an add-in registered in this way is also known as an *administrator add-in*. An HKEY_CURRENT_USER entry makes the add-in available to the user who creates the entry and is mirrored in the user settings under HKEY_USERS; not surprisingly, an add-in registered in this way is known as a *user add-in*. In either case, the name of the key is the ProgID of the class that implements *IDTExtensibility2*.

To register the Basic add-in for use by all users on a machine, run the Registry Editor utility (RegEdit) and create the following key (assuming that you have administrator privileges):

```
HKEY_LOCAL_MACHINE\SOFTWARE\Microsoft\VisualStudio\7.1\
AddIns\Basic
```

After you create this key, run Visual Studio .NET and choose Tools | Add-in Manager to display the dialog box shown in Figure 6-2. Notice that the Add-in Manager lists the add-in's name as Basic. By default, the Add-in Manager displays the ProgID it finds under the *AddIns* registry key. (In the section titled "Add-in Registry Named Values" later in this chapter, we'll cover the named values for this ProgID registry key that control the display name and other properties of the add-in.)

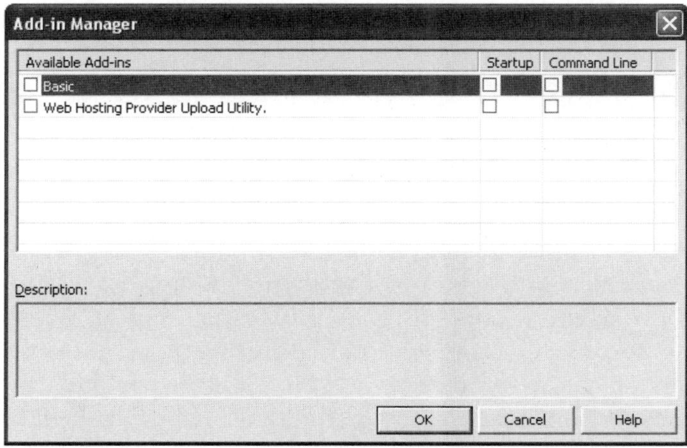

Figure 6-2 The Add-in Manager dialog box showing the Basic add-in

If you select the check box to the left of Basic and click OK, Visual Studio .NET loads the add-in. Assuming all goes well, Visual Studio .NET will call Basic's *OnConnection* method and you'll see the message box shown in Figure 6-3.

Figure 6-3 The message box displayed by the Basic add-in

And that's how you create an add-in from scratch. In the next section, we'll examine exactly what happens to an add-in in the Visual Studio .NET environment when the add-in loads, when the add-in unloads, and all the time in between.

Add-in Events

Add-ins are event-driven. Most everything an add-in does it does in response to some external prodding, and Visual Studio .NET prods add-ins with the *IDTExtensibility2* interface. We'll begin our exploration of add-in events by examining the sequence in which Visual Studio .NET calls the *IDTExtensibility2* methods.

The Add-in Event Sequence

Calls to the *IDTExtensibility2* methods, which we'll also refer to as *events*, occur at predictable points in the lifetime of an add-in. Figure 6-4 shows the sequence of events from the time an add-in is loaded to the time it is unloaded.

You can guess the actions that trigger the events just from the events' names, and the events occur pretty much in the order you would expect: *OnConnection* when an add-in loads, *OnDisconnection* when an add-in unloads, and so on. But however straightforward the event sequence might seem, it still holds a few surprises for the programmer who believes everything she reads in the documentation. The first surprise is the initial *OnAddInsUpdate* event. The documentation says that an add-in receives *OnAddInsUpdate* events only when other add-ins are loaded or unloaded; in truth, the add-in itself triggers the first *OnAddInsUpdate* it receives. This isn't a bug; instead, it turns out that the documentation is wrong, but you could argue that Visual Studio .NET should be smarter about which add-ins get notified. After all, an add-in already knows that it's being loaded when it receives the *OnConnection* event—it doesn't need an *OnAddInsUpdate* event to remind it of that.

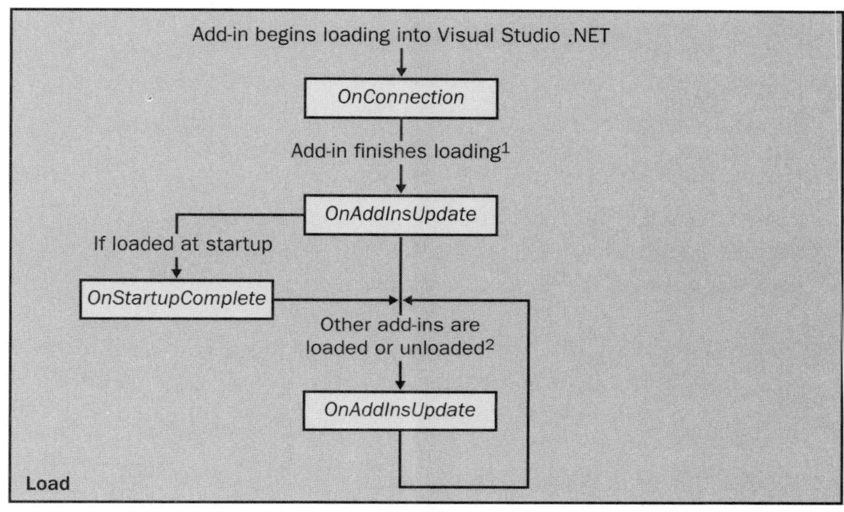

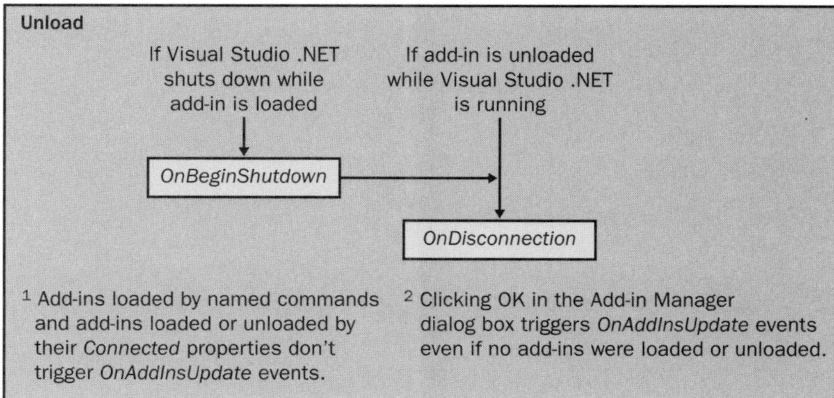

Figure 6-4 The add-in event sequence

The second surprise involves the Add-in Manager. The Add-in Manager triggers *OnAddInsUpdate* events whenever its OK button is clicked, regardless of whether an add-in was loaded or unloaded. This happens because clicking the OK button resets the add-ins list automatically, thereby triggering a round of *OnAddInsUpdate* events. This behavior is by design, for better or worse, so don't assume that every *OnAddInsUpdate* event after the first has something important to tell.

The third surprise is that add-ins loaded by commands don't trigger *OnAddInsUpdate* events, and neither do add-ins loaded or unloaded by way of their *Connected* properties. (We'll go over commands in detail in Chapter 7.) There's no nice way to describe this behavior, so we'll call a bug a bug and move on.

The LifeCycle Add-in

You can get a feel for the add-in event sequence by running the LifeCycle sample add-in. LifeCycle, shown in Listing 6-2, handles each *IDTExtensibility2* event by displaying the name of the event in the Output window. After you build and register LifeCycle, load it into Visual Studio .NET using the Add-in Manager. Then try loading and unloading other add-ins, such as Basic, to trigger the different *IDTExtensibility2* events. To fire the *OnStartupComplete* event, you first need to select the Startup check box for LifeCycle in the Add-in Manager, and then you must restart Visual Studio .NET. To fire the *OnBeginShutdown* event, close Visual Studio .NET while LifeCycle is loaded.

LifeCycle.cs

```
namespace InsideVSNET
{
    namespace AddIns
    {
        using EnvDTE;
        using Extensibility;
        using InsideVSNET.Utilities;
        using System;
        using System.Runtime.InteropServices;

        [GuidAttribute("D0C34F40-6A93-4601-B456-5A972E9C8D24")]
        public class LifeCycle : IDTExtensibility2
        {
            private string title = "LifeCycle";
            private OutputWindowPaneEx output;
            public void OnConnection(object application,
                ext_ConnectMode connectMode,
                object addInInst,
                ref Array custom)
            {
                this.output = new OutputWindowPaneEx((DTE)application,
                    this.title);
                this.output.WriteLine("OnConnection event fired");
            }
```

Listing 6-2 The LifeCycle add-in source code

```
            public void OnStartupComplete(ref Array custom)
            {
                this.output.WriteLine("OnStartupComplete event fired");
            }

            public void OnAddInsUpdate(ref Array custom)
            {
                this.output.WriteLine("OnAddInsUpdate event fired");
            }

            public void OnBeginShutdown(ref Array custom)
            {
                this.output.WriteLine("OnBeginShutdown event fired");
            }

            public void OnDisconnection(ext_DisconnectMode removeMode,
                ref Array custom)
            {
                this.output.WriteLine("OnDisconnection event fired");
            }
        }
    }
}
```

You already know how to build an add-in from scratch using the command line—now it's time to learn how to build an add-in from scratch using Visual Studio .NET. (After all, this isn't a book about how command-line programming can make your life easier.)

To construct the LifeCycle project, first create a new solution by choosing File | New | Blank Solution in Visual Studio .NET. Add a project named LifeCycle to the solution by choosing File | Add Project | New Project and selecting Visual C# Projects | Empty Project in the Add New Project dialog box. Finally, add a CS file named LifeCycle.cs to the project by choosing File | Add New Item and selecting Code File from the Add New Item dialog box.

Next you need to alter two of the project's properties: output type and COM interoperability. A blank project builds a console application by default; to change the project into one that creates a DLL, right-click on the project name in Solution Explorer and choose Properties from the shortcut menu. In the LifeCycle Property Pages dialog box, select Common Properties | General in the left pane and then select Class Library from the Output Type drop-down list in the right pane. The same dialog box lets you enable COM interoperability, which directs Visual Studio .NET to add the registry entries necessary to allow the add-in to function as a COM component. To enable COM interoperability for the add-in, select Configuration Properties | Build in the left pane of the LifeCycle Property Pages dialog box and select True from the Register For COM Interop drop-down list in the right pane.

> **Note** If you've just changed the output type, you have to click Apply before the Register For COM Interop drop-down list is enabled. If you switch to Configuration Properties | Build before you apply the new output type, you're out of luck—you'll have to close and reopen the dialog box before you can select a new Register For COM Interop setting.

Once you've set up your project, enter the code from Listing 6-2 into the CS file. If you try to build the project at this point, the compiler will complain that it can't find the *EnvDTE*, *Extensibility*, and *Utilities* namespaces and the types they define. To add references to these namespaces, right-click References in Solution Explorer and choose Add Reference from the shortcut menu. On the .NET tab of the Add References dialog box, select envdte, extensibility, and InsideVSNET.Utilities from the component list. Once you've done this, you can build LifeCycle.dll without a problem.

The *IDTExtensibility2* Interface

As you now know, an implementation of *IDTExtensibility2* lies at the core of every add-in. Visual Studio .NET calls the methods on this interface whenever it needs to apprise an add-in of important events, such as when another add-in is loaded or unloaded, or when Visual Studio .NET is about to shut down. The communication isn't just one-way, either: through the *IDTExtensibility2* interface, the add-in has access to and control over the entire Visual Studio .NET automation object model.

The *EnvDTE* Namespace

Before examining the individual *IDTExtensibility2* methods, we need to take a quick look at the real objective of add-ins—controlling the objects in the *EnvDTE* namespace. The name *EnvDTE* stands for *Environment Development*

Tools Extensibility, which pretty much describes its purpose: it defines the Visual Studio .NET automation object model. The Visual Studio .NET documentation includes a chart of the automation object model that displays a hierarchy of over 140 objects defined by the *EnvDTE* namespace. The add-ins in this book will make use of most of those objects, but a few of the objects are of special interest to add-ins:

- ***DTE*** The root object of the automation object model
- ***DTE.AddIn*** An object that represents an add-in
- ***DTE.AddIns*** A collection of *AddIn* objects that includes all add-ins registered with the Visual Studio .NET IDE
- ***DTE.Solution.AddIns*** A collection of *AddIn* objects associated with a solution

The next several examples will focus on the *DTE*, *DTE.AddIn*, and *DTE.AddIns* objects, which collectively give you control over your own add-in and others. We'll cover the *DTE.Solution.AddIns* object in Chapter 8.

Note The main purpose of an add-in class is to provide an implementation of *IDTExtensibility2*, but that doesn't have to be its only purpose. An add-in class is a class, after all, and it can define any number of non-*IDTExtensibility2*-related methods, properties, and events. The automation object model provides access to your add-in class through the *AddIn.Object* property, which returns the add-in's *IDispatch* interface. The following macro code shows how you would call a public method named *DisplayMessage* on the *MyAddIn.Connect* add-in class:

```
Dim dispObj As Object = DTE.AddIns.Item("MyAddIn.Connect").Object
dispObj.DisplayMessage("IDispatch a message to you.")
```

OnConnection

By far the most important of the *IDTExtensibility2* methods, *OnConnection* provides an add-in with the main object reference it needs to communicate directly with the IDE. The *OnConnection* method has the following prototype:

```
public void OnConnection(object application,
    ext_ConnectMode connectMode,
```

```
object addInInst,
ref Array custom);
```

The *application* parameter holds a reference to an instance of *EnvDTE.DTE*, which is the root object of the automation object model. Technically, *application* holds a reference to an instance of *EnvDTE.DTEClass*, which implements the *EnvDTE.DTE* interface, which in turn derives from the *EnvDTE._DTE* interface. This last interface contains the types you want. To get at the *_DTE* interface types, you can cast *application* to *DTE* or *_DTE*, according to your taste. (See the upcoming sidebar "Underscoring the Obvious" to find out where all those *EnvDTE* underscores come from.) Almost every add-in that does something useful has need of the *DTE* object, so the first statements in *OnConnection* typically cache the *DTE* object in a global variable.

Underscoring the Obvious

Staring at the underscores that litter the *EnvDTE* namespace, you might begin to wonder what the Visual Studio .NET programmers were smoking when they designed it. Most of the type names in the *EnvDTE* namespace bear little resemblance to type names found elsewhere in the .NET Framework; the name *EnvDTE* itself violates the .NET Framework's Pascal-casing rule. As it turns out, there's a legitimate reason for *EnvDTE*'s strange names (which implies that the programmers' smoking material probably was legitimate also): that reason is COM.

The original extensibility object model, Design Time Extensibility (DTE), began life as a COM component in previous versions of Visual Studio. Rather than rewrite the component as managed code, the Visual Studio .NET team chose to offer the component's functionality via COM interoperability. The *EnvDTE* assembly that shows up in the Add Reference dialog box was generated mechanically by running the extensibility component's type library (dte.olb) through the Type Library Importer utility (TlbImp). As it churns through a type library, TlbImp preserves the type library names exactly as it finds them—in the case of *EnvDTE*, the result is a namespace that carries its COM heritage in every underscore.

Of course, the Visual Studio team made the right decision not to rewrite the extensibility component for the earliest versions of Visual Studio .NET, so for now we'll just have to live with the funny names and hope our pinkies don't give out from typing Shift+<Underscore> all day.

The *connectMode* parameter tells an add-in the circumstance under which it was loaded. This parameter takes on one of the *Extensibility.ext_ConnectMode* enumeration values shown in Table 6-1.

Table 6-1 The *Extensibility.ext_ConnectMode* Enumeration

Constant	Value (Int32)	Description
ext_cm_AfterStartup	*0x00000000*	Loaded after Visual Studio .NET started.
ext_cm_Startup	*0x00000001*	Loaded when Visual Studio .NET started.
ext_cm_External	*0x00000002*	Loaded by an external client. (No longer used by Visual Studio .NET.)
ext_cm_CommandLine	*0x00000003*	Loaded from the command line.
ext_cm_Solution	*0x00000004*	Loaded with a solution.
ext_cm_UISetup	*0x00000005*	Loaded for user interface setup.

An add-in can check the *connectMode* value and alter its behavior accordingly. For example, when an add-in encounters *ext_cm_UISetup*, it knows that this is the first time it has run, so it can add its custom commands to the IDE menus and toolbars. (The Add-in Wizard generates code that handles the *ext_cm_UISetup* case in this manner.)

The *addInInst* parameter passes an add-in a reference to its own *AddIn* instance, which it can store for later use. (The *AddIn* instance proves invaluable for discovering the add-in's parent collection.) Finally, each of the *IDTExtensibility2* methods includes a *custom* parameter, which allows add-in hosts to pass in an array of host-specific data. Visual Studio .NET always passes an empty array in *custom*.

OnStartupComplete

The *OnStartupComplete* event fires only in add-ins that load when Visual Studio .NET starts. The *OnStartupComplete* prototype looks like this:

```
public void OnStartupComplete(ref Array custom);
```

An add-in that loads at startup can't always rely on *OnConnection* for its initialization—if the add-in arrives too early, it will fail when it tries to access a Visual Studio .NET component that hasn't yet loaded. In such cases, the add-in can use *OnStartupComplete* to guarantee that Visual Studio .NET is up and running first.

OnAddInsUpdate

The *OnAddInsUpdate* event fires when an add-in joins or leaves the Visual Studio .NET environment. An add-in can use this event to enforce dependencies on other add-ins. Here's the *OnAddInsUpdate* prototype:

```
public void OnAddInsUpdate(ref Array custom);
```

The lack of useful parameters reveals *OnAddInsUpdate*'s passive-aggressive nature—it interrupts your add-in to tell it that the state of some add-in has changed, but it withholds information about which add-in triggered the event and why. If you need to know the add-in responsible for the event, you have to discover its identity on your own. Fortunately, you have the *DTE.AddIns* collection to aid you in your investigation. This collection holds a list of *AddIn* objects (one for each registered add-in), and each *AddIn* object has a *Connected* property that exposes its connection status. You retrieve a specific add-in from the *AddIns* collection by passing the *AddIns.Item* method a ProgID or a 1-based index; if the requested index doesn't exist in the collection, the *Item* method throws an "invalid index" *COMException*; otherwise, it returns an *AddIn* reference. Here's one way to check InsideVSNET.AddIns.LifeCycle's connection status:

```
public void OnAddInsUpdate(ref Array custom)
{
    try
    {
        AddIn addIn =
            this.dte.AddIns.Item("InsideVSNET.AddIns.LifeCycle");

        if (addIn.Connected == true)
        {
            // InsideVSNET.AddIns.LifeCycle is connected
        }
        else
        {
            // InsideVSNET.AddIns.LifeCycle isn't connected
        }
    }
    catch (COMException)
    {
        // InsideVSNET.AddIns.LifeCycle isn't a
        // registered add-in
    }
}
```

Of course, whether InsideVSNET.AddIns.LifeCycle caused the event remains a mystery. The LoadUnload add-in, shown in Listing 6-3, does what the previous sample cannot: it deduces which add-in triggers the *OnAddInsUpdate* event.

LoadUnload.cs

```
namespace InsideVSNET
{
    namespace AddIns
    {
        using EnvDTE;
        using Extensibility;
        using InsideVSNET.Utilities;
        using Microsoft.Office.Core;
        using System;
        using System.Collections;
        using System.Runtime.InteropServices;

        [GuidAttribute("B2FCDEBF-1536-4EA2-9F1A-81878A9C028D"),
            ProgId("LoadUnload.Connect")]
        public class Connect : Object, IDTExtensibility2, IDTCommandTarget
        {
            private DTE dte;
            private AddIn addInInstance;
            private SortedList addInsList = new SortedList();
            private AddIns addInsCollection;
            private OutputWindowPaneEx output;
            private string title = "LoadUnload";

            public Connect()
            {
            }

            public void OnConnection(object application,
                ext_ConnectMode connectMode,
                 object addInInst,
                ref Array custom)
            {
                this.dte = (DTE)application;
                this.addInInstance = (AddIn)addInInst;
                this.addInsCollection = this.dte.AddIns;

                foreach (AddIn addIn in this.addInsCollection)
```

Listing 6-3 The LoadUnload source code

```
        {
            this.addInsList[addIn.ProgID] = addIn.Connected;
        }

        this.output = new OutputWindowPaneEx(this.dte, this.title);
        ⋮
    }

    public void OnDisconnection(ext_DisconnectMode disconnectMode,
        ref Array custom)
    {
    }

    public void OnAddInsUpdate(ref Array custom)
    {
        this.addInsCollection.Update();

        foreach (AddIn addIn in this.addInsCollection)
        {
            if (this.addInsList.Contains(addIn.ProgID))
            {
                if (addIn.Connected !=
                    (bool)this.addInsList[addIn.ProgID])
                {
                    string action = addIn.Connected ?
                        "loaded" : "unloaded";
                    this.output.WriteLine(addIn.ProgID +
                        " was " + action, this.title);
                }
            }
            else
            {
                string action = addIn.Connected ?
                    " and loaded" : String.Empty;
                this.output.WriteLine(addIn.ProgID +
                    " was added" + action, this.title);
            }

            this.addInsList[addIn.ProgID] = addIn.Connected;
        }
    }

    public void OnStartupComplete(ref Array custom)
    {
    }
```

```
            public void OnBeginShutdown(ref Array custom)
            {
            }
            ⋮
        }
    }
}
```

LoadUnload maintains a running list of add-ins and their connection statuses in its *addInsList* variable, which is declared as type *SortedList*. When *OnAddInsUpdate* fires, LoadUnload compares the connection statuses of the add-ins in its internal list with the connection statuses of the add-ins in the *DTE.AddIns* collection—if it finds a discrepancy, it knows which add-in to blame for the event. Here's the first part of the main loop from Listing 6-3:

```
this.addInsCollection.Update();

foreach (AddIn addIn in this.addInsCollection)
{
    if (this.addInsList.Contains(addIn.ProgID))
    {
        if (addIn.Connected !=
            (bool)this.addInsList[addIn.ProgID])
        {
            string action = addIn.Connected ?
                "loaded" : "unloaded";
            this.output.WriteLine(addIn.ProgID +
                " was " + action, this.title);
        }
    }
    ⋮
```

The *addInsCollection* variable holds a reference to the *DTE.AddIns* collection, and the call to *Update* synchs up the collection with the registry so that any newly created add-ins are included. (The Add-in Manager performs the equivalent of *Update* each time it runs.) After the call to *Update*, the main loop iterates through the current add-ins in *addInsCollection* and checks whether each add-in already exists in its internal list. If so, the *Connected* property of the add-in is compared with the corresponding value stored in the internal list; if they differ, the *Connected* property determines whether the add-in was just loaded (true) or unloaded (false).

If the current add-in doesn't exist in *addInsList*, the add-in was registered sometime between the previous *OnAddInsUpdate* event and this *OnAddInsUpdate* event. Here's the second part of the main loop, which handles new add-ins:

```
    ⋮
    else
    {
```

```
        string action = addIn.Connected ?
            " and loaded" : String.Empty;
        this.output.WriteLine(addIn.ProgID +
            " was added" + action, this.title);
    }

    this.addInsList[addIn.ProgID] = addIn.Connected;
}
```

The last statement either writes the current *Connected* value to an existing entry or creates a fresh entry for a newly registered add-in.

LoadUnload isn't foolproof—for example, add-ins loaded by commands arrive and leave unannounced—but it works well enough for demonstration purposes.

OnBeginShutdown

Here's the prototype for *OnBeginShutdown*:

```
public void OnBeginShutdown(ref Array custom);
```

This event fires only when the IDE shuts down while an add-in is running. Although an IDE shutdown might get canceled along the way, *OnBeginShutdown* doesn't provide a cancellation mechanism, so an add-in should assume that shutdown is inevitable and perform its cleanup routines accordingly. An add-in that manipulates IDE state might use this event to restore the original IDE settings.

OnDisconnection

This event is similar to *OnBeginShutdown* in that it signals the end of an add-in's life; it differs from *OnBeginShutdown* in that the IDE isn't necessarily about to shut down. *OnDisconnection* also provides more information to an add-in than *OnBeginShutdown* does. *OnDisconnection*'s prototype looks like this:

```
public void OnDisconnection(ext_DisconnectMode removeMode,
    ref Array custom);
```

The *removeMode* parameter passes in an *IDTExtensibility2.ext_Disconnect Mode* enumeration value that tells an add-in why it was unloaded. Table 6-2 lists the *ext_DisconnectMode* values.

Table 6-2 The *Extensibility.ext_DisconnectMode* Enumeration

Constant	Value (Int32)	Description
ext_dm_HostShutdown	*0x00000000*	Unloaded when Visual Studio .NET shut down
ext_dm_UserClosed	*0x00000001*	Unloaded while Visual Studio was running
ext_dm_UISetupComplete	*0x00000002*	Unloaded after user interface setup
ext_dm_SolutionClosed	*0x00000003*	Unloaded when solution closed

The *ext_DisconnectMode* enumeration serves a purpose similar to *ext_ConnectMode*: it allows an add-in to alter its behavior to suit its current circumstances. For example, an add-in that receives *ext_dm_UISetupComplete* probably would bypass its cleanup routines because it was loaded for initialization purposes only.

Add-in Registry Named Values

As you learned earlier in this chapter, an add-in makes itself known to Visual Studio .NET by creating a ProgID-named subkey under the *AddIns* registry key. This subkey can contain a number of named values that allow you to fine-tune the behavior of an add-in. The following several sections cover the named values you can apply to an add-in and describe the effects they produce.

CommandPreload and the *PreloadAddinState* Key

Many add-ins expose their functionality through menu items and toolbar buttons in the IDE—when selected or clicked, these user interface items load the add-in and pass along the appropriate command for processing. Of course, the user interface items don't appear magically; an add-in creates them and adds them to the IDE the first time that the add-in loads. But without user intervention, how does an add-in first get loaded in order to create the user interface item to load it? The solution to this "chicken or egg" problem begins with the *CommandPreload* named value and ends with the *PreloadAddinState* key. A newly installed add-in sets its *CommandPreload* value to *0x1* to tell Visual Studio .NET that it wants to be loaded once, the next time the IDE starts up, for the purpose of adding its user interface items to the IDE (a process known as *preloading*). Figure 6-5 illustrates how Visual Studio .NET preloads add-ins.

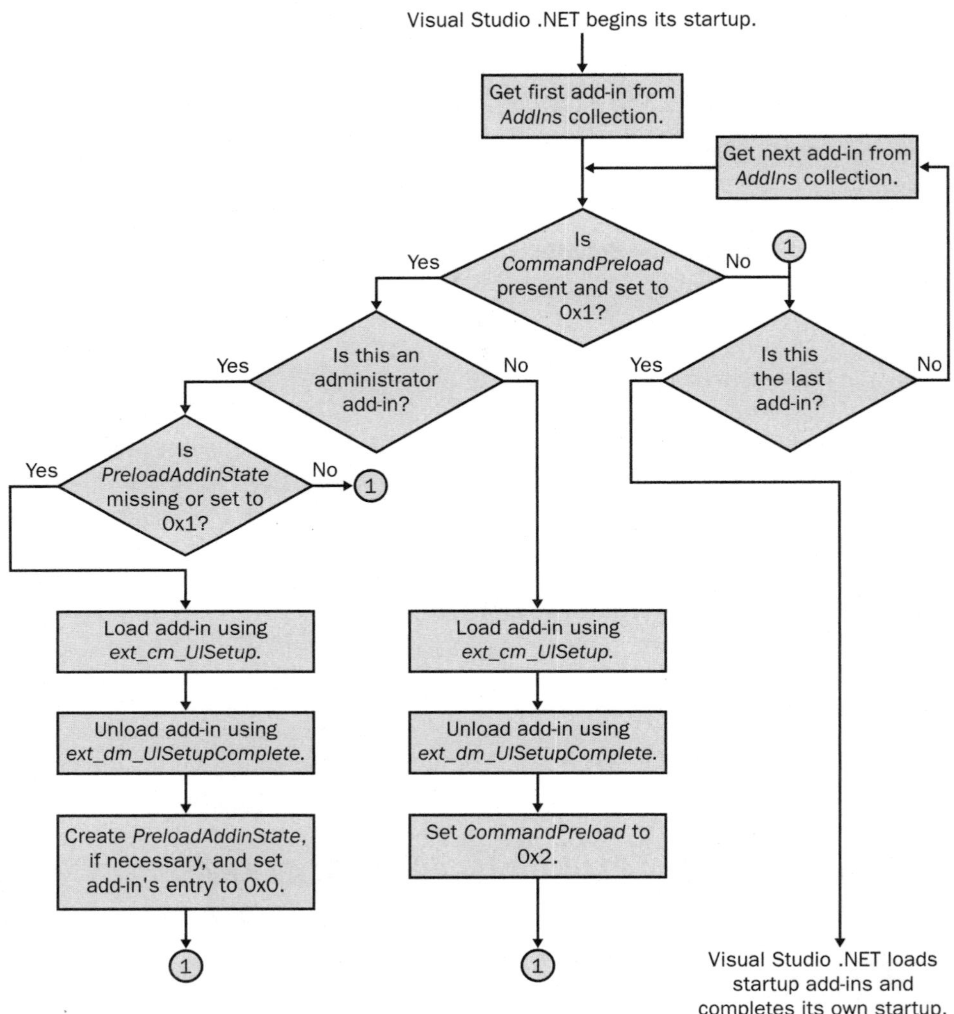

Figure 6-5 How add-ins are preloaded

> **Note** Actually, preloaded add-ins aren't required to create user interface items; they're free to perform any kind of "first load" initialization they need, such as creating data files, adding custom registry entries, and so forth.

At startup, Visual Studio .NET preloads each add-in that has a *CommandPreload* value of *0x1*, but only if the add-in hasn't yet been preloaded. The way Visual Studio .NET determines that an add-in hasn't been preloaded will differ a little depending on whether the add-in is an administrator add-in. As you can see from Figure 6-5, a user add-in's *CommandPreload* value alone determines whether it has been preloaded because Visual Studio .NET changes the value to *0x2* after preloading the add-in. An administrator add-in's *CommandPreload* value never changes, however, which means that Visual Studio .NET needs some other mechanism to keep track of whether the add-in has been preloaded. That's what the *PreloadAddinState* key is for: it holds a list of administrator add-ins and their preload statuses. Before Visual Studio .NET preloads an administrator add-in, it checks *PreloadAddinState*—if this key is missing, the add-in isn't in the list, or the add-in is in the list and its value is set to *0x1*, Visual Studio .NET knows that the add-in hasn't yet been preloaded.

For both administrator and user add-ins, Visual Studio .NET preloads the add-ins silently, passing them the *ext_cm_UISetup* value in their *OnConnection* events, and then unloads them immediately after *OnConnection* returns, passing them the *ext_dm_UISetupComplete* value in their *OnDisconnection* events. After preloading an administrator add-in, Visual Studio .NET creates the *PreloadAddinState* key, if necessary, and sets the add-in's value to *0x0*; after preloading a user add-in, Visual Studio .NET sets the add-in's *CommandPreload* value to *0x2*.

> **Warning** When we say that Visual Studio .NET preloads add-ins silently, we mean *silently*. Under normal circumstances, Visual Studio .NET tells you when your add-in fails to load, and it even offers you the choice of removing the offending add-in from the *AddIns* registry key. When preloading, however, Visual Studio .NET won't give you the slightest hint that your add-in bombed.

The *PreloadAddinState* key lives in the HKEY_CURRENT_USER branch of the registry at Software\Microsoft\VisualStudio\7.1\AddIns\PreloadAddinState. This key isn't created when you install Visual Studio .NET; instead, the key is created on demand the first time Visual Studio .NET preloads an administrator add-in for a particular user. In this way, an administrator add-in that sets *CommandPreload* to *0x1* gets preloaded automatically for each user—including users who are added after the add-in is installed.

> **Tip** If you need to restore an add-in's user interface items, set its *PreloadAddinState* value to *0x1* if it's an administrator add-in, or set its *CommandPreload* value to *0x1* if it's a user add-in, and it will get preloaded the next time Visual Studio .NET runs. If you prefer the shotgun approach, you can restore the user interface items of every add-in by executing the following command at the command prompt:
>
> ```
> devenv /setup
> ```
>
> This command resets the IDE to its original state (thereby removing every add-in user interface item, along with any other customizations to the IDE), changes the *CommandPreload* values of user add-ins from *0x2* to *0x1*, and deletes the *PreloadAddinState* key; the result is that Visual Studio .NET preloads each and every one of these add-ins the next time it runs. A bit crude, but effective.

LoadBehavior and *CommandLineSafe*

The *LoadBehavior* named value controls how an add-in is loaded and also reflects the add-in's current load state. Table 6-3 lists the possible *LoadBehavior* values. These values are bit flags, so in theory you can combine them to create your own custom load settings; in reality, with one exception, combinations of flags behave no differently from individual flags.

Table 6-3 *LoadBehavior* Values

Flag	Value	Description
ID_UNLOADED	*0x0*	Add-in currently is unloaded
ID_STARTUP	*0x1*	Add-in loads at startup
ID_LOADED	*0x2*	Add-in currently is loaded
ID_COMMAND_LINE	*0x4*	Add-in loads during command-line builds

The *ID_UNLOADED* and *ID_LOADED* values no longer serve a useful purpose. Use the *AddIn.Connected* property instead to discover the load state of an add-in.

The *ID_STARTUP* flag tells Visual Studio .NET to load the add-in when the IDE starts up. Add-ins that monitor IDE events, in particular, need to be up and running from the beginning—otherwise, they might miss some of the action. Add-ins that don't care about IDE events can omit this flag and wait to be loaded on demand.

The *ID_COMMAND_LINE* flag signals that an add-in should be loaded during command-line builds. Be aware that in Visual Studio .NET 2002 this flag doesn't work as advertised. In version 2002, the only effect this flag has is to disallow an add-in from being loaded by the Add-in Manager (and even this effect is overridden when the *ID_STARTUP* flag is present).

The optional *CommandLineSafe* named value is supposed to work hand-in-hand with the *ID_STARTUP* and *ID_COMMAND_LINE* flags to ensure the success of unattended builds. A *CommandLineSafe* value of *0x1* indicates that the add-in won't display a user interface that requires human interaction—at least, not when a build is started from the command line; a missing *CommandLineSafe* entry or a *CommandLineSafe* value of *0x0* marks the add-in as unsuited for command-line builds. Currently, the *CommandLineSafe* value doesn't affect whether Visual Studio .NET loads the add-in—the value is for informational purposes only.

Is It Safe?

Clearly, the Visual Studio .NET designers had something special in mind when they created the command line–related registry values. Long builds and overnight builds are staples of the software industry, so any feature that improves the odds for successful, unattended builds is worth a sys admin's weight in gold. As far as add-ins go, Visual Studio .NET 2002 includes all the components for the perfect command-line build—but the components just haven't been wired up yet. Here's how command-line builds work in Visual Studio .NET 2003:

1. A developer initiates a command-line build.
2. Visual Studio .NET loads the add-ins marked as *ID_COMMAND_LINE* and passes in an *ext_cm_CommandLine* value to each add-in's *OnConnection* event.
3. The add-ins use the *ext_cm_CommandLine* value as a signal to disable their user interfaces.

But command-line builds don't work this way in Visual Studio .NET 2002. Instead, *ID_COMMAND_LINE* doesn't affect whether an add-in is loaded; add-ins marked as *ID_STARTUP* are loaded by mistake; and Visual Studio .NET 2002 doesn't pass in *ext_cm_CommandLine* under any circumstances.

Not to worry, though—all these problems are fixed in Visual Studio .NET 2003. And you can work around these problems in Visual Studio .NET 2002 by marking the add-in as *ID_STARTUP* and using code like the following, which sifts through the *System.Environment.CommandLine* property looking for evidence of a command-line build:

```
if (Regex.IsMatch(System.Environment.CommandLine, "/build"))
{
    // Command-line build
    System.Console.WriteLine("Command-line build--phooey on GUI!");
}
else
{
    // Not a command-line build
    MessageBox.Show("GUI for you!");
}
```

By placing the previous code in your add-in's *OnConnection* event handler, your add-in can decide at startup whether to display its user interface.

SatelliteDLLPath and *SatelliteDLLName*

If you want to distribute your add-in internationally, you need to pay attention to the problem of localization. A worldly add-in doesn't force a particular language on its users—instead, it communicates with each user in his or her native tongue. Of course, a standalone add-in can't possibly accommodate every language; instead, an add-in that supports localization stores its localizable resources in *satellite DLLs*. At run time, the add-in searches for the satellite DLL that corresponds to the current locale and uses the localized resources from that DLL to populate its user interface. In this way, the same add-in can support any number of languages simply by providing a localized satellite DLL for each locale.

An add-in advertises the location of its satellite DLLs through the *SatelliteDLLPath* and *SatelliteDLLName* named values. *SatelliteDLLName* stores the satellite DLL name (which implies that all localized satellite DLLs share the same file name), and *SatelliteDLLPath* stores the satellite DLL root folder. Each localized satellite DLL lives in its own folder under the root, and the name of the folder is the locale identifier of the language that the DLL supports. For example, the locale identifier for U.S. English is 1033, so the U.S. English satellite DLL is found at <SatelliteDLLPath>\1033\<SatelliteDLLName>. At run time, you can locate an add-in's satellite DLL for the current locale by using either the *AddIn.SatelliteDllPath* property or the *DTE.SatelliteDllPath* method.

Lab: Probing for Satellite DLLs

The documentation claims that Visual Studio .NET locates an add-in's satellite DLL by looking in the following places, in the order listed:

```
<SatelliteDLLPath>\<Default system locale>\<SatelliteDLLName>
<SatelliteDLLPath>\<Default user locale>\<SatelliteDLLName>
<SatelliteDLLPath>\<OS setup locale>\<SatelliteDLLName>
<SatelliteDLLPath>\1033\<SatelliteDLLName>
<SatelliteDLLPath>\<SatelliteDLLName>
```

Problem is, the documentation is wrong—at least in part. So, how does Visual Studio .NET find satellite DLLs? See for yourself. The *SatelliteDLLProbing* macro creates a directory named *satellites* that contains subdirectories for 133 of your favorite locales—from Afrikaans to Zulu—and copies a satellite DLL into each locale's directory. The macro's main loop calls the *DTE.SatelliteDllPath* method repeatedly: after each call, the macro displays the satellite DLL path and corresponding locale in the Output window, and then it deletes the current satellite DLL, forcing *SatelliteDllPath* to search in a new location the next time through the loop.

If you run the *SatelliteDLLProbing* macro a couple of times, changing the user locale between runs, you'll notice that the user locale doesn't count for much. The system locale always overrides the user locale, which means the current user won't necessarily see his preferred locale. You'll also notice that *SatelliteDllPath* never finds the satellite DLL in <SatelliteDLLPath>, contrary to the claims made by the documentation. The most interesting result, however, is the stubborn determination with which *SatelliteDllPath* hunts down a stray satellite DLL. Instead of stopping after checking the system locale subdirectory and finding nothing, *SatelliteDllPath* starts rummaging through the other locale subdirectories like a raccoon digging through a trash can—the logic being, we suppose, that any language is better than no language at all. (Can't find English? Try Catalan instead!) In fact, *SatelliteDllPath* goes so far as to search through nonlocale subdirectories, and if it finds a satellite DLL there, it'll use it.

> Understand that localization is a complex issue and that Visual Studio .NET's satellite DLL search algorithm reflects that complexity—when the locales are set up correctly, the algorithm works just fine, but if a locale gets misplaced, the algorithm blows up spectacularly. The good news is that Visual Studio .NET uses the same mechanism for its own localization, which means that it will always find your add-in if your add-in uses the same locale as the Visual Studio .NET installation.

FriendlyName and *Description*

The *FriendlyName* and *Description* named values allow you to apply a meaningful name and a short description to your add-in. An example of an application that uses these values is the Add-in Manager, which populates its add-in list with *FriendlyName* values and displays the *Description* value of the selected add-in in its Description box.

FriendlyName and *Description* each store either a human-readable string or the ID of a string resource in the add-in's satellite DLL (in the form "#<resource ID>"). Pulling string resources out of satellite DLLs is fairly straightforward; you can find code for doing so in the Add-in Manager Plus sample add-in.

AboutBoxDetails and *AboutBoxIcon*

The *AboutBoxDetails* and *AboutBoxIcon* named values buy your add-in some real estate on the Visual Studio .NET About dialog box, as shown in Figure 6-6. The About dialog box displays *FriendlyName* values in the Installed Products list; when a user selects an add-in from this list, the dialog box displays the add-in's *AboutBoxIcon* under the Product Details label and its *AboutBoxDetails* information in the text box next to its icon.

> **Note** Both the *AboutBoxDetails* and *AboutBoxIcon* entries need to be in the registry before the About dialog box will display your add-in's information; however, either or both of the values can be bogus.

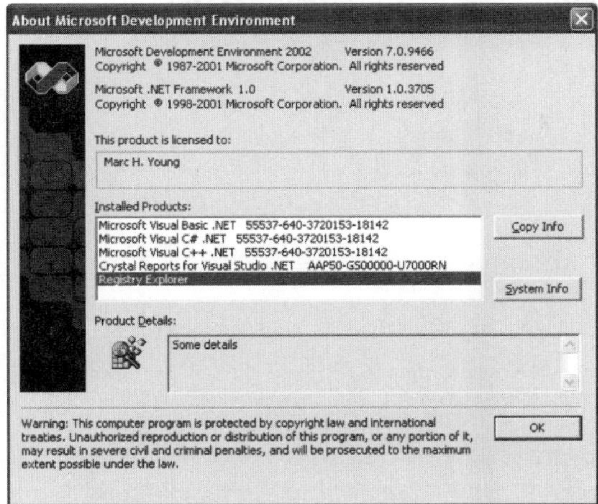

Figure 6-6 Add-in information displayed in the Visual Studio .NET About dialog box

The format of the *AboutBoxDetails* value is the same as that of the *FriendlyName* and *Description* values—a string that holds either a short description or the ID of a string resource in the add-in's satellite DLL (in the form "#<resource ID>").

The *AboutBoxIcon* value offers a bit more flexibility than its counterpart. An add-in can store its icon information in one of four formats:

- String data representing the ID of an icon resource in the add-in's satellite DLL (in the form "#<resource ID>").
- String data representing a path to an icon file.
- String data representing a path to an executable file and the ID of an icon resource within that file (in the form "<path>,<resource ID>"). For example, "C:\Program Files\Microsoft Visual Studio .NET 2003\Common7\IDE\devenv.exe,1200" refers to the Visual Studio .NET application icon.
- Binary data of an icon.

The last format gives an add-in the option of storing all its "personal" information—including *FriendlyName*, *Description*, and *AboutBoxDetails*—within the registry rather than distributed across separate files. Storing icon data in the registry is as easy as the following macro procedure, which takes the add-in's registry key and the pathname of the icon file as parameters:

```
Sub SetAboutBoxIcon(ByVal addInKey As RegistryKey, _
    ByVal iconPath As String)
```

```
    Dim iconFile As FileStream = File.OpenRead(iconPath)
    Dim iconData(iconFile.Length) As Byte
    Dim i As Integer

    For i = 0 To iconFile.Length - 1
        iconData(i) = iconFile.ReadByte
    Next

    addInKey.SetValue("AboutBoxIcon", iconData)
End Sub
```

Note Hats off to Kenny Kerr for his icon resource management classes! We're hard-pressed to think of a more thankless task than writing managed code to pull icons from Win32 executable files, but Kenny did it and saved us the trouble, so we're happy to give him all the thanks that can fit into one of these notes. (We put his classes to work extracting icons for the Add-in Manager Plus add-in and couldn't be more pleased with the results.) You can find his Icon Browser utility, for which the icon resource management classes were originally written, and lots more cool stuff by Kenny at his Web site: *http://www.kennyandkarin.com/kenny*.

Looking Ahead

The next chapter is for that little bit of drill instructor inside all of us—the part that wants to hear others shout "HOW HIGH?" when we say "JUMP!" As you'll soon learn, macros, add-ins, and Visual Studio .NET make the most loyal and obedient of soldiers, always at the ready and eager to do your bidding: all you have to do is give the right commands. If you turn the page, we'll show you how…"NOW!"

7

Commands

Commands are the most fundamental mechanism of communication between the user and the Microsoft Visual Studio .NET integrated development environment (IDE). In this chapter, we'll explore how you can use existing commands as well as create your own commands from add-ins and macros.

What Is a Command?

If you've written user interface software for the Microsoft Windows operating system, you're probably familiar with the event-driven programming model. When the user clicks a button on a form, chooses a menu item, or presses a key on the keyboard, your program receives a notification of that user action. If you're programming at the Windows SDK level, such as with the Visual C++ programming language, when the user performs this action your program receives a message detailing what happened. If you're using a language such as Microsoft Visual Basic .NET or Microsoft Visual C# .NET, this notification happens in the form of an event handler being called. These notifications are commands issued by the user, and the program carries out this command by performing some action for the user.

Visual Studio .NET uses a method of notification similar to that of Win32 message-passing to inform code as the user interacts with the IDE. However, because of the complexity and number of commands available in the Visual Studio .NET IDE, command *routing*, or passing a notification to the proper handler of that notification, isn't as simple as receiving a message. For instance, suppose the user chooses File | New | File. Because there are a number of different add-on programs (not to be confused with add-ins), such as Visual C++ .NET, Visual Basic .NET, and Visual C# .NET, Visual Studio .NET needs to determine which of these programs handles this menu item choice. When a Win32 program handles a message, one message loop handles that message, but because there are a number of possible handlers of a command in Visual Studio .NET, commands need to be routed to the correct code. Each of these add-on products reserves a globally unique identifier (GUID) to uniquely identify itself, and each command that is available associates itself with the GUID of a particular add-on. When a user executes a command, the GUID for that command is retrieved, the add-on program that handles that GUID is found, and the command is sent to that add-on.

A command also needs another part to identify itself. After all, if every command had just a GUID to identify it, and all the commands that belonged to an add-on had the same GUID, an add-on wouldn't be able to tell the difference between, for instance, the New File command and the New Project command. To disambiguate commands that all have the same GUID, a number, or ID, is assigned to each command in that group. An add-on is responsible for its own commands, so an ID can be assigned without conflicting with commands from a different add-on because the GUID for each add-on is different. When combined, this GUID and ID pair uniquely identifies each individual command.

> **Note** A command in Visual Studio .NET exists independently of any user interface elements (such as menu items) for that command. Commands can be created and destroyed, and a user interface element might have never been created for that command. But the opposite won't happen—a user interface element can't be created without having a corresponding command.

Locating Commands

In Visual Studio .NET, all the commands that a user can issue are represented in the object model by a *Command* object, and the *Commands* collection contains a list of these objects. Like other collection objects, *Command* objects allow the use of standard enumeration constructs such as the keywords *foreach* in Visual C# or *For Each* in Visual Basic .NET. Using these keywords, we can create a macro to walk the list of all *Command* objects:

```
Sub WalkCommands()
    Dim cmd As EnvDTE.Command
    For Each cmd In DTE.Commands
      'use the EnvDTE.Command object here
    Next
End Sub
```

The *Command* collection's *Item* method works a bit differently from the *Item* methods of other collection objects. *Commands.Item* accepts as a parameter the familiar numerical index, but it also accepts an additional optional argument. If you're using the numerical indexing method, you should set the second argument to *–1*. This method has an additional argument because, as mentioned earlier, a GUID and ID pair is used to uniquely identify a command. The GUID, in string format, is passed as the first argument, and the ID of the command is passed as the second argument when you're using the GUID and ID to index the *Commands* collection. The following macro demonstrates finding the command for opening a file using the GUID and ID pair:

```
Sub FindFileOpenCommand()
    Dim cmd As EnvDTE.Command
    cmd = DTE.Commands.Item("{5EFC7975-14BC-11CF-9B2B-00AA00573819}", 222)
End Sub
```

As you can see, code like this can be complicated to write because you need to find and learn the GUID and ID for every command (which would be hard to do because there are thousands of them), and then you must type this pair correctly every time, which can be a source of programming errors. To help with finding a *Command* object, the *Commands.Item* method accepts another format for indexing the collection, which is easier to remember: the name of a command.

Command Names

Remembering the GUID and ID for every command can be a huge waste of brainpower, so Visual Studio .NET defines an easier-to-remember textual representation for most commands. These names follow a general pattern: the text of the top-level menu on which the primary user interface element for the command is located, followed by a period, the text of all submenus combined, a period, and finally the text of the menu item. Any nonalphanumeric characters (except for the period separators and underscores) are then removed from this string. So, to use the earlier example of finding the *Command* object for the open file command and combine it with our newly found way of using a command name, a macro such as the following results:

```
Sub FindFileOpenCommandByName()
    Dim command As EnvDTE.Command
    command = DTE.Commands.Item("File.OpenFile")
End Sub
```

To find the GUID and ID pair of a command, you can use the *GUID* and *ID* properties of the *Command* object. We used these two properties to find the

GUID and ID pair used in the *FindFileOpenCommand* macro shown earlier. This is the macro we used to find them:

```
Sub FindGuidIDPair()
    Dim guid As String
    Dim id As Integer
    Dim command As EnvDTE.Command
    command = DTE.Commands.Item("File.OpenFile")
    guid = command.Guid
    id = command.ID
    MsgBox(guid + ", " + id.ToString())
End Sub
```

The Options dialog box, shown in Figure 7-1, lets you find all the available command names. You can select Environment | Keyboard in the left pane to display a list box that contains all the command names.

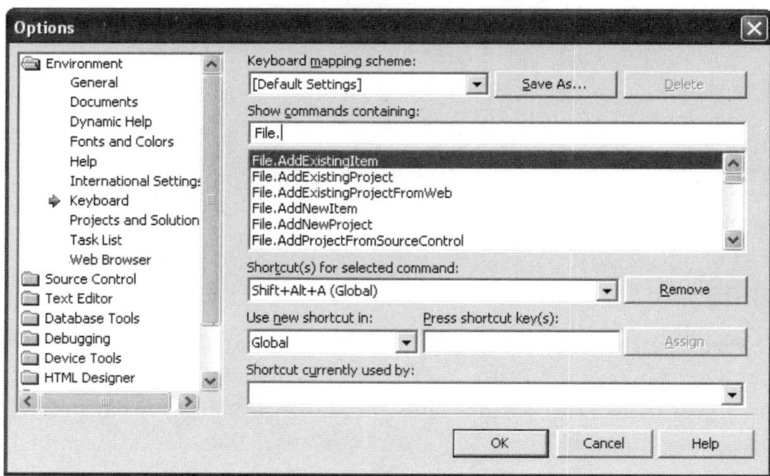

Figure 7-1 The Options dialog box

You can also use the object model to find available command names. We'll do this with the *EnvDTE.Commands* collection in this example macro:

```
Sub CreateCommandList()
    Dim command As EnvDTE.Command
    Dim output As New OutputWindowPaneEx(DTE, "Create Command List")

    For Each command In DTE.Commands
        If (command.Name <> Nothing) Then
            output.WriteLine(command.Name)
        End If
    Next
End Sub
```

When the macro is run, it places into the Output window the name of each command. If you examine the macro closely enough, you'll notice a special check to verify that the name of the command isn't set to *Nothing*. This check is done because if a command doesn't have a name set, it returns *Nothing* if it's using Visual Basic .NET or *null* if it's using C#. The .NET Framework is smart enough that if you try to use this *Nothing* string, it will construct a *System.String* object set to the empty string (""). For this macro, however, we want to filter out any unnamed commands, and we do this by checking for a *Name* set to *Nothing*. Commands that don't have a name are usually used internally by Visual Studio .NET for private communication, and the user generally shouldn't call them. We advise you not to use these commands because they can lead to unpredictable results.

Executing Commands

The purpose of a command is to provide a way for the user to direct Visual Studio .NET to perform some action. Commands can be invoked in a number of ways, the most common of which is for the user to choose a menu item or click a toolbar button. But commands can also be run in other ways. For example, if you write a macro that conforms to the standard macro notation (it is defined as public, doesn't return a value, and takes no arguments unless the arguments are optional strings), the macros facility detects that macro and creates a command for it. Double-clicking that macro in the Macro Explorer window executes the command associated with that macro, which is handled by the Macros editor. A third way to run a command is to use the *DTE.ExecuteCommand* method. This method runs a command, given by name, as if the user had chosen the menu item for that command.

To run our *File.OpenFile* command using the *ExecuteCommand* method, we would write code like this:

```
Sub RunFileOpenCommand()
    DTE.ExecuteCommand("File.OpenFile")
End Sub
```

When a call is made to the *ExecuteCommand* method, execution of the macro or add-in waits until the command finishes executing.

A final approach, which is useful for the power user, is to type the name of the command into the Command Window. As mentioned in Chapter 1, the Command Window is a text-based window in which you type the names of commands; when the user presses the Enter key, the command is run. The command name that you type into the Command Window is the same name that is returned from the *Command.Name* property, and it can be passed to the *ExecuteCommand* method.

Creating Macro Commands

As mentioned before, macros that follow a special format are automatically turned into commands, and these macro commands are given a named counterpart. The name of a macro command is calculated by combining the string *Macros*, the name of the macro project, the name of the module or class the macro is implemented in, and finally the name of the macro with each portion separated by a period. Using this format, the *TurnOnLineNumbers* in the Samples macro project that is installed with Visual Studio .NET takes on the name *Macros.Samples.Utilities.TurnOnLineNumbers*. You can enter this name in the Command Window or call it from another macro, like so:

```
Sub RunCommand()
    DTE.ExecuteCommand("Macros.Samples.Utilities.TurnOnLineNumbers")
End Sub
```

Creating an Add-in Command

Now that you know how commands are named, found, and run, it's time to create your own command. As we saw earlier, when a command built into Visual Studio .NET is invoked, the add-on program for that command is located because of the GUID assigned to the command, and it is asked to handle the command invocation. Likewise, commands that you create need a target that handles the command invocation. Commands can be dynamically created and removed, but creating them requires that an add-in be associated with the new command so Visual Studio .NET can find and use that add-in as the target. The method to create a command, *AddNamedCommand*, can be found on the *DTE.Commands* collection object; here is its signature:

```
public EnvDTE.Command AddNamedCommand(EnvDTE.AddIn AddInInstance,
    string Name, string ButtonText, string Tooltip, bool MSOButton,
    int Bitmap = 0, ref object[] ContextUIGUIDs,
    int vsCommandDisabledFlagsValue = 16)
```

Here are the arguments:

- ***AddInInstance*** The *AddIn* object that will act as the command invocation target.
- ***Name*** The name of the command. The name can contain only alphanumeric characters and the underscore character. Any invalid characters that are used are mapped to the underscore character.
- ***ButtonText*** The text that is displayed on any user interface elements such as buttons for the command that are placed on menus or command bars.

- ***ToolTip*** Descriptive text providing users information about the command.
- ***MSOButton*** True if the bitmap to display on user interface elements for this command should use the predefined command bar button graphics. If *False*, then the graphic for the button is retrieved from the satellite DLL that is specified in the registration information for the add-in.
- ***Bitmap*** If the *MSOButton* argument is *True*, then it is the index of the predefined command bar button graphic. See the HTML page in the CommandUIBmps folder included with the book's sample files for a listing of available images. If *MSOButton* is *False*, then this is the resource identifier of the bitmap picture in the satellite DLL.
- ***ContextUIGUIDs*** This parameter is unused for Visual Studio .NET 2003 and is reserved for a future version. An empty array of type *System.Object* should be passed for this value.
- ***vsCommandDisabledFlagsValue*** This is the default availability state of the button. If the add-in that handles the command invocation has not yet been loaded, rather than forcing the add-in to load to find how the command should be displayed, this argument provides a default availability state. This argument value is used in place of the value returned through the *StatusOption* argument of the *IDTExtensibility2.QueryStatus* method, which we'll discuss later in this chapter.

When called, this method adds an item to the internal list of commands maintained by Visual Studio .NET. The full name of the command, which you can use in the Command Window or as an argument to the *ExecuteCommand* method, is constructed by taking the ProgID of the add-in and concatenating a period, followed by the value of the *Name* parameter. So, for example, if the name you provide to the *AddNamedCommand* method is MyCommand and the ProgID of the add-in is *MyAddin.Connect*, the name of the command that's created is *MyAddin.Connect.MyCommand.*

All commands added with this method also have a GUID and ID pair assigned to them. The GUID that is used for all commands created with *AddNamedCommand* is defined by the constant *EnvDTE.Constants.vsAddInCmdGroup*; the ID value starts at the index 1 for the first call to *AddNamedCommand*, and it is incremented by 1 every time the *AddNamedCommand* method is called. Because of the data type used for IDs, a total of 4,294,967,296 commands can be created before conflicts arise between two add-in created commands.

Handling a Command

With a newly created command, our code now needs to provide a way for Visual Studio .NET to call back to the add-in to let it know when the command is invoked. Usually, when an add-in or macro wants to be informed when the user has performed an action, an event connection is made. But command handlers work a bit differently: rather than connecting to an event source, your add-in must implement a specific interface. The reason for not using events is simple. When an add-in command is invoked, if the add-in that handles that command hasn't been loaded, the code for the add-in is loaded into memory and run by calling the *OnConnection* and other appropriate *IDTExtensibility2* methods, just as if you were to go into the Add-in Manager dialog box and select the check box for that add-in. Because the add-in is demand-loaded (loaded when the command is run), code within that add-in could not have been run to connect to an event handler.

The interface to handle command invocations, named *IDTCommandTarget*, is modeled on the *IOleCommandTarget* interface of the Win32 SDK but has been changed to be *IDispatch*-compatible and easier to use. This is its signature:

```
public interface IDTCommandTarget
{
    public void Exec(string CmdName,
        EnvDTE.vsCommandExecOption ExecuteOption, ref object VariantIn,
        ref object VariantOut, ref bool Handled);

    public void QueryStatus(string CmdName,
        EnvDTE.vsCommandStatusTextWanted NeededText,
        ref EnvDTE.vsCommandStatus StatusOption,
        ref object CommandText);
}
```

When invoked, all commands that your add-in creates are dispatched through this interface, particularly through the *Exec* method. The *Exec* method has the following arguments:

- ***CmdName*** The full name of the command. Your add-in should do a case-sensitive compare on this string to determine which command is being asked to run because all commands that the add-in creates are sent to this method for handling.
- ***vsCommandExecOption*** For most situations, the value passed to this parameter is the *vsCommandExecOptionDoDefault* enumeration value, informing your add-in that it should do the work defined for that command.

- ***VariantIn*** As you'll see later in this chapter, commands can be passed data as an argument. If any arguments are passed to your command, they are passed through this argument. If your command is invoked through the user interface on a menu or a toolbar, the value of this parameter is *null* or *Nothing* (depending on the programming language used to write the add-in).
- ***VariantOut*** This argument is used to pass data from your add-in to the caller. However, Visual Studio .NET will ignore any value that your command returns.
- ***Handled*** This argument allows your add-in to pass back data to Visual Studio .NET signaling whether your add-in handled the command. If a *true* value is returned, it is assumed that no further processing for the command is necessary. If this value is set to *false* on return, Visual Studio .NET continues searching for a handler for the command. The search should fail because no other command handler will accept the same GUID and ID pair for the command your add-in has created.

Command State

A command and its user interface don't always need to be enabled and available to the user. For example, your add-in's command might be available only when a text editor is the currently active window. You can control whether your command is enabled, disabled, or in the *latched* state (which means a check mark is drawn next to the button if it is a menu item or appears with a box drawn around it if it is on a toolbar). You control this state by using the *QueryStatus* method of the *IDTCommandTarget* interface. If your add-in hasn't yet been loaded, the default status, or value passed as the last argument of *AddNamedCommand*, is used to control the default behavior. However, once you've loaded the add-in—by executing the command or manually through the Add-in Manager dialog box—*QueryStatus* is called to determine the state. The *QueryStatus* method has the following arguments:

- ***CmdName*** This argument has the same meaning as the *CmdName* argument passed to the *Exec* method of the *IDTCommandTarget* interface.
- ***NeededText*** This parameter is always *vsCommandStatusTextWantedNone*. Your add-in should always verify that this value is passed because the other values are reserved for future versions of Visual Studio .NET.

- ***StatusOption*** Your add-in should fill in this parameter, which lets Visual Studio .NET know whether the add-in command is supported (*vsCommandStatusSupported*) or unsupported (*vsCommandStatus-Unsupported*), whether the command is enabled and can be called (*vsCommandStatusEnabled*), whether the command user interface can't be seen (*vsCommandStatusInvisible*), or whether the user interface is drawn in the selected state (*vsCommandStatusLatched*). You can logically OR these values together to create the current status of the command and pass it back through this argument.
- ***CommandText*** This value currently isn't used by Visual Studio .NET, and shouldn't be modified.

Periodically, such as when the focus changes from one window to another or when a menu is displayed that contains an add-in command, Visual Studio .NET calls *QueryStatus* for that command to ensure that the user interface is synchronized with the command state. It is important to keep the code that implements *QueryStatus* as efficient as possible; otherwise, the user interface might become sluggish. Suppose you create a command that copies the currently active file to a network share. You might be tempted to have the *QueryStatus* method of a command check to ensure that a network connection is available and the share location can be found. If the network and shared location can be found, the command is enabled; otherwise, it is disabled. Testing for these connections can be time-consuming, taking up to a minute or more to complete. A user who has to wait more than a minute for your command to update itself would be much happier if the command were always enabled and he or she would receive an error message when the command was invoked.

Programmatically Determining Command State

At times, you might need to programmatically determine whether a command is enabled, such as when you want to invoke a command using *DTE.ExecuteCommand*. All commands, whether a macro command, one created by an add-in, or one built into Visual Studio .NET, support a *QueryStatus* method. When you invoke the *DTE.ExecuteCommand* and the command isn't enabled because the *QueryStatus* method returned a value indicating that isn't currently available, you'll get an exception if you're using a language supported by the .NET Framework.

To check whether a command is enabled and avoid this error condition, you can use the *Command.IsAvailable* property. For example, to make sure that the *Build.BuildSolution* command can be called before you invoke it, you can use the following code:

```
Sub CheckAvailability()
    If (DTE.Commands.Item("Build.BuildSolution").IsAvailable = True) Then
        DTE.ExecuteCommand("Build.BuildSolution")
    End If
End Sub
```

How an Add-in Command Handler Is Found

When a user invokes your command, Visual Studio .NET needs to know which add-in handles that command so it can call the methods of the *IDTCommandTarget* interface. It first inspects the command name; as noted earlier, the first part of the full command name is the ProgID of the add-in, and the remainder is the value passed for the *Name* parameter of the *AddNamedCommand* method. To locate the add-in, Visual Studio .NET extracts the ProgID from the command name and then checks the add-in corresponding to that ProgID to see whether it's loaded; if it isn't, it is told to load. Visual Studio .NET looks for the *IDTCommandTarget* interface (which must be implemented on the same object that implements *IDTExtensibility2*) on the add-in object instance, and then it calls the *Exec* method, passing the name of the command as the first parameter.

If, during this process, the add-in can't be found, the user is presented with the message box shown in Figure 7-2.

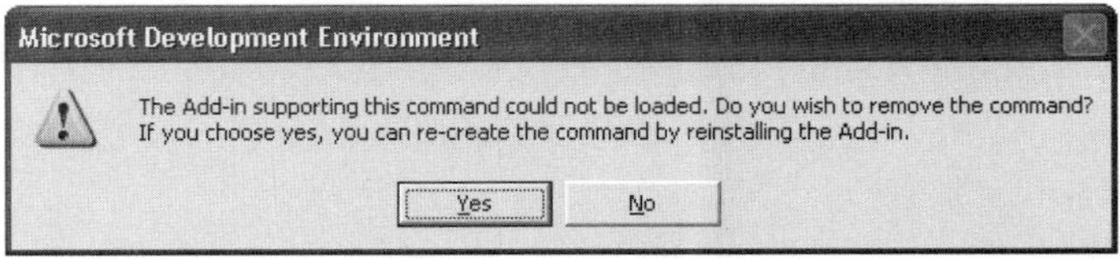

Figure 7-2 The message box displayed by Visual Studio .NET when a command's add-in doesn't load

If the user clicks the Yes button, the command is removed using the *Command.Delete* method, and any user interface elements for that command are removed. If the add-in is loaded but the *IDTCommandTarget* interface can't be found on the add-in object, the command is treated as if the *QueryStatus* method had returned the *vsCommandStatusUnsupported* flag.

The Command User Interface

Visual Studio borrows its toolbar and menu system from the Microsoft Office suite of applications. The command bars provide a common user interface experience across all of the Office applications as well as Visual Studio .NET. Because the command bars also support an object model, these applications also share a common programming model for accessing the command bar structure.

The main point of access to the command bar objects is through the *DTE.CommandBars* property. This property returns a *Microsoft.Office.Core.CommandBars* object, which is defined in the assembly Office.dll. The following macro code demonstrates retrieving this object:

```
Sub GetCommandBars()
    Dim commandBars As Microsoft.Office.Core.CommandBars
    commandBars = DTE.CommandBars
End Sub
```

The Command Bar Object Model

The command bar object model is arranged in a treelike hierarchy, in the same way as the Visual Studio .NET object model is. At the top of this tree is a collection of *Microsoft.Office.Core.CommandBar* objects that includes all the command bars and shortcut menus and the main menu bar. Each command bar contains a collection of controls that have the type *Microsoft.Office.Core.CommandBarControl*. Once a *CommandBarControl* is retrieved, it can be converted into one of three types. The first type, a *CommandBarButton*, is any item on a command bar that the user can click to perform an action; this is analogous to executing a Visual Studio .NET command. To get to a *CommandBarButton* object, a cast must be performed from the *CommandBarControl* object:

```
Sub GetCommandBarButton()
    Dim commandBarBtn As Microsoft.Office.Core.CommandBarButton
    Dim commandBarCtl As Microsoft.Office.Core.CommandBarControl
    Dim commandBarCtls As Microsoft.Office.Core.CommandBarControls

    'Find the View command bar
    commandBarCtls = DTE.CommandBars.Item("View").Controls
    'Retrieve the first control on the menu
    commandBarCtl = commandBarCtls.Item(1)
    'Convert the CommandBarControl to a CommandBarButton object
    commandBarBtn = CType(commandBarCtl, _
        Microsoft.Office.Core.CommandBarButton)
    MsgBox(commandBarBtn.Caption)
End Sub
```

The object returned from the *Controls* collection can be converted into a *CommandBarPopup* if the item is the root node of a submenu. An example of this is the New item on the File menu; when the user hovers the mouse cursor over this menu, a submenu appears. You can also retrieve a *CommandBar-*

Popup when the item is on a split-button drop-down menu, such as the New Project | New Blank Solution button on the Standard command bar:

```
Sub GetCommandBarPopup()
    Dim commandBar As Microsoft.Office.Core.CommandBar
    Dim cmdBarControl As Microsoft.Office.Core.CommandBarControl
    Dim cmdBarPopup As Microsoft.Office.Core.CommandBarPopup

    'Find the "Standard" command bar
    commandBar = DTE.CommandBars.Item("Standard")
    'Find the first control on the command bar
    cmdBarControl = commandBar.Controls.Item(1)
    'Convert the CommandBarControl to a CommandBarPopup
    cmdBarPopup = CType(cmdBarControl, _
        Microsoft.Office.Core.CommandBarPopup)
    MsgBox(cmdBarPopup.Controls.Item(1).Caption)
End Sub
```

A popup menu is itself a command bar. You can't cast directly to a *CommandBar* object on a popup menu, but this object does contain a *CommandBar* property, which returns a *CommandBar* object, which itself has a collection of controls (as you can see in the next-to-last line in the preceding macro code).

The Primary Command Bar

The *DTE.CommandBars* property returns the collection of all *CommandBar* objects available within Visual Studio .NET, but the most commonly used command bar is the main menu. Looking at the menu, you can see the File, Edit, and View items as well as a number of additional menu items; all of these are *CommandBar* objects within the *DTE.CommandBars* collection. But because there might be multiple items within the collection with the same name, indexing the collection using the name might not work. For example, there are multiple *CommandBar* objects with the title View, and you might not always get the one you want if you index the *CommandBars* collection with the string *View*. The following macro might return the View command bar for the SQL editor, a deployment project popup menu, or the View menu:

```
Sub GetView()
    Dim cmdbars As Microsoft.Office.Core.CommandBars
    Dim commandBar As Microsoft.Office.Core.CommandBar

    cmdbars = DTE.CommandBars
    commandBar = cmdbars.Item("View")
End Sub
```

To work around this, you can find the *CommandBar* object for the menu bar, called *MenuBar*, and then find the View submenu command bar:

```
Sub GetMenuCommandBar()
    Dim commandBar As Microsoft.Office.Core.CommandBar
    Dim cmdBarControl As Microsoft.Office.Core.CommandBarControl
    Dim cmdBarPopupView As Microsoft.Office.Core.CommandBarPopup
    Dim cmdBarView As Microsoft.Office.Core.CommandBar

    'Retrieve the MenuBar command bar
    commandBar = DTE.CommandBars.Item("MenuBar")
    'Find the View menu
    cmdBarControl = commandBar.Controls.Item("View")
    'Convert to a CommandBarPopup
    cmdBarPopupView = CType(cmdBarControl, _
        Microsoft.Office.Core.CommandBarPopup)
    'Get the CommandBar object for the view menu
    cmdBarView = cmdBarPopupView.CommandBar
    MsgBox(cmdBarView.Name)
End Sub
```

By default, if the Add-in Wizard generates an add-in and the option is selected to place an item on the Tools menu, code is generated to place a menu item on the Tools menu of the menu bar. If you want to move this command user interface to a different menu, you can simply change the string *"Tools"* to a different menu title; but be careful to select the correct menu. It's easy to make the mistake of selecting the wrong command bar, causing the command button to seemingly disappear because it was placed somewhere that you did not expect it to go.

Adding a New Command Bar User Interface

With a *Command* object in hand (found by either indexing the *Commands* collection or adding a new command) and after using the methods described earlier to find the proper command bar, you can add a new button to that command bar that invokes your command when clicked. You do this using the *Command.AddControl* method. When you add a command using the *AddNamedCommand* method, that command is persisted to disk and re-created automatically when Visual Studio .NET is next started. Likewise, when you place a control on a command bar using the *AddControl* method, that control and its placement are saved to disk and re-created when Visual Studio .NET is run. The first argument of the *AddControl* method is the *CommandBar* object that the button is to be placed on. The second argument defines the numerical position of the control in relation to the other controls on the command bar. (If this value is *1*, the control will be the first item on the command bar, and if the value is *2*, it will be the second item, and so forth.)

You can hard-code an index to place the control, but the control might not appear where you think it should go in relation to other controls. The reason is that a command bar might have one or more separators (or lines drawn between two controls) that divide controls into logical groups. These groups are also controls on the command bar, and they should be counted when you calculate the position. Not only are group controls counted as items in the index, but so are controls that are not visible because the value *vsCommandStatusInvisible* is returned from your *QueryStatus* method. If the control to be added should be placed at the bottom or end of the command bar, you can use the *Controls.Count* property to determine the final position:

```
Sub AddControl()
    Dim command As EnvDTE.Command
    Dim commandBar As Microsoft.Office.Core.CommandBar

    'Find the File.OpenFile command
    command = DTE.Commands.Item("File.OpenFile")
    'Find the Tools CommandBar
    commandBar = DTE.CommandBars.Item("Tools")
    'Add a control to the Tools menu that when
    ' clicked will invoke the File.OpenFile command
    command.AddControl(commandBar, commandBar.Controls.Count + 1)
  End Sub
```

Note that the index used doesn't fix a control to a particular position. If you add a control to position 1 and a second control is added to position 1, the first control is pushed into the second position.

At times, it might make sense to create a new command bar to place your buttons on because the default set of command bars don't suit your needs. The command bar object model allows you to create new command bars, but creating one in this way might not achieve the desired effects. Command bars created in this way are created in a temporary state, which means that when you exit and restart Visual Studio .NET, the command bar will have been destroyed. Because the button user interface for commands persists across instances, you'll want your command bars to also persist across instances. The Visual Studio .NET object model lets you do this, using the *Commands.AddCommandBar* method, which has this signature:

```
public object AddCommandBar(string Name, EnvDTE.vsCommandBarType Type, _
  Microsoft.Office.Core.CommandBar CommandBarParent = null, int Position = 1)
```

This method has the following arguments:

- ***Name*** The caption to display on the command bar.
- ***Type*** A value from the *vsCommandBarType* enumeration. If the value is *vsCommandBarTypeToolbar*, a command bar is created that can be docked to the top, left, bottom, or right of the Visual Studio .NET window. If the value is *vsCommandBarTypeMenu*, the command bar is added as a submenu to another command bar. If the value is *vsCommandBarTypePopup*, a shortcut menu is created.
- ***CommandBarParent*** If the value passed for the *Type* parameter is *vsCommandBarTypeToolbar* or *vsCommandBarTypePopup*, this value should be *null* or *Nothing* (depending on the language used). If the value passed to the *Type* parameter is *vsCommandBarTypeMenu*, the new menu should be rooted on the command bar object.
- ***Position*** This value is necessary only if the *Type* parameter is set to *vsCommandBarTypeMenu*. It defines the location on the parent command bar where the new menu command is placed. It has the same meaning as the *Position* parameter of the *AddControl* method.

How the newly created command bar is shown to the user depends on the type of command bar that's created. If the command bar type is a new menu, the menu item is hidden from the user until the command bar for that menu item is populated with buttons. If the command bar created is a new toolbar, the *Visible* property of the returned *CommandBar* object should be set to *True*. If a popup menu is created, you can show the menu to the user using the *CommandBar.ShowPopup* method, which takes two arguments, the *x* and *y* coordinates of the top left of where the popup menu should appear.

Using Custom Bitmaps

Visual Studio .NET has a number of predefined bitmaps that you can place on menu items and command bar buttons, but they might not always meet your needs. To use your own bitmap for the image on a button, you must register for your add-in a satellite DLL containing the bitmap in its resources (Chapter 6 has more information on creating satellite DLLs), and you must change the call to *Commands.AddNamedCommand* so Visual Studio .NET can find your bitmap. First, you should set the *AddNamedCommand* method's *MSOButton* parameter to *false* to tell Visual Studio .NET that the bitmap isn't among the default, built-in pictures but is in the satellite DLL. Second, you should change the *Bitmap* parameter to the resource ID of the bitmap in your satellite DLL.

The bitmap must have a specific format to be usable by Visual Studio .NET. It must be 16 pixels high and 16 pixels wide and must be saved so that it has 16 colors. Visual Studio .NET can also draw the picture so that a portion of it shows as transparent. To enable this, you must make the transparent area have the *RGB* (red, green, blue) color value of *0, 254, 0*. (Note that this color isn't the lime green color displayed in the color palette of the Visual Studio .NET image editor or the Paint application in Windows.)

Creating the bitmap so it has the correct size and color depth can be complicated. The CustomBitmap sample shows how this is done. The setup project has been modified to install the satellite DLL containing the custom bitmap into the correct place and to properly register the satellite DLL. When you install the sample using the setup project, you might find that the bitmap that appears on the button for the command on the Tools menu is blank. The reason is that the bitmap file used (in the file CustomBitmap\ CustomBitmapUI\untitled.bmp) is a blank template that uses the transparency color; you can use it as a starting point for creating your own custom bitmaps. The sample also shows how we modified the call to the *AddNamedCommand* method to reference the custom bitmap. As you can see in the following code, we changed the *MSOButton* argument from *true* to *false* and the *Bitmap* argument from *59* to *1*. (1 is the resource identifier for the bitmap in the satellite DLL.)

```
Command command = commands.AddNamedCommand(addInInstance, "CustomBitmap",
    "CustomBitmap", "Executes the command for CustomBitmap", false, 1,
    ref contextGUIDS, (int)vsCommandStatus.vsCommandStatusSupported +
    (int)vsCommandStatus.vsCommandStatusEnabled);
```

Restoring a Lost Command and Its User Interface

You might notice from time to time when you're developing an add-in (especially just after you've created the add-in) that the user interface for your command and the command itself have seemed to disappear. This happens because of the way the information for your command is stored. When Visual Studio .NET closes, all the information about the menu and toolbar placement, including the commands built into Visual Studio .NET and the ones you create, are saved to a file on disk. But if something happens that keeps Visual Studio .NET from saving this file, your commands and their user interface might be lost.

For example, suppose you create an add-in using the Add-in Wizard and you start debugging the resulting project. If you close the debugged instance of Visual Studio .NET by choosing File | Exit (or by using any other way of closing an application gracefully), its toolbar information is saved to a file on disk. When you close the instance of Visual Studio .NET that you used to develop the add-in, its toolbar information is saved as well, but the information defining your toolbar placements that was generated by the instance being debugged is overwritten. Thus, you lose any of the command information your add-in created.

You can lose this information in another way. Suppose you run the Add-in Wizard and generate an add-in, and then you start debugging that add-in by pressing the F5 key. Rather than closing down the debugged instance Visual Studio .NET (by choosing File | Exit or some other way), however, you choose to stop debugging in the debugger. That instance of Visual Studio .NET never has a chance to save its command information to disk, so that information is lost.

devenv /setup

You can re-create your command in a number of ways. First, you can close down all instances of Visual Studio .NET and from a command prompt window (the MS-DOS prompt), you can type **devenv /setup**. This will cause Visual Studio .NET to start and rebuild all the command bar information, removing any commands or *CommandBar* objects that were created by all add-ins. Running *devenv /setup* will also reset the appropriate flags to cause the add-in to rebuild its command information when Visual Studio .NET is started the next time.

> **Caution** Using *devenv /setup* can also produce undesired side effects: when command information is regenerated, all commands created by add-ins as well as customizations of commands (such as the moving of a button from one command bar to another) will be lost.

You can also re-create your command from the ResetCmdBarInfo add-in included with the book's sample files. ResetCmdBarInfo creates a command on the Tools menu. Choosing this menu item creates an instance of Visual Studio .NET that specifies the */setup* command-line option. When Visual Studio .NET is done re-creating the toolbar information, it closes. This has the same effect as typing **devenv /setup** from the command prompt.

Custom Registration

Another way to re-create a command is to reset the *CommandPreload* flag (first discussed in Chapter 6) that's registered for your add-in during build time. If the add-in you're building is written using Visual C++, you can easily modify the registration code for your add-in to reset this flag within the .rgs file, but a .NET assembly is not registered like Visual C++ COM objects are. To do custom system registry manipulation when an assembly is registered as a COM object, you can use .NET attributes. The .NET Framework libraries contain two attributes located in the *System.Runtime.InteropServices* namespace, named *ComRegisterFunctionAttribute* and *ComUnregisterFunctionAttribute*. These attributes, when placed on a static (for C#) or shared (for Visual Basic .NET) public method that takes an argument of type *System.Type*, are called during the RegAsm phase of registering a .NET component as a COM object (which happens every time the add-in project is built). Therefore, you can insert code that looks like this into your add-in's class declaration:

```
[ComRegisterFunctionAttribute]
public static void RegisterFunction(Type t)
{
    string progID = String.Empty;

    foreach (System.Attribute attrib in t.GetCustomAttributes(false))
    {
        if (attrib.GetType().FullName ==
            "System.Runtime.InteropServices.ProgIdAttribute")
        {
            ProgIdAttribute progIdAttrib = (ProgIdAttribute)attrib;
            progID = progIdAttrib.Value;
        }
    }

    if (progID != String.Empty)
    {
        RegistryKey key = Registry.CurrentUser.OpenSubKey(
            @"Software\Microsoft\VisualStudio\7.1\AddIns\" + progID,
            true);

        if (key != null)
        {
            if (((int)key.GetValue("CommandPreload", -1)) == 2)
            {
                key.SetValue("CommandPreload", 1);
            }
        }

        key = Registry.CurrentUser.OpenSubKey(
            @"Software\Microsoft\VSA\7.1\AddIns\" + progID, true);

        if (key != null)
        {
            if (((int)key.GetValue("CommandPreload", -1)) == 2)
                key.SetValue("CommandPreload", 1);
        }
```

(continued)

```
            key = Registry.CurrentUser.OpenSubKey(
                @"Software\Microsoft\VisualStudio\7.1\PreloadAddinState",
                true);

            if (key != null)
            {
                key.DeleteValue(progID, false);
            }

            key = Registry.CurrentUser.OpenSubKey(
                @"Software\Microsoft\VSA\7.1\PreloadAddinState", true);

            if (key != null)
            {
                key.DeleteValue(progID, false);
            }
        }
    }

    [ComUnregisterFunctionAttribute]
    public static void UnregisterFunction(Type t)
    {
        string progID = String.Empty;

        foreach (System.Attribute attrib in t.GetCustomAttributes(false))
        {
            if (attrib.GetType().FullName ==
                "System.Runtime.InteropServices.ProgIdAttribute")
            {
                ProgIdAttribute progIdAttrib = (ProgIdAttribute)attrib;
                progID = progIdAttrib.Value;
            }
        }

        if (progID != String.Empty)
        {
            RegistryKey key = Registry.CurrentUser.OpenSubKey(
                @"Software\Microsoft\VisualStudio\7.1\PreloadAddinState",
                true);

            if (key != null)
            {
                key.DeleteValue(progID, false);
            }
```

```
        key = Registry.CurrentUser.OpenSubKey(
            @"Software\Microsoft\VSA\7.1\PreloadAddinState", true);

        if (key != null)
        {
            key.DeleteValue(progID, false);
        }
    }
}
```

So, what does this code do? The first few lines of code in each function find the class that the function is implemented within, using reflection. The code then walks the list of attributes of that class, searching for the attribute that sets the ProgID of the add-in when it is registered as a COM object—the *ProgIdAttribute* attribute. Once this attribute is found, the ProgID for the add-in can be retrieved. The remainder of the code simply checks for certain registry values, which if present and set to the value *2* are reset back to *1*. Currently, the code resets values if they are present for the Visual Studio .NET Macros editor and Visual Studio .NET. If one or the other application isn't suitable for your application, you should remove that registry check. Also, if more applications based on Visual Studio .NET technology become available and you set your add-in to load for that application, you should add an appropriate check for that application's registry settings. You can find code that demonstrates resetting these flags in the ReRegisterCS add-in included with the book's sample files.

> **Note** This registration method will repair only a broken command creation and won't fully create all the necessary add-in registration settings. You can use this method to add your own registration code to register the add-in, but our example here doesn't do that.

These methods are useful for another situation besides repairing a lost command: moving the command bar user interface. Suppose you used the Add-in Wizard to create the default add-in code that places a button on the Tools menu. During development, however, you decide that the user interface for your command belongs on a different command bar—for example, the View menu. After rewriting the code to find the correct menu, you must reset the *CommandPreload* flag so the code will run to place the user interface elements.

Add-in Performance

To make sure your commands are created correctly and to work around the problems that we've discussed, you might be tempted to set your add-in to load on startup, call *AddNamedCommand* to create your commands after the add-in loads, and then call *Delete* to remove the commands when the add-in is unloaded. We advise you not to do this for one reason: performance. The Visual Studio .NET automation team designed commands so the user of an add-in is not penalized for having add-ins installed.

Suppose a user has 10 add-ins installed. If each of these add-ins were set to load on startup, you'd have to create, initialize, and execute the code of 10 separate components just to have the user interface for these add-ins available to that user, even if she never uses the add-ins. Also, it might not seem that bad to have your add-in load on startup, but the user will notice the additional time it takes to start Visual Studio .NET. The problems with commands not being saved from one instance of Visual Studio .NET to the next is a problem only for the developer and will rarely, if ever, be seen by the user.

A user once told Microsoft of a bug where Visual Studio .NET seemed to get slower over time, to where it was taking well over a minute to start. Microsoft looked for the standard performance-related problems, such as a badly fragmented disk drive, background processes that consume too much CPU bandwidth, and low memory conditions. The problem turned out to originate with an add-in that was set to load on startup and re-created its commands each time it was loaded. The third-party supplier of this add-in (which shall remain nameless) changed the code, and the user has been happily using the add-in ever since.

Removing a Command

Once created, if a command is no longer needed (for example, if your add-in is being uninstalled), you can delete it. Only commands created by add-ins can be deleted, however; commands defined by Visual Studio .NET or commands for macros can't be removed and an error is generated if a call is made to remove a non-add-in created command. To remove a command, you use the *Command.Delete* method; it removes not only the command name but also any user interface elements for that command, such as buttons on command bars.

```
Sub DeleteMyCommand()
    DTE.Commands.Item("MyAddin.Connect.MyCommand").Delete()
End Sub
```

Uninstalling an add-in should remove any commands that it has created, but by default, the code generated by the Add-in Wizard doesn't do this. You can add a *custom action* to your add-in component to remove these commands. A *custom action* is code that is run by the installer project created by the Add-in Wizard during install and/or uninstall time. During install and uninstall, the installer loads your add-in component and searches for a public class that derives from the *System.Configuration.Install.Installer* class and uses the *RunInstaller(true)* attribute. If a class meets these criteria, the methods *Install* and *Uninstall* are called, allowing any custom code to be run. Creating a component of this type is simple. In the Add New Item dialog box, you can insert an Installer Class project item, as shown in Figure 7-3.

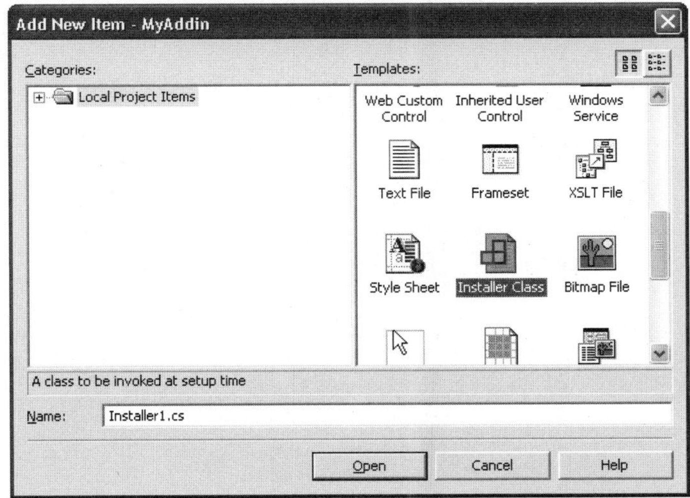

Figure 7-3 The Add New Item dialog box, with the Installer Class item selected

The following code implements the *Uninstall* and *Install* methods of the *Installer* class. These methods first check to make sure that no instances of the devenv.exe (the executable for Visual Studio .NET) process are running. These methods prompt the user to close any instances if any are running, and when they have been closed, the custom action starts a new instance of Visual Studio .NET through the automation model. The *Uninstall* method then continues on, calling the *Delete* method to delete the command. You can modify this code to find and delete the commands that your add-in has created.

This code also helps install an add-in using the *Install* method. When the *CommandPreload* flag is set in the registry, the next time Visual Studio .NET runs it starts the process of allowing add-ins to create commands. You've seen the problems that can arise if Visual Studio .NET is closed unexpectedly or if multiple instances are created before the command information can be written to disk. Using a custom action, you can create an instance of Visual Studio .NET through the automation model and then immediately close the process. This allows Visual Studio .NET to create any commands and save this data, allowing your user to avoid the trap of command information being overwritten.

```
bool IsVSRunning()
{
    System.Diagnostics.Process []processes =
        System.Diagnostics.Process.GetProcesses();
    foreach(System.Diagnostics.Process process in processes)
    {
        //Wrap in a try catch. If the process is not owned by
        //the user then an exception will be thrown trying to
        //get the ProcessModule
        try
        {
            if((process != null) && (process.MainModule != null))
            {
                //Get the file name of the process,
                // and compare it to 'devenv.exe'
                string fileName = process.MainModule.FileName;
                fileName = System.IO.Path.GetFileName(fileName);
                if(System.String.Compare(fileName, "devenv.exe") == 0)
                    return true;
            }
        }
        catch(System.Exception ex)
        {
        }
    }
    return false;
}

public override void Uninstall(System.Collections.IDictionary savedState)
{
    base.Uninstall(savedState);
    System.Windows.Forms.MessageBox.Show("Uninstall");
    while(IsVSRunning())
    {
        System.Windows.Forms.MessageBox.Show("A running instance of Visual " +
            Studio .NET was found.\n\nPlease close all copies of Visual " +
            "Studio .NET, then press OK.", "Uninstall...",
            System.Windows.Forms.MessageBoxButtons.OK);
    }
```

```
        EnvDTE.DTE dte = new EnvDTE.DTEClass();
        //Change the name of the command below
        //to the name of the command you have created
        // This can be called multiple times, once for each command created
        dte.Commands.Item("MyAddin1.Connect.MyAddin1", -1).Delete();
    }

    public override void Install(System.Collections.IDictionary stateSaver)
    {
        base.Install(stateSaver);
        System.Windows.Forms.MessageBox.Show("Install");
        while(IsVSRunning())
        {
            System.Windows.Forms.MessageBox.Show("A running instance of Visual " +
                "Studio .NET was found.\n\nPlease close all copies of Visual " +
                "Studio .NET, then press OK.", "Install...",
                System.Windows.Forms.MessageBoxButtons.OK);
        }
        EnvDTE.DTE dte = new EnvDTE.DTEClass();
    }
```

Once this component has been added to your add-in's project, the last step is to add it to the list of custom actions available to the installer. You do this by opening the Custom Actions editor of the installer project: right-click the setup project and choose View | Custom Actions. Next, you add the primary output of the add-in project to the Uninstall and Install nodes of this editor by right-clicking on each of these nodes in the Custom Actions window, choosing Add Custom Action, double-clicking on the Application Folder item in the Select Item In Project dialog box, and selecting Primary Output From Addin Project Name.

You don't need to add a custom action to your installer project to delete your commands during uninstall. Deleting commands that are no longer used results in the best user experience, but you don't need to manually remove the commands you create. When your add-in is uninstalled, it leaves behind any commands and the user interface for those commands. If the user chooses any of the commands for which the add-in that handles that command can't be found, the user is presented with the message box shown earlier in Figure 7-2. If the user clicks Yes, the command and any of its user interface elements are removed.

Command Parameters

Commands that you create for your add-in can accept parameters. You can pass these parameters to the command handler when they're invoked from the Command Window or by using the *DTE.ExecuteCommand* method. For example, suppose your add-in created a command with the name *MyAddin.Connect.Command*. If the user types into the Command Window the lines

```
MyAddin.Connect.Command
MyAddin.Connect.Command My Parameters
```

the *IDTCommandTarget.Exec* method of your add-in is called twice. The first time, the *VarIn* parameter is an empty string (*""*). The second time, *VarIn* contains the string *"My Parameters"*. Everything after the name of the command (except trailing and ending white space) is copied verbatim into the *VarIn* parameter. It's up to your add-in to parse the list of supplied parameters and handle them as needed. Parameters can also be passed using the *ExecuteCommand* method; up to this point, we've only seen *ExecuteCommand* being passed one argument—the full name of the command. However, you can pass an optional second argument, which is the parameter that's passed to your command handler the same way that data is passed when the command is invoked through the Command Window.

Commands that support parameters often require a specific syntax for what can be passed in. A user might be able to look up in the documentation exactly what that syntax is, but it would be easier for the user to ask the command directly for help. A common format for finding help from command-line utilities in Windows is to type the name of the program followed by a */?* argument. The Visual Studio .NET Command Window also supports help in a similar fashion. If the user types the command name followed by */?* into the Command Window, your *IDTCommandTarget.Exec* method is called with the *ExecuteOption* parameter set to a value OR'ed together with *vsCommandExecOption.vsCommandExecOptionShowHelp*. When this value is passed, your add-in can decide the best method of displaying help, such as displaying a Web page with documentation. The CommandHelp add-in included with the book's sample files demonstrates displaying a Help file when the */?* parameter is specified to a command.

Macros can also take parameters. To declare a macro that takes arguments, you must make all the arguments optional strings with a defined default value, as demonstrated in this macro:

```
Sub OptionalArguments(Optional ByVal optArg As String = "I am optional")
    MsgBox(optArg)
End Sub
```

This macro can be called from the Command Window or the *ExecuteCommand* method, using either just its name or the name and arguments. If the argument isn't specified when this macro is called, a message box with the text "I am optional" is displayed to the user. If an argument is specified, the message box uses that argument text. Macros don't provide special functionality for invoking help, but you can simulate this functionality by checking the argument value passed—if it's set to the string */?*, the user has requested help. You can rewrite the macro as follows to handle help:

```
Sub OptionalArguments2(Optional ByVal optArg As String = "I am optional")
    If (optArg = "/?") Then
      Dim helpString As String
      helpString = "Usage: OptionalArguments [optArg]"
      helpString = helpString + vbLf
      helpString = helpString + "This macro will display in " + _
          "a message box the passed argument."
      MsgBox(helpString)
    Else
      MsgBox(optArg)
    End If
End Sub
```

Key Bindings

You've seen the many ways that commands can be invoked, but each way requires either moving your hand from the keyboard to the mouse or typing a long string of commands. To aid in accessibility or just to make invoking these commands easier, many commands are assigned a shortcut keystroke, or key binding. For example, rather than picking up the mouse, opening the File menu, choosing the Open submenu, and then clicking File to open a file, you can use the keystroke Ctrl+O to quickly access the Open File dialog box.

Each command can have one or more key bindings assigned to it. The *Command.Bindings* property allows you to read or set the bindings assigned to that command. When you call this property to retrieve the set of bindings, an array of objects containing strings describing each binding is returned, which can be enumerated to find each binding. You can set bindings by using this property, and they can accept either a singular string to set a single keystroke or an array of strings to assign multiple bindings at once. You can see how these key bindings are retrieved in this macro:

```
Sub GetFileOpenBindings()
    Dim bindings As Object()
    Dim binding As Object
    bindings = DTE.Commands.Item("File.OpenFile").Bindings
    For Each binding In bindings
        MsgBox(CStr(binding))
    Next
End Sub
```

Each binding that is set has a specific format, and you must follow this format closely to avoid generating an error. Here's the format:

```
Scope::ModifierKeys+Key,ModifierKeys2+Key2
```

And here's a description of each piece of the binding:

- *Scope* is the context in which the key binding can be applied. For example, pressing the Ctrl+B key binding makes the selected text bold when you're using the HTML editor; if the image editor is active (a bitmap is loaded and is the active window), the brush tool is selected. If neither the HTML editor nor the image editor is active, pressing Ctrl+B displays the debugger breakpoints dialog box. A number of scopes are available, but the most common is the Global scope. In this scope, the command is available everywhere except when a more specific scope is active. The Ctrl+B keystroke for displaying debugger breakpoints is in the Global scope, while Ctrl+B for bolding text is in the HTML Editor Design View scope and takes precedence over the breakpoints dialog box if an HTML designer window is active.

- Modifier keys are system keys that are pressed while you're pressing another key. These modifiers include the Alt, Shift, and Ctrl keys. One or more modifier keys can be specified; they can appear in any order but must be separated by the + character.

- A key is any key on a standard 102-key keyboard (which excludes keys on newer Windows keyboards, such as the Windows key, multimedia keys, and the Fn key on some notebook keyboards). If a key is a system key, such as F1, F2, and so forth or the Esc key, a Modifier key isn't required. If the key is an alphanumeric key, a Modifier must be specified. It can't be Shift alone but must include either Alt or Ctrl or both because some keystrokes are reserved and can't be overridden. (For example, A and Shift+A are reserved by the text editor.) The keys available for use are the alphanumeric keys, the unshifted characters (such as the comma and period), and the values Bkspce, Del, Ins, Space, F1 to F24, Enter, Break, Up Arrow, Down Arrow, Left Arrow, Right Arrow, Tab, Home, End, PgUp, PgDn, Esc, NUM *, NUM -, NUM +, and NUM /. The Caps Lock, Print Screen, Num Lock, and Pause keys are reserved by the operating system, so you can't use them.

- ModifierKeys2 and Key2 make up another set of keystrokes. These are optional and can be used to refine command groups. For example, you can have your add-in use the key binding Ctrl+Shift+D, O to open a file into a tool window, while Ctrl+Shift+D, S can save that file. Key2 isn't restricted to being grouped with a modifier key, which means that ModifierKeys2 is optional.

Using this format, we can assign the keystroke Ctrl+Shift+D,O within the Global scope by using code like this:

```
Sub SetKeyBinding()
    Dim command As Command
    command = DTE.Commands.Item("File.OpenFile")
    command.Bindings = "Global::Ctrl+Shift+D,O"
End Sub
```

This call to the *Bindings* property sets one key binding, but you can also assign more than one key binding at a time by passing an array of *System.Object*, each set to a *System.String*:

```
Sub SetKeyBindings()
    Dim command As Command
    Dim bindings(1) As Object
    bindings(0) = "Global::Ctrl+Shift+D,O"
    bindings(1) = "Global::Ctrl+Shift+D,F"
    command = DTE.Commands.Item("File.OpenFile")
    command.Bindings = bindings
End Sub
```

When any changes are made to the key bindings for a command, all the bindings for that command are removed, and if the binding is in use with another command, that binding is also removed. After running a macro such as this, users who are accustomed to using Ctrl+O to open a file might become confused about why their familiar binding has been lost, but this setting can be preserved through code:

```
Sub SetKeyBindingsPreserve()
    Dim command As Command
    Dim bindings() As Object
    Dim preserveLength As Integer

    command = DTE.Commands.Item("File.OpenFile")
    'Retrieve the current bindings for the command
    bindings = command.Bindings
    'Find the number of current bindings
    preserveLength = bindings.Length
    'Add 2 elements to the array (remember, preserveLength
    ' will be 1 more than the number of elements, and this
    ' extra value with 1 added to it becomes 2 elements
    ReDim Preserve bindings(preserveLength + 1)
    'Assign our new bindings
    bindings(preserveLength) = "Global::Ctrl+Shift+D,O"
    bindings(preserveLength + 1) = "Global::Ctrl+Shift+D,F"
    command.Bindings = bindings
End Sub
```

When you attempt to modify the set of key bindings for a command, you might get an exception with the message "Setting key bindings valid only when using a non-built-in key binding scheme." This exception occurs because the key binding schemes that ship with Visual Studio .NET are read-only; to modify the keyboard scheme, you or your user must first switch to a user-defined key scheme. You can do this through the user interface in the Options dialog box on the Environment | Keyboard tab by clicking the Save As button or by assigning a path to the Environment | Keyboard property collection's *Scheme* property. If, when you're setting this value, the .vsk file (keyboard schemes are saved into a file with the extension .vsk) doesn't exist, a file is created for you.

The following macro creates a keyboard scheme file in the user's application data folder for Visual Studio .NET:

```
Sub ChangeKeyboardScheme()
    Dim props As EnvDTE.Properties
    Dim prop As EnvDTE.Property
    Dim path As String
    Dim folder As System.Environment.SpecialFolder

    'Find the Environment, Keyboard, scheme property
    props = DTE.Properties("Environment", "Keyboard")
    prop = props.Item("Scheme")
    'Set the path we wish to save information to
    folder = System.Environment.SpecialFolder.ApplicationData
    path = System.Environment.GetFolderPath(folder)
    path = path + "\Microsoft\VisualStudio\7.1\scheme.vsk"
    'Set the path
    prop.Value = path
End Sub
```

Lab: Creating a Command and Key Binding Cheat Sheet

I like to keep handy a printout of all commands and the bindings of those commands that Visual Studio .NET offers. When I find that I'm running a certain command repeatedly, I look up that command on my printout and then try to remember the keystroke shortcut for that command. Finding the command that I want to run might take a while because there are so many commands, but over time this approach has increased my productivity because I no longer need to hunt for a command on the menus—I can just press a keystroke. Here's the macro I used to create my command cheat sheet:

```
Sub GenerateCommandCheatSheet()
    Dim cmd As Command
    Dim selection As TextSelection
    Dim binding As String
    Dim newDocument As Document
    'Open a new document to store the information
    newDocument = DTE.ItemOperations.NewFile( _
        "General\Text File").Document
    selection = newDocument.Selection
    'Enumerate all commands:
    For Each cmd In DTE.Commands
        If (cmd.Name <> Nothing) Then
            Dim str As String
            'Get the command name, and format to
            ' make the output look nice:
            str = cmd.Name
            str = str.PadRight(70)
            'Output the command name, and the bindings for the command:
            If (cmd.Bindings.Length > 0) Then
                For Each binding In cmd.Bindings
                    str = str + binding
                    selection.Insert(str + vbLf)
                    str = ""
                    str = str.PadRight(70)
                Next
            Else
                selection.Insert(str + vbLf)
            End If
        End If
    Next
End Sub
```

Looking Ahead

In the next chapter, we'll focus on using the object model to create and modify solutions and projects that are loaded into Visual Studio .NET. We'll also look at how to work with those solutions, such as changing how a solution and projects are compiled into a running program.

8

Managing Solutions and Projects Programmatically

Microsoft Visual Studio .NET is rich with tools to help you manage and complete your programming tasks. One of these tools is the project management system. Projects are where files are created, managed, and compiled to create the resulting program. In this chapter, you'll discover how you can manipulate projects using the automation object model.

Working with Solutions

In Visual Studio .NET, a solution is the basic unit of project management. A solution is a container for any number of projects that work together to create the whole of a program. Each project within a solution can contain code files that are compiled to create the program, folders to make managing the files easier, and references to other software components that a project might use. You manage a solution through the Solution Explorer tool window, where you can add, remove, and modify projects and the files they contain. When a solution file is opened, a node is created within Solution Explorer that represents the solution, and each project added to this solution appears as a subnode of the top-level one.

Within the Visual Studio .NET object model, a solution is represented by the *EnvDTE.Solution* object, which you can retrieve using the *Solution* property of the *DTE* object, as shown in the following macro:

```
Sub GetSolution()
    Dim solution As EnvDTE.Solution
    solution = DTE.Solution
End Sub
```

Creating, Loading, and Unloading Solutions

To use the *Solution* object and its methods and properties, you don't need to create or open a solution file from disk. You can use the *Solution* object even though the solution node in Solution Explorer might not be visible. Visual Studio .NET always has a solution open, even if it exists only in memory and not on disk. If you open a solution file from disk and the in-memory solution is not *dirty* (modified but not saved to disk), this in-memory solution is discarded and the solution on disk is loaded. If the in-memory solution has been modified (such as by having a new or existing project added), when you close it you'll be prompted to save the solution to disk.

To save a solution programmatically, you can use the method *Solution.SaveAs*; you pass it the full path, including the filename and the .sln file extension, to where the solution should be stored on disk. However, using the *Solution.SaveAs* method might not always work and can generate an exception because you must first save a solution file to disk or load it from an existing solution file on disk before the *SaveAs* method can be used. To allow saving of the solution file, you can use the *Create* method. You use this method to specify information such as where the solution file should be saved and the name of the solution. By combining the *Create* and *SaveAs* methods, you can not only create the solution but also save it:

```
Sub CreateAndSaveSolution()
    DTE.Solution.Create("C:\", "Solution")
    DTE.Solution.SaveAs("C:\Solution.sln")
End Sub
```

Once you create a solution file and save it to disk, whether through the user interface or the object model, you can use the *Solution.Open* method to open it. Using the file path given in the CreateAndSaveSolution macro, we can open our solution as shown here:

```
DTE.Solution.Open("C:\Solution.sln")
```

When you call this method, the currently open solution is discarded and the specified solution file is opened. When an open solution is closed to make way for the solution file that is being loaded, you won't be notified that the current solution is being closed, even if the current solution has been modified. This means you won't be given the option to save any changes. A macro or an add-in can use the *ItemOperations.PromptToSave* property to offer the option of saving a solution. The *ItemOperations* object, which is accessed from the *DTE.ItemOperations* property, contains various file manipulation methods and properties. One property of this object, *PromptToSave*, displays a dialog box that gives you the option to select files to save and returns a value detailing which button you clicked. This property also saves the files you've chosen to save. This property won't show the dialog box if no files need to be saved—it will immediately return a value indicating that you clicked the OK button. You can combine the *PromptToSave* property with the *Open* method to properly save modified files and open a solution:

```
Sub OpenSolution()
    Dim promptResult As vsPromptResult
    'Offer to save any open and modified files:
    promptResult = DTE.ItemOperations.PromptToSave
    'If the user pressed anything but the Cancel button,
    ' then open a solution file from disk:
    If promptResult <> vsPromptResult.vsPromptResultCancelled Then
        DTE.Solution.Open("C:\Solution.sln")
    End If
End Sub
```

You've learned how to create, save, and open a solution—the only piece missing from the life cycle of a solution is closing it. The *Solution* object supports the method *Close*, which you can use to close a solution file. This method accepts one optional *Boolean* parameter, which you can use to direct Visual Studio .NET to save the file when you close it. If you pass the value *true* for this parameter, the solution file is saved before you close it; if you set it to *false*, any changes to the file are discarded.

Enumerating Projects

The *Solution* object is a collection of *Project* objects, and because it is a collection, it has an *Item* method that you can use to find a project within the solution. This method supports the numeric indexing method, like the *Item* method of other objects does, but it also supports passing a string to find a project. The string form of the *Solution.Item* method is different from that of other *Item* methods, however; rather than taking the name of a project, *Solution.Item* requires the unique name of a project. A unique name, as its name indicates, uniquely identifies a project among all other projects within a solution. Unique names are used to index the projects collection because Visual Studio .NET might eventually support loading two projects that have the same name but are located in different folders on disk. (Visual Studio .NET 2003 requires that all projects within a solution have a name that is different from all other projects.) Because loading two or more projects with the same name might be allowed in a version of Visual Studio .NET after version 7.1, the name alone isn't enough to differentiate one project from another when you call the *Item* method. You can retrieve the unique name of a project using the *Project.UniqueName* property. The following macro retrieves this value for all the projects loaded into a solution:

```
Sub EnumProjects()
    Dim project As EnvDTE.Project
    For Each project In DTE.Solution
        MsgBox(project.UniqueName)
    Next
End Sub
```

The *Solution* object isn't the only collection of all projects that are loaded. The *Solution* object has a *Projects* property, which also returns a collection of the available projects and works in the same way that the *Solution* object does for enumerating and indexing projects. It might seem redundant to have this same functionality in two places, but the Visual Studio .NET object model team, after performing usability studies, found that developers didn't recognize the *Solution* object as a collection. They therefore added this *Projects* collection to help developers find the list of projects more easily. The *EnumProjects* macro can be rewritten as follows to use the *Projects* collection:

```
Sub EnumProjects2()
    Dim project As EnvDTE.Project
    For Each project In DTE.Solution.Projects
        MsgBox(project.UniqueName)
    Next
End Sub
```

You can find the list of projects by using the *Solution* and *Projects* collections, but at times you'll need to find the projects that you've selected within Solution Explorer tree view window. You can do this using the *DTE.ActiveSolutionProjects* property. When you call this property, Visual Studio .NET looks at the items selected within Solution Explorer. If a project node is selected, the *Project* object for that selected project is added to a list of objects that will be returned. If a project item is selected, the project containing that item is also added to the list returned. Finally, any duplicates are removed from the list and the list is returned. The following macro demonstrates using this property:

```
Sub FindSelectedProjects()
    Dim selectedProjects As Object()
    Dim project As EnvDTE.Project
    selectedProjects = DTE.ActiveSolutionProjects
    For Each project In selectedProjects
        MsgBox(project.UniqueName)
    Next
End Sub
```

Capturing Solution Events

As you interact with a solution, Visual Studio .NET fires events that allow an add-in or a macro to receive notifications about which actions you perform. These events are fired through the *SolutionEvents* object, which you can access through the *Events.SolutionEvents* property. You can capture solution events in the usual way—by opening the *EnvironmentEvents* module of any macro project, selecting the *SolutionEvents* object in the left drop-down list at the top of the code editor window, and selecting the event name in the right drop-down list of this window.

Here are the signatures and meanings for the events available for a solution:

- ***void Opened()*** This event is fired just after a solution file has been opened.
- ***void Renamed(string OldName)*** This event handler is called just after a solution file has been renamed on disk. The only argument passed to this handler is the full path of the solution file just before it was renamed.
- ***void ProjectAdded(EnvDTE.Project Project)*** This event is fired when a project is inserted into the solution. One argument is passed to this event handler—the *EnvDTE.Project* object for the project that was inserted.
- ***void ProjectRenamed(EnvDTE.Project Project, string OldName)*** This event is fired when a project within the solution has been renamed. The event handler is passed two arguments. The first is of type *EnvDTE.Project* and is the object for the project that has just been renamed. The second parameter is a string that contains the full path of the project file before it was renamed.
- ***void ProjectRemoved(EnvDTE.Project Project)*** This event is fired just before a project is removed from the solution. This event handler receives as an argument the *EnvDTE.Project* object for the project that is being removed. Just as when you use the *BeforeClosing* event, you shouldn't modify the project being removed within this event because the project has already been saved to disk (if you specified that the file be saved) before being removed, and any modifications to the project will be discarded.
- ***void QueryCloseSolution(ref bool fCancel)*** This event is fired just before Visual Studio .NET begins to close a solution file. The

handler for this event is passed one argument—a reference to a *Boolean* variable. An add-in or a macro can block a solution from being closed by setting this parameter to *true*, or it can allow the solution to be closed by setting the parameter to *false*. You should take care when you choose to stop the solution from being closed—users might be unpleasantly surprised if they try to close the solution but a macro or an add-in disallows it.

- ***void BeforeClosing()*** This event is fired just before the solution file is about to close but after it has been saved (if you specified the option to save). Because this event is fired after the chance to save the file has passed, the event handler shouldn't make any changes to the solution because those changes will be discarded.
- ***void AfterClosing()*** This event is fired just after the solution file has finished closing.

The sample named SolutionEvents, which is among the book's sample files, demonstrates connecting to each of these events. Once you load this sample, as each event is fired the add-in displays a message box showing a bit of information about the event that was fired. The *QueryCloseSolution* event handler also offers the option of canceling the closing of the solution. The source code for this add-in sample is shown in Listing 8-1.

SolutionEvents.cs

```
namespace SolutionEvents
{
    using System;
    using Microsoft.Office.Core;
    using Extensibility;
    using System.Runtime.InteropServices;
    using EnvDTE;

    [GuidAttribute("1FF0C203-8036-4A54-A71A-B0F82BA60B0C"),
    ProgId("SolutionEvents.Connect")]

    public class Connect : Object, Extensibility.IDTExtensibility2

    {

        public Connect()
        {
        }
```

Listing 8-1 Source code for the solution events add-in

```
public void OnConnection(object application,
    Extensibility.ext_ConnectMode connectMode,
    object addInInst, ref System.Array custom)
{
    applicationObject = (_DTE)application;
    addInInstance = (AddIn)addInInst;

    //Set the solutionEvents delegate variable using the
    // DTE.Events.SolutionEvents property:
    solutionEvents = (EnvDTE.SolutionEvents)
        applicationObject.Events.SolutionEvents;

    //Set up all available event handlers by creating a new
    // instance of the appropriate delegates:
    solutionEvents.AfterClosing += new
        _dispSolutionEvents_AfterClosingEventHandler(AfterClosing);
    solutionEvents.BeforeClosing += new
        _dispSolutionEvents_BeforeClosingEventHandler(BeforeClosing);
    solutionEvents.Opened += new
        _dispSolutionEvents_OpenedEventHandler(Opened);
    solutionEvents.ProjectAdded += new
        _dispSolutionEvents_ProjectAddedEventHandler(ProjectAdded);
    solutionEvents.ProjectRemoved += new
        _dispSolutionEvents_ProjectRemovedEventHandler
        (ProjectRemoved);
    solutionEvents.ProjectRenamed += new
        _dispSolutionEvents_ProjectRenamedEventHandler
        (ProjectRenamed);
    solutionEvents.QueryCloseSolution += new
        _dispSolutionEvents_QueryCloseSolutionEventHandler
         (QueryCloseSolution);
    solutionEvents.Renamed += new
        _dispSolutionEvents_RenamedEventHandler(Renamed);
}

public void OnDisconnection(
    Extensibility.ext_DisconnectMode disconnectMode,
    ref System.Array custom)
{
    //The Add-in is closing. Disconnect the event handlers:
    solutionEvents.AfterClosing -= new
        _dispSolutionEvents_AfterClosingEventHandler(AfterClosing);
    solutionEvents.BeforeClosing -= new
        _dispSolutionEvents_BeforeClosingEventHandler(BeforeClosing);
    solutionEvents.Opened -= new
        _dispSolutionEvents_OpenedEventHandler(Opened);
    solutionEvents.ProjectAdded -= new
        _dispSolutionEvents_ProjectAddedEventHandler(ProjectAdded);
```

```
        solutionEvents.ProjectRemoved -= new
            _dispSolutionEvents_ProjectRemovedEventHandler
            (ProjectRemoved);
        solutionEvents.ProjectRenamed -= new
            _dispSolutionEvents_ProjectRenamedEventHandler
            (ProjectRenamed);
        solutionEvents.QueryCloseSolution -= new
            _dispSolutionEvents_QueryCloseSolutionEventHandler(
            QueryCloseSolution);
        solutionEvents.Renamed -= new
            _dispSolutionEvents_RenamedEventHandler(Renamed);
    }

    public void OnAddInsUpdate(ref System.Array custom)
    {
    }

    public void OnStartupComplete(ref System.Array custom)
    {
    }

    public void OnBeginShutdown(ref System.Array custom)
    {
    }

    //SolutionEvents.AfterClosing delegate handler:
    public void AfterClosing()
    {
        System.Windows.Forms.MessageBox.Show(
            "SolutionEvents.AfterClosing",
            "Solution Events");
    }

    //SolutionEvents.BeforeClosing delegate handler:
    public void BeforeClosing()
    {
        System.Windows.Forms.MessageBox.Show(
            "SolutionEvents.BeforeClosing",
            "Solution Events");
    }

    //SolutionEvents.Opened delegate handler:
    public void Opened()
    {
        System.Windows.Forms.MessageBox.Show("SolutionEvents.Opened",
            "Solution Events");
    }

    //SolutionEvents.ProjectAdded delegate handler.
```

```
//Display the UniqueName of the project that has been added.
public void ProjectAdded(EnvDTE.Project project)
{
    System.Windows.Forms.MessageBox.Show(
        "SolutionEvents.ProjectAdded\nProject: " + project.UniqueName,
        "Solution Events");
}

//SolutionEvents.ProjectRemoved delegate handler.
//Display the UniqueName of the project that has been added.
public void ProjectRemoved(EnvDTE.Project project)
{
    System.Windows.Forms.MessageBox.Show(
        "SolutionEvents.ProjectRemoved\nProject: " +
        project.UniqueName, "Solution Events");
}

//SolutionEvents.ProjectRemoved delegate handler.
//Display the UniqueName of the project that has been renamed,
// and the full path file before it was renamed.
public void ProjectRenamed(EnvDTE.Project project, string oldName)
{
    System.Windows.Forms.MessageBox.Show(
        "SolutionEvents.ProjectRenamed\nProject: " +
        project.UniqueName
        + "\nOld project name: " + oldName, "Solution Events");
}

//SolutionEvents.QueryCloseSolution delegate handler.
//Asks if closing the solution should be canceled.
public void QueryCloseSolution(ref bool cancel)
{
    if(System.Windows.Forms.MessageBox.Show(
        "SolutionEvents.QueryCloseSolution\nContinue with close?",
        "Solution Events",
        System.Windows.Forms.MessageBoxButtons.YesNo) ==
        System.Windows.Forms.DialogResult.Yes)

        cancel = false;
    else
        cancel = true;
}

//SolutionEvents.QueryCloseSolution delegate handler.
//Displays the full path the solution before and after it was renamed.
public void Renamed(string oldName)
{
    System.Windows.Forms.MessageBox.Show(
        "SolutionEvents.Renamed\nNew solution name: " +
```

```
                applicationObject.Solution.FullName + "\nOld solution name: "
                + oldName, "Solution Events");
        }

        private _DTE applicationObject;
        private AddIn addInInstance;

        //The delegate handler variable:
        private EnvDTE.SolutionEvents solutionEvents;
    }
}
```

Lab: Bug with Events Being Disconnected?

Over the years, I've often been asked if there is a bug with events because events can be unexpectedly lost and no longer fire even if code to disconnect an event is never run. This problem is due to a common programming mistake that reveals itself because of how the garbage collector works in the .NET Framework. Look at the following code, which connects to the solution renamed event:

```
public void ConnectSolutionEvents()
{
    EnvDTE.SolutionEvents solutionEvents;
    solutionEvents = (EnvDTE.SolutionEvents)
    applicationObject.Events.SolutionEvents;
    solutionEvents.Renamed += new
        _dispSolutionEvents_RenamedEventHandler(Renamed);
}
```

When this method is called to connect to the *Renamed* event, the *solutionEvents* variable is assigned to an instance of the *SolutionEvents* object. But the *solutionEvents* variable is local to the *ConnectSolutionEvents* method and, as a result, when *ConnectSolutionEvents* returns to the caller, *solutionEvents* is marked as available to be garbage collected. Usually the event fires once or twice, but when the garbage collector starts working, it sees that this variable can be removed from memory and removes it, thus disconnecting the event handler. To make your event handler code work correctly, you should move the *solutionEvents* variable outside the method and to class scope. This will ensure that the event handler isn't collected until the class is unloaded. Also note that this behavior applies to all event handlers when they're connected using the .NET Framework, not just the *Solution Renamed* event.

Solution Add-ins

As you saw in Chapter 6, Visual Studio .NET lets you write customization code by creating add-ins. Once you load an add-in, it will continue to run until you unload it or Visual Studio .NET is closed. Just as Visual Studio .NET can load and run add-ins, solutions can do so as well. As Visual Studio .NET starts to load a solution, it examines the solution file to see whether it contains a reference to any add-ins. If it does, it loads those add-ins and calls the same methods on the *IDTExtensibility2* interface (*OnConnection*, *OnDisconnection*, and so forth) as appropriate, just as if the add-in were loaded as a nonsolution add-in.

Creating a solution add-in can offer some benefits over creating a nonsolution add-in, such as when an add-in should be available only when a specific solution is open and running. For example, suppose you want to keep track of how many times a build of a solution is performed. You could create an add-in that would be loaded in the traditional way, but if the add-in were to count the number of times a specific solution is built, having this add-in loaded all the time would waste system resources.

The Add-in Wizard doesn't offer any options for creating solution add-ins, but by creating a nonsolution add-in and making a few modifications, you can generate all the necessary basic code. The only difference between a nonsolution add-in and a solution add-in is in how Visual Studio .NET is told to load the add-in. A standard add-in stores information in the registry; solution add-ins store their information directly in the solution (.sln) file. Knowing this, you can easily change the output for a standard add-in into a solution add-in. The first step is to run the Add-in Wizard, selecting the appropriate language but not changing any of the other options from their default. After the wizard finishes running and generating code, you delete the setup project for that add-in project. The setup project is used mainly to populate the system registry with values, and because these values aren't needed for a solution add-in, the setup project isn't necessary.

> **Note** If you follow these steps to create a solution add-in, this add-in will be available for loading as a nonsolution add-in on your development computer because the wizard creates the registry keys for a standard add-in when the code is generated. Having these extra keys in the system registry might be a little awkward for the developer of the solution add-in, but it won't cause any unwanted effects for the user of the solution add-in. If you do not want to clutter the Add-in Manager dialog box or if you want to remove the possibility of accidentally loading the solution add-in as a nonsolution add-in, you can safely remove these keys.

The next step is to register the add-in with the solution file. The property *Solution.AddIns* returns an *AddIns* collection—the same one that is returned from the *DTE.AddIns* property except that this collection contains only the add-ins registered with the solution file. To register the add-in with the solution, you use the *AddIns.Add* method, which has the following method signature and parameters:

```
public EnvDTE.AddIn Add(string ProgID, string Description, string Name,
    bool Connected)
```

Here's what the arguments that are passed to this method mean:

- ***ProgID*** The COM ProgID of the add-in to be associated with the solution.
- ***Description*** A description of the add-in. This value is used only for note keeping and isn't used by Visual Studio .NET.
- ***Name*** A short name for the add-in. Like the description, this value isn't used by Visual Studio .NET.
- ***Connected*** If this value is set to *true*, the add-in will be loaded after being associated with the solution and will be loaded again whenever the solution is reopened. If this value is *false*, the add-in will be associated with the solution but won't be loaded, and it won't be loaded when the solution is reopened.

Because you can't associate an add-in with a solution file through the registry—you must use code—you must decide on a way of running the code to insert the add-in into the solution. If it is running in a shared environment in which the source code is checked into a source code control system (such as Microsoft Visual SourceSafe), the project administrator can write and run a macro with the appropriate code and then check in the solution file, thus making the add-in load for everyone the next time the latest version of the solution is retrieved from source code control. Another approach is to create a wizard that makes the appropriate call to *AddIns.Add* after generating the code for the project. The easiest approach, however, might be to use something similar to the Add-in Manager dialog box to manage solution add-ins.

Visual Studio .NET doesn't provide a solution add-in manager, but you can build one using an add-in (a standard add-in, not a solution add-in). The SolutionAddinManager add-in, which is among the book's sample files, adds a command to the shortcut menu for the solution node in Solution Explorer. Choosing this command displays a dialog box in which you can load, unload, add, and remove solution add-ins.

Working with Project Items

Solutions manage a number of projects, and each project manages the files that are built into a program. Each project contains files that can be enumerated and programmed.

Enumerating Project Items

Files within a project are arranged hierarchically. A project can contain any number of files and one or more folders, which themselves can contain additional files and folders. To match this project hierarchy, the project object model is also arranged hierarchically, with the *ProjectItems* collection representing the nodes that contain items and the *ProjectItem* object representing each item within this collection. To enumerate this hierarchy, you use the *ProjectItems* and *ProjectItem* objects. The following macro walks the first level of the hierarchy of the *ProjectItems* and *ProjectItem* objects by obtaining the top-level *ProjectItems* object using the *Project.ProjectItems* property:

```
Sub EnumTopLevelProjectItems()
    Dim projItem As EnvDTE.ProjectItem
    Dim projectProjectItems As EnvDTE.ProjectItems
    Dim project As EnvDTE.Project

    'Find the first project in a solution:
    project = DTE.Solution.Projects.Item(1)
    'Retrieve the collection of project items:
    projectProjectItems = project.ProjectItems
    'Walk the list of items in the collection:
    For Each projItem In projectProjectItems
        MsgBox(projItem.Name)
    Next
End Sub
```

Some items within a project, such as a folder, are both an item within the project hierarchy and a container of other files and folders. Because these folders are both items and collections of items, a folder is represented in the project model hierarchy with both a *ProjectItem* object and a *ProjectItems* object. You can determine whether a *ProjectItem* node is also a container of more *ProjectItem* nodes by calling the *ProjectItem.ProjectItems* property, which returns a *ProjectItems* collection if the node can contain subitems. You can enumerate all the *ProjectItem* and *ProjectItems* objects within a project by writing a recursive macro function such as this:

```
Sub EnumProjectItems(ByVal projItems As EnvDTE.ProjectItems)
    Dim projItem As EnvDTE.ProjectItem
    'Find all the ProjectItem objects in the given collection:
    For Each projItem In projItems
        MsgBox(projItem.Name)
        'And walk any items the current item may contain:
        EnumProjectItems(projItem.ProjectItems)
    Next
End Sub

Sub EnumProject()
    Dim project As EnvDTE.Project
    'Find the first project in a solution:
    project = DTE.Solution.Projects.Item(1)
    EnumProjectItems(project.ProjectItems)
End Sub
```

The *EnumProject* macro first finds the *ProjectItems* collection of a given project, and then it calls the *EnumProjectItems* subroutine, which will find all the *ProjectItem* objects that the collection contains. If the *ProjectItem* object is itself a collection, it will recursively call the *EnumProjectItems* subroutine to display the items it contains.

Folders aren't the only items that can contain a collection of *ProjectItem* objects. Some files, such as Windows Forms and Web Forms files, are also collections of files. Each of these file types has associated resource files (in the form of .resx files), and Web Forms files also have an associated code-behind file. In the default state, Solution Explorer won't give any indication of whether these files are containers for other files, but you can modify it to show the files that these file types contain. Choose Show All Files from the Project menu to show all form files as expandable in the tree view that makes up Solution Explorer. When the *EnumProject* macro (shown earlier) is run, the *ProjectItem.ProjectItems* property returns a collection that contains the *ProjectItem* objects for these subitems. Code such as the *EnumProject* macro will return the same values whether or not the Show All Files menu command has been selected. This command affects only the Solution Explorer user interface.

You can combine the techniques for enumerating files and files within folders to find a specific item within a project. Suppose you've created a Windows Forms application solution and modified the project to look like that shown in Figure 8-1.

Figure 8-1 A Windows Forms application with nested resources

Using the *ProjectItem* object and *ProjectItems* collection, you can write a macro such as the following to locate the Bitmap1.bmp file:

```
Sub FindBitmap()
    Dim project As EnvDTE.Project
    Dim projectProjectItems As EnvDTE.ProjectItems
    Dim resourcesProjectItem As EnvDTE.ProjectItem
    Dim resourcesProjectItems As EnvDTE.ProjectItems
    Dim bitmapsProjectItem As EnvDTE.ProjectItem
    Dim bitmapsProjectItems As EnvDTE.ProjectItems
    Dim bitmapProjectItem As EnvDTE.ProjectItem

    'Get the project:
    project = DTE.Solution.Item(1)
    'Get the list of items in the project:
    projectProjectItems = project.ProjectItems
    'Get the item for the Resources folder:
    resourcesProjectItem = projectProjectItems.Item("Resources")
    'Get the collection of items in the Resources folder:
    resourcesProjectItems = resourcesProjectItem.ProjectItems
    'Get the item for the Bitmaps folder:
    bitmapsProjectItem = resourcesProjectItems.Item("Bitmaps")
    'Get the collection of items in the Bitmaps folder:
    bitmapsProjectItems = bitmapsProjectItem.ProjectItems
    'Get the item for the Bitmap1.bmp file:
    bitmapProjectItem = bitmapsProjectItems.Item("Bitmap1.bmp")
    MsgBox(bitmapProjectItem.Name)
End Sub
```

You can walk down the tree of the *ProjectItem* and *ProjectItems* hierarchy to find a specific file, but sometimes you might need a quicker and easier way of locating the *ProjectItem* object for a file with a specific filename in a project. You can use the *FindProjectItem* method of the *Solution* object to find an item by passing a portion of the file path to where the file is located on disk. For example, suppose two add-in projects have been created (using the Add-in Wizard) in a folder you created called Addins located in the root of drive C. Each of these two add-ins, MyAddin1 and MyAddin2, contains a file named Connect.cs. You could use the following macro to locate the Connect.cs file in either project:

```
Sub FindItem()
    Dim projectItem As EnvDTE.ProjectItem
    projectItem = DTE.Solution.FindProjectItem("Connect.cs")
End Sub
```

However, because *FindProjectItem* returns any file that matches this filename, you can't tell which *ProjectItem* will be returned—the *ProjectItem* object for the Connect.cs in MyAddin1 or the *ProjectItem* object for Connect.cs in MyAddin2. To refine the search, you can supply a bit more of the file path as the specified filename, as shown in the following macro, which adds the name of the folder on disk that contains the MyAddin1 version of Connect.cs:

```
Sub FindItemWithFolder()
    Dim projectItem As EnvDTE.ProjectItem
    projectItem = DTE.Solution.FindProjectItem("MyAddin1\Connect.cs")
End Sub
```

Of course, just as you can specify a portion of the path to find the *ProjectItem*, you can use the whole path to zero in on the exact item you want:

```
Sub FindItemWithFullPath()
    Dim projectItem As EnvDTE.ProjectItem
    projectItem = _
        DTE.Solution.FindProjectItem("C:\Addins\MyAddin1\Connect.cs")
End Sub
```

Adding and Removing Project Items

You can add new files to a project in two ways. The first way is to use the *AddFromDirectory*, *AddFromFile*, *AddFromFileCopy*, and *AddFromTemplate* methods of the *ProjectItems* interface (which we'll discuss in more detail in Chapter 9). The second way is to use the *ItemOperations* object. This object offers a number of file manipulation methods to help make working with files easier. The difference between using the methods of the *ProjectItems* object and the methods of *ItemOperations* is that the *ProjectItems* object gives an add-in or a macro more fine-grained control over where within a project the new file is created. The *ItemOperations* object is more user-interface-oriented; it adds the new file to the project or folder that is selected in Solution Explorer, or, if a file is selected, it adds the item to the project or the folder containing that file. These features help make macro recording possible. If you start the macro recorder and add a file using Solution Explorer, a call to one of the methods of the *ItemOperations* object is recorded into the macro. The selected item is where files are added when the proper method is called.

One method of the *ItemOperations* object, *AddExistingItem*, takes as its only argument the path to a file on disk and adds this file to the selected project or folder within a project. Depending on the type of project, the file might be copied to the project folder before being added or a reference might be added to the file without copying the file. Visual Basic .NET and C# projects are folder-based, which means that the project hierarchy shown in Solution Explorer is mirrored on disk, and any files within the project must be in the folder containing the project or in one of its subfolders. Visual C++ projects work a little differently: a file that is part of the project can be located anywhere on disk, and it doesn't need to be within the folder containing the project or a child folder. For instance, suppose a file named file.txt is located in the C:\ root folder. If we run the macro

```
Sub AddExistingItem()
    DTE.ItemOperations.AddExistingItem("C:\file.txt")
End Sub
```

and the item selected in Solution Explorer is a C# or a Visual Basic .NET project or one of its children, file.txt will be copied into the folder or subfolder containing the project file, and then added to the project. But if the selected item is a Visual C++ project, the file will be left in place and a reference will be added to this file.

While *AddExistingItem* inserts a file from disk into a project, *AddNewItem* creates a new file and adds it to the project. This method takes two arguments and has the following method signature:

```
public EnvDTE.ProjectItem AddNewItem(string Item = "General\Text File",
    string Name = "")
```

You can add a new item through the user interface by right-clicking a project and choosing Add | Add New Item from the shortcut menu item, which brings up the Add New Item dialog box. When you perform these steps for a C# project, you'll see the dialog box shown in Figure 8-2.

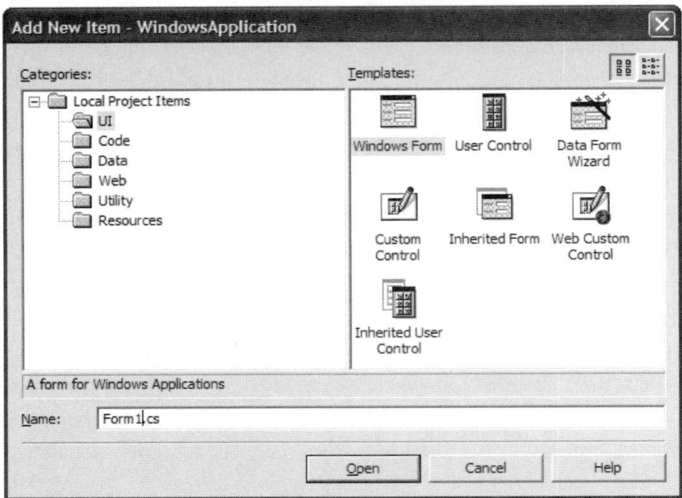

Figure 8-2 The Add New Item dialog box for a C# project

The Add New Item dialog box is related to the *AddNewItem* method in that the first parameter of *AddNewItem* is the type of file to be added and you can find this file type using the dialog box. The file type is calculated by taking the path to the item selected in the tree view, with each portion of the path separated by a backslash, and then taking the title of the item in the list on the right side of the dialog box. So, for example, when a Windows Forms file is added to the project, the top-most node of the tree view (Local Project Items) is concatenated with the backslash character. Next, the string "*UI*" is appended to this string because it is the tree node that contains the Windows Forms item to be added, followed by another backslash. Finally, the name of the item shown in the right panel of the dialog box, the string *"Windows Form"* is added, resulting in the string that can be passed to *AddNewItem*: *"Local Project Items\UI\Windows Form"*. The second argument of this method is simply the name of the file to create, with the file extension. If the filename parameter passed is an empty string, a default file name is generated and used.

You might occasionally need to remove an item that has been added to a project because you no longer need it. The *ProjectItem* object supports two methods for removing items from the project, *Remove* and *Delete*. These two methods both remove an item from the project, but *Delete* is more destructive because it also erases the file from disk by moving it into the computer's Recycle Bin.

Working with Language-Specific Project Objects

The Visual Studio .NET project object model was designed to provide functionality common to all project types. However, some projects can support additional, unique functionality. For example, a C# project has a references node within its project, but a Setup project does not. If you could programmatically add and remove these references, you'd get a lot of flexibility in writing add-ins, macros, and wizards. To enable such project-specific programming, the Visual Studio .NET project object model is extensible, allowing each project type to offer additional methods and properties beyond those defined by the *Project* object.

You can access the specific object type by using the *Object* property of the *Project* object. This property returns an object of type *System.Object*, which you can convert to the object model type supported by a specific language. The most commonly used project extension is the *VSProject* object, which is available for a Visual Basic .NET or C# project types.

VSProject Projects

VSLangProj.VSProject is the interface that defines extensions to the *EnvDTE.Project* object for Visual Basic .NET or C# projects. Once you've retrieved the *EnvDTE.Project* interface for one of these project types, you can get to the *VSLangProj.VSProject* interface by calling the *Project.Object* property. The following macro code, which assumes that the first project in the *Projects* collection is a Visual Basic or C# project, retrieves the *VSProject* object for that project:

```
Sub GetVSProject()
    Dim project As EnvDTE.Project
    Dim vsproject As VSLangProj.VSProject
    project = DTE.Solution.Projects.Item(1)
    vsproject = CType(project.Object, VSLangProj.VSProject)
End Sub
```

References

References are pointers to software components that a project can use to reduce the amount of code a programmer needs to write. A project uses the type information contained within a reference to display information in the form of IntelliSense statement completion. A reference also provides information to the compiler for resolving symbols used in programming code. A reference can be an assembly or another project loaded into the solution, and you can create references to COM components by wrapping the COM object type information library with an interop assembly. You can add references through the user interface by right-clicking the References node in a Visual Basic or C# project, choosing Add Reference from the shortcut menu, and then selecting a component in the dialog box that appears.

Using the *VSLangProj.References* object, you can enumerate, add, or remove references. To get to the *References* object, you use the *VSProject.References* property. For example, the following code retrieves the *References* object and then enumerates the references that have been added to a project:

```
Sub EnumReferences()
    Dim proj As EnvDTE.Project
    Dim vsproj As VSLangProj.VSProject
    Dim references As VSLangProj.References
    Dim reference As VSLangProj.Reference
    proj = DTE.Solution.Projects.Item(1)
    vsproj = proj.Object
    references = vsproj.References
    For Each reference In references
        MsgBox(reference.Name)
    Next
End Sub
```

You add a reference to an assembly by calling the *References.Add* method and passing the path to the assembly. The *Add* method copies the assembly into the project output folder unless a copy of the assembly with the same version and public key information is stored in the global assembly cache (GAC). This is done so that when the project output is run or loaded by another assembly, the correct assembly referenced can be loaded. The following macro code adds a reference to an assembly:

```
Sub AddReferenceToAssembly()
    Dim vsproj As VSLangProj.VSProject
    Dim proj As EnvDTE.Project
    proj = DTE.Solution.Projects.Item(1)
    vsproj = CType(proj.Object, VSLangProj.VSProject)
    vsproj.References.Add("C:\Program Files\Microsoft Visual Studio .NET " _
        & "2003\Common7\IDE\PublicAssemblies\extensibility.dll")
End Sub
```

This code finds the *VSProject* object for a project and then adds a reference to the Extensibility.dll metadata assembly (assuming that the default installation location of Visual Studio .NET was used)—the same assembly that contains the definition of the *IDTExtensibility2* interface, which is used for building add-ins. You can't add assemblies located within the GAC as references to a project because the Visual Basic and C# project systems maintain a separation between the files that are referenced for building against and files that are used during a component's run time.

During development, a component that is compiled by one project in a solution might be needed by a component in another project. You can create a reference from one project to another project by using the *References.AddProject* method. This method accepts a *Project* object and adds a reference to that project, as shown here:

```
Sub AddProjectReference()
    Dim vsproj As VSLangProj.VSProject
    Dim proj As EnvDTE.Project
    'Find the project the reference will be added to:
    proj = DTE.Solution.Projects.Item(1)
    vsproj = CType(proj.Object, VSLangProj.VSProject)
    'Find the referenced project:
    proj = DTE.Solution.Projects.Item(2)
    'Make the project to project reference:
    vsproj.References.AddProject(proj)
End Sub
```

Adding a reference to a COM object requires a few values that are COM-centric and might not be very intuitive to the non-COM programmer: the type library GUID, or library identifier (LIBID), of the type library that defines the COM component, and the version major and minor values of that type library. Using these values, you can add a reference to the type library of a COM component, and Visual Studio .NET will automatically create an interop assembly for that type library. The following macro code adds a reference to the type library for Windows Media Player:

```
Sub AddCOMReference()
    Dim vsproj As VSLangProj.VSProject
    Dim proj As EnvDTE.Project
    proj = DTE.Solution.Projects.Item(1)
    vsproj = CType(proj.Object, VSLangProj.VSProject)
    vsproj.References.AddActiveX( _
        "{22D6F304-B0F6-11D0-94AB-0080C74C7E95}", 1, 0)
End Sub
```

Web References

The .NET Framework not only makes traditional software development easier, but it also makes new software development methodologies possible. One of these new methodologies involves XML Web services. XML Web services enable software development across the Internet by placing software code on a server, which can then be accessed by software that is run on the user's computer. Visual Studio .NET makes connecting desktop software to XML Web services as easy as adding a Web reference. When a reference to an XML Web service is made, a special file written using the Web Services Description Language (WSDL) file is downloaded from the server computer and a proxy class (a class that contains the logic to translate a method or property call from the client computer across the Internet to the server computer) is generated from the WSDL file. This proxy class can then be used to call to the XML Web service.

The following macro adds a Web reference to a project. It retrieves the *VSProject* object for a project and then calls the *AddWebReference* method with the URL for the XML Web service. This example uses the TerraServer Web service provided by Microsoft, which offers detailed geographic information and satellite images for the United States. This Web service is located at *http://terraserver.homeadvisor.msn.com/TerraService.asmx*

```
Sub AddTerraServerWebRef()
    Dim vsProj As VSLangProj.VSProject
    Dim serviceURL As String
    'Set the URL to the TerraServer web service
    serviceURL = "http://terraserver.microsoft.net/TerraService.asmx"
    'Find the VSProject for a project
    vsProj = DTE.Solution.Projects.Item(1).Object
    'Add the web reference
    vsProj.AddWebReference(serviceURL)
End Sub
```

When this Web reference is made, the WSDL file describing the XML Web service is downloaded from the server computer and the proxy class for the service is generated and automatically added to the project. This class is placed in a namespace defined by the server's URL, but in reverse order. So, for example, if the XML Web service were located at *www.microsoft.com*, the namespace for the service would be *com.microsoft.www*. In this example, TerraServer is located at the server URL *terraserver.homeadvisor.msn.com* so the namespace used is *com.msn.homeadvisor.terraserver*. Once a reference to an XML Web service has been added to a project, using that service is as easy as calling methods on the generated proxy class.

Lab: Using an XML Web Service

While working on this book, I bought an electronic telescope that can automatically find and point to stars. But before I could use it, I needed to program the telescope with the latitude and longitude of my location—Redmond, Washington. But how could I find this information? The solution was to write a small program that can be run on any computer with an Internet connection to find my location through the TerraServer XML Web service—a kind of cheap, Web-enabled GPS locator.

After creating a new C# console application and adding a reference to the TerraServer Web service, I had all the pieces necessary to find the location of a city anywhere within the United Sates. To find a location, a variable of type *Place,* which is filled in with the name of a city, state, and country, is passed to the *TerraService.GetPlaceFacts* method. This method returns an object of type *PlaceFacts*, which holds, among other data, the latitude and longitude of the specified city. The following code is the same code I used to find my geographic location; all you do to find the latitude and longitude of your own location is to change the strings for the city, state, and country.

```
static void Main(string[] args)
{
    //Declare variables:
    com.msn.homeadvisor.terraserver.PlaceFacts placeFacts;
    com.msn.homeadvisor.terraserver.TerraService terraService;
    com.msn.homeadvisor.terraserver.Place place;

    //Create the necessary objects:
    terraService = new com.msn.homeadvisor.terraserver.TerraService();
    place = new com.msn.homeadvisor.terraserver.Place();

    //Find the Latitude and Longitude for Redmond, Washington:
    place.City = "Redmond";
    place.State = "Washington";
    place.Country = "USA";

    //Call to the web service, retrieving the requested information:
    placeFacts = terraService.GetPlaceFacts(place);

    //Display the information to the console:
    System.Console.Write(place.City + " Latitude and Longitude: ");
    System.Console.Write(placeFacts.Center.Lat.ToString());
    System.Console.Write(" ");
    System.Console.WriteLine(placeFacts.Center.Lon.ToString());
}
```

Imports

To make the programmer's life easier, Visual Basic .NET and C# source code can contain *using* and *Imports* statements to shorten the identifiers used to access the namespace defined by a library of code. For example, to display a message box, you could use the longer, more specific identifier to resolve to a class name:

```
System.Windows.Forms.MessageBox.Show("Hello World")
```

But if this code were repeated a number of times, you'd have to type the namespace identifier over and over, which could lead to programming errors. You can use an *Imports* statement in Visual Basic to shorten what you have to type:

```
Imports System.Windows.Forms
```

Later in the program, you can use this shorter form of the code:

```
MessageBox.Show("Hello World")
```

Visual Basic also allows you to enter import statements through a project's Property Pages dialog box (Figure 8-3) rather than typing the *Imports* statement into the source code. By using the dialog box instead of typing the statement into code, you can make the imports available for all the files within the project, not just the file that uses the *Imports* statement.

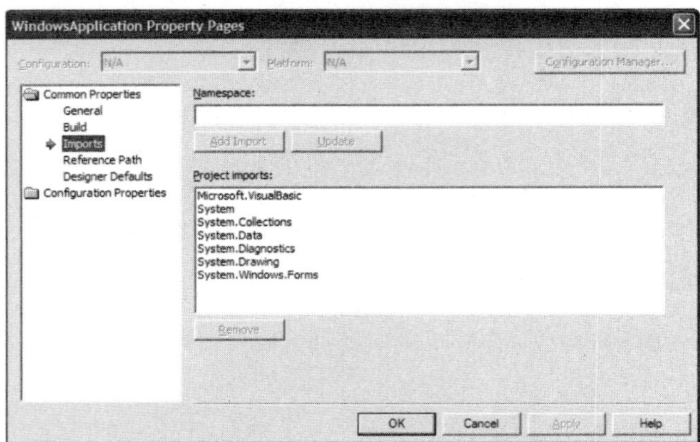

Figure 8-3 Entering import statements through the project's Property Pages dialog box

Using the *VSProject.Imports* collection, you can enumerate, remove, and add imports for the entire project. The following macro adds the *System.XML* namespace to a Visual Basic .NET project:

```
Sub AddSystemXMLImport()
    Dim vsProj As VSLangProj.VSProject
    Dim vsImports As VSLangProj.Imports
    vsProj = DTE.Solution.Projects.Item(1).Object
    vsProj.Imports.Add("System.Xml")
End Sub
```

> **Note** The *Imports* object is valid only for the Visual Basic .NET project type. Any attempt to access this object for another project type will return *null* if you're using C# to access this object or will return *Nothing* if you're using Visual Basic .NET.

ProjectProperties

Each project has a number of options associated with it that allow you to control how you interact with that project. You can set these options under the Common Properties node of a project's Property Pages dialog box. The options include the name of the component that the compiler should build, the kind of project to be generated (an .exe or a .dll), and layout options for the HTML designer. You can also set these options programmatically by using the *Properties* property of the *Project* object. This property returns the same *Properties* object that's used throughout Visual Studio .NET to set options. The following macro walks the list of properties available to a project as well as the values and types of each property:

```
Sub WalkVSProjectProperties()
    Dim project As EnvDTE.Project
    Dim properties As EnvDTE.Properties
    Dim [property] As EnvDTE.Property
    Dim owp As InsideVSNET.Utilities.OutputWindowPaneEx
    owp = New InsideVSNET.Utilities.OutputWindowPaneEx(DTE, _
        "Project properties")
    project = DTE.Solution.Projects.Item(1)
    properties = project.Properties
    For Each [property] In properties
        owp.WriteLine("Name: " + [property].Name)
        owp.WriteLine("Value: " + [property].Value.ToString())
        owp.WriteLine("Type: " + [property].Value.GetType().FullName)
        owp.WriteLine()
    Next
End Sub
```

You can use this *Property* object not only to read the values of properties but also to set the properties for a project. The following macro demonstrates this. It sets the icon to use for a project when it is compiled. This code assumes that an icon named Icon.ico is located in the folder containing the project file.

```
Sub SetProjectIcon()
    Dim project As EnvDTE.Project
    Dim [property] As EnvDTE.Property
    Dim projectPath As String
    project = DTE.Solution.Projects.Item(1)
    'Get the Property object for the icon:
    [property] = project.Properties.Item("ApplicationIcon")
    'Construct the path to the icon based off of the
    ' project path:
    projectPath = project.FullName
    projectPath = System.IO.Path.GetDirectoryName(projectPath)
    projectPath = projectPath + "\Icon.ico"
```

(continued)

```
    'Set the icon for the project:
    [property].Value = projectPath
End Sub
```

Leveraging Visual Studio .NET Utility Project Types

To help you more easily maintain files within a solution, Visual Studio .NET makes available various utility projects. These utility projects allow you to keep track of files that are not part of any other project that is loaded into a solution. Because any file type can be stored within these projects, such as program source files and Microsoft Word documents, these projects can't be compiled into a program. And because utility projects are part of Visual Studio .NET and are not associated with any particular programming language, they are available to all users of Visual Studio .NET and don't require Visual Basic .NET, C#, or Visual C++ to be installed.

Miscellaneous Files Project

When you're working with a solution, you might need to open files that are not part of an existing project. When you open such a file, it is automatically added to a project called Miscellaneous Files. A project file isn't created on disk for this project, as with other project types, but you get a convenient way of locating files that are open but are not part of any other project that is open within the solution. You can think of the Miscellaneous Files project as a list of most recently used open documents—when you open a file, an item for that file is added to the project, and when you close the file, it is removed. By default, the Miscellaneous Files project and the files it contains don't appear in the Solution Explorer tree hierarchy, but you can easily make them visible by opening the Tools Options dialog box, selecting the Environment | Documents node, and selecting the Show Miscellaneous Files In Solution Explorer check box.

The Miscellaneous Files project has a unique name associated with it that, unlike with other projects, doesn't change over time. This name, "<MiscFiles>", is defined by the constant *vsMiscFilesProjectUniqueName*. The following macro retrieves the *Project* object for the Miscellaneous Files project:

```
Sub FindMiscFilesProject()
    Dim project As EnvDTE.Project
    Dim projects As EnvDTE.Projects
    projects = DTE.Solution.Projects
    project = projects.Item(EnvDTE.Constants.vsMiscFilesProjectUniqueName)
End Sub
```

When the first file is opened within the Miscellaneous Files project, an item is added to the *Solution.Projects* collection that implements the *Project* interface. It works just like the *Project* interface implemented by projects such as Visual Basic .NET or C# projects, except that a few of the properties will return *null* or *Nothing* or throw a *System.NotImplementedException* when called. Table 8-1 lists the methods and properties of the *Project* object that return a meaningful value for the Miscellaneous Files project and the *ProjectItem* and *ProjectItems* objects contained within this project.

Table 8-1 Methods and Properties of the *Project*, *ProjectItems*, and *ProjectItem* Objects

Project	*ProjectItems*	*ProjectItem*
DTE	*DTE*	*DTE*
ProjectItems	*Parent*	*Collection*
Name (read-only)	*Item*	*Name* (read-only)
UniqueName	*GetEnumerator* / *_NewEnum*	*FileCount*
Kind	*Kind*	*Kind*
FullName	*Count*	*FileNames*
	ContainingProject	*SaveAs*
		Save
		IsOpen
		Open
		Delete
		Remove
		ExpandView
		ContainingProject
		IsDirty

You can add new files to the Miscellaneous Files project using the *ItemOperations.NewFile* method, which has the following method signature:

```
public EnvDTE.Window NewFile(string Item = "General\Text File",
    string Name = "", string ViewKind =
    "{00000000-0000-0000-0000-000000000000}")
```

By applying the techniques we used earlier to calculate the first parameter for the *ItemOperations.AddNewItem*, we can find the value that should be passed to the *NewFile* method. The second parameter also has the same meaning as the second parameter of the *ItemOperations.AddNewItem* method—the name of the file (with extension) that is to be added—and if the empty string is passed, a default name is calculated. The last argument specifies which view the file should be opened in when it is added. These values can be found within the *EnvDTE.Constants* class and begin with the name *vsViewKind*.

Solution Items Project

The Solution Items project works in a similar way to the Miscellaneous Files project but with a few small differences. Files that are opened in the Miscellaneous Files project are removed from that project when the solution is closed; items added to the Solution Items project stay with that project even after the solution is closed. Because these files stay within the project, you can think of the Solution Items project as a housekeeping project because you can keep items such as documentation, notes, and other files you might use in this project for easy access. Like the Miscellaneous Files project, the Solution Items project can't be built but supports an *EnvDTE.Project* object (with limited functionality, however). The same methods and properties shown in Table 8-1 apply to the Solution Items project. Also like the Miscellaneous Files project, the Solution Items project reserves a unique name for indexing the *Solution.Projects* collection, so you can find the Solution Items project within the list of projects maintained by the solution. You can use this constant, *vsSolutionItemsProjectUniqueName*, as shown in the following example:

```
Sub FindSolutionItemsProject()
    Dim project As EnvDTE.Project
    Dim projects As EnvDTE.Projects
    projects = DTE.Solution.Projects
    project = projects.Item( _
        EnvDTE.Constants.vsSolutionItemsProjectUniqueName)
End Sub
```

You add items to the Solution Items project by calling the *AddNewItem* and *AddExistingItem* methods of the *ItemOperations* object. This means you must first select the Solution Items project within Solution Explorer. And because the Solution Items project can be created only by the user manually adding a file to the project, you must be sure that the project exists before you attempt to add an item to it.

Unmodeled Projects

All the project types we've discussed so far have implemented a *Project* object that can be used by a macro or an add-in. However, a few project types, such as a database project or a project that has been unloaded using the Project | Unload Project command, don't implement the *Project* object themselves. To allow some programmability for these project types, Visual Studio .NET supports the unmodeled project type. An unmodeled project provides an implementation of the *Project* object that supports only the properties common among all project types, which are *DTE*, *Kind*, and *Name*. All other properties and methods on this implementation of the *Project* object return values that have no useful meaning or generate an exception when called and shouldn't be used by a macro or an add-in. You can distinguish an unmodeled project from other project types by checking the *Project.Kind* property, which returns the constant *EnvDTE.Constants.vsProjectKindUnmodeled* if the project is an unmodeled project. The following macro enumerates all the projects loaded into a solution and determines which ones are unmodeled:

```
Sub FindUnmodeledProjects()
    Dim i As Integer
    For i = 1 To DTE.Solution.Projects.Count
        Dim project As EnvDTE.Project
        project = DTE.Solution.Projects.Item(i)
        If (project.Kind = EnvDTE.Constants.vsProjectKindUnmodeled) Then
           MsgBox(project.Name + " is unmodeled")
        End If
    Next
End Sub
```

> **Note** You might notice that the *FindUnmodeledProjects* macro uses the numerical indexing method rather than the enumerator to find each project in a solution. It does this because of a bug in Visual Studio .NET that won't return a correct *Project* object when you use the enumerator. This bug applies only to unmodeled projects; using the enumerator works fine for other project types.

Project and Project Item Events

Just as a solution fires events to allow an add-in or macro to respond to the actions the user is performing, the various project types also fire events so that an add-in or a macro can be informed of what the user is doing. You connect to the events fired by the different project types in different ways, but each project type supports the same interfaces used to handle the event invocations. Each project type fires two classes of events: actions performed with the project and actions performed with the items within those projects. Here are the events and the signatures that the project will fire:

```
void ItemAdded(ByVal Project As EnvDTE.Project)
void ItemRemoved(ByVal Project As EnvDTE.Project)
void ItemRenamed(ByVal Project As EnvDTE.Project,
    ByVal OldName As String)
```

These are the available signatures of the project item events:

```
void ItemAdded(ByVal ProjectItem As EnvDTE.ProjectItem)
void ItemRemoved(ByVal ProjectItem As EnvDTE.ProjectItem)
void ItemRenamed(ByVal ProjectItem As EnvDTE.ProjectItem, _
    ByVal OldName As String)
```

Project events and project item events both fire three separate events—*ItemAdded*, *ItemRemoved*, *ItemRenamed*. These signify that a project or a project item was added, removed, or renamed, respectively.

Connecting to project items and projects events within a macro project requires more than connecting to other types of events supported by Visual Studio .NET. For example, to connect to solution events within a macro project, you first open the *EnvironmentEvents* module. Then, within this module, you select the *SolutionEvents* event object from the Class Name drop-down list on the left side of the text window and select a solution events handler method from the Method Name drop-down list. Connecting to project and project item events in a macro isn't this easy, however; you have to write a little glue code to connect the events. First, you declare the event variable by adding the following code to the *EnvironmentEvents* module. (This example uses the C# project events.)

```
<System.ContextStaticAttribute()> _
Public WithEvents csharpProjectItemsEvents As EnvDTE.ProjectItemsEvents
```

When you enter this code, an entry appears in the left drop-down list at the top of the code for the *EnvironmentEvents* macro module. Select the entry to fill the right drop-down list with the events for this object, and select each event to create the code necessary for capturing that event. At this point, the event handler won't be invoked for C# projects because the event variable, *csharpProjectItemsEvents*, has yet to be set to an instance of a *ProjectItemsEvents* object. You can set this variable to an instance of the correct event object by creating a handler for *DTEEvents.OnStartupComplete* and placing within it the code to connect to the event, much as you would within an add-in:

```
Private Sub DTEEvents_OnStartupComplete() _
    Handles DTEEvents.OnStartupComplete

    csharpProjectItemsEvents = _
        DTE.Events.GetObject("CSharpProjectItemsEvents")
End Sub
```

With this event handler in place, when Visual Studio .NET is closed and then restarted, the *OnStartupComplete* handler will be invoked, which will cause the event variable to be connected. Of course, you can insert this same code into a macro and run the macro; Visual Studio .NET doesn't need to be restarted for the event variable to be set. Here's an example of such a macro:

```
Sub ConnectCSharpProjectItemsEvents()
    csharpProjectItemsEvents = _
        DTE.Events.GetObject("CSharpProjectItemsEvents")
End Sub
```

You can connect to the project and project items events for project types other than the Miscellaneous File and Solution Items projects by changing the string passed to the *Events.GetObject* method. For example, to connect to Visual Basic .NET project and project item events, you can use the strings *VBProjectsEvents* and *VBProjectItemsEvents*. You can use the strings *VJSharpProjectsEvents* and *VJSharpProjectItemsEvents* to connect to events thrown by a Microsoft Visual J# project, and you can use *eCSharpProjectsEvents* and *eCSharpProjectItemsEvents* to capture events thrown by a C# smart device application. You can use *eVBProjectsEvents* and *eVBProjectItemsEvents* to capture events thrown by a Visual Basic .NET smart device application. The ProjectEvents sample demonstrates how to connect to all these project and project item events. It connects to the events provided by each project type, and as each event is fired, a message box is displayed containing information about that event.

Managing Build Configurations

Editing and manipulating a project is an important part of the development process, but most of your time is spent building and compiling a project, not moving around files within a project. Visual Studio .NET provides an object model for building a solution and controlling how the projects contained within that solution should be compiled. The root object for controlling how a solution should be built is named *SolutionBuild*; you access it by calling the *Solution.SolutionBuild* property, and you control how each project within the solution should be built by using the *ConfigurationManager* object, which is accessed through the *Project.ConfigurationManager* property.

Manipulating Solution Settings

Visual Studio .NET uses solution configurations to manage how a solution is built. A solution configuration is a grouping of project configurations that describe how the projects within the solution should be built. A project configuration, in the simplest terms, tells the various compilers how to create the code for a project. Each project can contain multiple project configurations that you can switch between within the solution configuration to control how the compilers build the code. The most common solution and project configurations are debug and release, which cause a project to be built with debugging information and with code optimizations, respectively. When a project such as a Windows Forms project is first created, Visual Studio .NET creates the debug solution configuration containing the Windows Forms debug project configuration and the release solution configuration containing the release Windows Forms project configuration. You can create new solution configurations that contain any of the available project configurations or new project configurations that can be loaded into any solution configuration.

SolutionConfiguration and *SolutionContext* Objects

Solution configurations are represented in the object model through the *SolutionConfigurations* collection, which contains *SolutionConfiguration* objects. Because the *SolutionConfigurations* object is a collection, you can use the standard techniques for enumerating this collection and use the *Item* method to find a specific *SolutionConfiguration* object by name. To create new solution configuration, you use the *SolutionConfigurations.Add* method, which makes a copy of an existing solution configuration and then renames it to the specified name. The signature of this method is

```
public EnvDTE.SolutionConfiguration Add(string NewName,
    string ExistingName, bool Propagate)
```

Here are the arguments that are passed to this method:

- ***NewName*** This is the name of the new solution configuration. It can't be the same as any existing solution configuration name, and it must follow the file system's file-naming rules. (It can't contain characters such as \, /, :, *, ?, ", <, or >.)
- ***ExistingName*** This is either the name of an existing solution configuration that is copied to create the new solution configuration or the string *"<Default>"*. If the name *"<Default>"* is used, the currently active solution configuration is used as the source of what is copied.
- ***Propagate*** If this parameter is *true*, when the new solution configuration is created, a copy of each project configuration referenced by the solution configuration is made and assigned the same name as the new solution configuration and each of these copies of project configurations is loaded into the new solution configuration. If this parameter is *false*, the new solution configuration is created and the same project configurations that were assigned to the solution configuration source are assigned to the new solution configuration.

The *SolutionConfiguration* object has one method and one property of note. One of these methods is named *Activate*; when a build is performed, whether through the user interface or through the object model by using the *SolutionBuild.Build* method, the currently active *SolutionConfiguration* is the configuration that is built. Therefore, activating a particular solution configuration causes any build actions to build the active solution configuration. The other item of importance is the *SolutionContexts* property. As discussed earlier, a *SolutionConfiguration* is a container of the projects within a solution and the project configuration associated with that solution configuration. The *SolutionConfiguration.SolutionContexts* property returns the list of those projects and which configuration of each project to build.

To set which project configuration is built when the solution is built, you can change the *SolutionContext* object's *ConfigurationName* to any project configuration name that the project supports. The following macro changes the debug solution configuration to build the release version of a project that is loaded into the solution:

```
Sub ChangeProjectConfiguration()
    Dim solutionBuild As EnvDTE.SolutionBuild
    Dim solutionCfgs As EnvDTE.SolutionConfigurations
    Dim solutionCfg As EnvDTE.SolutionConfiguration
    Dim solutionContext As EnvDTE.SolutionContext
    'Find the debug solution configuration:
    solutionBuild = DTE.Solution.SolutionBuild
    solutionCfgs = solutionBuild.SolutionConfigurations
    solutionCfg = solutionCfgs.Item("Debug")
    'Retrieve the solution context for the first project:
    solutionContext = solutionCfg.SolutionContexts.Item(1)
    'Change the debug solution context to build the
    ' Release project configuration:
    solutionContext.ConfigurationName = "Release"
    'Reset the build flag for this context:
    solutionContext.ShouldBuild = True
End Sub
```

Not only can you modify a *SolutionContext* to set the project configuration that should be built for a particular solution configuration, but you can also set values such as that specifying whether the project configuration should be built. This is done in the next-to-last line of the preceding macro, where the *ShouldBuild* property is set to *true*. In this macro, this property must be set because, as is expected, when the debug solution configuration is first created it doesn't contain the release project configuration. It therefore isn't set to build for that solution configuration, so when the debug solution configuration is set to build the release project configuration, that "do not build" state is carried along with it.

StartupProjects

When you start a solution running (usually by pressing the F5 key), the project builder first verifies that all the projects that need to be built are up-to-date, and then it starts walking the list of projects that are set as startup projects, running each project in turn. You can set the list of startup projects through the user interface by right-clicking the solution node in Solution Explorer and then choosing Set StartUp Projects from the shortcut menu. You'll see the Solution Property Pages dialog box (shown in Figure 8-4), in which you can set the startup projects for a solution containing four Windows Forms applications.

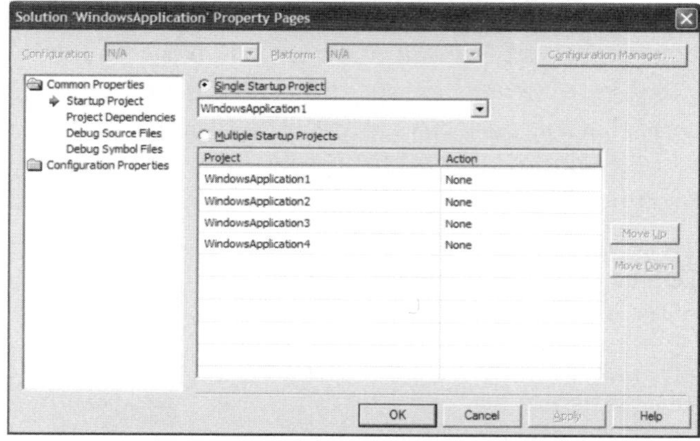

Figure 8-4 Setting the projects that will start when you run a solution

You can also set startup projects through the object model using the *SolutionBuild.StartupProjects* property. This property is set to a value of type *System.Object*, which is packed with the projects to start when you run a solution. The value passed to the *StartupProjects* property can take two forms: a single string that is the unique name of a project (which will set one single project to run) or an array of *System.Object* (which will be filled with one or more project unique names and will cause multiple projects to be run).

For example, suppose an open solution contains two projects, both of them to be designated as a startup project. You can use code such as the following to set these projects as startup projects:

```
Sub SetStartupProjects()
    Dim startupProjects(1) As Object
    startupProjects(0) = DTE.Solution.Projects.Item(1).UniqueName
    startupProjects(1) = DTE.Solution.Projects.Item(2).UniqueName
    DTE.Solution.SolutionBuild.StartupProjects = startupProjects
End Sub
```

If only one project should be set as a startup project, the code looks like this:

```
Sub SetStartupProject()
    Dim startupProject As String
    startupProject = DTE.Solution.Projects.Item(1).UniqueName
    DTE.Solution.SolutionBuild.StartupProjects = startupProject
End Sub
```

When you set the startup projects, you must be careful to supply only buildable projects. If one of the projects supplied to *SolutionBuild.StartupProjects* is, for example, the unique name for the Miscellaneous Files project or the Solution Items project, an error is generated.

> **Note** Visual Studio .NET contains a bug that affects using the *SolutionBuild.StartupProjects* property with multiple projects. When you change this property from starting only one project to starting multiple projects, the list of startup projects is modified. However, the Multiple Startup Projects option button won't be selected; you must select it yourself. Setting the *SolutionBuild.StartupProjects* property won't affect this button's state.

Project Dependencies

When you work with a solution that contains multiple projects, the components built by one project might rely on the output of another project. An example of this is a control project called UserControl, which is placed on the form of a Windows Forms application called WinForm. Because changes to the UserControl project might affect how that control is used by the Windows Forms project, the UserControl project must be compiled before the WinForm project is compiled. To enforce this relationship between the two projects, you can create a project dependency. The dependencies between two or more projects can be depicted using a dependency graph; the dependency graph for the projects WinForm and UserControl is shown in Figure 8-5. The arrow is pointing to the project that another project is dependent on.

Figure 8-5 A dependency graph showing a WinForm project dependent on a UserControl project

Suppose we add a new project to the solution—a class library called ClassLib that implements functionality used by both the WinForm and the UserControl projects. A dependency graph for this solution is shown in Figure 8-6.

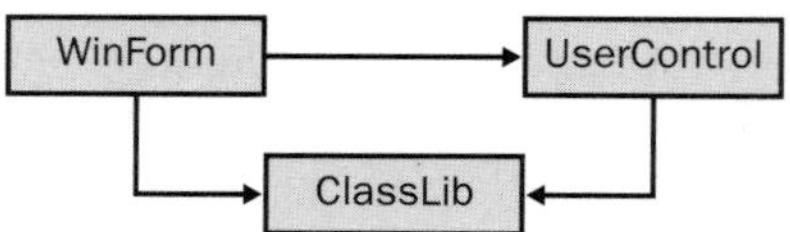

Figure 8-6 The dependency graph for three projects

You can see in this dependency graph that the WinForm project can't be built until the UserControl and ClassLib projects have been built. The UserControl project relies only on the ClassLib project being built first. When a build of this solution is started, if the build system chooses the UserControl project to start building first, this causes the ClassLib project to build. If the build system chooses the ClassLib project first, that project is built immediately because it doesn't depend on any other projects. When the UserControl project is built, the ClassLib project isn't built again because it is up-to-date. Regardless of which project the build system chooses to build first, the last project to be built is the WinForm project because it relies on the output of the other two projects.

A problem can occur with a dependency graph if you create a *cyclic dependency*, in which one or more projects are mutually dependent. Suppose the WinForm project relies on the UserControl project, the UserControl project relies on the ClassLib project, and the ClassLib project relies on the WinForm project. The cycle shown in Figure 8-7 is generated.

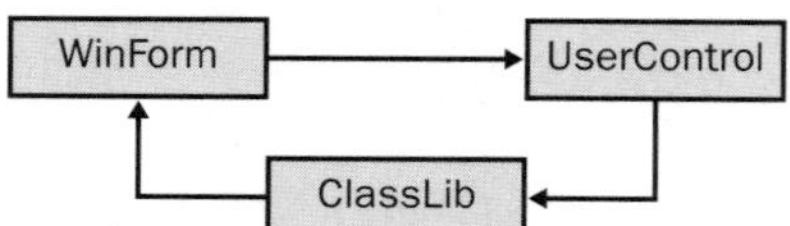

Figure 8-7 A dependency graph of three projects with a cycle

If the WinForm project is built, the build of the UserControl project is triggered because of the dependency. Building the UserControl project causes the building of the ClassLib project, which is dependent on the WinForm project. If the Visual Studio .NET build system were unable to detect this cycle, the loop would continue forever in an attempt to find the first project to build. But Visual Studio .NET is smart enough to detect dependency cycles, and it disallows them.

You can create dependencies between projects through the user interface by choosing Project | Project Dependencies, which will display the Project Dependencies dialog box (shown in Figure 8-8). The dialog box shows all the projects that can be set as a dependency for the UserControl project. The WinForm check box is shaded because a dependency is set from the WinForm project to the UserControl project and Visual Studio .NET won't allow a cycle between the WinForm project and the UserControl project to be created.

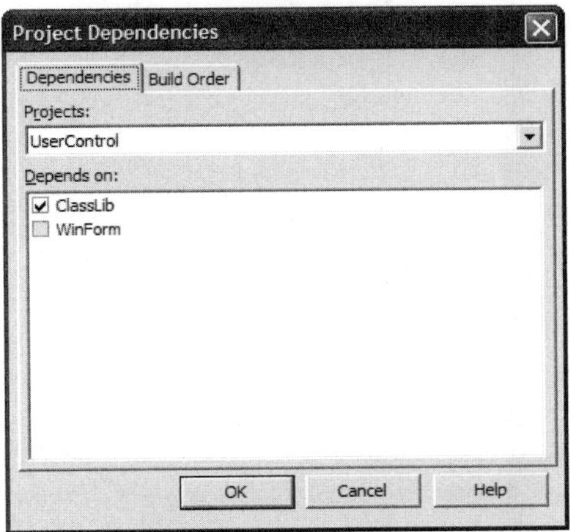

Figure 8-8 Setting project dependencies

You can also set build dependencies through the object model. The *SolutionBuild.BuildDependencies* property returns a *BuildDependencies* object, which is a collection of *BuildDependency* objects. You can index this collection using the *Item* method—you can pass a numeric index, an *EnvDTE.Project* object, or the unique name of a project. Each project in the solution has its own *EnvDTE.BuildDependency* object, whose *RequiredProjects* property you can use to add, remove, or retrieve dependencies for a project. The following macro displays in the Output window the available projects in the open solution, as well as all the projects it depends on.

```
Sub Depends()
    Dim projectDep As EnvDTE.BuildDependency
    Dim project As EnvDTE.Project
    Dim owp As New InsideVSNET.Utilities.OutputWindowPaneEx(DTE,
        "Build dependencies")

    For Each projectDep In DTE.Solution.SolutionBuild.BuildDependencies
        Dim reqProjects As Object()

        owp.Write("The project ")
        owp.Write(projectDep.Project.Name)
        owp.WriteLine(" relies on:")
```

```
            reqProjects = projectDep.RequiredProjects
            If (reqProjects.Length = 0) Then
                owp.WriteLine(vbTab + "<None>")
            Else
                For Each project In reqProjects
                    owp.WriteLine(vbTab + project.Name)
                Next
            End If
            owp.WriteLine()
        Next
    End Sub
```

Using the *BuildDependency* object, you can create a macro or an add-in that sets up the dependencies between two or more projects. Suppose, using our current example, that a solution with the projects WinForm, UserControl, and ClassLib is loaded and no dependencies have been set. The *BuildDependency* object supports three methods for modifying the projects that a project is dependent on: *AddProject*, *RemoveProject*, and *RemoveAllProjects*. *AddProject* and *RemoveProject* accept the unique name of a project that should be added or removed as a dependency for a specific project. *RemoveAllProjects* takes no arguments and removes all project dependencies. The following macro, *SetDependencies*, builds the correct dependencies for the three-project solution to conform to the dependency graph shown in Figure 8-6:

```
Sub SetDependencies()
    Dim buildDependencies As EnvDTE.BuildDependencies
    Dim buildDependency As EnvDTE.BuildDependency
    Dim project As EnvDTE.Project

    Dim winFormUniqueName As String
    Dim userControlUniqueName As String
    Dim classLibUniqueName As String

    'Gather up the unique name of each project
    For Each project In DTE.Solution.Projects
        If (project.Name = "WinForm") Then
            winFormUniqueName = project.UniqueName
        ElseIf (project.Name = "UserControl") Then
            userControlUniqueName = project.UniqueName
        ElseIf (project.Name = "ClassLib") Then
            classLibUniqueName = project.UniqueName
        End If
    Next

    buildDependencies = DTE.Solution.SolutionBuild.BuildDependencies
    For Each buildDependency In buildDependencies
```

```
        If (buildDependency.Project.Name = "WinForm") Then
            buildDependency.RemoveAllProjects()
            'Add all projects except the WinForm
            ' project as a dependency:
            buildDependency.AddProject(userControlUniqueName)
            buildDependency.AddProject(classLibUniqueName)
        ElseIf (buildDependency.Project.Name = "UserControl") Then
            buildDependency.RemoveAllProjects()
            'Add a dependency to the ClassLib project:
            buildDependency.AddProject(classLibUniqueName)
        End If
    Next
End Sub
```

Manipulating Project Settings

Solution configurations are used to group together project configurations. Each project contains a number of configurations that control how the compiler should create the program code for that project. Because a project can have multiple project configurations associated with it, you can generate different versions of a program.

ConfigurationManager Object

You manage project configurations through the *ConfigurationManager* object, which has a collection of *Configuration* objects and lets you create new configurations. Configurations for a project are arranged in a grid pattern, with the configuration type, such as debug or release, along one axis of the grid and the platform on which the configuration will be built for on the other axis. The platforms that Visual Studio .NET currently supports are Win32 for 32-bit Windows running on the x86 processor, .NET if the project is being compiled for the Microsoft .NET platform, and Pocket PC and Windows CE if the project is built for the Windows CE platforms. Because projects can build only one platform type at a time, the second axis will always have one dimension.

You can find a particular project configuration in several ways. The first way is to use the familiar *Item* method that's available on all collection objects. However, unlike other *Item* methods on most collection objects, the *ConfigurationManager.Item* method requires two parameters. The first parameter can be a numerical index and spans the entire grid of platforms and configurations. You can also use *Item* to directly locate a *Configuration* by passing the configuration name as the first parameter and the platform name as the second parameter. Suppose a Visual C++ project is open in Solution Explorer. To find the *Configuration* object for the Win32 debug build, you can use code such as the following:

```
Sub RetrieveDebugWin32Configuration()
    Dim config As Configuration
    Dim project As EnvDTE.Project
    project = DTE.Solution.Projects.Item(1)
    config = project.ConfigurationManager.Item("Debug", "Win32")
End Sub
```

Another way to retrieve specific configurations is to use the *ConfigurationManager.ConfigurationRow* and *ConfigurationManager.Platform* methods, which take the build type and the platform name, respectively. These methods return a collection of *Configuration* objects that you can iterate through to find a specific item. The *ConfigurationRow* method returns a list of all configurations with the passed name; the *Platform* method returns a list of all configurations belonging to a specific platform. These methods are most useful if you want to modify the settings of configurations that are closely related to one another, such as walking all the Win32 configurations of a Visual C++ project and enabling managed extensions, thus allowing your program to use the .NET Framework in C++ code. The following code sample does just that. After finding the Win32 configurations available to a project, it retrieves the *Properties* object for that configuration and sets the *ManagedExtension* property to *true*, allowing the compiler to generate code that can work with the .NET Framework.

```
Sub SetManagedExtensionsProperty()
    Dim configManager As ConfigurationManager
    Dim configs As Configurations
    Dim config As Configuration
    Dim project As EnvDTE.Project
    project = DTE.Solution.Projects.Item(1)
    configManager = project.ConfigurationManager
    configs = configManager.Platform("Win32")
    For Each config In configs
        Dim prop As EnvDTE.Property
        prop = config.Properties.Item("ManagedExtensions")
        prop.Value = True
    Next
End Sub
```

You can create new configurations based on an existing configuration in the same way that you can create new solution configurations by copying an existing solution configuration. You create new project configurations using the *ConfigurationManager.AddConfigurationRow* method. This method takes as its parameters the name of the new configuration and an existing configuration name, which is used as a template for creating the new configuration. *AddConfigurationRow* also accepts as an argument a *Boolean* value. This parameter, named *Propagate*, works in the same way as the *Propagate* parameter of the *SolutionConfigurations.Add* method, but in reverse. When the *SolutionConfigurations.Add* method is called with the *Propagate* parameter set to *true*, a copy of the solution configuration and all the project configurations it contains is made. If the *AddConfigurationRow* method is called with its *Propagate* parameter set to *true*, the currently active solution configuration is copied, its name is set to the name passed as the new project configuration, and the new solution configuration is modified to contain the newly created project configuration.

> **Note** The *ConfigurationManager* object contains the method *AddPlatform*, which works much like the *AddConfigurationRow* method but adds a platform row to the build type configuration grid. If you call this method for any of the current versions of the Microsoft-language products, an exception will be generated because new platforms can't be added for these project types. This doesn't mean that this method won't work for third-party programming language projects or future versions of Microsoft programming languages.

Most project types support only one platform type, and some projects, such as setup projects, do not support any platform—what is built is platform-agnostic. A setup project doesn't care whether its contents are intended for Win32 or .NET platforms; its role is to contain files to be installed onto the user's computer, so a platform is not a consideration when you build a setup project. Because the build type configuration grid can't be one-dimensional, a pseudo-platform is generated for these project types, and its name is set to *"<N/A>"*.

Project Configuration Properties

Project configurations differ in the property values that are set. For example, one difference between the debug and release configurations is that the debug configuration doesn't optimize the code, which makes debugging easier to perform, and optimization is turned on for the release configuration to make the code run faster. Such properties are set through the object returned by calling the *Configuration.Properties* property. As you saw earlier in the *SetManagedExtensionsProperty* macro example, this property returns an *EnvDTE.Properties* object—the same object that is used throughout Visual Studio .NET to set property values on various objects. The following macro retrieves the debug and release configurations for a project, reads the *Boolean Optimize* configuration property, negates it, and then stores it back into the configuration. This means that the *Optimize* property is inverted for all these configurations.

```
Sub SwapOptimizationSettings()
    Dim project As EnvDTE.Project
    Dim configManager As EnvDTE.ConfigurationManager
    Dim configs As EnvDTE.Configurations
    Dim config As EnvDTE.Configuration
    Dim props As EnvDTE.Properties

    'Find the ConfigurationManager for the project:
    project = DTE.Solution.Projects.Item(1)
    configManager = project.ConfigurationManager

    'Get the debug configuration manager
    configs = configManager.ConfigurationRow("Debug")
    'Walk each configuration in the debug configuration row
    For Each config In configs
        Dim optimize As Boolean
        'Get the Optimize property for the configuration
        props = config.Properties
        optimize = props.Item("Optimize").Value
        'Negate the value
        props.Item("Optimize").Value = Not optimize
    Next

    'Repeat for the release configuration
    configs = configManager.ConfigurationRow("Release")
    For Each config In configs
        Dim optimize As Boolean
        'Get the Optimize property for the configuration
        props = config.Properties
        optimize = props.Item("Optimize").Value
        'Negate the value
        props.Item("Optimize").Value = Not optimize
    Next

End Sub
```

Build Events

As each stage of a build is performed, Visual Studio .NET fires an event that can be captured by a macro or add-in, allowing custom code to be run. Four events are defined. Here are their signatures:

```
void OnBuildBegin(EnvDTE.vsBuildScope Scope, EnvDTE.vsBuildAction Action);
void OnBuildProjConfigBegin(string Project, string ProjectConfig,
    string Platform, string SolutionConfig);
void OnBuildProjConfigDone(string Project, string ProjectConfig,
```

```
    string Platform, string SolutionConfig, bool Success);
void OnBuildDone(EnvDTE.vsBuildScope Scope, EnvDTE.vsBuildAction Action);
```

These event handlers have the following meanings:

- ***OnBuildBegin*** This event is fired just before a build is started. Two arguments are passed to the handler of this event. The first argument is an enumeration of type *EnvDTE.vsBuildScope*, which can be either *vsBuildScopeBatch* (if you chose to start a batch build of one or more projects), *vsBuildScopeProject* (if you selected a single project to build by right-clicking on a project and choosing Build, or *vsBuildScopeSolution* (if you chose the active solution configuration to build). The second argument is of type *EnvDTE.vsBuildAction* and can be either *vsBuildActionBuild* (if the project or solution configuration is to be compiled), *vsBuildActionClean* (if the project or solution configuration's built output is to be deleted from disk), *vsBuildActionDeploy* (if the project or solution configuration is to be deployed to its target), or *vsBuildActionRebuildAll* (if the project or solution configuration is to be rebuilt, even if the project's dependencies do not warrant a rebuild).
- ***OnBuildProjConfigBegin*** This event is fired when a project's configuration starts to be built. It is passed four arguments, each of type *string*. The first argument is the unique name of the project being built, the second is the name of the configuration being built, the third is the name of the platform being built, and last is the name of the solution configuration being built.
- ***OnBuildProjConfigDone*** This event handler is fired after a project configuration has been built. It is passed the same arguments as the *OnBuildProjConfigBegin* event, with the addition of a *Boolean* value that signals whether the configuration was built successfully (*true*) or failed to build (*false*).
- ***OnBuildDone*** This event is fired after all build steps have been completed, whether successfully or unsuccessfully.

Among the samples that accompany this book is one called BuildEvents, which demonstrates connecting to each of the build events. As each event handler is called, the information passed to that event handler is displayed within the output window, which contains information about the arguments that were passed to each handler. For example, if we were to create a solution containing two projects, ClassLibrary1 and ClassLibrary2, load the sample add-in, and perform a build on the solution by choosing Build | Build Solution, the following information would be displayed:

```
OnBuildBegin
    Scope: vsBuildScopeSolution
    Action: vsBuildActionBuild

OnBuildProjConfigBegin
    Project: ClassLibrary1.csproj
    Platform: .NET
    Solution Configuration: Debug

OnBuildProjConfigDone
    Project: ClassLibrary1.csproj
    Platform: .NET
    Solution Configuration: Debug
    Success: True

OnBuildProjConfigBegin
    Project: ..\ClassLibrary2\ClassLibrary2.csproj
    Platform: .NET
    Solution Configuration: Debug

OnBuildProjConfigDone
    Project: ..\ClassLibrary2\ClassLibrary2.csproj
    Platform: .NET
    Solution Configuration: Debug
    Success: True

OnBuildDone
    Scope: vsBuildScopeSolution
    Action: vsBuildActionBuild
```

The information above outlines the steps performed to build this two-solution project. It starts with a call to the *OnBuildBegin* event handler and then builds each project configuration contained within the solution configuration, one after another, with the *OnBuildDone* event handler being fired to signal that the build process has been completed. With Visual Studio .NET 2003, the *OnBuildProjConfigBegin* and *OnBuildProjConfigEnd* events are fired one after another, with no other build events fired between them. However, a macro or add-in should not take advantage of this order of events if you plan to port this code to a future version of Visual Studio .NET because future versions might take advantage of multiprocessor computers, building one project configuration on one processor and another project configuration on another processor. If a macro or an add-in were to rely on this order of events, the code might not work properly.

Persisting Solution and Project Information Across IDE Sessions

At times, your add-in or macro might need to save some data that should be carried along with the solution or project file. The object model supports saving information into these files with the *EnvDTE.Globals* object. You can find this object by calling the *Globals* property of both of these objects:

```
Sub SolutionGlobals()
    Dim globals As EnvDTE.Globals
    globals = DTE.Solution.Globals
End Sub

Sub ProjectGlobals()
    Dim globals As EnvDTE.Globals
    globals = DTE.Solution.Projects.Item(1).Globals
End Sub
```

The *Globals* object of the *Solution* and *Project* objects works in much the same way as the *Globals* object found on the DTE object, with a few minor differences. First, if a macro or an add-in stores data into the solution or project file, even if the *VariablePersists* flag is set for that variable the data might not be written into the solution or project file. This is because making a change to a variable causes the project or solution file to be put into a modified state. If you close the solution or project file but do not choose to save the modified files, the data won't be written into that file. Second, unlike the *EnvDTE.Globals* object of the DTE object, which can store data into a wide variety of formats, data stored into a solution or project file can be stored only in string format. This is because project and solution files are text-based, so any data stored into these files must also be in a text format. This doesn't mean that nonstring data can't be stored into the solution or project *Globals* object. It just means that when the data is to be written into the solution or project files, an attempt will be made to convert the data into a string. If that fails, the data won't be stored. Also, because the data is converted into a string when it is stored into the solution or project files, when the *Globals* object is restored from the solution or project file this data will also be in a string format. It is up to the macro or add-in code to properly determine which format the data is in.

Earlier in this chapter, you saw a scenario of a solution add-in in which every time a build was performed a counter was incremented to keep track of the number of builds. The *Solution.Globals* object provides a good place to store this value, as is demonstrated in the BuildCounter sample. This sample, when loaded into a solution, first connects to the *OnBuildDone* event. As each *OnBuildDone* event is fired, the sample checks for the existence of the *BuildCounter* variable within the solution *Globals* object. If this value exists, it is incremented and stored back into the *Globals* object. If this value doesn't exist, the value *1* is stored. The code for the *OnBuildDone* event is shown here:

```
void OnBuildDone(EnvDTE.vsBuildScope Scope, EnvDTE.vsBuildAction Action)
{
    //Increment the build counter by storing a value in the
    // solution file through the Globals object:
    Globals globals;
    globals = applicationObject.Solution.Globals;
    if(globals.get_VariableExists("BuildCounter"))
    {
        //A counter has been set, increment it:
        System.Int32 int32;
        int32 = System.Int32.Parse((string)globals["BuildCounter"]);
        int32++;
        globals["BuildCounter"] = int32.ToString();
    }
    else
    {
        //The variable has never been set, seed the counter:
        globals["BuildCounter"] = 1.ToString();
        globals.set_VariablePersists("BuildCounter", true);
    }
}
```

Looking Ahead

In this chapter, we looked at how the pieces of the object model fit together to programmatically manage the many project types that can be loaded into a solution. We also examined the various objects that you can use to modify how those projects are built. In the next chapter, we'll apply these project management concepts to create wizards for Visual Studio .NET.

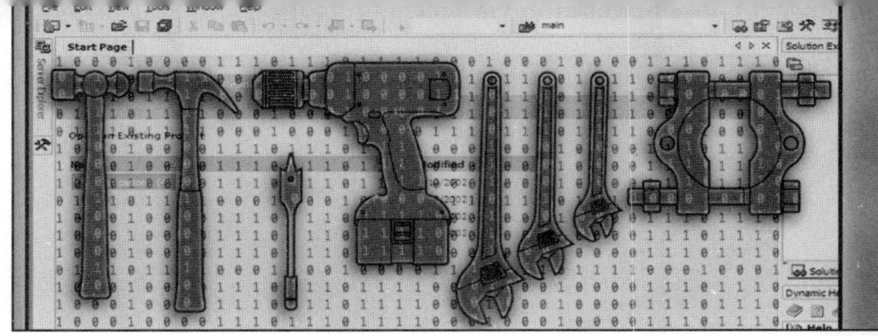

9

Visual Studio .NET Wizards

Wizards, which are familiar to users of Microsoft Windows, provide a simple, step-by-step way of making a complex task simple. In this chapter, we'll discuss how to create your own wizards to run within Microsoft Visual Studio .NET.

An Overview of Wizards

A programmer's work can be repetitive. There's plenty of new, innovative code to write, but a lot of code is common to all projects. Rather than writing this code over and over, you can use a wizard to generate the starter code and start writing the core implementation of a project. A wizard can display a dialog box to walk the user through a set of steps, asking questions, and it uses the answers to make a complicated or often-repeated task easier to complete. Alternatively, a wizard can skip displaying a dialog box and simply generate code without asking the user for any input. Windows is full of wizards, such as wizards that help connect to printers and networks and even ones to find help when something goes wrong. Visual Studio .NET, on the other hand, uses wizards to generate code.

Types of Wizards

You can build and run three types of wizards in Visual Studio .NET. The type that's probably the most familiar to developers is the New Project wizard. A New Project wizard, as its name suggests, generates the code for a project that gives the user a starting point for a new program. New Project wizards are invoked when the user selects an item in the right panel of the New Project dialog box, which is displayed by choosing File | New | Project.

The second type of wizard is an Add New Item wizard. Once a project has been created, a user often needs to add new files, such as classes, images, or Web pages, to that project. An Add New Item wizard can be used to create these new files. The common way to access this type of wizard is by right-clicking on a project in the Solution Explorer window and choosing Add | Add New Item. This displays the Add New Item dialog box, from which wizards can be run.

The third and least-often used wizard type is a Custom wizard. A Custom wizard isn't invoked directly by Visual Studio .NET; rather, it is explicitly called by a macro, an add-in, or another wizard. A Custom wizard can't be classified as an Add New Item wizard or a New Project wizard, but it can walk the user through a set of steps to accomplish some task. With a Custom wizard, you can add wizard-like functionality anywhere within Visual Studio .NET and not be limited only to creating new projects or adding new files to an existing project, as you are with New Project or Add New Item wizards.

Whether you choose to create a New Project, Add New Item, or Custom wizard, you implement it in the same basic way: you create a COM object that implements the wizard, you create a .vsz file to let Visual Studio .NET know about your wizard, and then you create the source code templates. We'll discuss each of these wizard types in this chapter as well as how to build them.

Creating the Wizard Object

Every wizard, whether it is a New Project wizard, an Add New Item wizard, or a Custom wizard, is simply a COM object that implements the *EnvDTE.IDTWizard* interface. *Execute*, the only method of this interface, is called when Visual Studio .NET loads the wizard. The signature for this interface is

```
public interface IDTWizard
{
    public void Execute(object Application, int hwndOwner,
        ref object[] ContextParams,
        ref object[] CustomParams,
        ref EnvDTE.wizardResult retval)
}
```

A number of arguments are supplied to the *Execute* method:

- ***Application*** The *DTE* object for the instance of Visual Studio .NET in which the wizard is being run
- ***hwndOwner*** A handle to a window that the wizard can use as a parent for any user interface elements that the wizard creates

- ***ContextParams*** An array of type *object* that describes the state Visual Studio .NET is in when the wizard is run
- ***CustomParams*** An array of type *object* containing data defined by the wizard writer and passed to the wizard object

The *Execute* method is where all the processing for a wizard takes place. Within this method, a wizard has complete control over how it performs its work. Visual Studio .NET places no restrictions on how a wizard is implemented other than that it must implement the *IDTWizard* interface on a COM object. A wizard can display a user interface to ask the user questions, or it can use the information provided through the various arguments of the *Execute* method to perform its work. You can think of the *Execute* method as similar to the *Main* function of a Visual Basic or Visual C# console application: once called, it can do whatever it wants.

The *ContextParams* argument passed to *Execute* is an array of elements that's populated with values the user enters in the Add New Item or New Project dialog box. It also contains a number of other values, provided by Visual Studio .NET, that give hints to your wizard about how it should generate code. The values in the array change depending on whether the wizard is run as a New Project wizard, an Add New Item wizard, or a Custom wizard. The arguments for the various project types and the order in which those types appear are listed in Table 9-1 and Table 9-2.

Table 9-1 *ContextParams* Array Values Passed to a New Project Wizard

Value	Description
Wizard Type	The value *EnvDTE.Constants.vsWizardNewProject*.
Project Name	The name of the project to create. This doesn't include the filename extension.
Local Directory	The directory in which to create the project or solution.
Installation Directory	The location on disk where Visual Studio .NET was installed.
Exclusive	If this value is *true*, a wizard should close the current solution and create a new one. If the value is *false*, the solution shouldn't be closed and the project should be added to the currently open solution file.

(continued)

Table 9-1 *ContextParams* Array Values Passed to a New Project Wizard *(continued)*

Value	Description
Solution Name	The name of the solution to create, if specified. This solution name is available if the Create Directory For Solution check box is selected in the New Project dialog box.
Silent	A Boolean flag indicating whether the wizard should run without displaying any user interface elements to the user. If this is *true*, use reasonable defaults when you generate code.

Table 9-2 *ContextParams* Array Values Passed to an Add New Item Wizard

Value	Description
Wizard Type	The value *EnvDTE.Constants.vsWizardAddItem*.
Project Name	The name of the project the item is being added to.
Project Items	The *EnvDTE.ProjectItems* collection the item should be added to.
New Item Location	The folder on disk in which the item should be created.
New Item Name	The name the user entered into the Name box in the Add New Item dialog box.
Product Install Directory	The folder in which the programming language is installed.
Silent	A Boolean flag indicating whether the wizard should run without displaying any user interface elements to the user. If this is *true*, use reasonable defaults when you generate code.

We didn't include a table that lists context parameters for a Custom wizard because these are not determined by Visual Studio .NET—they're supplied by an add-in, a macro, or even another wizard. We'll discuss the Custom wizard type and the *CustomParams* that Custom wizards are passed in more detail later in this chapter.

When run, a wizard should verify that the first element of the context parameter array is the constant *EnvDTE.Constants.vsWizardNewProject* if the wizard is a New Project wizard or the constant *EnvDTE.Constants.vsWizardAddItem* if the wizard is an Add New Item wizard. If the GUID doesn't match the type of wizard the object implements, the object should return the error code *wizardResult.wizardResultFailure* through the *retval* argument of *IDTWizard.Execute*.

Note When you check the GUID that is passed as the wizard type, you should perform a case-insensitive comparison because the constants *vsWizardNewProject* and *vsWizardAddItem* might have a different case than any value passed from Visual Studio .NET as the first value in the *ContextParams* array.

An example implementation of a wizard and the code to extract the elements from the *ContextParams* array are shown in Listing 9-1.

Wizard.cs

```
using System;
using System.Runtime.InteropServices;

namespace BasicWizard
{
    [GuidAttribute("E5D0A8B2-A449-4d3b-B47B-99494D23A58B"),
    ProgIdAttribute("MyWizard.Wizard")]
    public class Wizard : EnvDTE.IDTWizard
    {
        public void Execute(object Application, int hwndOwner,
                            ref object[] ContextParams,
                            ref object[] CustomParams,
                            ref EnvDTE.wizardResult retval)
        {
            EnvDTE.DTE application = (EnvDTE.DTE)Application;
            string wizardType = (string)ContextParams[0];

            if(System.String.Compare(wizardType,
                EnvDTE.Constants.vsWizardNewProject, true) == 0)
            {
                string newProjectName = (string)ContextParams[1];
                string newProjectLocation = (string)ContextParams[2];
                string visualStudioInstallDirectory =
                     (string)ContextParams[3];
                bool exclusiveProject = (bool)ContextParams[4];
                string newSolutionName = (string)ContextParams[5];
                bool runSilent = (bool)ContextParams[6];
            }
            else if(System.String.Compare(wizardType,
                EnvDTE.Constants.vsWizardAddItem, true) == 0)
            {
```

Listing 9-1 The wizard add-in source code

```
                string projectName = (string)ContextParams[1];
                EnvDTE.ProjectItems projectItems =
                     (EnvDTE.ProjectItems)ContextParams[2];
                string newItemLocation = (string)ContextParams[3];
                string newItemName = (string)ContextParams[4];
                string productInstallDirectory = (string)ContextParams[5];
                bool runSilent = (bool)ContextParams[6];
            }
            else
            {
                //ERROR! Unknown wizard type
            }
        }
    }
}
```

Creating the .vsz File

As you saw in Chapter 6, to create an add-in you must provide information to Visual Studio .NET to let it know that the add-in is available to be loaded. This information, which is stored in the system registry, includes the programmatic identifier (ProgID) as well as information detailing how the add-in should be loaded. Likewise, a wizard needs a way to announce itself as being available; but unlike with an add-in, you must rely on the file system to make a wizard available. You do this by creating a hierarchy of folders in a specific location on disk and placing files with the extension .vsz in within this folder hierarchy.

A .vsz file has a simple text-based file format. The file starts with the string "*VSWIZARD 7.0*", which tells Visual Studio .NET that the file declares a wizard and that the wizard should be run in Visual Studio .NET version 7 or later. The next line of text is a token that starts with "*Wizard=*" and is followed by the ProgID or the class identifier (ClassID) of the COM object implemented by the wizard. If we were to use the ProgID from the Wizard.cs code shown in Listing 7-1, the line in the .vsz file would appear as follows:

```
Wizard=MyWizard.Wizard
```

We could also use the ClassID format:

```
Wizard={E5D0A8B2-A449-4d3b-B47B-99494D23A58B}
```

After the line for the ProgID or ClassID, you can place a list of user-defined data. This data can be any string data that you want to pass to your wizard, and it can be static (hard-coded into the .vsz file during development) or generated when your wizard is installed by a setup program. Each line of this data starts with the token "*Param=*", and your wizard can require any number of these entries (including 0). Here's an example of this data:

```
Param=Hello World
Param=Second line of data
```

Each of these *Param* tokens is passed as an element of the *CustomParams* array when your wizard's *Execute* method is invoked and can be found within a wizard with code such as this C# snippet:

```
for(int i = 0 ; i < CustomParams.Length ; i++)
{
    string data = (string)CustomParams[i];
    System.Windows.Forms.MessageBox.Show(data);
}
```

When this code runs, the strings passed to *CustomParams* have the leading "*Param=*" stripped from each string; only the raw data is specified.

> **Note** Even if you're using Visual Studio .NET 2003 (version 7.1), the first line of a .vsz file must start with the string *'VSWIZARD 7.0'*, not *'VSWIZARD 7.1'*.

Where to Save .vsz Files

For a user to run your wizard, you must place the .vsz file in a specific location on disk so the New Project or Add New Item dialog box can find it and make that wizard available to be run. When the New Project or Add New Item dialog box is shown, a folder or number of folders on disk are read for the subfolders and files they contain. The names of these folders are inserted into the tree on the left side of the dialog box, and any subfolders are inserted as subitems of that tree node. As the user selects nodes in the tree, each file within the folder corresponding to the selected node is displayed in the list on the right side of the dialog box.

For example, Figure 9-1 shows the New Project dialog box with the file system modified to add a folder called A Sub Folder under the Extensibility Projects folder, which is the folder on disk where the .vsz files are stored for the Add-in Wizard. When the contents of the Extensibility Projects folder are copied into the A Sub Folder folder, they appear on the right side of the dialog box if this new folder is selected. The A Sub Folder folder was created in the folder C:\Program Files\Microsoft Visual Studio .NET 2003\Common7\IDE\Extensibility Projects (using the default installation location).

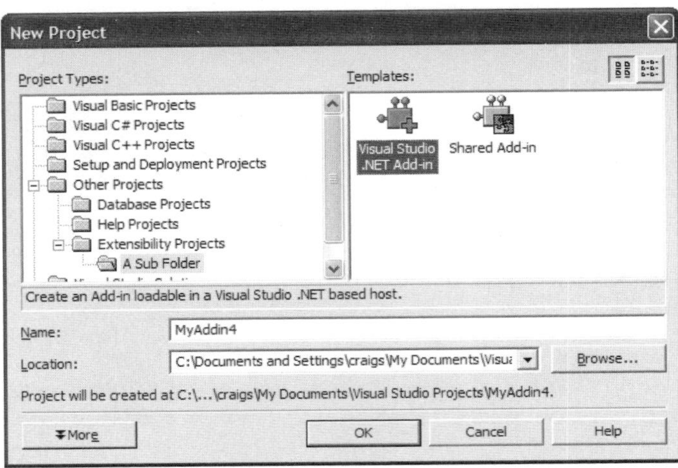

Figure 9-1 A new subfolder shown in the New Project dialog box

You can find the location to store your new project .vsz files programmatically using the *TemplatePath* property of the *Solution* object. The following macro displays message boxes showing the folder in which the .vsz files can be stored so that they will appear within the Visual Basic Projects and Visual C# Projects nodes on the right side of the New Project dialog box:

```
Sub VSZLocation()
    'Display the .vsz path for Visual Basic Projects
    MsgBox(DTE.Solution.TemplatePath( _
        VSLangProj.PrjKind.prjKindVBProject))

    'Display the .vsz path for C# Projects
    MsgBox(DTE.Solution.TemplatePath( _
        VSLangProj.PrjKind.prjKindCSharpProject))
End Sub
```

> **Note** The *TemplatePath* property was poorly named—a better name would be *VSZFilePath*. Don't confuse the word *Template* in the property name with file templates (which we'll discuss later in this chapter).

The constants *prjKindVBProject* and *prjKindCSharpProject*, which are defined in the metadata assembly VSLangProj.dll, are GUIDs in the form of a string. There are, as you probably know, project types other than those for Visual Basic and C#, but constants that can be passed to *TemplatePath* property for those projects types aren't found in any assembly. You can manually find the project type GUIDs for these other project types by poking around in the system registry. Under the registry key HKEY_LOCAL_MACHINE\SOFTWARE\Microsoft\VisualStudio\7.1\Projects is a list of GUIDs; each GUID defines a project type that Visual Studio .NET supports. Replacing the argument to *Solution.Template* path with one of these GUIDs returns the path in which to store your .vsz file so that an entry for the wizard appears in the New Project dialog box for that project type. If we search through this area of the registry for *vcproj* (the extension used for Visual C++ project files), we'll find that the GUID for the Visual C++ project type is {8BC9CEB8-8B4A-11D0-8D11-00A0C91BC942}. We can use this GUID to locate the path to where we can store .vsz files so they'll appear in the Visual C++ Projects node of the New Project dialog box:

```
Sub VSZLocation2()
    'Display the .vsz path for Visual C++ Projects:
    MsgBox(DTE.Solution.TemplatePath( _
        "{07CD18B1-3BA1-11d2-890A-0060083196C6}"))
End Sub
```

As you can see in Figure 9-1, a different image is shown for each .vsz file found. You can associate an image with a .vsz file by placing an icon (.ico) file in the same folder—one with the same name as the .vsz file but with the .ico extension. For the Add-in Wizard, the .vsz file on disk is called Visual Studio .NET Add-in.vsz. When the user selects the folder, a file called Visual Studio .NET Add-in.ico is searched for and, if found, used as the display image. If an icon for a .vsz file isn't found, the default icon for files as defined by Windows is used.

The Add New Item dialog box uses the directory structure in a similar way to the New Project dialog box. You can add new folders, and any files with a .vsz extension that the user selects will be run as a wizard. The only difference between the Add New Item dialog box and the New Project dialog box is that the template directories are located in different places. Figure 9-2 shows the directory structure after it was modified for the Add New Item dialog box and a text file template was placed in that folder.

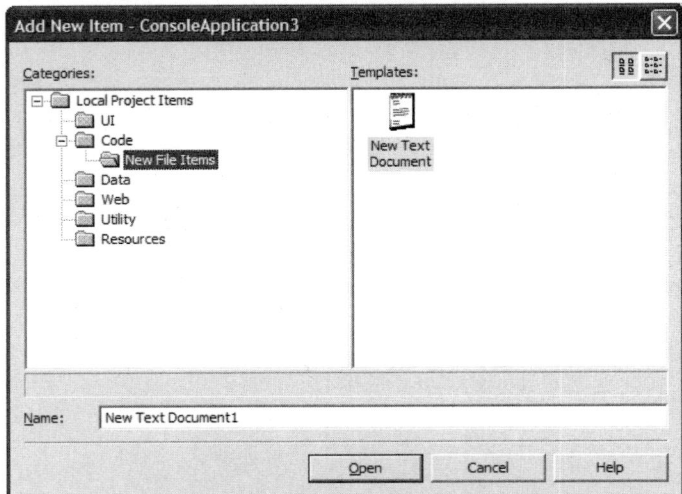

Figure 9-2 A custom folder in the Add New Item dialog box

You retrieve the location where the .vsz files are stored for this dialog box much like you retrieve the path for the New Project dialog box, but using a different method. Rather than using the *Solution.TemplatePath* method, you pass the project type GUID to the *Solution.ProjectItemsTemplatePath* method. You can use the following macro to find the path to where C# Add New Item .vsz files can be stored:

```
Sub ProjectItemVSZLocation()
    'Display the .vsz path for C# project items:
    MsgBox(DTE.Solution.ProjectItemsTemplatePath( _
        VSLangProj.PrjKind.prjKindCSharpProject))
End Sub
```

Creating Wizard Templates

A wizard's purpose is to create a new project or add code files to an existing project. But where does the code for these projects or project items come from? The answer is template files. Templates are the source code files that a wizard adds to a solution or an existing project. These files are placed on disk, and when a wizard wants to add the project or file, the template project and the files the project references or the file for an Add New Item wizard is copied into a folder the user specifies and is then added to the solution or project.

Templates are normally created using one of the wizards for generating a project or a project item, and then the file(s) of the new project are modified to fit the requirements of the project or project item you're trying to create. The code that's created and added to a solution when you run the Add-in Wizard is generated in this way. We used the C# and Visual Basic Class Library Wizard to generate the base project and then modified this project to implement the add-in. The Add-in Wizard locates this project and adds it to the solution, and then the files in this newly created project are modified to conform to the options the user selected when running the wizard.

Using Template Files

Once you've created the template files, you need a way to add them to the solution or project. Visual Studio .NET supports a number of methods to accomplish this. In Chapter 8, we explored the project model but purposely left out a discussion of two methods of the *Solution* object: *AddFromFile* and *AddFromTemplate*. These two methods are used to add project templates to a solution. *AddFromFile* adds a reference in the solution file to the project, keeping the project file where it exists on disk. Calling this method is analogous to right-clicking on the solution node in the Solution Explorer window, choosing Add | Add Existing Project, and browsing to a project file. Wizards, however, usually want to add a copy of a project template to the solution; otherwise, the user of the generated project would modify the template project and subsequent running of the wizard would add a reference to this same modified project. Wizards should normally use the *AddFromTemplate* method, which copies the project template and its associated files to a destination folder and then adds a reference of this copy to the solution. The signature for *AddFromTemplate* is

```
public EnvDTE.Project AddFromTemplate(string FileName, string Destination,
    string ProjectName, bool Exclusive = false)
```

Here are the arguments:

- ***FileName*** The full path to the project template.
- ***Destination*** The location on disk to which the project and the files it references are copied. The wizard should create this destination path before *AddFromTemplate* is called.
- ***ProjectName*** The name assigned to the project file and the name in Solution Explorer where it has been copied. Don't attach the extension of the project type to this argument.
- ***Exclusive*** If this parameter is set to *true*, the current solution is closed and a new one created before the template project is added. If this parameter is *false*, the solution isn't closed and the newly created project is added to the currently open solution.

> **Note** If the *Exclusive* parameter is set to *true* when *AddFromFile* or *AddFromTemplate* is called, the existing project is closed without the user being given the option to save any modified files. You should give the user the option to save by calling the *ItemOperations.PromptToSave* property before calling *AddFromTemplate* or *AddFromFile*.

AddFromTemplate and *AddFromFile* will add a template project from anywhere on disk; that is, the files don't need to be stored in a specific location—just a place that is convenient to find. A common place to store the template files is in a folder named Templates that has been placed in the same folder as the COM object implementing the wizard. If the wizard is built using a language supported by the .NET Framework, you can use reflection to calculate the path to the templates using code like this:

```
string templatePath =
    System.Reflection.Assembly.GetExecutingAssembly().Location;
templatePath = System.IO.Path.GetDirectoryName(templatePath) +
    "\\Templates\\";
```

The *AddFromTemplate* method adds a project template to a solution, but the *ProjectItems* collection has a series of methods for adding files to an existing project: *AddFromDirectory*, *AddFromFileCopy*, *AddFromFile*, and *AddFromTemplate*. *AddFromDirectory* accepts as a parameter the path to a folder on disk; this folder is searched recursively, causing all its contained files and subfolders to be added to the project. *AddFromFileCopy* and *AddFromFile* both perform the same basic operation, adding a reference to the specified file on disk to the project. However, *AddFromFileCopy* copies the file into the project's directory structure before adding this reference. *AddFromFileCopy* differs from the *AddFromTemplate* method of the *ProjectItems* collection (not to be confused with the *AddFromTemplate* method of the *Solution* object) in that *AddFromTemplate* copies the file into the folder on disk for the project and then the project might make some modifications to the file after the files are added.

Here are the signatures and parameters for these methods:

```
public EnvDTE.ProjectItem AddFromDirectory(string Directory)
public EnvDTE.ProjectItem AddFromFileCopy(string FilePath)
public EnvDTE.ProjectItem AddFromFile(string FileName)
public EnvDTE.ProjectItem AddFromTemplate(string FileName, string Name)
```

- ***Directory*** The source folder on disk. Searches for files and subfolders begin with this folder.

- ***FilePath / FileName*** The location of the file to copy or add a reference to.
- ***Name*** The resulting name of the file. This name should have the extension of the file type.

Each of these methods returns a *ProjectItem*, an object that can be used to perform operations on the file that was added (such as opening the file or accessing the file's contents).

Solution Filenames and the New Project Wizard

When a New Project wizard is run, a solution filename might or might not be specified within the *ContextParams* array, depending on whether the user has selected the Create Directory For Solution check box, which is visible after the user clicks More in the New Project dialog box. If the check box is selected, the New Solution Name box is enabled, allowing the user to specify a new directory name for the solution. If the user doesn't select the check box, when a project is created using *Solution.AddFromTemplate* you should use the name specified for the project in the *ContextParams* array as the name of the project, the name of the solution file (if the exclusive argument in the *ContextParams* array is *true* and a solution is not currently open), and the name of the folder on disk to contain those files. These solution and project files should also be stored in the same folder. If the user selects the check box, the solution name argument in the list of context parameters is valid and you should name the root directory for the solution and the solution file using the solution name argument.

To create and name a solution file, you can use the *Solution.Create* method (as discussed in Chapter 8) by passing in the path for where to store the solution file and the name of the solution as arguments. Under the directory for the solution file, you should create a new folder to contain the project file, and you should name both the folder and the project with the project name passed into the *ContextParams* array.

Replacements

When you use a template to create a new project or a new file, the code that's generated will most likely not match the requirements for your wizard. For example, if the C# Class Library Wizard is run, the class that is generated is named *Class1*. The user can modify this class manually to give it a different name, but it's better to dynamically give the class a name that reflects the kind of class the wizard is generating (such as the name *Wizard* if the class implements a wizard). You can do this by replacing specific textual tokens within the template files after they've been added to the solution or project. To make a replacement, you use the editor object model to search for the token, and then you modify the token's text. Tokens can be just about any text that is placed in the file, but normally they have a specific format that is distinguished from other text within the file. A common token used as a placeholder for the class name is *%CLASSNAME%*. The template for the class with the tokens added would look something like this:

```
public class %CLASSNAME%
{
    public %CLASSNAME%()
    {
        //
        // TODO: Add constructor logic here
        //
    }
}
```

The following macro, named *MakeReplacements*, replaces tokens in a file. Some of the concepts that this macro uses, such as the *EnvDTE.TextPoint* objects, might be unfamiliar to you, but we'll cover them in Chapter 11.

```
Sub MakeReplacements(ByVal projectItem As EnvDTE.ProjectItem, _
                     ByVal token As String, _
                     ByVal replaceWith As String)
    Dim window As EnvDTE.Window
    Dim textDocument As EnvDTE.TextDocument
    Dim textRanges As EnvDTE.TextRanges
    Dim findOptions As Integer
    findOptions = EnvDTE.vsFindOptions.vsFindOptionsFromStart + _
        EnvDTE.vsFindOptions.vsFindOptionsMatchCase + _
        EnvDTE.vsFindOptions.vsFindOptionsMatchWholeWord

    'Open the specified project item.
    ' This will open the file but show it hidden:
    window = projectItem.Open(EnvDTE.Constants.vsViewKindTextView)

    'Find the TextDocument object for the project item:
    textDocument = window.Document.Object("TextDocument")

    'Replace all the text that matches token with the replaceWith text:
    textDocument.ReplacePattern(token, replaceWith, _
                                findOptions, textRanges)
End Sub
```

Once you've opened the file that contains the class definition and made it the active document (by using the *ProjectItem* object returned by the *Add** methods of the *ProjectItems* collection), you can call the following macro to replace the *%CLASSNAME%* token with the class name *MyClass*:

```
Sub MakeReplacements()
    MakeReplacements(DTE.ActiveWindow.ProjectItem, _
        "%CLASSNAME%", "MyClass")
End Sub
```

Among the many variations on searching for tokens and replacing the text is deleting the text between two separate tokens. This technique is useful if the user selects an option in the user interface of a wizard that would cause a bit of code not to be needed. The Add-in Wizard uses this technique to remove the code for creating a command bar button when the Yes, Create A 'Tools' Menu Item check box on the Choose Add-in Options page of the Add-in Wizard has been cleared. The following macro deletes the text between two tokens:

```
Sub DeleteBetweenTokens(ByVal projectItem As EnvDTE.ProjectItem, _
                        ByVal token1 As String, _
                        ByVal token2 As String)
    Dim window As EnvDTE.Window
    Dim textDocument As EnvDTE.TextDocument
    Dim tokenEndPoint As EditPoint
    Dim tokenStartPoint As EditPoint
    Dim findOptions As Integer
    findOptions = EnvDTE.vsFindOptions.vsFindOptionsMatchCase + _
              EnvDTE.vsFindOptions.vsFindOptionsMatchWholeWord

    'Open the specified project item.
    ' This will open the file, but show it hidden:
    window = projectItem.Open(EnvDTE.Constants.vsViewKindTextView)

    'Find the TextDocument object for the project item:
    textDocument = window.Document.Object("TextDocument")

    'Create edit points for searching:
    tokenEndPoint = textDocument.StartPoint.CreateEditPoint()
    tokenStartPoint = textDocument.StartPoint.CreateEditPoint()

    'Loop while all start / end tokens can be found:
    While (tokenStartPoint.FindPattern(token1, findOptions))
        If (tokenEndPoint.FindPattern(token2, findOptions, tokenEndPoint)) _
            Then

            'Move the selection to bracket the start / end tokens:
            textDocument.Selection.MoveToPoint(tokenStartPoint, False)
            textDocument.Selection.MoveToPoint(tokenEndPoint, True)

            'Delete the selection:
            textDocument.Selection.Delete()
        Else
```

```
            Exit While
        End If
    End While
End Sub
```

If our template code were modified to look like this

```
public class %CLASSNAME%
{
    public %CLASSNAME%()
    {
        //
        // TODO: Add constructor logic here
        //
    }

%BEGINOPTIONALCODE%
    void SomeOptionalCode()
    {
    }
%ENDOPTIONALCODE%
}
```

after running this macro

```
Sub MakeReplacements2()
    MakeReplacements(DTE.ActiveWindow.ProjectItem, _
        "%CLASSNAME%", "MyClass")
    DeleteBetweenTokens(DTE.ActiveWindow.ProjectItem, _
                        "%BEGINOPTIONALCODE%", "%ENDOPTIONALCODE%")
End Sub
```

the following code would result:

```
public class MyClass
{
    public MyClass()
    {
        //
        // TODO: Add constructor logic here
        //
    }
}
```

Raw Add New Item Templates

An Add New Item wizard is generally used to add a file to a project and then modify the file by making replacements to it. However, sometimes a template file doesn't need to be modified after it's been inserted into a project. An example of this is a text file. When the user chooses to add a text file to a project, a blank file is added. Creating a wizard object just to insert a blank file is a waste of both disk space (to hold the wizard DLL) and time. To get around this, Visual Studio .NET allows what are called *raw templates*. When displaying the Add New Item dialog box, Visual Studio .NET not only searches for and shows .vsz files in the right panel of that dialog box but it also shows any other files within the folder where .vsz files can be placed. If the user selects one of these raw template files in the Add New Item dialog box, the equivalent of an *AddFromFileCopy* is performed on the file—the file is copied into the directory structure for the project that the item is being added to, and then the file is added to the project. To create a raw template, you simply create a file and place that file into the path returned by calling the *ProjectItemsTemplatePath* method and specifying the appropriate project type.

Custom Wizards

Visual Studio .NET has built-in support for creating only two types of wizards, New Project and Add New Item wizards. However, at times you might need to build a wizard that doesn't fit either of these types. Visual Studio .NET supports an extensible wizard architecture that allows you to create and invoke your own type of wizard, called a Custom wizard. An example of a Custom wizard is a wizard you can invoke to insert common code constructs, such as default implementations of classes, methods, or properties, directly into an existing source code file.

Why Custom Wizards?

The Visual Studio .NET automation group didn't add the ability to create Custom wizards simply to provide another way to extend a program with your own software creations; Custom wizards were born out of necessity. The Visual C++ group needed a way to add new functions and variables to classes from within the Class View tool window, and they wanted to do it in a wizard-like way. To make this possible, they added Custom wizards to the list of wizard types. They created wizards to add both functions and variables, and by calling the *DTE.LaunchWizard* method with the proper parameters to programmatically launch the wizards, they were able to allow the user to modify a class in a way that is familiar to them. So when you right-click on a C++ class within the Class View window and choose Add | Add Function or Add | Add Variable, you're really running a Custom wizard.

To create a Custom wizard, you build a COM object that implements the *IDTWizard* interface and you create a .vsz file for that wizard just as you would for a New Project or Add New Item wizard. However, unlike with the other types of wizards, you select the list of context parameters that your wizard takes, and a Custom wizard is invoked through your own code rather than through a dialog box. As you've seen, a list of context arguments is passed to a wizard when it is run, supplying information about how the wizard should do its work. If a wizard is to be run as a New Project or Add New Item wizard, Visual Studio .NET calculates the proper context parameters array and passes that array to the *IDTWizard.Execute* method. A Custom wizard is started programmatically, either from an add-in, a macro, or another wizard, and the calling application fills in the context parameters array.

> **Note** There are no restrictions on the context parameters that can be passed to a Custom wizard, but we recommend that you make the first argument a GUID that the caller and the wizard agree on beforehand. The wizard should then verify that the GUID passed is the expected GUID before proceeding. This approach helps keep the wizard from incorrectly using the context parameters and throwing an exception or crashing.

Running a Custom Wizard Programmatically

Your program could manually load a wizard COM object, find the *IDTWizard* interface of that wizard, and pass off the appropriate values to the *Execute* method, but it would be easier to let Visual Studio .NET handle much of this work for you. You can use the automation model to launch wizards programmatically using the *DTE.LaunchWizard* method. This method takes as its arguments the path to a .vsz file and an array of context parameters. Because the path to the .vsz file is passed to this method, the .vsz file for a Custom wizard can be stored anywhere on disk—it doesn't have to be in a specific location, as the other wizard types do. Once called, the *LaunchWizard* method instantiates the wizard COM object defined within the .vsz file and creates the custom parameters array that the .vsz file contains. The *LaunchWizard* method then passes off all the necessary values to the *Execute* method of that wizard.

You can see the *LaunchWizard* method in use in the sample CustomWizard. This wizard first verifies that the first argument of the *ContextParams* array is the expected wizard type GUID, and then it simply walks the list of context and custom arguments that it is passed, displaying a message box for each item that it finds in those arrays. Here's the macro that starts this wizard running:

```
Sub CallCustomWizard()
    Dim contextParams(1) As Object
    contextParams(0) = "{9A4B2CFF-7A69-4671-BFA5-AE0D0C44AEFB}"
    contextParams(1) = "Hello world!"
    DTE.LaunchWizard("C:\samples\CustomWizard.vsz", contextParams)
End Sub
```

If the wizard sample is placed in the folder C:\samples, this macro packs the wizard type and the string *"Hello world!"* into an array of type object and then calls *LaunchWizard*. The wizard defined the GUID {9A4B2CFF-7A69-4671-BFA5-AE0D0C44AEFB} and expects this string as the first element of the *ContextParams* array; if the wizard doesn't get this string, it will refuse to run and will return immediately with an error.

Chaining Custom Wizards

You can use the *LaunchWizard* method to chain wizards together, which means calling one wizard within another wizard to simplify creating a project. Suppose you need a solution that contains an XML Web service and you need a Windows Forms application to gather data from that XML Web service and display it to the user. Creating the form project is simple enough: you run the Windows Form Wizard to create the Windows Forms template project, and then you create the wizard object that will add the form template to a solution. But creating the XML Web service for the solution isn't as easy as creating a template and adding it to the solution. An XML Web service project, once created, is found only on a Web server. None of the files for that XML Web service except the project file are found on the local computer—the project file simply points to the server and the location on the server where the files can be found. A wizard could talk to the Web server through a protocol such as Front Page server extensions, giving it the proper commands to store the files of an XML Web service, but it would be easier to call on the Web Service Wizard to create the and store those files for you.

The sample project ChainWizard, which is included with the sample files for this book, demonstrates how to do this. Here's a portion of the *Execute* method of this wizard:

```
const string serviceName = "ChainWizardWebService";
object []contextParamsChain = new object[7];
EnvDTE.wizardResult wizardResultChain;
EnvDTE.DTE dte = (EnvDTE.DTE)Application;

// Add our web service by filling in the context parameters,
// and chain to the Web Service Wizard
```

```
contextParamsChain[0] = EnvDTE.Constants.vsWizardNewProject;
contextParamsChain[1] = serviceName;
contextParamsChain[2] = "http://localhost/" + serviceName;
contextParamsChain[3] = System.IO.Path.GetDirectoryName(dte.FullName);
contextParamsChain[4] = (bool)ContextParams[4];
contextParamsChain[5] = "";
contextParamsChain[6] = false;
string webSvcTemplatePath = dte.Solution.get_TemplatePath(
    VSLangProj.PrjKind.prjKindCSharpProject);
webSvcTemplatePath += "CSharpWebService.vsz";
wizardResultChain = dte.LaunchWizard(webSvcTemplatePath,
    ref contextParamsChain);
```

This code creates and fills in the context parameters that are sent to the wizard object, which is run with the call to *LaunchWizard*. You calculate the location of the .vsz file for the XML Web service by using the *TemplatePath* property and passing the project type for the C# project language. Note that this code makes no attempt to create a unique XML Web service name every time it is run. If the wizard is run multiple times, you should either delete the XML Web service created on the server or change the variable value *serviceName* to a unique value.

The result of running the ChainWizard sample is a solution containing an XML Web service project and a Windows Forms project that consumes the functionality of the XML Web service.

Lab: Decoding Wizard Parameters

How do you determine which arguments to pass to a wizard during chaining? You can do it by tricking Visual Studio .NET into calling a throwaway wizard whose sole use is to capture and let you debug the custom and context parameters passed to the wizard. This is what I did to find what should be passed to the ASP.NET Web Service Wizard in the ChainWizard sample.

To start, run the Visual Basic .NET or C# Class Library wizard from the New Project dialog box. Then modify that project to implement the *IDTWizard* interface and register the library as a COM object by assigning the code a GUID and a ProgID and setting the flag in the project Property Pages dialog box to register as a COM object, just as you would for other wizards. The next step is to change the .vsz file to point to this throwaway wizard; because our example chains to the C# Web Service Wizard, we'll modify the .vsz file for that wizard. Search in the Visual Studio .NET 2003\VC#\CSharpProjects folder for the file named CSharpWebService.vsz and open the file in Notepad. We're about to modify this file, so it might be a good idea to make a backup copy.

With this .vsz file open in Notepad, simply change the ProgID from VsWizard.VsWizardEngine.7.1 to the ProgID of the throwaway wizard, and then save the .vsz file. Now, back in Visual Studio .NET, where you have the wizard project open, place a breakpoint on the *Execute* method of your wizard and press F5. (You'll need to set Visual Studio .NET, or devenv.exe, as the debug target first.) In the new instance of Visual Studio .NET that appears, open the New Project dialog box and run the C# ASP .NET Web Service Wizard. Your wizard should be called in place of the ASP.NET Web Service Wizard, and when the breakpoint on the *Execute* method is hit, you can spy on what kind of data is passed to the wizard through the custom and context parameters.

Don't forget to restore the correct .vsz file—otherwise, the throwaway wizard will be run when you actually want to create an XML Web service.

The Wizard Helper Library

As you've seen, creating wizards isn't a very complicated task. By simply creating a COM object that implements the *IDTWizard* interface and placing a .vsz file on disk, you can create a wizard that the user can run by using the New Project or Add New Item dialog box. But creating and displaying the user interface for a wizard can be tedious, which is why we've avoided the topic of wizard user interfaces until now. To create the user interface for a wizard, you must create a Windows Form and the pages for the wizard. The Windows Form will display the pages of the wizard, and the Next, Back, Finish, and Cancel buttons must properly navigate between these pages.

Much of the code to display the user interface for a wizard is boilerplate code and is similar for all wizards. To make creating wizards with a user interface easier, we've included in the book's sample files the source code for a library that manages this user interface. Simply called WizardLibrary, the library implements the *IDTWizard* interface and also handles splitting the *ContextParams* array into separate variables, making wizard creation less error-prone. To use this library to implement a wizard, you simply create a user control for each page of the wizard, write a small amount of code to let the library know which pages are available, and then implement wizard-specific functionality such as creating and adding project code.

Let's use this library to build a wizard that generates the code for a wizard—a "Wizard Wizard." First, we create a C# class library project called WizardBuilder, and then we can add a reference to the WizardLibrary assembly (you must load and build this project from the example source files first so that the library code can be referenced) and then derive the class within our project from *InsideVSNet.WizardLibrary.WizardLibrary* (the base class that implements the functionality for the library). After making the changes to register the object for COM, our code will look like this:

```
[GuidAttribute("1EF6B85C-FD5C-4fb4-BA4D-
5ED221195DBF"), ProgIdAttribute("WizardBuilder.Wizard")]
public class Wizard : InsideVSNet.WizardLibrary.WizardLibrary
{
    public Wizard()
    {
    }
}
```

With this basic startup code, we can define the pages that the wizard displays to the user. The first page contains two options that the user can modify: an option to create an Add New Item or New Project wizard and an option to specify where the user can run the wizard. These options take care of creating the .vsz file and placing it in the correct place for the wizard that WizardBuilder generates. The second page allows the user to specify how many pages the resulting wizard code has. Since the library uses .NET user controls to implement each page of our wizard, we can use the Add New Item dialog box to add two user controls—Page1 and Page2—to our project and then add the appropriate windows controls to these forms.

With the two user controls, or pages, added to our project, we need some way for the wizard library to communicate with each page to let it do the work of generating the output project and modifying the source code files that are generated. We can do this by having each page implement the interface *InsideVSNet.WizardLibrary.IWizardPage*, which is defined by the library and has this signature:

```
public interface IWizardPage
{
    void PerformWork1(WizardLibrary WizardLibrary);
    void PerformWork2(WizardLibrary WizardLibrary);
    string HeadingLabel
    {
        get;
    }
    string DescriptionLabel
    {
```

```
        get;
    }
    System.Drawing.Image Icon
    {
        get;
    }
    void ShowHelp();
    void Initialize (WizardLibrary wizardLibrary);
}
```

Here are the methods and properties of this interface:

- ***PerformWork1*** This method is called when the user clicks the Finish button and the wizard page should start generating code. Each page is responsible for generating its own code within the project, and that work is done within this method.
- ***PerformWork2*** Each wizard page has its *PerformWork1* method called in the order that the pages are displayed. However, sometimes one page's output might depend on the output of another page. Information can be generated in the *PerformWork1* method, saved, and retrieved for further processing during the *PerformWork2* method. After the *PerformWork1* method for each page has been called, *PerformWork2* is called in the display order of each page.
- ***HeadingLabel*** This read-only property allows your wizard page to return information about the headline that's displayed in the top line of the wizard. In the Add-in Wizard's user interface, the top portion, or *banner*, of the user interface displays three pieces of information to the user: a headline displayed in bold text, descriptive text, and an icon for the page. This property returns the headline for the page.
- ***DescriptionLabel*** This property returns the description string to be displayed in the wizard banner.
- ***Icon*** This property returns a picture in the format of a *System.Drawing.Image* type to display in the banner of the wizard.
- ***ShowHelp*** This method is called when the Help button in the lower left of the wizard is clicked, signaling that the user is requesting help for the page.
- ***Initialize*** This method is called after the wizard page has been added to the list of pages maintained by the library.

With this interface implemented by each user control, we can tell the wizard library about the pages. The library implements the *IDTWizard* interface and its *Execute* method for us, but when the wizard is first run, it calls a method defined in the *WizardLibrary* class (from which we derived our wizard class), which is declared as abstract and is also called *Execute*. This method, which should be placed within the class that inherits from the *WizardLibrary* class, is defined as follows:

```
public override void Execute(EnvDTE.DTE applicationObject);
```

This version of *Execute* is where we set up the wizard library to let it know which pages are available to it. You add pages by calling the *WizardLibrary.AddPage* method, passing an instance of one of our user controls that implements the *IWizardPage* interface in the order that they should appear in the user interface for your wizard. We can create and add the two user controls we created earlier (*Page1* and *Page2*) within the *Execute* method using code such as this:

```
public override void Execute(EnvDTE.DTE applicationObject)
{
    Title = "Wizard Builder";
    AddPage(new Page1());
    AddPage(new Page2());
}
```

This code not only tells the library about the pages of our wizard but also sets the title of the wizard dialog box to *Wizard Builder*. The *WizardLibrary* class defines a property, *Title*, that sets the text of the user interface form for the wizard. When this *Execute* method returns, the wizard library has all the information it needs to run. The library then displays the Windows Form dialog box with the user control pages displayed and implements the proper navigation between pages of the wizard. The wizard library also manages the *wizardResult* parameter of the *IDTWizard.Execute* method, returning *wizardResultSuccess* if the Finish button is clicked, *wizardResultCancel* if the Cancel button is clicked, *wizardResultFailure* if an exception is thrown, and *wizardResultBackOut* if the first page of the wizard is displayed and the user clicks the Back button. With this code written, when the wizard is run, the dialog box in Figure 9-3 is shown with the first page of the wizard displayed.

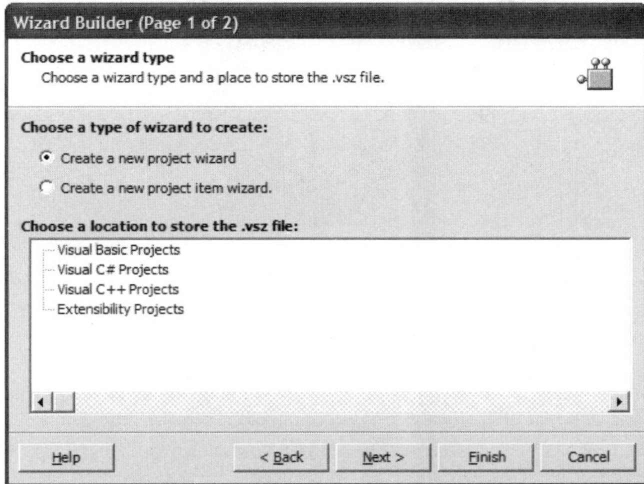

Figure 9-3 The first page of the WizardBuilder sample, with the first page displayed

Wizard Variables

As we've discussed, when the *IDTWizard.Execute* method is called, information is passed to the wizard through the *ContextParams* and *CustomParams* arguments. But the *Execute* method that your wizard implements isn't passed these arguments because the wizard library handles extracting the variables from the *ContextParams* array and storing them as member variables. The values of *CustomParams* aren't extracted in the same way as *ContextParams* because these variables are specific to your wizard and the library has no previous knowledge about what it contains. Table 9-3 and Table 9-4 list the variable names you can use, how they correspond to the values listed in Table 9-1 and Table 9-2, and the context in which you can use them.

Table 9-3 New Project Wizard Library Variables and Their Corresponding *ContextAttribute* Array Values

Variable	Corresponding Value
wizardType	Wizard Type
newProjectName	Project Name
newProjectLocation	Local Directory

(continued)

Table 9-3 New Project Wizard Library Variables and Their Corresponding *ContextAttribute* Array Values *(continued)*

Variable	Corresponding Value
visualStudioInstallDirectory	Installation Directory
exclusiveProject	Exclusive
newSolutionName	Solution Name
runSilent	Silent

Table 9-4 Add Item Wizard Library Variables and Their Corresponding *ContextAttribute* Array Values

Variable	Corresponding Value
wizardType	Wizard Type
projectName	Project Name
projectItems	Project Items
newItemLocation	New Item Location
newItemName	New Item Name
productInstallDirectory	Product Install Directory
runSilent	Silent

The variables listed in Table 9-3 and Table 9-4 are generated by extracting values from the context parameters array. Two other variables are available within the wizard library, and they are available to either New Project or Add New Item wizards:

- ***application*** The DTE object for the instance of Visual Studio .NET in which the wizard is running
- ***CustomArguments*** A list of the custom parameters, copied verbatim from the *CustomParam* arguments passed to the *IDTWizard.Exec* method

The wizard library provides one other variable that your wizard can use. We mentioned earlier that the *IWizardPage.PerformWork1* method can save information for later use in the *IWizardPage.PerformWork2* method. However, one page of a wizard doesn't have access to the data of another page because they are separate objects. For storing information, the wizard library contains a data member named *customData* that has the type *System.Collections.Specialized.ListDictionary*. This data member allows one page of the wizard to store a name and value pair for use by another page of the wizard. The sample wizard we're building here uses the *customData* member value to store information such as the *EnvDTE.Project* object, which was created with the call to *CreateProject* within the *PerformWork1* method of the first page of the wizard.

Wizard Helper Methods

The wizard library supports four helper methods that a wizard can use when generating the resulting project or file. You can use *CreateProject*, which has the following signature, to create a project based on a project template.

```
public EnvDTE.Project CreateProject(string templatePath)
```

This method creates a solution file if one is needed and places the project file in the correct folder on disk if the user specified creating separate folders for the project and solution files. The only parameter this project accepts is the path to the template project file. Values such as the name of the project and solution, as well as whether the solution file should be closed or the new project should be added to the currently open solution file, don't need to be passed to this method because these values are already known to the wizard. The final two methods, *DeleteBetweenTokens* and *MakeReplacements*, are C# versions of the macros of the same name shown earlier in this chapter; you can use them to modify the source files you create.

Completing the WizardBuilder Sample

Now that we've covered the techniques for building wizards using the library, we can complete the WizardBuilder sample. We've already created a class that derives from the *WizardLibrary* class, created the *Execute* method, added two pages in the form of user controls to the project, and implemented the *IWizardPage* interface in each of these pages. All that's left to do is to generate the output code. We'll start by creating the template files. We'll create a C# class library called WizardTemplate, specify the project setting to register as a COM object, and modify the code for the class to the following:

```
namespace %NAMESPACE%
{
    /// <summary>
    /// Summary description for Class1.
    /// </summary>
     [GuidAttribute("%GUID%"), ProgIdAttribute("%NAMESPACE%.Wizard")]
    public class Wizard : InsideVSNet.WizardLibrary.WizardLibrary
    {
        public Wizard()
        {
```

```
            //
            // TODO: Add constructor logic here
            //
        }

        public override void Execute(EnvDTE.DTE application)
        {
            Title = "My Wizard";
%WIZARDPAGES%
        }
    }
}
```

When run, the wizard replaces *%NAMESPACE%* with the name of the project specified in the New Project dialog box, and *%GUID%* is replaced with a new GUID. The token *%WIZARDPAGES%* is replaced with code generated to add an instance of the pages to the library. The next template to create is the template for the pages of the wizard. We'll do this by running the C# Windows Control Library Wizard, modifying the generated user control to implement *IWizardPage*, and changing the namespace and all instances of the class name with the tokens *%NAMESPACE%* and *%PAGENAME%*, respectively. We'll copy the file for the user control into the templates folder for our wizard.

The last step is to fill out the *PerformWork1* and *PerformWork2* methods for the two pages of the wizard. *PerformWork1* for the first page handles creating the project and making replacements within the file, as outlined earlier. *PerformWork2* for this first page handles building the .vsz file, placing a copy in the folder the user specified, and adding a reference to the WizardLibrary.dll assembly. *PerformWork1* for the second page isn't used; *PerformWork2* for this page handles adding one copy of the user control template for each of the number of pages the user specified while running the wizard, and then makes the proper replacements in the newly added page. Finally, the *PerformWork2* method sets up the code in the wizard.cs file to make the replacement to the *%WIZARDPAGES%* token.

Looking Ahead

In this chapter and the previous one, we have dealt with projects and their items—manipulating them through the object model and creating them using wizards. Next we'll move on to something a little different: windows within Visual Studio .NET and how to program them.

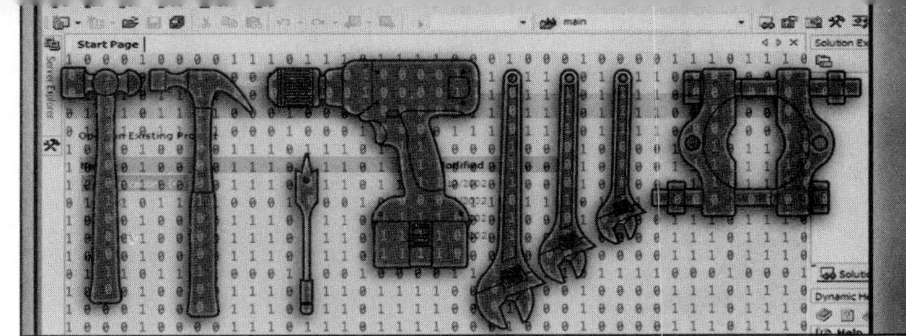

10 Programming the User Interface

Microsoft Visual Studio .NET is made up of many different windows that show data to the user, including the Task List, Solution Explorer, and the Windows Forms designer. You can manipulate these windows not only by using the mouse and keyboard but also through the object model by using a macro or an add-in. In this chapter, we'll discuss the many objects you can program in the user interface of Visual Studio .NET.

Window Basics

The user interface for each window in Visual Studio .NET is different from that of other windows, but they all share a few basic methods and properties. Let's look at the common parts of the object model.

The *Windows* Collection

Visual Studio .NET contains a number of tool and document windows that you can access through the automation model. Each of these windows is represented in the object model by a *Window* object and can be found in the *Windows* collection, which is accessible through the *DTE.Windows* property.

You can retrieve a *Window* object from the *Windows* collection in a number of ways. One way is to use the enumerator to walk the list of all available windows, as shown here:

```
Sub EnumWindows()
    Dim window As EnvDTE.Window
    For Each window In DTE.Windows
        MsgBox(window.Caption)
    Next
End Sub
```

Or you can use the numerical indexing method:

```
Sub EnumWindows2()
    Dim window As EnvDTE.Window
    Dim i As Integer
    For i = 1 To DTE.Windows.Count
        MsgBox(DTE.Windows.Item(1).Caption)
    Next
End Sub
```

However, using these formats for finding a window isn't optimal because you usually want to find one specific window, and looking at all the windows to find it is a waste of CPU cycles. The numerical indexing method isn't always best because the position of a window from one instance of Visual Studio.NET to the next might change, so you can't rely on using an index to return a specific *Window* object. In fact, you have no guarantee that calling the *Item* method two times in a row using a numerical index will return the same *EnvDTE.Window* object because new windows might be created in between calls to this method. In addition, the numerical indexing method might not find all the available windows. For example, creating a tool window can be an expensive operation. To increase performance, Visual Studio .NET won't create a tool window until one is specifically asked for, and because the numerical indexing method looks only for windows that have been created, a particular tool window might not be found.

A simple experiment shows how enumerating through the list of all tool windows slows down your code if all tool windows haven't been created. By default, the Server Explorer tool window is docked and hidden on the left side of the Visual Studio .NET main window. If you move the mouse pointer over the icon for this window, the Server Explorer window appears. If this window hasn't yet been shown for that instance of Visual Studio .NET, you'll see a couple-second delay as the window is created before being shown for the first time. If you run the *EnumWindows2* macro and some of the *Window* objects need to be created, creating those windows will consume a lot of processor time, causing the macro to run very slowly.

Another way to find a window is to index the *Windows* collection by using the name of the window. The following macro demonstrates this approach; it uses the name of the Task List tool window to find the *Window* object for the Task List.

```
Sub FindTaskListWindow()
    Dim objWindow As EnvDTE.Window
    objWindow = DTE.Windows.Item("Task List")
End Sub
```

This is also not the best way of finding a particular *Window* object, as this example clearly shows. During a search for a window, the string passed to the *Windows.Item* method is compared to the title of each window until a window with a matching title is found. If you right-click on the Task List and choose Show Tasks | Comment, the title of this window becomes "Task List – X Comment tasks shown (filtered)," where *X* is a number. Because the string *"Task List"* passed to the *Item* method doesn't exactly match the title of the Task List window, the code *Windows.Item("Task List")* won't find the *Window* object. This isn't to say you can't use the title indexing method in some situations. Some windows, such as the Properties window or Object Browser window, have names that don't change (unless the user is using a different language), and finding such windows by using the window title as the index works. Another reason why passing the title of a window isn't the best choice for the *Item* method is because, just as in the case of a numerical index, if the tool window hasn't been created, the *Window* object won't be found.

The best way to find a *Window* object is to use an index that is unique and independent of both the position within the *Windows* collection and the title of the window. Each tool window has a constant GUID assigned to it; you can pass this GUID to the *Item* method to find the window you need. Because a GUID might be hard to remember, most of the tool windows that Visual Studio .NET can create have constants defined that are easier to remember and recognize. These constants all start with the prefix *vsWindowKind* and are static (shared if you're using the Visual Basic .NET language) members of the *EnvDTE.Constants* class. The following macro finds the Task List tool window:

```
Sub FindTaskListWindow2()
    Dim objWindow As EnvDTE.Window
    objWindow = DTE.Windows.Item(EnvDTE.Constants.vsWindowKindTaskList)
End Sub
```

Because the GUID is unique to a specific tool window and doesn't change over time, you don't need to worry about either the caption of a window or its position within the *EnvDTE.Windows* collection changing. One other benefit of using the GUID is that even if the window you're searching for hasn't yet been created, Visual Studio .NET is smart enough to create the tool window when it's asked for.

You might occasionally run across a window that doesn't have a constant GUID defined for it. The Favorites window is an example. When you need such a window, you can use the GUID in the form of a string in place of one of the predefined constants, as shown in the following example, which retrieves the *Window* object for the Favorites window:

```
Sub FindTheFavoritesWindow()
    Dim window As EnvDTE.Window
    window = DTE.Windows.Item("{E8B06F43-6D01-11D2-AA7D-00C04F990343}")
End Sub
```

You can find the GUID that can be passed to the *Item* method by using the *ObjectKind* property. The following macro takes this approach to display the GUID for the Favorites window:

```
Sub FindTheFavoritesWindow2()
    Dim window As EnvDTE.Window
    'You should show the Favorites window
    ' before calling this code!
    window = DTE.Windows.Item("Favorites")
    MsgBox(window.ObjectKind)
End Sub
```

When you run this macro, the GUID for the Favorites window is displayed in a message box. You can then define a constant set to this GUID, and use this constant in any code that needs to find this window. This is how we found the GUID for the *FindTheFavoritesWindow* macro.

Using the *Object* Property

Many windows in Visual Studio .NET have an object model that you can use to manipulate the data contained in that window. You can find these window-specific objects using the *Object* property of the *Window* object. For example, calling the *Object* property of the *Window* object for the Task List window returns the *TaskList* object, which allows you to enumerate, add, and change properties of task items in the Task List window. The following macro retrieves the *TaskList* object:

```
Sub GetTaskListObject()
    Dim window As EnvDTE.Window
    Dim taskList As EnvDTE.TaskList
    window = DTE.Windows.Item(EnvDTE.Constants.vsWindowKindTaskList)
    taskList = CType(window.Object, EnvDTE.TaskList)
End Sub
```

A number of types are available as the programmable object for the different windows, not just the *TaskList* object, as shown in the macro. Table 10-1 lists the GUID constant you pass to the *Item* method to find a *Window* object, as well as the programmable object for that window.

Table 10-1 Windows and Their Programmable Objects

Window	GUID Constant	Object Type
Command Window	*vsWindowKindCommandWindow*	*EnvDTE.CommandWindow*
Macro Explorer	*vsWindowKindMacroExplorer*	*EnvDTE.UIHierarchy*
Output window	*vsWindowKindOutput*	*EnvDTE.OutputWindow*
Server Explorer	*vsWindowKindServerExplorer*	*EnvDTE.UIHierarchy*
Solution Explorer	*vsWindowKindSolutionExplorer*	*EnvDTE.UIHierarchy*
Task List	*vsWindowKindTaskList*	*EnvDTE.TaskList*
Toolbox	*vsWindowKindToolbox*	*EnvDTE.ToolBox*
Web browser window	*vsWindowKindWebBrowser*	*SHDocVw.WebBrowser*
Text editor	<None>	*EnvDTE.TextWindow*
Forms designer	<None>	*System.ComponentModel.Design.IDesignerHost*
HTML designer	<None>	*EnvDTE.HTMLWindow*

Not only do some of the tool windows in Visual Studio .NET have an object model, but a couple of the document windows have an object model as well. The *Window.Object* property of the text editor, .NET Forms designer, and HTML designer windows returns an object appropriate for programming that window object. The object for programming the .NET Forms designer windows is discussed later in this chapter; the objects for programming the text editor and HTML editor windows are discussed in Chapter 11.

The Main Window

Each tool and document window in Visual Studio .NET has a *Window* object available. However, Visual Studio .NET is also a window, so it's only fair that a *Window* object be available for that window as well. Rather than indexing the *EnvDTE.Windows* collection to find this *Window* object, you use the *MainWindow* property of the *DTE* object:

```
Sub FindTheMainWindow()
    Dim mainWindow As EnvDTE.Window
    mainWindow = DTE.MainWindow
End Sub
```

When you work with the *Window* object for the Visual Studio .NET main window, a few methods and properties don't work as they do when you work with tool or document *Window* objects. The differences between tool and document *Window* objects and the *Window* object for the main window are as follows:

- The *Document*, *Selection*, *Object*, *ProjectItem*, and *Project* methods return *null* if you're using C#, and they return *Nothing* if you're using Visual Basic .NET.
- The set versions of the *Caption* and *Linkable* properties generate an exception if called.
- *IsFloating* and *AutoHides* generate an exception if you call the *get* or *set* versions of these properties.
- The *Close* method generates an exception if called.

A number of methods and properties don't work on the *Window* object for the main window, and one property is available only for the main window. If an add-in or a macro needs to display a dialog box, you should supply a parent window when the dialog box is shown to correctly manage focus and set the "modalness" of the new window. You can use the main Visual Studio .NET window as the parent window by using the *Window.HWnd* property. This property returns a handle to a window—a Windows platform SDK *HWND* data type. This property is hidden, so when you develop your add-in or macro it doesn't appear within statement completion. Because the .NET Framework can't use *HWND* values as a parent, this handle must first be wrapped by a class that implements an interface that the .NET library can accept as a parent. You can implement this interface, *System.Windows.Forms.IWin32Window*, on your add-in class or on a separate class within a macro project. The *IWin32Window* interface has one property named *Handle*; this property returns a *System.IntPtr*, which contains the handle to a parent window and, in this case, is the value returned from the *Window.HWnd* property. When it's time to show a form using the *Form.ShowDialog* method, you can pass the class that implements the *IWin32Window* as an argument to this method.

To implement *IWin32Window* for an add-in, you must first add it to the interface list for your add-in, as shown here:

```
public class Connect : Object, Extensibility.IDTExtensibility2,
System.Windows.Forms.IWin32Window
```

Next, you add the implementation of the *Handle* property:

```
//Implementation of the IWin32Window.Handle property:
public System.IntPtr Handle
{
    get
    {
        return new System.IntPtr (applicationObject.MainWindow.HWnd);
    }
}
```

Finally, you can display the form (assuming that a form class named *Form1* exists within an add-in project) using code such as this:

```
Form1 form1 = new Form1();
form1.ShowDialog(this);
```

Implementing this interface within a macro is even easier; the macro samples project that is installed with Visual Studio .NET already contains the code for a class that implements this interface. Located in the Utilities module of the Samples project, this class, named *WinWrapper*, can be instantiated and passed to any code that requires a parent window, such as the standard Open File dialog box:

```
Sub ShowFileOpenDialog()
    Dim openFile As New OpenFileDialog
    openFile.ShowDialog(New WinWrapper)
End Sub
```

All you do is copy the *WinWrapper* class into your macro project, and it's ready to use.

Explorer Windows and the *UIHierarchy* Object

User interface hierarchy (or UI hierarchy) windows are tool windows that use a tree-like structure to display their data. Examples include the Solution Explorer, Server Explorer, and Macro Explorer windows. The *UIHierarchy* object and its associated objects *UIHierarchyItems* and *UIHierarchyItem* are so named because they represent a hierarchy of objects displayed in a tool window. The *UIHierarchy* object is used extensively by the macro recorder, allowing it to record the correct code to modify the selection within a UI hierarchy window; you can also use the *UIHierarchy* object as a valuable source of information about what is contained within these tool windows.

The *UIHierarchy* Object Tree

The *UIHierarchy, UIHierarchyItems,* and *UIHierarchyItem* objects work recursively. The *UIHierarchy* object is used to find the *UIHierarchyItems* collection, which contains all the root items of the tree within a UI hierarchy window. Each root tree item is represented by a *UIHierarchyItem* object within the *UIHierarchyItems* collection, and because all of these tree items can themselves contain subitems, the *UIHierarchyItem.UIHierarchyItems* property returns a *UIHierarchyItems* collection. This pattern of tree nodes returning a collection of other nodes continues until that branch of the tree ends. The following macro uses the *UIHierarchy* object to find and display the name of the top-level node of Macro Explorer:

```
Sub GetTopLevelUIHierItems()
    Dim macroExplWin As Window
    Dim uiHierarchy As EnvDTE.UIHierarchy
    Dim uiHierarchyItems As EnvDTE.UIHierarchyItems
    'Find the macro explorer window, and the UIHierarchy
    ' object for this window:
    macroExplWin = DTE.Windows.Item(Constants.vsWindowKindMacroExplorer)
    uiHierarchy = macroExplWin.Object
    'Get the top level collection of items:
    uiHierarchyItems = uiHierarchy.UIHierarchyItems
    'Display the name of the first node in this collection:
    MsgBox(uiHierarchyItems.Item(1).Name)
End Sub
```

Here, Macro Explorer's *UIHierarchy* object is found and the collection of *UIHierarchyItems* is retrieved. The name displayed is that of the first item in the collection, which in this case is Macros because the top-level node in Macro Explorer is always the Macros node.

Continuing with our example, the Macros node in the Macro Explorer window contains a number of macro projects. Because this node can have subitems, it is a container of *UIHierarchyItem* objects, so the *UIHierarchyItem.UIHierarchyItems* property returns a collection object. This *UIHierarchyItems* collection contains a list of all the macro projects, and if we modify the earlier macro, we can walk the list of the macro projects:

```
Sub WalkMacroProjects()
    Dim macroExplWin As Window
    Dim uiHierarchy As EnvDTE.UIHierarchy
    Dim uiHierarchyItems As EnvDTE.UIHierarchyItems
    Dim uiHierarchyItem As EnvDTE.UIHierarchyItem
    Dim uiHierarchyItem2 As EnvDTE.UIHierarchyItem
    'Find the Macro Explorer window, and the UIHierarchy
    ' object for this window:
    macroExplWin = DTE.Windows.Item(Constants.vsWindowKindMacroExplorer)
    uiHierarchy = macroExplWin.Object
    'Get the first node in this collection, the Macros node:
    uiHierarchyItem = uiHierarchy.UIHierarchyItems.Item(1)
    'Walk all the items in this collection, which is
    ' the list of macro projects:
    For Each uiHierarchyItem2 In uiHierarchyItem.UIHierarchyItems
        MsgBox(uiHierarchyItem2.Name)
    Next
End Sub
```

These sample macros show how to walk the hierarchy shown in the Macro Explorer window. To use this code to look at what is contained in the Solution Explorer and Server Explorer windows, you can simply change the value passed to the *Windows.Item* method to *Constants.vsWindowKindSolutionExplorer* or *Constants.vsWindowKindServerExplorer*.

> **Note** Do the *UIHierarchy* objects seem familiar? Walking the *UIHierarchy*, *UIHierarchyItems*, and *UIHierarchyItem* objects to find an item in a UI hierarchy window is similar to using *ProjectItems* and *ProjectItem* to walk a project to find a project item. The reason for this similarity is that the *UIHierarchy* objects were designed to reflect how you would use the *ProjectItem* and *ProjectItems* objects.

The *UIHierarchy* Object

Finding a specific node within a UI hierarchy window can involve a great deal of code, especially if the node is nested more than a couple levels deep. Using the *UIHierarchy.GetItem* method, you can directly find a *UIHierarchyItem* object of a node rather than writing a lot of code to traverse the tree of nodes. For example, if you want to get to the *UIHierarchyItem* object of the *InsertDate* macro located in the VSEditor module of the Samples macro project, you can write code such as this:

```
Sub FindUIHierItemForInsertDateMacro()
    Dim macroExplWin As Window
    Dim uiHierarchy As EnvDTE.UIHierarchy
    Dim uiHierarchyItem As EnvDTE.UIHierarchyItem
    Dim uiHierarchyItems As EnvDTE.UIHierarchyItems
    macroExplWin = DTE.Windows.Item(Constants.vsWindowKindMacroExplorer)
    uiHierarchy = macroExplWin.Object
    uiHierarchyItems = uiHierarchy.UIHierarchyItems
    uiHierarchyItem = uiHierarchyItems.Item("Macros")
    uiHierarchyItems = uiHierarchyItem.UIHierarchyItems
    uiHierarchyItem = uiHierarchyItems.Item("Samples")
    uiHierarchyItems = uiHierarchyItem.UIHierarchyItems
    uiHierarchyItem = uiHierarchyItems.Item("VSEditor")
    uiHierarchyItems = uiHierarchyItem.UIHierarchyItems
    uiHierarchyItem = uiHierarchyItems.Item("InsertDate")
    MsgBox(uiHierarchyItem.Name)
End Sub
```

This bit of code is quite verbose, however, and we can shorten it by using the *UIHierarchy.GetItem* method:

```
Sub FindUIHierItemForInsertDateMacro2()
    Dim macroExplWin As Window
    Dim uiHierarchy As EnvDTE.UIHierarchy
    Dim uiHierarchyItem As EnvDTE.UIHierarchyItem
    macroExplWin = DTE.Windows.Item(Constants.vsWindowKindMacroExplorer)
```

```
    uiHierarchy = macroExplWin.Object
    uiHierarchyItem = _
        uiHierarchy.GetItem("Macros\Samples\VSEditor\InsertDate")
    MsgBox(uiHierarchyItem.Name)
End Sub
```

UIHierarchy.GetItem accepts a string, which is the path to an item that pinpoints a node within the hierarchy. This path is calculated by taking the names of each node in the branch to the tree node that you want to find, separated by the forward slash character. Although the *UIHierarchy.GetItem* method finds nodes within the Macro Explorer and Solution Explorer windows, a bug in Visual Studio .NET doesn't allow you to find a *UIHierarchyItem* object in the Server Explorer window.

The *UIHierarchy.SelectedItems* property returns an array of *UIHierarchyItem* objects for items that are selected within the UI hierarchy tree. Like other arrays returned by the object model when you're using a language supported by .NET, this property returns an array of untyped objects—an array of *System.Object*.

```
Sub GetUIHierSelectedItems()
    Dim macroExplWin As Window
    Dim uiHierarchy As EnvDTE.UIHierarchy
    Dim selectedItems As Object()
    Dim uiHierarchyItem As EnvDTE.UIHierarchyItem
    macroExplWin = DTE.Windows.Item(Constants.vsWindowKindMacroExplorer)
    uiHierarchy = macroExplWin.Object
    selectedItems = uiHierarchy.SelectedItems
    For Each uiHierarchyItem In selectedItems
        MsgBox(uiHierarchyItem.Name)
    Next
End Sub
```

To help the macro recorder record the movement of selections in a UI hierarchy window, the *UIHierarchy* object has two methods, *SelectUp* and *SelectDown*, that simulate the user selecting nodes within the tree. Both methods take as arguments two parameters. The first parameter is of type *EnvDTE.vsUISelectionType*, which denotes how nodes should be selected and closely reflects how the keyboard and mouse can be used to select particular nodes. *EnvDTE.vsUISelectionTypeSelect* selects a single node within the tree, causing any other selected node or nodes to lose their selection state. *EnvDTE.vsUISelectionTypeExtend* selects from the last selected node to the chosen node, much as if the user had clicked on a node while holding down the Shift key. *EnvDTE.vsUISelectionTypeSetCaret* doesn't select a node—it moves the caret within the tree to the specified node. Lastly, *EnvDTE.vsUISelectionTypeToggle* swaps the selection state of a node, setting the selection if the node isn't selected or clearing the selection if it is selected. The second parameter of the *SelectUp* and *SelectDown* methods is a count parameter. By default, only one item is selected in either the up or down direction, but you can supply a different value so more than one node can be selected at one time.

The *UIHierarchy* object also has a method named *DoDefaultAction*. This method simulates the user pressing the Enter key with one or more nodes selected in the tree. For example, if a macro node is selected in Macro Explorer and the *UIHierarchy.DoDefaultAction* method is called, that macro runs.

The *UIHierarchyItems* Object

The *EnvDTE.UIHierarchyItems* object is a collection of *EnvDTE.UIHierarchyItem* objects and works like any other collection object in the Visual Studio object model. This object supports one property that is not part of the standard set of methods and properties of other collection objects: the *Expanded* property. This property is of type *Boolean* and returns whether the nodes underneath the *UIHierarchyItem* collection are shown in the user interface. Setting this property to *True* has the same effect as the user clicking the plus symbol next to a tree view item; setting it to *False* is the same as the user clicking the minus symbol.

The *UIHierarchyItem* Object

The *EnvDTE.UIHierarchyItem*, being a collection item, supports the standard collection item methods and properties, such as *Collection* and *Name*. It also supports a method named *Select*. This method is similar to the *UIHierarchy.SelectUp* and *UIHierarchy.SelectDown* methods, except that it works on only one node at a time—the *UIHierarchyItem* that the *Select* method was called on. Because the *Select* method modifies only the current *UIHierarchyItem*, it doesn't accept a number of items to select.

Calling the *UIHierarchyItem.Object* property returns the extensibility object, if one is available, for that node. For example, when you're using Solution Explorer, you can retrieve a *EnvDTE.Project* or *EnvDTE.ProjectItem* object behind that node by using the *Object* property. The following code finds the *UIHierarchyItem* for the first project and second item within that project (the second item is searched for because the first item, when a .NET project is loaded, is the References node) and gets the *EnvDTE.Project* and *EnvDTE.ProjectItem* objects for those nodes:

```
Sub GetUIHierItemObject()
    Dim uihier As EnvDTE.UIHierarchy
    Dim uihierProj As EnvDTE.UIHierarchyItem
```

```
    Dim uihierProjItem As EnvDTE.UIHierarchyItem
    Dim project As EnvDTE.Project
    Dim projItem As EnvDTE.ProjectItem
    uihier = DTE.Windows.Item( _
        Constants.vsWindowKindSolutionExplorer).Object
    uihierProj = uihier.UIHierarchyItems.Item(1).UIHierarchyItems.Item(1)
    project = uihierProj.Object
    uihierProjItem = uihierProj.UIHierarchyItems.Item(2)
    projItem = uihierProjItem.Object
End Sub
```

The Toolbox Window

The Toolbox stores controls and code snippets that you can drag onto the Forms Designer window, text editor windows, and anything else that can be a drag-and-drop target. The Toolbox is made up of a set of tabs where items can be stored and grouped into related categories. The items on a Toolbox tab are relatively static, but one tab, the Clipboard Ring, changes often and collects text that has been cut or copied from a text editor window.

Tabs and Items

To find the Toolbox window, you can pass the constant *vsWindowKindToolbox* to the *Windows.Item* method, which returns a *Window* object. The *ToolBox* object is then found by calling the returned object's *Window.Object* property, as shown here:

```
Sub FindTheToolBox()
    Dim toolBoxWindow As EnvDTE.Window
    Dim toolBox As EnvDTE.ToolBox
    toolBoxWindow = DTE.Windows.Item(Constants.vsWindowKindToolbox)
    toolBox = toolBoxWindow.Object
End Sub
```

Because the Toolbox can contain more than one tab, a collection is available to enumerate all these tabs. You find this collection, the *ToolBoxTabs* object, by calling the *ToolBox.ToolBoxTabs* property. Using the *ToolBoxTabs* collection, you can enumerate each *ToolBoxTab* object in the Toolbox and even create new tabs to house components or text fragments of your choosing. To create a new tab, you use the *ToolBoxTabs.Add* method, which takes as an argument the name of the new tab to create and returns a *ToolBoxTab* object for the newly created tab. The following macro adds a new Toolbox tab:

```
Sub AddNewToolBoxTab()
    Dim toolBoxWindow As EnvDTE.Window
    Dim toolBox As EnvDTE.ToolBox
    toolBoxWindow = DTE.Windows.Item(Constants.vsWindowKindToolbox)
    toolBox = toolBoxWindow.Object
    toolBox.ToolBoxTabs.Add("My commonly used items").Activate()
End Sub
```

This code creates a new tab called My Commonly Used Items, and the *Activate* method of the *ToolBoxTab* object makes sure it's the selected tab.

Not only is the Toolbox a collection of tabs, but each tab is also a collection of items. Each collection item is represented in the object model by a *ToolBoxItem* object and can be enumerated using the *ToolBoxItems* object, which is found by calling the *ToolBoxTab.ToolBoxItems* property. You can walk the entire contents of the Toolbox using the *EnumerateToolBoxContents* macro, shown here:

```
Sub EnumerateToolBoxContents()
    Dim toolBoxWindow As EnvDTE.Window
    Dim toolBox As EnvDTE.ToolBox
    Dim toolBoxTab As ToolBoxTab
    Dim outputWindow As New _
        InsideVSNET.Utilities.OutputWindowPaneEx(DTE, "Toolbox contents")
    toolBoxWindow = DTE.Windows.Item(Constants.vsWindowKindToolbox)
    toolBox = toolBoxWindow.Object
    For Each toolBoxTab In toolBox.ToolBoxTabs
        Dim toolBoxItem As ToolBoxItem
        outputWindow.WriteLine(toolBoxTab.Name)
        For Each toolBoxItem In toolBoxTab.ToolBoxItems
            outputWindow.WriteLine(vbTab + toolBoxItem.Name)
        Next
    Next
End Sub
```

Once you find a *ToolBoxItem* object, you'll see that you can't do much with it. You can call the *Select* method to make sure it's the active item in the Toolbox, you can remove the item using the *Delete* method, and you can find the label that's displayed in the user interface by using the *Name* property. Although the object model of a *ToolBoxItem* is a functional dead end, the real power that the Toolbox object model offers you is the ability to create new items.

Adding Items to the Toolbox

The Toolbox can hold different types of objects, such as text, HTML, COM components, and .NET components. You can add your own items by using the *ToolBoxTab.Add* method, which takes three parameters. The first parameter, *Name*, is the name of the item to add; this string is the text that will be displayed within the Toolbox user interface. The second parameter, *Data*, defines the information stored in the Toolbox for the item. How this data is formatted depends on the third parameter, *Format*, which is of type *vsToolBoxItemFormat*.

The simplest data type that can be stored is raw text. The string passed to the *Data* parameter is copied verbatim into the Toolbox item, and when the text is dragged onto a window that supports drag-and-drop with a Clipboard format of type *text* (such as a text editor window), it is copied into that window. To add a text fragment, you can use code like this:

```
Sub AddTextToTheToolBox()
    Dim toolBoxWindow As EnvDTE.Window
    Dim toolBox As EnvDTE.ToolBox
    Dim toolBoxTab As EnvDTE.ToolBoxTab
    Dim toolBoxItems As EnvDTE.ToolBoxItems
    toolBoxWindow = DTE.Windows.Item(Constants.vsWindowKindToolbox)
    toolBox = toolBoxWindow.Object
    toolBoxTab = toolBox.ToolBoxTabs.Item("General")
    toolBoxItems = toolBoxTab.ToolBoxItems
    toolBoxItems.Add("My Text", "This is some text", _
        vsToolBoxItemFormat.vsToolBoxItemFormatText)
End Sub
```

This code starts by walking the object model and finding the General tab of the Toolbox. It ends by calling the *ToolBoxItems.Add* method and adding an item labeled *My Text* with the text *This is some text* that has the Clipboard format of type *text*.

Adding text in the HTML format is similar to adding text—the differences are that rather than passing raw text, you need to pass a fragment of HTML code, and the format of the data is marked as HTML by using *vsToolBoxItem-FormatHTML*:

```
Sub AddHTMLToTheToolBox()
    Dim toolBoxWindow As EnvDTE.Window
    Dim toolBox As EnvDTE.ToolBox
    Dim toolBoxTab As EnvDTE.ToolBoxTab
    Dim toolBoxItems As EnvDTE.ToolBoxItems
    toolBoxWindow = DTE.Windows.Item(Constants.vsWindowKindToolbox)
    toolBox = toolBoxWindow.Object
    toolBoxTab = toolBox.ToolBoxTabs.Item("General")
    toolBoxItems = toolBoxTab.ToolBoxItems
    toolBoxItems.Add("My HTML", "<b>This is bold HTML</b>", _
        vsToolBoxItemFormat.vsToolBoxItemFormatHTML)
End Sub
```

After you run this code, a fragment of HTML is placed onto the Toolbox; if you drag that Toolbox item into the HTML designer, text will appear in bold style.

> **Note** Remember that HTML is really just an application of XML that follows a particular schema. Because HTML is XML, you can also store XML fragments as HTML on the Toolbox. Visual Studio .NET not only lets you drag-and-drop these HTML/XML fragments into an HTML document, but it also allows you to drag them into an XML document.

Along with these two text formats, the Toolbox can also store ActiveX controls, which can be dragged onto HTML files or Win32 applications (such as an MFC dialog box) that support hosting ActiveX controls. To add an ActiveX control, you supply the *vsToolBoxItemFormatGUID* data type. The format of the *Data* argument is the CLSID GUID of the ActiveX control or (despite the name of the format type) the ProgID of the control. The following macro adds two copies of the Windows Media Player control to the Toolbox. The first one is added using the CLSID of the control, and the second is added based on its ProgID:

```
Sub AddCOMObjectToTheToolBox()
    Dim toolBoxWindow As EnvDTE.Window
    Dim toolBox As EnvDTE.ToolBox
    Dim toolBoxTab As EnvDTE.ToolBoxTab
    Dim toolBoxItems As EnvDTE.ToolBoxItems
    toolBoxWindow = DTE.Windows.Item(Constants.vsWindowKindToolbox)
    toolBox = toolBoxWindow.Object
    toolBoxTab = toolBox.ToolBoxTabs.Item("General")
    toolBoxItems = toolBoxTab.ToolBoxItems
    toolBoxItems.Add("Name", "{22D6F312-B0F6-11D0-94AB-0080C74C7E95}", _
        vsToolBoxItemFormat.vsToolBoxItemFormatGUID)
    toolBoxItems.Add("Name", "MediaPlayer.MediaPlayer.1", _
        vsToolBoxItemFormat.vsToolBoxItemFormatGUID)
End Sub
```

When you run this code, you'll notice that the *Name* parameter is ignored. This is because the Toolbox extracts the name from the control.

The last type of item you can add to the Toolbox is a .NET Framework component. You use the *vsToolBoxItemFormatDotNETComponent* type format and supply the path location of a .NET assembly. That assembly is searched for controls, and if any are found, they're added to the Toolbox tab. For example, suppose you have an assembly called WindowsControlLibrary.dll at the root of your C: drive. The following code adds all the controls contained within that assembly to the Toolbox:

```
Sub AddDotNetComponentToTheToolBox()
    Dim toolBoxWindow As EnvDTE.Window
    Dim toolBox As EnvDTE.ToolBox
    Dim toolBoxTab As EnvDTE.ToolBoxTab
    Dim toolBoxItems As EnvDTE.ToolBoxItems
    toolBoxWindow = DTE.Windows.Item(Constants.vsWindowKindToolbox)
    toolBox = toolBoxWindow.Object
    toolBoxTab = toolBox.ToolBoxTabs.Item("General")
    toolBoxItems = toolBoxTab.ToolBoxItems
    toolBoxItems.Add("Control", "C:\WindowsControlLibrary.dll", _
        vsToolBoxItemFormat.vsToolBoxItemFormatDotNETComponent)
End Sub
```

Often, an assembly that contains a control is placed into the global assembly cache (GAC) so it is available to all .NET Framework programs. Because the path to an assembly in the GAC isn't easy to find, you can load that assembly, ask it for its path, and then pass the path to the Toolbox add function. For example, suppose you have a user control with the assembly name *WindowsControlLibrary*, version number 1.0.795.38182, and a public key of 6fc70375761725c0. Using the *System.Reflection.Assembly.Load* static method, you can load the assembly by passing in the assembly name, version number, and public key. This method returns a *System.Reflection.Assembly* object, which supports a *CodeBase* property that returns the path in the *file:///* format.

```
Sub AddDotNetComponentToTheToolBox2()
    Dim toolBoxWindow As EnvDTE.Window
    Dim toolBox As EnvDTE.ToolBox
    Dim toolBoxTab As EnvDTE.ToolBoxTab
    Dim toolBoxItems As EnvDTE.ToolBoxItems
    Dim asm As System.Reflection.Assembly
    toolBoxWindow = DTE.Windows.Item(Constants.vsWindowKindToolbox)
    toolBox = toolBoxWindow.Object
    toolBoxTab = toolBox.ToolBoxTabs.Item("General")
    toolBoxItems = toolBoxTab.ToolBoxItems
    asm = System.Reflection.Assembly.Load("WindowsControlLibrary1, Version=1.0.
795.38182, Culture=neutral, PublicKeyToken=6fc70375761725c0")
    toolBoxItems.Add("Control", asm.CodeBase, _
        vsToolBoxItemFormat.vsToolBoxItemFormatDotNETComponent)
End Sub
```

Just as when you add an ActiveX control, when you add a .NET component to the Toolbox, the *Name* parameter is ignored and the name of the control is derived from the control itself. This might seem like a bug in Visual Studio .NET, but adding an assembly to the Toolbox differs slightly from adding the other formats. When you add text, HTML, or an ActiveX control, an *EnvDTE.ToolBoxItem* object for the newly added item is returned. However, when you add an assembly, a *null* or *Nothing* value (depending on the programming language used) is always returned. This is because an assembly can contain zero, one, or multiple controls. If the assembly contains zero controls, this *null* or *Nothing* return value makes sense because nothing was added and there's no *ToolBox-Item* object to return. Multiple items cannot be returned because the method returns only a single *EnvDTE.ToolBoxItem* object, not an array. If the assembly has only one control, it can return an *EnvDTE.ToolBoxItem*, but it would seem odd to return an item in this case and not in the others, so the design team decided to also return *null* or *Nothing* in this case.

The Task List Window

As you saw earlier, the programmable object behind the Task List window is the *EnvDTE.TaskList* object. Using the *TaskList* object, you can add new task items to provide information to the user about work that needs to be performed, as well as examine tasks added by a compiler or other tool.

Task List Items

The *EnvDTE.TaskList* object lets you get to the items in the Task List by calling the *TaskItems* property, which returns a *TaskItems* collection containing one item for each task item in the Task List window. You can view subsets of the items in the Task List by filtering out items that don't belong to a particular grouping, or category, but items that are hidden because of this filtering will still have an item in the *EnvDTE.TaskItems* collection.

As with any other collection, you can index *EnvDTE.TaskItems* by its numerical position, which returns an *EnvDTE.TaskItem* object. You can use a number as an index to this collection, but it doesn't have a string format as an index.

Adding New Tasks

You can add new items to the Task List to build a wide range of new tools. Here are examples of tools you can build that use the Task List:

- Code analysis tools that find common programming errors, letting you find a bug before your customer does. You can place details about these errors in the Task List alongside compiler errors.
- Scheduling tools that pull information from other software such as Microsoft Project and create task items to let programmers know when a specific portion of their work is due. When the check box next to a task item is selected, the corresponding item in Project is marked as completed.

- An add-in that searches through compiler errors and fixes as many as it can. Remember the last time you compiled a C# project, only to have errors generated because you forgot a semicolon? Wouldn't it be great to have a tool to fix this automatically?
- A macro that synchronizes your calendar in Microsoft Outlook with the Visual Studio .NET Task List, reminding you to, among other things, pick up a gift on your way home from work for an anniversary or a birthday. (Such a tool can save you from a lot of grief.)

You can build such tools because you insert new task items into the Task List using the *TaskItems.Add* method. *TaskItems.Add* offers a great deal of flexibility in what elements are displayed for new task items and how they're displayed. As a result, this method has one of the most complex argument signatures of all the methods in Visual Studio .NET:

```
public EnvDTE.TaskItem Add(string Category,
    string SubCategory,
    string Description,
    EnvDTE.vsTaskPriority Priority = vsTaskPriorityMedium,
    object Icon,
    bool Checkable = false,
    string File = "",
    int Line = -1,
    bool CanUserDelete = true,
    bool FlushItem = true)
```

You can use the sample add-in AddTaskListItems to see the output generated by the many combinations of these parameters. We'll look at each parameter in turn over the next few sections.

Category and *SubCategory*

All tasks, whether they're created by the automation object model or by Visual Studio .NET itself, belong to a category. Categories are used simply to group tasks and relate them to one another. Common category types are compile errors, user tasks, and shortcuts. When the user right-clicks on the Task List and chooses Show Tasks, either all tasks can be shown or they can be filtered to show only the tasks belonging to a category group. You can create new category groups using the *Category* parameter of the *Add* method. When you call the method, the list of currently known categories is searched for a category with a name that matches this argument. If one is not found, a new category is added and the new task item is added to this category. If a category with a matching name is found, the new task is added to that existing category group.

Visual Studio .NET doesn't currently use the *SubCategory* argument of the *Add* method; your add-in or macro can leave it blank.

Description

The description of a task appears in the Description column of the Task List, and the *Description* argument of the *Add* method sets this column. This parameter of the *Add* method and the *Category* and *SubCategory* parameters are the only required parameters. Ignoring the optional parameters for now, we'll create our first Task List item using the following macro code:

```
Sub TLAddItems()
    Dim taskList As EnvDTE.TaskList
    taskList = DTE.Windows.Item(Constants.vsWindowKindTaskList).Object
    taskList.TaskItems.Add("Category", "", "Description2")
    taskList.TaskItems.Add("Category", "", "Description1")
End Sub
```

After you run this macro and choose Sort By | Category from the Task List shortcut menu, the Task List appears as shown in Figure 10-1.

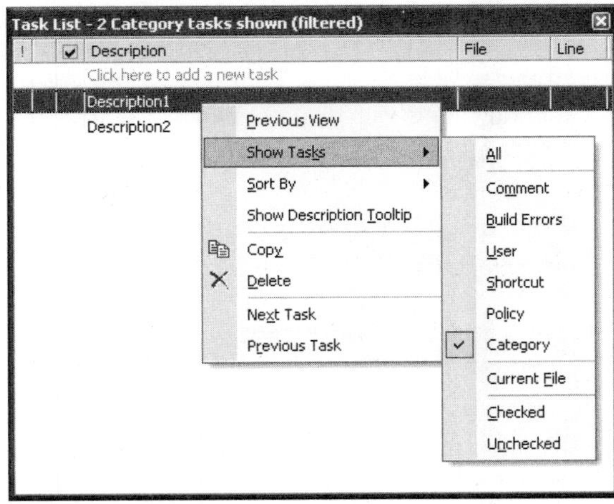

Figure 10-1 Task List items added by a macro and the categories they're sorted by

Priority

The next argument you can pass to the *Add* method is the *Priority* argument. This argument is optional when you use the Visual Basic .NET programming language, but if it's supplied, an icon appears in the first column of the Task List—the priority column—to remind the user of the importance of completing that task. A high-priority task has a red exclamation point next to it, a low-priority task has a blue downward-pointing arrow, and a medium-priority task has no priority icon. The following macro adds new task items to the Task List, each with a different priority. The Task List should appear as shown in Figure 10-2 after you run the macro.

```
Sub TLAddItemsPriority()
    Dim taskList As EnvDTE.TaskList
    taskList = DTE.Windows.Item(Constants.vsWindowKindTaskList).Object
    taskList.TaskItems.Add("Category", "", _
        Description1", vsTaskPriority.vsTaskPriorityHigh)
    taskList.TaskItems.Add("Category", "", _
        "Description2", vsTaskPriority.vsTaskPriorityLow)
    taskList.TaskItems.Add("Category", "", _
        "Description3", vsTaskPriority.vsTaskPriorityMedium)
End Sub
```

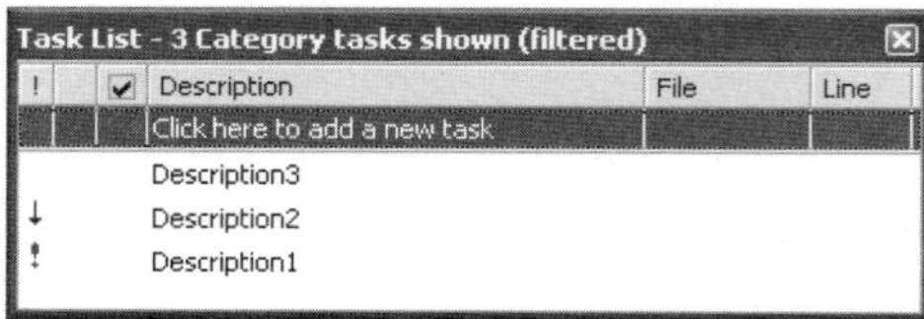

Figure 10-2 The Task List showing items with different priority values

Icon

The *Icon* parameter allows you to place an icon next to a newly added task item to identify that task item. The five predefined icons are described in Table 10-2.

Table 10-2 Predefined Icons for Task List Items

Icon Image	Constant
	vsTaskIcon.vsTaskIconComment
	vsTaskIcon.vsTaskIconUser
	vsTaskIcon.vsTaskIconSquiggle
	vsTaskIcon.vsTaskIconShortcut
	vsTaskIcon.vsTaskIconCompile

Left out of this table is the default icon, *vsTaskIconNone*—a blank icon—which appears if this parameter is not specified.

> **Note** If you call the *TaskItems.Add* method and supply the value *vsTaskIconShortcut* as the icon, a shortcut in a file isn't created. The icon is used for display purposes only. This applies to the other values that can be passed as the *Icon* parameter; using *vsTaskIconCompile* doesn't create a compiler error, *vsTaskIconComment* doesn't add a comment to a source file, and so forth.

If these predefined images don't suit the task item you're creating, you can create your own image to display next to the task. You need a 16-by-16-pixel bitmap image with a color depth of 16. Any pixel in the image that has a background RGB color of 0,255,0 will bleed through the image, showing the background of the Task List. To set the image, you must first load the bitmap into an *IPictureDisp* object and then pass it as the *Icon* parameter. An *IPictureDisp* is the COM way of passing around a bitmap object. To create an *IPictureDisp* object in a .NET add-in, you must write a little P/Invoke code to create this object type. (P/Invoke is the technology the .NET Framework uses to call unmanaged code from .NET programs.) The system DLL, oleaut32.dll, exports a method called *OleLoadPictureFile* that takes a path to a bitmap file, which can be the bitmap to show in the Task List, and returns the necessary *IPictureDisp* object. Before you call the *OleLoadPictureFile* method, you must add some code to the class that implements your add-in that might seem magical:

```
[DllImport("oleaut32.dll", CharSet=System.Runtime.InteropServices.CharSet.Auto,
SetLastError=true)]
internal extern static int OleLoadPictureFile(object fileName,
[MarshalAsAttribute(UnmanagedType.IDispatch)] ref object ipictrueDisp);
```

This code defines the method signature for code that's exported from the COM DLL OleAut32.dll, and with this P/Invoke method declared, you can call the *OleLoadPictureFile* method with the filename of the custom bitmap:

```
object objIPictureDisp = null;
string filename = "C:\SomeImage.eps";
int nret = OleLoadPictureFile(fileName, ref objIPictureDisp);
```

When this method call returns, the *objIPictureDisp* variable is set to an *IPictureDisp* object that can be passed as the *Icon* parameter of the *TaskItems.Add* method.

If you try to call the *Add* method from within a macro and pass as the *Icon* parameter an *IPictureDisp* object, an exception is generated. This happens because the Visual Studio .NET Macros editor runs your macros in a separate process. When a method or property is called on the Visual Studio .NET object model, all data must be marshaled, or translated from the memory being used by the Macros editor program to the memory used by the Visual Studio .NET program, across the process boundaries. However, objects such as *IPicture* and *IPictureDisp* can't be marshaled across processes, so if you try to create an *IPicture* and *IPictureDisp* and pass it to the *TaskItems.Add* method from a macro, an exception will be generated. This limitation prevents you from creating a task with a custom image from a macro, but you can create and use a custom bitmap from within an add-in because add-ins are loaded into the same process as Visual Studio .NET.

Checkable

The *Checkable* parameter of *TaskListItems.Add* controls whether the check box appears next to a task item. If it's set to *true*, the check box is available; if it's set to *false*, the check box does not appear.

File and *Line*

File and *Line* are a string and integer, respectively, that fill out the File and Line columns of the Task List. These can contain any values you want—they're not used in any way other than for information to display within the Task List. If the user later performs the default action on the task (either double-clicking or pressing the Enter key when the task item is selected), the file won't open and the caret won't be placed on the line specified in the *Line* argument. This is because the object model makes no assumptions about the data in the file; if the file points to a binary file, opening and placing the caret on a line might not do what you expect; rather than do something that might be incorrect, it does nothing. However, you can still connect an event handler onto the task item that was created, watch for a *TaskNavigate* event (discussed later), and then manually open the file using code.

CanUserDelete

The *CanUserDelete* parameter controls whether the user can delete the task item by pressing the Delete key when the task is selected in the user interface. If this value is set to *false*, the user cannot delete the item, but you can still delete it through the object model by calling the *TaskItem.Delete* method.

FlushItem

The last parameter of *TaskListItems.Add* is a Boolean value called *FlushItem*. As each new item is inserted into the Task List, the Task List must be updated to show the new task. If you add a large number of tasks, redrawing the Task List each time an item is added will slow down your application's performance. If you pass a *false* value as the *FlushItem* argument, no updates are made to the Task List until either another task item is added that does an update or the method *TaskItems.ForceItemsToTaskList* is called.

The *TaskItem* Object

Once an item has been added to the Task List—whether it was created using the *TaskItems.Add* object or created by Visual Studio .NET itself and obtained by the *TaskItems* collection—you can use the *TaskItem* object's methods and properties to examine and modify the data displayed for that task item. The properties *Category, SubCategory, Checked, Description, FileName, Line,* and *Priority* each can be read programmatically to see what data is stored for those columns of the Task List. You can also set these properties as long as they're not read-only. Some task items that Visual Studio .NET creates have their columns marked as read-only so they can't be modified. To test whether a particular column can be set, you can make a call to the *IsSettable* property, which accepts as a parameter the column within the Task List (a *vsTaskListColumn* enumeration value), and if the column can be modified the *IsSettable* property returns true; otherwise, it returns false. For example, to change a task item's description value, you can write code such as this, which first verifies that the description can be changed:

```
Sub ModifyTaskDescription()
    Dim taskList As EnvDTE.TaskList
    Dim task As EnvDTE.TaskItem
    taskList = DTE.Windows.Item(Constants.vsWindowKindTaskList).Object
    task = taskList.TaskItems.Item(1)
    If (task.IsSettable(vsTaskListColumn.vsTaskListColumnDescription)) Then
        task.Description = "A new description"
    End If
End Sub
```

Delete deletes the item, if deletion is possible, from the list of items. As mentioned earlier, all items added through the object model can be deleted whether the *CanUserDelete* parameter is *true* or *false* when you call the *TaskItems.Add* method. Other task items can be deleted depending on who created them. For example, if the task item was added by the user clicking on Click Here To Add A New Task Item in the Task List, it can be deleted using the object model. If the item was created by IntelliSense or by a compiler, an exception is generated when this method is called because the only way to remove the task item is to modify the source code that's causing the task item to appear.

The *Navigate* method simulates the user double-clicking or pressing the Enter key when the task has the focus. If the task was added by Visual Studio .NET or by a compiler or if the task is a shortcut task, this opens the target file and places the caret on the line specified by the task. If the task was added through the automation model, no action is taken unless you write code to manually navigate to the proper file and line location using the *TaskNavigated* event.

Task List Events

As the user interacts with the Task List, events are fired to allow your add-in or macro to respond to those user interactions. Possibly the most important event of your add-in or macro that adds task list items is the *TaskNavigate* event. This event is fired when the user double-clicks on a Task List item, presses the Enter key when a task has the focus, or chooses Next Task or Previous Task from the Task List's shortcut menu. To capture this event, you can connect to the *TaskListEvents.TaskNavigated* event. This event is passed the *TaskItem* object of the item that the user wants to navigate to, plus a reference to a Boolean value called *NavigateHandled* that you can use to tell Visual Studio .NET whether your code has handled the navigation of the task item. If the value *false* is passed back through the *NavigateHandled* argument and no one else handles the navigation of the task, Visual Studio .NET plays a bell sound for the user.

Connecting to this event within a macro project is as simple as opening the *EnvironmentEvents* macro module, selecting the TaskListEvents item from the drop-down list at the top left of the editor window for this module, and then selecting the *TaskNavigated* event from the top right drop-down list. Using this event and the arguments that are passed to it, you can write a macro event handler for the *NavigateHandled* event that opens the file (if specified) that the task item refers to and select the line in the source file that the task item points to. The code for this event handler would look like this:

```
Private Sub TaskListEvents_TaskNavigated(ByVal TaskItem As EnvDTE.TaskItem, _
    ByRef NavigateHandled As Boolean) Handles TaskListEvents.TaskNavigated
    'If the file argument has been specified for this task...
    If (TaskItem.FileName <> "") Then
        Dim fileWindow As EnvDTE.Window
        Dim textWindow As EnvDTE.TextWindow
        Dim textPane As EnvDTE.TextPane

        'Then open the file, find the TextWindow and TextPane objects...
        fileWindow = DTE.ItemOperations.OpenFile(TaskItem.FileName, _
            EnvDTE.Constants.vsViewKindTextView)
        textWindow = CType(fileWindow.Object, EnvDTE.TextWindow)
        textPane = CType(textWindow.ActivePane, EnvDTE.TextPane)
```

```
        'Then move the caret to the correct line:
        textPane.Selection.MoveTo(TaskItem.Line, 1, False)
        textPane.Selection.SelectLine()
        NavigateHandled = True
    End If
End Sub
```

Connecting to this event within an add-in is almost as simple as connecting to it within a macro, but a little more code is needed. The first step is to declare a variable to connect the event handler to. In this case, we're connecting to Task List events, so we'll use the *EnvDTE.TaskListEvents* class:

```
private EnvDTE.TaskListEvents taskListEvents;
```

Next you declare the event handler method, which must follow the method signature as declared in the Object Browser. You can also convert the macro code shown earlier into C# for an add-in:

```
public void TaskNavigated(EnvDTE.TaskItem taskItem,
    ref bool navigateHandled)
{
    //If the file argument has been specified for this task...
    if(taskItem.FileName != "")
    {
        EnvDTE.Window fileWindow;
        EnvDTE.TextWindow textWindow;
        EnvDTE.TextPane textPane;

        //Then open the file, find the TextWindow and TextPane objects...
        fileWindow = applicationObject.ItemOperations.OpenFile(
            taskItem.FileName, EnvDTE.Constants.vsViewKindTextView);
        textWindow = (EnvDTE.TextWindow)fileWindow.Object;
        textPane = (EnvDTE.TextPane)textWindow.ActivePane;

        //Then move the caret to the correct line:
        textPane.Selection.MoveTo(taskItem.Line, 1, false);
        textPane.Selection.SelectLine();
        navigateHandled = true;
    }
}
```

Finally, you must set the *taskListEvents* variable to an instance of a *TaskListEvents* object, which you find by calling the *Events.TaskListEvents* property. This property takes one argument—a category that's used as a filter. If you pass the empty string as an argument, your event handler is called when any task item generates an event—whether the item was added by an add-in or macro or by Visual Studio .NET itself. But if you specify a category for this argument—the same category string you can pass as the first argument to the *TaskItems.Add* method—only events for a task item that have this same category are sent to your event handler. This filtering mechanism can help cut down on the number of events that are fired, thereby increasing the performance of your code. Because we want our code to handle events for all task items, we'll pass the empty string to the *Events.TaskListEvents* property:

```
EnvDTE.Events events = applicationObject.Events;
taskListEvents = (EnvDTE.TaskListEvents)events.get_TaskListEvents("");
```

The last step is to associate the event object with the event handler. You do this by creating a new *EnvDTE._dispTaskListEvents_TaskNavigatedEventHandler* object and adding it to the *taskListEvents.TaskNavigated* collection of event handlers:

```
taskListEvents.TaskNavigated += new
    _dispTaskListEvents_TaskNavigatedEventHandler(this.TaskNavigated);
```

TaskNavigated isn't the only Task List event your code can capture. *TaskAdded* and *TaskRemoved* events are fired when a new task item is added or just before it's removed, respectively. The last event, *TaskModified*, is fired when one of the columns of the Task List is modified. For instance, the user can check or uncheck an item or change the priority or descriptive text for a task item. To let your code know when these tasks are changed, the *TaskModified* event is fired, passing the task item and the column that was modified.

Comment Tokens

Developers commonly leave portions of their code incomplete as they work, with the intention of adding it later. This omitted code might include error-checking, some parameter validation, or notes to themselves to handle a few additional code paths. Of course, unless you specifically search through the code for these tokens, either by visually inspecting it or by using the Visual Studio .NET search tools, you might never revisit these notes and make the corrections. However, if you use a special notation, the Task List can find and report these notes for you automatically. When you open a source file, the file is scanned for these special tokens, and if any are found, an entry is made in the Task List. The tokens in the source file have the format of a language comment marker followed by the comment token, the colon character, and finally the note that is to appear within the Task List. For example, the comment *//TODO: Fix this later* creates a Task List item for Visual C++ and C# with the description *Fix this later*, and the comment *'TODO: Fix this later* does the same for a Visual Basic .NET file.

The special tokens that the Task List searches for are defined in the Options dialog box, where you can add new tokens and remove or modify existing tokens. Figure 10-3 shows the available tokens: HACK, TODO, UNDONE, and UnresolvedMergeConflict.

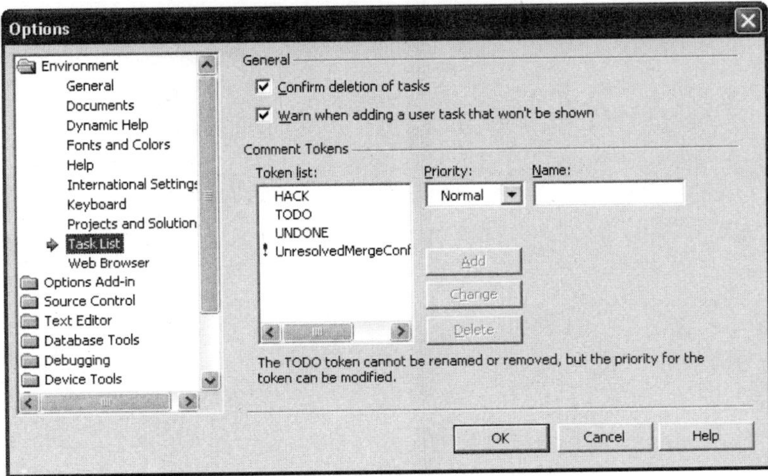

Figure 10-3 Task List token options

You can add a new token by typing a token name in the Name box, selecting a priority, and then clicking the Add button. You can also add, remove, and modify these tokens through the object model. To program these tokens, you use the *Properties* collection. You'll find more details about the *Properties* collection later in this chapter—for now, we'll overlook the details of how to use the *Properties* collection and look only at how to change the tokens using this object. The first step is to find the *CommentTokens* property using code such as the following:

```
Sub GetTokensArray()
    Dim tokens As Object()
    Dim prop As EnvDTE.Property
    Dim props As EnvDTE.Properties
    props = DTE.Properties("Environment", "TaskList")
    prop = props.Item("CommentTokens")
    tokens = prop.Value
End Sub
```

The *CommentTokens* property returns an array of strings that have a special format, and when this macro is run, it finds all the available tokens in the format *TokenName*: *Priority*, where *TokenName* is what should appear after the comment notation for the given language and *Priority* is the numerical value of an item in the *EnvDTE.vsTaskPriority* enumeration. In the preceding macro, the string for the TODO token is *"TODO:2"* because the string to search for in the text editor is *"TODO"* and the priority that appears in the Task List for this token is *vsTaskPriorityMedium* (whose numerical value is 2).

Adding your own token to the list of tokens is a three-step process. Setting the list of tokens clears the current list (at least the tokens that are not read-only), so you need to preserve the known tokens so you don't overwrite the known tokens that the user might have created. First, you need to retrieve the list of current Task List tokens. You add your own token to the array of existing tokens, and then you set the property with the expanded array. You can see this in the following macro, which adds a high-priority *SECURITY* token to the list of comment tokens:

```
Sub AddSecurityToken()
    Dim tokens As Object()
    Dim token As String
    Dim prop As EnvDTE.Property
    Dim props As EnvDTE.Properties
    'Find the property holding the known tokens
    props = DTE.Properties("Environment", "TaskList")
    prop = props.Item("CommentTokens")
    tokens = prop.Value
    Add one to the list of known tokens to hold
    ' the new SECURITY token
    ReDim Preserve tokens(tokens.Length)
    'Add the new token
    tokens(tokens.Length - 1) = "SECURITY:3"
    'Set the list of known tokens
    prop.Value = tokens
End Sub
```

To delete a token, you run similar code, but instead of adding an element to the array you remove an element:

```
Sub RemoveSecurityToken()
    Dim tokens As Object()
    Dim newTokens As Object()
    Dim token As String
    Dim i As Integer = 0
    Dim found As Boolean = False
    Dim prop As EnvDTE.Property
    Dim props As EnvDTE.Properties
    props = DTE.Properties("Environment", "TaskList")
```

```
    prop = props.Item("CommentTokens")
    tokens = prop.Value
    'Don't want to shrink the array if
    '  the token is not available
    For Each token In tokens
        If token = "SECURITY:3" Then
            found = True
            Exit For
        End If
    Next
    'If the SECURITY token was not found, then
    ' there is nothing to remove so we can exit
    If found = False Then
        Exit Sub
    End If
    'Resize the newTokens array
    ReDim newTokens(tokens.Length - 2)
    'Copy the list of tokens into the newTokens array
    ' skipping the SECURITY token
    For Each token In tokens
        If token <> "SECURITY:3" Then
            newTokens(i) = token
            i = i + 1
        End If
    Next
    'Set the list of tokens
    prop.Value = newTokens
End Sub
```

If your add-in generates code to place in the text buffer and you want to insert a comment token that gives the user additional information about how to modify the code, you can use the *TaskList.DefaultCommentToken* property to find which token to insert. The following code creates a string containing a class, with the default comment token directing the user to where to insert code:

```
Sub InsertTLTokenCode()
    Dim classString As String
    Dim taskList As EnvDTE.TaskList
    taskList = DTE.Windows.Item(Constants.vsWindowKindTaskList).Object
    classString = "Public Class AClass" + Chr(13)
    classString = classString + Chr(9) + "'" + taskList.DefaultCommentToken
    classString = classString + ": Insert your code here" + Chr(13)
    classString = classString + "End Class"
End Sub
```

The Output Window

The Output window is where Visual Studio .NET displays text information generated by tools such as compilers or the debugger. The Output window is also a perfect place for any tools you create that generate text information that might be useful to the user. In fact, throughout this book the sample macros and add-ins use the class library OutputWindowPaneEx to display text in the Output window as these samples do their work.

The object behind the Output window is called *OutputWindow*, and you can find this object using code such as this:

```
Sub FindOutputWindow()
    Dim window As EnvDTE.Window
    Dim outputWindow As EnvDTE.OutputWindow
    window = DTE.Windows.Item(EnvDTE.Constants.vsWindowKindOutput)
    outputWindow = CType(window.Object, EnvDTE.OutputWindow)
End Sub
```

Output Window Panes

The user interface of the Output window consists of a number of view ports, or panes, each of which displays text. You can switch between these panes by selecting a pane by name from the drop-down list at the top of the Output window. You can enumerate the panes using the *OutputWindowPanes* object, as shown here:

```
Sub EnumOutputWindowPanes()
    Dim window As EnvDTE.Window
    Dim outputWindow As EnvDTE.OutputWindow
    Dim outputWindowPanes As EnvDTE.OutputWindowPanes
    Dim outputWindowPane As EnvDTE.OutputWindowPane
    'Find the OutputWindow object
    window = DTE.Windows.Item(EnvDTE.Constants.vsWindowKindOutput)
    outputWindow = CType(window.Object, EnvDTE.OutputWindow)
    'Retrieve the OutputWindowPanes object
    outputWindowPanes = outputWindow.OutputWindowPanes
    'Enumerate each OutputWindowPane
    For Each outputWindowPane In outputWindowPanes
        MsgBox(outputWindowPane.Name)
    Next
End Sub
```

You can also use the *OutputWindowPanes* object to create new panes. The method *Add* takes as its only argument the name of the new pane to create:

```
Sub CreateOutputWindowPane()
    Dim window As EnvDTE.Window
    Dim outputWindow As EnvDTE.OutputWindow
    Dim outputWindowPanes As EnvDTE.OutputWindowPanes
    Dim outputWindowPane As EnvDTE.OutputWindowPane
    'Find the OutputWindow object
    window = DTE.Windows.Item(EnvDTE.Constants.vsWindowKindOutput)
    outputWindow = CType(window.Object, EnvDTE.OutputWindow)
    'Retrieve the OutputWindowPanes object
    outputWindowPanes = outputWindow.OutputWindowPanes
    'Add a new pane:
    outputWindowPane = outputWindowPanes.Add("My New Pane")
End Sub
```

This macro creates a new output window pane named My New Pane that's ready to be filled with the text output of your add-in or macro code. You can inject code into this window using the *OutputWindowPane.OutputString* method, which takes a string that's appended to the end of other text in the appropriate pane. As strings are placed into the Output window pane, they're injected without a line break between them; this means that if a new line character needs to be placed between each string, you must write the code to do this. The following macro sample displays the contents of the folder containing the solution file that's currently open; as each file path is displayed in the Output window pane, a line break (or ASCII value 13) is inserted:

```
Sub DisplaySolutionDirectory()
    Dim files As String()
    Dim file As String
    Dim directoryOutputWindowPane As OutputWindowPane
    Dim fullName As String
    Dim outputWindow As OutputWindow
    outputWindow = DTE.Windows.Item(Constants.vsWindowKindOutput).Object

    'Find the folder the solution is in, as well as the files that are
    ' in that folder:
    fullName = System.IO.Path.GetDirectoryName(DTE.Solution.FullName)
    files = System.IO.Directory.GetFiles(fullName)

    'Try to find a "Solution Directory" pane, if one does not exist,
    ' create it:
    With outputWindow.OutputWindowPanes
        Try
            directoryOutputWindowPane = .Item("Solution Directory")
            'Show the pane:
            directoryOutputWindowPane.Activate()
        Catch
            directoryOutputWindowPane = .Add("Solution Directory")
```

```
        End Try
    End With
    'Clear the pane:
    directoryOutputWindowPane.Clear()
    For Each file In files
        'Display the file path, with a line break between each line
        directoryOutputWindowPane.OutputString(file + Chr(13))
    Next
End Sub
```

This macro demonstrates the use of a few methods and properties of the *OutputWindowPane* object. The *Activate* method makes sure the pane corresponding to the instance of the *OutputWindowPane* that it's being called on is the same pane displayed to the user; it simulates selecting that pane from the drop-down list in the Output window. *OutputString* dumps a string into the pane, and *Clear* removes all text from that pane. Another property, *TextDocument*, which isn't shown in this macro, deserves special note. It returns an *EnvDTE.TextDocument* object for the pane that's read-only—you can retrieve the contents of this window, but not change it. (You can only use *OutputString* to modify the contents.) We'll discuss this object in further detail in the next chapter.

The Forms Designer Window

You visually create the user interface for your .NET Framework program in the Visual Studio .NET Forms designer. By simply dragging and dropping controls from the Toolbox onto a form and setting a few properties in the Properties window, you can build the user interface for your program. The Forms designer was built with .NET components and uses the *System.Windows.Forms* assembly to display and create the form. Because the *System.Windows.Forms* assembly is used, programming a form in the designer is similar to programming a form as it executes at run time.

The *IDesignerHost* Interface

A Forms designer window exposes an object model, as many of the other windows do. The object hierarchy returned from calling the *Window.Object* property of a Forms designer window is of type *System.ComponentModel.Design.IDesignerHost*. To examine and modify a form within the designer, you must find the *System.Windows.Forms.Control* object for that form. You can do this by calling the *IDesignerHost.RootComponent* property and casting the object returned into a *Forms.Control* object, as shown in this code snippet:

```
System.Windows.Forms.Control control;
System.ComponentModel.Design.IDesignerHost designerHost;
designerHost =(System.ComponentModel.Design.IDesignerHost)
    applicationObject.ActiveWindow.Object;
control = (System.Windows.Forms.Control)designerHost.RootComponent;
```

> **Note** The *System.Windows.Forms.Form* class derives from the *System.Windows.Forms.Control* class. The code shown here demonstrates how to manipulate a user control, but you can use the same unmodified code to program a Windows Form.

Using the *System.Windows.Forms.Control* object, you can connect events to determine when the form was modified, to find and modify properties such as the dimensions of the form, and place, modify, and remove controls n the form.

Marshaling

If you try to use the *IDesignerHost* interface from within a macro, a *System.Runtime.Remoting.RemotingException* exception is thrown. This is because user interface elements, such as the *System.Windows.Control* object, cannot be remoted across process boundaries. Remember that the Macros IDE runs in a process separate from the Visual Studio .NET process. Because of this restriction, the designer object model can be used only within an add-in and not from a macro.

Adding Controls to a Form

Once you find the *IDesignerHost* interface for a Forms designer, you can easily add new controls to the form. To add a control, you need the *System.Type* object that describes the control. You can find this object using the *Type.GetType* static method, which is passed the full class name of a control. For example, to add a list view control to a form, you can use code such as this:

```
System.Type type;
type = System.Type.GetType("System.Windows.Forms.ListView");
```

You can then pass this *Type* object to the *IDesignerHost.CreateComponent* method to create the control. This method has two overloads, the first of which takes two parameters. The first parameter is the *Type* object we just found, and the second parameter is the variable name of the control we want to create. This variable name must be unique among variables contained within the form's class; otherwise, a name collision will occur and an exception will be generated. The second overload of this method takes as an argument only the *Type* object; the Forms designer examines the form code to find a unique variable name to use. Both of these overloads emit the appropriate code to instantiate a control of the specified type. The following code creates a list view control with the variable name *listViewControl*:

```
System.ComponentModel.IComponent component;
component = designerHost.CreateComponent(type, "listViewControl");
```

If you were to add this code to an add-in and execute it, you wouldn't see the control appear on the form. This is because the control, while instantiated, hasn't been parented to the form and added to the form's *Controls* collection. To add the control to the form's *Controls* collection, you must set the *Parent* property of the control to the form that should contain the control. You can set the *Parent* property (or any property of a control, for that matter) using the *System.ComponentModel.PropertyDescriptorCollection* object. This object contains a collection of properties available for a control; as values are set for the properties they contain, code is generated within the form's class that corresponds to the property you set. You can set the *Parent* property as follows:

```
System.ComponentModel.PropertyDescriptorCollection props;
System.ComponentModel.PropertyDescriptor propParent;
//Find the properties for the listViewControl control:
props = System.ComponentModel.TypeDescriptor.GetProperties(component);
//Get the Parent property
propParent = props["Parent"];
//Set the Parent property to the form:
propParent.SetValue(newControl, designerHost.RootComponent);
```

Finding Existing Controls

You now know how to create controls and place them on a form. But how do you find existing controls on a form? As mentioned earlier, the *IDesignerHost.RootComponent* property returns an object that can be cast into a *System.Windows.Forms.Control* object. Using this object, you can call methods and properties just as you would at run time to find information about a form. For example, the following code walks the list of controls contained in a *System.Windows.Forms.Control* object:

```
System.ComponentModel.Design.IDesignerHost designer;
System.Windows.Forms.Control rootControl;

//Set the designer variable here from the Window.Object property

rootControl = (System.Windows.Forms.Control)designer.RootComponent
foreach (System.Windows.Forms.Control control in rootControl.Controls)
{
    //Retrieve desired control information
}
```

You can use the *PropertyDescriptorCollection* object to find properties of a control much as you would to set properties on the form, except you use the *PropertyDescriptor.GetValue* method:

```
System.ComponentModel.Design.IDesignerHost designer;
System.ComponentModel.PropertyDescriptor propControls;
System.ComponentModel.PropertyDescriptorCollection props;
System.ComponentModel.IComponent component;
System.Windows.Forms.Form form;
System.Drawing.Size size;
designer = (System.ComponentModel.Design.IDesignerHost) applicationObject.Activ
eWindow.Object;
component = designer.RootComponent;

//Get the Size property using the forms designer:
props = System.ComponentModel.TypeDescriptor.GetProperties(component);
propControls = props["Size"];
size = (System.Drawing.Size)propControls.GetValue(component);

//Get the Size property directly from the form:
form = (System.Windows.Forms.Form)component;
size = form.Size;
```

A Form Layout Sample

Visual Basic 6 and earlier has a tool window called Form Layout that shows the size of a form being designed as it would appear on the desktop of your computer. Visual Studio .NET doesn't have this feature, but you can easily add it using the automation model of the Forms designer. You can find the source code for this sample, called FormView, among the book's sample files.

When the add-in starts, it creates a tool window that draws a virtual monitor representing your computer monitor. The screen of the virtual monitor matches the display resolution of your monitor. (If your computer uses multiple monitors, the resolution of the primary monitor is used.) After connecting to the *WindowActivated* event, it waits for a Forms designer window to become active, and then it looks at the available controls in the form and draws the form and its controls on the virtual screen. For example, if you create a form that has the calendar and button controls on it, as shown in Figure 10-4, the Forms designer window, shown in Figure 10-5, appears.

Figure 10-4 A Windows Form with a calendar control and a button control

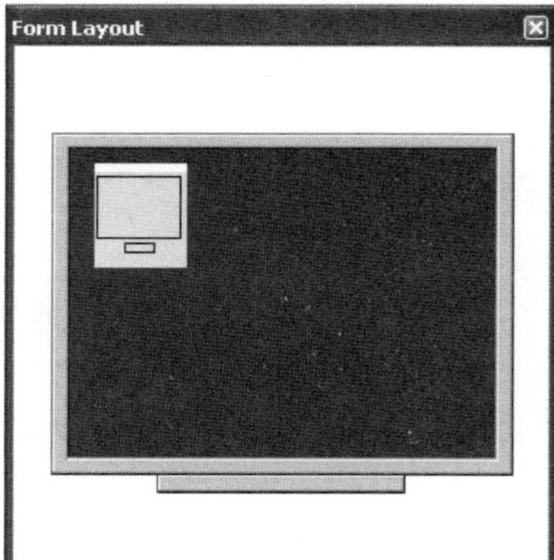

Figure 10-5 The Form Layout window showing the form from Figure 10-4

Creating Custom Tool Windows

As you know, most of the windows in Visual Studio .NET have an object model that you can use to program the contents and present data that your code generates. However, at times you might need to display data in a way that the existing tool windows cannot handle. To allow you to display data in a way that is most suitable for your add-in, the Visual Studio .NET object model allows creation of custom tool windows.

To create a tool window, all you need is an ActiveX control and an add-in that makes a call to the *Windows.CreateToolWindow* method. *CreateToolWindow* has the following method signature:

```
public EnvDTE.Window CreateToolWindow(EnvDTE.AddIn AddInInst,
    string ProgID,
    string Caption,
    string GuidPosition,
    ref object DocObj)
```

This method returns a Window object that behaves like any tool window that Visual Studio .NET creates. Here are the arguments for this method:

- **AddInInst** An add-in object that's the sponsor of the tool window. When the sponsor add-in is unloaded, all tool windows associated with that add-in are automatically closed and the ActiveX control is unloaded.
- **ProgID** The ProgID of the ActiveX control that's hosted on the newly created tool window.
- **Caption** The text to show in the title bar of the new tool window.
- **GuidPosition** A GUID in string format. As you'll recall, the *Windows.Item* method can be indexed by a GUID, and that GUID uniquely identifies a specific window. The GUID assigned to your tool window and the GUID passed to the *Windows.Item* method are set using this parameter. This GUID must be different from the GUID used by other tool windows; if you call *CreateToolWindow* multiple times, you must use a different GUID for each window.
- **DocObject** Most ActiveX controls have a programmable object in the form of a COM *IDispatch* interface, which is mapped to a *System.Object* when you're using the .NET Framework. The programmable object of the ActiveX control is passed back to the caller through this parameter, which allows you to program the control as you would any other tool window. You can also retrieve the programmable object of the ActiveX control by calling the *Object* property of the *Window* object for the tool window that's created using the *CreateToolWindow* method.

To demonstrate using the *CreateToolWindow* method, the samples that accompany this book include an add-in project called VSMediaPlayer. This sample creates a tool window using Windows Media Player as the ActiveX control and then, by using the programmable object of the control, plays an audio file. The code that does the work of creating the tool window looks like this:

```
void CreateMediaPlayerToolWindow()
{
    EnvDTE.Windows windows;
    EnvDTE.Window mediaPlayerWindow;
    object controlObject = null;
    string mediaPlayerProgID = "MediaPlayer.MediaPlayer";
    string toolWindowCaption = "Windows Media Player";
    string toolWindowGuid = "{AB5E549E-F823-44BB-8161-BE2BD5D698D8}";

    //Create and show a tool window that hosts the
    // Windows Media Player control:
    windows = applicationObject.Windows;
    mediaPlayerWindow = windows.CreateToolWindow(addInInstance,
                                                 mediaPlayerProgID,
                                                 toolWindowCaption,
                                                 toolWindowGuid,
                                                 ref controlObject);
    mediaPlayerWindow.Visible = true;

    //Play the Windows "Tada" sound:
    //Can only get the system directory (Eg: C:\windows\system32),
    // need to change this to the Windows install dir
    string mediaFile = System.Environment.GetFolderPath(
        System.Environment.SpecialFolder.System);
    mediaFile += "\\..\\media\\tada.wav";
    MediaPlayer.IMediaPlayer2 mediaPlayer =
         (MediaPlayer.IMediaPlayer2)controlObject;
    mediaPlayer.AutoStart = true;
    mediaPlayer.FileName = mediaFile;
}
```

The *CreateMediaPlayerToolWindow* method is called in two places in the sample add-in—once in the *OnConnection* method and once in the *OnStartupComplete* method. It must be called twice because of the way add-ins are loaded by Visual Studio .NET. If an add-in is set to load on startup, when Visual Studio .NET starts, the add-in starts loading. This loading process includes calling the *OnConnection* method. But the *OnConnection* method is called just before the Visual Studio .NET main window is created and shown. If you call the *CreateToolWindow* method within *OnConnection* before the main window is shown, creating the tool window will fail because creating an ActiveX control requires its parent window to be visible. You can check to make sure that the main window has been created by examining the *connectMode* argument passed to the *OnConnection* method. If this is set to *ext_cm_AfterStartup*, the add-in was loaded through the Add-in Manager or by means other than the load on startup flag being set and Visual Studio .NET being started. Therefore, the tool window can be shown when an add-in is loaded using an *OnConnection* implementation such as this:

```
public void OnConnection(object application,
    Extensibility.ext_ConnectMode connectMode, object addInInst,
    ref System.Array custom)
{
    applicationObject = (_DTE)application;
    addInInstance = (AddIn)addInInst;

    //If the add-in is loaded from the Add-in Manager dialog, then
    // create and show the tool window:
    if(connectMode == Extensibility.ext_ConnectMode.ext_cm_AfterStartup)
    {
        CreateMediaPlayerToolWindow();
    }
}
```

If the load on startup flag is set and you want to show the tool window when an add-in is loaded, you can create the window in the *OnStartupComplete* method. This method is called when initialization of Visual Studio .NET is complete, which includes creating and showing the main window. It's as simple as this code snippet:

```
public void OnStartupComplete(ref System.Array custom)
{
    //If the add-in is loaded at startup, then
    // create and show the tool window:
    CreateMediaPlayerToolWindow();
}
```

The *CreateToolWindow* method can be a powerful aid in creating an add-in's user interface, but it does add one complication. As mentioned earlier, when a tool window is created, an ActiveX control is instantiated and hosted within the new window; but ActiveX controls cannot be created using the .NET Framework. To allow use of a .NET user control within a tool window, you need a *shim control.*

Shim Controls

To enable hosting of a .NET Framework user control in a tool window, you can use a specialized ActiveX control called a shim control. A shim control is simply an ActiveX control written in an unmanaged language (such as Visual C++) that creates an instance of the .NET common language runtime (CLR). Using a small amount of code, you can direct the instance of the CLR to create the user control to display in the tool window and then parent the control onto the shim ActiveX control. You can add new user controls to an existing project by choosing Project | Add User Control, or you can create a new Windows Control Library project, which will create a user control object.

The book's sample files include an implementation of a shim control called VSUserControlHost and a sample that uses the shim control, CSHostedControl. To create and host an instance of a user control on a tool window, two steps are needed. First, to host the shim ActiveX control in a tool window, you call the *CreateToolWindow* method, supplying the ProgID of the shim, as shown in this line of code taken from the CSHostedControl sample:

```
toolWindow = applicationObject.Windows.CreateToolWindow(addInInstance,
    "VSUserControlHost.VSUserControlHostCtl", "C# Hosted Control",
    "{C4E8F504-E3FB-4828-82F4-DDD1CAE13D39}", ref obj);
```

The next step is to tell the shim control where the Windows control can be found and the name of the class that implements the control. You do this through the *VSUserControlHostLib.IVSUserControlHostCtl* interface, which you can obtain by casting the programmatic object of the shim control:

```
shimControl =
     (VSUserControlHostLib.IVSUserControlHostCtl)toolWindow.Object;
```

The *IVSUserControlHostCtl* interface has four methods that you can call to pass the control's location and class name as well as other bits of information. Here's the signature of the interface:

```
System.Object HostUserControl(System.String Assembly, System.String Class);
System.Object HostUserControl2(System.Int32 HWnd);
```

Each of these methods returns the programmable object of the .NET control that's hosted by the shim control. The arguments passed to these methods are as follows:

- **Assembly** The location of the assembly that contains the control that is to be hosted. This location can be in one of three formats. The first is the full path to the assembly of the user control, such as C:\Assembly.dll. The second format is the URL of an assembly located on a Web server, such as *http://localhost/Assembly.dll*. The third format is the full name of an assembly located within the GAC, such as *System.Windows.Forms, Version=1.0.5000.0, Culture=neutral, PublicKeyToken=b77a5c561934e089, Custom=null* for the assembly implementing the *System.Windows.Forms* namespace.

- **Class** The full name of the class that implements the control that is to be hosted. If the assembly location is the full name of the *System.Windows.Form* assembly, as given above, and the name of the class is *System.Windows.Forms.Button*, an instance of the Windows Forms *Button* object is created and hosted in the tool window.
- **HWnd** The handle of a .NET control that is to be hosted within the shim control. Using this form of hosting a control is useful if the control has already been created or if the control code is located in the same assembly as the add-in calling *CreateToolWindow* because you can create the control and pass its window handle rather than passing information such as the location of the assembly and the class name.

Add-in developers commonly add a user control class to an add-in and then place that control on a tool window. You can do this using the shim control in two ways. The first way is to find the location of the assembly that implements the add-in and pass this as the first parameter to the *HostUserControl* method, as shown here:

```
VSUserControlHostLib.IVSUserControlHostCtl shimControl;
string assemblyPath;
EnvDTE.Window toolWindow;
object obj = null;
toolWindow = applicationObject.Windows.CreateToolWindow(addInInstance,
    "VSUserControlHost.VSUserControlHostCtl", "Hosted Control",
    "{A71654EC-A72E-40cf-9CD6-63FA3C52C307}", ref obj);
toolWindow.Visible = true;
shimControl =
    (VSUserControlHostLib.IVSUserControlHostCtl)toolWindow.Object;
assemblyPath = System.Reflection.Assembly.GetExecutingAssembly().Location;
shimControl.HostUserControl(assemblyPath, "MyAddin1.UserControl1");
```

The second way is to instantiate the control directly and pass the control's window handle to the *HostUserControl2* method:

```
VSUserControlHostLib.IVSUserControlHostCtl shimControl;
string assemblyPath;
EnvDTE.Window toolWindow;
object obj = null;
toolWindow = applicationObject.Windows.CreateToolWindow(addInInstance,
    "VSUserControlHost.VSUserControlHostCtl", "Hosted Control",
    "{A71654EC-A72E-40cf-9CD6-63FA3C52C307}", ref obj);
toolWindow.Visible = true;
shimControl =
    (VSUserControlHostLib.IVSUserControlHostCtl)toolWindow.Object;
assemblyPath = System.Reflection.Assembly.GetExecutingAssembly().Location;
UserControl1 uc = new UserControl1();
shimControl.HostUserControl3(uc.Handle.ToInt32());
```

Lab: Setting Up a Web Server to Host a User Control for a Tool Window

The *HostUserControl* method of the shim control takes as its first argument the full path to a .NET Framework user control on disk, the full name of an assembly in the computer's GAC, or a URL to a control that's on a Web server. If you put a user control for a tool window on a Web server, you can modify the control to provide new functionality and bug fixes to the user, but the user must connect to the Internet to download the control. If the user isn't connected to the Internet or if your Web server is down when a request for the control is made and the control has previously been downloaded, the control is loaded from the computer's download cache.

You can use the Microsoft Internet Information Services (IIS) Web server running on your computer as a test server. To set up your project to place your user control on the Web server, simply right-click on the project for the user control you want to place on a tool window and choose Properties to display the Property Pages dialog box for that project. Select the Configuration Properties | Build node, change the Configuration drop-down list selection to All Configurations, and then enter the path to your IIS Web server directory (usually C:\Inetpub\wwwroot) as the Output Path property. To cause the shim control to load your control from the Web server, change the path to the control from a location on disk or the name of an assembly on disk to http://localhost/*assemblyname*.dll.

You should keep a few things in mind when you load a control from a Web server. First, any assemblies that the control references, except ones within the GAC of the computer that load the control, must be placed in the same folder on the Web server so the .NET Framework loader can find those references. Second, you can't program the object exposed through the control unless you use the *Type.InvokeMember* method. This is because of the way the .NET Framework resolves types when methods and properties are invoked. Third, before giving your add-in to a user, you must copy the user control to a server that the user can access and change the URL passed to the *HostUserControl* method to point to that server.

Setting the Tab Picture of a Custom Tool Window

When two or more tool windows are tab-linked together, an image is displayed so the user can quickly recognize the tool windows that are linked together. Figure 10-6 shows the Macro Explorer, Solution Explorer, and Properties windows docked to one another.

Figure 10-6 The pictures displayed on the tabs of the Macro Explorer, Solution Explorer and Properties windows

To set the tab picture for a tool window that's created by an add-in, you use the *Window.SetTabPicture* method. *SetTabPicture* takes as its argument a COM *IPictureDisp* type, which is mapped to the .NET Framework as a *System.Object* type. To create an *IPictureDisp* object, you can use the same technique described earlier of calling the *OleLoadPictureFile* method and then passing the returned *IPictureDisp* object to the *SetTabPicture* method.

The bitmap to place onto a tool window tab must have a specific format, and any deviation from this format can cause the bitmap to appear with incorrect colors or not appear at all. This bitmap must be 16 by 16 pixels, with a color depth of 16. If any portion of the bitmap is to show as transparent, the transparent pixels must have the RGB value 0,254,0. The format for this bitmap is the same format used for displaying custom pictures on command bar buttons (as discussed in Chapter 7); a bitmap can be shared for these two uses.

You can call the *Window.SetTabPicture* method only on a tool window created using the *Windows.CreateToolWindow* method. Windows defined by Visual Studio .NET already have their bitmaps set; if you try to change them, an exception will be generated. If you want to set the bitmap for your own tool window, you should set it before setting the *Visible* property of your window to *true*; otherwise, the picture might not be displayed immediately. Lastly, if a custom picture is not set, Visual Studio uses a default picture—the Visual Studio .NET logo.

Setting the *Selection* Object

As you select different windows in Visual Studio .NET, you see the Properties window update itself with properties available for those windows. For example, if you select a file in Solution Explorer, a set of properties is made available—such as the file path, when the file was modified, or how the file should be built. When you create a tool window, you might also want to have properties for your tool window appear in the Properties window. You set items to appear in the Properties window using the *Window.SetSelectionContainer* method, which takes as a parameter an array of type *System.Object*. These items are displayed in the Properties window when the window that has this method called on it becomes the active window. The sample VSMediaPlayerAdv, an extension to the VSMediaPlayer sample, displays a property set in the Properties window by calling the *SetSelectionContainer* method with the programmable object of Windows Media Player, which was returned through the *DocObj* parameter of the *CreateToolWindow* method. This portion of code shows how this is done:

```
object []propertiesWindowObjects = {mediaPlayer};
mediaPlayerWindow.SetSelectionContainer(ref propertiesWindowObjects);
```

You can call the *SetSelectionContainer* method only on tool windows that you create. If you call this method on a *Window* object for, say, the Solution Explorer tool window, an exception will be generated.

The Options Dialog Box

Developers can be a finicky bunch—they want Visual Studio .NET to work the way they want down to the finest detail; if even one option is set up in a way they didn't expect, they can become quite unproductive. The Options dialog box is full of options that you configure—everything from how many spaces are inserted when the Tab key is pressed in the text editor to whether the status bar is shown along the bottom of the main window of Visual Studio .NET.

Changing Existing Settings

Many settings in the Options dialog box can be controlled through the automation model using the *Properties* and *Property* objects. To find a *Properties* collection, you must first calculate the category and subcategory of the settings you want to modify. On the left side of the dialog box is a tree view control that's rarely more than two levels deep. The top-level nodes in this tree, such as Environment, Source Control, and Text Editor, are the categories of options you can manipulate. Each category contains a group of related Options pages, each containing a number of controls you can manipulate to customize your programming environment. The subitem nodes are the subcategories of the Options dialog box; if you select one of these nodes, the right side of the Options dialog box changes to show the options for that category and subcategory. The category and subcategory used to find a *Properties* collection are based on the category and subcategory displayed in the Options dialog box user interface, but their names might be slightly different from the category and subcategory names. To find the list of categories and subcategories, you must use the Registry Editor. First, you find the item in the Options dialog box that you want to edit. For our example, we'll modify the tab indent size of the Visual Basic .NET source code editor, which is found on the page of the Text Editor category and Basic subcategory.

> **Note** The Text Editor category is a bit different from other categories in the Options dialog box in that it has three levels, with the third level being a sub-subcategory. However, in the automation model, the General and Tabs sub-subcategories are combined into one and have the same name as the programming language.

After running regedit.exe, you must navigate the key *HKEY_LOCAL_MACHINE\SOFTWARE\Microsoft\VisualStudio\7.1\AutomationP* properties. Underneath this key is a list of all the property categories accessible to a macro or an add-in. We're looking for the Text Editor category—the key whose name most closely matches this category name in the user interface is TextEditor (without a space). After expanding this item in the Registry Editor, you'll see list of subcategories; one of those subcategories, Basic, matches the subcategory displayed in the user interface of the Tools Options dialog box, so this is the subcategory we'll use.

Now that we've found the automation category and subcategory TextEditor and Basic, we can plug these values into the *DTE.Properties* property to retrieve the *Properties* collection:

```
Sub GetVBTextEditorProperties()
    Dim properties As Properties
    properties = DTE.Properties("TextEditor", "Basic")
End Sub
```

The last step in retrieving a *Property* object is to call the *Item* method of the *Properties* collection. The *Item* method accepts as an argument the name of the property, but this name is not stored anywhere except within the object model. Remember that the *Properties* object is a collection, and like all other collection objects it can be enumerated to find the objects it contains and the names of those objects. You can use the following macro to examine the names of what will be passed to the *Properties.Item* method. The macro walks all the categories and subcategories listed in the registry and then uses the enumerator of the *Properties* collection to find the name of *Property* object contained in that collection. Each of these category, subcategory, and property names are then inserted into a text file that the macro creates:

```
Sub WalkPropertyNames()
    Dim categoryName As String
    Dim key As Microsoft.Win32.RegistryKey
    Dim newDocument As Document
    Dim selection As TextSelection
    'Open a new document to store the information
    newDocument = DTE.ItemOperations.NewFile("General\Text File").Document
    selection = newDocument.Selection
    'Open the registry key that holds the list of categories:
    key = Microsoft.Win32.Registry.LocalMachine
    key = key.OpenSubKey( _
        "SOFTWARE\Microsoft\VisualStudio\7.1\AutomationProperties")
    'Enumerate the categories:
    For Each categoryName In key.GetSubKeyNames()
        Dim subcategoryName As String
        selection.Insert(categoryName + vbLf)
        'Enumerate the subcategories:
        For Each subcategoryName In _
            key.OpenSubKey(categoryName).GetSubKeyNames()
            Dim properties As Properties
            Dim prop As [Property]
            selection.Insert("  " + subcategoryName + vbLf)
            Try
                'Enumerate each property:
                properties = DTE.Properties(categoryName, subcategoryName)
                For Each prop In properties
                    selection.Insert("    " + prop.Name + vbLf)
                Next
            Catch
            End Try
        Next
    Next
End Sub
```

Using the output from this macro, we can find the TextEditor category and the Basic subcategory and then look in the Options dialog box for something that looks like the name Tab Size. The closest match is TabSize. Using this name, we can find the *Property* object for the Visual Basic .NET text editor Tab Size:

```
Sub GetVBTabSizeProperty()
    Dim properties As Properties
    Dim prop As [Property]
    properties = DTE.Properties("TextEditor", "Basic")
    prop = properties.Item("TabSize")
End Sub
```

Now all that's left to do is retrieve the value of this property using the *Property.Value* property:

```
Sub GetVBTabSize()
    Dim properties As Properties
    properties = DTE.Properties("TextEditor", "Basic")
    MsgBox(properties.Item("TabSize").Value)
End Sub
```

This macro displays the value *4*, which is the same value in the Tools Options dialog box for the Tab Size option of the Basic subcategory of the Text Editor category. You set this value the same way you retrieve the value, except the *Value* property is written to rather than read:

```
Sub SetVBTabSize()
    Dim properties As Properties
    properties = DTE.Properties("TextEditor", "Basic")
    properties.Item("TabSize").Value = 4
End Sub
```

By simply changing the category and subcategories passed to the *DTE.Properties* property and looking at the list of property names generated by the *WalkPropertyNames* macro, you can modify many of the options shown in the Tools Options dialog box.

Is It What It Says It *Is*?

When you use the Visual Studio .NET object model, you might use the Visual Basic .NET *Is* operator or the .NET Framework *Object.Equals* method to try to determine whether two objects are the same. But the *Is* operator and the *Equals* method might not always return what you expect because of how the Visual Studio .NET object model was built. If you run a macro such as this

```
Sub CompareWindowsObjects()
    Dim window1 As Window
    Dim window2 As Window
    window1 = DTE.Windows.Item(Constants.vsWindowKindTaskList)
    window2 = DTE.Windows.Item(Constants.vsWindowKindTaskList)
    MsgBox(window1 Is window2)
End Sub
```

a message box with the value *True* is displayed. When you ask for a *Window* object, the object model checks to see whether a *Window* object has been created for the specific window; if not, a new *Window* object is constructed and returned to the calling code. If a *Window* object has already been created, that object is recycled and returned to the caller. This is both a performance and memory consumption optimization because new objects are not unnecessarily created (which consumes memory) and initialized (which consumes processor time). But if you run code such as this

```
Sub ComparePropertyObjects()
    Dim props1 As Properties
    Dim props2 As Properties
    props1 = DTE.Properties("Environment", "General")
    props2 = DTE.Properties("Environment", "General")
    MsgBox(props1 Is props2)
End Sub
```

the message box displays *False* because the *Properties* collection must be reconstructed each time you call the *DTE.Properties* property to be sure it has the most up-to-date information.

Calling the *DTE.Properties* property multiple times can cause huge memory consumption problems. Suppose you call the *DTE.Properties* property repeatedly in a tight loop; every time the property is called, a new *Properties* collection is created, initialized, and then returned to the calling code. This object consumes memory for the COM object that Visual Studio .NET creates, and if you're using a programming language supported by the .NET Framework, a .NET wrapper class that allows you to program this object is constructed. You can see the memory consumption grow almost boundlessly if you run the following macro and watch the vsmsvr.exe process (the process that hosts the instance of the .NET Framework and runs macro code) on the Processes tab of Windows Task Manager:

```
Sub RepeatedConstruct()
   Dim i As Long
    Dim props As Properties
    For i = 1 To Long.MaxValue
        props = DTE.Properties("Environment", "General")
    Next
End Sub
```

When you run this macro, the loop never allows a garbage collection to occur because the .NET Framework is focused on running your code, not searching and removing unused objects. To make sure your program doesn't waste more memory than it should, you should be sure you're not creating more objects than necessary by using the *Is* operator or the *Object.Equals* method and optimizing accordingly. For example, you can rewrite the *RepeatedConstruct* macro as follows and avoid system memory stress by simply moving the call to *DTE.Properties* outside of the loop:

```
Sub OptimizedRepeatedConstruct()
    Dim i As Long
    Dim props As Properties
    Dim showStatusbar As Boolean
    props = DTE.Properties("Environment", "General")
    For i = 1 To Long.MaxValue
        showStatusbar = props.Item("ShowStatusBar").Value
    Next
End Sub
```

An unscientific measurement (consisting of opening up Windows Task Manager and noting of the amount of memory consumed before and after running the macro) shows that moving the one line outside of the loop saves almost 35 MB of memory—something your users will appreciate.

Creating Custom Settings

Not only can you examine and modify existing settings, but you can also create your own options for your add-ins. Creating a page in the Options dialog box for your add-in requires an ActiveX control and making modifications to the system registry to let Visual Studio .NET know to load your Options page. An add-in is also required because Visual Studio .NET uses registry keys located under the registry keys for your add-in to find which Options pages are available. When the user opens the Options dialog box, the registry keys for each add-in is examined, and if the registry settings for a custom tools options page is found, the ActiveX control is instantiated and shown in the Options dialog box.

You can create the registry keys for a Options page by modifying the registry settings of the setup project created when you ran the Add-in Wizard. To make the necessary modifications, right-click on the setup project for your add-in in the Solution Explorer tool window and choose View | Registry. The Registry editor window for the setup project will open. Expand the tree view on the left side of this window until you find the ProgID key for the add-in you created using the wizard, and select that item. If you call the add-in you created using the wizard—OptionsAddin—and use all the default options except you select the Yes, Create A "Tools" Menu Item option, the left panel of the registry editor should look like that in Figure 10-7.

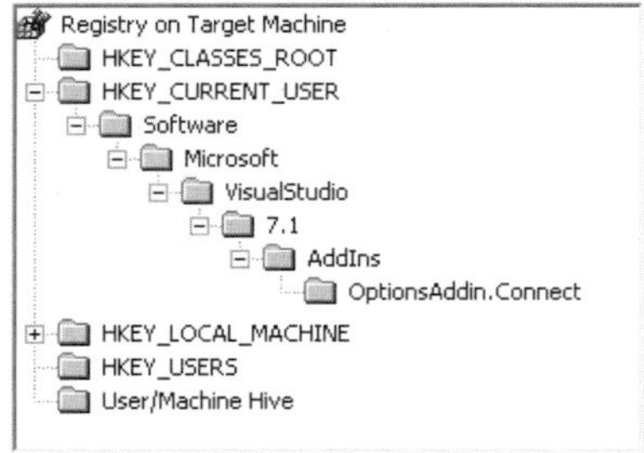

Figure 10-7 The Registry editor of an add-in called OptionsAddin

To declare an Options page, you must add three registry keys to this selected key, each one a child of the previous one added. The first key you create is called Options. As Visual Studio .NET displays the Options dialog box, every add-in's registry keys are examined and if the Options key is present, the Options dialog box knows that an add-in might have a Options page associated with it. To create the Options key, right-click on the registry key for the ProgID of the add-in, choose New | Key, and then type **Options**. The next two registry keys to create for the tools options are the category and subcategory of the Options page. To create the registry keys for the category and subcategory, simply repeat the steps you performed to create the Options key, with the category as a child of the Options key and the subcategory as a child of the category key. You can name the keys anything you want; the name that you use will be the text displayed in the Options dialog box tree. If you were to use the name Options Add-in for the category of your page and General for the subcategory, the registry editor should appear as shown in Figure 10-8.

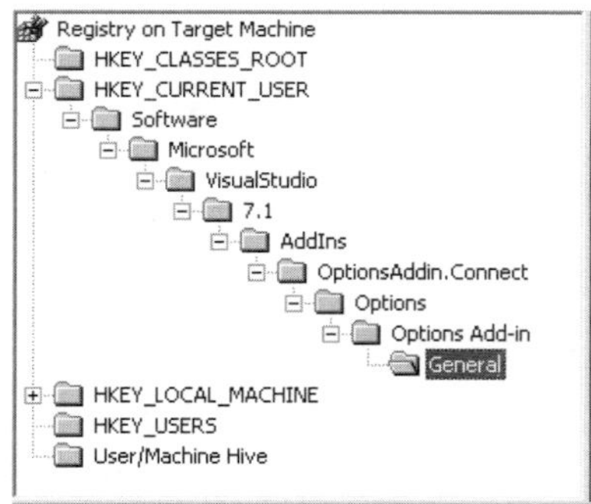

Figure 10-8 The Registry editor of an add-in with the registry keys for an Options page

The last step in setting up the registry for an Options page is to declare the ProgID of the ActiveX control hosted in the Options dialog box when the appropriate category and subcategory are selected. To do this, select the subcategory node in the left side of the registry editor window, right-click on the right side of this window, choose New | String Value, and the type the name **Control**. To set this registry key's value, with the value Control selected, look in the Properties window and type the ProgID of the ActiveX control into the Value property. We haven't yet created the ActiveX control that we'll host, but if you're following along with this sample, enter the value *OptionsAddinPage.OptionsAddinPageCtl*. (This is the ProgID of the control that we'll soon create.)

Creating the ActiveX Control

When the registry editor of the setup project is populated with the registry keys necessary to declare the tools options page, the next step is to create the ActiveX control. This step is not as easy as it might seem. When we were trying to create a tool window using the *Windows.CreateToolWindow* method and we wanted to use a .NET Framework user control as the user interface for the window, we had to use a shim ActiveX control to host the user control because a .NET control is not an ActiveX control. The problem with using a user control as a Tools Options page is that, first, it is not an ActiveX control, and second, you cannot use the shim control because you need to be able to run code to tell the shim where to find the user control. Because Visual Studio .NET creates Tools Options pages for you instead of you creating it as you did with a tool window, code never has the chance to run to program the shim control.

For all these reasons, a .NET user control cannot be used as an Options page. That leaves the option of using an unmanaged programming language that can create ActiveX controls—such as Visual C++. To create this control, you first add an ATL project to the project that contains your add-in; for this example, we'll call it OptionsAddinPage. Next, you implement an ActiveX composite control, hook up some additional interfaces, and write additional code to wire up the page. Because this is a book about programming Visual Studio .NET, we'll use our bag of tricks to create an Options page wizard. This wizard, OptionsPageWizard, will generate all the code necessary to create a Tools Options page for us. After building the wizard sample and copying the .vsz file into the Extensibility Projects folder, as you did in Chapter 9 for the WizardBuilder sample, you can right-click on the solution node in Solution Explorer, enter the project name **OptionsAddin**, and then run the wizard to create the starter code. The only option this wizard asks for is the ProgID of the add-in that the Options page is for so the correct location within the system registry to store options can be computed.

The *IDTToolsOptionsPage* Interface

An Options page has three stages in its lifetime: creation, interaction, and dismissal. To allow your page to know about these three stages, you can optionally implement the *IDTToolsOptionsPage* interface on the ActiveX control of your page. This interface has the following signature:

```
public interface IDTToolsOptionsPage
{
    public void GetProperties(ref object PropertiesObject);
    public void OnAfterCreated(EnvDTE.DTE DTEObject);
    public void OnCancel();
    public void OnHelp();
    public void OnOK();
}
```

When the user first displays the Options dialog box, Visual Studio .NET sees in the registry that you've declared a page, and it creates an instance of your ActiveX control. If the *IDTToolsOptionsPage* interface is implemented on that control, the *OnAfterCreated* method is created and is passed the *DTE* object for the instance of Visual Studio .NET that is creating the control. The implementation of this method can perform any initialization steps needed, such as reading values from the system registry and using these values to set up the user interface of the control. The default page that the OptionsPageWizard generates does this very thing—reading a value from the registry, and if set to a certain value, selecting the check box.

The Options dialog box has three buttons the user can click: OK, Cancel, and Help. If the user clicks OK, the *IDTToolsOptionsPage.OnOK* method is called, giving your page a chance to store back into the system registry any values that the user might have selected. The code generated by the wizard stores the state of the check box into the registry at this time. You should also perform any cleanup work in the *OnOK* method because the Options page is about to be dismissed. If the user clicks the Cancel button, the *OnCancel* method is called. No values that the user selected in the page should be persisted, and this method is called so you can perform any cleanup necessary because, as when the user clicks OK, the Options dialog box is about to be closed. If the user clicks Help, the *OnHelp* method is called, giving your page a chance to display any help necessary to the user. Unlike the other buttons, Help doesn't dismiss the dialog box, so you shouldn't do any cleanup or store or discard values during this method call.

The last method of the *IDTToolsOptionsPage* interface is the *GetProperties* method. This method allows users to retrieve a *Properties* object for the options on your page in the same way they could retrieve a *Properties* object for other Options pages.

Exposing a *Property* Object

As you saw earlier, many of the values in the Options dialog box are programmable through the *Properties* collection. You can also allow the user to set and retrieve the values of your page through the *Properties* collection using the *GetProperties* method. This method returns an *IDispatch* interface, which is wrapped up into a *Properties* collection by Visual Studio .NET and handed back to the user when the *DTE.Properties* property is called with the category and subcategory of your page. By default, the OptionsPageWizard wizard creates one property, called *CheckBoxOption*, of the *IDispatch* interface. It corresponds to the check box on the user interface of the control. Using our example of the OptionsAddinPage page, you can call to this property using a macro such as this:

```
Sub GetSetCustomOptions()
    Dim properties As EnvDTE.Properties
    Dim prop As EnvDTE.Property
    'Retrieve the Properties object of our custom page:
    properties = DTE.Properties("Options Add-in", "General")
    prop = properties.Item("CheckBoxOption")
    'Display the options value:
    MsgBox(prop.Value)
    'Change the value, then display the new value:
    prop.Value = True
    MsgBox(prop.Value)
End Sub
```

In your add-in, when you need to retrieve the value of an option, you can use code such as that shown in GetSetCustomOptions to find how the add-in can act according to the user's preferences. For example, suppose you want to add a Tools Options page for the VSMediaPlayer tool window to allow the user to set a multimedia file that is played when the window is activated. You can use a line of code such as this to find that file path:

```
DTE.Properties("VSMediaPlayer", "General").Item("MediaFile").Value
```

It's important that you not cache the values you retrieve from a *Property* object because the user might modify these options at any time, and if you did not retrieve the value when the window became active, the cached file to play will be out-of-date.

Looking Ahead

In this chapter, you learned how you can program many of the windows available in Visual Studio .NET. In the next chapter, we'll show you how to program the data in one specific window type: the text editor window.

11

Text Editing Objects and Events

Much of what a programmer does during the workday (and worknight) involves editing text. In fact, editing text is so much a part of programming that many a successful business has been built around creating a better Notepad, and the popularity of these editors has grown in direct proportion to the number of mundane tasks that they automate and the extent to which they can be customized. As you learned in Chapter 3, Visual Studio .NET boasts a first-class code editor, and the automation object model lets you leverage the editor's functionality to create all the editing features that would've been included had you been in charge at Microsoft.

Editor Windows

If you want to edit text in the IDE, you need a document; if you have a document, you also have an editor window. In Visual Studio .NET, documents and editor windows are like Siegfried and Roy—together, they work magic; apart, they're just a couple of sequined guys with pet tigers. (OK, we admit the analogy isn't perfect.) The point is that you can't have one without the other, so it pays to know a little about editor windows even if editing text in documents is your ultimate goal. Figure 11-1 gives a sneak preview of the editor windows of interest to us in this chapter.

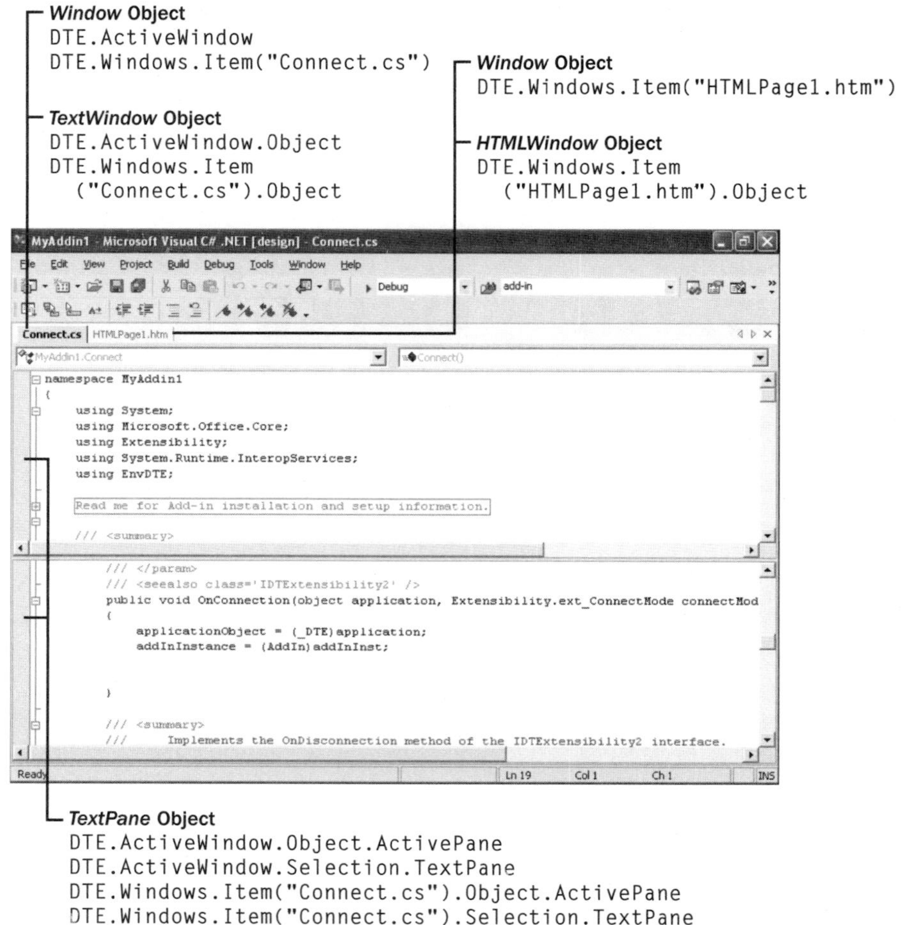

Figure 11-1 Editor windows

The *Window* Object

There's not much to say about the *Window* object—it's just a short stop on the way to more specialized windows. Finding a window is straightforward: if you want the window that has the focus, the *DTE.ActiveWindow* property returns it to you; if you want some other window and you know its caption, use *DTE.Windows.Item(<caption>)*. (Figure 11-1 shows the code for retrieving the Connect.cs and HTMLPage1.htm windows.)

Once you have a *Window* object, the most important property for finding other windows is *Object*, which returns the corresponding *TextWindow* or *HTMLWindow* object for editor windows. If you don't know for certain which type the *Object* property holds, you'll have to check using the *TypeOf...Is* (Visual Basic) or *is* (C#) keyword, as in

```
If TypeOf DTE.ActiveWindow.Object Is TextWindow Then
    ⋮
End If
```

Of course, if you don't check and you use the wrong object, you'll receive an exception courtesy of the common language runtime (CLR).

The *TextWindow* and *HTMLWindow* Objects

The *TextWindow* and *HTMLWindow* objects represent the editor windows in the IDE. Each type offers a small set of properties that give you access to editor-window-specific features. Table 11-1 lists the *TextWindow* properties. The two properties of note are *ActivePane* and *Panes*, which give you access to the panes in a given editor window.

Table 11-1 *TextWindow* Properties

Property	Description
ActivePane	Returns the *TextPane* object associated with the active pane.
DTE	Returns the top-level *DTE* object.
Panes	Returns a *TextPanes* collection containing the panes in the window.
Parent	Returns the parent *Window* object.
Selection	Returns the *TextSelection* object for the active pane. (It is equivalent to *Parent.Selection*.)

Essentially, an *HTMLWindow* object is just a *TextWindow* object—except when it isn't. Table 11-2 shows the *HTMLWindow* properties.

Table 11-2 *HTMLWindow* Properties

Property	Description
CurrentTab	Sets or returns the currently selected tab (HTML or Design)
CurrentTabObject	Returns a *TextWindow* object when the HTML tab is selected or returns an *IHTMLDocument2* interface when the Design tab is selected
DTE	Returns the top-level *DTE* object
Parent	Returns the parent *Window* object

The *CurrentTab* property uses values from the *EnvDTE.vsHTMLTabs* enumeration: *vsHTMLTabsSource* when setting or returning the HTML tab and *vsHTMLTabsDesign* when setting or returning the Design tab. The *CurrentTabObject* property returns a *TextWindow* object when the HTML tab is selected, which is why we suggested earlier that an *HTMLWindow* is just a *TextWindow* in disguise. When the Design tab is selected, however, *CurrentTabObject* returns an *mshtml.IHTMLDocument2* interface, which provides access to the Dynamic HTML (DHTML) object model of the underlying document. Be aware that the views offered by the Design tab and HTML tab aren't synchronized: changes in one view won't propagate to the other until you switch views. In practical terms, this means that you should use references only to the current view.

> **Note** To use the *mshtml* namespace, you need its primary interop assembly: Microsoft.mshtml.dll. You can find this assembly at (of all places) Program Files\Microsoft.NET\Primary Interop Assemblies. Add-in writers can add a reference to this assembly by browsing to it from the Add Reference dialog box; macro writers first need to copy the DLL file to Visual Studio .NET's PublicAssemblies folder before they can access the assembly.

As you now know, it takes several steps to discover whether a text window hides inside an arbitrary window. If you think it would be nice to have a function that takes care of these steps for you, you're in luck:

```
Function GetTextWindow(ByVal win As Window) As TextWindow
    ' Description: Returns the TextWindow object for a given window,
    '              or Nothing if not a text window

    Dim txtWin As TextWindow = Nothing

    ' Check for TextWindow
    If TypeOf win.Object Is TextWindow Then
        txtWin = win.Object

    ' Otherwise, check for HTMLWindow, then TextWindow
    ElseIf TypeOf win.Object Is HTMLWindow Then
        Dim htmlWin As HTMLWindow = win.Object

        If htmlWin.CurrentTab = vsHTMLTabs.vsHTMLTabsSource Then
            txtWin = htmlWin.CurrentTabObject
```

```
        End If
    End If

    Return txtWin
End Function
```

The *TextPane* Object

The *TextPane* object represents a pane in an editor window. Every editor window can be split into two panes to allow you to juxtapose two locations in a text file. You can split the view manually either by double-clicking the splitter bar—the thin rectangle at the top of the scroll bar—or by clicking and dragging the splitter bar to the desired location. Afterwards, you can make changes to the same document through either pane.

Finding *TextPane* Objects

The automation object model makes it easy to find *TextPane* objects if you already have a *TextWindow* object: just use the *ActivePane* property or iterate through the *Panes* collection until you find the *TextPane* you want. Unfortunately, the *TextWindow* object's alter ego, *HTMLWindow*, doesn't offer similar properties directly, so you first have to use logic like that found in the *GetTextWindow* function from the previous section to extract a *TextWindow* from an *HTMLWindow*.

An alternative way of retrieving a *TextPane* is through the *TextSelection* object. *TextSelection* has a *TextPane* property that returns the pane to which the selection belongs. (*TextPane* has an orthogonal property, *Selection*, that returns the *TextSelection* in the pane.) *TextWindow* and *HTMLWindow* both have a *Selection* property, as does *Window*, which means there's an indirect path to *TextPane* that all window objects can travel. For most purposes, however, using a *TextWindow* to find a *TextPane* works just fine.

One pane-related question you might ask is whether a second pane is open in an editor window. The following code gives you the answer:

```
Function IsSecondPaneOpen(ByVal txtWin As TextWindow) As Boolean
    ' Description: Returns whether a second pane is open in a text window

    Return (txtWin.Panes.Count = 2)
End Function
```

The *TextPanes* collection returned by *Panes* has one *TextPane* object for each pane in the window, so its *Count* property returns 2 when a second pane is open.

Here's a more interesting problem—finding the top or bottom pane in a window. The problem would be intractable except for the fact that the bottom pane is always at index 1 of its *TextPanes* collection. Given that bit of information, here are two functions that return the appropriate pane:

```
Function GetTopPane(ByVal txtWin As TextWindow) As TextPane
    ' Description: Returns the top pane in the text window

    Dim txtPane As TextPane = Nothing

    If txtWin.Panes.Count = 1 Then
        ' Only one pane, so return it
        txtPane = txtWin.ActivePane
    Else
        ' Top pane is always index 2
        txtPane = txtWin.Panes.Item(2)
    End If

    Return txtPane
End Function

Function GetBottomPane(ByVal txtWin As TextWindow) As TextPane
    ' Description: Returns the bottom pane in a text window. Returns
    '              top pane if only one pane is open

    ' Bottom pane is always index 1
    Return txtWin.Panes.Item(1)
End Function
```

The *ActivateTopPane* and *ActivateBottomPane* macros included with the book's sample files let you test the previous code on live windows.

One last question you might want answered is which pane a given *TextPane* belongs to. At first, it might seem easy enough to compare the given *TextPane* with its corresponding member in the *TextPanes* collection, but for the reasons given in the Chapter 10 sidebar "Is It What It Says It Is?" you can't compare *TextPane* references and expect a straight answer. Fortunately, you can compare *TextSelection* references successfully, which is all the help you need to write the following functions:

```
Function IsTopPane(ByVal txtPane As TextPane) As Boolean
    ' Description: Returns whether the given TextPane is the top pane

    Dim result As Boolean = False

    If txtPane.Collection.Count = 1 Then
        result = True
    Else
        If txtPane.Selection Is txtPane.Collection.Item(2).Selection Then
            result = True
        End If
    End If
```

```
    Return result
End Function

Function IsBottomPane(ByVal txtPane As TextPane) As Boolean
    ' Description: Returns whether the given TextPane is the bottom pane

    Dim result As Boolean = False

    If txtPane.Collection.Count = 2 Then
        result = _
            (txtPane.Selection Is txtPane.Collection.Item(1).Selection)
    End If

    Return result
End Function
```

A Splitting Headache

Search all you want, but you won't find a *Split* method in the automation object model. However, Visual Studio .NET defines a *Windows.Split* command that works on the active window. For fun, here's a macro that splits every splittable window in the IDE. (If you don't think it's fun to have to unsplit all those windows, you'll find the corresponding *UnsplitAllWindows* macro in the book's sample files):

```
Sub SplitAllWindows()
    ' Description: Splits all text windows

    Dim win As Window
    Dim txtWin As TextWindow
    Dim saveWin As Window = DTE.ActiveWindow

    For Each win In DTE.Windows
        txtWin = GetTextWindow(win)

        If Not txtWin Is Nothing Then
            SplitWindow(txtWin)
        End If
    Next

    saveWin.Activate()
End Sub
```

```
Sub SplitWindow(ByVal txtWin As TextWindow, _
        Optional ByVal restoreActive As Boolean = False)
    ' Description: Splits a text window and optionally restores the
    '              active window when finished

    Dim split As Command = DTE.Commands.Item("Window.Split")
    Dim saveWin As Window

    If restoreActive Then
        saveWin = DTE.ActiveWindow
    End If

    txtWin.Parent.Activate()

    If split.IsAvailable And Not IsSecondPaneOpen(txtWin) Then
        DTE.Commands.Raise(split.Guid, split.ID, Nothing, Nothing)
    End If

    If restoreActive Then
        saveWin.Activate()
    End If
End Sub
```

Documents

At the risk of stating the obvious (and possibly the painfully obvious), the Visual Studio .NET text editor operates on documents. When you program, it's easy to think that you're typing in a file: you load source code from a file when you begin editing and you save the changes to a file when you finish, so it's natural to assume that all the time in-between is spent working on a file. However, a file is a something that exists on disk—the document you work with in the text editor is something less permanent but infinitely more malleable. This section introduces you to the two objects that capture these qualities of documents and make them available to you through automation: the *Document* and *TextDocument* objects.

The *Document* Object

The *Document* object serves as a general-purpose wrapper for text data; it provides methods and properties that give you high-level control over both the data and the windows in which that data appears.

Creating and Finding Documents

You can create a document programmatically by using methods of the *ItemOperations* object, which is covered in Chapter 8, and the *ProjectItems* object, which is covered in Chapter 9. For example, the *ItemOperations.NewFile* method, which corresponds to the File | New | File menu command, lets you create a file that isn't associated with a particular project. The following macro shows how to create a text file using the *NewFile* method:

```
Sub CreateNewTextFile()
    ' Description: Shows how to use the ItemOperations.NewFile method
    '              to create a new text file

    Dim Item As String = "General\Text File"
    Dim Name As String = "MyTextFile"
    Dim ViewKind As String = Constants.vsViewKindPrimary
    Dim win As Window

    win = DTE.ItemOperations.NewFile(Item, Name, ViewKind)
End Sub
```

One peculiarity of the *NewFile* method's *Name* parameter is that it specifies the name of the new document indirectly. With an existing file, the document name and the window caption both correspond to the filename. With a document created by *NewFile*, however, the *Name* parameter serves as the caption of the new document's window only—the document acquires the name of the temporary file created by Visual Studio .NET to store the new document. The "indirectly" part happens when you save the document: Visual Studio .NET displays the *Name* value as the default name of the file to save.

You have three main ways of finding and retrieving an existing *Document* object: the *DTE.Documents* collection, the *Window.Document* property, and the *DTE.ActiveDocument* property. The *DTE.Documents* collection contains a reference to every open *Document* object. Just like any other collection in the automation object model, you can iterate through the *Document* objects in the collection looking for the one you want, or if you know the name of the document, you can retrieve it by using the *Documents.Item* method, like so:

```
Dim doc As Document = DTE.Documents.Item("MyFile.cs")
```

If you have a *Window* object, its *Document* property returns the associated *Document* object. Some of the tests for this chapter use the following macro to retrieve the *Document* object of a *Window*; if the window doesn't exist, the macro creates a new text file with the requested caption and returns its *Document* object:

```
Function GetDocument(ByVal caption As String) As Document
    ' Description: Retrieves the Document object associated with
    '              the specified window, or creates a text file in
    '              a new window and returns its Document object

    Dim win As Window = DTE.Windows.Item(caption)

    ' Check whether window is open
    If win Is Nothing Then
        win = DTE.ItemOperations.NewFile("General\Text File", caption)
    End If

    Return win.Document
End Function
```

Managing Document Windows

The relationship of *Document* objects to windows is one-to-many: a window always has one associated *Document*, but a *Document* can be open in many windows. You can open a new window on a document by using the *Document.NewWindow* method, which works the same as the Window | New Window menu command. Each of the windows associated with a particular document will have as its caption the document name followed by a colon (:) and the window number. (For example, "Connect.cs:1," "Connect.cs:2," and so on.) Because the windows have the same underlying data, changes in one window can be seen by all other related windows.

> **Warning** Visual Basic files don't support *Document.NewWindow* and throw a "not implemented" exception when you call this method.

The ability to have multiple windows means that you won't find a *Document.Parent* property that returns the containing window. (Which window would it return?) Instead, you can find all the windows associated with a particular document by iterating through the *Document.Windows* collection, as shown by the following macro:

```
Sub ListDocumentWindows()
    ' Description: Lists all the windows associated with
    '              each open document

    Dim output As New OutputWindowPaneEx(DTE, title)
```

```
    output.Clear()
    output.WriteLine("--- ListDocumentWindows ---")
    output.WriteLine()

    Dim doc As Document

    For Each doc In DTE.Documents
        Dim win As Window

        output.WriteLine(doc.Name & " windows:")

        For Each win In doc.Windows
            output.WriteLine("    " & win.Caption)
        Next
    Next
End Sub
```

You can find the active window for the *Document* object by using its *ActiveWindow* property, which returns the active window, if applicable, or the top-most window associated with the document if none of the document's windows is active.

> **Warning** The *Document.ActiveWindow* property has a bug—it always returns the first document window, regardless of which window has the focus.

Managing Document Changes

The coarsest means available to the *Document* object for managing changes is its *ReadOnly* property, which allows you to get or set the document's read-only state. Methods that modify a document's text throw an exception if the document is read-only, so it's worth checking the *ReadOnly* property before you make text changes.

You can undo and redo changes to a document by using the *Document.Undo* and *Document.Redo* methods, respectively. These two methods offer the same functionality as their Edit menu counterparts. The *Undo* and *Redo* methods both return a Boolean value indicating whether the operation took place.

> **Warning** You can call *Document.Undo* or *Document.Redo* on a read-only document all you want, so long as the corresponding undo or redo stack is empty; in such cases, the method returns *False*. Problem is, you can change the *Document.ReadOnly* property on the fly, which means you can have undoable (or redoable) changes in your document when you switch from read-write to read-only. If you call *Undo* or *Redo* on a nonempty undo or redo stack of a read-only document, you get an exception.

The *Document.TextSelection* property returns the *TextSelection* object associated with the active window, or the top-most window if none of the document's windows has the focus. You can use the *TextSelection* object's myriad editing methods and properties to automate just about any editing task you can think of. (You'll learn all about *TextSelection* objects in the upcoming section titled "The *TextSelection* Object.")

Saving and Closing Documents

The *Document.Save* method saves the document and optionally lets you choose the name and the location to save to. The *Save* method throws an exception if the location you specify doesn't already exist; if you give a correct location but no name, the *Save* method uses the current name of the document. (A bug in the Visual C++ implementation causes the *Save* method to ignore any new filename you give it.) If you want to save every open document in one call, use the *SaveAll* method of the *Documents* collection. What you gain in convenience you give up in control—you can't specify new names or locations for the files as you can with the *Save* method.

The *Document.Close* method closes a document and also lets you pass in a *vsSaveChanges* value that signals whether to save changes (*vsSaveChanges*), discard changes (*vsSaveChangesNo*), or let the user decide whether to save changes (*vsSaveChangesPrompt*, which is the default). The *Documents* collection has a corresponding *CloseAll* method that lets you close every document and also specify a *vsSaveChanges* value to apply to every document.

The *Document.Saved* property indicates whether the document has changes that haven't yet been saved—a value of *False* means that the document is dirty, as indicated by an asterisk in the document window's title bar. Essentially, this property controls whether the IDE prompts you to save a document when the document is closed. You can write to this property, but be aware that you will lose changes if you close a dirty document after setting its *Saved* property to *True*.

The *TextDocument* Object

Whereas a *Document* object can represent any document in the IDE, the *TextDocument* object represents text documents only. You retrieve a *TextDocument* object by using the *Document.Object* method and passing in an empty string or a value of "*TextDocument*"; the method returns *null* or *Nothing* for nontext documents.

The most important *TextDocument* properties and methods are those related to the *TextPoint*, *EditPoint*, and *TextSelection* editing objects. The *TextDocument.Selection* property returns the text document's selection and behaves just the same as the *Document.Selection* property. The *StartPoint* and *EndPoint* properties return *TextPoint* objects that mark the beginning and end, respectively, of the text document buffer. The *CreateEditPoint* method returns an *EditPoint* object at the location of the *TextPoint* passed into the method; passing in *null* or *Nothing* creates an *EditPoint* at the beginning of the document.

> **Note** Calling *TextDocument.CreateEditPoint* with a *TextPoint* parameter makes little sense because a *TextPoint* object already has its own *CreateEditPoint* method. However, passing null to *TextDocument.CreateEditPoint* is the only way to create an *EditPoint* without first creating an intermediary point object.

Point Objects

As you might guess, a point object represents a position in a text document. The automation object model gives you three point objects to choose from: *TextPoint*, *VirtualPoint*, and *EditPoint*.

TextPoint

The *TextPoint* object embodies the fundamental attributes of a text document location; *VirtualPoint* and *EditPoint* implement the *TextPoint* interface, so all point objects have these fundamental attributes in common. The following list gives you an idea of what these attributes might be:

- **Line information** The *Line* property returns which line of the document the point is in.

- **Offset information** The *AbsoluteCharOffset* and *LineCharOffset* properties return the number of characters between the point and the beginning of the document and the beginning of the current line, respectively.
- **Extreme information** The *AtStartOfDocument*, *AtEndOfDocument*, *AtStartOfLine*, and *AtEndOfLine* properties allow you to determine whether the point is at the beginning or end of a document or line.

The *TextPoint LessThan*, *EqualTo*, and *GreaterThan* methods also let you discover the relation of one point with respect to another.

The *TextPoint* object doesn't have methods that allow you to edit text directly. Instead, you either pass these point objects to editing methods or use them to create an *EditPoint* at a particular location, which you can then use to edit text. Table 11-3 shows you the different ways to find a *TextPoint* object.

Table 11-3 How to Retrieve a *TextPoint* Object

Returned By	Applies To
StartPoint property	*TextDocument*
	TextPane
	TextRange
EndPoint property	*TextDocument*
	TextRange

VirtualPoint

A *VirtualPoint* object represents a point in *virtual space*, which, sorry to disappoint, has nothing to do with *The Matrix*. Virtual space is a text editor feature that allows the insertion point to move indefinitely past the end of a line; typing a character at a point in virtual space causes the editor to automatically fill in the space between the end of the line and the new character. You can enable virtual space for all languages by opening the Tools Options dialog box, selecting Text Editor | All Languages | General, and selecting the Enable Virtual Space check box in the Settings area. (See Figure 11-2.)

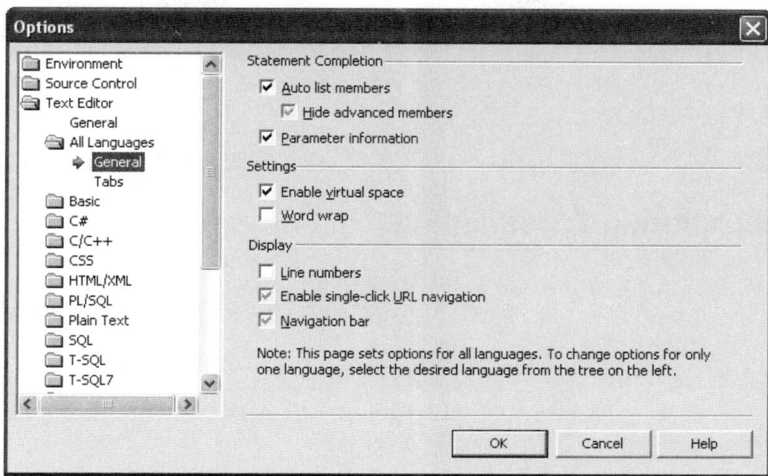

Figure 11-2 Enabling virtual space

Table 11-4 shows the different ways you can find a *VirtualPoint* object. As you can see from the table, *VirtualPoint* objects spring from *TextSelection* objects, which gives you a clue to their function; selections can extend into virtual space, so the *TextSelection* object needs *VirtualPoint* objects to keep track of endpoints that fall outside the text buffer.

Table 11-4 How to Retrieve a *VirtualPoint* Object

Returned By	Applies To
ActivePoint property	*TextSelection*
AnchorPoint property	
BottomPoint property	
TopPoint property	

As with the *TextPoint* object, one of the *VirtualPoint* object's main uses involves the creation of *EditPoint* objects. Be aware, however, that a *VirtualPoint* object can't create an *EditPoint* object in virtual space—if you try, the *EditPoint* gets created at the end of the current line instead. You can avoid those situations by using the following function, which tells you when a *VirtualPoint* has strayed into virtual space:

```
Function IsVirtualSpace(ByVal vrtPoint As VirtualPoint) As Boolean
    ' Description: Returns whether the VirtualPoint lies in virtual space

    Return vrtPoint.LineCharOffset <> vrtPoint.VirtualCharOffset
End Function
```

The *VirtualPoint* object defines a property named *VirtualCharOffset* that returns how far the point is from the beginning of the line. The *VirtualCharOffset* property always has the same value as the *LineCharOffset* property except when the point is in virtual space.

Lab: Exploring Virtual Space

The best way to understand virtual space and its effects on point objects is to test it for yourself. Here's a quick experiment:

1. Turn off virtual space in the editor.
2. Open a new text file and type **I am a fish.** without hitting Enter.
3. Select the entire sentence by dragging the mouse from left to right. Notice that the editor won't extend the selection beyond the period.
4. Open the Output window and run the *DisplayTextSelectionEditPoints* macro. Observe that the *DisplayColumn* entries for *TopPoint* and *BottomPoint* are 1 and 13, respectively.
5. Run the *DisplayTextSelectionVirtualPoints* macro. Notice that the *DisplayColumn* entries for *TopPoint* and *BottomPoint* match those from the previous step.
6. Run the *DisplayTextSelectionText* macro and observe that the output is '*I am a fish.*'

When you disable virtual space, you confine *VirtualPoint* objects to the limits of the text buffer. Enable virtual space, however, and those same *VirtualPoint* objects can wander off to parts unknown:

1. Enable virtual space in the text editor.
2. Reselect the entire sentence, but this time extend the selection beyond its end.
3. Rerun the *DisplayTextSelectionEditPoints* and *DisplayTextSelectionVirtualPoints* macros. Notice that the *EditPoint* values remain unchanged but the *VirtualPoint*'s *VirtualCharOffset* and *VirtualDisplayColumn* values exceed those of the corresponding *LineCharOffset* and *DisplayColumn* values.

4. Run the *DisplayTextSelectionText* macro and observe that its output is the same as before.

That last step shows that virtual space exists outside the text buffer; it also shows that virtual space doesn't count as selected text. Instead, virtual space allows for what you might call WYSINWYG editing—what you see isn't necessarily what you get.

EditPoint

The *EditPoint* is the workhorse of the point objects. In addition to the *TextPoint* methods and properties, *EditPoint* has methods that let you automate every possible modification of the text buffer. Table 11-5 shows the different ways you can get an *EditPoint* object.

Table 11-5 How to Retrieve an *EditPoint* Object

Returned By	Applies To
CreateEditPoint method	*EditPoint*
	TextPoint
	VirtualPoint
	TextDocument

We'll examine *EditPoint*'s methods shortly, in the section titled "A Comparison of *TextSelection* and EditPoint."

The *TextSelection* Object

The *TextSelection* object pulls double duty as a representation of the caret in the editor window as well as a representation of the currently selected text. (You can think of the caret as a zero-length selection.) Because there can be only one selection in an editor window, there can be only one *TextSelection* object per document. Figure 11-3 breaks down a *TextSelection* into its constituent parts.

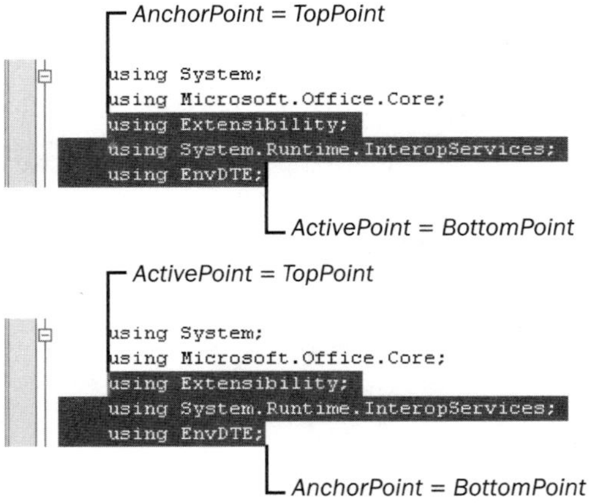

AnchorPoint = TopPoint

```
using System;
using Microsoft.Office.Core;
using Extensibility;
using System.Runtime.InteropServices;
using EnvDTE;
```

ActivePoint = BottomPoint

ActivePoint = TopPoint

```
using System;
using Microsoft.Office.Core;
using Extensibility;
using System.Runtime.InteropServices;
using EnvDTE;
```

AnchorPoint = BottomPoint

Figure 11-3 Anatomy of a *TextSelection*

As you can see in Figure 11-3, four properties delineate a *TextSelection*: *TopPoint*, *BottomPoint*, *AnchorPoint*, and *ActivePoint*. Each of these properties returns a *VirtualPoint* object from one of the ends of the selected range. The *TopPoint* and *BottomPoint* properties always refer to the upper-left and bottom-right of the selection, respectively. The *AnchorPoint* and *ActivePoint* properties refer to the equivalent of the start and end points of a mouse-drag selection; for example, the top selection in Figure 11-3 would result from dragging the mouse from the beginning of *using Extensibility;* to the end of *using EnvDTE;*. You can determine the orientation of a *TextSelection* by checking its *IsActiveEndGreater* property, which returns *True* when *ActivePoint* equals *BottomPoint*. If the orientation isn't to your liking, you can flip it by calling the *TextSelection.SwapAnchor* method, which exchanges the positions of *AnchorPoint* and *ActivePoint*.

The *TextSelection.IsEmpty* property lets you know whether there's a selection, and you can retrieve the selected text from the *Text* property. If there's no selection, *Text* always returns an empty string. The converse doesn't hold, however, because *Text* returns an empty string for a virtual space selection. When a selection spans multiple lines, the *TextRanges* property holds a collection of *TextRange* objects, one for each line of the selection.

Table 11-6 lists the different ways you can get a *TextSelection* object.

Table 11-6 Properties Returning a *TextSelection* Object

Property	Applies To
Selection	*Document*
	TextDocument
	TextPane
	TextWindow
	Window

A Comparison of *TextSelection* and *EditPoint*

The *TextSelection* and *EditPoint* objects offer a bewildering array of editing methods, which are listed in Table 11-7. Looking at the table, you'll see that *TextSelection* and *EditPoint* share the majority of their methods and have only a few seemingly minor differences, which makes choosing one over the other akin to choosing between the 52-feature Swiss army knife that comes with scissors and the 52-feature Swiss army knife that comes with a saw. In most circumstances, either knife will do just fine—it's only in those particular moments when you need to gather firewood or do a little personal grooming that you suddenly realize that you can't cut down branches with scissors and you can't trim nose hairs with a saw. Using the editing objects is much the same in that you won't know whether you've chosen the right one for the job until it fails you.

Table 11-7 *TextSelection* and *EditPoint* Methods

Task	Methods in Common	*TextSelection* Only	*EditPoint* Only
Moving the insertion point	*CharLeft*, *CharRight*, *EndOfDocument*, *EndOfLine*, *LineDown*, *LineUp*, *MoveToAbsoluteOffset*, *MoveToLineAndOffset*, *MoveToPoint*, *StartOfDocument*, *StartOfLine*, *WordLeft*, *WordRight*	*Collapse*, *GoToLine*, *MoveToDisplayColumn*, *PageDown*, *PageUp*	
Finding and retrieving text	*FindPattern*	*FindText*	*GetLines*, *GetText*
Selecting text		*SelectAll*, *SelectLine*	
Modifying text	*ChangeCase*, *Copy*, *Cut*, *Delete*, *DeleteWhitespace*, *Indent*, *Insert*, *InsertFromFile*, *PadToColumn*, *Paste*, *ReplacePattern*, *SmartFormat*, *Unindent*	*DeleteLeft*, *DestructiveInsert*, *NewLine*, *Tabify*, *Untabify*	*ReplaceText*

Table 11-7 *TextSelection* and *EditPoint* Methods *(continued)*

Task	Methods in Common	*TextSelection* Only	*EditPoint* Only
Managing bookmarks	*ClearBookmark, NextBookmark, PreviousBookmark, SetBookmark*		
Miscellaneous	*OutlineSection*	*SwapAnchor*	*ReadOnly*

The fundamental difference between the two objects is that the *TextSelection* object is view-based and the *EditPoint* object is buffer-based. The *TextSelection* object exists primarily to model user actions within the text editor—if you can do it by hand in the editor, you can do it with the *TextSelection* object. (You can see this demonstrated every time you record a macro: the Macro Recorder translates changes that you make to text documents into sequences of *TextSelection* statements.) This emphasis on WYSIWYG functionality, however, means that the global view state can affect the behavior of a *TextSelection* method. For example, when line wrapping is enabled, you can't count on *TextSelection.LineDown* moving the insertion point to the next line of text in the buffer—if the line wraps underneath the insertion point, then moving the insertion point to the next line in the view serves only to move the insertion point further down the same line in the buffer.

The *EditPoint* object, on the other hand, knows nothing about the view, so its operations are immune from the view's effects. Therefore, a call to *EditPoint.LineDown* always moves the *EditPoint* to the next line in the buffer, regardless of the line wrapping state. The only drawback of this insulation from the view is that you can't use *EditPoint* objects to affect virtual space.

So there you have it—if you want your add-ins and macros to make use of the view state automatically, use *TextSelection*; if you want complete control over the text buffer, use *EditPoint*.

Undo Contexts

The modern user interface has come a long way toward fulfilling one of humankind's greatest hopes—to be saved from its own stupidity. The undo facility you find in most of today's applications represents the crowning achievement of this pursuit. The next best thing to a time machine, undo allows you to roll back your most recent mistakes—usually with considerable relief—so that you can start making new ones in their place. The automation object model gives you full access to Visual Studio .NET's undo manager, allowing you to define your own sets of mistakes that can be undone at the click of a button.

Automatic Undo Contexts

The basic unit of "undoability" is the *undo context*. (We'll use this term to mean both an undoable unit—the named entity that appears on the undo list—and the mechanism by which you group individual actions to create an undoable unit.) The Visual Studio .NET IDE creates undo contexts automatically as you program, allowing you to undo and redo edits to your code. Try the following experiment to see some of the automatic undo contexts created by Visual Studio .NET:

1. Open a blank text file in Visual Studio .NET.
2. *Type* **spelled backwards is epyT** and press Enter.
3. Copy a block of text from some document and paste it into the text file.

When you've finished, click the drop-down list on the Undo button and you'll see the list of undo contexts shown in Figure 11-4. (The drop-down list represents the document's *undo stack*, which is the internal data structure that stores the undoable changes.) The three undo contexts named Paste, Enter, and Type each represent one or more individual actions that can be undone as a whole. You can appreciate the ability to group multiple actions under a single name when it comes to large paste operations, where the alternative would be undoing the pasted characters one by one.

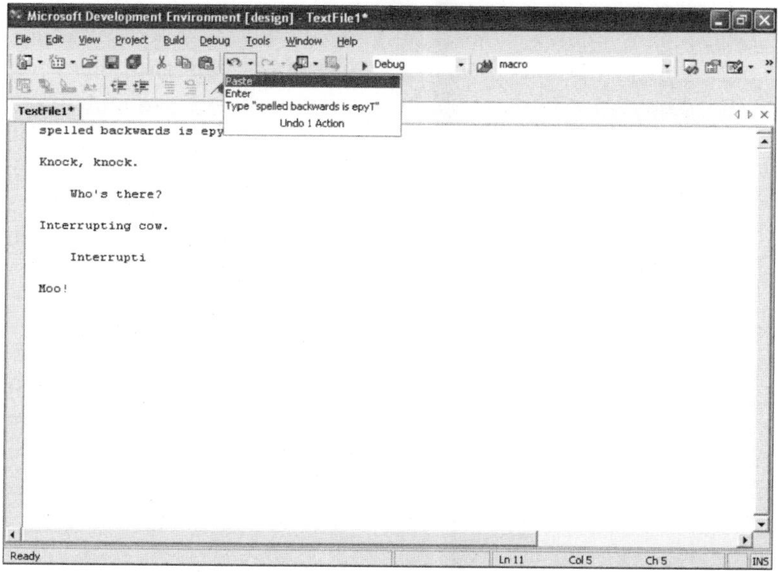

Figure 11-4 A list of undo contexts

Creating Undo Contexts

An undo context is an atomic transaction: you open the undo context and give it a name, make changes to one or more documents, and then either commit the changes by closing the undo context or abort all the changes. Once committed, the changes can be undone as a group only. You create your own undo contexts by calling methods of the *DTE.UndoContext* object: *Open* begins an undo context, *SetAborted* discards all changes made within the current undo context, and *Close* commits the changes and pushes the undo context onto the undo stacks of the participating documents.

The undo manager in Visual Studio .NET allows only one undo context at a time to be open, and to share that undo context you must follow a few rules. First, always call *Open* within a *try* block because this method throws an exception if an undo context is already open. Although you can check the availability of the undo context by using the *UndoContext.IsOpen* property, which returns *True* when an undo context is open, a *False* value won't guarantee that the undo context will still be free by the time your code executes *Open*. Second, if you open an undo context, you should close it when you're finished with it by calling *Close* or *SetAbort*. (Use just one or the other because *SetAbort* closes the undo context for you and calling *Close* on a closed undo context raises an exception.) Third, you should never call *SetAbort* or *Close* on someone else's undo context. That's just not nice.

> **Important** Macro writers, be aware that the undo manager doesn't trust you to close your own undo contexts. Instead, it automatically closes any undo context opened by a macro when execution returns to Visual Studio .NET. (Add-ins are free to keep their undo contexts open as long as they want, regardless of the consequences.) If you find that somewhat demeaning, then don't give the undo manager the satisfaction—instead, always use *SetAbort* or *Close* to tidy up your undo contexts.

Because only one undo context can be open at a time, if you don't acquire the undo context, any changes you make will belong to some other context. If the changes you need to make absolutely positively must be in their own context, you'll have to poll the *UndoContext.IsOpen* property until the undo context becomes free. Listing 11-1 shows one way to do this.

UndoContextTimer

```
<System.ContextStaticAttribute()> Public WithEvents UndoTimer _
    As System.Timers.Timer

Private Const title As String = "Text Editor"

Sub UndoContextTimer()
    ' Description: If undo context is busy, creates a timer that
    '              polls the UndoContext.IsOpen property until the
    '              undo context becomes free

    ' Start timer if undo context is busy
    If Not AddText() Then
        UndoTimer = New System.Timers.Timer()
        UndoTimer.Interval = 100
        UndoTimer.Enabled = True
    End If
End Sub

Private Function AddText() As Boolean
    ' Description: Adds text to the "Text File" document within
    '              the "Timer" undo context

    Dim success As Boolean = True

    Try
        ' Open the undo context
        DTE.UndoContext.Open("Timer")

        ' Open the "Text File" document for editing
        Dim txtDoc As TextDocument = GetTextDocument("Text File")
        Dim editPnt As EditPoint = txtDoc.StartPoint.CreateEditPoint

        ' Add some text
        editPnt.Insert("Here's text in the 'Timer' undo context." _
            + System.Environment.NewLine)

        ' Close the undo context
        DTE.UndoContext.Close()
    Catch
        success = False
    End Try

    Return success
End Function
```

Listing 11-1 Grabbing the undo context when it becomes free

```
Public Sub UndoTimer_Elapsed(ByVal sender As Object, _
    ByVal e As System.Timers.ElapsedEventArgs) Handles UndoTimer.Elapsed

    ' Check whether the undo context is free
    If Not DTE.UndoContext.IsOpen Then
        UndoTimer.Enabled = False

        ' Kill timer if AddText is successful, otherwise re-enable it
        If AddText() Then
            UndoTimer.Dispose()
            UndoTimer = Nothing
        Else
            UndoTimer.Enabled = True
        End If
    End If
End Sub

Function GetTextDocument(ByVal caption As String) As TextDocument
    ' Description: Retrieves the TextDocument object associated with
    '              the specified window, or creates a text file in
    '              a new window and returns its TextDocument object

    Dim doc As Document = GetDocument(caption)

    Return doc.Object("TextDocument")
End Function

Function GetDocument(caption As String) As Document
    ' Description: Retrieves the Document object associated with
    '              the specified window, or creates a document in
    '              a new window

    Dim win As Window

    Try
        ' Check whether window is open
        win = DTE.Windows.Item(caption)
    Catch
        ' Create a new text file
        win = DTE.ItemOperations.NewFile("General\Text File", caption)
    End Try

    Return win.Document
End Function
```

Normally, you shouldn't have to resort to the measures taken in Listing 11-1 because the undo context shouldn't be open for long periods of time. However, it's good to know that it can be done.

Stack Linkage

Sooner or later, when you edit multiple documents within the same undo context, you run across the problem of desynchronized undo stacks. Suppose you edit Document1 and Document2 within the Link undo context. After you close Link, it gets pushed onto the tops of the two documents' undo stacks. Then, if you undo Link in Document1, you also undo Link in Document2 because their edits belong to the same atomic operation. So far, so good.

Suppose you add some text to Document2. These new edits get pushed onto the top of Document2's undo stack. What happens now when you try to undo Link in Document1? To respect Link's atomicity, you have to undo Link in Document2, and there's the problem—you can't undo Link in Document2 without first undoing the text that was just added. The undo stacks have become desynchronized.

The undo manager solves this synchronization problem by introducing the concept of *stack linkage*. By default, an undo context that involves more than one document has a *nonstrict stack linkage*, which allows the atomicity of the undo context to be broken across documents; when the break happens, each document ends up with its own undo context containing only changes to itself. In our previous example, if the Link undo context were created with a nonstrict stack linkage, you could undo Link in Document1 without affecting Document2. Link would disappear from Document1's undo stack but remain on Document2's undo stack, minus the changes to Document1. A *strict stack linkage*, on the other hand, enforces the undo context's atomicity with extreme prejudice. If our previous example were to involve a strict stack linkage, the undo manager would kill any attempt to undo Link in Document1.

You specify the strictness of the stack linkage through the second parameter to *UndoContext.Open*, passing *True* for strict. You can identify undo contexts with strict stack linkage by the plus (+) sign that precedes their names on undo lists.

Lab: Strict and Nonstrict Stack Linkage

The *UndoContexts.StackLinkage* macro lets you test the differences between strict and nonstrict stack linkages. This macro creates three documents and adds text to them within an undo context; an optional *Boolean* parameter controls whether the undo context's stack linkage is strict. Follow these steps to see a nonstrict stack linkage in action:

1. In the Command Window, type **Macros.InsideVSNET.Chapter11.UndoContexts.StackLinkage** and press Enter. The macro creates three files—Nonstrict1, Nonstrict2, and Nonstrict3—and adds text to them within the NonstrictLinkage undo context.
2. In any of the files, click the Undo button, and then click the Redo button. You'll see that the changes to the documents are undone and redone as a group.
3. Add some additional text to the Nonstrict2 file.
4. Select the Nonstrict3 file and click its Undo button.

The changes disappear from Nonstrict3 and its Undo button turns gray. The undo lists for Nonstrict1 and Nonstrict2 still show NonstrictLinkage, however, which means that the atomicity of NonstrictLinkage has been broken. You'll find that Nonstrict1's NonstrictLinkage undoes the changes in Nonstrict1 without affecting Nonstrict2, and vice-versa.

Now, close all the documents and redo the previous steps, but add **True** to the macro command in step 1. The *True* parameter tells *StackLinkage* to create files named Strict1, Strict2, and Strict3, and to add text to them within the StrictLinkage undo context. This time, when you try step 4, you'll get the error message "The application cannot undo." That's the essence of strict stack linkage.

The *LineChanged* Event

The automation object model defines a single event specific to editing: the *LineChanged* event. Having only one text-editing event at your disposal is both a blessing and a curse, analogous to owning a single flat screwdriver when half the world is built using Phillips screws—you always know which tool you're going to use and you can disassemble just about anything, given time, but you sometimes find yourself wishing for a more varied toolbox.

The *LineChanged* event has three parameters to help you figure out why the event fired. The first two parameters, *StartPoint* and *EndPoint*, mark the beginning and end of the changes to the text buffer. You can use these *TextPoint* values to retrieve the changes, like so:

```
Dim text As String
text = StartPoint.CreateEditPoint.GetText(EndPoint)
```

And if you're ever curious about which document the changes belong to, you can follow the object hierarchy up a couple of levels to find the parent document:

```
Dim doc As Document
doc = StartPoint.Parent.Parent
```

The third parameter, *Hint*, is a bit flag that holds values from the *vsTextChanged* enumeration (shown in Table 11-8). The flags set in *Hint* are evidence from the crime scene that you can piece together to recreate the actions leading up to the event. (In practice, the *Hint* parameter doesn't give you quite enough information to figure out exactly what led to the event—but then, if it did, it wouldn't be called a *hint*.)

Table 11-8 The *vsTextChanged* Enumeration

Field	Description
vsTextChangedMultiLine	The changes affected multiple lines of text.
vsTextChangedSave	The changes were saved to disk.
vsTextChangedCaretMoved	The insertion point moved off the line containing the changes.
vsTextChangedReplaceAll	The entire text buffer was replaced by an insertion.
vsTextChangedNewLine	A new line was entered.
vsTextChangedFindStarting	A find operation moved the insertion point off the line containing changes.

The *LineChanged* event doesn't really fire when the line changes—that is, it doesn't fire for each new character added or deleted from a line. Instead, the event fires when changes to a line are committed in some way, such as when the insertion point moves off the line, changes are saved to disk, or the document window loses focus. An undo context effectively disables this event until the undo context closes; afterwards, the event fires if any of the changes made within the undo context would have caused it to fire under normal circumstances (the insertion point moves off a changed line, the entire text buffer is replaced by an insert, and so forth). The event handler receives *StartPoint* and *EndPoint* values that reflect all uncommitted changes from before and during the undo context. Listing 11-2 demonstrates this effect.

UndoContexts and *LineChanged* Events

```
Private Const title As String = "Text Editing Events"

<System.ContextStaticAttribute()> Public WithEvents _
    TextEditorEvents1 As EnvDTE.TextEditorEvents

Sub LineChangedAndUndoContexts(Optional ByVal useUndoContext _
        As String = "False")
    ' Description: Demonstrates the effect of undo contexts on the
    '              LineChanged event

    TextEditorEvents1 = DTE.Events.TextEditorEvents()

    Dim useUndo As Boolean = ToBoolean(useUndoContext)

    ' Create a new document
    Dim txtDoc As TextDocument = GetTextDocument("LineChanged Test")
    Dim editPnt As EditPoint = txtDoc.EndPoint.CreateEditPoint

    ' Insert text. Not a new line, so won't trigger LineChanged
    editPnt.Insert("Beginning of document.")

    If useUndo Then
        Try
            DTE.UndoContext.Open("LineChangedAndUndoContexts")

            ' Inside undo context, so new lines won't trigger
            ' LineChanged until the undo context closes
            editPnt.Insert(Environment.NewLine)
            editPnt.Insert("Here's a new line." + Environment.NewLine)

            DTE.UndoContext.Close()
        Catch
        End Try
    Else
        ' No undo context, so new lines trigger LineChanged immediately
        editPnt.Insert(Environment.NewLine)
        editPnt.Insert("Here's a new line." + Environment.NewLine)
    End If
End Sub
```

Listing 11-2 Testing the effect of undo contexts on the *LineChanged* event

```
' LineChanged event handler
Public Sub TextEditorEvents1_LineChanged( _
        ByVal StartPoint As EnvDTE.TextPoint, _
        ByVal EndPoint As EnvDTE.TextPoint, _
        ByVal Hint As Integer) Handles TextEditorEvents1.LineChanged
    Dim output As New OutputWindowPaneEx(DTE, title)

    output.WriteLine("--- TextEditorEvents1_LineChanged ---")
    output.WriteLine("Changed text:")
    output.WriteLine(StartPoint.CreateEditPoint.GetText(EndPoint))
    output.WriteLine()
End Sub

Function ToBoolean(ByVal val As Object) As Boolean
    Dim bool As Boolean = False

    Try
        ' Convert the bool parameter
        bool = System.Convert.ToBoolean(val)
    Catch
    End Try

    Return bool
End Function
```

The *LineChangedAndUndoContexts* macro in Listing 11-2 creates a new document and adds a couple lines of text to it. Figure 11-5 shows the result of running this macro without using undo contexts—the *LineChanged* event fires once for each new line of text, which is the same as if you had typed in the lines by hand. Figure 11-6 shows what happens when you wrap the changes in an undo context. Because the new lines are created within an undo context, all the changes, including the ones before the undo context started, get rolled into one *LineChanged* event that fires after the undo context closes.

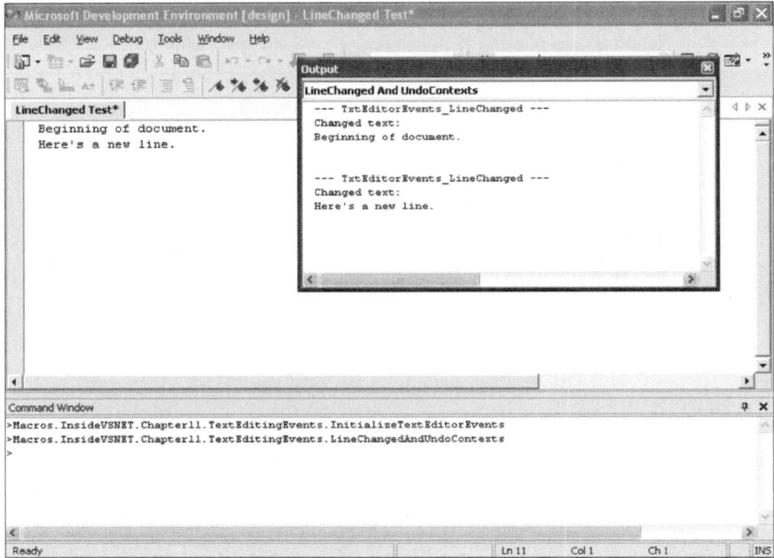

Figure 11-5 Text changes without an undo context generate two *LineChanged* events.

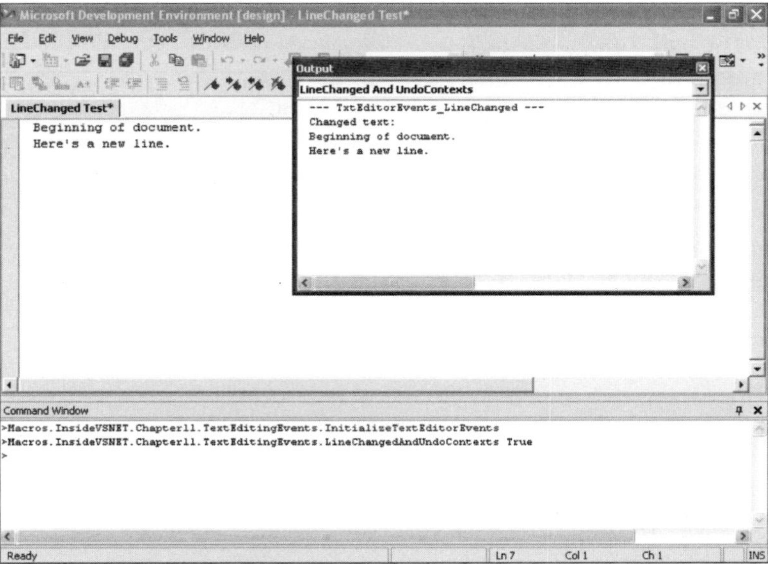

Figure 11-6 Text changes with an undo context generate one *LineChanged* event.

Multiple *LineChanged* Event Handlers

A *LineChanged* event handler can modify the text buffer without triggering *LineChanged* events, which allows you to add changes without fear of reentry. When multiple event handlers are involved, any changes that one event handler makes are seen by all event handlers downstream; the same *Hint* parameter gets passed along to each succeeding event handler, but the *StartPoint* and *EndPoint* parameters expand or contract to include any changes made by previous event handlers.

Lab: Using Multiple *LineChanged* Event Handlers

The *MultipleHandlers* add-in included with the book's sample files lets you experiment with the changes that pass down the chain of multiple *LineChanged* event handlers. *MultipleHandlers* defines three *LineChanged* event handlers, whose names reflect the order in which they fire: *LineChanged1*, *LineChanged2*, and *LineChanged3*. (Note that an add-in's event handlers fire in the same order in which they subscribe to the event. Multiple macro event handlers, however, fire in reverse order of declaration.) Each of these event handlers displays information about its parameters; in addition, *LineChanged1* and *LineChanged2* modify the document so you can see how the changes are passed along to *LineChanged2* and *LineChanged3*, respectively.

MultipleHandlers also defines a command named *ReplaceAll*, which accepts an optional *Boolean* parameter that controls the changes made by *LineChanged2*. Passing a *False* parameter (or no parameter) to *ReplaceAll* directs *LineChanged2* to add a line of text, whereas a *True* parameter causes *LineChanged2* to replace all text in the document with the document's last two lines. Note that one call to *ReplaceAll* buys you one *LineChanged* event—*LineChanged3* unsubscribes the event handlers so you don't accidentally modify important files when you're done with the lab.

Here's experiment #1:

1. Open a new text file.
2. In the Command Window, type **MultipleHandlers.Connect.-ReplaceAll** and press Enter.
3. In the text file, type in a line of text (such as **Here's a line**) and press Enter.

Pressing Enter triggers the *LineChanged* event, and the Text Editing Event Output Window pane displays the event handlers' output. You'll see that the changed text grows from *LineChanged1* to *LineChanged3* as new text is added by intervening event handlers.

Experiment #2 demonstrates the constancy of the *Hint* parameter:

1. Open a new text file and add three lines of text.
2. In the Command Window, type **MultipleHandlers.Connect.-ReplaceAll** and press Enter.
3. Run the *TextEditingEvents.ReplaceTextWithLastTwoLines* macro. In the Text Editing Event Output Window pane, verify that one of the hints is *vsTextChangedReplaceAll*.

The *ReplaceTextWithLastTwoLines* macro copies the last two lines of text in a document and then replaces all the text in the document with those two lines. *LineChanged* passes along the *vsTextChangedReplaceAll* value to let you know that a wholesale replacement triggered the event. But see what happens when *MultipleHandlers* performs the same operations in its *LineChanged2* event handler:

1. Open a new text file and add two lines of text.
2. In the Command Window, type **MultipleHandlers.Connect.-ReplaceAll True** and press Enter.
3. Add a third line of text and press Enter.

When you examine the output, you'll see that every event handler received *vsTextChangedCaretMoved* and *vsTextChangedNewline* as the hints for the event, even though *LineChanged2* performed actions that otherwise would have garnered a *vsTextChangedReplaceAll*. Keep this in mind if you're tempted to use the *Hints* parameter in your event handler's logic—if your event handler isn't first in line, the information in *Hints* might be as stale as month-old biscotti.

Looking Ahead

The automation object model makes it easy to edit text. And because source code is just text, the automation object model makes it easy to edit source code, right? Well, yes and no. Editing source code as if it were just a large array of characters works well enough for many problems, and you can use the objects and events in this chapter to solve those, but as programmers we know there's plenty of structure to be found in that array of characters if we look at it from a higher level. In the next chapter, we'll show you the higher-level view provided by the automation object model: the code model.

12

The Code Model

The Visual Studio .NET code model promises to be nothing less than the programmer's Universal Translator, the macro writer's Babel fish, the hacker's Esperanto. The idea is simple—define a single API that captures the essence of the most common programming constructs, and have each of the languages in Visual Studio .NET implement that API in its native tongue. The result is a single set of objects—the code model—that a programmer can use to read or write code in any of the languages in Visual Studio .NET.

Discovering Code

One of the basic uses of the code model is to find code that's already there. The code model gives you the tools to enumerate all the code constructs in a project as well as zero in on a code construct in a specific source file at the user's request.

A Quick Tour Through a Source File

Let's look at an example file to see how the code model represents it. Listing 12-1 shows a (somewhat) typical C# source file.

```
namespace CMNamespace
{
    delegate void CMDelegate(int delParam);

    struct CMStruct
    {
        int field;
    }
```

Listing 12-1 An example C# source file

```
    enum CMEnum
    {
        Member
    }

    interface CMInterface
    {
        int CMInterfaceMethod();
    }

    [ CMAttribute("CMVal") ]
    class CMClass
    {
        object memberVar;

        void CMCallbackFunction(int param)
        {

        }

        int CMProperty
        {
            get
            {
                return 0;
            }
            set
            {
            }
        }
    }
}
```

The code in Listing 12-1 defines a namespace that holds a menagerie of code constructs, including a delegate, a structure, an enumeration, an interface, and a class. The interface and the class each define members of their own: the interface defines a method, and the class defines a member variable, a method, and a property.

The code model gives you different ways of looking at these constructs, depending on your needs. We'll begin with the most basic representation: the *CodeElement*. The *CodeElement* object exposes a number of properties that allow you to determine the specific kind of code construct being represented. Figure 12-1 shows how the code model wraps each of the code constructs in Listing 12-1.

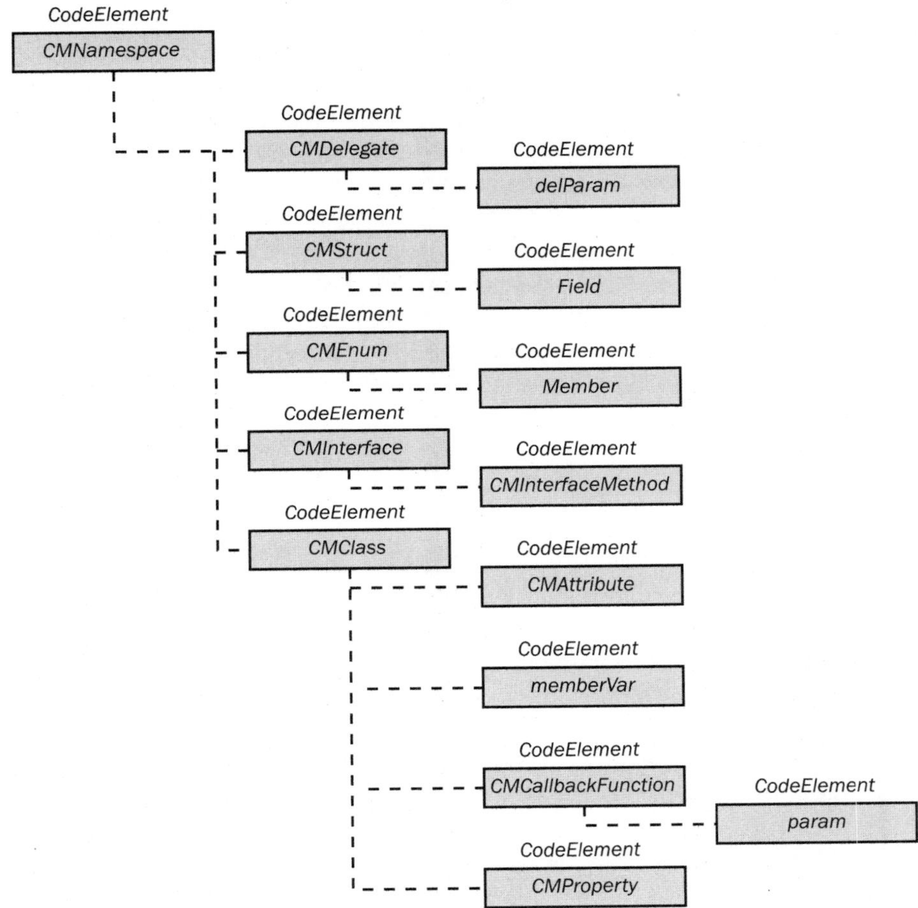

Figure 12-1 The *CodeElement* objects that the code model generates for Listing 12-1

Figure 12-1 illustrates the hierarchical relationship between the different *CodeElement* objects, starting with *CMNamespace*. The dotted lines are to remind you that the *CodeElement* objects have no direct connections linking them together—you'll need a more refined view before you can navigate the hierarchy.

Note As a programmer, you know that modern programming languages have complexity to spare—so much so that the 21 days to mastery promised by some programming books hardly seems enough time to teach yourself *cout << "Hello, world";*, much less all of Visual C++. Now try to imagine the complexity of the code model, which strives to distill the functionality of four major languages—Visual C++, Visual C#, Visual J#, and Visual Basic—into a single, comprehensive API. If you think one chapter might not be enough to cover all the code model, you're right, and this chapter doesn't even try. Instead, this chapter gives merely a short introduction to the two main uses of the code model—code discovery and code generation; we'll defer complete coverage of the code model until the Appendix.

Navigating the Hierarchy

Before you can navigate the hierarchy shown in Figure 12-1, you need access to the top-level *CodeElement* objects. The *FileCodeModel* object represents a source file and its code constructs, and the *FileCodeModel.CodeElements* property holds the collection of top-level *CodeElement* objects that we want. In our example, the only top-level object is *CMNamespace*, so you'd expect to find only one *CodeElement* object in the *FileCodeModel.CodeElements* collection. (Alternatively, you could use the *CodeModel.CodeElements* collection, which holds the top-level *CodeElement* objects for an entire project, but then you'd have to search the items in the collection to find the one representing *CMNamespace*.) To get you started on your code model journey, Listing 12-2 provides functions that return the *FileCodeModel* object or the *CodeModel* object associated with the active window.

```
Function GetFileCodeModel() As FileCodeModel
    ' Description: Returns the FileCodeModel object of the active window

    Dim txtWin As TextWindow = GetTextWindow(DTE.ActiveWindow)
    Dim fcm As FileCodeModel

    If Not txtWin Is Nothing Then
        Try
            fcm = txtWin.Parent.ProjectItem.FileCodeModel
        Catch e As Exception
        End Try
    End If
```

Listing 12-2 The *GetFileCodeModel* and *GetCodeModel* functions

```
    Return fcm
End Function

Function GetCodeModel() As CodeModel
    ' Description: Returns the CodeModel object of the active window

    Dim txtWin As TextWindow = GetTextWindow(DTE.ActiveWindow)
    Dim cm As CodeModel

    If Not txtWin Is Nothing Then
        Try
            cm = txtWin.Parent.ProjectItem.ContainingProject.CodeModel
        Catch e As Exception
        End Try
    End If

    Return cm
End Function
```

We established already that you can't travel directly from one *CodeElement* object to another, so how do you find the rest of the *CodeElement* objects from the *CMNamespace CodeElement* object? The answer is that you query the *CodeElement* object for the interface that corresponds to the underlying code construct and then use that interface to find the related *CodeElement* objects. The code model defines interfaces for each of the major code constructs: *CodeNamespace*, *CodeStruct*, *CodeInterface*, *CodeClass*, *CodeEnum*, *CodeVariable*, *CodeDelegate*, *CodeProperty*, *CodeAttribute*, *CodeFunction*, and *CodeParameter*. Each of these interfaces offers properties and methods specific to its underlying code construct; for example, *CodeFunction* has a *Parameters* collection that contains a *CodeParameter* object for each formal parameter of the underlying function. The *CodeElement.Kind* property returns a value from the *vsCMElement* enumeration that indicates the specific type of the underlying code construct. For the *CodeElement* that wraps *CMNamespace*, the *Kind* property returns *vsCMElementNamespace*, which means you can retrieve a *CodeNamespace* interface from that *CodeElement* object.

Once you have the *CodeNamespace* interface, you can retrieve its children in the hierarchy by iterating through its *Members* collection. Most of the interfaces also contain a *Members* collection, which allows you to access their children. Navigating the code hierarchy, then, requires successive iterations of querying the *CodeElement* object for a specific interface and then finding the child *CodeElement* objects through the *Members* property of the interface. Figure 12-2 shows a more detailed view of our example hierarchy. The solid lines in Figure 12-2 represent the child code elements reachable through the *Members* collections.

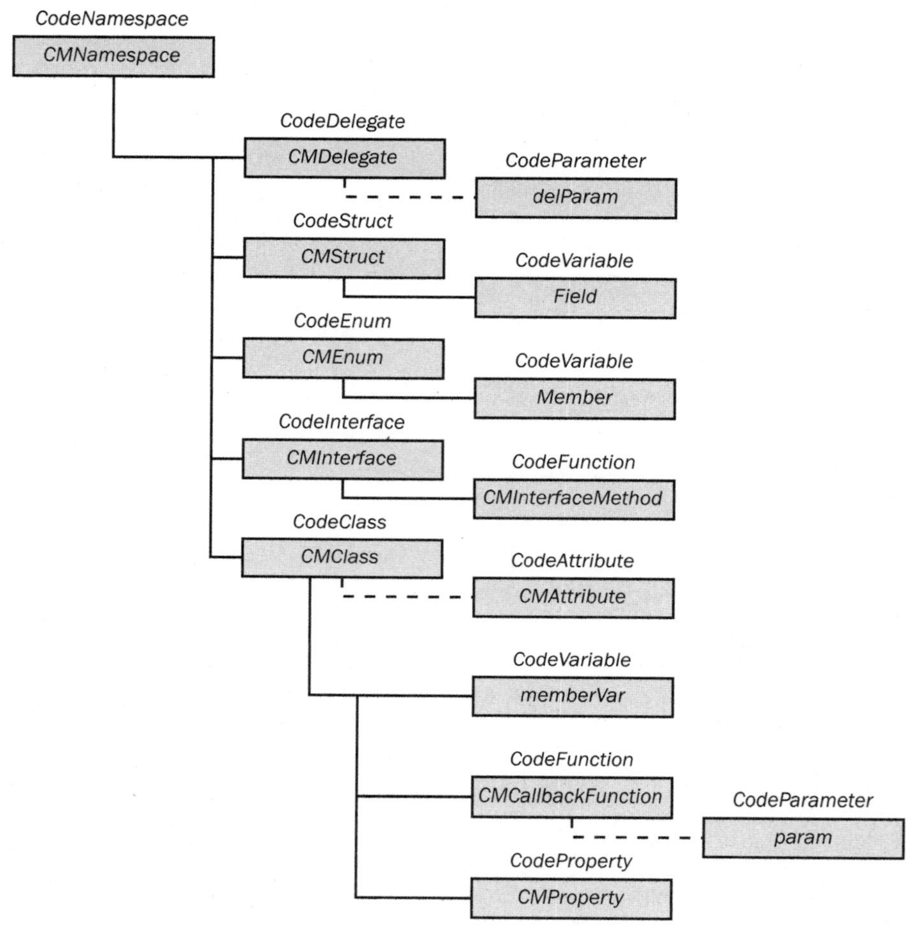

Figure 12-2 A detailed view of the example hierarchy

Listing 12-3 shows one way of traversing the hierarchy. You pass in a *CodeElements* collection to the *RecurseCodeElements* routine, which iterates through the collection, writing the names of each item to the Output window and calling itself recursively whenever the current item sports a *Members* collection.

```
Sub TestRecurseCodeElements()
    Dim output As New OutputWindowPaneEx(DTE)

    output.Clear()
    output.WriteLine("--- TestRecurseCodeElements ---")
    output.WriteLine()

    Dim fcm As FileCodeModel = GetFileCodeModel()

    If Not fcm Is Nothing Then
        RecurseCodeElements(fcm.CodeElements, 0)
    End If
End Sub

Sub RecurseCodeElements(ByVal elements As CodeElements, _
        ByVal level As Integer)
    Dim output As New OutputWindowPaneEx(DTE)

    Dim indent As New String(" ", 4 * level)
    Dim members As CodeElements
    Dim elem As CodeElement

    ' Iterate through each item in CodeElements collection
    For Each elem In elements
        ' Display element name
        output.WriteLine(indent & elem.Name)

        members = GetMembers(elem)

        If Not members Is Nothing Then
            ' Call macro recursively
            RecurseCodeElements(members, level + 1)
        End If
    Next
End Sub

Function GetMembers(ByVal elem As CodeElement) As CodeElements
    Dim members As CodeElements = Nothing

    If Not elem Is Nothing Then
        ' Determine the element type and retrieve its Members collection
        Select Case elem.Kind
            Case vsCMElement.vsCMElementNamespace
                Dim cdeNamespace As CodeNamespace = elem
                members = cdeNamespace.Members
```

Listing 12-3 Navigating the hierarchy recursively

```
                Case vsCMElement.vsCMElementClass
                Dim cdeClass As CodeClass = elem
                 members = cdeClass.Members

            Case vsCMElement.vsCMElementStruct
                Dim cdeStruct As CodeStruct = elem
                members = cdeStruct.Members

            Case vsCMElement.vsCMElementDelegate
                Dim cdeDelegate As CodeDelegate = elem
                members = cdeDelegate.Members

            Case vsCMElement.vsCMElementEnum
                Dim cdeEnum As CodeEnum = elem
                members = cdeEnum.Members

            Case vsCMElement.vsCMElementInterface
                Dim cdeInterface As CodeInterface = elem
                members = cdeInterface.Members
        End Select
    End If

    Return members
End Function
```

The *GetMembers* function in Listing 12-3 determines the type of the *CodeElement* passed to it, assigns the *CodeElement* to a variable of the correct type, and returns the type's *Members* collection. In Visual Basic, you could just as easily return *Members* from the *CodeElement* variable itself, assuming that the underlying object also implemented a *Members* property. However, strongly typed languages require that you explicitly cast the *CodeElement* variable to the correct type (or *QueryInterface* for the correct interface), so we tried to use code comparable to that used by such languages.

The *GetMembers* function illustrates some of the complexities involved with managing the code model interfaces. To help manage this complexity, the code model defines a generic interface named *CodeType*, which you can retrieve from any object that also supports one of the following interfaces: *CodeClass*, *CodeStruct*, *CodeInterface*, *CodeEnum*, and *CodeDelegate*. (Incidentally, *CodeType* defines the *Members* property, which is why you can find this property on objects that support the previous interfaces.) If you have a *CodeElement* object, you can check for the availability of the *CodeType* interface directly by using the *CodeElement.IsCodeType* property.

So, *CodeType* gives us yet another way to view our example hierarchy, as shown in Figure 12-3; *CodeType* also simplifies the logic needed to traverse the code hierarchy, as shown in Listing 12-4. The one "gotcha" in the *CodeType* approach is that *CodeNamespace* objects don't support the *CodeType* interface. In the *RecurseCodeElementsByCodeType* macro, solving this "gotcha" requires an extra *If* branch to check for *CodeNamespace* elements specifically.

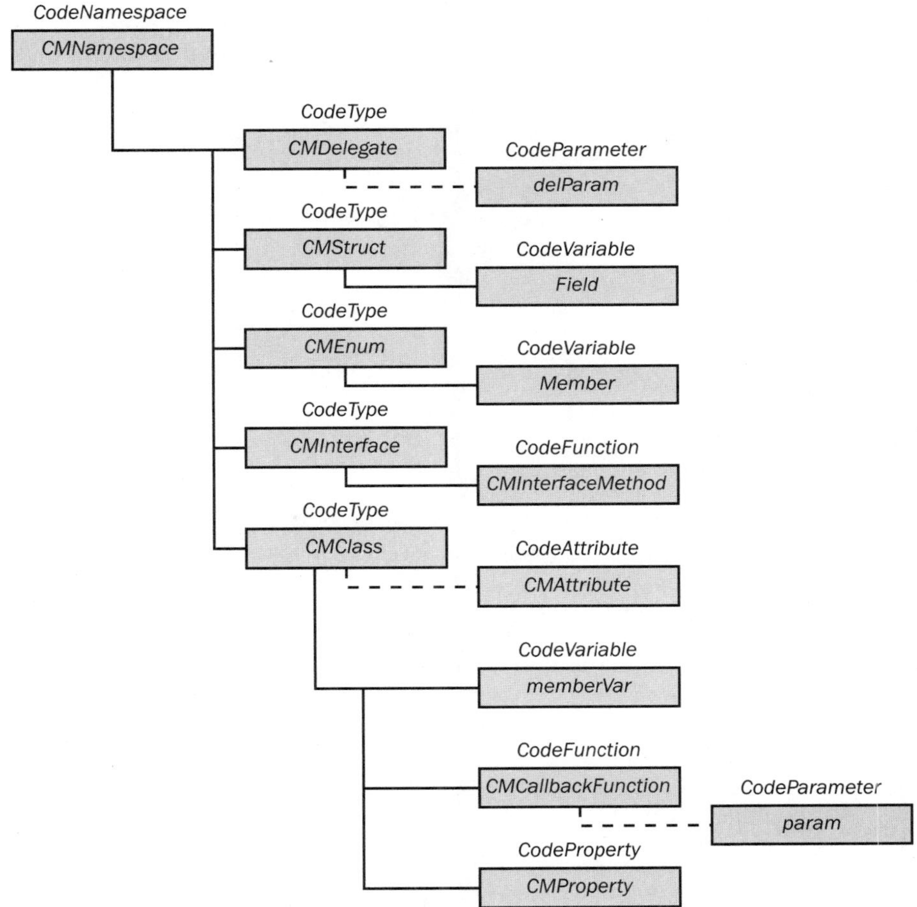

Figure 12-3 A *CodeType* view of the example hierarchy

We're almost at the end. You can see from Figure 12-2 and Figure 12-3 that the *Members* collections let you reach all *CodeElement* objects except the attribute on the class and the parameters in the delegate and the class member function. The *CodeClass* interface defines an *Attributes* collection that holds the

CodeAttribute objects that apply to the class, and the *CodeDelegate* and *CodeFunction* interfaces define a *Parameters* collection of *CodeParameter* objects; iterating through those collections allows you to complete the journey through the code hierarchy.

```
Sub TestRecurseCodeElementsByCodeType()
    Dim output As New OutputWindowPaneEx(DTE)

    output.Clear()
    output.WriteLine("--- TestRecurseCodeElementsByCodeType ---")
    output.WriteLine()

    Dim fcm As FileCodeModel = GetFileCodeModel()

    If Not fcm Is Nothing Then
        RecurseCodeElementsByCodeType(fcm.CodeElements, 0)
    End If
End Sub

Sub RecurseCodeElementsByCodeType(ByVal elements As CodeElements, _
        ByVal level As Integer)
    Dim output As New OutputWindowPaneEx(DTE)

    Dim indent As New String(" ", 4 * level)
    Dim elem As CodeElement

    ' Iterate through each item in CodeElements collection
    For Each elem In elements
        ' Display element name
        output.WriteLine(indent & elem.Name)

        ' Check whether element is a namespace
        If elem.Kind = vsCMElement.vsCMElementNamespace Then
            Dim cdeNamespace As CodeNamespace = elem

            ' Call macro recursively
            RecurseCodeElementsByCodeType(cdeNamespace.Members, level + 1)

        ' Check whether CodeType is available
        ElseIf elem.IsCodeType Then
            Dim cdeType As CodeType = elem

            ' Call macro recursively
            RecurseCodeElementsByCodeType(cdeType.Members, level + 1)
        End If
    Next
End Sub
```

Listing 12-4 Using *CodeType* to recurse through the code hierarchy

Lab: Using the Code Model Explorer Add-in

The Code Model Explorer (CME) add-in provides a handy interface for exploring the code model objects that represent your Visual Studio .NET projects. In this lab, you'll use the CME add-in to examine a typical add-in project. Follow these steps to get started:

1. Create a new Visual C++ add-in project.
2. Choose Tools | Code Model Explorer to display the CME add-in's main form.
3. Open the Output window.
4. Select the definition of *CConnect*, as shown in Figure 12-4.

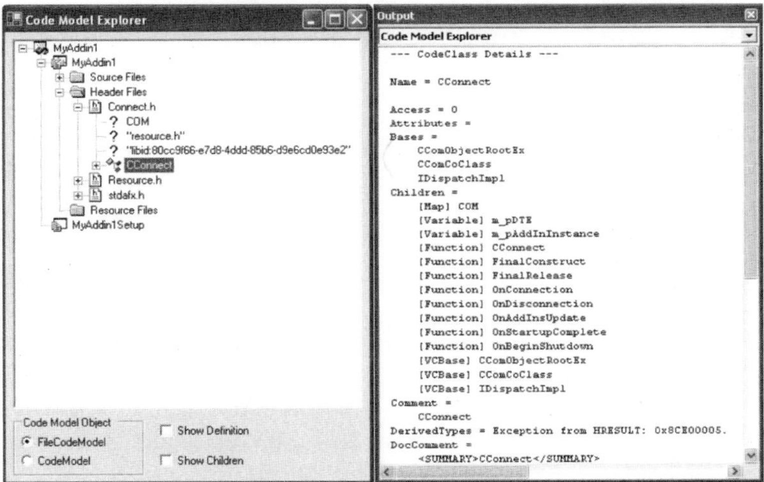

Figure 12-4 The CME add-in output

When you select a *CodeElement* node in the CME add-in tree view, the add-in dumps information about the *CodeElement* to the Output window. For example, in the Output window shown in Figure 12-4, the "---CodeClass Details ---" header indicates that *CConnect* is represented by a *CodeClass* object; the "Bases" entry shows *CConnect*'s three base classes—*CComObjectRootEx*, *CComCoClass*, and *IDispatchImpl*; and the "Children" entry lists the 14 *CodeElement* objects in *CConnect*'s *Children* collection.

When you select the Show Definition check box, the CME add-in will do its best to display the source code for the selected *CodeElement* node. If you select the Show Definition check box, expand the *CConnect* node, and select the *OnConnection* node, you'll see the *OnConnection* source code highlighted in the Connect.cpp file (as shown in Figure 12-5).

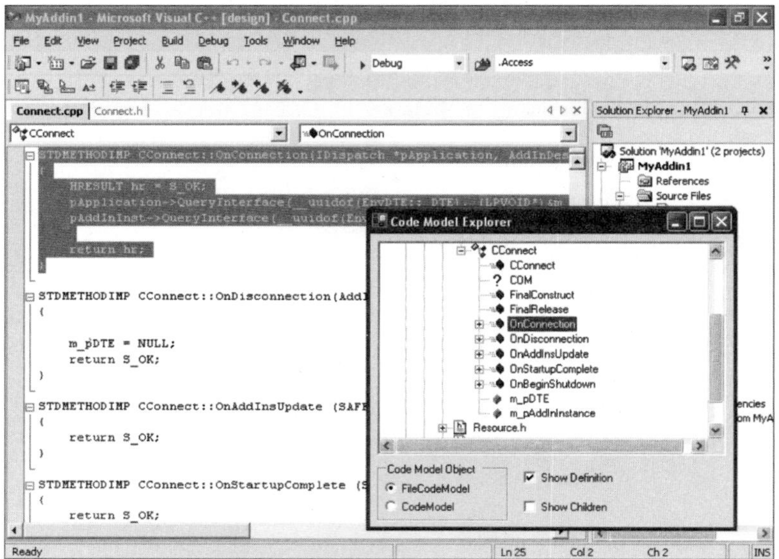

Figure 12-5 The CME add-in Show Definition feature

Selecting the Show Children check box tells the CME add-in to display the *CodeElement* objects from the *Children* collection. For Visual C++ *CodeElement* objects, the *Children* collection is a superset of the *Members* collection and includes objects such as the bases for the parent *CodeElement*. Select Show Children and then collapse and reexpand the *CConnect* node, and you'll see its *Children* nodes highlighted in red (as shown in Figure 12-6). Notice that the corresponding *COM* node from the *Members* collection doesn't have any child nodes, which means that the red *COM* node has *Children* nodes of its own. Expand the red *COM* node and you'll see that its children consist of two *COM_INTERFACE_ENTRY* nodes; select the first *COM_INTERFACE_ENTRY* node to see the output shown in Figure 12-7.

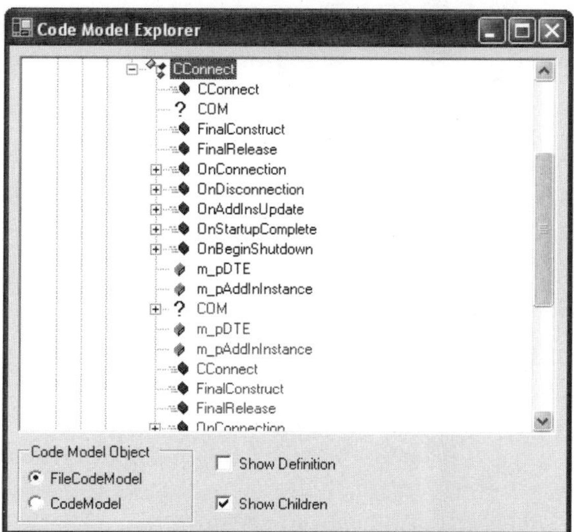

Figure 12-6 The Show Children feature

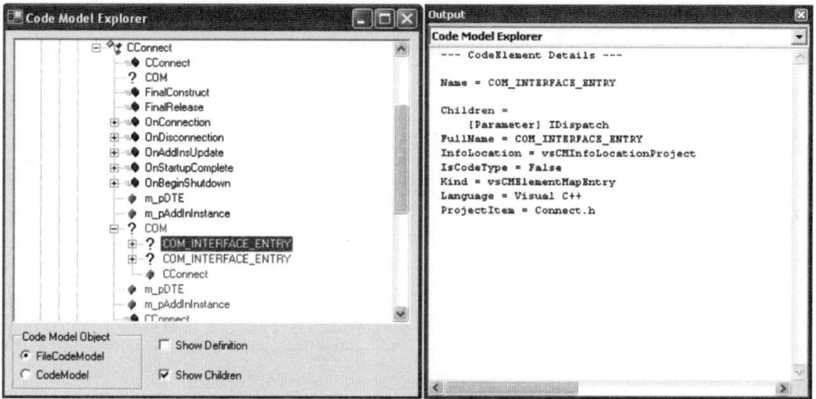

Figure 12-7 *COM_INTERFACE_ENTRY* details

Finally, select the CodeModel option, which displays the *CodeElement* objects available through the *CodeModel.CodeElements* property. In addition to the top-level objects available through the *FileCodeModel* object, you'll find *CodeElement* objects representing everything from macros to IDL libraries.

Getting a *CodeElement* from a Point Object

You've seen how to start at the top of a *CodeElement* hierarchy and visit every child. The code model also allows you to find a *CodeElement* from a point object in a source file. This ability enables you to create interactive features that respond to the programmer's input.

The code model offers two ways of retrieving a *CodeElement* object from a point: the *CodeElementFromPoint* method of the *FileCodeModel* object and the *CodeElement* property of the *TextPoint*, *EditPoint*, and *VirtualPoint* objects. Here's the prototype for *CodeElementFromPoint*:

```
CodeElement CodeElementFromPoint(TextPoint Point, vsCMElement Scope);
```

The *CodeElementFromPoint* method takes a *TextPoint* object that specifies a location in a source file and a *vsCMElement* value that determines which of the enclosing code elements to return. For example, in Listing 12-1, if you had a *TextPoint* located on the *param* parameter of *CMCallbackFunction*, calling *CodeElementFromPoint* with a *vsCMElement* value of *vsCMElementParameter* would return the *CodeElement* representing *param*; calling *CodeElementFromPoint* with a *vsCMElement* value of *vsCMElementClass* would return the *CodeElement* representing *CMClass*.

The *CodeElement* property takes a *vsCMElement* value that serves the same purpose as the *Scope* parameter of *CodeElementFromPoint*. You might wonder why the code model would bother with *CodeElementFromPoint* when point objects already have a way to get a *CodeElement*. The answer is that the *CodeElement* property is implemented in terms of *CodeElementFromPoint* and is just a concise way of calling *xxxPoint.Parent.Parent.ProjectItem.FileCodeModel.CodeElementFromPoint*.

Lab: Finding *CodeElement* Objects from Point Objects

The *TestCodeElementFromPoint* and *TestCodeElementProperty* macros let you get a feel for how the *Scope* parameter affects the *CodeElement* returned by the *CodeElementFromPoint* method and the *CodeElement* property. To use either of the macros, open the Output window, place the insertion point anywhere in a source code file, and run the macro. The macro calls *CodeElementFromPoint* or the *CodeElement* property with each possible *vsCMElement* value in the *Scope* parameter and sends information about the returned *CodeElement* to the Output window.

If you run these macros on different code constructs in source files from different languages, you'll soon notice that Visual C++ does the best job of returning the element you request. However, best doesn't mean perfect. For example, suppose you have the Visual C++ equivalent of Listing 12-1. If you were to place the insertion point on the *param* parameter of *CMCallbackFunction* and run the *TestCodeElementFromPoint* macro, Visual C++ would correctly return *CMCallbackFunction* for *vsCMElementFunction*, *CMClass* for *vsCMElementClass*, and *CMNamespace* for *vsCMElementNamespace*, but it would miss *param* entirely when asked for *vsCMElementParameter*! The same test for the other languages yields the following results: Visual C# ties Visual J# at 2 for 3 (*vsCMElementParameter* and *vsCMElementFunction*), and Visual Basic is 1 for 3 (*vsCMElementParameter*). What's worse are the false positives—the incorrect *CodeElement* objects that are returned in place of the correct ones. You might order a *vsCMElementParameter*, but don't be surprised if the waiter brings you a *vsCMElementFunction* instead.

So what are you to make of all this? Basically, you can't trust *CodeElementFromPoint* and *CodeElement* in the general case—at least not yet. At best, you might be able to get by in certain situations, when you know that only a particular language will be used.

Generating Code

The other main use of the code model is to generate source code programmatically. This aspect of the code model reveals most clearly the promise of a universal programming language: the same *AddClass* method that generates a Visual C# class when run against a .cs file will generate a Visual C++ class when run against a .cpp file, and will generate a Visual J# class when run against a .jsl file. In this section, we'll show how to generate the source file in Listing 12-1 by using the code model. Note that the following example provides only the briefest of introductions to this subject—for details about the objects and methods used in this section, please refer to the Appendix.

Building a Source File

All of the code model methods that generate code begin with *Add*, as in *AddNamespace*, *AddClass*, *AddVariable*, and so on. By calling an *Add* method on a *CodeElement*, you create a new code construct within the *CodeElement*. Note that *CodeElement* objects can't adopt other existing *CodeElement* objects—they can have children only by bearing their own; a consequence of this is that you have to create your code hierarchy from the top down. The top-most element in Listing 12-1 is *CMNamespace*, so you begin by creating a new namespace, as shown in the following code:

```
Sub CreateListing_12_1()
    Dim fcm As FileCodeModel = GetFileCodeModel()

    If Not fcm Is Nothing Then
        Dim cdeNamespace As CodeNamespace

        ' Try to create a new namespace
        Try
            cdeNamespace = fcm.AddNamespace("CMNamespace")
        Catch e As Exception
        End Try

        ' If successful, create the rest of the code elements
        If Not cdeNamespace Is Nothing Then

            ⋮

        End If
    End If
End Sub
```

The *FileCodeModel.AddNamespace* method generates the source code for a new top-level namespace and returns a reference to its corresponding *CodeNamespace* object. The call to *AddNamespace* takes place within a *Try/Catch* block because *Add* methods throw an exception if they're unable to create the requested code element. Assuming all goes well, you'll have a reference with which to create the namespace's child elements.

The first child element to create is *CMDelegate*. *CMDelegate* defines an integer parameter, and you can create both the delegate and the parameter in the same *Try/Catch* block:

```
Try
    Dim cdeDelegate As CodeDelegate

    ' Try to create a new delegate
    cdeDelegate = cdeNamespace.AddDelegate("CMDelegate", _
        vsCMTypeRef.vsCMTypeRefVoid)

    ' Try to add a new parameter to the delegate
    cdeDelegate.AddParameter("delParam", vsCMTypeRef.vsCMTypeRefInt)
Catch e As Exception
End Try
```

AddDelegate and *AddParameter* both take a parameter that specifies the code element's type; the *vsCMTypeRef.vsCMTypeRefVoid* value represents a void type, and the *vsCMTypeRef.vsCMTypeRefInt* value represents an integer type. The previous code doesn't declare a variable to store *AddParameter*'s return value because nothing further needs to be done with the delegate's parameter.

Next you create the structure and its field:

```
Try
    Dim cdeStruct As CodeStruct

    ' Try to create a new structure
    cdeStruct = cdeNamespace.AddStruct("CMStruct", -1)

    ' Try to add a new field to the structure
    cdeStruct.AddVariable("field", vsCMTypeRef.vsCMTypeRefInt)
Catch e As Exception
End Try
```

By now the rhythm should be familiar: define a variable for the new code element, assign the return value of the *Add* method to the variable, and call methods on the variable to alter the new code element. The *-1* parameter to *AddStruct* tells the method to insert the source code for the new structure after every other sibling code element; all the *Add* methods accept this optional parameter. Here's the code for creating the enumeration and the interface:

```
Try
    Dim cdeEnum As CodeEnum

    ' Try to create a new enumeration
    cdeEnum = cdeNamespace.AddEnum("CMEnum", -1)

    ' Try to add a new member to the enumeration
    cdeEnum.AddMember("Member")
Catch e As Exception
End Try

Try
    Dim cdeInterface As CodeInterface

    ' Try to create a new interface
    cdeInterface = cdeNamespace.AddInterface("CMInterface", -1)

    ' Try to add a new method to the interface
    cdeInterface.AddFunction("CMInterfaceMethod", _
        vsCMFunction.vsCMFunctionFunction, vsCMTypeRef.vsCMTypeRefInt)
Catch e As Exception
End Try
```

The second parameter to *AddFunction* lets you specify what kind of function to create, such as a constructor, a destructor, a pure virtual function, and so on; the value of *vsCMFunction.vsCMFunctionFunction* for *CMInterfaceMethod* creates a vanilla function. Finally, here's the code that creates the class, its attribute, and all its members:

```
Try
    Dim cdeClass As CodeClass

    ' Try to create a new class
    cdeClass = cdeNamespace.AddClass("CMClass", -1)

    Try
        ' Try to add a new attribute to the class
        cdeClass.AddAttribute("CMAttribute", "CMVal")
    Catch e As Exception
    End Try

    Try
        ' Try to add a new member variable to the class
        cdeClass.AddVariable("memberVar", vsCMTypeRef.vsCMTypeRefObject, -1)
    Catch e As Exception
    End Try

    Try
        Dim cdeFunction As CodeFunction

        ' Try to add a new member function to the class
        cdeFunction = cdeClass.AddFunction("CMCallbackFunction", _
            vsCMFunction.vsCMFunctionFunction, _
            vsCMTypeRef.vsCMTypeRefVoid, -1)

        ' Try to add a new parameter to the member function
        cdeFunction.AddParameter("param", vsCMTypeRef.vsCMTypeRefInt)
    Catch e As Exception
    End Try

    Try
        ' Try to add a new property to the class
        cdeClass.AddProperty("CMProperty", "CMProperty", _
            vsCMTypeRef.vsCMTypeRefInt, -1)
    Catch e As Exception
    End Try
Catch e As Exception
End Try
```

Now that you're done writing the code that writes the code, it's time for some bad news: none of the language implementations will generate a complete simulacrum of Listing 12-1 from this code, either because the language doesn't support a particular code construct or because the language hasn't yet implemented a particular *Add* method. You can verify this for yourself by running the *CreateListing_12_1* macro on different language source files—if you do, you'll find that Visual C# generates everything but the attribute; Visual C++ generates everything but the delegate and the property; Visual J# generates everything but the delegate, structure, enumeration, attribute, and property; and Visual Basic doesn't generate anything. Again, that's the bad news—the good news is that the code model is a young branch of the automation object model, so you can expect major improvements in its next version.

Looking Ahead

The code model brings us to the end of Part II of this book. Part III takes you into territory mostly uncharted by other programming books: in it you'll learn how to set up Setup, find help on Help, hotwire the V12 command-line engine hidden under the unassuming hood of the Visual Studio .NET IDE, and keep your source safe from everyone, including yourself.

Part III

Deployment, Help, and Advanced Projects

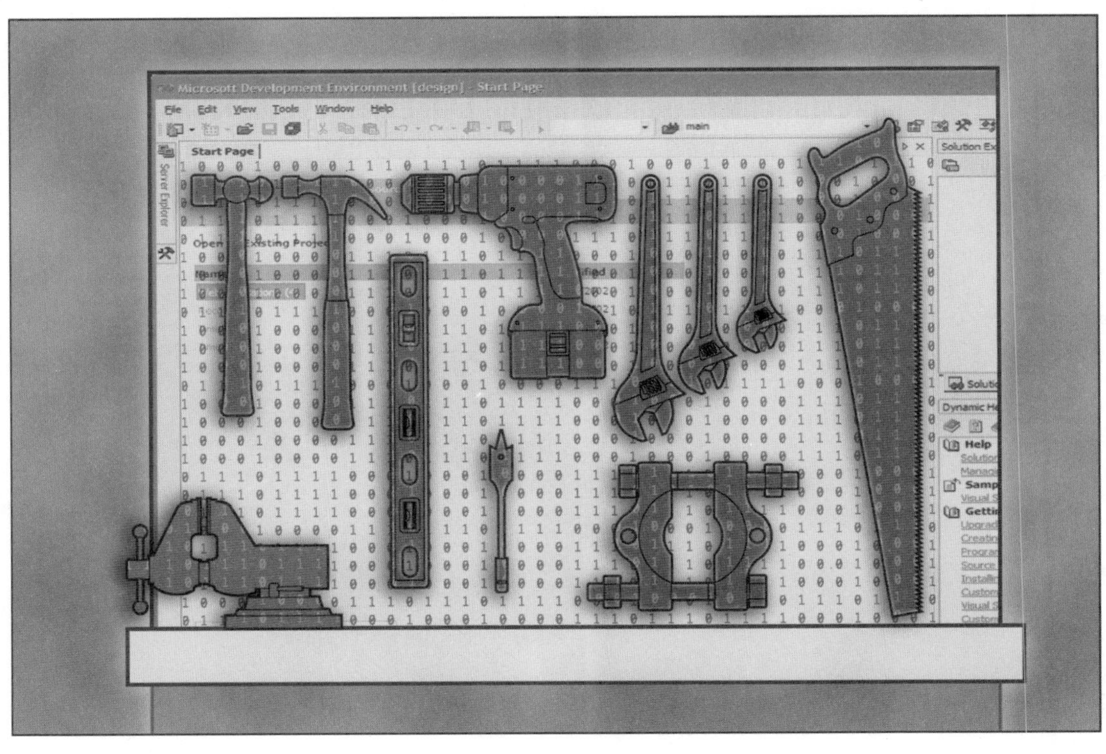

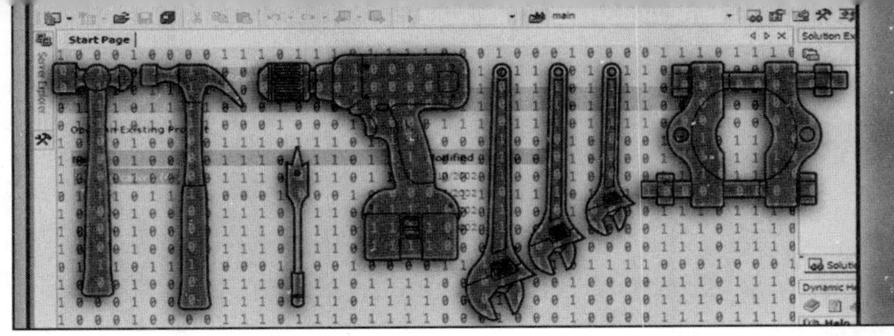

13 Designing Setup Projects

When creating a new application, the last thing a developer usually thinks about is how to get the application onto the user's computer. In this chapter, we'll explore the tools in Microsoft Visual Studio .NET that help you create setup files for use with Windows Installer.

Microsoft Windows Installer (MSI) Background

In the early days of Microsoft Windows development, an application rarely consisted of more than a single executable file and maybe a DLL or two, so installing the application was as simple as copying the files from a floppy disk onto the computer. Changes to the system settings were rare, and when necessary they were simply a few changes to the win.ini and system.ini files in the C:\Windows folder.

Much has changed since those days; preparing even the simplest of applications so the user can run it on modern versions of Windows requires many changes to the user's computer. The setup process for a modern Windows application must modify the system registry to associate files with your application so when the user double-clicks on the file it automatically opens. It must place COM DLLs in various locations on disk and register them, causing changes to the system registry. It must modify the Start menu so the user can conveniently find and run your application. In the case of Web applications and XML Web services, installing an application on a Web server requires not only placing the files on the server's hard drive but also configuring Microsoft Internet Information Services (IIS) to serve the Web application to the user.

Since those early days of Windows development, countless setup development tools have become available. One of the most popular ones, which

Microsoft used, was called Acme Setup; it was used in programs such as Microsoft Office 95 and Microsoft Visual Studio 6.0. Acme Setup and many of the other setup technologies got the job done, but they were complicated to develop for and didn't provide the user with a consistent experience from one application to another. These setup technologies could also be dangerous to the user's computer. If a problem occurred during installation, such as an error in installing a component, or if the user canceled the installation, the state of the computer would become unstable; some components or registry settings would be left behind or incorrectly removed.

To make developing setup programs easier and to solve the problems associated with existing setup programs, the Office product group set out to develop a new type of setup program. This technology is called Windows Installer. When a Windows Installer setup program is built, a file with the .msi extension is created; the user can double-click on this file to start installing a program. The files that make up the program to be installed can be either compressed and stored within the .msi file or stored loosely (on a distribution medium such as a floppy disk, CD, or DVD that's separate from the .msi file).

Because logic is built into Windows Installer for handling the system registry, COM objects, and (with version 2.0 of Windows Installer, the same version used by Visual Studio .NET and the .NET Framework) .NET components and .NET Web applications, installing these components is easy. Windows Installer also takes care of mundane setup chores such as making sure the computer has enough disk space, and it creates an entry in Control Panel's Add Or Remove Programs applet for uninstalling the program. Lastly, Windows Installer is transactional, which means the state of the computer is preserved when you install a component or a registry key. If a problem occurs during setup, a rollback is performed that restores the computer to the state it was in before setup was started.

Creating Custom Installation Projects

With the tools in Visual Studio .NET, you can easily create a setup project that, when built, generates an .msi file. You can find the templates for creating a setup project in the New Project dialog box, by selecting the Setup And Deployment Projects node in the Project Types tree. The Setup Project type is used to install client software, such as a .NET or Win32 program, onto a user's computer, and the Web Setup Project type is used to install a Web application or Web service onto a server computer. The Merge Module template (discussed later in this chapter) is used to create setup project components.

If you were to add a setup project to an existing solution and then choose Build | Build Solution to build your solution, the setup project wouldn't build because in the Configuration Manager dialog box the setup project isn't selected by default to build. Setup projects can take a while to build, and because you usually don't need to recompile the .msi file each time you want to debug a project, not building the setup project each time you compile the solution saves you some time. When you're ready to test your setup project, you can right-click on it in Solution Explorer and choose Build or you can select the Build check box in the Configuration Manager dialog box. If you're creating a setup project in a new solution file, the Build check box is selected by default because no other projects are in the solution.

Once a setup project has been added to a solution, you can choose among six editors to build your setup project: File System, Registry, File Types, User Interface, Custom Actions, and Launch Conditions. You can use any of these editors to configure how your software is installed onto a user's computer. You can display any of these editor windows by selecting a setup project in Solution Explorer and then clicking the appropriate button on the command bar or right-clicking on the project in Solution Explorer and choosing View and then the editor.

File System Editor

You use the File System editor to graphically indicate where files that make up your software project should be placed on disk when the .msi file is installed. In this editor, you can add folders and files compiled by a project to create a directory structure that's logical for your application.

Specifying an Installation Folder

To install your program, you must create the directory structure that will contain the program's files. Many default installation folders are available in the File System editor, giving you a starting point for a directory structure. To add a file to a folder, right-click on the appropriate folder, point to Add, and then select one of the file types—Folder to create a subfolder, Project Output to add a file generated by another project in the solution, File for a file on disk, or Assembly for an assembly file. Visual Studio .NET defines the following folders that you can add files or folders to:

- **Common Files Folder** For files that are common among all programs installed on the computer. This folder can be found at C:\Program Files\Common Files.

- **Fonts Folder** For all the font files installed on the computer. The default location of this folder is C:\Windows\Fonts.
- **Program Files Folder** The folder where all programs installed on the computer should be stored. It can be found at C:\Program Files.
- **System Folder** For storing operating system components. This folder should be modified only in the rarest of situations. It can be found at C:\Windows\System32.
- **User's Application Data Folder** The folder where applications can store data files that the user shouldn't manipulate. It can be found at C:\Documents and Settings*username*\Application Data.
- **User's Desktop** For all the items shown on the user's desktop. The default location for this folder is C:\Documents and Settings*username*\Desktop.
- **User's Favorites Folder** For links to favorite items. The default location for this folder is C:\Documents and Settings*username*\Favorites.
- **User's Personal Data Folder** For documents that the user creates. This folder can be found at C:\Documents and Settings*username*\My Documents.
- **User's Programs Menu** For shortcuts to programs that will be shown on the Start menu. This folder can be found at C:\Documents and Settings*username*\Start Menu\Programs.
- **User's Send To Menu** For Send To menu items, which you can see by clicking on a file in Windows Explorer and selecting the Send To menu. This folder can be found at C:\Documents and Settings*username*\SendTo.
- **User's Start Menu** For Start menu items. This folder can be found at C:\Documents and Settings*username*\Start Menu.
- **User's Startup Folder** For all programs (or shortcuts to programs) that will run when the user logs in to the operating system. This folder can be found at C:\Documents and Settings*username*\Start Menu\Programs\Startup.
- **User's Template Folder** For templates to create new files. This is the source folder where the items on the New menu of the desktop's shortcut menu are located. This folder can be found at C:\Documents and Settings*username*\Templates.

- **Windows Folder** For operating system files. A typical location is C:\Windows.
- **Global Assembly Cache Folder** For the computer's global assembly cache (GAC). Any files placed in this folder are accessible by the .NET Framework for all users of the computer.
- **Application Folder** The folder where you should store most of the files and project output you're installing onto the user's computer. This folder defaults to C:\Program Files*Manufacturer**ProductName*, where *Manufacturer* and *ProductName* are the property values in the Properties window when the setup project is selected in Solution Explorer.
- **Web Application Folder** A folder that's available only if the setup project is a Web Setup Project. Items added to this folder are installed in the IIS virtual folder and are available (security settings permitting) to users of your Web server.

You can also create a new folder on the computer that's not a child of any of the default folders. To do this, right-click on the File System On Target Machine node in the File System editor and choose Add Special Folder | Custom Folder. The name you enter for the folder is not the path for the folder that will be created on the computer—it's for display purposes in the File System editor only. You set the folder path by selecting the newly created custom folder and typing the path to create in the *DefaultLocation* property in the Properties window. However, be careful when you create a custom folder and give it a hard-coded path; if you enter a disk drive that's not available on the computer, an error is generated. Later in this chapter, you'll see how you can set the path of the folder dynamically at installation time.

Project Output

Once you create a program and the directory structure to hold the program, you need a way to add the files to the File System editor. You could build your code project and then manually select each file generated by the project and add them to the File System editor. However, this approach can lead to problems. For example, if you switch the project type from Debug to Release, you must manually modify the setup project to make sure the correct build version of the files is copied into the setup project. Another problem is that you might inadvertently omit a file or add a file that is not needed, causing the program to not function properly or causing the .msi file to be bigger than it needs to be. To make selecting files to install for a project easier, you can include the project output in a setup project.

To add a project's output to the File System editor, right-click on the folder that should contain the output and choose Add | Project Output. The Add Project Output Group dialog box opens and lists the projects that generate output and lists output types you can add to the setup project. The project output types you can add to a setup project are:

- **Documentation Files** This type adds any files generated by IntelliDoc to the File System editor. IntelliDoc files can be generated only from C# projects, so this option appears only if the project selected in the Project box is a C# project.
- **Primary Output** This group contains the DLL or EXE file that the project creates when compiled. You must add this output to the File System editor to enable the user to run your program.
- **Localized Resources** If you add this output type to the File System editor, all resource satellite DLLs are copied into the selected folder.
- **Debug Symbols** This output type contains all the debug symbols, such as .pdb files, that are used to debug the application. If you want users of your application to be able to debug problems, you should add this output type to the File System editor. However, placing debugging symbols on the user's computer increases the size of the .msi file. In addition, you make it easier for people to reverse-engineer your application and possibly gain access to your intellectual property.
- **Content Files** This output type includes all files within the selected project that were added as content files.
- **Source Files** This project output type includes all the source files used to build a project.
- **Built Outputs** This output type is available only if the selected project is another setup project. Adding this output type to a setup project allows you to install an .msi file onto the installer's disk.

When a project's output is added to a setup project, Visual Studio .NET automatically scans the output and adds to the setup project any files (such as assemblies, unmanaged DLLs, or type libraries) that the project is dependent on. When the setup project is compiled, these dependent DLLs are packaged up into the .msi file and installed alongside the code that's dependent on those DLLs. These dependent DLLs appear in the File System editor alongside the file or project output that is dependent on them, and they're added to Solution Explorer underneath the Detected Dependencies folder of your setup project.

You can control which dependencies are installed on the user's computer by excluding a dependency; you simply right-click on a dependency file and choose Exclude. There can be many reasons for excluding a file, the most common of which is that the user has the dependency file on her computer and therefore you don't need to package that file into the .msi file. In addition, when a project's output is added to the File System editor, a project dependency is created from the setup project to the project generating output. As a result, when a solution build is started, the project, which has its output in the setup project, is built before the setup project is compiled, which ensures that the files in the setup project are up-to-date.

Have Your Wizards Stopped Working?

When you test your setup project to make sure it installs and uninstalls properly, you might find that some programs have stopped working—especially after you uninstalled the .msi file. This problem is common when you're building a setup program for wizards or add-ins. Suppose you reference the assembly *VSLangProj* within your add-in project. When you build the setup project for the add-in, the setup project sees that you referenced the *VSLangProj* assembly and automatically adds it to the setup project as a dependency. Also, because *VSLangProj* is a Primary Interop Assembly (PIA) for the type library VSLangProj.tlb, the type library is added to the setup project as a dependency. This last file is where you can run into trouble. When COM objects (including type libraries) are added to the File System editor, they're automatically set to be registered when installed.

If the .msi file for your add-in or wizard is uninstalled, Windows Installer removes all the files that it installed on the system. Because the VSLangProj.tlb type library is being uninstalled, it also unregisters itself as a type library. Other components, such as Visual Studio .NET wizards, use this type library, and if the type library is not registered, the wizards cannot run.

To fix this problem and prevent it from recurring, you can scan your setup project after adding a new project output to the File System editor, to look for components added as dependencies that aren't part of your project. If you find such a file, right-click on that file and choose Exclude, or if you know that the dependency is located within a merge module, add the merge module to your setup project. This ensures that the component is properly installed on the computer. (*VSLangProj* is not in a merge module, so this is not an option for a wizard or an add-in.)

If you've already uninstalled an .msi file that contains a dependency that shouldn't have been installed and you want to repair your computer, you have a few options. The first is to run the repair option of the application that has stopped working. If the application is Visual Studio .NET, the repair process will be lengthy and you might not want to go through it. An alternative way of fixing the problem is to find and then manually reregister the type libraries and COM objects that were unregistered. You can do this only if you have the necessary tools. The third option is to create a throwaway setup project, add the necessary components (such as VSLangProj.tlb) to the setup project, and then build and install that setup project. This causes the file to be registered, and as long as you do not uninstall this .msi file, everything should once again work fine.

Registry Editor

With the Registry editor, you can point and click your way to creating entries in the system registry when the .msi file is installed. During installation, the registry keys and values you create within this editor are copied into the system registry, mirroring the structure you create. You can see an example of the Registry editor being used to help set up an add-in when you run the Add-in Wizard. The purpose of a setup project being added to a solution when you run this wizard is not to install files (although the setup project also helps do that) but to create the registry keys necessary for Visual Studio .NET to find, load, and run your add-in.

You'll notice that the Registry editor window closely resembles the Registry Editor program (regedit.exe) that's installed with Windows. Just as you can edit the system registry using regedit.exe, you can edit the registry using the Registry editor, except that registry settings declared in the Visual Studio .NET Registry editor window are created at install time.

If you use a setup project to install a COM object created with the C++ programming language, you must decide whether to define the registry keys for that COM object within the Registry editor or let the COM object register itself during installation. When the output of a COM object project is added to the File System editor, the *Register* property in the Properties window for that output is set to *vsdrpCOM*, which means the COM object knows how to register itself, and the *DllRegisterServer* and *DllUnregisterServer* methods are called on installation or uninstallation of that object. However, if a COM object registers itself, the keys it creates aren't included in the transactional feature of Windows

Installer. If installation fails, the *DllUnregisterServer* method is called to try and roll back the registry key creation; if that fails, some registry entries might be left behind. On the other hand, creating the registry entries for a COM object can be a tedious, error-prone chore. If all you need to do is copy the entries in an .rgs file to the Registry editor, it isn't a problem, but you must create multiple registry keys and values for every interface defined by that COM object so the proxy and stub DLL for that interface are set up correctly. The choice is yours, but you should consider the options carefully.

The User/Machine Hive

The Registry editor lets you modify the registry settings for the four main registry root sections, or hives: HKEY_CLASSES_ROOT, HKEY_CURRENT_USER, HKEY_LOCAL_MACHINE, and HKEY_USERS. However, the Registry editor for an .msi setup project has one additional node that's not a root key within the system registry: the User/Machine Hive key. This key is used to conditionally modify the HKEY_LOCAL_MACHINE key or HKEY_CURRENT_USER key and is dependent on an option the user selects when installing an .msi file. If you create a setup project and then build and install the resulting .msi file, the second page of the setup user interface appears as shown in Figure 13-1. On the bottom left of this dialog box are two options, Everyone and Just Me. If the user selects Everyone, all the registry keys you create in the User/Machine Hive key are placed in the system registry under the HKEY_LOCAL_MACHINE key. If the user selects Just Me, all these settings are placed in the HKEY_CURRENT_USER key of the system registry. If the person running the .msi file has reduced permissions, such as Guest, these two option buttons are not displayed and the setting defaults to Just Me.

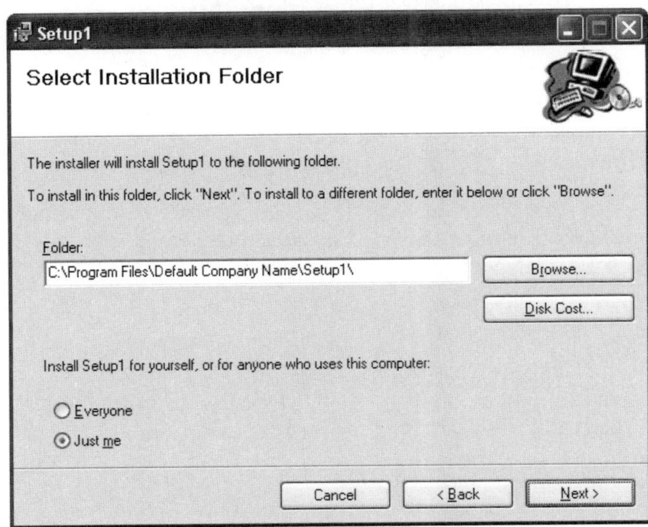

Figure 13-1 The Select Installation Folder page of an .msi setup file

Installer Properties

Although the Registry editor provides an easy-to-use, point-and-click way to create registry settings for your program, the registry modifications you make are static. That is, the key names, value names, and data values you enter are copied into the registry during setup exactly as you've typed them. However, at times you'll need to create a registry key with a name or value that's dynamic, reflecting the state of the computer when the user installs an .msi file. Such dynamic values are known as *installer properties*. Using an installer property in the Registry editor is as simple as placing the installer property name within square brackets; when the .msi file is run, Windows Installer notices these installer properties and replaces them with the appropriate values.

Table 13-1 lists the most commonly used installer properties of the nearly 200 that are available. New ones are being added with each new version of Windows Installer. You should consult MSDN for an up-to-date listing of the available installer properties. As an example, to place the date on which the user installed the .msi file into the registry, you use *[Date]* as the registry key name, value name, or value. You can combine installer properties by placing them next to one another, and you can add string data where appropriate. For example, the value *[Time]-[Date]* is expanded to create the value *17:54:35-11/10/2002* for November 10, 2002, at 5:54:35PM. You can see one of these installer properties being used when you first create a setup project. If you look in the Registry editor of a setup project, you can see that the keys HKEY_LOCAL_MACHINE\Software\[Manufacturer] and HKEY_CURRENT_USER\Software\[Manufacturer] are automatically created for you. These keys are where you can place data specific to your company's software; the token *[Manufacturer]* expands into the name of your company, which you can enter as the *Manufacturer* property in the Properties window when the setup project is selected in Solution Explorer.

Table 13-1 Commonly Used Installer Properties

Installer Property	Description	Example
AdminToolsFolder	Folder where tools to administer the computer are stored.	C:\Documents and Settings*username*\Start Menu\Programs\Administrative Tools\
AdminUser	This value is 1 if the installing user has administrator privileges, 0 if not.	1
AppDataFolder	Folder where application-specific data is stored.	C:\Documents and Settings*username*\Application Data\

Table 13-1 Commonly Used Installer Properties *(continued)*

Installer Property	Description	Example
ARPCONTACT	The name of the technical support contact person. This value is set using the Author property in the Properties window when the setup project is selected.	Default Company Name
Author	The author of the installer. The value of this property is set in the Properties window when the setup project is selected in Solution Explorer.	Default Company Name
CommonAppDataFolder	The folder shared by all users for storing application-specific data.	C:\Documents and Settings\All Users\Application Data\
CommonFilesFolder	The folder where shared software components are stored.	C:\Program Files\Common Files\
ComputerName	The network name of the computer.	CRAIGS4000
Date	The date on which the .msi file is installed.	11/10/2002
DesktopFolder	The folder for installing user's desktop items.	C:\Documents and Settings*username*\Desktop\
FavoritesFolder	The folder where Internet Explorer favorites are stored.	C:\Documents and Settings*username*\Favorites\
FontsFolder	The folder where fonts are stored.	C:\Windows\Fonts\
Intel	If setup is running on a computer with one or more Intel processors, this value is the processor class being used: 4 for a 486, 5 for a Pentium, 6 for a P6, and so on.	6
LocalAppDataFolder	The folder for nonroaming, application-specific user data.	C:\Documents and Settings*username*\Local Settings\Application Data\
LogonUser	The user name of the person running the .msi file.	Craig Skibo
Manufacturer	The name of the company that created the .msi file.	Default Company Name
MyPicturesFolder	The folder where user images are stored.	C:\Documents and Settings*username*\My Documents\My Pictures\

Table 13-1 Commonly Used Installer Properties *(continued)*

Installer Property	Description	Example
MsiNTProductType	The type of the operating system installed. A value of 1 means that the computer is a workstation, 2 means that the computer is a domain controller, and 3 means it's a server.	1
NetHoodFolder	The Network Neighborhood folder.	C:\Documents and Settings*username*\NetHood\
PersonalFolder	Folder where user documents are stored.	C:\Documents and Settings*username*\My Documents\
PhysicalMemory	The amount of memory, in megabytes, on the computer where the .msi file is being run.	384
PrintHoodFolder	The folder where printers are installed.	C:\Documents and Settings*username*\PrintHood\
Privileged	This value is 1 if the installation is performed under elevated user privileges.	1
ProductID	The serial number entered in the Serial Number edit box in the User Information dialog box (described later in this chapter).	111-7000000
ProductName	The name of the product being installed. You set this value by changing the ProductName property in the Visual Studio .NET Properties window when the setup project is selected.	Setup1
ProductVersion	The version of the .msi file being installed. You set this value in the Version property in the Properties window when the setup project is selected in Solution Explorer.	1.0.0
ProgramFilesFolder	The Program Files folder.	C:\Program Files\
ProgramMenuFolder	The folder where Start menu program shortcuts are stored.	C:\Documents and Settings*username*\Start Menu\Programs\
RecentFolder	The folder where shortcuts to recently used documents are stored.	C:\Documents and Settings*username*\Recent\

Table 13-1 Commonly Used Installer Properties *(continued)*

Installer Property	Description	Example
RemoteAdminTS	This value is 1 if the computer has terminal services installed and configured.	1
ROOTDRIVE	The drive on which to install the program.	C:\
ScreenX	The width, in pixels, of the user's primary monitor.	1024
ScreenY	The height, in pixels, of the user's primary monitor.	768
SendToFolder	The folder containing items shown on the context menu when you right-click on a file in Windows Explorer and choose Send To.	C:\Documents and Settings*user-name*\SendTo\
ServicePackLevel	The current service pack version installed on the computer.	1
ServicePackLevel-Minor	The minor version number of the service pack installed.	0
SourceDir	The folder containing the .msi file.	C:\Documents and Settings*username*\My Documents\Visual Studio Projects\Setup1\Debug\
StartMenuFolder	The folder where Start menu shortcuts are stored.	C:\Documents and Settings*username*\Start Menu\
StartupFolder	The folder containing links to programs that are started when the user logs in to the operating system.	C:\Documents and Settings*username*\Start Menu\Programs\Startup\
SystemFolder	The Windows system folder.	C:\Windows\System32\
SystemLanguageID	The locale identifier (LCID) of the operating system.	1033
TARGETDIR	The folder where the setup project is being installed.	C:\Program Files\Default Company Name\ Setup1\
TempFolder	The folder for temporary files.	C:\ Documents and Settings\ *username*\Local Settings\Temp\
TemplateFolder	The folder where templates are stored. Templates are the items shown on the New menu when the context menu of the desktop is displayed.	C:\Documents and Settings*username*\Templates\

Table 13-1 Commonly Used Installer Properties *(continued)*

Installer Property	Description	Example
Time	The time when the .msi file is being installed, in the format HH:MM:SS.	17:54:35
UserLanguageID	The locale identifier (LCID) in use by the user.	1033
USERNAME	The logon name of the user installing the .msi file.	craigs
VersionNT	The version of operating system being used if the operating system is 32-bit NT class.	501
VirtualMemory	The amount of memory, in megabytes, assigned to the virtual memory page.	576
WindowsBuild	The build number of the operating system.	2600
WindowsFolder	The folder in which the operating system is installed.	C:\Windows\
WindowsVolume	The hard disk drive on which Windows is installed.	C:\

You can use these installer property values not only in the Registry editor but also in the File System editor. The previous section described how you can define custom folders that are created when the .msi file is installed, but the path to those folders was hard-coded. Using installer properties, you can specify that the path of a custom folder be determined at install time.

Suppose you need to create a folder for storing application-specific data. The installer property *AppDataFolder* is typically set to the value *C:\Documents and Settings*\username*\Application Data*\, which is the folder where user-specific data for a program, such as configuration options, should be stored. The installer property *ProductName* is set to the name of the product being installed, which defaults to the name of the setup project. You could set the custom folder's location to point to the path C:\Documents and Settings*username*\Application Data*ProductName*, but if the user installs the operating system to the D drive or changes the application data path, this won't be the correct location to store data. You can combine the installer properties *AppDataFolder* and *ProductName* and set the *DefaultLocation* property for the folder to create within the Properties window into *[AppDataFolder][ProductName]*. This automatically creates the folder C:\Documents and Settings*username*\Application Data\Setup1 (where the name of the setup project is Setup1).

File Types Editor

Of all the technologies built into Windows to help users get started using their computers, file associations are probably the most overlooked. Back in the days of MS-DOS, if you wanted to view or edit a data file, you had to know which application could be used to edit that file, and then you had to know how to start that application to view it. With Windows, all you need to know is how to double-click, because when you double-click the icon in Windows Explorer, the application associated with that file is automatically run and the data file is loaded. You create associations by creating a set of system registry keys and values that link the extension of a data file to the program that views or edits that file. You can use the Registry editor of a setup project to define your file associations, but this can be complicated. The File Types editor in Visual Studio .NET lets you easily define your file associations.

Suppose you create a new way of storing image data in a compressed format that's better than any other image format available. You've also created a .NET program named MyImageViewer to make viewing, printing, and editing that file format possible. If the user of this file format wants to print the image, she can open your viewer application, choose File | Open, browse to the image (which has the file extension .myimage), and then choose File | Print to print the image. Or, she can let Windows handle all the work for her using a file association. For the purposes of this example, we'll leave the theories about image file formats to other books and use a bitmap file, renamed to have the .myimage extension, as our file format.

To create a .myimage file association within a setup project, first open the File Types editor for the setup project by right-clicking the setup project in Solution Explorer and choosing View | File Types. Right-click on the File Types On Target Machine node, and select Add File Type. This creates a file association for the Open verb. A verb is an action you take against the file; the default verb (denoted within the File Types editor using boldface) is the action performed when the user double-clicks on the file in Windows Explorer. Other common verbs are Print and Edit. For our example, we'll add both of these.

To add the Print verb, right-click on the file type node you just created, choose Add Action, and then type **&Print**. The verb name is preceded by an ampersand because this text will be displayed to the user when a .myimage file is right-clicked in Windows Explorer and the P key will be the shortcut key for printing. Next, you set how the verb will tell your program that it has been invoked. Select &Print and, in the Properties window, type the command-line argument for the Print verb in the *Arguments* property. For this example, the command-line argument is *–print "%1"*. The *–print* value is a command-line switch that tells your program it should print a file. Windows Explorer replaces the *%1* token with the file path of the image that is to be printed. This token should be surrounded by double quotes. If it isn't and the file path has an embedded space, two or more strings will be passed as the filename to the program's command line arguments, not just one, thereby confusing the program that handles the verb. Next, in the Properties window, type the name of the verb, **Print**, in the *Verb* property. For the purposes of this example, you should also repeat the process to create another verb, using the verb Edit in place of Print where appropriate.

Now you need to tell the setup project which program to run when the user selects one of these verbs. Select the file type node you created underneath the File Types On Target Machine node, and then open the Properties window. The *Command* property specifies the program that will run when the verb is invoked; you can set the target of the verb to any file that's been added to the File System editor, including project output such as the primary output. To specify an extension that is associated with the program, type one or more extensions, separated by semicolons, in the *Extensions* property. For this sample, type **myimage**; a period preceding the extension isn't required. If you want to use a custom icon for your file format when the file is viewed in Windows Explorer, you can add an icon to the File System editor and then browse to that icon using the *Icon* property.

The last step is to modify your program to accept the command-line parameters passed to the program. If your program is a Windows Forms application and the main form in the program is called Form1, you can add the following constructor to the *Form1* class:

```
public Form1(string []args)
{
    InitializeComponent();
    if(args.Length == 1)
    {
        pictureBox1.Image = System.Drawing.Bitmap.FromFile(args[0]);
        this.Text = this.Text + " - " +
                    System.IO.Path.GetFileName(args[0]);
    }
    else if (args.Length == 2)
    {
        //The two command line switches that are recognized:
        string printCommand = "-print";
        string editCommand = "-edit";
        if(System.String.Compare(printCommand, args[0], true) == 0)
        {
            //We were asked to print the image. Load the image, then use
            // the PrintDocument class to print
            pictureBox1.Image = System.Drawing.Bitmap.FromFile(args[1]);
            PrintDocument printDocument = new PrintDocument();
            printDocument.PrintPage += new
                PrintPageEventHandler(printDocument_PrintPage);
```

```
            printDocument.Print();
            System.Diagnostics.Process.GetCurrentProcess().Kill();
        }
        else if(System.String.Compare(editCommand, args[0], true) == 0)
        {
            //We were asked to edit the image.
            //Spawn off to MSPaint to edit:
            System.Diagnostics.Process.Start("mspaint.exe", "\""
                                             + args[1] + "\"");
            System.Diagnostics.Process.GetCurrentProcess().Kill();
        }
    }
}
```

Next, change the *Main* function to the following:

```
static void Main(string []args)
{
    Application.Run(new Form1(args));
}
```

When the Edit or Print verbs are invoked, the command line to the program is –edit *filename* or –print *filename*. This code examines the parameters, and if *–print* or *–edit* is specified, it takes the appropriate action, either printing the image or calling to mspaint.exe to display the image passed on the command line, and then it exits. If neither verb is specified and the user wants to view the image, the image file is loaded and displayed on the form. The MyImageViewer sample contains the complete source code for a .myimage viewer and a setup project that includes the settings to register a file extension.

User Interface Editor

When an .msi file is installed, a setup wizard walks the user through the install process. The wizard's dialog boxes do little more than tell the user which program he's installing, ask for the name of the folder on disk in which to install the program, and provide feedback during installation. Using the setup tools built into Visual Studio .NET, you can add dialog boxes that ask for more information about how to configure your program's installation.

You can customize any dialog box within a setup project by modifying two properties in its Properties window: *BannerText* and *BannerBitmap*. *BannerText* specifies the text in the banner at the top of the dialog box, which describes that step of the setup wizard. *BannerBitmap* specifies a bitmap file to show along the top of the dialog box; you must add this bitmap to the File System editor before you can browse to it, and it must be 496 pixels wide and 68 pixels high. The bitmap can look any way you want, but keep in mind that the value of the *BannerText* property will appear on top of the bitmap; you should use a color that will allow this text to be visible.

In the User Interface editor, you'll notice two branches of a tree, Install and Administrative Install. The Install branch is where you do most of the work to design the user interface of a setup project. The dialog boxes shown in this branch make up the user interface that most users see; they walk users through the steps of setting up your application. The Administrative Install branch, as its name suggests, is for system administrators. If a network administrator runs an .msi file with the *–a* switch on a command line, such as *msiexec.exe –a msifile.msi*, the files contained in the .msi file are installed so the users of the network can perform a network installation of the program. Only a subset of the dialog boxes available in the Install branch can be used in the Administrative Install branch. In most situations, you don't need to make changes to the Administrative Install branch of the User Interface editor; Windows Installer handles all the details of an administrative install for you.

Splash Screen

The purpose of a splash screen page is simply to display an image to users that identifies what program they're installing. The image must be a bitmap or JPG file that's 480 pixels wide and 320 pixels high. To set the image to display in this dialog box, first add the image to an appropriate folder in the File System editor, select the Splash dialog box in the User Interface editor, and then set the *Splash-Bitmap* property in the Properties window to the image file you just added to the File System. Figure 13-2 shows a splash screen of a setup project with the cover of this book used as the image.

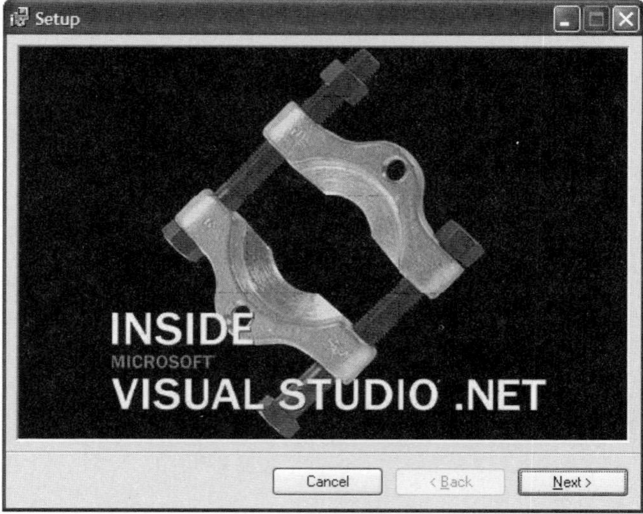

Figure 13-2 A splash screen for a setup project showing the Inside Microsoft Visual Studio .NET book cover

Options Dialog Boxes

The options dialog boxes—RadioButtons (2 Buttons), RadioButtons (3 Buttons), RadioButtons (4 Buttons), Checkboxes (A), Checkboxes (B), and Checkboxes (C)—give you a way to offer users installation options. The RadioButtons dialog boxes display 2, 3, or 4 option buttons that the user can choose from, respectively; the Checkboxes dialog boxes display between 0 and 4 check boxes. (See Figure 13-3.)

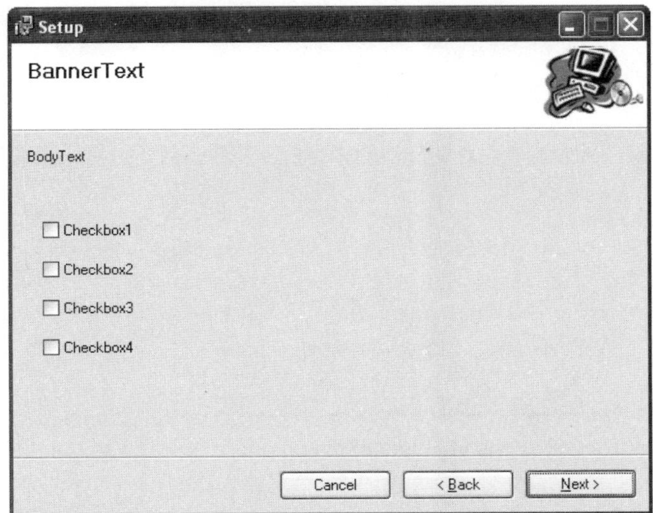

Figure 13-3 One of the Checkboxes dialog boxes

You can manipulate the settings for each option button and check box in these dialog boxes in the Properties window. You can set an option's default state (selected or unselected, checked or unchecked), installer property name, and label. The most interesting value is the installer property name, which is denoted in the Properties window as *ButtonProperty* for RadioButtons dialog boxes and *CheckBoxXProperty* (where *X* is a number from 1 to 4) for Checkboxes dialog boxes. You can use the value of these properties in other editors, such as the Registry editor, as key names, value names, or values, just as you would for the installer properties listed earlier in Table 13-1.

You can use the value of an option in a RadioButtons dialog box (shown in Figure 13-4) in the Registry editor in the same way you use a check box value. Only one option can be selected at a time, so only one property is available for each dialog box; the value of *ButtonXValue* is used when the installer populates the system registry. For example, the RadioButtons (2 Buttons) dialog box has two value properties, *Button1Value* and *Button2Value*, which are set to *1* and *2*, respectively. The property name of these buttons is *BUTTON2*, so in the Registry editor you can use the value *[BUTTON2]* for a registry key name, value name, or value. If the first radio button (*Button1*) is selected, the data placed into the registry is *1*; if the second button (*Button2*) is selected, the data is *2*.

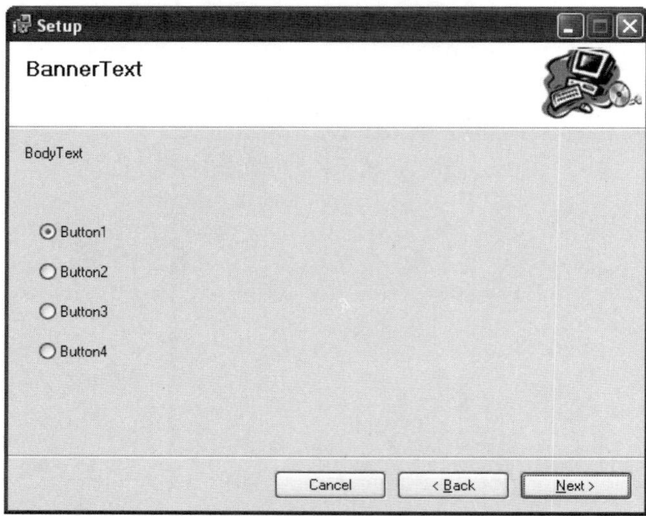

Figure 13-4 The RadioButtons (4 Buttons) dialog box

Later in this chapter, we'll discuss how you can use the options dialog boxes to conditionally install the registry keys and files you place in the Registry and File System editors.

Data Entry Dialog Boxes

You use the data entry dialog boxes—Textboxes (A), Textboxes (B), and Textboxes (C)—to ask the user for text data. Figure 13-5 shows one of these dialog boxes. Each data entry dialog box has four text boxes. For example, if you need to show only two of the text boxes, you can hide the other two text boxes by selecting the appropriate data entry dialog box in the User Interface editor and then, in the Properties window, setting the *Edit*X*Visible* property (where *X* is the edit box number) to *False*. Each text box in a dialog box has a name, and this name is listed in the Properties window using the *EditXProperty* property. You can use the value of this property, surrounded by square brackets, in the Registry Editor just as you use the other installer properties. For example, the first text box in the Textboxes (A) dialog box has the value *EDITA1* for the

Edit1Property property, so you can enter the registry key name, value name, or the value *[EDITA1]* to represent what the user typed in the text box.

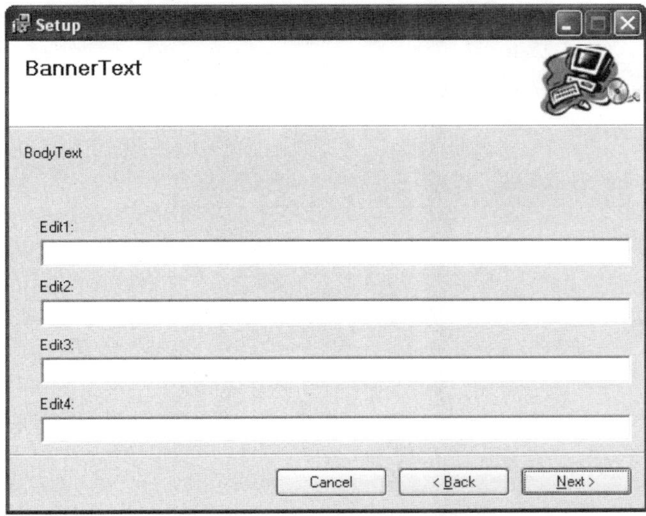

Figure 13-5 One of the TextBoxes dialog boxes

Customer Information Dialog Box

You use the Customer Information dialog box to gather information from users such as their name, the company they work for, and optionally a serial number for the program. To verify that a user has entered a correct serial number, a validation algorithm is performed on the serial number, with the algorithm being based on the value of the *SerialNumberTemplate* property in the Properties window. The value of the *SerialNumberTemplate* property creates the user interface for the serial number in the Customer Information dialog box and verifies that the serial number entered is valid. To define the serial number that the user can enter, you string together a special set of tokens to create a template. This template is surrounded by the less-than and greater-than symbols. Between these two characters, you can place any number of the characters #, %, ?, ^, and -. The # and % symbols are placeholders for digits, and ? and ^ are placeholders for alphanumeric characters, with ^ denoting an uppercase character. When a dash character is encountered within the template, a new text box is created in the dialog box. The dialog box determines whether the serial number entered is valid by adding all the numbers appearing in place of % in the template and dividing by seven. (The dialog box ignores all other characters in the template.) If the remainder is 0, the number entered by the user is considered valid and the user is allowed to continue installing the application;

otherwise, an error message is shown and the user must either reenter the serial number to continue or exit the installation program. The dialog box shown in Figure 13-6 uses the default serial number template of <###-%%%%%%%>; the number entered is invalid because the sum of the numbers 4, 5, 6, 7, 8, 9, and 9 is 48, which is not evenly divisible by 7. Once the serial number has been validated, the value of the serial number entered is stored in the installer *ProductID* property.

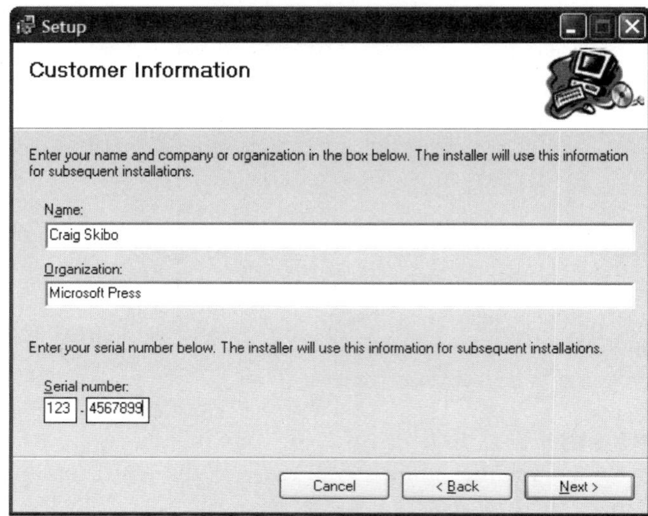

Figure 13-6 The Customer Information dialog box

License Agreement and Read Me Dialog Boxes

Just about every software program comes with some legal restrictions on how the program can and cannot be used. These restrictions, in the form of a license agreement, generally inform the user that the software cannot be illegally copied, cannot be reverse-engineered, and so forth. You can use the License Agreement dialog box to display license information to the user; unless the user selects an option to accept the license agreement, the user cannot continue installing the software. The options for accepting or not accepting the terms of the license agreement are shown in Figure 13-7. If the user selects the I Do Not Agree option, the Next button is disabled. Selecting the I Agree option is legally binding; a user who accepts the license agreement can continue installing the program.

To create the text to display in the License Agreement dialog box, you must create a rich text format (RTF) text file. You can use tools such as Microsoft Word or even WordPad, the better-than-Notepad text editor installed with Windows, to create an RTF file. After creating this file, you can add it to the File System editor and then set the text to appear in the License Agreement dialog box by first adding and then selecting the License Agreement dialog box in the User Interface editor and then in the Properties window browsing to the RTF file with the *LicenseFile* property.

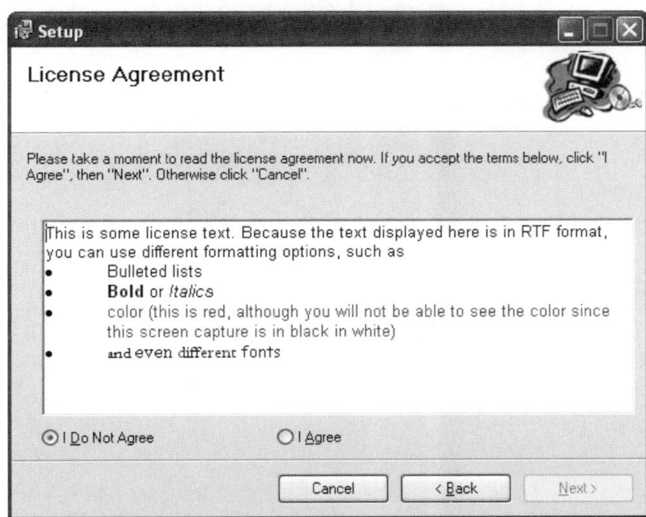

Figure 13-7 The License Agreement dialog box with richly formatted text

The Read Me dialog box looks and works much like the License Agreement dialog box, except it doesn't have I Do Not Agree and I Agree options. Text in the Read Me dialog box, like that in the License Agreement dialog box, is defined using an RTF file, so it can contain text that's formatted with colors, fonts, and styles.

Register User Dialog Box

Many software packages ask users for personal information such as name and e-mail address so when new versions or bug fixes are available, the software company can send them upgrade information. You can add the Register User dialog box, shown in Figure 13-8, to your setup program to gather this information. This dialog box doesn't contain entries for users to type their name, e-mail address, land-based address, or other data; instead, it contains a simple button that, when clicked, invokes any executable program that has been added to the File System editor of your setup project.

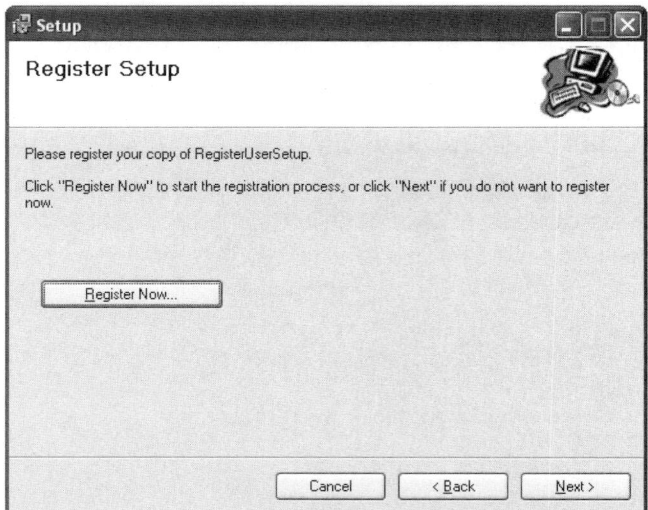

Figure 13-8 The Register User dialog box

To associate your registration program with the Register Now button, you must first create a registration program and add the primary output of this program to your setup project's File System editor. Next, select the Register User dialog box in the User Interface editor, and in Visual Studio .NET's Properties tool window, browse to the executable using the *Executable* property.

Creating the registration program isn't complicated—you can simply run the C# Windows Application Wizard and use the executable file—but you can find the source code for a registration project among the book's sample files. This project, RegisterUser, gathers the appropriate information from the user. Another sample project, called ProductRegistration, is a .NET Web application that you can install on a Web server. When the RegisterUser program is run and the user clicks the Register Online button, the information entered is packaged up into a HTTP request header and then posted to the ProductRegistration Web application. The Web application then unpacks this information from the request header and sends a message back to the RegisterUser project that can be displayed to the user.

To use the RegisterUser and ProductRegistration samples, install the ProductRegistration sample onto your Web server and add the output of the RegisterUser project to your setup program. Within the ProductRegistration code, open the code-behind file for the ProductRegistration.aspx file and find the TODO comment toward the end of this file. You should replace this comment with custom code to store the user's information for later use, such as within a database. You can also modify the text message returned to the user, customizing the message to suit your needs. The second step is to modify the Register-User Form1.cs file to point to the server containing the ProductRegistration Web application. To do this, search for the string *localhost* and change it to point to the server and virtual directory where the ProductRegistration Web application is installed.

Custom Actions

Windows Installer offers a lot of functionality to help you install your application, but at times you might need to run code during an installation to help get your program onto the user's computer. This helper code is called a *custom action*. We looked briefly at a custom action in Chapter 7 to help create and remove commands for Visual Studio .NET, but you can create a custom action to do anything you want. You can build three types of custom actions for a setup project: .NET Custom Actions, Script Custom Actions, and Win32 Custom Actions. The samples for this book include the CustomActions sample, which demonstrates creating and using each of these custom action types.

You add custom actions to the Custom Actions editor by first adding the primary output of the project implementing the custom action to the File System editor and then right-clicking on the appropriate installation action in the Custom Actions editor and browsing to the project output. Four installation actions are defined: Install, Commit, Rollback, and Uninstall. Which one you add your custom action to will depend on the work your custom action performs. An Install custom action is called when an .msi file is being installed. If an error occurs during installation, custom actions in the Rollback group are called. A Rollback custom action is run when an error occurs during installation; it can be used to repair a computer, removing data such as files or registry keys created within the Install action. If the installation completed successfully, custom actions in the Commit group are called, allowing you to complete setup on the computer. When a program is uninstalled, custom actions in the Uninstall group are called, giving your custom action the chance to clean up any data that might have been left behind by your program.

.NET Custom Actions

You can build custom actions by using the .NET Framework with an executable program, such as a Windows Forms application or a console application, or with a .NET class library that derives from a class found in the .NET base class libraries. Choosing which type of custom action to create is a tradeoff between how your user interacts with your custom action and how easy it is for you to develop and test your custom action.

If you want your custom action to display a user interface, the best option is to create a Windows Forms custom action. You simply add a Windows Forms application to your solution, add the output of this project first to your setup application's File System editor and then to the Custom Actions editor, and then select the appropriate installation stage in which the custom action should be run. When that stage is run, the custom action program is called, allowing the user to interact with the user interface the custom action displays. Creating a Windows Forms custom action is also a good choice for ease of developing and testing your custom action. Because a Windows Forms custom action is a program, you can run, test, and debug the custom action without needing to build and install the .msi file; this increases your productivity. Creating a custom action with a Windows Forms application is not the best choice if you don't intend to display a user interface because the form will block the install progress until dismissed, and you don't want to display a dialog box to the user that simply says "Click me to continue installing"—that's just poor style.

The second option is to create a console application custom action. This custom action type offers the benefits of a Windows Forms custom action in terms of the ease of testing and debugging, and it displays a user interface to the user. Depending on what your custom action does, the user interface can be either a blessing or a curse. Users don't like seeing console windows—they're not pretty to look at and are hard to use. If the custom action you're creating does its job quickly, the screen will flash with a console application, causing the user to question what the installer is doing to his computer. However, if you need to display text information such as the output of another console application, a console custom action is a good choice. If you've created a custom action using either a Windows Forms or console application using a language supported by the .NET Framework, you must change the *InstallerClass* property in the Properties window from *True* to *False* when the custom action is selected in the Custom Actions editor. If this property is *False*, Windows Installer knows it should invoke the custom action as a program. If this property is *True*, Windows Installer searches the program for a class with a specific attribute, which is used by the third type of .NET custom action—a .NET class library.

A .NET class library is a good choice if your custom action should run silently in the background without any user interaction. A custom action of this type is more complicated to test and debug because a class library isn't a free-standing executable that you can run without a hosting application. To create a class library custom action, you create a class library using your favorite .NET-enabled programming language, right-click on that project in Solution Explorer, choose Add | Add New Item, and then add an Installer Class item to the project. The item added is a class that derives from the class *System.Configura-*

tion.Install.Installer and uses the attribute *RunInstaller*. When the .msi project is run and starts to run custom actions, it examines all classes within an assembly that implement the custom action; if it finds a class with the *RunInstaller* attribute, the class is instantiated and a proper method of the class is called. The class *System.Configuration.Install.Installer* defines four methods you can override that are called during certain actions of the install process: *Commit*, *Install*, *Rollback*, and *Uninstall*. You can add these to the class from the Class View window.

Script Custom Actions

Creating a custom action by using script code involves little more than creating a VBScript or JScript file, adding that file to the File System editor, and then adding it as a custom action in the Custom Actions editor. A script custom action is just a list of commands that the ActiveX Scripting engine loads and runs. When these script custom actions start running, one global variable of type *Session* named *Session* is created so you can find out information about the currently installing .msi file. Listing 13-1 shows a simple VBScript custom action, and Listing 13-2 shows its JScript equivalent. The custom action does little more than show a message box to the user containing these custom actions.

VBScriptCustomAction.vbs

```
'Can use the object Session to peek into the MSI
' file being installed. See the MSDN topic located at
' ms-help://MS.VSCC.2003/MS.MSDNQTR.2003FEB.1033/msi/vref_8xis.htm
' for information about how to use this object.
msgbox("VBScript Custom Action")
```

Listing 13-1 Source code for a VBScript custom action

JScriptCustomAction.js

```
//Can use the object Session to peek into the MSI
// file being installed. See the MSDN topic located at
// ms-help://MS.VSCC.2003/MS.MSDNQTR.2003FEB.1033/msi/vref_8xis.htm
// for information about how to use this object.
var wshShell = new ActiveXObject("WScript.Shell");
wshShell.Popup("JScript Custom Action");
```

Listing 13-2 Source code for a JScript custom action

You might choose to create a script custom action rather than another type of custom action for a couple reasons. First, you might have built up a library of scripts written using VBScript or JScript to help configure a computer. Rather than rewriting these into a .NET custom action, you can simply add the scripts to the setup project and run them. Another reason you might want to create a custom action using script is ease of development. Scripts are lines of text that are interpreted, which means you don't need to compile them. To create and test a script custom action, you simply open any text editor (even Notepad), write code, and then run that script code by double-clicking on the file in Windows Explorer.

Win32 Custom Actions

If the software you're trying to install is not a .NET application and the user doesn't have the .NET Framework installed on his computer, your choices are either script or Win32 custom actions. Script custom actions are easy to write but don't have full access to the Windows API and therefore might not be an option. The only remaining choice is to use a language such as Visual C++ to create a Win32 custom action. To create a Win32 custom action, you must first create a Visual C++ Win32 DLL and export a function that uses the *__stdcall* calling convention. This exported function must return a value of type *unsigned int*, which is a status code. If the custom action returns anything other than *ERROR_SUCCESS*, Windows Installer thinks it failed and rolls back the installation. The exported function takes as its only argument a value of type *MSIHANDLE* that can be used to query the setup project for information. To let Windows Installer know which exported function it should call within a DLL when a custom action is run, you must set the *EntryPoint* property in the Properties window when the custom action is selected in the Custom Actions editor. If you were to write a custom action like that shown in Listing 13-3, for example, you would enter **Install** for the *EntryPoint* property because that's the exported function for handling the custom action invocation.

Win32CustomAction.cpp

```
#include "stdafx.h"
#include <tchar.h>
#include <msi.h>
#include <Msiquery.h>

BOOL APIENTRY DllMain(HANDLE hModule, DWORD ul_reason_for_call,
                      LPVOID lpReserved)
{
    return TRUE;
}

__declspec(dllexport) unsigned int __stdcall Install(MSIHANDLE hInstall)
{
    MessageBox(NULL, "CustomAction", "VC++", MB_OK);
    return ERROR_SUCCESS;
}
```

Listing 13-3 Source code for a Win32 custom action

Lab: Debugging Custom Actions

Debugging a custom action when it's running inside an .msi file isn't as simple as it might seem. An .msi file doesn't run code—it's a collection of compressed files with data describing how those files should be installed. To debug a custom action, you must start installing the .msi file and attach the debugger at just the right time—after the code has started executing but before the code you want to debug has run. As you can guess, getting the timing just right can be nearly impossible. A trick I use to debug custom actions is to place a message box inside the custom action just before the code that I want to debug and then build and install the .msi file. When the message box appears, I know I can attach the debugger to that code and start debugging. Execution of the custom action stops while the message box is shown, so I know I'm connecting the debugger at the correct time. But what program do you attach the debugger to? It depends on which type of custom action you created. If the custom action is a .NET class library and you open the debugger's Processes dialog box, you'll see that three msiexec.exe processes are running that you can attach to. One of these processes will have the word *.NET* in the Type column of this dialog box. This is the process to attach to because it has the .NET Framework loaded and is executing your custom action.

If the custom action you created is a .NET Windows Forms application or a .NET console application, you'll see the programs listed in the Processes dialog box by their executable names; you can attach to those processes without attaching to the msiexec.exe process. To debug a Win32 DLL custom action, you must look in the Processes dialog box for an msiexec.exe process that has the same title you used for your message box in the Title column. Currently, there's no way to debug a script custom action; you have to use an alternative method of debugging, such as displaying a message box with information so you can trace through the code.

When you're done debugging, don't forget to remove your message boxes; otherwise, the user will see them when installing an .msi file.

Launch Conditions Editor

Sometimes the software you create will have special requirements for running. For instance, suppose you take advantage of the latest technology in Windows XP and therefore the user must run that operating system to run your program.

Or suppose your program is an add-in and therefore cannot run without Visual Studio .NET installed on the computer. You could write a custom action that checks for these requirements during install time, but it's better to let the .msi file ensure that these requirements are met before the files are placed on the user's computer.

You can define the requirements in a setup project with a launch condition in the Launch Conditions editor. To add a launch condition, open the Launch Conditions editor, right-click on the Launch Conditions node, and choose Add Launch Condition. In the Properties window, you can type an expression in the *Condition* property that must evaluate to *true* for the .msi file to install. If this expression doesn't evaluate to *true*, the user cannot install your program and sees the error message contained in the *Message* property. If the *InstallURL* property for the condition is set to anything other than an empty string and the condition evaluates to *false*, the user has the option to go to a Web page to find more information about why installation failed. A condition expression must use a special syntax, or condition algebra, in order for Windows Installer to be able to evaluate the expression.

Condition Algebra

To define a condition, you must use a Visual Basic .NET–like syntax to define an expression. The variables you can use in an expression are the same installer properties listed earlier in Table 13-1 or those found in the various dialog boxes in the User Interface editor. However, when you define a condition, you don't need to include the brackets around the installer property names as you do in other editor windows.

Table 13-2 lists the operators you can use in an expression. These operators, when combined with string or integral constants (floating-point comparisons aren't supported) and installer property names, create the algebra you use to create a condition.

Table 13-2 Condition Algebra Operators

Operator	Description
Not	Logically negates the term.
And	*True* if the two terms evaluate to *True*, *False* otherwise.
Or	*True* if one of the two terms is *True*.
Xor	*True* if only one of the two terms is *True*.
Eqv	Logical equivalence operator. *True* if both terms are *True* or both are *False*.

Table 13-2 Condition Algebra Operators *(continued)*

Operator	Description
Imp	Implication operator. *True* if the left term is *False* or the right term is *True*.
=	Equality operator. *True* if both terms are equal; otherwise evaluates to *False*.
<>	*True* if the two terms are not equivalent.
>	*True* if the left term is greater than the right term.
>=	*True* if the left term is greater than or equal to the right term.
<	*True* if the left term is less than the right term.
<=	*True* if the left term is less than or equal to the right term.
><	Bitwise *And* operator. *True* if any bits in the two terms match.
><	String comparison operator. *True* if the left string contains the right string.
<<	Bitwise comparison operator. *True* if the high 16 bits of the left integer term equal the right term integer.
<<	String comparison operator. *True* if the left string starts with the right string.
>>	Bitwise comparison operator. *True* if the low 16 bits of the left integer term equal the right term integer.
>>	String comparison operator. *True* if the left string ends with the right string.

Here are some examples of using these operators and installer Properties in the *Condition* property:

- ***Not Privileged*** *True* if the user isn't running under elevated privileges.
- ***(VersionNT = 501) And (ServicePackLevel = 1)*** *True* if the .msi file is being installed on Windows XP (version 501) and with Service Pack 1 installed.
- ***(VersionNT = 500) Or (VersionNT = 501)*** *True* if the .msi file is being installed on Windows 2000 (version 500) or Windows XP (version 501).
- ***(ScreenX >= 800) And (ScreenY >= 600)*** *True* if the user is running at a screen resolution of 800 × 600 or greater.

- ***PhysicalMemory > 128*** *True* if the computer has more than 128 MB of memory installed.
- ***PhysicalMemory >= 128*** *True* if the computer has 128 MB or more of memory installed.
- ***"Hello World" >< "Hello"*** *True* if the string on the right is contained in the first string.
- ***"Hello World" << "Hello"*** *True* if the string on the left starts with the string on the right.
- ***"Hello World" >> "World"*** *True* if the string on the left ends with the string on the right.
- ***Intel > 4*** *True* if the computer's processor is an Intel Pentium or later. This rule is useful if your software is compiled to use only the Pentium (or compatible) processor instruction set.
- ***Intel = "5"*** *True* if the computer's processor is an Intel Pentium. This expression is similar to the previous one, except with the number 5 is surrounded by quotes, the greater-than operator cannot be used because you cannot evaluate a string that includes a numerical operator.
- ***BUTTON2 = 1*** *True* if you added the RadioButtons (2 Buttons) dialog box to the User Interface editor and the user has selected the first option button in that dialog box.

Defining Custom Installer Properties

You've seen the use of installer properties in the Registry, Launch Conditions, User Interface, and File System editors. However, these installer properties, defined by either Windows Installer or dialog boxes added to the setup project, might not always meet your needs. Using the Launch Conditions editor, you can create custom installer properties to use wherever installer properties are allowed. To create a custom installer property, right-click on the Search Target Machine node in the Launch Conditions editor and choose File Search or Registry Search.

A File Search installer property searches the computer for a file, and if the file is found, the property is set to the path of that file. To specify the file to search for, add a File Search launch condition and then set the folder in which to start the search and the file to search for (in the Properties window's *Folder* and *FileName* properties, respectively). If you know that the file to search for is somewhere in one of the subfolders of the folder specified, you can set the *Depth* property to the number of folder levels into the folder hierarchy that should be searched.

For example, suppose you need to set an installer property to the path of the file dte.olb, which contains the type library for the Visual Studio .NET object model. Because Visual Studio .NET installs this file in the Program Files folder, you set the *FolderName* property of a file search launch condition to *[ProgramFilesFolder]*, the *File* property to *dte.olb*, and the *Depth* property to *20* (an arbitrary value that will ensure that all the necessary folders are searched). If the installer property name of the file search launch condition is *FILEEXISTS1* (the default installer property name of the first file search launch condition created), you can use the installer property *FILEEXISTS1* in the File System editor, Registry editor, or any other place that installer properties can be used where the path to dte.olb is needed.

A Registry Search launch condition works much like a File Search launch condition, except it searches the system registry rather than the user's disk drive, and an installer property is set to a registry value rather than a file path. For example, suppose you want to verify that Visual Studio .NET 2003 is installed before you try to install an add-in. You can do this by using a Registry Search condition. First, create a Registry Search condition by right-clicking on the Search Target Machine node, choosing Add Registry Search, and typing a name for the condition. In the Properties window, type the registry key hive for Visual Studio .NET in the *RegKey* property, which is **SOFTWARE\Microsoft\VisualStudio\7.1**, and type **InstallDir** as the Value property. The *InstallDir* registry value holds the location on disk where Visual Studio .NET has been installed. The other values can be left as their defaults, but you should note the value of the *Property* property. This is the installer property you'll use for creating the condition. (By default, this value is *REGISTRYVALUE1* for the first registry search condition.) Next, create a condition by right-clicking on the Launch Conditions node in the Launch Conditions editor and choosing Add Launch Condition. Open the Properties window, type **REGISTRYVALUE1 <> ""** for the *Condition* property, and type any message you want in the *Message* and *InstallURL* properties. When the .msi file for the Add-in is run, it creates an installer property called *REGISTRYVALUE1* that's set to the installation location of Visual Studio .NET. If this installer property is anything other than an empty string, the expression is *True* and setup continues; otherwise, a message is shown to the user with the value you entered in the *Message* property.

Installing an Assembly in the PublicAssemblies Folder

As we've said a couple times in this book, if you build an assembly that you want to call from a macro, you must put the assembly into a specific folder so you can add a reference to that assembly in the Macros editor. If you use the default installation location of Visual Studio .NET, which is C:\Program Files\Microsoft Visual Studio .NET 2003\Common7\IDE\PublicAssemblies, you cannot assume it's correct because the user might have selected a different installation location for Visual Studio .NET. You can use the custom *Registry Search* installer property we just described to verify that Visual Studio .NET is installed, and then install the assembly in the correct location so it can be used by a macro.

To place the assembly in the correct place, open the File System editor, right-click on the File System On Target Machine node, and choose Add Special Folder | Custom Folder. In the Properties window for this custom folder, type the name of the custom *Registry Search* installer property surrounded by square brackets (in this case, *[REGISTRYVALUE1]*), and then type **\PublicAssemblies** in the *DefaultLocation* property. Then add the primary output of the assembly to the custom folder. When the .msi file is installed, it places the assembly in the correct location so it can be referenced in the Macros editor.

Conditions

If you looked closely at the Properties window while working with the File System, Registry, Custom Actions, or File Types editors, you might have noticed the *Condition* property. This property controls whether a project output, registry key, or file type is installed on the computer or if a custom action is run. You can use the same condition algebra you use to create a launch condition to set the *Condition* property. For example, suppose you want to give the user the option of installing the source code for an add-in that you created. To do this, you run the Add-in Wizard to completion, and after the source files have been generated, you open the User Interface editor for the setup project. Insert a RadioButtons (2 Buttons) dialog box into the User Interface editor, open the Properties window, and set the *Button1Label* property to **Yes, install source code** and set the *Button2Label* property to **No, do not install source code**. Make note of the installer property name of this dialog box, *BUTTON2*, and the values of the buttons in the dialog box, *1* and *2*.

Next, open the File System editor for the setup project, right-click on the Application Folder node, choose Add | Folder, and then enter **source**. This creates the folder to hold the source files for the add-in. To add the source files output, right-click on the source folder, choose Add | Project Output, and select the Source Files output. If you build and install the .msi file for the add-in after making these changes, the source files are always installed because the condition on the source files output isn't connected to the option the user selects in the RadioButtons (2 Buttons) dialog box. To connect the dialog box to the source files folder you created, select the source folder in the File System editor, and in the Properties window enter the expression **BUTTON2 = 1** in the *Condition* property. Now if you install the .msi file and if the user selects the first option button, the sources are installed in a folder called sources. But if the user selects the second option button—the one that corresponds to the value *2*—the expression *BUTTON2 = 1* evaluates to *False* and the source folder isn't created. Because the source file output is contained in the source folder, that project output is also not installed. You could place the condition *BUTTON2 = 1* on the source file project output so that if the user selects the second option button, the source files are not installed, but the source folder will have been created, leaving an empty folder on the user's computer. The samples for this book contain the setup project for the SourceFilesAddin sample, which demonstrates how you can optionally install the source code to an add-in project.

Merge Modules

When creating software for the Windows operating system, developers commonly place code into DLLs so it can be shared among multiple applications. To distribute software to your customers, you could install the DLLs you create with a .msi setup project, but this would be a less-than-ideal way to install the code. Suppose you've built a .NET user control library that you want to sell; your customers can use this library to build their own applications. How can customers redistribute this library to their own customers? You could provide detailed instructions that explain to your users how to include the component in their own .msi setup. However, this could be problematic because if they don't install your component properly, other software that uses your component might stop functioning. Alternatively, you could create a setup project that installs and uninstalls your library, but that's not a good option because your users would have to give their customers two .msi files and make sure they were installed in the correct order.

To make installing your library easy and reduce the risk of a user incorrectly installing and uninstalling a component, you can store your library in a merge module (.msm file). Merge modules are like the DLLs of a setup project. You can use a DLL to store code shared among different applications; a merge module contains installation logic shared among many .msi files. Merge module projects are similar to setup projects, except you cannot use the User Interface and Launch Conditions editors. One other difference between a setup project and a merge module project is that with a merge module project, the File System editor adds the folders Web Custom Folder and Module Retargetable Folder. If you place files in these folders, the user consuming your merge module can choose which location on disk to place the files. The user can change the installation path of the merge module contents by selecting the merge module in Solution Explorer and modifying the *ModuleRetargetableFolder* property in the Properties window. Consuming a merge module in a setup project is easy; you select the setup project in Solution Explorer and choose Project | Add | Merge Module.

Setup for .NET Programs

Suppose you're taking the setup-building capabilities of Visual Studio .NET out for a spin, trying out the various features. You've built a .NET application, added the project output to a setup project, built the solution, and tested the .msi file by installing the project. Everything has installed perfectly, and you were able to run your application. Being the good developer you are, and because you want to be sure your program works in all scenarios, you try installing the same .msi file on a clean computer—a computer with nothing more than the base operating system installed. When you run the setup project on the clean computer, you're presented with the dialog box shown in Figure 13-9. What went wrong, and why did it work fine on the development computer but not the clean computer? Visual Studio .NET cannot run without the .NET Framework installed, and the clean computer, with only the operating system installed, doesn't have the .NET Framework.

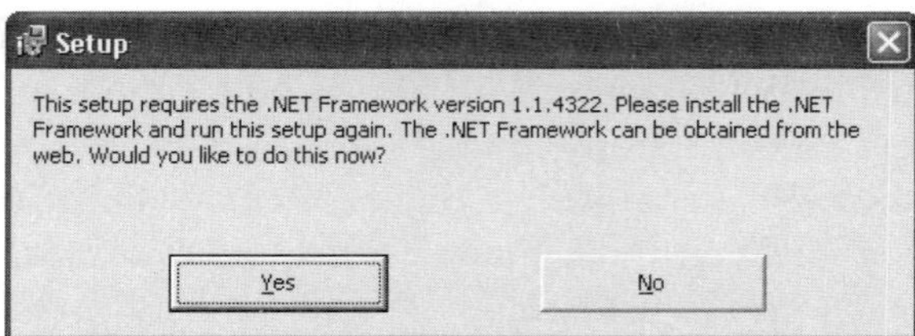

Figure 13-9 The error message you see when you try to install a .NET program on a computer that doesn't have the .NET Framework installed

When you add output from a C# or Visual Basic .NET project to the File System editor, Visual Studio .NET automatically adds a condition to the Launch Conditions editor that verifies that the .NET Framework is installed. Because the clean computer doesn't have the .NET Framework installed, the launch condition was not satisfied and an error was displayed to the user to that effect.

To run an .msi file that contains components that use the .NET Framework, you have two options. The option you choose will depend on how you plan on distributing your software. The first option is to let the user click the Yes button in the dialog box shown in Figure 13-9 and then install the .NET Framework manually. This option is best if you're distributing your software on the Internet or using a limited-size medium such as a floppy disk that doesn't have enough room to hold the .NET Framework redistributable files.

If you're shipping your program on a large media format such as a CD, another option is better. You store the .NET Framework redistributable files on the CD, and use a bootstrapping program to install the .NET Framework and then your .msi file. A bootstrap program is a small bit of code that takes care of getting the installation up and running. The bootstrap program makes sure the .NET Framework is installed and then starts installing the .msi file. To install a program, you should run the bootstrap program but not run the .msi file. By default, when you build a setup project, a bootstrap program named Setup.exe is generated and placed in the output folder for your setup project. This bootstrap program only makes sure that the Windows Installer program is installed, and not the .NET Framework. You don't need to redistribute this bootstrap program if you're trying to install the .NET Framework because the setup program for the .NET Framework installs the .msi installer if it isn't on the user's computer, and you can turn off generating this bootstrap file in the setup project Properties dialog box.

When you first add a .NET component to a setup project, a dependency to the merge module dotnetfxredist_x86.msm is added to your project and is marked to be excluded. You might assume that you can include this merge module in your setup project (instead of exclude it) to set up the .NET Framework if needed, but this is not what this merge module does. This merge module contains assemblies that are part of the .NET Framework—such as System.XML, System.Web, and so forth—and should be on the user's computer if the use has the .NET Framework installed. This merge module doesn't contain files that make up the common language runtime (CLR), so if you were to include this merge module in your setup project, you'd be including many assemblies that the user should already have installed but not everything the user needs to run a .NET program.

To make installing the .NET Framework with your program easier, you can use the Bootstrapper sample, which is included with the samples for this book. This sample, written using Visual C++, performs a couple of steps when it first runs. First, it checks to make sure another instance of the bootstrapping program isn't running because if one is already running, errors can arise if the other instance is started. To ensure that another instance is not running, the bootstrap program creates a mutex; mutexes are shared across process boundaries, so an error is generated if the mutex has already been created by another instance of the bootstrap program. This error condition signals that another instance is running; a message is displayed to the user and then the bootstrap program exits. The second step the bootstrap program performs is to read a file called Setup.ini, which needs to be located in the same folder as the bootstrap executable. This file describes to setup where it can find, among other things, the .NET Framework redistributable file. An example Setup.ini file is shown here:

```
[Setup]
InstallName=Setup
FrameworkVersionRequired=v1.1
UseLocaleForFindingRedist=1
FrameworkRedistName=DotNetfx
FrameworkInstallPath=FrameworkRedist
MSIFilePath=Setup.msi
```

All the values in this INI file are optional; if a particular key and value aren't found, the value as shown in this example is used. The meanings of these values are:

- ***InstallName*** The name of the product being installed. The value defaults to *Setup* if a name is not supplied. This string is used to display the name of your program in the user interface of the bootstrap program.
- ***FrameworkVersionRequired*** The version of the .NET Framework in use by the program being installed. If a currently installed .NET Framework with the version that matches this string is found, installation of the .NET Framework is skipped. This value can be *v1.0* (the letter *v* must precede the version number, and the trailing *0* is required) or *v1.1*. *v1.0* is the version of the .NET Framework installed with Visual Studio .NET 2002, and *v1.1* is the version of the .NET Framework installed with Visual Studio .NET 2003.
- ***FrameworkRedistName*** The name of the executable file (without the .exe filename extension) that holds the .NET Framework

redistributable file. The name of this executable is always DotNetfx, so in most situations you don't need to specify this value.

- ***UseLocaleForFindingRedist*** If this value is *1*, the bootstrap program attempts to find and install a localized version of the .NET Framework redistributable from the CD. Up to this point, the .NET Framework has been localized into nine languages: English, French, German, Italian, Japanese, Spanish, Chinese Traditional, Chinese Simplified, and Korean. If a localized version needs to be installed, the bootstrap program retrieves the language used by the operating system and uses this language, or *locale*, when searching for the redistributable. If this value is *0*, the bootstrap program doesn't use the operating system language when searching for the redistributable file. If your program is not localized into different languages, you should distribute the localized version of the .NET Framework that your user customer would use and set this value to *0*.
- ***FrameworkInstallPath*** The path relative to the bootstrap program where the .NET Framework redistributable file can be found. Suppose you have the bootstrap code in the folder D:\MyProgramSetup and the *FrameworkInstallPath* value is set to its default value, *FrameworkRedist*. The bootstrap program will look for the .NET Framework redistributable file in the path C:\MyProgramSetup\FrameworkRedist\DotNetfx.exe. If the value of *UseLocaleForFindingRedist* is set to *1*, the language identifier is inserted into this path between the value for *FrameworkInstallPath* and the *FrameworkRedistName* value. Table 13-3 shows the language identifiers for the various languages used; if the language is English, for example, the redistributable is searched for at D:\MyProgramSetup\FrameworkRedist\9\DotNetfx.exe. If the redistributable is not found in the path with the language identifier or if a language being used by the operating system is not supported, the path without the language identifier is searched. If all the search options have been exhausted and the redistributable hasn't been found, an error is given and setup exits.
- ***MSIFilePath*** The path relative to the bootstrap program where the setup .msi file can be found. If the bootstrap program is in the folder D:\MyProgramSetup and the default value of *Setup.msi* is used for this key, the path searched is D:\MyProgramSetup\Setup.msi.

Table 13-3 Languages and Their Identifiers

Language	Language Identifier
English	*9*
French	*12*
German	*7*
Italian	*16*
Japanese	*17*
Spanish	*10*
Chinese	If the operating system is using Chinese Traditional, the language identifier is 1228. Otherwise, Chinese Simplified is used, which is language ID 2052.
Korean	*18*

Note Installing the proper language version of the .NET Framework is important because although it might seem that only the program being installed will be affected, your users have to live with the language of the .NET Framework you install unless they uninstall and then install a new version of the language they want to use.

Creating a Setup CD

Today, most computers have a CD burner installed, and you can find blank CDs at your local discount store for well under 50 cents each. The availability of CD burners, cheap media, and the setup development tools available with Visual Studio .NET make distributing your software programs easy. To create a CD with your .msi file on it, you must combine the bootstrap program, the .msi file to install your program, and a few other files to make installation as seamless as possible for your users.

Note If you intend to place the .NET Framework redistributable on the CD for your program or make it available for download from a non-Microsoft Web site, you must read and agree to the Microsoft .NET Framework SDK end user license agreement (EULA) before redistributing the .NET Framework.

The Windows operating system simplifies installing software on a CD with AutoPlay. When a CD is inserted into the computer's CD drive, Windows examines the root folder of the CD, and if it finds a file called autorun.inf, it reads, parses, and then does the work as described in that file. Here's an example autorun.inf file that you can place in the root folder of a CD to automatically start running the bootstrap program when the CD is inserted into the drive:

```
[autorun]
open=setup.exe
icon=setup.ico
label=My Setup
shell\launch\command=Setup.exe
shell\launch=&Install this program
```

The meanings of each entry in this file are:

- ***open*** When the CD is inserted into the CD drive, this is the path to a file (without the drive letter) that will be run. If you're using the bootstrap program to install the .NET Framework and your program, you should give the path to the bootstrap program; otherwise, you can specify the relative path to the .msi file.
- ***icon*** The path to an icon on the disk (without the drive letter) that's displayed in Windows Explorer for the CD. The path can point to an .ico file or to an executable or DLL file. If the path is to an executable or DLL file, the path should be followed by a comma and then the zero-based index of an icon within the resources of that file.
- ***label*** The text to display as a label next to the CD drive in Windows Explorer.
- ***shell*\verbname** If the user right-clicks on the CD drive in Windows Explorer, the text following this entry is shown on the shortcut menu. The text *verbname* is arbitrary and can be any string, as long as it contains only alphanumeric characters. The text following this key name can contain any character, and if the ampersand character is used, the accelerator key follows; use a double ampersand if you want the string to contain the ampersand character.
- ***shell*\verbname*command*** If the user right-clicks on the CD drive in Windows Explorer and chooses the command specified in the *shell*\verbname line, the program pointed to by the path specified is run. The *verbname* string here is also arbitrary, but it

should match the name used in the previous line. The autorun.inf file can contain any number of these *shell*\verbname pairs (including 0 entries), with each item appearing on the CD drive shortcut menu, but each pair of items should use a matching but unique pair.

Once you create your autorun.inf file, you must gather all the files that will be placed on the CD; this requires you to download the .NET redistributable files from Microsoft's Web site. Because the redistributable file is over 20 MB in size, this file (or files, if you intend to offer your users localized versions of the redistributable files) is not included with the samples for this book. Figure 13-10 shows the layout of the CD with the typical components necessary to install your program. This layout (without the .NET Framework redistributable files) can be found among the samples for this book in the folder SetupCD. To build a setup CD, you simply copy your .msi file into this folder, burn its contents to a writable CD, and you're done! You've just created a professional setup for your software.

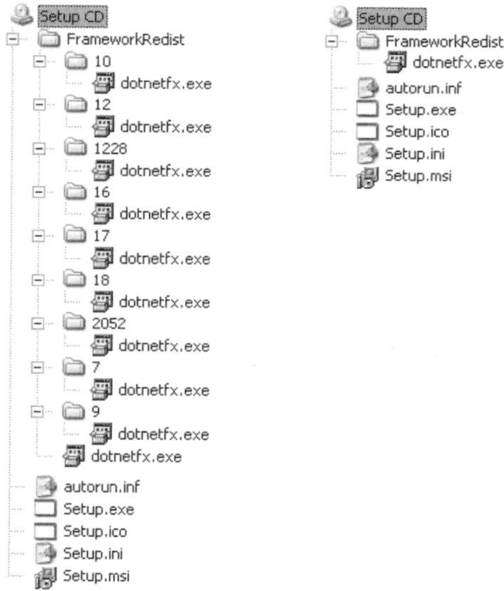

Figure 13-10 The directory structure of a setup CD if you offer localized versions of the .NET Framework (left) and a nonlocalized setup (right)

Setting Up the Book's Samples

If you downloaded and installed the sample files that accompany this book, you ran an .msi file that was built with the setup tools in Visual Studio .NET. This setup .msi file was built using many of the concepts described in this chapter, including installer properties, custom actions, the Registry editor, Web setup projects, and more. The source code for the setup project and the custom actions used can be found in the folder InsideVSNetSetup. For details about how to rebuild the Inside Visual Studio .NET 2003 samples .msi file, consult the Readme.htm file in the InsideVSNetSetup folder.

Looking Ahead

All users, regardless of their skill level, sometimes need help completing a task. Visual Studio .NET provides a full-featured help system to display MSDN contents. In the next chapter, we'll look at how you can use that system and how you can customize it to include your own help topics.

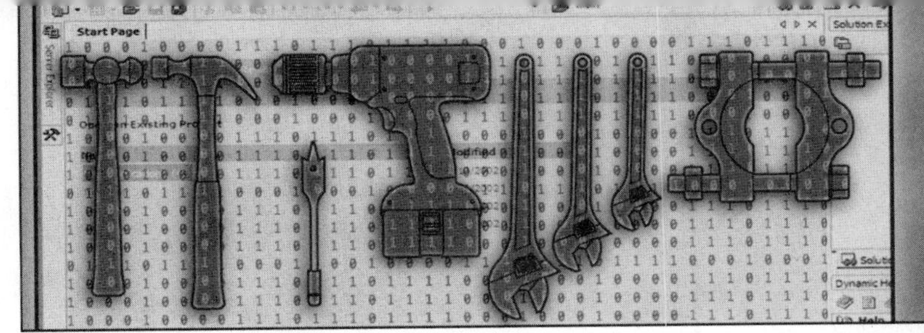

14

Visual Studio .NET Help

The MSDN Library that ships with Microsoft Visual Studio .NET contains a huge amount of data that developers can use in building their solutions in the IDE. It contains so much data, in fact, that finding what you're looking for can be a chore. Fortunately, the Help facility in Visual Studio .NET is extremely extensible. You can customize it to improve search performance and to ensure you're getting the exact information you need. You can also use it to publish context-sensitive help for your own libraries, assemblies, and add-ins and have that information available to developers from within the IDE. You can even add your documentation to the Visual Studio .NET Help Table of Contents, Search, and Index windows, making it extremely easy for other programmers to access your information.

In this chapter, we'll spend some time describing how to customize the Help facility in Visual Studio .NET and how to build your own Help collections in Visual Studio .NET.

Navigating the Help System

The Help system in Visual Studio .NET is one of the best features of the IDE. It's context-sensitive, well indexed, and completely searchable. It covers the entire MSDN Library, which includes some 1.5 GB of data. In fact, the Help system is so big that it's worth discussing how you can customize it to get just the data you're looking for.

As part of the multistep Visual Studio .NET installation process, you have the opportunity to install the MSDN documentation that ships with the product. Installing this documentation is a separate step because it allows developers to install the latest MSDN Library from Microsoft. (If you're an MSDN subscriber, be sure to check for the latest MSDN Library if you're installing Visual Studio .NET 2003 soon after its release.)

If you have multiple Help collections installed, you can choose the one you want in the Options dialog box. The default Help collection for Visual Studio .NET 2003 is called the Visual Studio .NET 2003 Combined Help Collection. This is the recommended Help collection because it includes extra documentation to help you with certain add-in features and miscellaneous other features in the product.

You can see the Help page in the Environment folder in the Options dialog box in Figure 14-1. Notice that you can set a preferred language along with the collection you want as the default. You must have the specific language documentation installed on your machine to get an alternative choice for this setting.

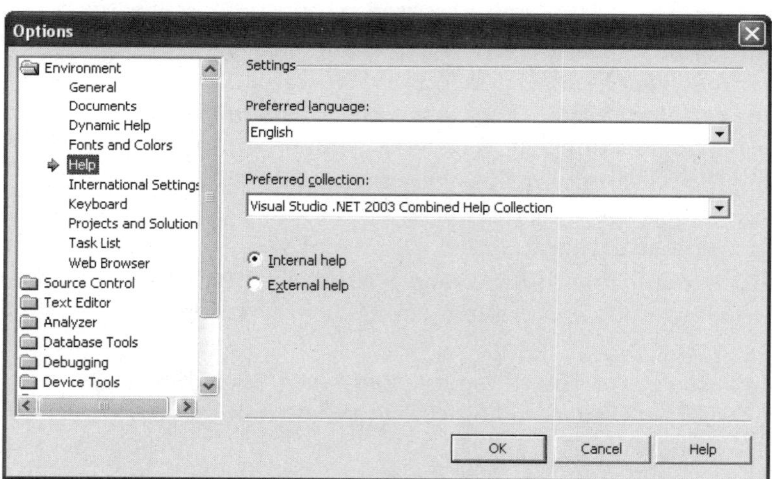

Figure 14-1 You can set the preferred Help collection in the Visual Studio .NET Options dialog box.

A final setting you can specify is whether to display help internally or externally. If you choose to display it internally, you'll see the help information inside the IDE. If you choose the external option, help will be displayed in a window outside the IDE. The external option makes a lot of sense if you're working in a multimonitor environment. Using an external window, you can keep the help open in one screen and your IDE open in another.

Help Windows

Whether you use help that's integrated into the IDE or you use the standalone viewer, you need to be familiar with three organizational windows. The Contents window contains a hierarchical display of the available help topics. The Index window contains a list of the index terms found in the Help collection. And the Search window lets you perform a search of the entire help system for a particular term or phrase. The results of searches are displayed in the Search Results window. Searches have a limit of 500 returns, so it pays to narrow your searches whenever possible. Figure 14-2 shows the Microsoft Document Explorer window, which contains all these same features. You can open this window by clicking the Microsoft Visual Studio .NET 2003 Documentation link in the Microsoft Visual Studio .NET 2003 folder on the Start menu.

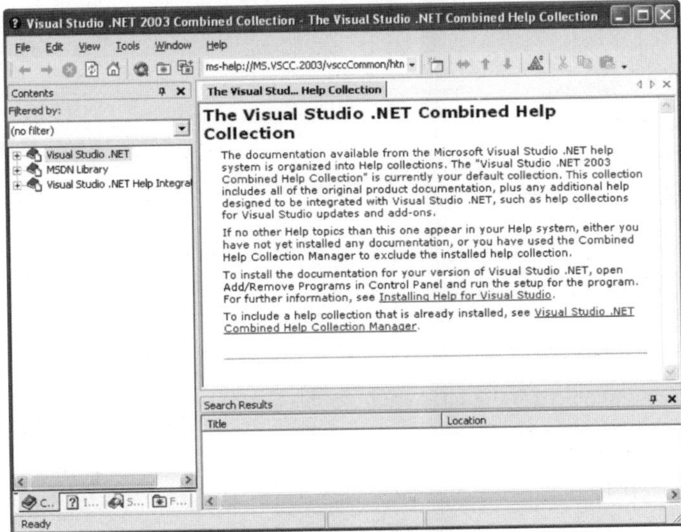

Figure 14-2 Visual Studio .NET 2003 Help as displayed in Document Explorer

The Document Explorer features don't require a lot of explanation. They're pretty straightforward and they've been part of Visual Studio and MSDN for years. As we mentioned, though, the documentation collection is quite large and you can use some techniques and settings to make your searches and index lookups more efficient.

Search and Index Options

What you select as the Filtered By option in the Search window (as shown in Figure 14-3) has a major effect on what information is presented when you enter a string in the Look For box. For example, typing **CString** while the Visual Studio Macros filter is activated returns the DataSet Class item from the .NET Framework Class Library as the first hit in the Search Results window. If Visual C++ is the active filter, the first hit returned is the CString Operation Relating To C-Style Strings topic from Visual C++ Concepts. With no filter at all, these two items appear in the list together, with no real contextual information. Both results are valid, but the filter helps you pinpoint the specific topic you're searching for.

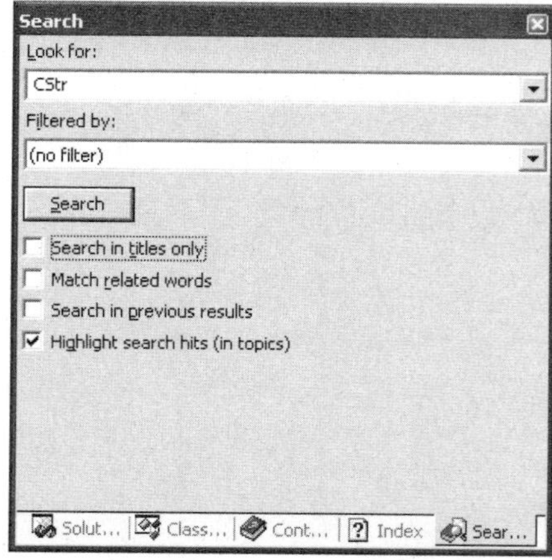

Figure 14-3 You should set the filter value to the topic you're interested in to obtain better search results.

The Search In Titles Only option limits returns to terms found only in the document titles. You can put this option to good use if you're looking for top-level documentation on a particular subject. Match Related Words causes your search terms to be matched to variations of those terms. For example, searching for *link* with the Match Related Words option selected might return *linked*, *linking*, and *linker*. The Search In Previous Results option causes your search to be confined to the results of the last search. This lets you drill down in your list of current results.

When you select the Highlight Search Hits (In Topics) option, the terms you're searching for are highlighted in the document window when you view a topic in the search results. This is a fantastic option that helps you easily find the term you're looking for. The highlighting can get annoying when you want to just read the document you're looking at, however, so to clear the document of highlighted search items, deselect this option and refresh the window by clicking the Refresh button on the Web toolbar. Alternatively, you can just double-click the item again in the Search Results window.

Narrowing Search Results

The Search window lets you enter words, phrases, and logical operators to help find the information you're seeking. You can also use certain wildcard characters to refine your search.

Let's take a minute to go through some of the general rules regarding help searches. We'll assume that you generally know what you're looking for but that you don't want to sift through hundreds of hits to get the information you need. To search for a string consisting of multiple terms, you should enclose your search phrases in quotes. Doing so will return an exact match for the phrase you're searching for. For example, searching for *CString* returns 500 matches (the maximum number returned from any search). Searching for *"CString object"* returns just over 170 hits. Knowing just what you're looking for and making your searches more specific has obvious advantages.

You can use logical operators to include or exclude certain types of results. For example, you're probably aware that placing an *OR* between your search terms returns all pages that include either term in the search. Table 14-1 lists the logical operators you can use to narrow searches in Visual Studio .NET.

Table 14-1 Logical Search Operators

Operator	Description
AND	Returns all pages that include both search terms.
OR	Returns pages that include either search term.
NOT	Returns pages that include the term on the left only if the term on the right is not in the same document.
NEAR	Returns pages where the term on the left appears within eight words of the word on the right.
THRU	Returns pages that contain terms that are part of a numeric range.

One of the more interesting logical operators is the *THRU* operator. Using this operator, you can search for a range of numbered terms. You might use this operator to search for a range of constants or a set of error values. Note that numeric searches using the *THRU* operator tend to take a long time, especially if you combine that search with a second operator.

You can broaden or narrow your searches by employing wildcards—for example, to search for terms that might have different spellings or extensions. Table 14-2 lists the two available wildcard characters.

Table 14-2 Wildcard Search Characters

Character	Description
*	Broadens the results of your search to words that contain a prefix or suffix in place of the character. For example, **String* returns *string*, *CString*, and *ToString*, among others.
?	Used as a substitute for any single character in a search. For example, *?String* returns *aString*, *bString*, and *CString* but not *ToString* (which has a prefix length outside the search parameter). Using *??String* returns *ToString* but not the others.

Creating Custom Help Filters

If you find yourself searching for related terms from different help topics, you might want to create a custom help filter. For example, if you plan to work with both COM and .NET in a solution you're creating, you might find it easier to create a custom filter that returns hits from these two topics rather than creating a more specific help string under a broader search filter.

To create a custom help filter, open the Edit Help Filters window by typing **Help.EditFilters** in the Command Window or by choosing the Edit Filters command from the Help menu. You can see the Edit Help Filters window in Figure 14-4.

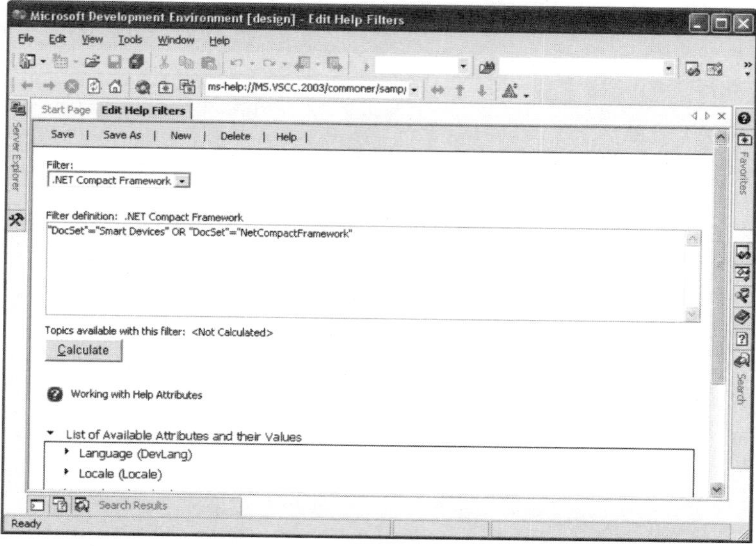

Figure 14-4 You create custom Help filters in the Edit Help Filters window.

In the Filter Definition box, you can enter a set of attributes that narrows the list of items returned in an index or a search. You can enter search attributes that specify the language, product, target operating system, or even the technology you want to search. The possible attributes are listed in the List Of Available Attributes And Their Values box at the bottom of the Edit Help Filters window. Attributes are grouped using parentheses, and you can use logical operators to specify the type of inclusion in the string.

To create a simple COM/.NET subset, we can string together two *DocSet* attributes with two *Technology* attributes:

```
("DocSet"="NETFramework" OR "DocSet" =
"NETFrameworkExtender") or("Technology"="COMt" OR "Technology"="COMt" )
```

You have a large number of attributes to choose from when you create attributes. For the most part, you'll probably want to string together document sets, languages, and technologies, but other attributes are available. You can click on individual attributes in the List Of Available Attributes window and they'll be added to the currently open set automatically.

As you create the list of attributes you want to use, click the Calculate button to see how many topics will show up in your new list. You can use this number to determine whether your attributes are too broad or exclusive to be useful.

Searching from the Command Window

A feature that will be popular with programmers who are used to the Vim editor is the ability to search for a help topic from the Command Window. The *Help.F1Help* command is aliased to help by default in the Command Window. *The F1Help* command takes one argument—a string representing the F1 keyword you want to search for. If the term you're searching for is an F1 keyword, you get the specific help topic for that keyword when you type **>help *term*** in the Command Window, where *term* is the word you're searching for. If the term you're searching for is not an F1 keyword, the term is placed in the Index window and the index results are displayed.

If you're looking for help on a named command in Visual Studio .NET, the F1 keyword for that command is usually the command itself, so if you know the command name, you can easily get to the help topic. For example, to get help on the Find command, you type **>help Edit.Find** in the Command Window. You can try this with any of the named commands you've worked with in this book, and you should immediately get the topic you're searching for. The terms you might search for include:

- Edit.ReplaceInFiles
- Help.Index
- File.NewFile
- Debug.Start

If you start to get used to this function and you're curious about how to determine the F1 keywords for particular help topics, you can turn on debugging in the Dynamic Help window by adding an entry to the registry. The key is:

```
HKCU\Software\Microsoft\VisualStudio\7.1\Dynamic Help
```

To turn on debugging, you must add the string key "*Display Debug Output in Retail*" if it doesn't exist and set its value to "*Yes*". Figure 14-5 shows the Dynamic Help window after debugging has been enabled. Keep in mind that only topics assigned to F1 help work this way. Other search terms open the Index window.

Figure 14-5 Turning on debugging in the Dynamic Help window

Customizing the Dynamic Help Window

You can do a couple of things to customize the way the Dynamic Help Window presents data. First, you can control what data is presented through the Dynamic Help page of the Options dialog box (shown in Figure 14-6). All the options for the Dynamic Help window are turned on by default; you won't get extra information by setting options, but you can get more focused on what you want. Also, because the Dynamic Help window is small, you can make sure you can see the important information without having to scroll up or down. For example, deselecting the Samples option moves the Getting Started topic just below the Help topic (as shown in Figure 14-7).

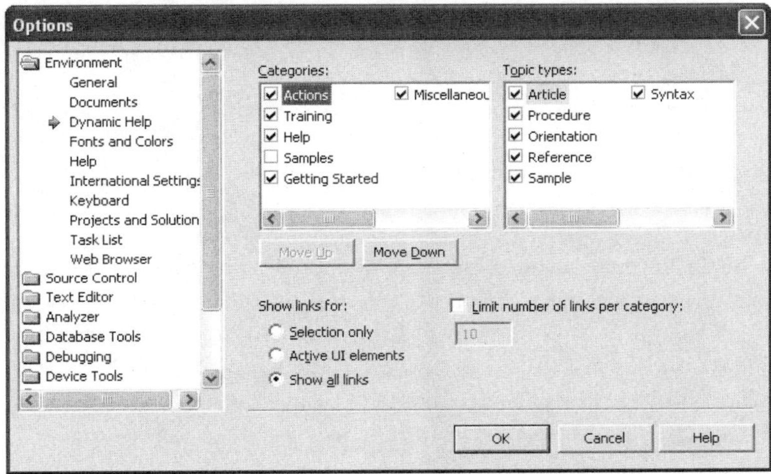

Figure 14-6 Setting the options for Dynamic Help in the Options dialog box

Figure 14-7 The Dynamic Help window with the Samples topic filtered out

The second way you can customize Dynamic Help is by adding your own custom links to the Dynamic Help window through the XML Help Provider service, which we'll discuss next.

Using the XML Help Provider Service

The dynamic links that you display can open any kind of help, including plain text, HTML, and even Microsoft Word documents, so this can be an effective alternative to creating the more complex help that we'll discuss later in the chapter.

To add your own links to the Dynamic Help window, you must create an XML file and place it in the appropriate folder. The next instance of Visual Studio .NET 2003 that you open will display your information when the specified context criteria are met. You have to meet just a few requirements to have your information displayed properly. Let's go over these one at a time.

Location

Your XML file can be named anything you want, but it must be placed in the folder C:\Program Files\Microsoft Visual Studio .NET 2003\Common7\IDE\HTML\XMLLinks\1033. If you install Visual Studio .NET to another folder or if you're using Visual Studio 2002, your path will be a little different, but the Common7\IDE\HTML\XMLLinks\1033 path is the one that's important. The file must have an .xml extension.

> **Note** In Windows, 1033 is the code for U.S. English. If your copy of Visual Studio .NET is localized for another region, the folder you copy your XML file to will have a different code number.

In the 1033 folder, you'll find at least one existing XML file. This file, Context.xml, contains the link groups that have been set up in advance for Visual Studio .NET. You can add your own link groups by editing this file or by specifying them in your own XML file.

Schema

The XML Help that you add to the Dynamic Help window requires a specific schema in order to work properly in the IDE. This schema looks like the following:

```
<DynamicHelp xmlns="http://msdn.microsoft.com/vsdata/xsd/vsdh.xsd"
xmlns:xsi="http://www.w3.org/2000/10/XMLSchema-instance"
xsi:schemaLocation="http://msdn.microsoft.com/vsdata/xsd/vsdh.xsd">
```

Link Groups

Link groups are the groupings of topics in the Dynamic Help window. You can create your own link groups or you can add your help links to one or more of the existing help groups. You specify link groups using the *LINKGROUP* tag. In this example, we'll create a new link group with an *ID* of "*InsideVSNET*" and a *Title* value of "*Inside Visual Studio .NET*". The *ID* value will be used when we create a link to some information.

```
<LINKGROUP ID="InsideVSNET" Title="Inside Visual Studio .NET"
  Priority="300">
  <GLYPH Collapsed="1" Expanded="2" />
</LINKGROUP>
```

The *Priority* is a number that's added to other scored attributes to move a link higher or lower in the list of links in the Dynamic Help window. You can see these scores if you look at the debug output shown earlier in Figure 14-5.

The *GLYPH* tag lets you specify the icons that are displayed for your link group. You can specify one icon for the collapsed view and another for the expanded view of your group. Table 14-3 shows the built-in icons.

Table 14-3 Link Group Icons

Index	Icon
1	
2	
3	
4	
5	
6	
7	
8	

Table 14-3 Link Group Icons *(continued)*

Index	Icon
9	
10	
11	
12	
13	
14	

Context

The *Context* tag contains the body of the information you're adding to Dynamic Help. This tag contains all the other context-related tags for your information, so it's essentially the body of the information you want to present. The rest of the tags we'll discuss in this section are found in the *Context* tag.

Inside the *Context* tags are two tags that determine what gets shown in Dynamic Help. The *Keywords* and *Attributes* tags contain *KItem* and *AItem* subtags, respectively, which let you specify when a particular topic comes into context. The item tags in these sections are weighted based on factors such as the type of project currently open or the window that has focus. The online documentation has some information about these tags and how they're scored, but we suggest you use the debug output to determine what's going on.

We'll keep our example really simple. Because we want the information to be available to the user in all circumstances, we'll use the *"VS.Ambient" KItem* value. This value displays a topic at all times, as opposed to something like the *"VS.SolutionExplorer" KItem*, which displays a topic only when Solution Explorer gets the focus. You can see the code for this item here:

```
<Keywords>
  <!-- KItems contain keywords for a topic.-->
  <KItem Name="VS.Ambient" />
</Keywords>
```

The final thing we need to do is to create some links. These are held in the *Links* tag using *LItem* tags, as shown here:

```
<Links>
  <!-- LItems contain links to the topics you wish to display.-->
  <LItem URL="file:///C:\InsideVSNET\Info.htm"
  LinkGroup="InsideVSNET">Macro Information</LItem>
  <LItem URL="http://www.microsoft.com/mspress/books/6425.asp"
  LinkGroup="InsideVSNET">Web Page</LItem>
  <LItem URL="http://www.microsoft.com/mspress/support/"
  LinkGroup="InsideVSNET">Support</LItem>
</Links>
```

Each *LItem* contains a number of attributes. The *URL* attribute is the link to the help topic you want to display. The *LinkGroup* attribute contains the *ID* of the *LinkGroup* under which you want to display the link. In this case, we created three links. The first is a link to a file on the C: drive. The second and third links are to this book's Web page and to the Microsoft Press Support Web site.

Listing 14-1 shows the file InsideVSNET.xml, which is in the 1033 folder, as mentioned earlier.

InsideVSNET.xml

```
<?xml version="1.0" encoding="utf-8" ?>
<!-- These schema are required for Dynamic Help.-->
<DynamicHelp xmlns="http://msdn.microsoft.com/vsdata/xsd/vsdh.xsd"
  xmlns:xsi="http://www.w3.org/2000/10/XMLSchema-instance"
  xsi:schemaLocation="http://msdn.microsoft.com/vsdata/xsd/vsdh.xsd">
  <!-- Create a link group in which to display our information.-->
  <LINKGROUP ID="InsideVSNET" Title="Inside Visual Studio .NET"
    Priority="500">
    <GLYPH Collapsed="1" Expanded="2" />
  </LINKGROUP>
  <Context>
    <Keywords>
      <!-- KItems contain keywords for a topic.-->
      <KItem Name="VS.Ambient" />
    </Keywords>
    <Links>
      <!-- LItems contain links to the topics you wish to display.-->
      <LItem URL="file:///C:\InsideVSNET\Info.htm"
        LinkGroup="InsideVSNET">Macro Information</LItem>
      <LItem URL="http://www.microsoft.com/mspress/books/6425.asp"
        LinkGroup="InsideVSNET">Web Page</LItem>
      <LItem URL="http://www.microsoft.com/mspress/support/"
        LinkGroup="InsideVSNET">Support</LItem>
    </Links>
  </Context>
</DynamicHelp>
```

Listing 14-1 Adding links to Dynamic Help

Figure 14-8 shows Visual Studio .NET after you link to the book's Web page from the Dynamic Help window.

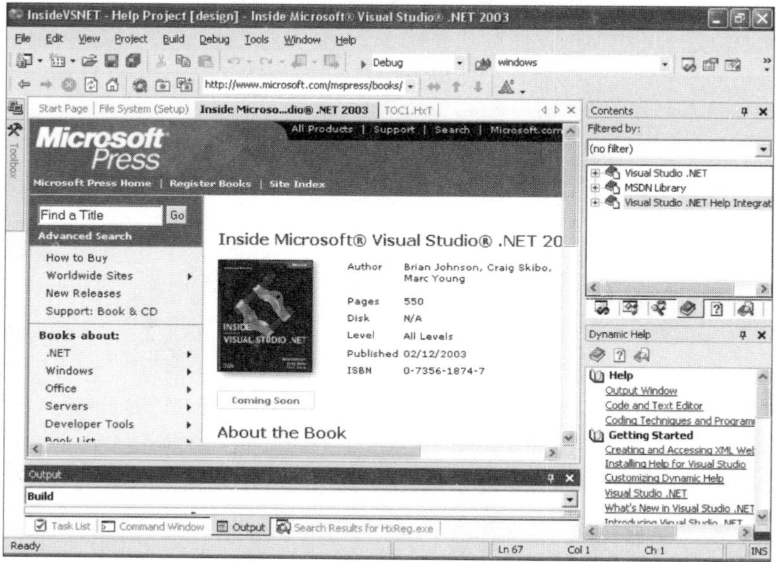

Figure 14-8 Linking to custom information from the Dynamic Help window

Creating Custom Help Files

This section serves as an introduction to creating help. To do this, you must install the Visual Studio .NET Help Integration Kit (VSIK) 2003, which you should be able to download from MSDN around the time Visual Studio .NET 2003 launches.

In this example, we'll create a simple Help file and integrate it into Visual Studio .NET 2003. In a way, creating help is much like using a new programming language, so we'll leave out some of the creation details in favor of the integration details.

After you install the Visual Studio .NET Help Integration Kit 2003, you'll find a new project category in the Visual Studio .NET New Project dialog box. The Help Projects category provides templates for new Help projects, Help conversion, and Help decompilation. You can see the new project templates in Figure 14-9.

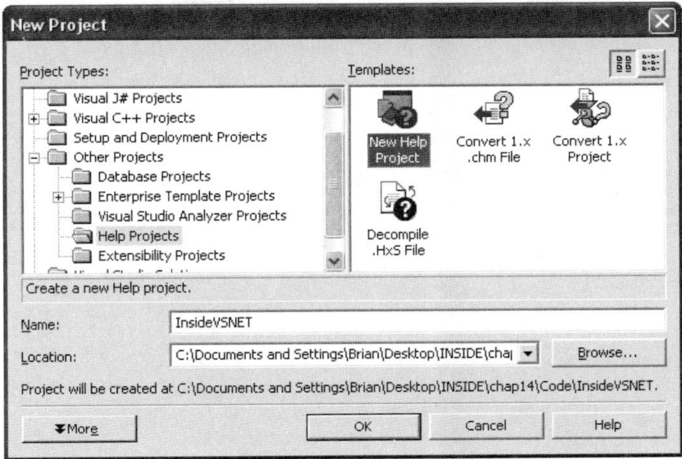

Figure 14-9 Help project templates in Visual Studio .NET 2003

One of the best features of the Help Integration Kit is that it lets you work on your Help project files from within Visual Studio .NET and therefore take advantage of the editors and the Help system in the IDE as you work.

The version of Help we'll use in this section is Microsoft Help 2. A number of files are used to organize an average Help 2 project. These files generally have an .Hx? extension, where *?* represents a letter specific to the work that the file does. For example, the Help collection definition file extension is .HxC and the Help include file extension is .HxF. In Visual Studio .NET, Help 2 projects have an .HWProj extension. You can add a help project to any solution you create. Table 14-4 lists the extensions you should be familiar with.

Table 14-4 File Extensions Used in Microsoft Help 2

Extension	Description
.HxS	The compiled Help file
.HxC	Help collection file
.HxF	Help include file
.HxT	Help table of contents file
.HxK	Help index file
.HxA	Help attribute file
.HxE	Help sample definition file
.html, .htm, .txt, and others	Help topic files and content

When you create a new project, you start with an .HxC (collection) file and an .HxF (include) file. If you were building these files by hand, you'd normally edit them yourself, but in Visual Studio .NET you can do this using the project's Property Pages dialog box, as shown in Figure 14-10.

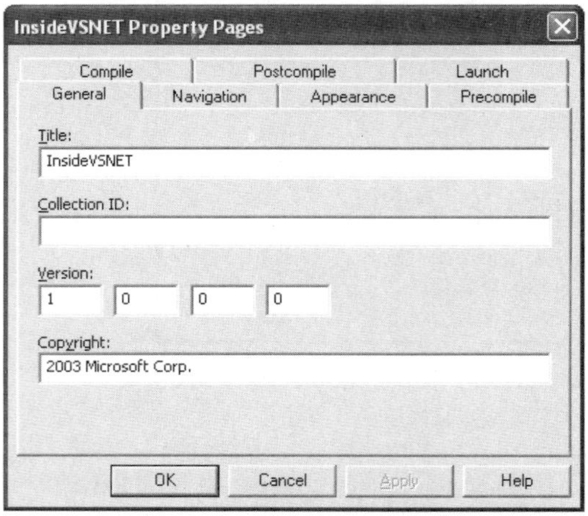

Figure 14-10 A Help project Property Pages dialog box

Templates for the file types you can add to a project are available in the Add New Item dialog box, as shown in Figure 14-11. You normally want to add a least one .HxT (TOC) file and one .HxK (Index) file.

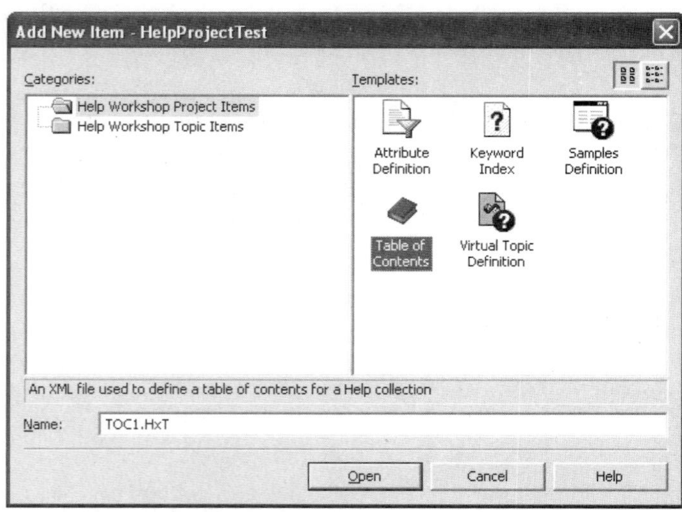

Figure 14-11 The Add New Item dialog box

Once you've added an .HxT file and an .HxK file to your project, you use the project's Property Pages dialog box to set a couple of important options. On the Navigation tab of the dialog box, select the TOC and Index files you want to use in your project from their respective drop-down lists, as shown in Figure 14-12. Then you can add some content to the project.

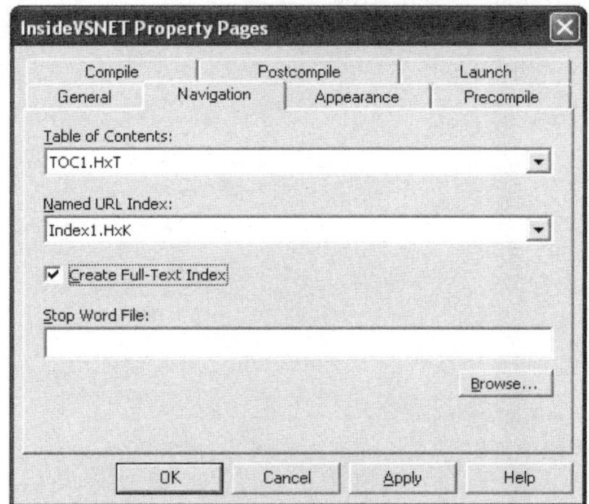

Figure 14-12 Setting the navigation options for the project

Next, we'll use the Add New Item dialog box to add an .htm file named Intro.htm. We'll use this file as the default page for the project. You can see in Figure 14-13 how our project stands. We have the .htm page open in the editor, and the files we've created are all listed in the Project Explorer window. At this point, we can add nearly any content that we want to the project and make it available through the TOC.

After you create and save a number of content files, you can add them to the TOC by dragging and dropping them. Figure 14-14 shows the open TOC file. You can drag your content files to the tree and set their order by using the arrows on the toolbar or by using the context menu for the individual items. In this case, we've added a second TOC to the Global TOC.

Notice that in addition to the compiled content, you can add links in the TOC to external Web sites and to file system items. In this case, we added a link to the book's home page and set the Icon property to 22 to display a Web icon. You can customize the icon for any topic in the TOC in the Properties window for each topic. There are 45 icons available for use in the TOC, so you can get pretty specific with your content. To see the complete list, search on *Default TOC Icons* in VSHIK Help.

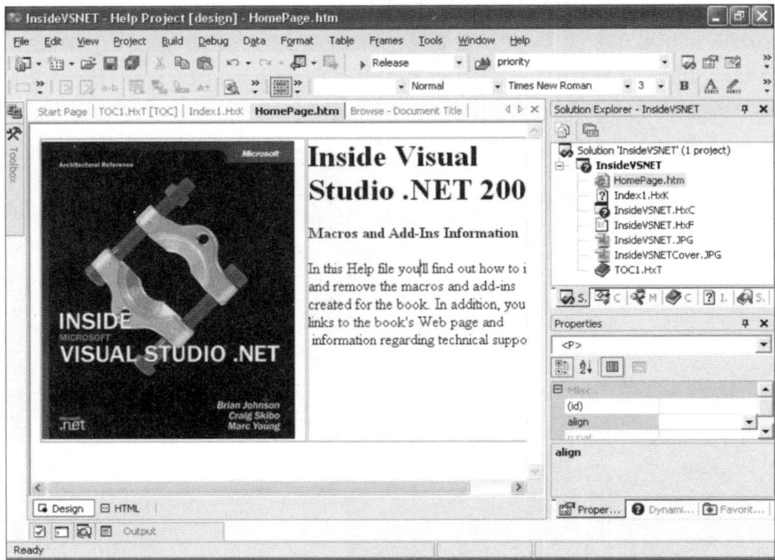

Figure 14-13 Visual Studio .NET with a help topic open for editing

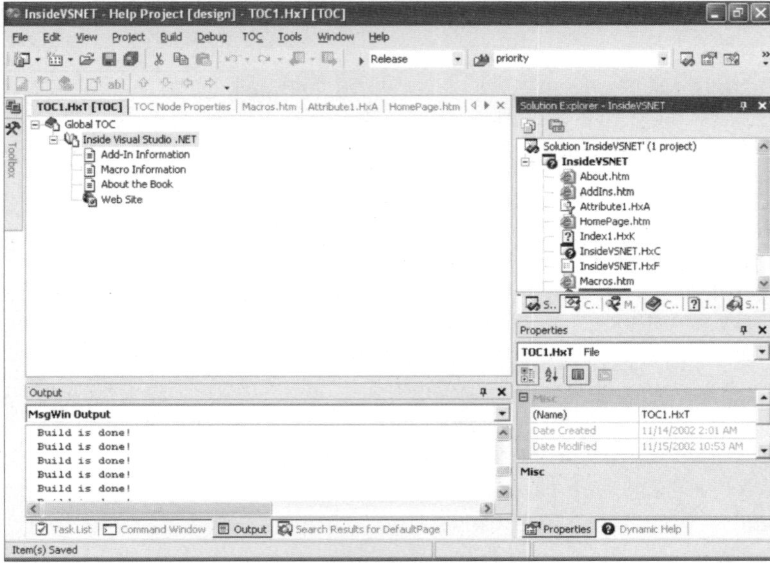

Figure 14-14 Working with the TOC in Visual Studio .NET

We now need to add some code to the file to get it to do some specific things. First, we want a default page to show up when we open our new Help file. If we don't set one, we'll just get our default Microsoft Internet Explorer

Web page, which isn't what we want. We also want to add the appropriate help topics to the Index. To do both of these things, we need to add some code to the .HxK (Index) file.

First, let's talk about what we need to do to get a default page up and running. To get a default page to show up in help, you must create a *Keyword* index entry with a particular keyword and point that entry at the file you want to make the default. The *Keyword* for the default page in a Help file is *"HomePage"*. The code to set this keyword in the .HxK (Index) file is shown here:

```
<Keyword Term = "HomePage">
  <Jump Url = "HomePage.htm"/>
</Keyword>
```

To add topics to the index, you can use the *Keyword* syntax we just described or add XML data to your topics, which adds them to the index automatically. Our example is short, so we just added a few entries to the Index file. The complete listing for the Index1.HxK is shown in Listing 14-2.

Index1.HxK

```
<?xml version="1.0"?>
<!DOCTYPE HelpIndex SYSTEM "ms-help://hx/resources/HelpIndex.DTD">

<HelpIndex DTDVersion="1.0" Name="K">
  <!-- Insert keywords here -->
  <Keyword Term = "Macros">
    <Jump Url = "Macros.htm"/>
  </Keyword>

  <Keyword Term = "Web Site">
    <Jump Url = "http://www.microsoft.com/mspress/books/6425.asp"/>
  </Keyword>

  <Keyword Term = "About">
    <Jump Url = "About.htm"/>
  </Keyword>

  <Keyword Term = "Add-Ins">
    <Jump Url = "AddIns.htm"/>
  </Keyword>

  <Keyword Term = "HomePage">
    <Jump Url = "HomePage.htm"/>
  </Keyword>

</HelpIndex>
```

Listing 14-2 Help index file

With all that in place, running the project should result in a complete Help collection like the one shown in Figure 14-15. You can compile and launch a Help collection by issuing the *Debug.Start* command from the Command Window or by pressing F5. This runs the compiler that creates the .HxS file and then starts a copy of Document Explorer (Dexplorer.exe) using the arguments supplied on the Launch page of the Project Properties dialog box.

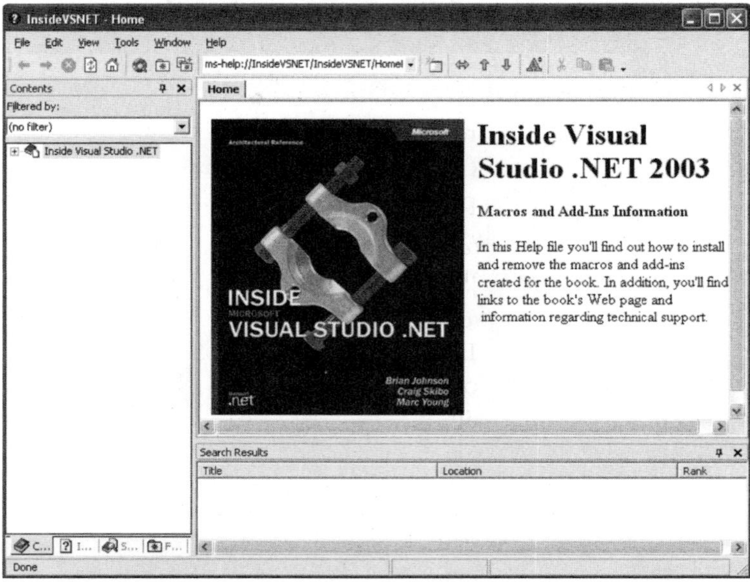

Figure 14-15 The compiled Help collection in Document Explorer

Registering Your Help Collection

Before the help topic can be addressed by Dexplorer, it must be registered. There are a couple ways to register your Help collection so it can be viewed. The recommended way is to set up a Windows Installer package. This involves a fairly complicated set of steps that requires you to edit a merge module with the Orca tool from the Windows SDK. This method is described in a document that ships with the Help 2 SDK entitled *Visual Studio .NET Help Integration*. Here we'll describe an alternative method of registering a Help collection using the HxReg.exe utility for testing purposes.

To register the Help collection we just created, we need to run the HxReg.exe utility, specifying the namespace of the collection (*-n*), the name of the collection file (*-c*), and a description of the namespace (*-d*). To accomplish this, you probably need to add the Help 2 SDK to your path (C:\Program

Files\Microsoft Help 2.0 SDK). To run the registration commands, navigate to the folder containing the .HxS file and run the following commands from the Command Window. The first one registers a namespace for your Help collection:

```
HxReg.exe -n MS.InsideVSNET.1033 -c InsideVSNET.HxC
-d "Inside Visual Studio .NET Help Sample"
```

Next, you register the compiled Help file:

```
HxReg.exe -n MS.InsideVSNET.1033 -i InsideVSNET
-s InsideVSNET.HxS -l 1033
```

Notice that we wrapped the namespace with *MS. And .1033*. The convention for namespaces in this regard is (*Company*).Namespace.(*Language*).

Finally, to create a link to the newly registered Help file, create a shortcut that contains the following path in the Target text box:

```
"C:\Program Files\Common Files\Microsoft Shared\Help\dexplore.exe"
/helpcol ms-help://MS.InsideVSNET.1033
```

You can also use the topics in your Help file from within Dynamic Help. To do this, just add the URL to the topic you want to display in the *LItem* tag that we discussed earlier. For the Macro topic in the help sample, the XML for the link would look something like this:

```
<LItem URL="ms-help://MS.InsideVSNET.1033/InsideVSNET/Macros.htm"
  LinkGroup="InsideVSNET">Macro Information</LItem>
```

This won't integrate your Help collection into Visual Studio .NET. You must create an installer and edit the appropriate merge module to do that. But this gives you enough information so you can test your help topics from the Web toolbar and from Dynamic Help.

Looking Ahead

In the next chapter, the last one in the book, we'll revisit projects and solutions and discuss using Visual Studio .NET from the command line and how you can secure your source using Microsoft Visual SourceSafe.

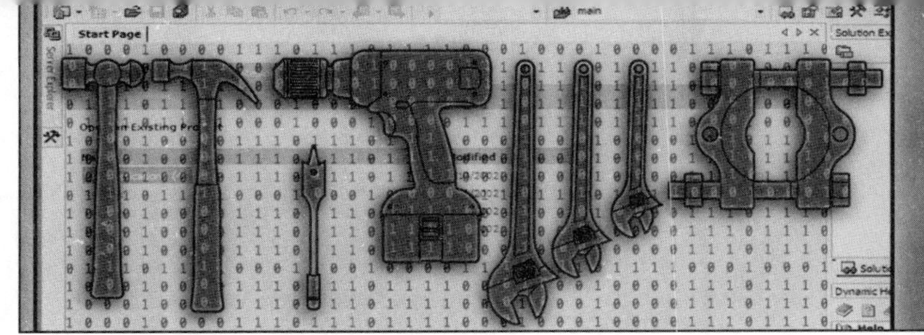

15

Advanced Projects in Visual Studio .NET

Understanding the concept of projects and solutions is central to success with Microsoft Visual Studio .NET. We presented these concepts in Chapter 2 and then moved on to discuss other features of the IDE and how to extend the IDE through macros and add-ins. In this chapter, we'll look at how to customize and use projects and solutions in advanced scenarios. We'll build projects and solutions from the command line, and we'll talk about using Microsoft Visual SourceSafe (VSS) for source code management.

Visual Studio .NET from the Command Line

You can use Visual Studio .NET from the command line to build solutions and projects in much the same way that you might have used NMake.exe to build make files in the past. By using Visual Studio .NET from the command line, you can conveniently build your projects without opening the IDE. The obvious benefit of this approach is that you can automate your build processes through scripting and batch files.

The easiest way to use Visual Studio .NET from the command line is to place the path to Devenv.exe into your *PATH* environment variable or to do your work from the Visual Studio .NET 2003 Command Prompt window. By default, the *PATH*, *INCLUDE*, *LIBPATH*, and *LIB* environment variables are the ones set in the IDE, but you can set Visual Studio .NET to use the current variables by specifying the *\useenv* option on your command line.

Building Projects and Solutions from the Command Line

Building a solution or project from the command line is fairly straightforward, but it's worth reviewing the options you need to specify to do this correctly. To build a solution from the command line, open a command window with Devenv.exe set in the path and navigate to the folder containing the solution file. Then execute the Devenv.exe command on the solution file by using the */build* switch followed by the name of the build type you want to run. In most cases, this will be debug or release. If you've created custom build types as described in Chapter 2, you can specify one of these. A typical debug build command for a solution looks something like this:

```
devenv SCTestVCS1.sln /build debug
```

Build information is returned to the command window, but you can also send that output to a build log. To do so, specify the */out* option with a filename. To review the output of the build process, open the output file in Notepad or run the Type command as shown in Figure 15-1.

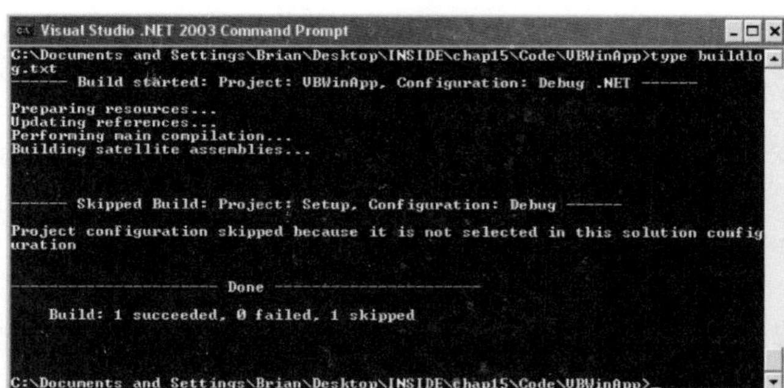

Figure 15-1 The Type command lets you take a quick look at the build output file you've created.

To perform a build of a particular project within a solution, use the */project* switch. To build a single project that's part of a multiproject solution, your command line might look like the following:

```
devenv SCTestVCS1.sln /project JSConsoleApp /build debug
```

In this case, the solution has multiple projects, but only the specified project file is built. If you want to open a solution in the IDE to a particular project configuration, you can specify the configuration using the */projectconfig* switch. Opening the IDE in this way lets you get straight into a project and configuration within a particular solution.

You should note a couple of idiosyncrasies when you work with Devenv.exe from the command line. First, you should specify the solution or project file before the other switches in the command. In some cases, you can specify the switches first, but that doesn't work for all switches, so it's easier to just get the solution specification out of the way. Second, you must place any paths with spaces within quotation marks.

The build switches work just like the named commands do in the IDE. The */rebuild* switch performs a clean operation on the target folder before the build or forces all the targets to be rebuilt, depending on the language. The */clean* switch runs the *Build.CleanSolution* command on the solution. The behavior of the clean command is dependent on the implementer of the language. It works well for Visual C++ projects, but Visual Studio .NET 2003 doesn't support cleaning the other included project types. As with the build command, you need to specify the build type that you want to clean at the command line:

```
devenv SCTestVCS1.sln /clean debug /out clean.txt
```

Here's the output of this command on a solution with multiple project types. (In this case, only one project actually performs the clean command.)

```
------ Clean started: Project: CPPConsoleNet,
Configuration: Debug Win32 ------

Deleting intermediate files and output files for project
'CPPConsoleNet', configuration 'Debug|Win32'.



---------------------- Done ----------------------

    Clean: 1 succeeded, 0 failed, 0 skipped
```

If you want to run the target file that your solution or project creates, use the */run* option. This option opens the IDE and runs your program as if you had run the *Debug.Start* command. If you set a breakpoint that gets hit when your application runs, program execution stops at the breakpoint. This fact can be useful if you find yourself opening and closing the IDE a lot and you want to get straight back to the point where you left off while debugging.

To take a quick look at the output from a particular solution, you can use the */runexit* option. This option opens the IDE in a minimized state and runs your executable. The minimized IDE closes automatically when the target process exits. Debugging isn't enabled in the */runexit* scenario, so if you have breakpoints set in your code, they're ignored.

The command line for a solution that you want to run within the IDE will look something like this:

```
devenv VBWinApp.sln /run
```

If your solution contains a deployment project, you can use the */deploy* option to build the solution and run the deployment. This switch has two requirements. First, you must have a deployment project in your solution. Second, you must add your deployment project to the configuration you want to build with. The default for new deployment projects added to projects is to have the project's Build check box cleared. To use the */deploy* command, you must open the Configuration Manager dialog box by choosing Configuration Manager from the Build menu. Figure 15-2 shows the dialog box with the appropriate check box selected in the Release configuration for the solution.

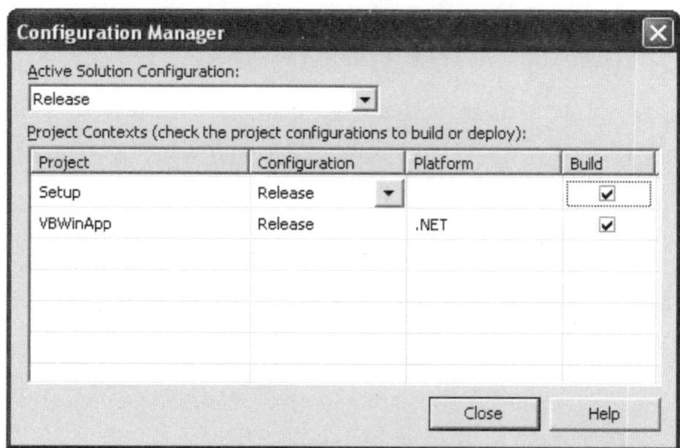

Figure 15-2 Selecting the Setup project in the Configuration Manager dialog box

To build and deploy a solution like this, close the IDE and enter your command with the */deploy* switch, like this:

```
devenv VBWinApp.sln /deploy release
```

This should start the deployment program you've created.

One command-line switch you'll find valuable as an add-in developer or macro writer is the */command* switch. This switch lets you run a named command as you open the IDE. For example, if you want to open the Code Model Add-in from Chapter 12 when you start the IDE, you simply enter a command line that looks something like this:

```
devenv /command CMEAddIn.Connect.CMEAddIn
```

It's not that easy to remember *CMEAddIn.Connect.CMEAddin*, but one useful feature of this switch is that you can use an alias in place of that named command, making it a lot easier to enter your command. To alias the *CMEAddIn* line (assuming you have it installed), in the IDE press Ctrl+Alt+A to open the Visual Studio .NET Command Window and then enter the following:

```
alias cme CMEAddIn.Connect.CMEAddIn
```

You can then run the add-in from the Windows command line by entering the following:

```
devenv /command cme
```

If you have a command that takes arguments, you can place the command within quotes and it will usually be executed correctly. The following command line executes the *help* alias with the term *command* as the argument:

```
devenv /command "help command"
```

The */command* switch works equally well for running macros and aliases to macros. As you can imagine, this gives you access to quite a bit of functionality from the command line. You can use this switch for testing add-ins and macros, for performing operations on solutions, and for setting up batch files that give you access to your own custom IDE setups.

The */debugexe* switch opens an executable file in the Visual Studio .NET debugger as a new solution. To run the executable and attach to the process, you can execute the *Debug.Start* command. At this point, you're prompted to save a new solution and the executable is run in the debugger. You can then break into the source or disassembly for the executable, depending on whether you're debugging a release or debug version of the executable and whether Visual Studio .NET can find the source code for the executable and dependent files. The command line for opening an executable in Visual Studio .NET will look something like the following:

```
devenv /debugexe VBWinApp.exe
```

If the last build on this file was a debug build, Visual Studio .NET should have no trouble breaking into the source for the file. If the build was a release build, you can break only into disassembly. The build type is usually a little easier to determine in Visual C# and Visual C++ because the outputs are placed in debug or release folders, depending on the build.

Finally, the */useenv* switch is specific to Visual C++. It lets you direct the IDE to use the environment variable set for the command session from which Devenv.exe is run. The setting is helpful if you want to create builds with specific versions of the installed runtime libraries. For example, you might want to use files from a particular version of the Windows SDK or you might want to test beta versions of the DirectX libraries. The */useenv* switch lets you do this without having to set these options in the IDE.

Table 15-1 contains a list of the Devenv.exe command-line build options.

Table 15-1 Devenv.exe Command-Line Build Options

Option	Description
/build <build>	Specifies the build type to use.
/clean <build>	For project types that support this option, build outputs of the specified build type are deleted.
/command <command>	Specifies a named command, a macro, or a Command Window alias to run when the IDE is started.
/debugexe <exename>	Specifies an executable to be debugged in the IDE.
/deploy	For solutions that have associated deployment projects, the application is deployed after the targets are built.
/out <filename>	Specifies a log file to use to get information about command-line builds.
/project <project>	Specifies the project within a solution to open or build.
/projectconfig <projectconfiguration>	Specifies the project configuration when you open a project within a solution.
/rebuild <build>	For projects that support the clean command, the projects are cleaned before a build is done. Otherwise, all project targets are rebuilt.
/run	The output of a solution is run from within the IDE.
/runexit	The IDE is opened minimized and the solution outputs are run.
/useenv	For Visual C++ builds, this option lets you specify that the environmental variables set in the command session be used by the IDE.

Setting GUI Options at the Command Line

The GUI options let you change some of the settings of the IDE from the command line. Some of these might not seem particularly useful at first, but you can use them to test tool windows that you build in your add-ins under different GUI scenarios.

The */mdi* and */mditabs* switches let you toggle between the use of MDI windows or tabs for document windows in the IDE. Keep in mind that your choice sticks with the IDE, so if you're playing with */mdi* and you forget to run Devenv.exe with the */mditabs* switch, your tabs will go missing the next time you open the IDE.

There are two font switches, but these affect only the IDE itself and not the document windows. The */fs* switch lets you specify the point size for the text displayed in the IDE. The */fn* switch lets you specify a particular font name if you want. Again, these settings are sticky, so you should use them with care; you can make the IDE quite unusable if you specify unreasonable values. Figure 15-3 shows the IDE with the */fn* switch set to 14.

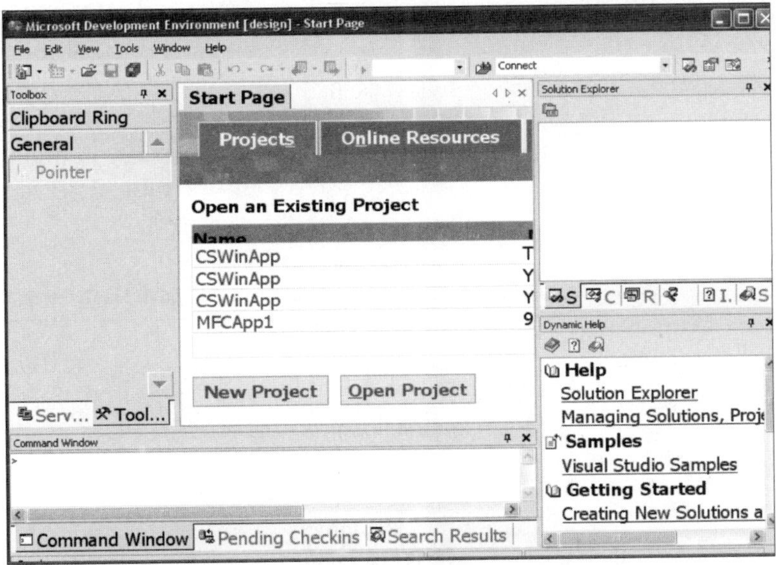

Figure 15-3 Don't try this at home: *Devenv.exe /fn 14*

Finally the */LCID* switch lets you run the IDE with a specified language. This switch can be helpful if you're localizing your add-ins. You must have the version of Visual Studio .NET specific to the language you want to use installed on the machine on which you're running the IDE. You can use this option to test your add-ins in different languages without having to set up a bunch of different test machines. MSDN Universal subscribers will have access to these different Visual Studio .NET builds.

Table 15-2 lists the different command-line GUI options.

Table 15-2 Devenv.exe Command-Line GUI Options

Option	Description
/mditabs	Opens the IDE with tabbed document windows
/mdi	Opens the IDE with MDI windows
/fn <fontname>	Uses the specified font in the IDE

Table 15-2 Devenv.exe Command-Line GUI Options *(continued)*

Option	Description
/fs	Uses the specified font size in the IDE
/migratesettings	Migrates some user settings from an earlier version of Visual Studio .NET
/LCID <languageID>	Opens the IDE in the specified language

VSIP Options

The remaining options are used by Microsoft Visual Studio Integration Program (VSIP) partners to test their VSIP solutions. They won't do you much good without access to this program, but we've listed them in Table 15-3 for the sake of completeness.

Table 15-3 Devenv.exe Command-Line Environment Options

Option	Description
/noVSIP	Turns off the VSIP license key for testing purposes
/safemode	Loads a stable default environment for testing
/resetskippkgs	Reenables packages that were flagged to be skipped in the IDE

Source Control with Visual SourceSafe

Visual Studio .NET ships with support for VSS, and the Enterprise Developer and Enterprise Architect editions of Visual Studio .NET ship with the bits required to set up a VSS server.

In this section, we'll talk about getting up and running with a VSS server and how you can put your projects under source control for versioning and protection and to help manage team development.

Setting Up VSS

Even if you're a single developer, you should try to set up a VSS server on a machine separate from your workstation. That way, even if your workstation hard drive dies, you have a fairly recent version of your project under source control on another server.

Placing Files Under Source Control

To use VSS with Visual Studio .NET, you should set up the version of VSS that ships with Visual Studio .NET. Here we'll assume that you've set up your VSS database properly and that you want to access that database using the tools built into Visual Studio .NET 2003.

When you first run Visual Studio .NET on a workstation, you'll notice that the Source Control menu items are grayed out. To take advantage of the VSS features built into Visual Studio .NET, you must first install the VSS client on the workstation. You can usually install the client from the share containing the server. Look for the file Netsetup.exe in the shared VSS folder on the server. Run this file to install the client.

You can use the VSS client to do your initial setup with VSS. First open the VSS database that you'll be using to maintain your code. After installing the VSS client, you'll find a link to the executable in the Microsoft Visual SourceSafe folder on the Start menu. Open the client and press Ctrl+P to display the Open SourceSafe Database dialog box. Browse to your VSS database share and open the srcsafe.ini file there. Figure 15-4 shows how this dialog box looks after you specify the appropriate file.

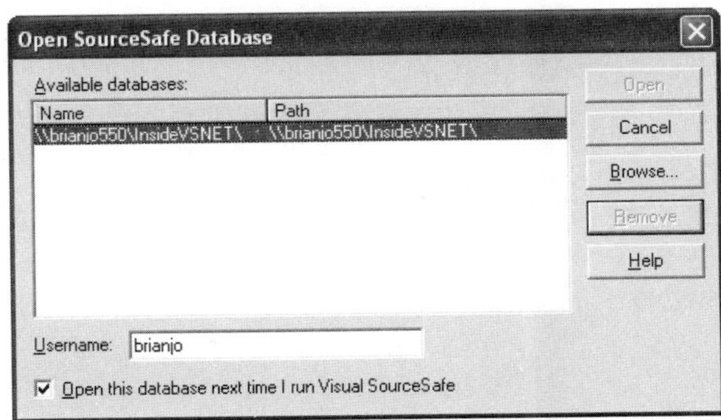

Figure 15-4 The Open SourceSafe Database dialog box after you select the appropriate database

When prompted, enter the username and password that you or your administrator have set up, and you should be in business. Figure 14-5 shows a VSS database set up to help manage the code and chapters written for this book. At this point, you can close the VSS client application. From here, we'll do most our work in Visual Studio .NET.

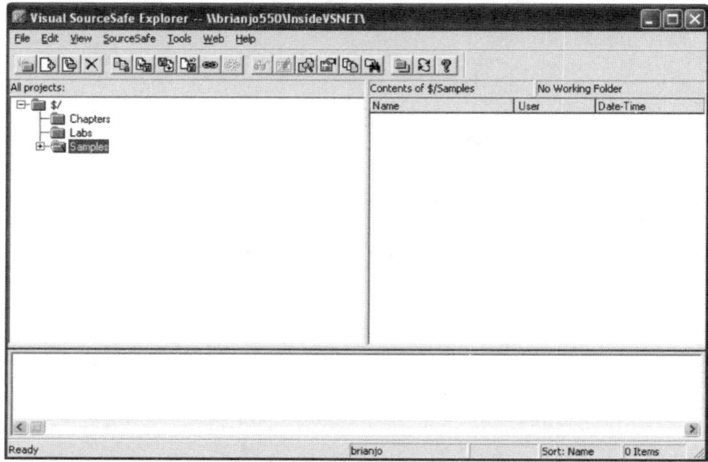

Figure 15-5 A VSS database open in the VSS client application

Once your database is set up and you have access from your workstation, you can start putting solutions and projects under source control. First open a solution in the IDE or create a new solution. On the Visual Studio .NET File menu, choose Source Control and then choose Add Solution To Source Control, as shown in Figure 15-6.

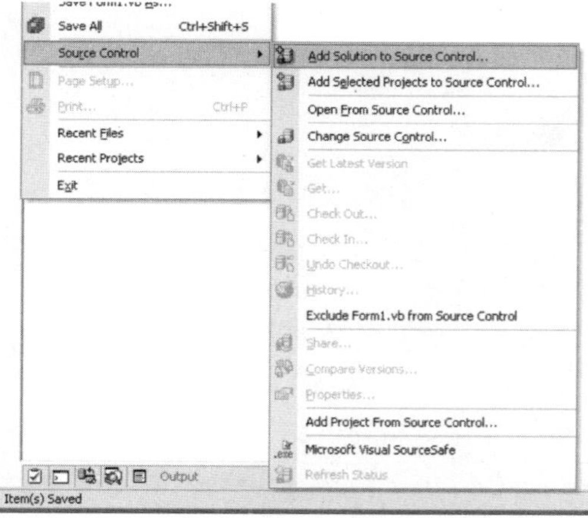

Figure 15-6 Adding a solution to VSS through the Visual Studio .NET Source Control menu

You'll see the Visual SourceSafe Login dialog box, followed by the Add To SourceSafe Project dialog box (shown in Figure 15-7), which lets you select or create a folder for the project.

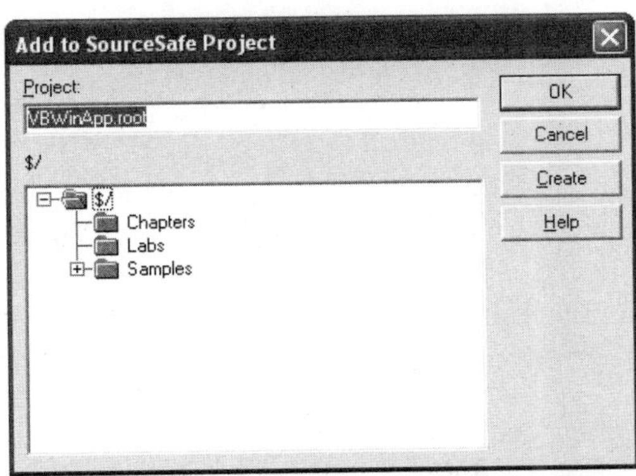

Figure 15-7 The Add To SourceSafe Project dialog box

Placing a solution under source control results in the solution being added to the VSS server. The solution you started with is now considered a working copy, and you must check out the files from VSS to make changes. You can see the Solution Explorer window for a project under source control in Figure 15-8. The lock icons in Solution Explorer indicate that the files are copied locally but aren't checked out for editing. A checked out file has a check mark next to its name.

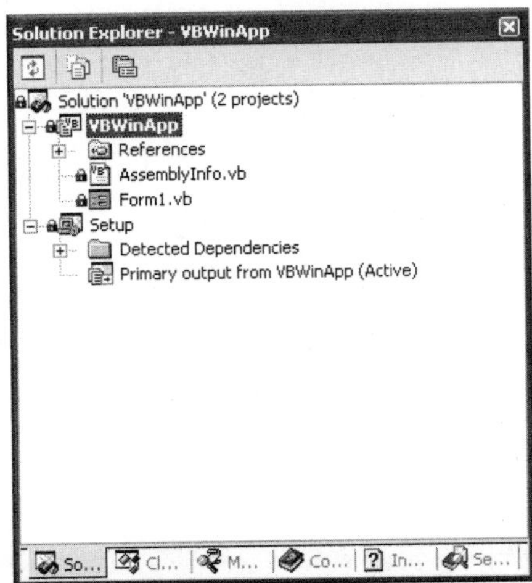

Figure 15-8 A solution under source control

Working with Files Under Source Control

Once you place a solution under source control, you and your team members can access the solution through Visual Studio .NET. On the machine where the initial solution was created, the files added to VSS become the working copy for that particular developer. Alternatively, you can delete the local folder and open the VSS version of the solution, copying it to a new location on the workstation.

To open a project from a VSS server, from the File menu choose Source Control and then choose Open From Source Control, or enter **File.OpenFromSourceControl** in the Command Window. This opens a Visual SourceSafe Login dialog box, where you can enter your credentials and select the VSS database you want to access. After logging in, you're presented with a Create Local Project From SourceSafe dialog box like the one shown in Figure 15-9.

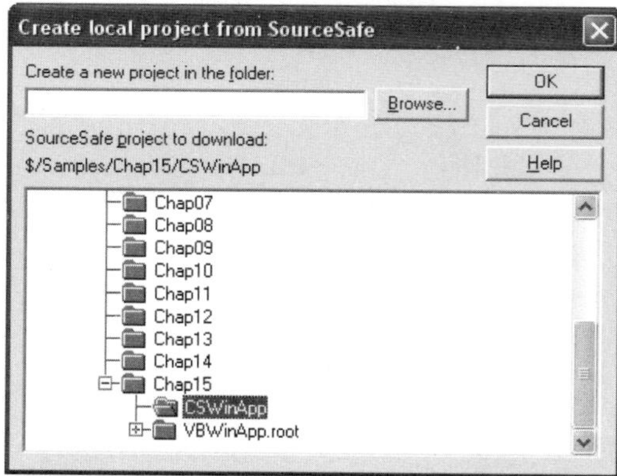

Figure 15-9 Selecting a project from a VSS database

Select a project and click OK, and you'll see a Browse Folder dialog box that lets you select the working folder for the solution. The program adds the folder you select to the Create A New Project In The Folder box. Click OK a second time to copy the solution files to your local machine and display the Open Solution dialog box, which contains the .sln file for your solution. Select the .sln file from this dialog box, and you'll be working with the local copy of the solution.

> **Note** You can set a network share as your working folder for the solution. With VSS, it's often easiest to map a network share to a drive letter and use that when you work with older-style common dialog boxes.

Working with files under source control is fairly straightforward. When you begin to edit a file, you lock that file on the server so no other developer can make changes at the same time. This is the "control" in source control.

Let's look at what happens when two developers work on a single solution using source control. Both developers have the solution open through VSS to a local folder or network share and are working on these projects in Visual Studio .NET. Let's say Marc is in the process of adding a button to a dialog box. When he attempts to make a change to the file, a Check Out For Edit dialog box (shown in Figure 15-10) appears and gives him the opportunity to add a note about what he's doing before checking out the file.

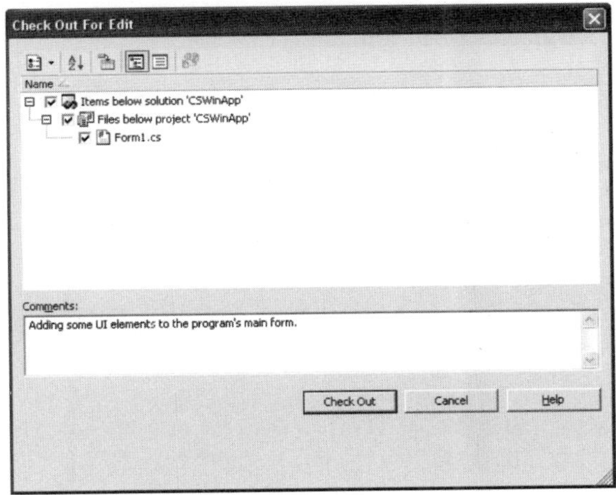

Figure 15-10 Checking a file out of VSS for editing

Keep in mind that both developers are working in Visual Studio .NET the whole time and are prompted to check out files as they work. Almost everything about working with VSS databases in Visual Studio .NET is automatic, so you don't have to go hunting for files using the VSS client.

At this point, Brian wants to make a change to the form that Marc has checked out. Marc hasn't checked in his changes yet, and he still has exclusive access to the files. This means Brian can't make a change until that file is checked in. When Brian tries to check out this file for editing, he's prompted with the cancellation dialog box shown in Figure 15-11.

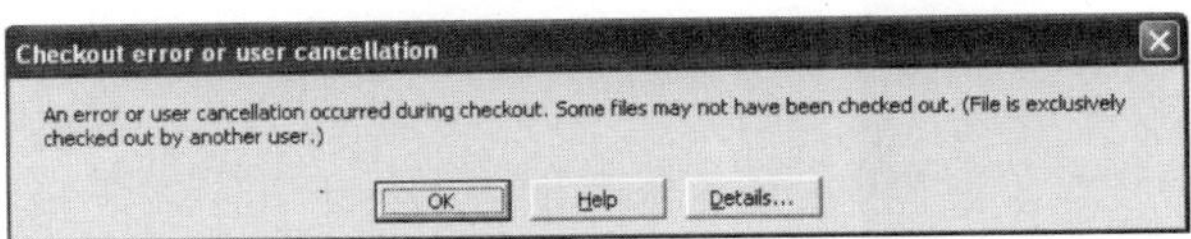

Figure 15-11 The message that appears if you try to check out a file that's been checked out by another user

If Brian really needs this file, he can ask Marc to check it in. Small teams can work informally in this way, but with larger teams, you most likely won't touch each other's code. As you can see, though, the source control features make it clear who has control of the source file at any given moment and that changes aren't permitted on that file until the person who has control of that file checks it back into the database.

Let's say Marc has made his changes to the file and is ready to check the changes back in. He can check the files in by right-clicking on the checked out files in Solution Explorer and choosing Check In from the shortcut menu. This opens the Check In dialog box shown in Figure 15-12. Here, he can enter a comment about the files that he's checking in. This comment can be directed to the program manager or to other developers on the project.

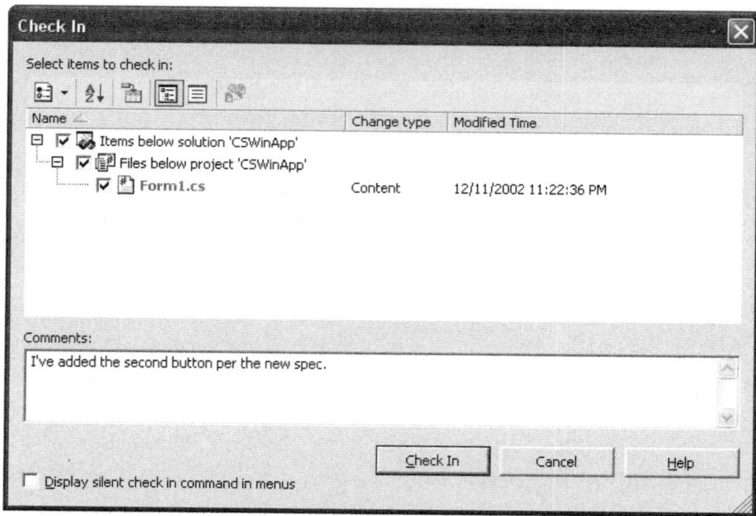

Figure 15-12 Checking a file back in to VSS

At this point, Brian is working with an out-of-date copy of the source files. What happens if he tries to edit the old form on his machine? The answer is that when VSS checks out the file for editing, it replaces the out-dated version of the file on Brian's machine with the updated file from the database.

To update the files on a local machine to the latest available in the database, you use the *File.GetLatestVersion* command. This command is also available from the shortcut menu in Solution Explorer. If you've made changes to a file that you've checked out, you can either merge those changes back into the database or you can keep working without merging your changes back in. In either case, changes checked in by other developers are applied to the source files in your solution.

A couple of VSS features that are available from within Visual Studio .NET are worth noting. The first is the History command (*File.History*). This command works on a file-by-file basis; you access it from the Source Control submenu of the File menu or from the Command Window. The History command opens a dialog box (shown in Figure 15-13) that lists who has checked out a file and when. You can double-click on any of the versions listed to display the History Details dialog box shown in Figure 15-14, which contains any notes that were added when the file was checked in.

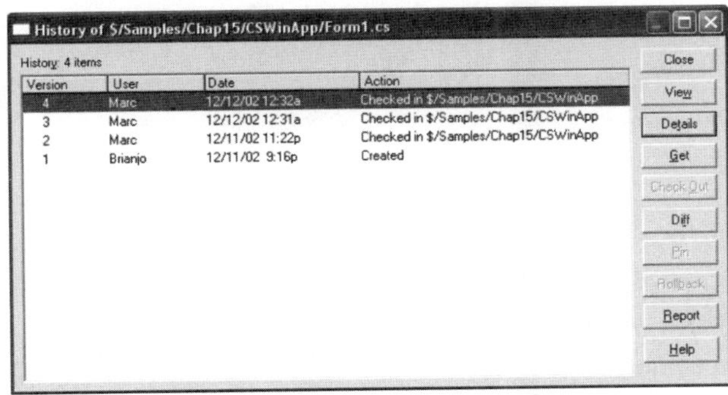

Figure 15-13 Viewing the history of a file in VSS

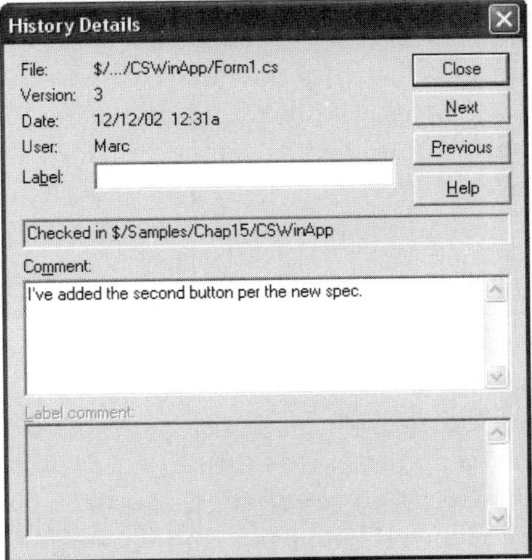

Figure 15-14 The details of a particular version of a file

Another interesting feature is the Pending Checkins tool window (shown in Figure 15-15). This dockable window is available only when you have files currently checked out. You can access this dialog box through the Source Control submenu of the File menu or through the shortcut menu in Solution Explorer. This tool window offers some features that aren't as easy to find in the other available dialog boxes. For example, you can click the Option button on the Pending Checkins toolbar to keep a file checked out while you check a version in. You can thus make changes available to others while ensuring that you keep control of the file.

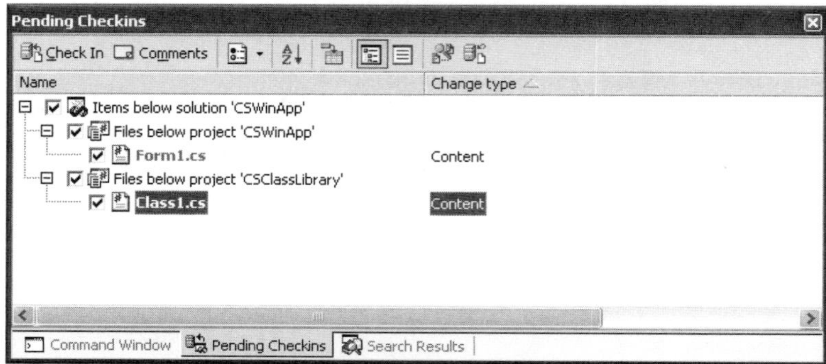

Figure 15-15 The Pending Checkins tool window

Lab: Cleaning Up Source Control

When you download a solution that someone has uploaded to the Web, you might find error messages reporting that the solution has been under source control. Opening a zipped solution that someone has had under source control can be an annoying experience, but you can easily remove source control from a solution through the Source Control submenu of the Visual Studio .NET File menu.

Open the CSWinApp solution in the Chapter 15 folder of the book's companion content. You'll see a couple of dialog boxes informing you that the files in the solution have been under source control. To get rid of these messages, you must unbind the solution and projects from the source control they were under. To do that, press Ctrl+Alt+A to display the Command Window and enter **File.ChangeSourceControl**. This command opens the Change Source Control dialog box shown here:

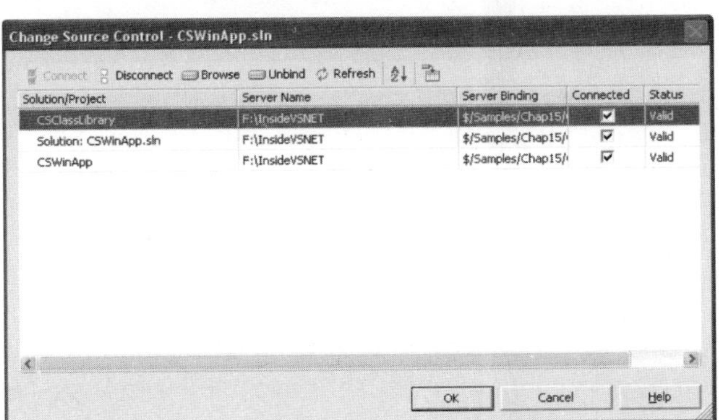

To unbind the solution, select the components listed and click the Unbind button. You'll get a message telling you that after you unbind the solution, these files will no longer be under source control. Click OK, save the solution, and the annoying source control messages will be gone. You can do this with any such solutions you come across on the Web. If you share source code, remember to unbind source control yourself before you pass it on. The developers you share your code with will appreciate it.

Planning Your Solutions Carefully

When you work with more complex, multiproject solutions in VSS, it's important to plan your solutions carefully before checking them in for the first time. This planning can save you a lot of grief later on. The most important thing to remember before performing that initial check-in is to keep your main solution file in a parent folder that contains individual folders for each of the projects in your solution. For example, say you want to create a solution that contains three separate components. It has a GUI of some sort written in Visual Basic .NET. It has a class library written in Visual C#, and it has a COM component written in Visual C++. (We talked a bit about combining these types of projects in a single solution in Chapter 2.)

To combine all of these project types into a single solution, you should first create a folder to hold the solution. You can do this by creating an empty solution in some convenient location. From there, you should add new projects to the blank solution and place the folders for these projects in the same folder that contains the main solution file.

Once you have all your projects in place in your solution, you can check that solution into VSS, as described earlier in the chapter. Now it will be a little easier for VSS to maintain the links within your project, and it will be easier for developers assigned to the different components in the solution to maintain their own projects under source control.

> **Note** For those planning to do a lot of large-team development under VSS, Microsoft has an excellent document with a lot of great information about how to plan solutions, builds, and source control. The document is titled "Team Development with Visual Studio .NET and Visual Source-Safe" and is available on MSDN at *http://msdn.microsoft.com/library/default.asp?url=/library/en-us/dnbda/html/tdlg_rm.asp*.

Don't Break the Build

One of the most important things about source control is that it helps you perform regular builds so you can continually run and test the product. These kinds of builds should be performed as often as is reasonable given the size and scope of the overall project and the size of the project team. To that end, you should make sure that your new code builds before you add it to source control.

The idea behind source control is that you keep a good version of the product going all the time. If code that you check in to the VSS database breaks the build, it might interfere with the efforts of the other development teams working on components. You therefore shouldn't check in code until it's in a state where it can be compiled into the product without causing problems. Source control in a multideveloper scenario shouldn't be used as the backup repository for your ongoing work. Rather, you should back up the projects on your workstation nightly and check in code when it's ready to run.

> **Note** Of course, in a single-user scenario, VSS makes an excellent backup solution, and it's perfectly legitimate to work in that way.

Looking Ahead

In this book, we've presented a range of topics related to the use and customization of Visual Studio .NET. As you explore this amazing tool and the automation object model, you'll probably start to see completely new and exciting ways that you can customize and automate the IDE. We sincerely hope that we'll start seeing solutions that have in some way been helped along by the ideas and topics discussed here.

Appendix

Code Model Reference

Chapter 12 gave you a peek at the Visual Studio .NET code model but left out the troublesome details. Here, we'll provide those details in an up-to-date reference of all the code model objects, properties, and methods.

Code Model Objects

This section explains the workings of the code model objects and their properties. We'll defer an examination of the code model methods until the section titled "Generating Code."

FileCodeModel and *CodeModel*

The *FileCodeModel* object and the *CodeModel* object are the two entryways into the code model; each contains a collection of top-level code elements in addition to methods that allow you to add, delete, and modify those code elements. Table A-1 lists the *FileCodeModel* properties.

Table A-1 *FileCodeModel* Properties

Property	Description
CodeElements	Returns a collection of top-level *CodeElement* objects defined in the associated source file
DTE	Returns the *DTE* object
Language	Returns a GUID representing the source file's programming language
Parent	Returns the *ProjectItem* object for the associated source file

A *FileCodeModel* object always belongs to a specific source file in a project. You retrieve the *FileCodeModel* object by using the *FileCodeModel* property of the *ProjectItem* object that wraps the source file; once you have a

FileCodeModel object, you can use its *Parent* property to get back to the parent *ProjectItem*. The most important *FileCodeModel* property in terms of the code model is *CodeElements*, which gives you access to the top-level code elements in the corresponding source file.

The *Language* property returns a GUID that represents the programming language of the source file. The *EnvDTE.CodeModelLanguageConstants* enumeration defines constants for the Visual Basic, Visual C#, and Visual C++ GUIDs. (The enumeration leaves out the Visual J# GUID: E6FDF8BF-F3D1-11D4-8576-0002A516ECE8.) If you have trouble remembering which GUID goes with which language, you can use code like the following to translate the *Language* GUIDs into English:

```
string LanguageFromGUID(string langGuid)
{
    string language = String.Empty;

    switch (langGuid.ToUpper())
    {
        case CodeModelLanguageConstants.vsCMLanguageCSharp:
            language = "Visual C#";
            break;

        case CodeModelLanguageConstants.vsCMLanguageVB:
            language = "Visual Basic";
            break;

        case "{E6FDF8BF-F3D1-11D4-8576-0002A516ECE8}":
            language = "Visual J#";
            break;

        case CodeModelLanguageConstants.vsCMLanguageVC:
            language = "Visual C++";
            break;

        default:
            language = "Other";
            break;
    }

    return language;
}
```

> **Important** You can't just open an arbitrary source file in Visual Studio .NET and access its code elements through the code model. (For example, you can't get a *FileCodeModel* object from a source file in the Solution Items folder.) Only if you assign the source file to a project of the same language does the code model get built for the source file.

Table A-2 lists the *FileCodeModel* methods. We'll cover the *Addxxx* methods and the *Remove* method in the section titled "Generating Code"; for a complete treatment of the *CodeElementFromPoint* method, see the section titled "Getting a *CodeElement* from a Point Object" in Chapter 12.

Table A-2 *FileCodeModel* Methods

Method	Description
AddAttribute	Creates a new top-level attribute
AddClass	Creates a new top-level class
AddDelegate	Creates a new top-level delegate
AddEnum	Creates a new top-level enumeration
AddFunction	Creates a new top-level function
AddInterface	Creates a new top-level interface
AddNamespace	Creates a new top-level namespace
AddStruct	Creates a new top-level structure
AddVariable	Creates a new top-level variable
CodeElementFromPoint	Returns the code element containing the given *TextPoint* object
Remove	Removes the specified code element

The *CodeModel* object returned by the *Project.CodeModel* property provides a more comprehensive view than does the *FileCodeModel* object. For one thing, the *CodeModel* operates at the project level instead of at the project item level, so you can expect to see a greater number of top-level source code elements in its *CodeElements* collection than you'd see in the typical *FileCodeModel.CodeElements* collection. Also, depending on the project type, the *CodeModel* object reveals information that isn't included by the *FileCodeModel* object, such as assembly-level attributes and external namespaces. The *CodeModel* properties are shown in Table A-3.

Table A-3 *CodeModel* Properties

Property	Description
CodeElements	Returns a collection of top-level *CodeElement* objects defined in the associated project
DTE	Returns the *DTE* object
IsCaseSensitive	Returns whether the project's programming language is case-sensitive
Language	Returns a GUID representing the project's programming language
Parent	Returns the parent *Project* object

Most of the *CodeModel* properties mirror those of the *FileCodeModel* object but provide project-level information. This higher-level perspective comes in handy sometimes; the *CodeModel.Language* analogue, for example, can tell you the project's programming language even when the project has no files (and, therefore, has no *FileCodeModel*). The *IsCaseSensitive* property is unique to *CodeModel*; this property allows you to determine the case-sensitivity of the project's programming language, which can make all the difference when you have to generate a new code element name.

The *CodeModel* methods are listed in Table A-4. We'll postpone a closer examination of the *Addxxx* and *Remove* methods until the section titled "Generating Code."

Table A-4 *CodeModel* Methods

Method	Description
AddAttribute	Creates a new top-level attribute
AddClass	Creates a new top-level class
AddDelegate	Creates a new top-level delegate
AddEnum	Creates a new top-level enumeration
AddFunction	Creates a new top-level function
AddInterface	Creates a new top-level interface
AddNamespace	Creates a new top-level namespace
AddStruct	Creates a new top-level structure
AddVariable	Creates a new top-level variable
CodeTypeFromFullName	Returns a *CodeType* object representing the given code element

Table A-4 *CodeModel* Methods *(continued)*

Method	Description
CreateCodeTypeRef	Returns a *CodeTypeRef* object representing the type of the fully qualified name
IsValidID	Returns whether a specified name is a valid programmatic identifier for the current language
Remove	Removes the specified code element from the source file

The *CodeTypeFromFullName* method allows you to retrieve a *CodeType* object for a particular code element, given its fully qualified name.

The *CreateCodeTypeRef* method lets you create a *CodeTypeRef* object based on a fully qualified name or a *vsCMTypeRef* enumeration value. (See Table A-5.) All of the languages except Visual Basic support this method.

Finally, the *IsValidID* method lets you check whether a given identifier is valid for a particular language. All of the languages implement this method.

Table A-5 The *vsCMTypeRef* Enumeration

Constant	Description
vsCMTypeRefOther	Data type not in this table
vsCMTypeRefCodeType	*CodeType*
vsCMTypeRefArray	Array
vsCMTypeRefVoid	Void
vsCMTypeRefPointer	Pointer
vsCMTypeRefString	String
vsCMTypeRefObject	Object
vsCMTypeRefByte	Byte
vsCMTypeRefChar	Character
vsCMTypeRefShort	Short integer
vsCMTypeRefInt	Integer
vsCMTypeRefLong	Long integer
vsCMTypeRefFloat	Floating point
vsCMTypeRefDouble	Double-precision floating point
vsCMTypeRefDecimal	Decimal
vsCMTypeRefBool	Boolean
vsCMTypeRefVariant	Variant

CodeElement

The *CodeElement* object serves as a kind of "base class" for the other code model objects by providing a set of properties common to all of the kinds of programming constructs. Table A-6 lists the *CodeElement* properties.

Table A-6 *CodeElement* Properties

Property	Description
Children	Returns a collection of all *CodeElement* objects related to this code element
Collection	Returns the parent *CodeElements* collection
DTE	Returns the *DTE* object
EndPoint	Returns a *TextPoint* object that marks the end of the code element definition
*Extender**	Returns the requested extender object
ExtenderCATID	Returns the extender category ID
ExtenderNames	Returns the names of the available extender objects
FullName	Returns the fully qualified name of the code element
InfoLocation	Returns a *vsCMInfoLocation* value that describes where the code element is defined
IsCodeType	Returns whether the code element is a *CodeType*
Kind	Returns a *vsCMElement* value that describes the specific type of the code element
Language	Returns the programming language used to create the code element
Name	Sets or returns the name of the code element
ProjectItem	Returns the *ProjectItem* that contains the code element
StartPoint	Returns a *TextPoint* object that marks the beginning of the code element definition

* C# won't allow you to reference this property using property syntax because its *get* accessor takes a parameter. Use an explicit call to the *get* accessor instead.

The three most important *CodeElement* properties are *Name*, *FullName*, and *Kind*. The *Name* property—*CodeElement*'s only read/write property—allows you to retrieve and change the code element's name programmatically. (Visual Basic doesn't implement the *Name* property's write functionality.) Note, however, that you can't always change the name of a code element—for example, you can't change the name of a constructor because a constructor must have the same name as its parent class. The *FullName* property returns the code element's fully qualified name. The *Kind* property returns a *vsCMElement* value that identifies the underlying code construct. The *vsCMElement* enumeration has 40 constants representing the most common code constructs you'll encounter (as well as some of the more obscure ones that we hope you'll never have to deal with).

The *Children* property returns a *CodeElements* collection that contains all the code elements related to this one. Languages aren't required to support this property—and most languages don't support it. Of the four languages that come in the Visual Studio .NET box, only Visual C++ uses the *Children* property.

Note As you learn more about the code model, you'll find that Visual C++ contributes to many of its idiosyncrasies. When Visual Studio .NET invited the different language groups to join the code model party, Visual C++ showed up with a code model of its own. For the most part, Visual C++ did its job implementing the Visual Studio .NET code model (by way of its own code model, of course), but some accommodations were made in the Visual Studio .NET code model to allow more access to the Visual C++ native code model. The result is the occasional oddball property, such as *CodeElement.Children*, and the overrepresentation of Visual C++ in different areas of the code model, such as the constants in the *vsCMElement* enumeration.

The *InfoLocation* property returns a value from the *vsCMInfoLocation* enumeration that lets you know where to find the code construct. Table A-7 lists the *vsCMInfoLocation* constants.

Table A-7 *vsCMInfoLocation* Constants

Constant	Description
vsCMInfoLocationProject	Code element lives in a project file.
vsCMInfoLocationExternal	Code element lives in an external file.
vsCMInfoLocationVirtual	This constant isn't used in Visual Studio .NET 2003.
vsCMInfoLocationNone	Code model is unable to determine the location of the code element.

When the *InfoLocation* value is *vsCMInfoLocationProject*, the *StartPoint* and *EndPoint* properties return *TextPoint* objects that delimit the code element in the source file.

The *Extender*, *ExtenderCATID*, and *ExtenderNames* properties allow you to access the extender objects related to the code element. (Extender objects let you add, hide, or replace properties of the underlying code element when you view them in the integrated development environment [IDE].)

The *Language* and *ProjectItem* properties are equivalent to the *FileCodeModel.Language* and *FileCodeModel.Parent* properties, respectively. The *Collection* property returns the parent *CodeElements* collection. The *IsCodeType* property returns *true* when the *CodeElement* object also supports the *CodeType* interface. (You'll learn all about *CodeType* later in this chapter.)

Table A-8 lists the *CodeElement* methods.

Table A-8 *CodeElement* Methods

Method	Description
GetEndPoint	Returns a *TextPoint* object that marks the end of the code element definition
GetStartPoint	Returns a *TextPoint* object that marks the beginning of the code element definition

The *GetStartPoint* and *GetEndPoint* methods return a *TextPoint* object that marks the start or end, respectively, of some aspect of the code element definition. You specify which aspect to return by passing a *vsCMPart* enumeration value to the appropriate method. (See Table A-9.) The *GetStartPoint* and *GetEndPoint* methods offer more flexibility than do their *StartPoint* and *EndPoint* counterparts; in fact, *CodeElement.StartPoint* and *CodeElement.EndPoint* are equivalent to *CodeElement.GetStartPoint(vsCMPartWholeWithAttributes)* and *CodeElement.GetEndPoint(vsCMPartWholeWithAttributes)*, respectively. You can see for yourself how just how flexible the *GetStartPoint* and *GetEndPoint* methods are by running the *Chapter12\CodeDiscovery\TextFromStartAndEndPoints* macro, which calls the two methods with each of the *vsCMPart* values and displays the results.

Table A-9 The *vsCMPart* Enumeration

Constant	Returns
vsCMPartName	The name of the code construct
vsCMPartAttributes	The attributes that apply to the code construct, minus the attribute delimiters
vsCMPartHeader	The header of the code construct
vsCMPartWhole	The entire code construct
vsCMPartBody	The body of the code construct, minus the body delimeters
vsCMPartNavigate	The location in the source code to which the caret moves when you double-click on an element in Class View
vsCMPartAttributesWithDelimiter	The applicable attributes and the attribute delimiters
vsCMPartBodyWithDelimiter	The body of the code construct and its delimiters
vsCMPartHeaderWithAttributes	The code construct's header and its attributes
vsCMPartWholeWithAttributes	The entire code construct and its attributes

Specialized Code Model Objects

This section describes the various objects that correspond directly to specific code constructs. Each of these objects aggregates its specific members with the *CodeElement* members, which makes for pretty long member lists in the Help files. In the following tables, we factored out the common *CodeElement* members so we could concentrate on the members specific to each type. We also factored out the properties in Table A-10—they're not part of the *CodeElement* properties, but they're common to all the types described in this section.

Table A-10 Properties Common to All Code Model Types

Property	Description
Comment	Sets or returns the comment associated with the code element
DocComment	Sets or returns the code element's document comments
Parent	Returns the parent *CodeElements* collection

The *DocComment* property allows you to create XML document comments for languages that support them (such as C# and J#). The string you pass to *DocComment* must contain valid XML enclosed within *<doc></doc>* elements.

The *Comment* property creates normal, run-of-the-mill comments. (C# and J#, however, implement the write functionality of their *Comment* properties by turning a normal string into a *<summary>* XML document comment.)

CodeNamespace

The *CodeNamespace* object corresponds to a .NET namespace construct (*package* in J#, *namespace* in C# and C++, and *Namespace* in Visual Basic). *CodeNamespace* includes the properties listed in Table A-11.

Table A-11 *CodeNamespace* Properties

Property	Description
CodeElement properties	See Table A-6.
Other common properties	See Table A-10.
Members	Returns the top-level code elements contained by the namespace.

As you can see from Table A-11, the only property specific to *CodeNamespace* is *Members*, which lets you access the namespace's top-level code elements.

Table A-12 shows the *CodeNamespace* methods, which are discussed in detail in the section titled "Generating Code."

Table A-12 *CodeNamespace* Methods

Method	Description
CodeElement methods	See Table A-7.
AddClass	Creates a new class within the namespace.
AddDelegate	Creates a new delegate within the namespace.
AddEnum	Creates a new enumeration within the namespace.
AddInterface	Creates a new interface within the namespace.
AddNamespace	Creates a new namespace within the namespace.
AddStruct	Creates a new structure within the namespace.
Remove	Removes the specified code element.

CodeType

The *CodeType* object is a kind of generic object, like *CodeElement*, that corresponds roughly to what would be a type in the .NET Framework. The *CodeType* object allows you to treat certain code model types—*CodeClass*, *CodeStruct*, *CodeDelegate*, *CodeInterface*, and *CodeEnum*—as if they were the same kind of object. Table A-13 lists the *CodeType* properties.

Table A-13 *CodeType* Properties

Property	Description
CodeElement properties	See Table A-6.
Other common properties	See Table A-10.
Access	Sets or returns the access modifiers.
Attributes	Returns a collection of attributes.
Bases	Returns a collection of base types.
DerivedTypes	Returns a collection of derived types.
*IsDerivedFrom**	Returns whether this type has another type as a base.
Members	Returns a collection of top-level code elements contained by this type.
Namespace	Returns a *CodeNamespace* object representing the parent namespace.

* C# won't allow you to reference this property using property syntax because its get accessor takes a parameter. Use an explicit call to the get accessor instead.

The *Access* property sets or returns a *vsCMAccess* value that determines the code element's access (such as public, private, and so on). Be aware that the *CodeType.Access* write functionality doesn't work for Visual C++ and Visual Basic. Table A-14 lists the *vsCMAccess* enumeration constants.

Table A-14 The *vsCMAccess* Enumeration

Constant	Description
vsCMAccessPublic	Public access
vsCMAccessPrivate	Private access
vsCMAccessProject	Project access
vsCMAccessProtected	Protected access
vsCMAccessProjectOrProtected	Combination of project and protected access
vsCMAccessDefault	Default access
vsCMAccessAssemblyOrFamily	Assembly or family access
vsCMAccessWithEvents	*WithEvents* access

The *Attributes* property returns a collection of *CodeElement* objects of type *CodeAttribute*, one for each attribute that applies to the *CodeType*. The *Bases* property returns a collection of *CodeElement* objects of type *CodeClass*; each *CodeClass* represents a base class of the *CodeType*.

The *IsDerivedFrom* property lets you discover whether the *CodeType* has another code element from the current project as one of its bases. Currently, the Visual C++ implementation works correctly for both class and interface bases, the C# and J# implementations work correctly for classes only, and the Visual Basic implementation doesn't work at all.

The *DerivedTypes* property returns a collection of *CodeElement* objects that specify which other code constructs in the current project derive from this object. Currently, none of the languages implements *DerivedTypes*.

The *Members* property returns a collection of *CodeElement* objects representing the top-level code constructs contained by the *CodeType*. Finally, the *Namespace* property returns the parent namespace.

Table A-15 shows the *CodeType* methods, which are explained in the section titled "Generating Code."

Table A-15 *CodeType* Methods

Method	Description
CodeElement methods	See Table A-7.
AddAttribute	Creates a new attribute.
AddBase	Adds a new base type.
RemoveBase	Removes a base type.
RemoveMember	Removes a member code element.

CodeClass and *CodeStruct*

The *CodeClass* and *CodeStruct* objects represent classes and structures, respectively. In the C family of programming languages, classes and structures are intimately related—beginning C++ programming books often introduce the *class* construct as a *struct* whose members are private by default. The code model also treats the *CodeClass* and *CodeStruct* similarly; in fact, the two objects share exactly the same properties and methods, which is why we group them together here, beginning with Table A-16.

Table A-16 *CodeClass* and *CodeStruct* Properties

Property	Description
CodeElement properties	See Table A-6.
CodeType properties	See Table A-11.
Other common properties	See Table A-10.
ImplementedInterfaces	Returns a collection of implemented interfaces.
IsAbstract	Sets or returns whether this item is abstract.

The *ImplementedInterfaces* property returns a *CodeElements* collection that contains the interfaces implemented by the class or structure. C#, J#, and Visual Basic implement the *ImplementedInterfaces* property correctly; Visual C++ includes its implemented interfaces in its *Bases* collection, so its *ImplementedInterfaces* property always returns an empty collection.

The *IsAbstract* property returns whether the object is an abstract class or structure. All of the languages implement the read functionality of *IsAbstract*; only C# and J# implement the write functionality.

Table A-17 lists the *CodeClass* and *CodeStruct* methods, which are explained in the section titled "Generating Code."

Table A-17 *CodeClass* and *CodeStruct* Methods

Method	Description
CodeElement methods	See Table A-7.
CodeType methods	See Table A-12.
AddClass	Creates a new class within the class or structure.
AddDelegate	Creates a new delegate within the class or structure.
AddEnum	Creates a new enumeration within the class or structure.
AddFunction	Creates a new function within the class or structure.
AddImplementedInterface	Adds an implemented interface to the class or structure.
AddProperty	Creates a new property within the class or structure.
AddStruct	Creates a new structure within the class or structure.
AddVariable	Creates a new variable within the class or structure.
RemoveInterface	Removes an implemented interface from the class or structure.

CodeInterface

The *CodeInterface* object encapsulates an interface code construct. Table A-18 shows the *CodeInterface* properties; as you can see from the table, *CodeInterface* doesn't define any interface-specific properties.

Table A-18 *CodeInterface* Properties

Property	Description
CodeElement properties	See Table A-6.
CodeType properties	See Table A-11.
Other common properties	See Table A-10.

The *CodeInterface* methods are shown in Table A-19. You can find an explanation of the *Addxxx* methods in the section titled "Generating Code."

Table A-19 *CodeInterface* Methods

Method	Description
CodeElement methods	See Table A-7.
CodeType methods	See Table A-12.
AddFunction	Creates a new function within the interface.
AddProperty	Creates a new property within the interface.

CodeEnum

The *CodeEnum* object represents an enumeration code construct. *CodeEnum* doesn't define any enumeration-specific properties, as you can see from Table A-20.

Table A-20 *CodeEnum* Properties

Property	Description
CodeElement properties	See Table A-6.
CodeType properties	See Table A-11.
Other common properties	See Table A-10.

The *CodeEnum* methods, shown in Table A-21, have explanations in the "Generating Code" section.

Table A-21 *CodeEnum* Methods

Method	Description
CodeElement methods	See Table A-7.
CodeType methods	See Table A-12.
AddMember	Creates a new enumeration constant.

CodeDelegate

The *CodeDelegate* object represents a delegate code construct. Table A-22 lists the *CodeDelegate* properties.

Table A-22 *CodeDelegate* Properties

Property	Description
CodeElement properties	See Table A-6.
CodeType properties	See Table A-11.
Other common properties	See Table A-10.
BaseClass	Returns a *CodeClass* object that represents the delegate's base class.
Parameters	Returns a *CodeElements* collection containing the delegate's parameters.
*Prototype**	Returns the delegate's prototype.
Type	Sets or returns a *CodeTypeRef* object representing the delegate's type.

* C# won't allow you to reference this property using property syntax because its get accessor takes a parameter. Use an explicit call to the get accessor instead.

The *BaseClass* property always returns a *CodeClass* object that represents *System.Delegate*. Every language except Visual C++ implements the *BaseClass* property.

The *Parameters* property returns a collection of *CodeElement* objects that contains an item for each parameter of the delegate; Visual C++ doesn't implement this property.

The *Prototype* property returns the delegate's prototype as a string. The *Prototype* property accepts values from the *vsCMPrototype* enumeration that determine which aspects of the prototype to return. The *vsCMPrototype* constants listed in Table A-23 are bit flags, so you can combine them to customize the string returned by *Prototype*. For example, the combination of *vsCMPrototypeFullname*, *vsCMPrototypeType*, *vsCMPrototypeParamNames*, and *vsCMPrototypeParamTypes* would return all information about a particular delegate. All of the languages except Visual C++ implement this property.

Table A-23 The *vsCMPrototype* Enumeration

Constant	Description
vsCMPrototypeFullname	Returns the fully qualified name
vsCMPrototypeNoName	Omits the name
vsCMPrototypeClassName	Returns the name and class prefix
vsCMPrototypeParamTypes	Returns the parameter types
vsCMPrototypeParamNames	Returns the parameter names
vsCMPrototypeParamDefaultValues	Returns the parameter default values
vsCMPrototypeUniqueSignature	Returns a unique string based on the prototype
vsCMPrototypeType	Returns the type
vsCMPrototypeInitExpression	Returns the initialization expression

Finally, the *Type* property lets you read or write a *CodeTypeRef* value that represents the delegate's type. Currently, none of the *Type* property's write implementations works, and read works only for C#, J#, and Visual Basic.

The *CodeDelegate* methods are shown in Table A-24; you can find explanations for them in the section titled "Generating Code."

Table A-24 *CodeDelegate* Methods

Method	Description
CodeElement methods	See Table A-7.
CodeType methods	See Table A-12.
AddParameter	Creates a new delegate parameter.
RemoveParameter	Removes a delegate parameter.

CodeVariable

A *CodeVariable* object represents a variable declaration. Table A-25 lists the *CodeVariable* properties.

Table A-25 *CodeVariable* Properties

Property	Description
CodeElement properties	See Table A-6.
Other common properties	See Table A-10.
Access	Sets or returns the variable's access modifiers.
Attributes	Returns a collection of the variable's attributes.
InitExpression	Sets or returns the variable's initialization code.
IsConstant	Sets or returns whether the variable is constant.
IsShared	Sets or returns whether the variable is a shared class variable.
Prototype[*]	Returns the variable's declaration.
Type	Sets or returns a *CodeTypeRef* object representing the variable's type.

* C# won't allow you to reference this property using property syntax because its get accessor takes a parameter. Use an explicit call to the get accessor instead.

The *Access* property is similar to the *CodeType.Access* property and takes the same *vsCMAccess* values found in Table A-14. All languages implement the *Access* property's read functionality; only C# and J# implement the write functionality.

The *Attributes* property returns a *CodeElements* collection that contains an item of type *CodeAttribute* for each attribute of the variable.

The *InitExpression* property lets you read or write the variable's initialization expression. All languages support the *InitExpression* read functionality, and all languages but Visual Basic support the *InitExpression* write functionality. The expression you pass to the *InitExpression* property shouldn't contain an initialization operator because the correct operator is supplied by the language. Also, be aware that *InitExpression* won't validate the expression you specify.

The *IsConstant* property lets you read or write whether the variable is declared as a constant. All languages implement the *IsConstant* read functionality, but the J# implementation always returns *False*. Every language except Visual Basic implements the *IsConstant* write functionality.

The *IsShared* property lets you read or write whether a variable is a class shared variable (*True*) or a class instance variable (*False*). The read functionality of *IsShared* works for all languages and the write functionality works for C# and J#.

The *Prototype* property returns a string that represents the variable's declaration. This property works the same way as the *CodeDelegate.Prototype* property—you pass it a combination of values from the *vsCMPrototype* enumeration (listed in Table A-23), and it returns those parts of the declaration that you request. Unlike the *InitExpression* property, the *Prototype* property returns the initialization operator along with the initialization expression when passed a value of *vsCMPrototypeInitExpression*. All languages implement this property.

The *Type* property sets or returns a *CodeTypeRef* object that represents the variable's type. All languages implement the *Type* property's read functionality, but only Visual C++ implements the write functionality.

Table A-26 lists the *CodeVariable* methods. You can find an explanation of these methods in the section titled "Generating Code."

Table A-26 *CodeVariable* Methods

Method	Description
CodeElement methods	See Table A-7.
AddAttribute	Creates a new attribute for the variable.

CodeProperty

The *CodeProperty* object represents a property code construct. Table A-27 lists the *CodeProperty* properties. Note that the J# implementation doesn't recognize property declarations—instead, J# interprets the property's *get_xxx* and *set_xxx* methods as *CodeFunction* objects. Consequently, the explanations that follow Table A-27 won't include mention of J#.

Table A-27 *CodeProperty* Properties

Property	Description
CodeElement properties	See Table A-6.
Other common properties	See Table A-10.
Access	Sets or returns the property's access modifiers.
Attributes	Returns a collection of the property's attributes.
Getter	Sets or returns a *CodeFunction* object representing the property's getter function.
Prototype	Returns the property's prototype.
Setter	Sets or returns a *CodeFunction* object representing the property's setter function.
Type	Sets or returns a *CodeTypeRef* representing the property's type.

The *Access* property allows you to read or write the access modifiers of the property. (See Table A-14.) All of the languages implement the read functionality, but only C# implements the write functionality—Visual Basic returns "not implemented" and Visual C++ only allows properties to have public access, so it always returns "read-only".

The *Attributes* property returns a *CodeElements* collection containing an item of type *CodeAttribute* for each attribute that applies to the property.

The *Getter* and *Setter* properties let you read or write the property getter and setter, respectively. *Getter* and *Setter* each take or return a *CodeFunction* object that represents the corresponding getter or setter of the property code construct. C# and Visual Basic implement the read functionality of these properties. None of the languages implements the write functionality, but you can achieve the same effect in some of the languages by retrieving the *CodeFunction* object for the getter or the setter and making changes through the *CodeFunction* methods.

The *Prototype* property returns the property's prototype as a string. This property takes a combination of values from the *vsCMPrototype* enumeration (listed in Table A-23) and returns the requested information about the prototype. Note that *CodeProperty.Prototype* returns information about the property declaration only and doesn't include prototype information about the property's getter and setter functions. All the languages implement the *Prototype* property.

The *Type* property allows you to read or write a *CodeTypeRef* value that represents the property's type. All of the languages implement the *Type* property's read functionality, and none of the languages implements the write functionality. However, although you can't change a Visual C++ property's type directly, you can change it indirectly by changing the types of the underlying getter and setter functions.

Table A-28 lists the *CodeProperty* methods, which are explained in the section titled "Generating Code."

Table A-28 *CodeProperty* Methods

Method	Description
CodeElement methods	See Table A-7.
AddAttribute	Creates a new attribute for the property.

CodeAttribute

The *CodeAttribute* object corresponds to an attribute as defined by the .NET Framework. Table A-29 shows the *CodeAttribute* properties.

Table A-29 *CodeAttribute* Properties

Property	Description
CodeElement properties	See Table A-6.
Other common properties	See Table A-10.
Value	Sets or returns the attribute's value.

The *Value* property lets you read or write the attribute's value. All the languages implement the read functionality, but J# returns the wrong information if the attribute has more than one parameter. Only Visual C++ implements the write functionality.

Table A-30 shows the *CodeAttribute* methods, which are explained in the section titled "Generating Code."

Table A-30 *CodeAttribute* Methods

Method	Description
CodeElement methods	See Table A-7.
Delete	Removes the attribute.

CodeFunction

The *CodeFunction* object represents a function or sub procedure code construct. Table A-31 lists the *CodeFunction* properties.

Table A-31 *CodeFunction* Properties

Property	Description
CodeElement properties	See Table A-6.
Other common properties	See Table A-10.
Access	Sets or returns the function's access modifiers.
Attributes	Returns a collection of the function's attributes.
CanOverride	Sets or returns whether the function can be overridden.
FunctionKind	Returns a *vsCMFunction* enumeration value that describes what kind of function the function is.
IsOverloaded	Returns whether this function is overloaded.
IsShared	Sets or returns whether the function is statically defined.
MustImplement	Sets or returns whether the function is abstract.
Overloads	Returns a *CodeElements* collection containing the function's overloads.

Table A-31 *CodeFunction* Properties *(continued)*

Property	Description
Parameters	Returns a *CodeElements* collection containing the function's parameters.
Prototype[*]	Returns the function's declaration.
Type	Sets or returns a *CodeTypeRef* representing the function's type.

* C# won't allow you to reference this property using property syntax because its get accessor takes a parameter. Use an explicit call to the get accessor instead.

The *Access* property lets you read or write the function's access modifiers. (See Table A-14.) All languages implement the read functionality, and all languages but Visual Basic implement the write functionality.

The *Attributes* property returns a *CodeElements* collection containing an item of type *CodeAttribute* for each attribute that applies to the function.

The *CanOverride* property lets you read or write whether the function is overridable. All the languages implement the read functionality, but Visual C++ always returns *True*. C# and J# implement the write functionality; however, J# will only let you change from a nonoverridable (*final*) function to an overridable function.

The *FunctionKind* property returns one of the *vsCMFunction* values from Table A-32. Every language implements this property.

Table A-32 The *vsCMFunction* Enumeration

Constant	Description
vsCMFunctionOther	A kind of function not listed in this table
vsCMFunctionConstructor	A constructor
vsCMFunctionPropertyGet	A property getter
vsCMFunctionPropertyLet	A property letter
vsCMFunctionPropertySet	A property setter
vsCMFunctionPutRef	A put reference
vsCMFunctionPropertyAssign	A property assign
vsCMFunctionSub	A *Sub* procedure
vsCMFunctionFunction	A function
vsCMFunctionTopLevel	A top-level function
vsCMFunctionDestructor	A destructor

Table A-32 The *vsCMFunction* Enumeration *(continued)*

Constant	Description
vsCMFunctionOperator	An operator
vsCMFunctionVirtual	A virtual function
vsCMFunctionPure	A pure virtual function
vsCMFunctionConstant	A constant
vsCMFunctionShared	A shared function
vsCMFunctionInline	An inline function

The *IsOverloaded* property returns whether the function is overloaded. When *IsOverloaded* returns *True*, the *Overloads* property returns a collection that contains the function's overloads. Note that the C# and J# *Overloads* properties hold overloads only, whereas the Visual C++ and Visual Basic *Overloads* properties include the function in addition to its overloads.

The *IsShared* property lets you read or write whether a member function is a class shared function (*True*) or a class instance function (*False*). The read functionality of *IsShared* works for all languages, and the write functionality works for Visual C++, C#, and J#.

The *MustImplement* property lets you read or write whether the function is abstract. All languages support the read functionality. Visual C++ implements the write functionality fully, but C# and J# only allow you to convert an abstract function into a real function.

The *Parameters* property returns a collection that contains an item for each parameter of the function. All of the languages support this property.

The *Prototype* property returns a string that represents the function's prototype. This property accepts a combination of values from the *vsCMPrototype* enumeration in Table A-23 and returns the requested parts of the function's declaration. All of the languages implement this property.

The *Type* property allows you to read and write a *CodeTypeRef* value that represents the function's return type. All of the languages implement the read functionality, but only Visual C++ implements the write functionality.

Table A-33 lists the *CodeFunction* methods, which are explained in the section titled "Generating Code."

Table A-33 *CodeFunction* Methods

Method	Description
CodeElement methods	See Table A-7.
AddAttribute	Creates a new attribute.
AddParameter	Creates a new parameter.
RemoveParameter	Removes a parameter.

CodeParameter

The *CodeParameter* object represents a parameter of a function, sub procedure, or delegate. Table A-34 lists the *CodeParameter* properties.

Table A-34 *CodeParameter* Properties

Property	Description
CodeElement properties	See Table A-6.
Other common properties	See Table A-10.
Attributes	Returns a collection of the parameter's attributes.
Type	Sets or returns a *CodeTypeRef* representing the parameter's type.

The *Attributes* property returns a *CodeElements* collection containing an item for each attribute that applies to the parameter. C#, J#, and Visual Basic implement this property.

The *Type* property allows you to read or write a *CodeTypeRef* value that represents the parameter's type. All of the languages implement the read functionality, but only Visual C++ implements the write functionality.

Table A-35 lists the *CodeParameter* methods, which are explained in the section titled "Generating Code."

Table A-35 *CodeParameter* Methods

Method	Description
CodeElement methods	See Table A-7.
AddAttribute	Creates a new attribute.

CodeTypeRef

The *CodeTypeRef* object represents the type of a function, delegate, property, variable, or parameter. Table A-36 lists the *CodeTypeRef* properties.

Table A-36 *CodeTypeRef* Properties

Property	Description
AsFullName	Returns the type's fully qualified name
AsString	Returns the language's keyword for the type
CodeType	Sets or returns the *CodeType* associated with the type
DTE	Returns the *DTE* object
ElementType	Sets or returns the type of the array's elements
Parent	Returns the parent *CodeElement*
Rank	Sets or returns the number of dimensions of the array
TypeKind	Returns the base type

The *AsFullName* property returns the type's fully qualified name. All of the languages support this property, but the Visual C++ implementation returns the same value as the *AsString* property.

The *AsString* property returns the language's keyword that corresponds to the type. (For example, in C#, *AsString* returns *int* for *System.Int32*.) All of the languages support this property, but the Visual Basic implementation returns the same value as the type name part of the *AsFullName* property.

The *CodeType* property returns a *CodeType* object that represents the type. C#, J#, and Visual Basic support this property, although Visual Basic always returns a *vsCMElementOther CodeType*.

When the *CodeTypeRef* represents an array, the *ElementType* property sets or returns the type of the array's elements, and the *Rank* property sets or returns the number of dimensions of the array. Currently, none of the languages implements either of these properties.

When the *CodeTypeRef* represents a *CodeElement* in a source file, the *Parent* property returns that *CodeElement*. All of the languages implement this property.

The *TypeKind* property returns a *vsCMTypeRef* value from Table A-5 that signifies the type of the *CodeTypeRef*. All of the languages implement this property.

Generating Code

In this section, we'll explore the active side of the code model—generating code. In most uses of the code model, code discovery isn't an end unto itself; instead, finding a source code element is just the first step toward changing that code element in some way. Conceptually, generating code with the code model is simplicity itself: you find the code element you want to modify, and then you call the appropriate *Addxxx* method to add a child code element or call a *Removexxx* method to delete a child code element. The devil is in the disassembly, however, and the code-generating methods have quirks to spare in each of the language implementations. The rest of this section provides an up-to-date reference on what does and doesn't work.

> **Note** The documentation claims that all the code model languages recognize fully qualified type names that use the dot (.) operator; in truth, the Visual C++ implementation understands only type names that use the double-colon [::] scope resolution operator. As a rule, if you pass a type name that uses the dot operator to a Visual C++ code model *Addxxx* method, Visual C++ adds the name as is, which results in syntactically incorrect source code.

Common Parameters

Most of the *Addxxx* methods have a few parameters in common. To not repeat each of these parameters in the following sections, we'll list the parameters most often used and give each a generic description. We'll refer to these parameters in the following sections only if there's additional information specific to the method being discussed.

- ***Name*** A string value that represents the name of the code construct. The Visual C++ implementation verifies the legality of the names you use, but the other languages use the name as is, which means it's up to you to make sure the name is valid. You can validate a name for a particular language by using the *CodeModel.IsValidID* method.
- ***Type*** The *Type* parameter governs the new code construct's type. This value takes either a *CodeTypeRef* object or a *vsCMTypeRef* enumeration value and sometimes a string containing a fully qualified

type name. Be aware that some implementations substitute aliases for the types you give. For example, in the *AddFunction* method, even if you specify a function's return value as "*System.Int32*" or "*System.Boolean*", C# generates a return type of *int* or *bool*, respectively.

- ***Position*** The *Position* parameter determines where the new code element is placed in the source file relative to its sibling code elements. A value of 0 indicates that the new code element appears before any other sibling code elements, and a value of –1 indicates that the new code element appears after all other sibling code elements. To place a new code element after a particular sibling code element, you either pass in the sibling's *CodeElements* index or pass in a *CodeElement* that represents the sibling code element. (As of this version of Visual Studio .NET, none of the languages supports passing a *CodeElement* to the *Position* parameter.)
- ***Access*** The *Access* parameter controls the accessibility of the new code element. This parameter takes on one of the *vsCMAccess* enumeration values listed in Table A-14. The different implementations won't verify the appropriateness of the access you give a code element, so it's up to you to do so.

CodeModel Variations

If you skim the Visual Studio .NET Help, you'll notice that the *Addxxx* methods come in two flavors, which Help calls Variant1 and Variant2. A better description would be to call one set the "*CodeModel* variants"—the *CodeModel* object isn't associated with any particular source file, so the *CodeModel Addxxx* methods have an extra *Location* parameter that specifies which file receives the generated code.

The name you pass to the *Location* parameter doesn't have to reference an existing file; if the file can't be found, a new one is created, so long as the name isn't an invalid filename. The most important thing to remember about the *Location* value is that it has to specify a correct source file for whatever language you're working with. (For example, "*myfile.cpp*" for Visual C++, "*myfile.cs*" for C#, and so on.) We'll ignore the *CodeModel* variants in the sections that follow.

Main Add Methods

This section describes the behavior of the code model methods that create the most basic code constructs, such as namespaces, classes, functions, and so on.

AddNamespace

The *AddNamespace* method applies to the *CodeModel*, *FileCodeModel*, and *CodeNamespace* objects and has the following prototype:

```
CodeNamespace AddNamespace(
    string Name,
    object Position
);
```

Note that you can create nested namespaces only by using the *CodeNamespace* object; the *CodeModel* and *FileCodeModel* objects can create top-level namespaces only. Otherwise, there's not really anything more to say—*AddNamespace* is about as straightforward a method as you'll find in the code model. Be thankful.

AddClass and *AddStruct*

The *AddClass* and *AddStruct* methods apply to the *CodeModel*, *FileCodeModel*, *CodeNamespace*, *CodeClass*, and *CodeStruct* objects and have the following prototypes:

```
CodeClass AddClass(
    string Name,
    object Position,
    object Bases,
    object ImplementedInterfaces,
    vsCMAccess Access
);

CodeStruct AddStruct(
    string Name,
    object Position,
    object Bases,
    object ImplementedInterfaces,
    vsCMAccess Access
);
```

The *Bases* parameter allows you to specify one or more base types for the new class or structure by passing in a 1-based array of *CodeClass* objects representing the bases. (The Visual C++ implementation also allows you to pass in an array of strings containing type names.) Of course, the common language runtime (CLR) doesn't support multiple implementation inheritance, so if you're generating managed code, you'll want to restrict yourself to a single base type. Currently, only the Visual C++ implementation supports the *Bases* parameter.

The *ImplementedInterfaces* parameter lets you add one or more interfaces to the class or structure's list of inherited types. *ImplementedInterfaces* takes a 1-based array of *CodeInterface* objects representing the interfaces to implement. As with the *Bases* parameter, the Visual C++ implementation also allows an array of strings representing type names. Only Visual C++ supports the *ImplementedInterfaces* parameter.

AddInterface

The *AddInterface* method applies to the *CodeModel*, *FileCodeModel*, and *CodeNamespace* objects and has the following prototype:

```
CodeInterface AddInterface(
    string Name,
    object Position,
    object Bases,
    vsCMAccess Access
);
```

The *Bases* parameter adds one or more interfaces to the new interface's list of inherited types. *Bases* takes a 1-based array of *CodeInterface* objects or strings representing the interfaces to implement. None of the implementations supports the *Bases* parameter, but you can achieve the same functionality in some of the implementations by using the *CodeInterface.AddBase* method.

AddDelegate

The *AddDelegate* method applies to the *CodeModel*, *FileCodeModel*, *CodeNamespace*, *CodeClass*, and *CodeStruct* objects and has the following prototype:

```
CodeDelegate AddDelegate(
    string Name,
    object Type,
    object Position,
    vsCMAccess Access
);
```

Currently, only C# implements this method.

AddFunction

The *AddFunction* method applies to the *CodeModel*, *FileCodeModel*, *CodeClass*, *CodeStruct*, and *CodeInterface* objects and has the following prototype:

```
CodeFunction AddFunction(
    string Name,
    vsCMFunction Kind,
    object Type,
    object Position,
    vsCMAccess Access,
);
```

The *Name* parameter controls the name of the function, except in the case of constructors and destructors (which take the name of the class to which they belong).

The *Kind* parameter determines what kind of function to create, such as a constructor or pure virtual function. This parameter takes one or more of the constants from the *vsCMFunction* enumeration, which are listed in Table A-32. Not every combination of *vsCMFunction* values is meaningful; even so, some implementations do their best to create a "getter constructor" when asked, so it's up to you to ensure that the value you pass to *AddFunction* makes sense.

AddProperty

The *AddProperty* method applies to the *CodeClass*, *CodeInterface*, and *CodeStruct* objects and has the following prototype:

```
CodeProperty AddProperty(
    string GetterName,
    string PutterName,
    object Type,
    object Position,
    vsCMAccess Access,
    object Location
);
```

Currently, only the C# *AddProperty* implementation works. The *GetterName* and *PutterName* parameters represent the names of the property getter and property setter, respectively. For a C# read/write property, the *GetterName* and *PutterName* values must be the same. You can create a read-only property by passing *null* to the *PutterName* parameter and create a write-only property by passing *null* to the *GetterName* parameter.

The *Location* parameter allows you to specify a new file into which this property will go; it has the same semantics as the *CodeModel*-variant *Location* parameters. (See the section titled "*CodeModel* Variations.") The C# implementation ignores this parameter.

AddEnum

The *AddEnum* method applies to the *CodeModel*, *FileCodeModel*, *CodeNamespace*, *CodeClass*, and *CodeStruct* objects and has the following prototype:

```
CodeEnum AddEnum(
    string Name,
    object Position,
    object Bases,
    vsCMAccess Access
);
```

The *Bases* parameter takes a 1-based array of *CodeType* objects or strings representing the underlying type of the enumeration. None of the implementations uses the *Bases* parameter.

AddVariable

The *AddVariable* method applies to the *CodeModel*, *FileCodeModel*, *CodeClass*, and *CodeStruct* objects and has the following prototype:

```
CodeVariable AddVariable(
    string Name,
    object Type,
    object Position,
    vsCMAccess Access
);
```

The *AddVariable* method works for all implementations, but because C# and J# don't allow top-level variable declarations, the *CodeModel.AddVariable* and *FileCodeModel.AddVariable* methods for these languages throw exceptions.

AddAttribute

The *AddAttribute* method applies to the *CodeModel*, *FileCodeModel*, *CodeClass*, *CodeDelegate*, *CodeEnum*, *CodeFunction*, *CodeInterface*, *CodeParameter*, *CodeProperty*, *CodeStruct*, *CodeVariable*, and *CodeType* objects (did we leave any out?) and has the following prototype:

```
CodeAttribute AddAttribute(
    string Name,
    string Value,
    object Position
);
```

Currently, C# and J# don't implement *AddAttribute*. The Visual C++ *CodeDelegate* and *CodeProperty* objects are read-only and won't allow you to add an attribute. Of the writable *Codexxx* objects that Visual C++ supports, only the *CodeParameter* object doesn't implement *AddAttribute*.

Other Add Methods

This section describes the remainder of the code model add methods, which allow you to flesh out the basic constructs created by the add methods in the previous section.

AddBase

The *AddBase* method applies to the *CodeClass*, *CodeStruct*, *CodeDelegate*, *CodeInterface*, *CodeEnum*, and *CodeType* objects and has the following prototype:

```
CodeElement AddBase(
    object Base,
    object Position
);
```

The *Base* parameter represents the new base type for the particular object; in the case of a C# *CodeEnum*, the *Base* parameter represents the underlying type of the enumeration. (Currently, the C# *CodeEnum.AddBase* implementation is broken.)

Each of the languages implements *AddBase* in its own special way; Table A-37 summarizes the combinations of language, object, and base type. (It doesn't make sense to add a new base to a delegate, so you won't find an implementation of *CodeDelegate.AddBase* in any of the languages.)

Table A-37 Valid Types for the *AddBase* Method's *Base* Parameter

	Visual C++	Visual C#	Visual J#
CodeClass.AddBase			
CodeClass	No	Yes	Yes
CodeInterface	No	No	No
CodeTypeRef	No	Yes	Yes
CodeType	No	Yes	Yes
Fully qualified name	Yes	Yes	Yes
CodeStruct.AddBase			
CodeClass	No	No	N/A
CodeInterface	No	Yes	N/A
CodeTypeRef	No	No	N/A
CodeType	No	No	N/A
Fully qualified name	Yes	Yes	N/A
CodeInterface.AddBase			
CodeClass	No	No	N/A
CodeInterface	No	Yes	N/A
CodeTypeRef	No	Yes	N/A
CodeType	No	Yes	N/A
Fully qualified name	Yes	Yes	N/A
CodeEnum.AddBase			
CodeClass	N/A	N/A	N/A
CodeInterface	N/A	N/A	N/A
CodeTypeRef	N/A	N/A	N/A
CodeType	N/A	N/A	N/A
Fully qualified name	N/A	N/A	N/A

AddImplementedInterface

The *AddImplementedInterface* method applies to the *CodeClass* and *CodeStruct* objects and has the following prototype:

```
CodeInterface AddImplementedInterface(
    object Base,
    object Position
);
```

The *Base* parameter takes either a *CodeInterface* object or a string with a fully qualified type name representing the interface that the class or structure will implement. Only J# implements this method.

AddMember

The *AddMember* method applies to the *CodeEnum* object and has the following prototype:

```
CodeVariable AddMember(
    string Name,
    object Value,
    object Position
);
```

You use this method to add a new member to an enumeration. The *Name* parameter becomes the name of the new member, and the *Value* parameter becomes the initial value of the member. You can pass a numeric value to the *Value* parameter using either a string or an object and the method will insert the correct operator for the member's initialization; however, it's up to you to ensure the validity of the member's value.

AddParameter

The *AddParameter* method applies to the *CodeDelegate* and *CodeFunction* objects and has the following prototype:

```
CodeParameter AddParameter(
    string Name,
    object Type,
    object Position
);
```

The *AddParameter* method doesn't allow you to create optional parameters.

CreateArrayType

The *CreateArrayType* method applies to the *CodeTypeRef* object and has the following prototype:

```
CodeTypeRef CreateArrayType(
    int Rank
);
```

This method returns a *CodeTypeRef* that you can use to create an array. The *Rank* parameter determines the number of dimensions in the array described by the new *CodeTypeRef*. Here's an example of how to use this method to create a new array (assuming you have a *CodeModel* reference in the *cdeModel* variable and a *CodeClass* reference in the *cdeClass* variable):

```
Dim cdeVariable As CodeVariable
Dim cdeTypeRef As CodeTypeRef
Dim cdeTypeRefArray As CodeTypeRef

' Create a reference to an int type
cdeTypeRef = cdeModel.CreateCodeTypeRef(vsCMTypeRef.vsCMTypeRefInt)

' Turn the reference into an int array type
cdeTypeRefArray = cdeTypeRef.CreateArrayType()

' Create a new int array variable within a class
cdeVariable = cdeClass.AddVariable("myIntArray", cdeTypeRefArray)
```

Currently, none of the languages supports this method.

Remove Methods

This section describes the code model methods that allow you to rid your source code of unwanted code constructs.

Delete

The *Delete* method applies to the *CodeAttribute* object and has the following prototype:

```
void Delete();
```

None of the languages supports this method.

Remove

The *Remove* method applies to the *CodeModel*, *FileCodeModel*, and *Code-Namespace* objects and has the following prototype:

```
void Remove(
    object Element
);
```

The *Element* parameter takes either a *CodeElement* or *CodeType*. The C# and J# implementations remove the corresponding source code from the file; the Visual C++ implementation takes a more conservative approach and simply comments out the code element—the one exception being the *CodeParameter* object, which Visual C++ deletes.

In C# and J#, only the identifier of a *CodeVariable* is deleted, which can be a little awkward when all that's left of your declaration is *object;*.

RemoveBase

The *RemoveBase* method applies to the *CodeClass*, *CodeDelegate*, *CodeEnum*, *CodeInterface*, *CodeStruct*, and *CodeType* objects and has the following prototype:

```
void RemoveBase(
    object Element
);
```

The *RemoveBase* method is the inverse of the *AddBase* method. The *Element* parameter takes a *CodeElement* representing the base to remove. (The C# implementation also allows a *CodeType* for this parameter.) Note that *RemoveBase* won't let you remove *System.Object* if it's the only base class.

For C# enumerations, *CodeEnum.RemoveBase* works—but barely. As with the *AddBase* method, the C# *CodeEnum.RemoveBase* method takes a 1-based array of *CodeType* or *CodeTypeRef* objects that represents the underlying type of the enumeration.

RemoveInterface

The *RemoveInterface* method applies to the *CodeClass* and *CodeStruct* objects and has the following prototype:

```
void RemoveInterface(
    object Element
);
```

The *Element* parameter takes a *CodeInterface* object representing the interface to remove from the *ImplementedInterfaces* collection. Only J# implements this method.

RemoveMember

The *RemoveMember* method applies to the *CodeClass*, *CodeDelegate*, *CodeEnum*, *CodeInterface*, *CodeStruct*, and *CodeType* objects and has the following prototype:

```
void RemoveMember(
    object Element
);
```

The *Element* parameter takes a *CodeElement* representing the child code construct to remove. A *RemoveMember* has no meaning for the *CodeDelegate* object because a delegate never has elements in its *Members* collection.

RemoveParameter

The *RemoveParameter* method applies to the *CodeDelegate* and *CodeFunction* objects and has the following prototype:

```
void RemoveParameter(
    object Element
);
```

The *Element* parameter takes a *CodeParameter* object representing the parameter to remove from the corresponding delegate or function. Only C# and J# implement this method.

Index

Symbols

A

B

C

D

E

G

H

K

L

M

N

O

P

T

X

About the Authors

Photo by Jason E. Fish

Left to right, Brian Johnson, Craig Skibo, and Marc Young

Brian Johnson works as a programming editor at Microsoft Press. He lives in Redmond, Washington, with his wife, Kathryn, and their three children, Will, Hunter, and Buffy. He was a technical editor for *Microsoft Office and VBA Developer* magazine and has written for *MSDN* and *Microsoft Visual J++ Informant* magazines. He is a former Marine Corps combat correspondent and a graduate of the University of Wisconsin.

Craig Skibo, a resident of Redmond,Washington, has worked at Microsoft for seven years on the programmability features of Visual Studio. He often lectures at industry conferences about the Visual Studio automation model and consults with developers to help them learn how to use the latest Visual Studio technologies. He is a graduate of Penn State University.

Marc Young has worked as a programming editor at Microsoft Press for nearly a decade. He has worked on programming titles covering the gamut of Microsoft and Microsoft-related technologies—everything from VGA video systems in the MS-DOS world to the latest in .NET server-side components. Marc lives in Seattle with his beautiful wife, cute-as-a-button son, and two wretched cats.

Muffler clamp

An automobile's exhaust system carries exhaust gases from the engine's combustion chamber to the atmosphere and reduces, or muffles, engine noise. The conventional muffler is an enclosed metal tube packed with sound-deadening material. Most conventional mufflers are round or oval-shaped with an inlet and outlet pipe at either end. Some contain partitions to help reduce engine noise. A muffler clamp holds the muffler on the tailpipe.*

At Microsoft Press, we use tools to illustrate our books for software developers and IT professionals. Tools very simply and powerfully symbolize human inventiveness. They're a metaphor for people extending their capabilities, precision, and reach. From simple calipers and pliers to digital micrometers and lasers, these stylized illustrations give each book a visual identity, and a personality to the series. With tools and knowledge, there's no limit to creativity and innovation. Our tag line says it all: the tools you need to put technology to work.

The manuscript for this book was prepared and galleyed using Microsoft Word. Pages were composed by Microsoft Press using Adobe FrameMaker+SGML for Windows, with text in Garamond and display type in Helvetica Condensed. Composed pages were delivered to the printer as electronic prepress files.

Cover Designer:	Methodologie, Inc.
Interior Graphic Designer:	James D. Kramer
Principal Compositor:	Kerri DeVault
Interior Artist:	Michael Kloepfer
Copy Editor:	Ina Chang
Proofreader:	nSight, Inc.
Indexer:	Bill Meyers

Get a **Free**
e-mail newsletter, updates, special offers, links to related books, and more when you

register on line!

Register your Microsoft Press® title on our Web site and you'll get a FREE subscription to our e-mail newsletter, *Microsoft Press Book Connections.* You'll find out about newly released and upcoming books and learning tools, online events, software downloads, special offers and coupons for Microsoft Press customers, and information about major Microsoft® product releases. You can also read useful additional information about all the titles we publish, such as detailed book descriptions, tables of contents and indexes, sample chapters, links to related books and book series, author biographies, and reviews by other customers.

Registration is easy. Just visit this Web page and fill in your information:

http://www.microsoft.com/mspress/register

Microsoft®

Proof of Purchase

Use this page as proof of purchase if participating in a promotion or rebate offer on this title. Proof of purchase must be used in conjunction with other proof(s) of payment such as your dated sales receipt—see offer details.

Inside Microsoft® Visual Studio® .NET 2003

0-7356-1874-7

____

CUSTOMER NAME

Microsoft Press, PO Box 97017, Redmond, WA 98073-9830